B 813

FATHERS OF
THE VICTORIANS

FATHERS OF
THE VICTORIANS

THE AGE OF WILBERFORCE

BY

FORD K. BROWN

CAMBRIDGE
AT THE UNIVERSITY PRESS
1961

PUBLISHED BY
THE SYNDICS OF THE CAMBRIDGE UNIVERSITY PRESS

Bentley House, 200 Euston Road, London, N.W. 1
American Branch: 32 East 57th Street, New York 22, N.Y.
West African Office: P.O. Box 33, Ibadan, Nigeria

Printed in Great Britain at the University Press, Cambridge
(Brooke Crutchley, University Printer)

CONTENTS

Never, perhaps, since the first age of Christianity, has a holier zeal existed than at the present moment, for the moral and religious improvement of mankind.

THE BIBLE SOCIETY OF MASSACHUSETTS, 1815

I live in a region in which I would have you also move.

CHARLES SIMEON, 1828

FOREWORD

The timid defensive state, in which christians have long been contented to stand, in respect of the gentile world, has tended greatly to extinguish the spirit of zeal for the conversion of sinners at home...but if once the servants of God should...declare offensive war against the kingdom of the devil...zeal for pure christianity in our own country and in our own hearts, will revive in proportion.

THE REVEREND THOMAS SCOTT, 1801

You have, *as yet*, not met *every where*, with equal success; but it has, however, uniformly been such that all intelligent Christians agree, that with the NINETEENTH century, A NEW ERA *has begun betwixt* CHRIST *and* BELIAL. THE ADHERENTS OF BOTH ARE ARMING *on either side*.

The Calvinists' Convention at Herrnhuth to the London Missionary Convention; communicated by BROTHER STEINKOPFF, 1807

If the Lord wills, our work goes on. If it be his pleasure that we should exist, still let his enemies and ours, against whom we have drawn the sword, know this, that we... are still the adversaries of the uncircumcised in purpose of heart.

The Christian Review and Clerical Magazine, 1829

I

This is the story of a movement of national reform that took place in England from the 1780's to the early years of the Princess Victoria, or roughly through the lifetime of Lord Byron. Begun by a handful of men and women shocked at the decay of English religion and the corruption of English morals, it grew rapidly into huge proportions. In thirty years it had covered England with reforming institutions and made its leader one of the foremost moral figures of the world. It left a lasting impression on all English-speaking countries.

The moral scene in England as these people saw it at the beginning of what has been called the Age of Elegance was a spectacle of horror, a nightmare of depravity, vice, sin and infidelity. In 1785 William Wilberforce, the young Member of Parliament for Hull, recorded his 'despair of the republic', caused by 'the universal corruption and profligacy of the times, which taking its rise amongst the rich and luxurious has now extended its baneful influence and spread its destructive poison through the whole body of the people'.[1] Others who felt that despair saw the sign of an approaching retribution in the national complacency that went with the universal corruption. 'I fear the Lord has a controversy with us', wrote the Reverend John Newton, a homely old divine who had been converted from a life of sin in the African slave trade. '...I see the nation in general hardened into that spirit of insensibility and blind security, which in all former ages and nations has been the token and forerunner of judgment.'[2] Those statements were made by men who would have denied with profound sadness that they were exaggerating. To their mind there was a horror even worse than the overwhelming tide of evil, their Established Church's lack of any spirituality.

By 1785 the small group Newton belonged to, probably not a hundred people all told, who came to be called 'the Evangelicals' or the 'Evangelical Party', had made some kind of beginning beyond setting individual examples of devoutness and virtue. Besides some forty or fifty clergymen scattered over England, none above the rank of a parish incumbent and only two with London livings, they included a few influential people of means and standing who were doing what they could to advance 'true religion': Baron and Lady Smythe, Sir Charles and Lady Middleton, Sir Richard Hill, the Earl of Dartmouth, the London Russia-merchant John Thornton. They were already educating 'truly religious' young men for Holy Orders and buying church livings, in as prominent and influential locations as they could manage, for their 'religious clergymen'. But as a group they had no clear direction, no organization, no programme, no means, no resources, no propaganda, no numbers, no power. Above all, they had no leader. When William Wilberforce was 'converted' in 1785 from the 'mere nominal Christianity' of the great majority of churchmen to the 'vital Reformation Christianity' of Newton's group, it was clear that God had provided one. When he entered in his diary in 1787 'God has set before me as my object the reformation of manners' and in the next

---

[1] *The Life of William Wilberforce.* By his sons Robert Isaac Wilberforce and Samuel Wilberforce (5 vols., London, 1838), vol. I, p. 84. This is the 'official' biography of the Evangelical leader, cited here as *Wilberforce*.

[2] *Works of the Reverend John Newton* (6 vols., New York, 1810), vol. VI, pp. 283–4. Cited as *Newton*.

year established the first of many Evangelical reforming institutions, the Society to Effect the Enforcement of his Majesty's Proclamation Against Vice and Immorality, an extraordinary campaign for national righteousness had begun.

A particular situation here called for abilities far beyond those canonically necessary in the leader of any reform cause. It had already been shown that in eighteenth-century England an idealistic reform movement based only on moral and religious principle was doomed in advance. The leader of this movement had to have the ability to use worldly means for spiritual ends, a genius for expediency, opportunism and 'accommodation', steadfastness in taking calculated moral risks, willingness to practise in a great cause what enemies of the right and the good in this campaign—'emissaries of Satan'—were to call 'moral equivocation'. We shall see in how extraordinary a way Wilberforce had those qualities. He was twenty-eight years old in 1787, already a noted speaker in Parliament. The prime minister William Pitt thought he had 'the greatest natural eloquence in England'. A gentle, bright, vivacious man of great charm and sweetness of character, a 'winged being in airy flight'—seraphic, his friends said—he had earnest moral principle of course, with Evangelical love for his fellow Christians, warm sympathy for virtuous people who were unfortunate or oppressed. One other qualification as leader could not have been more vital: a rich man, a favourite of London society and one of the young prime minister's closest friends, he had access to those circles of the ruling class that were closed to John Newton and had been closed to the Methodist leaders John Wesley and George Whitefield who had already tried to reform the nation.

As England was constituted at the end of the eighteenth century a national reform of morals was unthinkable without support from the ruling class and the Established Church. Both were terrified by the French Revolution into hostility to all change. Through twenty of the reform campaign's first thirty years, England was fighting the greatest war of its history. But this movement led by William Wilberforce touched something basic in the nature of large numbers of Englishmen no matter how disturbed the times or how great the spiritual poverty and sophisticated barrenness of the Age of Enlightenment; perhaps an antipathy to moral corruptness, perhaps a desire for a 'religion of the heart' not offered by the Church of England in the eighteenth century. We should probably not be wrong in believing that an important factor of the Evangelicals' success, as astonishing to them as it was to everybody else, was simply Wilberforce's incomparable leadership.

As this movement has been described in conflicting ways and the present way appears to conflict with all the rest, what are taken here as the basic facts are summarized, in the interests of clarity, even perhaps of understanding.

1. The unmistakable improvement in manners and morals of early nine-teenth-century England that has generally been ascribed to the Methodists can be credited to them only in the most indirect way. It would not have taken place without the work of these Evangelical reformers of the Established Church. By keeping alive a religion of the heart that had died in the rest of the church John Wesley provided a vague but pervasive background— probably foundation—for the work of succeeding reformers with superior methods. Considered as a reform of the moral and religious life of the nation his work was obviously a failure.

2. The earnest but slight efforts of Wilberforce and his lieutenants round 1790 grew in twenty-five years into an immense reform movement, well organized and superbly directed, conducted with the most practical strategy and tactics on the most practical principles, and using agencies and resources of a size, number and power not yet fully recognized. This movement was so organic as to have the appearance of being from the outset unerringly de-signed and constructed to be precisely what it became in nearly every part (and it is convenient to treat it as such).

3. One element of it was basic in so absolute a way that without it there would not have been any reform. That was the clear recognition that an idealistic procedure (such as Wesley's) is a mere waste of time and that the reform of this world can only be brought about by the ways and means of this world. One fact in particular the Evangelical leadership saw from the beginning in the most realistic way: their attempt to reform the nation was certain to fail unless they won over a substantial number of the ruling class that to so great an extent set the moral tone of the people.

4. As it was obvious that as many as possible of the ruling class, 'the great', had to be drawn into the reforming ranks, it was obvious that Evangelical reform could not have characteristics that were basically offensive to them and could offer them no social, moral or economic views fundamentally opposed to their own views, manners and tastes. (Thus it would have been folly in

the Society for the Suppression of Vice to attack any of the particular vices of the upper classes.)

5. It had to be, and was, a cardinal principle of the reformers' strategy not to allow themselves to be confused with the Calvinistic or any dissenters, with radicals or liberals, or with the Methodists. The great were strongly opposed to Calvinism, were not fond of dissenters, owned an immense part of all English property, had a strong sense of their financial well-being, and thought the Methodists were fanatical in religion and subversive in politics and economics. The frequently expressed belief that Evangelicals were liberals, still more the frequently expressed belief that Evangelicals and Methodists can be lumped together into something called 'the Evangelical Revival', wholly miss the nature and accomplishment of this reform movement.

6. Not political reformers, not dissenters and not Methodists but deeply conservative members of the Established Church, the Evangelicals were concerned with no reform but the reform of vice and sin and of the infidelity that to their mind was the sole cause of vice and sin. Their only object was to have a nineteenth century peopled by Evangelical Christians leading moral lives of a puritanical kind.

7. With those principles the Evangelicals attempted the moral reform of the nation by the following chief means, nearly all of them struck on at the beginning of the campaign, all of them exploited to an almost unbelievable extent:

(*a*) Carefully planned, ceaseless proselytizing in the ranks of the great—as the eighteenth century said, of *those who count*.

(*b*) The establishment of societies for religious and moral reform, and societies for charity, benevolence and education that could be made contributory to moral reform, with the capture of already existing societies controlled by others if they could be made 'useful'.

(*c*) The capture of the Established Church by 'converting' High Church (Regular, Orthodox) clergymen to true (Evangelical) Christianity, encouraging and helping Evangelical young men to enter Holy Orders, and employing all possible means to get Evangelical clergymen into lectureships, livings and church offices.

(*d*) Immense religious and moral propaganda.

(*e*) The creation of proper subsidiary causes of a popular nature to attract to participation in the reform of the nation people who had not been immediately and directly brought into it.

(*f*) The relentless (and, to the minds of their opponents, unscrupulous) use of Evangelical money.

8. In their attempt to make all England 'truly religious' and puritanically

moral, Wilberforce and his associates failed, as may be noticed. They failed too in their attempt to wrest control of the Established Church from the High Church party. But in defeat they had forced their antagonists to be seriously religious and they had spread their puritanical morality far beyond the bounds of England. Their opponents might well have thought 'One more such victory and we are lost'.

9. When the conflict had so ended it was doubtful if there was any further need of an Evangelical Party (except possibly in purely theological terms). In anything that vitally concerned England, it had done its work.

10. In the course of forcing the Church of England to be Christian and the nation so far as humanly possible to be moral in their puritanical way, the Evangelicals who came to be dominant in the Party before Wilberforce's death (with exceptions, but by and large) had lost to a distressing extent, as means came to be taken for ends and genuine beliefs degenerated into doctrinaire pedantries, the taste, culture and intellectual interest that had marked many of the dominant Evangelicals of Wilberforce's generation. No better evidence could be presented than that Wilberforce, who more than any other man formed the Evangelical Party and who led it for nearly forty years, at the end of that time left it to go over to High Church. Frankenstein's giant creation had got out of all control.

There is an impressive roll of Victorian notables who were Evangelical in their youth, through parental influence or early teaching or both. It includes Charlotte, Emily and Anne Brontë, Henry Thomas Buckle, Mark Pattison, Samuel and Robert Isaac Wilberforce, Sir James Stephen and Sir George Stephen, Lord Glenelg, Sir Gilbert Scott, Samuel Butler, Benjamin Jowett, Elizabeth Barrett, George Eliot, Kingsley, De Quincey, Ruskin, Macaulay, Peel, Gladstone, Pusey, Manning and Newman. Of those men nine were sons of the Evangelical high command.[1] It is not meaningless that the eminent Victorians of that list should have had the strong discipline one would expect of a later Puritanism in their early training. But it is not meaningless either that not one of them stayed an Evangelical.

II

In the size and scope of this movement, the variety of its means and devices, its deliberate and resourceful use of worldly methods and the violent opposition of its enemies, the story of Evangelical reform

---

[1] What can be thought of as the Evangelical directorate included, besides Wilberforce, Charles Grant (father of Lord Glenelg), Zachary Macaulay, James Stephen, Sir Robert Peel, William Manning, and Philip and Lady Emily Pusey.

reaches a massive breadth and depth so rich in detail that the following
pages present only two minor episodes of it in more than outline form.
Those episodes are the fight to establish a branch of the British and
Foreign Bible Society at Cambridge, and the fight down in Somerset
over the great Evangelical propagandist Mrs Hannah More's so-called
schools. They perhaps show in a peculiarly dramatic way the intensity
and bitterness of the conflict between the forces of good, the Evangelicals, and the forces of irreligion, reaction and obscurantism, the High
Church party, defenders of the old order. In those local engagements
of the great national struggle to make all Englishmen moral and pious
in the Evangelical way we see the marshalling and deployment of
influence, 'interest' and social power, the intense zeal and passionate
fervour of moral suasion, the subtlety of ecclesiastical intrigue, the
obduracy, wiliness and 'Evangelical cunning'—so the High Church
group said; even 'Evangelical duplicity'—with all the animus and
rancour and the *odium theologicum*. They also serve to make it clear that
the methods and principles of this campaign are at least as interesting
as its outcome. In the complexities of this great movement, as troublesome questions seem to rise—Can a purely virtuous act be accomplished
by those quite unvirtuous means of the world? Can expediency and
deviousness support Christian integrity?—there seems eventually to
come to view an extraordinary example of an end shaped by its means.

The principles and even the events of this campaign have been misunderstood in later years, but not more than they were during Wilberforce's lifetime. There may have been somewhere a more determined
attempt at the moral reform of a nation, by people burning with more
single-minded devotion and using greater means. There can hardly
have been one more misunderstood even by many of those taking part
in it or combating it. From its earliest days the history of Evangelical
reform is one of incredible misconceptions. The *Anti-Jacobin Review*,
standing grimly for order, government and property, violently attacks
an Evangelical Party standing for order, government and property in
precisely the same way. William Hazlitt, a thoughtful observer, is
wholly unable to understand the Evangelical commander who wishes
to free the African natives but does not wish to free the English natives.
A maiden lady's anonymous volume of sermons—with twelve thousand
clergymen on the Register—has forty-odd editions and wins its author

the offer of a church living from the Bishop of London; the mistress of a corrupt sovereign raises a young Evangelical to one of the highest offices of the church; the most violent opposition to Sunday schools comes from clergymen, the Bishop of Ely labours grimly to suppress the Reverend Charles Simeon's religious evening lectures, which indeed are saved only by the divine interposition, and the first Evangelical bishop is raised to his office quite literally in spite of his piety. Evangelical clergymen obtain by ruse High Church pulpits from which to preach doctrine well known to be profoundly hostile to that of the hoodwinked incumbent glowering up at them; other clergymen entitled to occupy pulpits are kept out of them by illicit devices or bodily force of church authorities; cures of souls are bought and sold in the market-place in religious jockeyings for power. A society to print and distribute religious tracts is attacked by sincere Christians; deeply religious people unite with atheistic radicals in fighting the Society for the Suppression of Vice. The archbishops and most of the bench of bishops lead a determined opposition to a society whose stated object is to distribute the Bible; the archbishops and many of the bench refuse for forty years to join a society whose object is to send missionaries to the heathen.

The Lock Hospital for Persons Afflicted with the Venereal Disease, the Lock Asylum for the Reception of Penitent Females, and the London Female Penitentiary have as patron and president, Evangelically nominated, King George IV and the Marquis of Hertford, two of the most notoriously impenitent debauchees of the age. The great democrat of the age, William Cobbett, opposes the abolition of Negro slavery because the Evangelicals are for it, the great Christian philanthropist of the age, William Wilberforce, supports the Repressive Acts and the suspensions of Habeas Corpus, and historians attribute political liberalism to moral reformers who in respect of such a taint were spotlessly pure.

Most confusing and most slowly understood of all was the Evangelical success in the most vitally important matter. How could it be possible that such substantial and conservative people, such numbers of the noble and respectable—as Dean Isaac Milner expressed it to the archbishop, such 'masses of property'—were coming forward to the side of 'the Fanatics', the 'Methodists in the church'? Before the turn of the century the Evangelical commanders had begun to win over to their campaign important peers and peeresses, Members of Parliament and government, High Church clergymen, affluent merchants, bankers and industrialists, influential men in the services and the professions. Rich converts, converts of great social prestige, politically useful converts, were pouring into the moral ranks from the 1790's on, in many cases deliberately selected and carefully acquired, to take part in the fight against the High Church party and other reactionaries, to suppress a lost century and establish one not so far this side Jordan. In 1788 the Society for the Relief of Poor, Pious Clergymen, Residing in the Country was founded. The wish to help the virtuous needy, and the outspoken and to the minds of their enemies arrogant distinction between clergymen and pious clergymen, which meant quite simply High Church clergymen and Evangelical clergymen, are equally characteristic. In 1792, the first year for which a subscription list has survived,[1] the Society was composed of some sixty clergymen and a handful of laymen of the upper and upper-middle classes. The clergymen were probably almost the entire roll of known Evangelicals in Holy Orders, those that is who were known to the Evangelicals to have 'happily emerged from their brethren'. The laymen included the Earl of Dartmouth, Henry Hoare of Mitcham, Thomas Hayter of London, Sir Richard Hill and Sir Charles Middleton, Lady Catherine Murray, Lady Robert Manners, Lady Mary Fitzgerald, Mrs Bouverie, and five residents of Clapham, a village just across the river from London: Charles Elliott, Samuel, Henry and Robert Thornton, and William Wilberforce. Those Evangelical pioneers were, in the order named, a leading peer (Cowper's 'one who wears a coronet and prays'), the head of the Fleet Street banking house, a London merchant, a country gentleman, a naval officer, four women of the great families, a London manufacturer, three young financiers (sons of John Thornton the Russia-merchant), and the young leader. Thirty years later, the Evangelical Party established the Society for the Relief of Distressed Widows, to give 'discreet relief to Widows of character'. This institution, intensely pietistic and admitting dissenters to membership, was doubly unlikely to be supported in the 1820's by High Churchmen

[1] Here and elsewhere that means: 'is to be found in the Reading Room of the British Museum or in other libraries used by the present writer'.

and was a trivial society in the size and scope of Evangelical operations of that period. Its officers included the Duchess of Kent (the mother of Victoria), the Duchess of Gloucester (a sister of the king), the Duchess of Beaufort, the Marchioness of Cholmondeley, Countesses Morley, Harrowby and Darnley, the Dowager Countess Morton, Viscountess Bernard; the Duke of Gloucester, the Marquis of Cholmondeley, Earls Spencer, Bexley, Harrowby, Egremont, Morley, Cardigan and Listowel, the Bishops of Winchester, Lichfield and Coventry, and Salisbury, and Lords Barham, Teignmouth and Calthorpe; and the list of subscribers from Sir Thomas Dyke Acland and Lady Acland to Lord and Lady Willoughby de Broke is a long and glittering muster-roll of the wealthy, highly placed and socially powerful.

III

The suppression of an evil eighteenth century and establishment of a righteous nineteenth was not to be done without a struggle. The foremost champion of the old age was Property, its second champion the Established Church as controlled at the end of the century. It was itself a large section of the vested interest of the ruling class, a subsidiary of Property, entrusted by it, in a tolerably formal way, with the guardianship of the morals and manners of a large majority of the people. The Lords Spiritual and their clergy could hardly have been expected to welcome the intrusion of an outspokenly hostile element. The violence and even hatred of more than a little of this struggle was not lessened by the circumstance that the alleged antagonism of the Evangelicals to Property, vested interest, the economic and political *status quo* and all the privilege of the great was a contrived fiction. With both sides strong and determined—when vested strength, intelligence, common sense and scholarly culture on the High Church side were offset, as Evangelicalism gathered numbers, by energy, Christian zeal and not least Christian money and 'Evangelical cunning' —the odds were even, and it should not have surprised a detached observer to see a curiously drawn battle.

But to make the odds even required an Evangelical triumph. The Party's growth in power, in the thirty years that followed Wilberforce's conversion, was unimaginable; so also, as it seemed to them, what they had accomplished. Not that the Victorian Age was without immorality, vice and infidelity. But to remove all visible evidence of Original Sin was never the Evangelical aim; if that could have been done, Hannah More, Evangelicalism's greatest publicist, wisely pointed out, this would be not earth but heaven. In the 1830's many a person described his difficulty in realizing that only a few years earlier, almost unrebuked except by the Evangelicals, there was the torpor or actual irreligion of the church that he could dimly remember, and among the great (rebuked by the Evangelicals only in a general way) public dissoluteness and unashamed vice. Before George IV's life came to an end in 1830 he was a painful moral anachronism, regarded with open contempt by nearly everyone, even by members of his court. In 1815 Miss Jane Porter (*Thaddeus of Warsaw, The Scottish Chiefs*) was congratulating Hannah More on her leading part in 'the reformation of the country'. If that was premature, it was not many years later that Mrs More could echo her friend Dr Johnson's 'Where is the world in which I was born?' On her lips that question could have been a cry of triumph. Changes in the moral and religious tone of a nation such as she could see some years before her death in 1833 have not often taken place in a generation.

If the changes that took place in the spiritual life in England were not solely the work (humanly speaking) of the Evangelicals, as they tended to believe, their belief was understandable. They saw very much that they favoured flourish and spread over the land, much that they were opposed to in the nation's moral life languish and sicken in the disapproval of an English public become 'serious'.

PART I

WAR ON THE GENTILE WORLD

CHAPTER 1

FAT BULLS OF BASHAN

I

The Evangelicals were not alone in seeing flagrant and dangerous evil about them in the Age of Elegance. There were pastimes and diversions, even some conspicuously of the world and the flesh, that High Church-men had little or no objection to. All violations of the Sabbath—newspapers, travel and the transacting of any business, but especially amusements such as cards, balls, assemblies or Sunday music, even walks in the country—seemed shockingly unchristian to the Evangelicals. On any day, the theatre, opera and masquerade, village fairs and rural sports, country dances, fiddlers and mountebanks, horse races, boat races, prize fights, 'low' gambling, the fives court and the public house, bear-baiting and bull-baiting, jolly songs, immodest feminine dress, jewellery and other adornment, French fashions (or anything French), improper literature (Shakespeare, Cervantes, Byron) and proper but unreligious literature (Walter Scott), with other things that will appear in the following pages, were abhorrent to the truly religious character and generally not condemned by High Church. But there were other evils opposed by all thoughtful persons. In its mere nominal Christian way the *Anti-Jacobin Review and Magazine*, for example, a High Church journal that was the most violent enemy of 'the Fanatics' for some years of the reform period, had moral standards as stern as the Evangelicals'. It was opposed to useless violations of the Sabbath, to the introduction of corrupt French manners and to some kinds of dancing. It condemned the fearful gambling of the day, honoured Sir Richard Hill (in spite of his Evangelical religion) for his attempts in Parliament to put down bull-baiting, and looked on many other aspects of the moral life of England with dread. Its horror at the growth of prostitution, for instance, was as great as the Evangelicals'. This 'extensive evil' might 'at least be made to hide its head', a review of the Proclamation Society's *Report of 1800* says. 'If only one-tenth of the Bow-street patrols were employed in clearing the public streets of these wretched females, those "open outrages on decency public", which are nightly committed in the Strand, the Haymarket, Charing Cross, Whitehall, &c. which are a disgrace to the police of the metropolis, would be easily prevented.'[1]

'That a great and general increase of moral corruption has taken place within a century, and, more particularly, within the last ten years', the *Anti-Jacobin* quoted in 1802 from a pamphlet of John Bowles, a High Church writer, 'is too obvious to need any proof....Luxurious habits, dissipated manners, and shameless profligacy, are the characteristics of the age.' In the same year it cited not only such social calamities as the enormous increase of claimants for parochial relief, the dreadful development of pauperism and the fostering of indolence by poor administration of the laws, but the prevalence of illicit intercourse in the lower ranks of society, and the general disregard there of all moral and religious obligations. 'Bastardy is now scarcely deemed a disgrace.' The baseborn of paupers in many parishes outnumbered their legitimate offspring; even poorhouses kept pauper girls in indolence 'and so lead to an increase of this public calamity'. 'This species of profligacy, so detestable in itself, and so pernicious in its consequences, both to the individuals, and to the community at large, has increased of late years, especially in the metropolis, to an extent that is almost incredible. Adultery and concubinage in the lower classes of society are unhappily most prevalent, and culprits of this description so rarely attend divine worship, and so seldom become objects of legal punishment, that little hopes of reformation remain.—Yet how can we expect a nation to flourish where the people are so abandoned?'[2]

Yet the *Anti-Jacobin Review*, High Church and bitterly anti-puritanical, was not only shockingly lax in many respects; failing to understand the real source of all evil it had no true realization of the moral corruption of the age. The rising tide of vice, immorality and infidelity so dreadfully in the nature of the Age of Elegance was far more pervasive, destructive and terrifying than appeared to this spiritually shallow journal. It was not only too obvious to need proof. It came close to being too obvious to be noticed, particularly when so many of the nation's guardians of morality, the priesthood, were themselves

[1] *The Anti-Jacobin Review and Magazine*, 1802, pp. 184–5.
[2] *Ibid.* p. 287.

wanting even in the outward observance of decency. To the Evangelicals it was a frightening aspect of the evil about them that professing Christians should sink into coarseness, gross manners or actual viciousness; that clergymen of the Established Church should do so was a compounded horror.

It was not merely a matter of the High Church clergy's playing whist on Sundays, officiating as master of ceremonies at balls, drinking many bottles of port at a sitting, or even going to the theatre—though how a Christian clergyman could do that was incomprehensible. Beyond such things, many of the Orthodox clergymen were spectacularly lacking in spiritual dedication. In the swarm of anecdotes bearing witness to the clerical character of the age, the point often is not that a story is demonstrably true but that it was accepted as having some kind of agreement with a general truth. Samuel Rogers the banker-poet recorded once asking Lord Dudley and Ward if he was going to a dinner of the princess's. Ward explained that he had not been invited. 'The fact is, when I dined there last, I made several rather free jokes; and the Princess, taking me perhaps for a clergyman, has not asked me back again.'[1] The clergy in fact included one or two of the more noted practitioners of evil, in addition to such cool hands as the Reverend John Horne Tooke who is described as living in genial retirement with his illegitimate daughters. One of the infamous Barrymores, usually pictured as the last of the hell-fire rakes, was in Holy Orders. In *Harriette Wilson's Memoirs*, a scandalous chronicle of the period, there is a 'good clergyman', 'the little parson', one of Harriette's hangers-on; 'a sly, shy, odd creature, not communicative unless one talks about cricket'. Harriette did not go into particulars about her clients' theology, but in assuming that the 'good clergyman' was not Evangelical we are on solid ground.

Nothing testified more eloquently to a hardened indifference or callousness that was the very triumph of sin than that in the age's matter-of-fact acceptance of an evil coarseness of manners such unhappy parts should be played by ministers of the Gospel. It was bad, for example, that Thurlow, the Lord Chancellor, had illegitimate children, but it was worse that a published account of him should say so in the least disturbed way. It was worse still that the account should be published in

[1] *Recollections of the Table-Talk of Samuel Rogers* (2nd ed., London, 1856), p. 264.

a periodical of considerable circulation conducted in part by clerics. *Public Characters*, an annual series of sketches of contemporaries edited and largely written by dissenting divines, also had more than an occasional 'pleasantry' that to the Evangelical mind was inexcusable. One of the most celebrated women of the day, Jane Duchess of Gordon, a hilarious and witty figure, was noted for the coarseness of her talk. A sample of it, probably restrained, has interest as appearing in such a publication. The duchess frequently dealt in 'bon mots', we are told, 'some of them sportive'. 'One evening a party of friends being engaged at some amusement resembling questions and commands, it is said that the Marquis [of Huntly, her son] being asked what trade he would choose, answered, making garters for ladies' stockings; and that the duchess observed, "Ah, George! you would soon be *above* your trade".' To that outrage the editors of *Public Characters* coolly added a worse, in a footnote: 'A certain Scotch methodistical lady, of considerable beauty, was so fond of scripture passages, that she had some of them marked on different parts of her dress. The motto of her garters was, *set your affections on things above*.'[1]

Those witticisms about the flesh were opposed to good morality, but it was worse that the offence, with added profanation of Holy Writ, should have been unconcernedly committed by ministers, in public print. As the moral campaign of Wilberforce and his associates had no illusions about obliterating wickedness, but had as a prime Evangelical purpose its removal from public view to avoid the further contagion of evil example, all conspicuous vice was peculiarly important. Hence an emphasis that at first seems exaggerated on the thoughtless or deliberately wicked vulgarity, 'freedom' or actual foulness of speech that was so much a matter of course in 'good society' at the beginning of this period that it was hardly noticed until the Evangelicals pointed it out. It was not found in the lower classes only. The speech of some ladies and gentlemen of the upper ranks, and even of the High Church clergy, was likely to contain expressions that the following generation was to consider extremely offensive. Only a few years later such language was barred in circles of any respectability. Early in the reform campaign it was to be found not only in references to physiological and biological functions that should never be mentioned, but in religious matters. In

[1] *Public Characters*, 1799, pp. 519–20.

1815 Miss Jane Porter wrote to Hannah More to praise the blessing her pen had been to her country. 'I need only call to the mind of Mrs Hannah More, what was the state of morals and religious opinions, amongst all ranks of persons in this country, twenty years ago! The poor were in profligate ignorance—the rich in presumptuous arrogance. I cannot give the latter a milder name; for I remember that about that period (then a very young person) I burst into tears at a large table after dinner, from horror and pity of some persons present, who were scoffing at religion, without a reprimand from any one.' 'Such conduct now', Miss Porter could add as early as 1815, 'would not be tolerated a moment in any company; and the one I speak of, was then what was called a most respectable circle.'[1]

The *Anti-Jacobin Review*, dedicated to morality and religion and except for its editor written almost entirely by clergymen, allowed itself occasionally to use language that Dickens could not have used in print and that could not safely have been printed for some years before he published. Such language in the *Anti-Jacobin* was what is called 'thinly disguised', as: 'Peter [Pindar], thou art a very puff....And like that other puff, a f—t.' In that form vulgar words were likely to appear without restraint in the first decade of the century, more rarely in the second. They can be seen in undisguised forms even in such publications intended for the young as school dictionaries. The 'corrected edition' of Boyer's *Royal Dictionary* (French–English, English–French, abridged) of 1803 contains, with French equivalents or used in defining French words, at least some fifty or so expressions such as 'to hang an arse', 'a short-arse', 'his arse makes buttons' ('il chie de peur'), 'a shitten girl', 'he came off very shittenly', 'he is the crack-fart of the nation' ('c'est un homme qui tranche hautement sur les affaires d'état, ou un homme qui se mêle de régler l'état'), 'turdy', 'to piss upon one', 'they piss through one quill' (act in concert; the Latin is 'in one quill': 'ex compacto agere'). In a work of the kind perhaps such expressions as to leap, to tup, to cover, to line, to horse and to couple are reasonable. Few of those words are indicated as 'mean, vulgar, or used in a comic or burlesque style'. They were probably vestiges of an earlier day, as the edition of 1803 was the twenty-third. The *Royal Dictionary* was

---

[1] *Memoirs of the Life and Correspondence of Mrs Hannah More.* By William Roberts Esq. (4 vols., London, 1834), vol. III, pp. 431–2. Cited here as *More*.

'specially designed to afford help to young students'. A similar work 'designed for the use of schools', Morell's abridgment of *Ainsworth's* (English–Latin) *Dictionary* (seventh edition, 1806), contains all basic forms of those terms in Boyer and adds variants and many other expressions: 'bugger', 'to have a desire to skite', 'pissed out'.

Life in the poorer classes, at least in the cities, was far under the comparative refinement of the Victorians. The *Reports* of Sir Edwin Chadwick, written after the Evangelical reform, give an idea of domestic sanitation that must have been as bad at the turn of the century. The matter of 'conservancy' (disposal of domestic sewage) is hard to learn anything about, but there is enough casual reference to it to show that partly through necessity the early nineteenth century looked on the matter with great frankness. A moral consequence of that state of sanitation is described in a strange Evangelical work of a later and Evangelically different period, Charlotte Elizabeth's *Wrongs of Women* published in 1842–3. John Smith, looking for work in a screw manufactory,

observes one thing that makes him fully resolve never to let any female of his family work there. The arrangement of outhouses is such as to set common decency at defiance; the honest rustic's cheek burns with shame and indignation as he notices the constant outrage to which modesty must be exposed, for lack of a very obvious needful separation in that department.

'I'll tell you what,' he says to his new acquaintance [the foreman of the manufactory], 'we poor folks down in the country are not over nice; but this beats all the indecency I ever heard of down there. I've done with this manufactory, at any rate.'

'If you mean to wait till you find a place where they manage any better, you'll be long out of work. 'Tis the same all over the town.'

'It's a shame to any christian land.'

'I've heard say so, and maybe, if I hadn't been brought up to it, I might think the same. As it is, nobody minds it here.'

But Smith minds it; and with indignant sorrow of heart he ascertains the truth of the declaration that the same scandalous disregard of morality, and, indeed, of right manly feeling, prevails in all directions; not to save money, for it would have cost nothing more to commence on a right plan; but to avoid the trouble of making a regulation, or of enforcing it when made.[1]

---

[1] Charlotte Elizabeth, *Collected Works* (New York, 1849), vol. II, pp. 421–2.

Fat Bulls of Bashan

Chadwick's *Report of 1842* also described living conditions, particularly housing, that were probably not much better or worse than could have been found forty years earlier; in place after place over England, ten or twelve people living in one tiny apartment, eight persons sleeping in one room, a family of eleven in two small rooms, 'three or four families occupying the same bedroom, and young men and women promiscuously sleeping in the same apartment'. 'I have known 14 individuals of one family together in a small room, the mother being in labour at the time, and in the adjoining room seven other persons sleeping, making 21 persons, in a space which should be occupied by six persons only at most.' Reports edited by Chadwick mention eleven persons sleeping in three beds—married, single, adult, young, lodgers— and a man and his wife in one bed in the same room with two grown females and two unmarried young men. 'I have met with instances of a man, his wife, and his wife's sister, sleeping in the same bed together. I have known at least half-a-dozen cases in Manchester in which that has been regularly practised, the unmarried sister being an adult.... I have frequently met with instances in which the parties themselves have traced their own depravity to these circumstances....In all of these cases the sense of decency was obliterated.'[1]

The lax sexual morality of the age was particularly a source of horror to the Evangelicals. One of the worst of sins, sexual promiscuity was taken as a matter of course beyond other immoralities. In the lower classes prostitution was so widespread as to alarm all but the callous or thoughtless, while seduction by members of the upper ranks was described, and by many non-Evangelicals, as a major evil of the day. There were many infanticides, the newspapers continually printing notices of serving-maids in particular destroying their infants, usually by thrusting them down privies, in many cases their only means of disposing of them. An unusual incident of the year 1782 shows the matter-of-fact attitude of one famous institution toward this promiscuity. On 19 August occurred one of those catastrophes that send a thrill of horror over a nation. Caught by a squall at Spithead with metal shifted, the *Royal George*, the most celebrated of His Majesty's men-of-war, turned turtle and went under, fully manned, as the eighteenth century said, from admiral to chaplain, a death trap

[1] Sir Edwin Chadwick, *Report of 1842*, pp. 123-6.

for fourteen hundred souls. 'Toll for the brave!' the poet Cowper wrote.

> His sword was in its sheath;
> His fingers on the pen
> When Kempenfelt went down
> With twice four hundred men.

It was nearer twice five hundred counting marines, and the poet did not mention two discordant elements of the tragedy that were juxtaposed for an instant as the great ship sank. There also went down on the *Royal George*, the papers reported, four hundred prostitutes or other women of the town, and by what perhaps demands to be called an odd coincidence four hundred Bibles just received, the day before, from the Naval and Military Bible Society. The presence of the prostitutes was not unusual. It was common practice to allow them on board, to stay for days, when ships were in harbour. They were still allowed on men-of-war as late as 1844. 'Lieutenant Rivers and Montmorency...assured me...they had actually seen more unfortunate females on board than there were men.'[1] The Bibles were the first shipment ever made to a British man-of-war. Two ages met when the *Royal George* went down.

The tide of evil, clearly in view on all sides, was so huge in London alone, or in any great city, that from time to time the Evangelicals came close to despair. They should have accomplished so much, with their hundreds upon hundreds of moral societies, their religious tracts and other literature, their Bible distributors, home missionaries, district visitors and other reforming agencies. 'Sin wears a front of brass among us', the editors of the *Christian Guardian* said in 1809. They had particularly in mind 'the illicit commerce that subsists between the sexes'. 'It...walks with shameless impudence through our public streets in open day.'[2] In 1809 came the revelation that the mistress of the Duke of York, second son of the king and commander-in-chief, had established a lucrative sideline selling military appointments. While Parliament solemnly held that the duke did not know about it, terrible harm had been done, to the mind of the Evangelicals, in the exposure of the traffic, of the mistress, and of the manners of the great generally. It was a 'beautiful lesson in morality to the lower classes', who promptly

---

[1] J. Beard Talbot, *The Miseries of Prostitution* (1844), p. 14.
[2] *Christian Guardian*, February 1809, p. 65.

substituted 'Duke or Darling' for the common expression 'head or tail'.[1] It was on this occasion that the *Christian Guardian* rose to a unique place of distinction in Evangelical ranks: in the passage cited above, it attacked the Duke of York by name for grossly scandalous conduct. No other such attack is to be found in the body of Evangelical writings of this period. The *Christian Guardian* was a provincial journal at that time (Bristol). The London Evangelicals had a clearer view of the great strategy.

Such conduct as the Duke of York's, which was not spectacular in the flagrant immorality of the day, was generally accepted with a deeply ingrained public callousness. One of the chief wickednesses of the corruption the Evangelicals saw on all sides was that it existed open and unashamed. The ruinous gaming debts of many a public figure, the drunkenness of the great prime minister, of the greatest dramatist of the age, of the greatest scholar of the age, the varied mistresses and general lubricities of scores of public figures including some of the royal dukes, the assorted vices of the Prince Regent, were all matters of public knowledge, ribald amusement and little concern. They were as unconcealed and unabashed as the prostitutes plying their trade in London streets and in the boxes of theatres during performances.

Nearly everywhere, it seemed to sober and thoughtful men, there was a scandalous or dangerous antagonism, blindness or indifference to good manners, good morals, upright living and true religion, the most unmistakable evidence of a luxurious and profligate corruption of the upper classes, a general debauchery and corruption of the lower. The evil of the England of the earnest people whom this study is concerned with was not simple but compounded. Prostitution, for example, was dreadful in its wickedness and its dimensions; and this 'extensive evil' was complicated and multiplied by its obvious connection with juvenile delinquency and with crime. Apart from the 'dreadful immorality' of the brothels, which flourished, by hundreds, everywhere and which the magistrates were believed to be powerless against, the business of contributing to the corruption of young girls and boys flourished too. 'The city swarms with prostitutes', the *Anti-Jacobin* reported in January 1816, 'who now pick up men, in the most public streets, Cheapside, for instance, in the middle of the day; while within its precincts, thieves,

---

[1] M. W. Patterson, *Sir Francis Burdett* (London, 1931), vol. I, p. 226.

receivers of stolen goods, and keepers of brothels, find, if not a sure refuge, a ready protection.' There were 'swarms of beggars, children were sent out by their mothers and corrected at night if they returned with less than two shillings'.[1]

Throughout the period institution after institution—societies, asylums, refuges, homes, hospitals, penitentiaries—rose up against the 'open female debauchery of the age', many of them founded by the Evangelicals, the rest taken over by them by the end, or the middle, of the period, to attempt to 'check the progress of female depravity', which 'is every day increasing'. There were 30,000 prostitutes in and about London, it was claimed—or 40,000, or 50,000; if the last estimate was correct, one in four of the city's total population of unmarried women.[2] 'In some of the daily papers it was last season estimated at 100,000.' The widespread 'licentiousness among the lower orders' has 'so very much destroyed the class of servant girls in London'; 'without a male protector a respectable and virtuous female dare scarce set her foot in the streets during the day, far less attempt it at night...even guarded, she must shut her eyes and ears to avoid infection...she is forced to abstain from visiting almost every public place of amusement'.[2] 'Loose women' are 'allowed to prowl over' the theatres, 'exhibiting the most indecent appearance and gestures with perfect impunity';[3] in particular the saloons of theatres are 'dreadful hot beds of vice and immorality' where shocking scenes occur nightly 'that can only be conceived by those who witness them'.[4]

The increase of the number of infamous houses throughout London is 'truly alarming'; there is a 'torrent of profligacy which pervades, not only the metropolis, but every part of the kingdom'. In some parts of London the number of prostitutes has 'doubled in twenty years'.[5] Women 'of the most lady-like appearance, attend at the various Common Register Offices for obtaining servants, and actually hire

---

[1] *Anti-Jacobin*, January 1816, p. 66; quoted from *Minutes of the Evidence taken before the Committee appointed by the House of Commons to inquire into the State of Mendicity and Vagrancy in the Metropolis and its Neighbourhood* (1815).

[2] S.T., *An Address to the Guardian Society* (London, 1817), pp. 36–7.

[3] *Ibid.* pp. 47–8.   [4] *Ibid.* pp. 52–3.

[5] *The Fund of Mercy; or, an Institution for the Relief and Employment of Destitute and Forlorn Females* (London, 1813).

females merely by their personal figure, for no other purpose than to gain money by their seduction from the paths of virtue. One of this class actually became subscribed to the "London Society for the Improvement of Female Servants".[1]

There was an unmistakable connection of crime and prostitution, in particular the fatal corruption of juvenile prostitution. In the London Female Penitentiary the average age of prostitutes 'appears to be only sixteen'.[2] The non-Evangelical Committee for Investigating the Causes of the Alarming Increase of Juvenile Delinquency in the Metropolis came to believe—while such judgments were 'very indefinite'—that some thousands of boys under seventeen were daily engaged in the commission of crime, frequented houses of 'the most infamous description' and associated 'with professed mature thieves, and with girls who lived by prostitution'. 'The number of abandoned children, from the age of *twelve to fourteen years*, living in a state of *prostitution*, who are brought daily before the magistrate for petty crimes, are increased to an alarming degree within these few years; "and the depredations committed on the public by these little miscreants, who unite with boys about the same age, in gangs of from twenty to thirty, are become a terror to every house-keeper in the neighbourhood of their haunts," (Vide the Times Newspaper, Nov. 7, 1812.).'[3] There were schools for the instruction of youth in every species of theft and immorality, intoxication and debauchery. Upwards of four hundred individuals made their living by getting females from eleven to fourteen years old for prostitution.[4] One brothel, 'in Crispin-street, Spitalfields, is kept particularly for the reception and seduction of female infants under fourteen'.[5]

This picture was heightened by allied practices. Decency was

---

[1] *Report of the Provisional Committee of the Guardian Society*, 13 December 1815, which also asserts that in three London parishes alone there were 362 houses of prostitution (London, 1816), pp. 8, 9.

[2] *By-Laws and Regulations of the London Female Penitentiary* (1809); quoted in *Cursory Remarks on a Recent Publication, etc.* By Juvenis (1809).

[3] *The Fund of Mercy.*

[4] *The Refuge* (London, 1835); quoted from a *Report of the London Society for the Suppression of Juvenile Prostitution* (no date, apparently early in the century).

[5] *Part the Second of an Address to the Public* (of the Vice Society) (London, 1804), p. 51.

'grossly violated', the first *Address to the Public from the Society for the Suppression of Vice* said in 1803, 'by the open exposure of indelicate and obscene prints, in the windows of many print-shops in the Metropolis';[1] and there was the publication of obscene books, a particular market for which (as for the obscene prints) according to the Vice Society was girls' schools, and the sale of obscene objects, whose manufacture was a speciality of French prisoners of war, allowed to pursue their art in English prisons, no doubt with some reasonable division of profits with their guardians. To those traffics can be added the introduction of disaffected or seditious books into schools, the horror of which was greater as all of them were written by infidels and blasphemers,[2] and the publication of immoral and blasphemous literature in general—a special province of the Vice Society, one of whose more controversial verdicts was obtained, under Wilberforce's direction, against the poet Percy Bysshe Shelley. There was also the great evil of disaffection and insubordination, a sure accompaniment, to the Evangelical mind, of immorality and infidelity.

II

Even with respect to those unmistakable evils on which all responsible persons agree, there was a vital difference between High Church and Evangelicalism. One basic principle in particular of the Evangelical reform that constitutes a major difference between these reformers and perhaps all others has to be understood literally to see the Age of Elegance as the Evangelicals saw it and to understand the peculiar nature of this reform movement. It is indicated by the *Anti-Jacobin's* belief that 'the causes of moral corruption' are evident and visible. The 'luxurious habits, dissipated manners, and shameless profligacy' that were 'the characteristics of the age' were in its opinion a product of the mismanagement of social institutions, or came from other sources that the Evangelicals held to be the merest *second causes*, explaining nothing and to be explained themselves in terms of a first cause. One such, the *Anti-Jacobin* believed, was 'our intimacy with profligate Paris' which

---

[1] *Address to the Public from the Society for the Suppression of Vice* (1803), p. 42, note.

[2] *Address to the Public from the Society for the Suppression of Vice, Part the Second* (London, 1804), pp. 24-7.

'seems to increase, as that country advances in profligacy'. After the spread of 'French ideas' across the Channel in the early 1790's and again in 1802 and after 1814, it was customary to put many immoralities down to French Jacobinism. It was radical and subversive, consequently it favoured and produced moral turpitude. The French in general—'that nation of baboons', the Bishop of Derry said—had long been known to be an immoral people. In its review of the Proclamation Society's *Report for 1800* the *Anti-Jacobin* noted the existence in England of an organization for circulating obscene books and prints that employed 'a great number of emissaries' to introduce such wares into private families and 'places of female education'. 'We are, in all probability, indebted for the existence of this truly infernal society to the *great nation* which all descriptions of persons seem now so fond of visiting.' The Society for the Suppression of Vice found that the peddlers of obscene prints and books were not French but Italian. But in any case to attribute English sin to the French, or to any social institution, was simply the deeply erroneous thinking of irreligious people. The Evangelicals knew that the cause of all depravity, vice and sin is the lack of true religion, and the cause of that is the evil heart of man.

When John Newton took a trip to Greenwich and looked back from the park at the cloud of smoke hanging over London, it seemed to him 'an emblem of the accumulated stock of misery, arising from all the trials and afflictions of individuals within my view'. If it were possible for us to know those afflictions, we would not be mirthful again. 'A person would hazard his reputation for humanity, who was disposed to be merry among the lunatics in Bethlehem, or in the midst of a group of agonizing sufferers in Bartholomew's Hospital, or on a field of battle. And what is the world at large but a more extensive and diversified scene of wretchedness, where phrensy and despair, anxiety, pain, want, and death, have their respective *wards* filled with patients?' It was also a symbol of another kind. 'I thought it likewise an emblem', Newton continues, 'of that cloud of sin which is continually ascending with a mighty cry in the ears of the Lord of hosts. Sin overspreads the earth; but in London the number and impunity of offenders, joined with the infidelity and dissipation of the times, make it a kind of hot-bed or nursery for wickedness. Sin is studied as a science, and there are professors and inventors of evil things in a variety of branches, who have an unhappy address in teaching others to sin with an *eclat*. Could we have knowledge of the monstrous enormities and villanies which are committed in a single day, within the compass of the prospect I had... it would make us groan and tremble.'[1]

In those lines Newton was describing the sole Evangelical enemy. Wilberforce mustered a great strength, in his campaign to make England a virtuous land, and it was all directed against profligacy, callousness, vice, sin and the cause of all such things, infidelity. No social institution as such gave the Evangelicals a moment's concern. They were concerned solely with the *best interests* of the English people. To do away with the irreligion that is the cause of vice and sin was the whole Evangelical purpose. Every part of every Evangelical activity and institution was to give to England, immediately or in the long run, the true religion that leads to righteousness and salvation. Human institutions that seemed to other people to create sin, vice and depravity had no immediate or primary interest. They were not even *second causes*. In so far as they were bad—that is, were not divinely ordered—they did not produce but came from the depravity of the human heart.

This basic point of view is stated in a sermon preached by Joseph Milner on 18 October 1785 that is incomprehensible without an understanding of the Evangelical attitude and purpose. Milner's subject was 'Various Degrees of Accountableness at the Day of Judgment', his theme that 'unto whomsoever much is given, of him shall be much required' and that much has been given to Englishmen of all ranks. 'There is not a nation under heaven, to whom the maxim may with more justice be applied. Even to the poorest of us God may say, Much is given to you, and therefore much will be required of you at my great day of account. The advantages we all have in this country for light, for instruction, for civilization, are equal, or more than equal to what any nation under the sun enjoys.'[2] This matter seems difficult. How those greatly fortunate members of the upper class were given much, in England in the eighteenth century, is clear. George Wyndham, Earl of Egremont, for instance, is said to have received an annual sixty to eighty thousand pounds in rents for the seventy-odd years he held the

---

[1] *Newton*, vol. VI, p. 164.

[2] *Works of the late Rev. Joseph Milner, etc.*, edited by Isaac Milner (8 vols., London, 1810), vol. VIII, p. 429. Cited as *Joseph Milner*.

title.[1] But how could Joseph Milner, a humane man, believe that the chimney sweepers' apprentices, whom there was no need for Parliament to be concerned about as they were all illegitimate, had been given much, in England in 1785, to have much required of them by a just God at the Day of Judgment? In an ordinary view they had been given nothing except a life that could hardly be more literally poor, nasty, brutish and short. In particular, what advantages for light, instruction and civilization had they been given? No Climbing Boy could read or write and no one had ever thought he should be taught. In Van Diemen's Land they would have been no more remote from the advantages of British civilization than they were in London.

But in the Evangelical way Milner was right. This matter concerned the Climbing Boys' *best interests*. They like all Englishmen had great advantages for light, instruction and civilization—that is, for Christian light, Christian education and Christian civilization. Those advantages fell short of what they ought to be, in England in 1785, for the Established Church was in the hands of Orthodox clergy—apathetic, coldly formal, only moral at best, at worst theologically wrong and sickeningly corrupt. But after forty years of the Methodist Revival and with the Evangelical Reformation beginning, the Climbing Boys (and every Englishman) were offered more for their *best interests* than they would find in any other country. They could hardly go into a church and there were not yet any Sunday schools, but in the church they would only hear a High Church clergyman anyhow, the Sunday schools were being instituted in this year 1785, there were already a few chapels and even a church or two where true religion was to be found, and in the streets and market-places, at fairs and in the fields, anywhere, they could hear the preaching of truly religious men: John Berridge, Rowland Hill and others whose parishes were limited by no fixed lines and contained no small areas. In Spain or Italy they would be welcome in the church or the cathedral. What Christian light would they find there, or instruction, or civilization?

With one institution that was social and political by a perversion of its nature the Evangelicals were forced to have the deepest concern, for

[1] Said also to have given £20,000 annually to philanthropic causes for sixty years, Egremont was a powerful 'associate in the holy war', or sharer in Evangelical enterprises without being himself a truly religious man.

in these desperate circumstances of their country they saw in its Established Church the horrifying spectacle of religious leaders false to their charge. We shall see the 'mere nominal Christian' section of this church—everybody except the Evangelicals—divided into two kinds of presumed Christians, both kinds bad: what were known in Hannah More's phrase as 'good sort of people', and what were known in the phrase of Joseph Milner as 'false prophets and ravening wolves'. The members of the first group meant well and thought they were Christians. From the second group might be expected anything at all except piety. It was impossible to say which did the more harm. The Scribes and Pharisees were described by the Reverend Rowland Hill as 'the Regular clergy of the day', and his older sister Jane seems to have included both kinds of the Orthodox clergy and laity indifferently in her terse description of them as 'fat bulls of Bashan'.[1] It was clear to all Evangelicals that this was one institution of the Age of Elegance that had to be made over.

III

At the end of the eighteenth century there were many parishes in England—John Newton would have agreed—where the curate, or even the incumbent, was a kindly, moral and well-meaning man; with all the attributes of a Christian priest, Newton would have added, except Christianity. The English writers have given us many pictures of honest country parsons, if 'not at all heavenly-minded' at least 'of a more decent cast'. George Eliot's Mr Gilfil, for example, was born some time round 1762 and in his old age, when he was vicar of Shepperton, used to smoke very long pipes and preach very short sermons. 'You already suspect that the Vicar did not shine in the more spiritual functions of his office; and indeed, the utmost I can say for him in this respect is, that he performed those functions with undeviating attention to brevity and despatch. He had a large heap of short sermons, rather yellow and worn at the edges, from which he took two every Sunday, securing perfect impartiality in the selection by taking them as they came, without reference to topics; and having preached one of those sermons at Shepperton in the morning, he mounted his horse and rode hastily with the other in his pocket to Knebley'—where, as at Shepperton, if

[1] The Rev. Edwin Sidney, A.M., *The Life of Rowland Hill*, p. 33.

the sermon was not wholly audible it did not make much difference, as the congregation knew it about as well as the vicar did. '"We've had a very good sermon this morning", was the frequent remark, after hearing one of the old yellow series, heard with all the more satisfaction because it had been heard for the twentieth time.'[1]

Some of the bishops too in the eighteenth century seemed to be men of good will, and even virtue. The early pre-Evangelicals were indebted to the broadmindedness, or possibly the Christian love, of more than one of them. Scott, Newton, Atkinson and others got themselves ordained without formal training, Charles Simeon's diocesan Bishop Yorke was uniformly kind, or forbearing, Hannah More's friend Bishop Horne seems clearly an intelligent, good and pious man. At the beginning of Wilberforce's campaign the bench included Beilby Porteus, then at Chester, translated to London in 1787, and Shute Barrington, in 1791 and for long years after Bishop of Durham. Both were sympathetic and friendly, to the point of playing an extremely helpful if cautious part in the national reform, and Porteus seems to have been as close to an actual member of the group as he believed his office allowed.[2] Barrington is a fine example of the harmless and even meritorious clergyman who owed great preferment entirely to family interest. His father was Lord Barrington, his brother Lord Barrington was Chancellor of the Exchequer, and he was Bishop of Llandaff at thirty-one, having never had a parish, and translated to Salisbury and to Durham (where his predecessor was Thurlow, brother of the Lord

---

[1] *Scenes of Clerical Life: Mr Gilfil's Love Story.*
[2] Because Porteus was not a Calvinist some church historians have held that he was not an Evangelical. By that reasoning Thomas Adam of Wintringham, an open Arminian, was not an Evangelical, the leader of the Party was not an Evangelical, its great propagandist was not an Evangelical and Wilberforce's chosen parliamentary successor (Fowell Buxton) was not an Evangelical. Porteus was indistinguishable in politics and morality from the Evangelicals, was an extreme and wholly unqualified admirer of Hannah More, had as chaplain a noted Evangelical, John Owen, steadfastly opposed the good sort of people including his own clergy, steadfastly refused to take action against the Evangelical lecturers of his diocese though angrily attacked by the High Church clergy for not doing so, at once joined the Bible Society and was angrily attacked for that. It is true he gave preferment to Paley and other non-Evangelicals. If on that ground he was not an Evangelical neither was the Earl of Shaftesbury.

Chancellor). The case of Brownlow North is similar. A half-brother of Lord North, he was Dean of Coventry at twenty-eight, Bishop of Lichfield and Coventry at thirty-three and translated to Worcester and to Winchester. Lord North is said to have pointed out, with that cool humour the century is justly celebrated for, when Brownlow North's elevation was opposed because of his youth, that when he was older he might not have a brother who was prime minister.[1]

Bishop North was 'noted for the suavity of his manners and his elegant deportment'. Barrington was perhaps even more noted for such qualities. But if not spiritually eminent he was a superb example of the English gentleman become priest. Thoroughly good-hearted, he not only gave large parts of his fortune to moral and religious causes— £200,000, it is said—but was a moral and religious man. In so far as he had any theology, a church historian remarks, it was not strongly opposed to Evangelicalism, and he had a steady and large share in the great campaign. Apart from his high office he was particularly valued by the Evangelicals for his riches (he was wealthy himself and married two heiresses), his important connections, particularly at Windsor, and 'the sober magnificence in which he occupied his princely see'.

But there were not many such on the bench when Wilberforce set out, and there were many clergymen who were not like Mr Gilfil. The 'fox-hunting parsons' have often been described, who worked little and were likely to drink hard, and the absentee incumbents, pocketing as much church revenue as they could and leaving their parishes to wretchedly paid curates who officiated as seldom as possible. On Sunday mornings battalions of them, known as 'the gallopers', hurried off to perform hasty services in two or three parishes and few congregations, probably, were surprised at hearing the same sermon year after year, like Mr Gilfil's, perhaps cribbed in the first place from some preacher of repute. To publish volumes of sermons designed for just such a practice was one of the ways in which a clergyman could increase his income. It was carried to an ingenious length with great profit by at least one clergyman, the Reverend Dr John Trusler, who in 1771 established a business in 'abridging the Sermons of eminent divines, and printing them in the form of manuscripts, so as not only to save

[1] *Dictionary of the Living Authors*, p. 253, which also says Bishop North was 'the youngest prelate known to have been consecrated since the Reformation'.

clergymen the trouble of composing their discourses, but even of transcribing them'.[1]

If a clergyman had a family, no rich parish, no other income and did not wish to starve, it was a necessity for him to hold plural livings; and it soon became an accepted practice, recognized by the age in the most matter-of-fact way, to accumulate pluralities of parishes for the more pleasant purpose of amassing a comfortable livelihood. If a man could not get hold of a bishopric or other high church office, one of the fat rectories, a cathedral stall or other ecclesiastical sinecure, it was the only possible course of making a decent living. When Thomas Sedgwick Whalley, an important figure in the Blagdon Controversy of 1801 and 1802, went down from Cambridge, the Bishop of Ely, a friend of his father, gave him the living of Hagworthingham in Lincolnshire on the express understanding that he was not to reside, as it was considered very unhealthy for anyone but a native. Whalley hired a native, went to live in Somerset, and though married to a wealthy wife appears to have kept the living through more than fifty years of devotion to belles-lettres and the life of a country gentleman, until the very end of that time not paying the slightest attention to his parish. Few incumbents disturbed the unfortunate curates, unprovided with interest, who were everywhere. Arthur Young the agriculturalist pointed out that 'country towns abound with curates who never see the parishes they serve but when they are absolutely forced to it by duty: that several parishes are often served by the same person, who, in order to double or treble his curacy, hurries through the service in a manner perfectly indecent; strides from the pulpit to his horse and gallops away as if pursuing a fox'.[2]

'The clergy of the Church of England at that period (why should the painful truth be disguised?) were, as a body, lamentably defective.' This is an Evangelical clergyman writing in 1831. 'Some rose little higher than heathen moralists; and too many, though not obviously heterodox in their creed, were wholly secular in their spirit, exhibiting nothing beyond the frigid decencies of professional character, and utterly opposed to that spirit which determines to know nothing among

[1] *Ibid.* p. 355.

[2] *Autobiography*, pp. 421, 436; *Enquiry into the State of the Public Mind Amongst the Lower Classes* (London, 1798), pp. 22–3.

men but Jesus Christ and him crucified.... A person eagerly in quest of spiritual truth might have entered scores of churches in succession, without hearing a discourse which clearly set forth such topics as the lapsed and guilty and helpless condition of man by nature.'[1] When the lawyer Blackstone had heard all the celebrated London preachers 'he declared that not one of the sermons contained more Christianity than the writings of Cicero'. 'Mr Laurence Sterne, prebendary of York, published, a few weeks since, two volumes of sermons', Henry Venn, one of the foremost of the early Evangelical clergymen, wrote to John Thornton's sister Mrs Knipe of Clapham. 'They are much commended by the Critical Reviewers. I have read them; and, excepting a phrase or two, they might be preached in a synagogue or mosque without offence.'[2]

Under such conditions, the Evangelicals saw the Regular clergy as so ignorant of real Christianity or so indifferent to it as to present the terrifying spectacle of shepherds who would neither save their flocks nor be saved themselves.

An account of the spiritual state of the nation written in the early 1780's by Joseph Milner introduces the peculiar Evangelical distinction between ordinary bad clergymen and those 'of a more decent cast', and the basic Evangelical belief that as all true virtue must be founded on Christianity the advance in wickedness in England in the eighteenth century and the advance in 'infidel principles' are inseparably connected.

'Practice has grown as corrupt as principle. This must be the case. The preaching of morality is not God's appointed way of making men holy in their lives. It has a place, an extremely necessary place, in doctrine, but not a prominent one. Christ crucified is the chief Gospel-theme. Who does not see what an increase of wickedness has prevailed among us! Look at the Clergy. I would be tender in speaking of my brethren; but is there not a loud call for it, in charity? That sermons should be sold to them by a person advertising in the newspapers, is a flaming proof of the low state of their religious views and studies.... That we are a selfish, profane, licentious people, is evident. *The whole*

---

[1] S. C. Wilks, *Memoirs of the Rev. Basil Woodd* (1831), p. 19.

[2] *The Life...of Henry Venn*, by [John Venn and] the Rev. Henry Venn (New York, 1855), from the 6th London edition, p. 71 (June 1760). Cited as *Venn*.

head is sick, and the whole heart faint.'[1] 'It is an affecting consideration', Milner wrote in 1789, 'to reflect what a number of Clergymen there are, whose lives demonstrate them to be totally void of any religious sensibility whatever, with whom "to pray and to sermonize" is the same thing as to till the ground, or to navigate the seas, a mere secular trade, and unconnected with any concern for their own salvation, or that of the flocks committed to their charge.'[2] In Milner's second group too there was a considerable number, 'many Clergymen not at all heavenly-minded, though of a more decent cast'. To the mind of the Evangelicals these clergymen of a more decent cast were as harmful as the openly faithless, perhaps more so. Having the appearance of a truly religious man with no more of the reality than an infidel, it was a simpler matter for them to lead others into 'mere nominal Christianity' than for a vicious person to seduce others into following his example. 'O! it is awful to think what a sinner a man may be', Hannah More points out, 'and yet retain a decent character!'[3]

The spiritual torpor and fear of 'enthusiasm' of these respectable but not truly religious clergymen, probably a better testimony to the state of the Established Church than lurid examples of clerical neglect and pillage, is to be seen in the Charges of Archdeacon Paley, one of the most respected and rewarded clergymen of the century. Eminently of a more decent cast, the foremost spokesman of a sensible and reasonable religion, Paley's instructions, with their sober commonplaces and complete acceptance of the clerical office as a 'mere secular employment', show perfectly what the Evangelicals meant by the term 'mere nominal Christian'. In his diocese (Carlisle) it is evident that the clergy were not expected to be much concerned with the influences of the Spirit. A Charge on 'Amusements Suitable to the Clergy' is a peculiarly good monument to such priests. 'I have repeatedly said from this place, that if there be any principal objection to the life of a clergyman...it is this— that it does not supply sufficient engagements to the time and thoughts of an active mind.' That more than any other of Paley's beliefs might have struck the Evangelical clergy there at Carlisle in 1785, men whose complaint was always that there are only twenty-four hours in a day. One

---

[1] *Joseph Milner*, vol. VIII, pp. 190, 191.   [2] *Ibid.* p. 279.
[3] Hannah More, *Stories for the Middle Ranks of Society, and Tales for the Common People* (2 vols., London, 1818), vol. I, p. 285. Cited as *Stories 1818*.

subject to while the time away with is the study of natural history. 'As a mere amusement, it is of all others the most ingenuous; the best suited, and the most relative, to the profession of a clergyman.' Botany is 'an extremely important and entertaining part of the science of nature.... We most of us become gardeners or farmers. It is not for me to censure these employments indiscriminately, but they may be carried on (the latter especially) to such an extent as to be exceedingly degrading; as so to engross our time, our thoughts and our cares, as to extinguish almost entirely the clerical character.' To collect and read 'at least the elementary books upon the subject...is the precise thing which will dignify our employments in the field and the garden; and will give to both the appearance, and not only the appearance, but the real character, of an intellectual and contemplative, as well as of an active manual employment'.

Electrical experiments are satisfactory and useful, and the use of a microscope 'is also another endless source of novelty, and by consequence, of entertainment and instruction'. Astronomy is a proper and perhaps the most proper 'of all possible recreations to a clergyman', chemistry may be pursued at a very moderate expense and with advantage. Two articles of investigation were particularly useful in the diocese in which the archdeacon was speaking: the admeasurement of the height of mountains, and meteorological observations, such as the quantity of rain that falls in a year. 'There is no man of liberal education who need be at a loss to know what to do with his time.' Leisure need never be a burden; if we sink into sloth, it is our fault, not that of our situation.[1]

Those observations were made in the year in which William Wilberforce despaired of the republic because of its universal corruption. It is a pity that Paley took his duties with such sobriety, restraint and probably clear understanding of the capacities of his hearers, for he had a wit of the first order. When Pitt, just made prime minister at the age of twenty-four, came back to Cambridge for a visit and attended the university church, Paley suggested as a fitting text 'There is a lad here who hath five barley loaves and two small fishes; but what are they among so many'? It was reported, and the times were such that people saw no reason for not believing it, that he had 'actually preached the sermon'.

[1] *Works of William Paley, D.D.* (London, 1830), vol. VI, pp. 35–41.

The better kind of mere nominal Christian, the superior good sort of person and person of a decenter cast, is easy to recognize in the Evangelical descriptions. At Lord Muncaster's in Cumberland in 1818 Wilberforce met a Mr Morritt, 'very cheerful, unassuming, full of anecdote, and a good deal of knowledge—literary—of the old-fashioned Church of England religion, and high-spirited as to integrity, generosity, gratitude, friendly attachment, &c.' When Wilberforce adds, no cruelty intended, 'most kind to his family and friends', the account is complete. This man does not come up to scratch in any important respect. He is a 'better sort' of mere nominal Christian.

IV

While the clerical gentlemen whom Archdeacon Paley had sized up so realistically may have been working more severe harm to the cause of Christianity, those clergymen who were neither heavenly minded nor more decent in cast at least contributed to the corruption of manners and morals in a spectacularly offensive way. To the reformers (and to others) the Established Church exhibited everywhere lax morality, mercenary interest and actual bad practice if not actual moral corruptness. It was part, and a large part, of the ruling class's vested interest, its holdings enormous, its revenues of the most satisfactory kind, to any fortunate member or servitor of the great who had entered Holy Orders and whose family or 'patron' was powerful enough to get him into a lucrative office or amass handsome multiple holdings for him. Joseph Milner did not exaggerate the callousness with which the church was regarded simply as a means of providing for one's younger son or brother, tutor, secretary, schoolmaster or son-in-law, or, more simply, one's self. In this arena of avidity and complicated intrigue, great plums were to be contended for: the rich livings or clusters of livings, the golden cathedral stalls, lucrative deaneries, bishoprics replete with wealth and power—all, in the higher range, immediately or indirectly in the gift of the great or of some substantial institution or person, and the appointment to all of them in the higher range subject to the purest consideration of personal favour or political expediency, bestowed, with few exceptions indeed, without any regard to the capacity or merit of the receiver.

In this churchly drama the most vigorous efforts were naturally made for the disposal of the fattest prizes. The indecent rush to get esteemed livings or offices on the death of their holder, or often, when particularly desirable preferments were concerned, when the holder was dying or reported to be dying, was taken as wholly natural. In that scramble for more profitable places and additional emoluments the bishops, with few exceptions, were well in the lead. 'The hostility of the worldly part of our hierarchy to true religion is deep and inveterate', Zachary Macaulay, one of Wilberforce's right-hand men, wrote as late as 1818, and if he had been asked to name the unworldly part of the bench for the past thirty years or so only five or six names would have occurred to him. Some of these worldly prelates were amiable gentlemen, a few were scholars or men of intellect, a few had some kind of religious belief. Nothing could have been more idealistic than to expect any reform of the system from them. Invariably connected with influential people, in nearly every case they were members by birth of the great families or had been attached to one of them as tutor or secretary.

That spiritual situation is perhaps eloquent not so much in the handing out of ecclesiastical rewards by the great to their relatives, employees and tutors as in its unquestioning acceptance by the age as wholly proper. The great nobleman or influential politician who failed to look out for the clergyman he was connected with as a youth, or whom his sons were connected with, would have been thought of as uncivilized. 'To the honour of Mr Pitt it must be spoken', says *Public Characters*, 'that he has been duly sensible of the care taken of his rising years.' To think of that and many such statements of the age as ironic would be to misunderstand its ecclesiastical attitude. 'His instructors have received repeated marks of his acknowledgements. Dr Wilson, his first instructor, is now canon of Windsor; and one of his sons has a lucrative sinecure in Jamaica. The worthy Dr Turner is Dean of Norwich; Dr Pretyman has received the Bishopric of Lincoln, and the Deanery of St Paul's, and will, doubtless, not be overlooked in future promotions.'

No better account of this aspect of the Established Church in the eighteenth century could be wished for than that provided by the career of John Moore, described in detail in *Public Characters*. He was the son of a Gloucestershire butcher, or innkeeper, and educated at the Gloucester free schools. At Oxford he had 'no higher prospect before him than that of a country curacy, till one of those lucky circumstances happened, which sometimes occur in the great game of human life, and bring the obscurest individual to the most unlikely of all situations'. Given accidentally the position of tutor to the Marquis of Blandford, he was so much disliked by the boy's mother, the Duchess of Marlborough, that he had to take his place at the second table. When shortly thereafter she became a widow, the duchess had changed her mind about Moore and proposed marriage to him. 'Few men in Mr Moore's circumstances would have scrupled how to act on such an occasion. His prudence, however, made him foresee that no real good could well result to him from an acceptance of the proposal; and he accordingly declined it. This generous conduct endearing him to his pupil and the whole family, every exertion was made to promote his advancement in the church.'

The exertions were successful. The young duke made him an annuity and got him, as a beginning, a 'golden prebend' at Durham, with a 'valuable living'. He was then successively made Dean of Canterbury and Bishop of Bangor, a very profitable office, and when Cornwallis died in 1783, John Moore was raised to the throne of Canterbury. Lowth and Hurd had declined the office, and it was reported that both had recommended Moore. That story *Public Characters*, simple and forthright, saw no reason to accept. It was neither necessary nor likely. 'We are inclined to believe that the real fact is otherwise, and that his advancement to the primacy was the effect of the same patronage which first raised him in the church. Most undoubtedly he had not evinced any of those strong powers which could have produced so remarkable a predilection in his favour in the minds of his learned brethren.'

As Archbishop of Canterbury Moore was inoffensive and decorous. It was noticed, however, that with him 'generous patronage and friendliness to merit' were most lavishly exercised in his own immediate circle. The *Dictionary of National Biography* remarks that he 'appears to have dispensed his patronage with somewhat more than due regard to the interest of his own family'. It did not seem more than due regard to the mind of his century. 'Dr Moore no sooner began to taste the sweets of prosperity, than he eagerly hastened to communicate a portion of them to his family; and as he advanced in preferment, his attention to them was proportionately increased. This is an eulogy far more honourable than that derived from the most illustrious talents or the most splendid actions.' It was *Public Characters'* opinion that Moore had happily avoided a failing too frequently found in men of obscure origin who reached 'an elevation for which they were in no way prepared by family connexions', namely that of forgetting former friendships and poor relatives. 'He who rises superior to this common failing is a true philosopher, and worthy of our esteem.'

This story of the fortunate rise of Archbishop Moore was told in faithful detail in a biography written by his chaplain and published in his lifetime. To the mind of the Age of Elegance it was wholly admirable.

There was nothing novel in Moore's regard for the interests of his family. Archbishop Manners Sutton, his successor, 'showered preferment' on sons and sons-in-law; Moss, Beadon, Tomline, Sparke and others bestowed livings and offices in their gift lavishly on sons and nephews. The bishop whose son was not archdeacon or chancellor, with a prebendal stall or other lucrative sinecure, was a rarity. It would be wrong too to assume that bishops' sons were given all the prizes. Cleaver kept the bishopric of Bangor while Principal of Brasenose, Mansel was Master of Trinity and Bishop of Bristol, Majendie is said to have had eleven parochial preferments, and Bishop Watson of Llandaff probably outdid them all. His autobiography is a prolonged and bitter lament at the gross neglect that kept him from becoming a rich man; because of Pitt's callous political nominations and the king's stubborn dislike—George clung to the mistaken idea that Watson was a republican—he was never rewarded, in spite of what appeared to him unequalled merits, with one of the profitable bishoprics. Thirty years before his death he devoted himself to the life of a prosperous agriculturalist, keeping however his diocese of Llandaff, where he never resided, his professorship of divinity at Cambridge and the archdeaconry of Ely, while he 'was Rector at one and the same time of two parishes in Shropshire, two in Leicestershire, two in the Isle of Ely, three in Huntingdonshire, and seven in Wales'.[1] 'I thought that the improvement of a man's fortune by cultivating the earth was the most useful and honourable mode of providing for a family.'[2]

[1] G. R. Balleine, M.A., Vicar of St James's, Bermondsey. *A History of the Evangelical Party in the Church of England* (London, 1908), p. 18. Cited as 'Balleine'.

[2] *Anecdotes of the Life of Richard Watson, Bishop of Landaff, etc.* (London, 1817), p. 189.

V

Some years after the Evangelical reform had got under way an *Edinburgh* reviewer complained of a contemporary description of England by an American writer, deliberately one-sided, that showed only the unhappy conditions to be found in any large industrial country. 'Accustomed, as we have long been, to mark the vices and miseries of our countrymen, we really cannot say we recognize any likeness in this distorted representation; which exhibits our fair England as one great lazar-house of moral and intellectual disease—one hideous and bloated mass of sin and suffering—one festering heap of corruption, infecting the wholesome air which breathes upon it, and diffusing all around the contagion and terror of its example.' With allowance for 'the social evils always with us' probably most people at the time thought it as unquestionably an age of moral distinction as an age of great prosperity— a view held by the Evangelicals too, who saw that all English men and women were prosperous to whose station in life prosperity was fitting. Gilbert White wrote his *Natural History of Selborne* at the beginning of this age of universal corruption and William Hazlitt had 'had a happy life' by its end. It was the age of the Gurneys of Earlham, Horatio Nelson, Jenner, Cavendish, Humphry Davy and Charles Lamb; it saw the noble philanthropies of Howard and Romilly. Obviously it would be as preposterous to suggest there were no conspicuously moral Englishmen in 1785 as to suggest there were no conspicuously immoral Victorians. Thousands of eighteenth-century families lived sober and at least what they thought were pious lives, and in Victorian days the later Evangelicals found giant masses of moral corruption to work against (which it was easy for many of them to attribute to the fatal removal of Roman Catholic disabilities in 1829). There was probably a general improvement in the moral tone of English society up to something like the beginning of Pitt's ministry. A classic illustration is furnished by Walter Scott's story of his grandmother who toward the end of her life found herself blushing as she read in privacy a novel of Aphra Behn that she could remember having read aloud in mixed company when she was a girl. London street names provide examples of an increasing propriety. Codpiece Row next to Breeches Yard near Cold Bath Fields, later swallowed up in King's Cross Road,

41

became Coppice Row, an ingenious delicacy, during the century, and Black Mary's Hole north-east of it, near Merlin's Cave, lost its name altogether, at least on the maps, around 1790.[1]

Even then there was some reason for William Wilberforce to despair of the republic, and perhaps more reason than he knew. As the cause of all vice and sin is infidelity, the rapid moral decline in England at the end of the century, before the French Revolution, could be explained, it seemed to the Evangelicals, by one single, simple fact: the nation had fallen away from true religion. If a *second cause* was wanted, it was the spiritual failure of the Established Church. Others have felt it had some connection with the unwholesome wealth of the great, the corrupt constitution of Parliament, the unregulated Industrial Revolution, the violence of the working population at the time of the French Revolution and the harsh repressions of the great. In this society government took no responsibility for education or public health, almost none for the protection of the weak except a badly mismanaged parochial relief, and in practice next to none for public morals. Sober and orderly living was not likely to be promoted by the extremes of wealth and indigence of the new industrial system. In an age in which the most powerful word was the word Property, any social Christian attitude was likely to rouse alarm in the ruling class. This, a chief cause of the noble failure of John Wesley, led to a pervasive callousness toward human rights.

Four aspects of this society are particularly striking. The first is the contrast between the immense wealth of the great and the degrading indigence and squalor of a large mass of the 'lower orders'. The second is the shocking increase in crime and in savage legal punishment, though the criminal code was so barbarous that juries sometimes refused to convict even when evidence of guilt was clear (the bankers, for example, petitioning for the removal of the death penalty for forgery, as in cases involving small amounts juries were likely to acquit no matter what the evidence). A committee for investigating juvenile delinquency in 1816 claimed that over two hundred crimes carrying the death penalty were on the statute books.[2] The Evangelical clergyman Rudge mentions

[1] John Rocque, *Plan of London*, 1769. Chamberlain, *History of London and Westminster; A New and Correct Plan of London, Westminster, & Southwark, etc.* (1770).
[2] *Report of the Committee for Investigating the Causes of the Alarming Increase of Juvenile Delinquency in the Metropolis* (London, 1816), p. 21.

the execution of fourteen people in London in one week, and Charles Wesley once preached to a group of fifty-two men, including a ten-year-old boy, who were about to be executed.[1] Miss Martha More's journal called *Mendip Annals* mentions a village woman who was condemned to death in 1795 'for attempting to begin a riot, and purloining some butter from a man who offered it for sale at a price they thought unreasonable'.[2] 'When I was a lad', Samuel Rogers said, 'I recollect seeing a whole cartful of young girls, in dresses of various colours, on their way to be executed at Tyburn. They had all been condemned, on one indictment, for having been concerned in (that is, perhaps, for having been spectators of) the burning of some houses during Lord George Gordon's riots. It was quite horrible.—Greville was present at one of the trials consequent on those riots, and heard several boys sentenced, to their own amazement, to be hanged. "Never," said Greville with great naïveté, "did I see boys cry so."'[3] From 1817 to 1820 particularly, at the height of the dreadful period after Waterloo, crime and its punishment rose to terrible proportions. According to figures compiled and published by the *Christian Pocket Magazine* in August 1822, 5107 persons were sentenced to death in England in those four years and 427 executed.

The third striking aspect of this society during the early part of the Age of Wilberforce is the ruling class's fear of the lower orders, eventually a chief cause of the passing of the Reform Bill. More striking still, on greater familiarity, is the patience, or resignation, or moral serenity of some kind, with which even good-hearted members of the upper and middle classes were able to bear the manifest sufferings of the poor as necessary in a pre-established and unchangeable divine order. That religious view is seen in many people of the day whose belief in a divine order is otherwise hard to make out.

This was the Age of Elegance. Looking about him in the Brighton Pavilion the Prince Regent, an unfortunate person trained from youth

---

[1] Balleine, p. 15.

[2] *Mendip Annals: or, A Narrative of the Charitable Labours of Hannah and Martha More in their Neighbourhood. Being the Journal of Martha More*, edited, with additional matter, by Arthur Roberts, M.A. (London, 1858), p. 167. The fourth edition (1861) is cited here.

[3] *Recollections of the Table-Talk of Samuel Rogers*, pp. 183–4.

in the practice of assorted vices, a little gilded over by good nature and some of the outward bearing of a gentleman, would have thought that was a very proper name for it. So would the faro queens and petits-maîtres. Mr Turveydrop would have agreed. The surviving rips and rakes would have thought so, and the proprietors of the gaming clubs, Harriette Wilson and her colleagues and clientele, probably Rundell the goldsmith who died leaving one and a half million sterling. John Thornton the Russia-merchant, founder of Evangelical reform, did not think so, neither did its leader who despaired of the republic because of the universal corruption that taking its rise among the rich and luxurious had spread its destructive poison through the whole body of the people. That description of England that the *Edinburgh Review* objected to would not have seemed distorted to Wilberforce and John Newton, for a reason different from its writer's. To the Evangelical way of thinking it was true that England was a festering heap of corruption. It was only too clear that it was a hideous and bloated mass of sin and suffering. The shocking thing was that any other view could be held by Christian men. Indeed that the *Edinburgh* reviewer did hold another view was evidence that he was not a truly Christian man. He had the complacent ignorance of a mere nominal Christian. He was blind to the *best interests* of his countrymen.

CHAPTER 2

THE MOSES OF THE ISRAELITES,
A COURTIER OF PHARAOH

All armed prophets have conquered, all unarmed have been destroyed.
MACHIAVELLI

I

That state of the spiritual life of England had at least brought about one circumstance that could be useful to new leaders of a movement of national reform if they were level-headed and practical. At the end of the century they had directly before them not only the inspiring example of two great religious reformers but their giant errors. It would have been hard to overlook those errors and fantastic, in any sensible person, to repeat them. That the Evangelicals did neither made the difference between complete failure as a more gentlemanly continuation of the Wesleyan Revival and the success they won—qualified as it was, great nevertheless.

There is no wish here to undervalue John Wesley's contribution to the quickening of English spiritual life. But when Wilberforce, seeing the corruption and profligacy, the destructive poison, that had culminated in the Age of Elegance, set out on his divinely appointed mission to reform the land, George Whitefield had been dead nearly twenty years and Wesley had four years to live. Merely to observe that the Methodist Revival had then been preached for half a century is enough to make the point that no matter what he accomplished, Wesley left very much to be done. The simplest examination of his Revival shows why that was so. It was designed to appeal to the wrong people. Wesley's mission was 'chiefly to the poor', what he did was 'in the meeting, and amongst the multitude'. In terms of national reform in eighteenth-century England such a mission and such an accomplishment was not only not enough: it was hopeless.

Wesley's blunder was his conviction that one soul is as good as another. There is a spiritual way of looking at this matter and a practical way. Wesley chose the wrong one. It was not a morally reprehensible choice, but if one has in mind large and permanent results in national reform there is nothing commendable about it. In the course of the Revival, it is true, thousands of English men and women, almost all of the middle and labouring classes, were converted to Christian belief and conduct. Who were converted by the converted Methodists? In what way were they fitted to prosecute the reform of their unconverted fellow-Englishmen? By what power and influence did they exert social authority over the rest of the nation? How were they capable of appealing successfully to the ruling class that by its authority and example so largely prescribed the morals of the country?

It may be admirable, in some abstract manner, that to the mind of Wesley, John Fletcher of Madeley and their associates it was as good to rescue from sin and infidelity a miner, orange-girl or cobbler as a banker, great merchant, duchess, East India magnate or Member of Parliament. If one is planning on the reform of a nation such as England in the eighteenth century it is not admirable at all; it is mere folly. It shows a heart concerned only with the love of God and his creatures, a true wish to serve God without thought of worldly necessities, a resoluteness to compromise and to accommodate his word to no one, a spiritual disregard of all the values of this world. By virtue of just such qualities and in the most obvious way, indeed by definition, how unworldly, how impractical, how fruitless! How certain to accomplish nothing in a campaign of national reform!

At the end of the century Methodism had been preached, in the ways of Wesley, Whitefield and Selina Lady Huntingdon, for sixty years. Who were the people of influence, authority and social power in the Methodist connections in 1800? There was a large body of followers of Wesley, a smaller body of Whitefield's Calvinists, still fewer followers of Lady Huntingdon. Some of them, probably many, were respectable and respected, sober, orderly and pious. But such qualities are not enough. At the end of the century the Methodists had almost no representation in Parliament and no place in government. They had no members among the great landlords and few, if any at all, in the peerage or lesser ranks of titled persons and in the country gentry.[1] They had next to no members among the great merchants, traders,

[1] Virtually all (if not all) titled persons who had been Methodists and were living when Wilberforce's campaign got under way became Evangelicals.

bankers and other financial people and moneyed commoners. And with no influence, no interest, no patronage, no social authority and no funds, they had deliberately set themselves up in opposition to that Established Church without whose active co-operation a reform of the nation was a sheer impossibility.

'The Clergy are less powerful from their rank and industry than from their *locality*', William Cobbett wrote in May 1802, at the height of the Blagdon Controversy. 'They are, from necessity, *everywhere*; and their aggregate influence is astonishingly great. When, from the top of any high hill, one looks round the country, and sees the multitude of regularly distributed spires, one not only ceases to wonder that order and religion are maintained, but one is astonished that any such thing as disaffection or irreligion should prevail. It is the equal distribution of the clergy, their being in every corner of the kingdom, that makes them a powerful and a formidable corps.'[1] Cobbett was an enemy of all that is good and true, in the Evangelical belief, a supporter of evil in many forms and a recognizable emissary of Satan; but he was probably right about that. It can also be categorically asserted that no Evangelical who is on record during this period questioned the determining influence of the great, for better or worse, on the morals of the nation, through the church and by their own example and authority. There seems in fact to be no expressed belief at all opposed to the belief that the middle class and the poor imitated the manners of their superiors. One aspect of those manners was peculiarly easy to imitate, the depravity of their superiors. 'It is only when the nerve of virtue is relaxed among the great, that the contagion of vice descends with accelerated violence among the imitating multitude', says a decidedly non-Evangelical source.[2] That an example of virtue would operate similarly was universally accepted. The most formal and elaborate statement of the principle is contained in the manifesto of the Evangelical campaign, Hannah More's *Thoughts on the Importance of the Manners of the Great to General Society*. It is stated over and again in the moral writings of the age and long after it. 'It should be a very serious reflection to those who occupy the higher ranks of life', says a mid-Victorian spiritual handbook for District Visitors, 'that their influence and example, by

[1] Melville, *Life and Letters of William Cobbett* (1913), vol. I, pp. 156-7.
[2] *Public Characters* (on Sir Robert Peel), vol. VI, pp. 38-9.

a natural tendency, descend to the lower ranks, thus making them to an untold extent, responsible for the character and habits of those beneath them.'[1]

That being a matter of knowledge to all reflecting persons, there could not be a difference of opinion among practical men setting out to reform the morals of England over what their attitude toward the church, and toward the great, should be. We see why the Evangelical leader in a remarkable passage in his diary thanked God for having kept him from becoming a Methodist (and why the confusion of Methodist and Evangelical has caused such serious misunderstanding). No reform movement could succeed unless it could make use, by proselytizing, of a working section of the Established Church and of the ruling class. After the experience of John Wesley it would have been folly indeed to set out on a seriously intended moral reform without accepting that stubborn and intractable fact. If the Evangelicals had made one mistake here, they would have done little or nothing worth recording. They would have done much less than Wesley instead of going on from where he left off.

Being the practical men of affairs that they were, the reforming commanders at no time thought of doing anything else. From the earliest days of the campaign to its end, it was steadily clear to them that success could come only by a practically formulated appeal to the socially powerful. Visionary Methodism, Arminian and Calvinistic, rigid, inflexible, unworldly, scorned such a thing as earthy until it had so constituted itself that it could not have adopted it if it had wished to do so. John Wesley said to his preachers, 'You are no more concerned to have the manners of a gentleman than a dancing master'. To the great Evangelicals such a statement would have been incomprehensible.

In 1825 the Reverend Edward Irving, not Evangelical,

delivered a sermon on the missionary character which startled everybody.... Irving chose for his theme the history of our Lord's sending forth the twelve, without gold or silver, without scrip or purse, without shoes or staves, and he held up the twelve as an example for missionaries.... He seemed going back to the days of Francis of Assisi.... He said: 'I remember in this metropolis to have heard it uttered with great applause in a public meeting, where the heads and leaders of the religious world were present, "If I were asked what

---

[1] Mrs Sewell, *Thy Poor Brother* (London, 1863), p. 33.

was the first qualification for a missionary, I would say, Prudence; and what the second? Prudence; and what the third? I would say, Prudence." Money, money, money is the universal cry. Mammon hath gotten the victory, and may triumphantly say (nay, he may keep silence, and the servants of Christ will say it for him), "Without me ye can do nothing".' Irving threw prudence to the winds, and cared not a straw about money; with wild aberrations of genius he had something of the old Hebrew prophet.

What did the Evangelical leaders think of that? 'He did a courageous deed that night, but most of his hearers looked on him as mad. I distinctly remember deliverances to that effect uttered by some who were distinguished amongst Evangelical ministers, as leaders of opinion and main pillars of our religious societies.'[1]

In a second vital matter too, a sensible 'accommodation' was obligatory. To the error of John Wesley, George Whitefield added an almost equally serious error. The soundest practical criticism of the kind of Christianity known as High Calvinism was uttered when Charles II observed, 'Say what you will, it is no religion for a gentleman'. Charles was right. It is true that gentlemen have been known to be Calvinists, and it may be true (particularly in the long run) that it is better to be a Calvinist than a gentleman. But in the late eighteenth century at any rate the class of gentlemen were temperamentally and by all their training at considerable odds with Calvinism. A powerful form of Christian belief, its peculiar doctrines are of an outwardly forbidding nature, and some of them not only outwardly. Hardly any one has gone beyond Calvin in establishing Christian doctrine in a true light rather than a pretty one. John Newton was using a good Calvinistic figure when he wrote to Wilberforce, about the troubled state of the times in 1797, 'I trust we are like Noah in the ark. I think his voyage was not very *pleasant*, but he had the comfort of knowing he was *safe*.'[2] There have been few kinds of Christianity that in their pure form are less adapted to be successfully brought to persons of the cultivated rational formality and abhorrence of fanaticism, the polished worldliness of morals and manners, the temporal power and great self-respect,

[1] John Stoughton, *History of Religion in England*, vol. vii, pp. 378–9.
[2] *The Correspondence of William Wilberforce*, edited by his sons Robert Isaac Wilberforce and Samuel Wilberforce. Revised and enlarged from the London edition (2 vols., Philadelphia, 1841), vol. i, p. 138. Cited as *Correspondence*.

self-esteem and general satisfaction with their world, of the English ruling class of the eighteenth century.

In John Wesley's anti-Calvinistic, Arminian scheme of Christian matters there was plain language too, for unheavenly minded creatures of the Gentile world; but it was not of the seemingly sombre and harsh cast of the whole of Calvin's thinking, and it did not require the rigorous acceptance, by an uncompromising act of faith, of an extreme set of views that on the face of them celebrate an unjust and unmerciful God. To Wesley's mind, Christianity did not hold that by nature and because of the Fall mankind was wholly evil. A Calvinist held of mankind that 'Whether Greek or Barbarians, wise or ignorant, bond or free, the bent and disposition of their minds, while unrenewed by grace, is black and implacable enmity against the blessed God'.[1] Wesley did not believe that by unconditional and irrevocable decrees man was doomed to everlasting torture unless he had instead been chosen for salvation by an act of the Deity that had no reference to his merits (and could have none, as until it had been performed he had no merits). It was not, in Wesley's system, impossible for any sinner to be saved; the mercy of God was extended to all. In the High Calvinistic faith, those who had not by a purely arbitrary act been elected could never receive salvation.

There is no wish here to argue that Calvinism is or is not the true teaching of the Scriptures, but only to indicate that in a century in which the upper classes honoured common sense and sobriety and condemned extremeness and fanaticism, it was no religion by means of which to try to convert them into taking part in the reform of the country. It was not opposed to the rank, wealth or privileges of a gentleman, though that too was not understood at the beginning of the Evangelical campaign; but to his tastes and modes of thinking it was greatly more antagonistic than sober Anglicanism. It was also much less suitable for 'accommodation' to social necessities.

II

Wesley made no attempt to convert the great until it was too late, Whitefield made none and if he had done would have offered them a religion uselessly antagonistic to their accepted mode of existence. It

[1] *Newton*, vol. III, p. iii.

appeared for a while that the new reformers could fall into both of those errors. The early clerical leaders of the group that came to be known as the Evangelical Party were greatly influenced by Whitefield and in a broad way by Wesley, virtually all of them were Calvinists, and their talk about wealthy, obviously 'useful' people was full of sentiments of a harmful kind. 'What miserable work it is to preach at the rich', Rowland Hill exclaimed, and some such remark is common in the writings of the Party clergy before the leadership of Evangelicalism had come into the hands of laymen.[1] This is particularly true of the older clergy bred in the full eighteenth-century manner, many of them closely associated with Wesley or Whitefield. 'Give no way to any conciliatory schemes, which vainly attempt to unite the interests of God and Mammon', Joseph Milner exhorted true believers.[2] Converted from mere nominal Christianity to true religion around 1770, Milner constantly expressed this embarrassingly wrong attitude toward the great. 'Can riches feed the immortal spirit? Do we not see the more men have of them, the more greedy they are after filthy lucre?...The health of the soul is holiness, conformity to God.—This your wealth would be so far from promoting, that it would hinder it exceedingly.'[2] In 1754 Henry Venn the elder, assuming the curacy of Clapham at the age of twenty-nine, wrote to Wesley asking from him 'a personal charge, to take heed to feed the flock committed unto me'. 'And if you consider, sir, the various snares a curate is exposed to, either to palliate the doctrines of the gospel, or to make treacherous allowances to the rich and great, or at least to sit down well satisfied with doing the least, more than the best, among the idol shepherds—if you consider these things, you will not, I hope, condemn this letter, as impertinently interrupting your noble employment.'[3] 'In 1759 Venn "accepted a living unexpectedly offered me by my very affectionate friend, the Earl of Dartmouth";...throughout his curacy he had been constantly grieved at the obstinate rejection of the gospel during five years by almost all of the rich (and there were still very few poor in the place)...'. Forty years later there were still 'very few poor' in Clapham, but nearly all the rich, not driven off by that attitude of the early Evangelicals, had joined to make Clapham for a time the heart of the Evangelical reform.

[1] Sidney, *Life of Rowland Hill*, p. 73.   [2] *Joseph Milner*, vol. VIII, p. 191.
[3] Quoted in J. Telford, *A Sect that Moved the World*, pp. 19–20.

Henry Venn became a shining light among Evangelical clergymen of the eighteenth century, but his later letters too show how great a change had to take place before progress could be made among useful people. 'I took my children to see Harewood House; but how little, how despicable is the superb mansion, and all that pomp can procure, if the Builder of all things is Himself unknown! My children were much pleased with the great man's toy; whilst Mr Marshall and myself could unfeignedly thank the Lord, who had been pleased to provide so much better things for us.'[1]

This point of view is constantly met in the writings of the older, un-worldly, school of Evangelical divines, and once in a while of those who lived into the early nineteenth century. 'We are sometimes temp-ted to accommodate the representation of evangelical truth to great hearers', the Reverend Robert Storry said, on this vital point, at a meeting of the Eclectic Society as late as April 1806. 'But—*I am the voice of one crying in the wilderness.* My business is with the middle and the poor.'[2] After the death of the Reverend Thomas Scott, Wilberforce wrote to his son John Scott about the good old Calvinist's many valu-able qualities, in particular his admirable financial unworldliness. Among the 'Christian principles which shone most conspicuously in his character' was 'his generous contempt of this world's wealth in comparison with those heavenly treasures on which his heart was supremely set. He conceived it to be peculiarly the duty of a Christian minister to be a pattern of disinterestedness, and to render it clear that he was governed by higher motives than those of worldly gain or advancement.—It may be an illustration of this part of his character, that, in opening his heart to a friend on the marriage of one of his children, he expressed his gratification that the lady had little or no fortune.'[3]

Such sentiments are praiseworthy, and good when unworldly think-ing can be afforded. But it is noticeable that Joseph Milner's brother

[1] *Venn*, p. 117.

[2] *Eclectic Notes*, edited by John H. Pratt, M.A. (2nd ed., London, 1865), p. 386. (These are Josiah Pratt's notes of the Eclectic Society's meetings.)

[3] John Scott, A.M., *The Life of the Rev. Thomas Scott* (London, 1822; 9th ed., revised 1836), p. 420. This long and interesting letter, which describes Wilberforce's great indebtedness to Scott, is not printed in *Wilberforce*.

The Moses of the Israelites

Isaac 'never met with any person who resembled him in...an extreme ignorance of the ways and manners of mankind in their ordinary intercourse with each other,—and an utter and absolute rejection of disguise in all its shapes.'[1] It was all very well for Milner to be 'gladly heard by the common people' and for Robert Storry's business to be with the middle and the poor. Milner and Storry did not have to lead a moral campaign in which success depended on the attraction of substantial numbers of the powerful. William Wilberforce, the most important figure of the Evangelical world and a man of large wealth, married an heiress.

This is a point so weighty that the reform cause could not afford a mistake about it (and so obvious there is no need to belabour it). If it adds up to saying among other things that no 'unaccommodated' clergyman, of the Milner–Venn–Storry sort, would do as a leader or even prominent representative of this movement, it would be unjust to the Evangelical clergy of this early period not to note one service they did perform without which the Evangelical cause would have failed. For practical purposes their attitude toward the great was harmfully wrong. But in the beginning their attitude toward religion too was harmfully wrong. Though it was not clear enough to some of them—in a few cases throughout the campaign—the simplest common sense demanded that their Calvinism should be *accommodated*. A pure unadulterated religion of such outward ferocity could not suddenly be thrown at people such as those who constituted the English ruling class. It was even questionable if presenting such a religion to them at all, no matter how gradually and subtly, was the best way to entice them into a great reform movement.

In any case, there was good precedent for not presenting all of Calvin in a lump, including, for example, the explicit belief that only a tiny remnant of all human beings who are born will be saved, the rest being condemned to everlasting torture, that remnant consisting of an Elect chosen without the use of the divine foreknowledge and with no regard to their goodness or piety, which are qualities they could not have until they had been chosen. Only as a matter of good sense and without any consideration of Evangelical expediency, several of the soberer Calvinistic divines of the Party—among them Thomas Scott, John Newton

[1] *Joseph Milner*, vol. VI, p. lxiii.

and Robinson of Leicester—saw that such Christian truths must be disclosed very gradually; a practice, Scott held, established by St Paul himself. 'Indeed they are not at all proper subjects to insist on, when we preach to...newly awakened persons....Let it not then be thought *carnal policy* to adapt our discourses to the occasions and wants of the hearers, while nothing inconsistent with truth is spoken, nothing profitable held back.'[1] It is true that to some this seemed a watering down of the pure milk of the Gospel. Joseph Milner and other veteran Calvinists probably would not have agreed that such a thing was not carnal policy. 'A great trust is indeed reposed in us, *the everlasting gospel of Jesus Christ*. We are to set it forth...in its primitive purity, and to make no deductions or concessions on account of the fashions of the times.'[2] In a sermon on hell and its punishments Milner made a particular point of the probability that Jesus ('in practice at least') has no pity for eternally tortured sinners,[3] a part of the Calvinistic doctrine that probably cannot be thought of as well suited to attract a pleasure-loving duchess or a successful member of the financial world (to mention no other kinds of people).

There is a difficulty here that might well have seemed insurmountable. If all the Evangelicals of John Newton's persuasion had been like him the problem would have been simpler. This remarkable man, whose heart brimmed over with abounding good will for his fellow human creatures, is one of the surely very few known Calvinists who did not insist that everybody else had to be a Calvinist. He held to all of Calvin, as a personal necessity that he could not get along without; but if someone else was a vital Christian in another way, it made no difference to Newton what theological label he applied to himself. 'Though a man does not accord with my views of election, yet if he gives me good evidence that *he is effectually called of God*, he is my brother: though he seems afraid of the doctrine of final perseverance; yet if grace enables him to persevere, he is my brother still.'[4] Elsewhere Newton says the same thing more vigorously: he would not walk the length of his study to convert such a brother.

As he was unique among the Evangelicals in that respect, however, the difficulty was great, for while it is easy to be a Calvinist, and

---

[1] *Life of Thomas Scott*, p. 443.   [2] *Joseph Milner*, vol. VIII, p. 435.
[3] *Ibid.* vol. VII, p. 10.   [4] *Newton*, vol. VI, p. 199.

probably easier not to be one, it is not so much hard as impossible to be part of one. 'If you mean by a rigid Calvinist', Newton wrote, 'one who is fierce, dogmatical, and censorious...I hope I am no more such a one than I am a rigid Papist. But as to the doctrines which are now stigmatized by the name of Calvinism, I cannot well avoid the epithet rigid, while I believe them: for there seems to be no medium between holding them and not holding them.'[1] Such a medium had to be found, just the same, and the process was begun at an early point in the period by Henry Venn. Soon after the end of the century, the 'Evangelical religion' had been adequately stated. The early rigorous view passed gradually into a happy blending of the incompatible positions, and shortly came to be a really felicitous reconciliation of irreconcilables, after a fashion that has also been thought to have been established by St Paul.[2] The road to heaven is no tortuous path but a noble highway, a Roman road, straight, elevated and unmistakable; *panta ta anagkaia estin dela*,[3] all things needful are obvious; difficulties should quite simply be disregarded. William Romaine, Joseph Milner and Henry Venn, unaccommodatable Calvinists, were dead before the end of the century. Soon Charles Simeon at Cambridge, the 'Old Apostle', could say openly he was now Calvinist, now Arminian: 'I am free from all the trammels of human systems';[4] and the Party's great publicist Hannah More held 'no doctrine that is *exclusively* Calvinist'. The Reverend Legh Richmond had managed for himself '*a modified Calvinism*, remote from all objectionable extremes' that seems to resemble closely the 'curious and beautiful mean between Arminianism and High Calvinism' he described in another practical religionist;[5]

[1] *Ibid.* pp. 245–6.

[2] 'He exhorts as if he were an Arminian in addressing men. He prays as if he were a Calvinist in addressing God and feels no inconsistency in the two attitudes. Paul makes no attempt to reconcile divine sovereignty and human free agency, but boldly proclaims both.' A. T. Robertson, *Word Pictures in The New Testament* (New York, 1931; itself a fine Evangelical exegesis), vol. IV, p. 446, on Philippians ii. 12.

[3] *Venn*, p. 415.

[4] William Carus, *Memoirs of the Life of the Rev. Charles Simeon, M.A.* (2nd ed., London and Cambridge, 1847), p. 563. ('You well know that though strongly Calvinistic in some respects, I am as strongly Arminian in others.') This book will be cited as *Simeon*.

[5] T. S. Grimshawe, *Memoir of the Rev. Legh Richmond, A.M.* (4th ed., London, 1837), pp. 96, 63.

Thomas Robinson, Thomas Gisborne and many other respected Evangelical ministers were 'moderated' or 'modern' Calvinists evading some, most or all of the harshest of the basic tenets; the leader of Evangelicalism denied he was a Calvinist while not subscribing to High Church Arminianism; and in this gradual process John Newton the old slaver had been made to look ingenuous. His belief that there is no medium between holding the Calvinistic doctrine and not holding it was right, but there was nothing else to be said for it.

Once matters were organized and basic principles understood, there was no difficulty about a sensible attitude toward the great. To offend potentially valuable people because they happened to have wealth, rank, position, authority, power, in other words immense use for reform, was at once seen as no way to act, when laymen had assumed the Evangelical leadership. The practical wisdom and desirability of the great strategy was questioned, in the recorded body of Evangelical writings, public and private, of this period, one solitary time, and that in a mild and tentative way. 'If ever the success of the Bible Society could have been doubtful', the Rt Hon. Nicholas Vansittart wrote to Isaac Milner in April 1813,

the events of the past year must have placed it beyond dispute, as far as public opinion and extensive patronage can decide it. I am, however, sometimes, a little disposed to reflect on the situation of the Church under Constantine; and to ask myself whether so much imperial and royal patronage will really promote the simplicity and godly sincerity in which alone the cause of a Society like ours can prosper. We have, however, to look to our own hearts, or rather to Him to whom all hearts are open, that our internal improvement may correspond with our external splendour. The Society is becoming every day a more powerful instrument of good; and it will be our own fault if we do not fully participate in the blessings which it is the instrument of conveying to others.[1]

That momentary doubt stated by an Evangelical Chancellor of the Exchequer does not appear again in the Party's literature, and 'little Van' does not seem to have distressed himself further about the church under Constantine. After all, the British and Foreign Bible Society's

---

[1] *The Life of Isaac Milner, etc.*, by his niece Mary Milner (London and Cambridge, 1842), p. 558. Cited as *Isaac Milner*.

external splendour—that is, its patronage by the great—and its becoming every day a more powerful instrument of good were hardly unconnected. It is the absolute foundation of the Evangelical success that that fact was clear to realistic leaders. One mistake about this matter, one decision to rest the reform of the nation on simplicity and godly sincerity, would have been enough. The Evangelical 'reform' would have consisted of another handful of Calvinistic divines and a few congregations in the middle ranks. Wesley had relied on simplicity and godly sincerity.

Still another fact of vital importance had to be seen clearly. The attitude of Milner, Venn, Storry and many others of the early, unworldly, Evangelical clergy was doubly wrong. What Henry Venn would write in a private letter about the country gentleman who became the Earl of Harewood he would say openly. To offend needlessly the class represented by this man would if carried far enough be fatal to a national reform. But it was wrong too in a profounder sense. No human being was in a position to know that Edward Lascelles of Harewood might not himself become a truly Christian man. To hold otherwise was the height of spiritual arrogance. If such a man needed only instruction and guidance, perhaps, to bring him from a nominal High Church religion to true religion, what could be more fantastic than to set out by reproaching him with his superb country seat?

In a sermon on the death of John Thornton, Thomas Scott, pointing out that Thornton 'observed a strict frugality in his expences', which would not offend anyone and needed no amplification, could not keep from adding that Thornton did not consider it 'necessary for him to live in that style, which those that are distinguished by titles, or high offices, deem requisite to their rank and character; and he had no relish for parade and magnificence'.[1] How unnecessary, how wrong, how harmful! If Thomas Scott feared the love of money, there were resolute (and virtuous) Englishmen who did not. Why should it be thought that only those who have no title, no high office, no rank, no position, no wealth, no influence, no power for reform, can be Christians? Only a few years after that funeral sermon hundreds of Evangelical English-

---

[1] *Theological Works, Published at Different Times, and Now Collected into Volumes.* By Thomas Scott, Rector of Aston Sandford, Bucks. Printed for the author (Buckingham, 1805, etc.), vol. III (1807), p. 54.

men living in a style requisite to their rank and fully relishing one degree or another of magnificence (of a sober kind; 'not more than I believe God himself approves of', the Reverend Charles Simeon said of his own) were showing that a rational avoidance of apostolic poverty is in no way opposed to serious religion, puritanical morality and reforming fervour. Many of the recognized Evangelical leaders lived in such a style as a matter of deliberate policy, if they were financially able to do so (and nearly all of them were), to make it plain to the upper ranks that Evangelicals were not 'methodistical' but respectable and substantial. At the very time Scott wrote those words Sir Richard Hill was testifying, in Parliament and whatever other conspicuous place he could manage, that the profession of the staunchest Evangelicalism was fully consonant with wealth, rich hospitality, the complete tone of the great (barring a distressing religiosity) and the possession of the most beautiful of the smaller country seats in England. Such sentiments as those of Venn, Milner, Storry, Scott and other early divines are not to be found in the preserved writings of any leader of the later, accommodated, 'useful' Evangelicalism, lay or clerical, and there are repeated expressions of exultation over the handsome establishment, 'great affluence', 'vast fortune', and the like of many a chosen vessel as it was realized that a true spiritual radiance may be quite in harmony with the rich gleam of gold.

An example or two of the later, 'useful', Evangelical attitude may help to make this matter as simple, clear and uncontrovertible as it is. In 1827 William Wilberforce paid a visit to Wentworth House. 'No visit gave him greater pleasure', his biographers say. This was not a stronghold of true religion and there were reflections he would like to make 'at some future opportunity', he wrote to his son Samuel; 'I will now only say it is quite a palace, and the whole apparatus in proportion. The domestic chaplain, a truly good, and from age a venerable man' (how could Wilberforce say more clearly, in his gentle way, that this clergyman, like the great earl himself, was a mere nominal Christian?) 'told me that they dined daily in the servants' hall about seventy-six of Lord Fitzwilliam's own household.'...'Lord Fitzwilliam is all benevolence; really there is a seraphic benignity about him.'...'The old gentleman, (gentleman I may truly term him, for a finer gentleman cannot be conceived,) has behaved to us with an unaffected, unassuming friendliness, that at times has brought tears into my eyes.'[1] The man whose leadership of Evangelical reform had made him years before 1827 the foremost moral citizen of the world did not think of Wentworth House as a great man's toy, neither would he have assumed, as Henry Venn did, that one of the great country gentlemen was a 'confirmed castaway' (in the happy phrase of a later Gentile, Wilkie Collins).

In 1814 the Reverend Legh Richmond after preaching at Knaresborough for the Church Missionary Society, one of the most powerful of the Evangelical reforming agencies and one of the most violently opposed by the idol shepherds, 'started for Harewood....The Earl's family...were all present in the beautiful church, and after service the preacher [that is, Richmond] was invited to dine with them, a compliment which he hoped betokened some good-will to his cause, which he understood had not before been regarded with favour.' The cause of the new good will is soon apparent. This is how Evangelicalism worked. The rector of the parish is the Earl of Harewood's nephew—'an estimable character', Richmond describes him, 'breaking out into an honest, ardent, fearless profession of religion'.[2] Richmond would peculiarly understand this High Church rector who was 'becoming religious', as he himself had been 'converted' after he had entered into Holy Orders.

That there was a constant danger here goes without saying. In these procedures, no matter for what great end, there is an assumption of grave risks, perhaps not wholly calculated. In this element of the high strategy there had to be the finest discrimination; for every potentially useful person always a consummate suiting of the treatment to the occasion. De Quincey, whose mother was a good Evangelical and who knew about these matters, left a superb account of an opening talk on religious concerns between Hannah More, whose 'approach' Wilberforce always spoke of with admiration and Christian envy, and Mrs Siddons, at the end of which the great actress, who thought she was a Christian, had no idea that to Mrs More's mind she was thus far (humanly speaking) a doomed creature.

What approach, for instance, what attitude, toward the Prince Regent? Of course a condemnation of the manifold and outrageous

[1] *Wilberforce*, vol. v, pp. 279–81.
[2] The Rev. Charles Hole, *Early History of the Church Missionary Society for Africa and the East* (London, 1896), p. 571. Cited as 'Hole'.

vices (which does not have to be expressed) is to be combined with a perfect respect for the office. But the situation involved more than that. Vicious and debauched, to human eyes irredeemable, his country's foremost confirmed castaway, George had in the most obvious way the greatest possibilities for good. No more than a single episode is needed to show how correct the Evangelical thinking was in this matter. In 1815 Wilberforce spent the winter in Brighton. He was well known by then as the Evangelical commander-in-chief. In Brighton was the Regent's Pavilion, and the Regent, and his excessively Gentile entourage. The prince and the Duke of Clarence 'too very civil', Wilberforce's private diary says (from him a strong condemnation: they had both opposed the abolition of the slave trade). 'The Prince came up to me and reminded me of my singing at the Duchess of Devonshire's ball in 1782, of the particular song, and of our then first knowing each other.' 'We are both I trust much altered since, sir', Wilberforce said. 'Yes, the time which has gone by must have made a great alteration in us.' That kind of change was not what Wilberforce meant. 'Something better than that, too, I trust, sir.' 'He then asked me to dine with him the next day', Wilberforce's conversational memorandum goes on, 'assuring me that I should hear nothing in his house to give me pain.'

'The Prince Regent has done himself great credit by the respect, I had almost said reverence, with which he has behaved to Mr Wilberforce, at Brighton, where both have passed the winter', Hannah More wrote to J. S. Harford of Bristol in February 1816. 'His invitations to him to dinner were incessant; finding him often evading them, he assured him that he should never hear a word at his table which could give him a moment's pain. He kept his word. He went frequently, and was on the whole much pleased....It is pleasing to see how consistency in religion ultimately beats down all hostility. Oh that it were more frequently seen in religious people!' 'The papers told us—not your honours—but those of the Regent', she wrote to Wilberforce, '—for surely he never did himself so much credit as in seeking your society; and though it does YOU no good, yet it will do good in too many ways for me to specify.'[1]

Let us specify one of the ways. Of course Wilberforce's example of

[1] *Wilberforce*, vol. IV, pp. 277; *More*, vol. III, pp. 444–5.

religious consistency would strengthen others; but Mrs More had a far greater 'use' than that in mind. On the death of the old insane king this man would be George IV. His name at the head of the list of officers of the London Female Penitentiary testified to the respectability of Wilberforce's lieutenants who were directing that and scores of other Evangelical institutions. But beyond that, this man was the head of the Established Church. Who could tell what 'use' he might provide?

In the summer of 1814, a year and a half before the Brighton episode, a young clergyman and second cousin of Wilberforce, Charles Richard Sumner of Trinity College, Cambridge, went on a Continental trip in charge of two sons of the Marquis of Conyngham, the elder, Lord Mount-Charles, an undergraduate of his college. In Geneva they met a professor of surgery, M. Maunoir, and his young daughter. Sumner became engaged to this girl and married her in January 1815. It was believed he had taken the step to prevent Mount-Charles from marrying the girl and that his extraordinary career was wholly due to the gratitude of Lord and Lady Conyngham.[1] They were in a position to be of some service to a young clergyman, as Lady Conyngham was the Regent's mistress. In 1820, when George came to the throne, the marquis introduced Sumner to him at the Pavilion. Between 1821 and 1826 he was made historiographer to the king, the king's private chaplain at Windsor, vicar of St Helen's, Abingdon, a canon of Worcester Cathedral and a canon of Canterbury, chaplain in ordinary to the king, and Deputy Clerk of the Closet. In 1826 he was made Bishop of Llandaff, holding at the same time a prebendal stall and the deanery of St Paul's, and in December 1827, Charles Richard Sumner was translated, at the age of thirty-seven, to Winchester. The last of the prince-bishops, he held that immense and immensely lucrative see for forty-two years. And this man was an Evangelical. At the end of his tenure

[1] S. Baring-Gould, M.A., Hon. Fellow of Clare College, Cambridge, *The Evangelical Revival* (London, 1920), pp. 263–5; Lady Charlotte Bury, *The Diary of a Lady-in-Waiting* (London, 1908), vol. II, pp. 218–19 (this 'gossip', which gives the story in a still less attractive form, adds (in 1820) that Sumner had been promised a bishopric); Charles Greville, *A Journal of the Reigns of King George IV and King William IV*, edited by Henry Reeve (London, 1874), vol. I, pp. 45–6 (this describes the prime minister Lord Liverpool's threatened resignation on the first attempt of the king to give high preferment to Sumner; 'the man was only a curate, and had never held a living at all'); G. W. E. Russell, *Seeing and Hearing* (London, 1907), p. 201.

of Winchester he had named Evangelical clergymen to almost every office and every living of the huge territory that was in his gift, and he was influential in 1828 in the elevation of his brother John Bird Sumner, an Evangelical, to the diocese of Chester and twenty years later to the archbishopric.

The total absence of Evangelical shame, regret or even embarrassment that one of their clergymen was raised to the bench in such a fashion is perhaps in itself a kind of indication of the strongly practical nature of this reform movement.

III

Calvinism is no religion for a gentleman, the reform of a nation socially dominated by the great can be attempted in no more hopelessly ineffectual way than by methods repellent to the great. In 1785 that was tantamount to saying, among other things, that the leader of a national reform could not be a Methodist or dissenter (or like them), a member of the lower ranks, or a clergyman. The Evangelical clergy were in fact disqualified on several counts. In the early days of the campaign almost none of them came from the upper classes and almost all of them were unaccommodated Christians. To a lack of the manners suitable to a gentleman they were likely to add an inflexible assurance of their Christian rightness and their opponents' error that seems often to accompany the Calvinistic faith and is hardly ingratiating. Let us suppose for an instant that the leadership of Evangelicalism had been assumed by Thomas Scott. He was an admirable, faithful man, scrupulous and steadfast. He had an earnest conviction of the Evangelical truth, solid intelligence, a deep basic integrity. Without any formal training he had made himself the most learned of the Evangelical divines. How could such a man, of 'low' origin—he had been a shepherd in Lincolnshire—externally harsh and uncouth, without polish or suavity of manners and still less any desire for them, carry a successful appeal to the great? He was also a firm if slightly 'modern' Calvinist, he had a conspicuously wrong attitude toward wealth, and like Joseph Milner he was strongly marked by 'ignorance of the ways of men and an absolute rejection of disguise'.

There were still other peremptory disqualifications of a clerical leader. While these religious men of the eighteenth century were devoted and zealous, with many of the qualities of the admirable dissenters (from whom most of them were hardly distinguishable except by actual adherence), their attitude toward their religion was uncompromising and their presentation of it unyielding. They had no talent for accommodation. For one thing, their antagonism to the Regular clergy was not only bitter but undisguised and expressed publicly, often, and in no conciliatory way. From pre-Evangelical days the demarcation between clergymen and pious clergymen was a chasm. The Regular clergy were either Archdeacon Paley Christians or venal characters of the Gentile world; the Evangelicals were true shepherds, 'gospel-preaching' ministers; in the gulf between there was no resting place. Between false shepherd and true shepherd there was nothing.

The Evangelical clergy's outspokenness about that awful difference was a cause of deep resentment and active hostility. It seemed to the Evangelicals a dreadful perversion of true religion that the Regular clergy should believe there was a connection between 'a strict moral correctness of conduct' and 'a real conversion of the heart to God'. That confusion—pointed out again and again with explicit reference to the idol shepherds—was 'the destruction of vital Christianity'.[1] A further practice seemed even more, to the High Church group, the very essence of spiritual arrogance. It was clear to the Evangelicals that their opponents even of a decenter cast were not Christians at all. 'In this place, where I now am,' Henry Venn wrote from Helmsley (he was visiting John Thornton's brother-in-law Conyers who was preaching twenty-one times a week), 'the Lord Jesus has a Church; and many souls, who were lost and dead, have been called, by Sovereign Grace, to partake of eternal life, in the precious Saviour.'[2] It would have appeared to a High Churchman that the Lord had several churches in Helmsley; not so to the Evangelicals, for it was their belief that among the High Church clergy there were very many (or could it be all?) who had 'presumed to enter upon the work of the ministry while a stranger to true religion'.[3] Consequently the Party, particularly their clergy, always spoke of a mere nominal, High Church, Christian who had

[1] The Reverend C. E. Kennaway, *Funeral Sermon...on the Death of Sir John Kennaway*, p. 28, note.
[2] *Venn*, p. 118.   [3] *Christian Observer*, November 1816, p. 691.

become an Evangelical as having been 'converted'; and the happiest form of such an occurrence was the 'conversion' of a clergyman of the Established Church. For all of them it had to be hoped, in charity, that they could have an 'experience', 'the illumination or conversion of a minister who had been walking in darkness'.[1] Such an event gave rise to as much joy in the Party as the conversion of a merchant prince, a duke of the royal blood or a great industrialist. Virtually all the death notices printed in the *Christian Guardian*, one of the best Evangelical periodicals, describe the conversion of their subject after he had been a member of the church for years. The Orthodox *Christian Remembrancer* indignantly cited an obituary of the Reverend W. Fanshawe according to which Fanshawe, pictured as blameless and actively charitable, did justly for thirty years after he entered Holy Orders, loved mercy and walked humbly with his God—'and at the end of that period *was converted*'.[2]

From an early point in the campaign the words 'religious', 'sincere', and 'pious' were used by the Evangelicals to designate Evangelicals only. When Wilberforce spoke of 'religious men', he meant men of his Party; 'true religion' meant Evangelical religion. Archbishops Moore and Manners Sutton were not 'truly religious' men, or 'religious men'. Bishop Tomline's religion was not 'true religion'. 'Sincere' and 'serious' men were not High Churchmen. When Legh Richmond described the nephew of the Earl of Harewood as 'breaking out into a profession of religion' he had not forgotten he was the rector of the parish. When Mrs De Quincey wrote to tell her son Henry that Sir James Stonhouse's *Assistant* was a very valuable book and a group of 'religious clergymen' had printed a thousand copies of it[3] she was uttering no tautology, and there was none in the name of the Society for the Relief of Poor, Pious Clergymen.

How could an upper class devoted to sense, reason and propriety respect men in Holy Orders who publicly referred to nineteen-twentieths of their fellow priests, including with special emphasis their Lords Spiritual, as Scribes and Pharisees, fat bulls of Bashan, priests walking in darkness? But the bitterness of their antagonism to High

[1] *Christian Observer*, November 1816, p. 691.
[2] *Christian Remembrancer*, July 1819, pp. 432–7.
[3] Alexander H. Japp, *De Quincey Memorials* (New York, 1911), vol. I, p. 226.

Church and their zeal to advance true religion had led many of the early Evangelical ministers into another serious error—enough in itself to show their unfitness for the direction of this movement. A good number of them, including many who regretted it, had not hesitated to extend their ministry beyond the bounds of their parish. This 'itineration', a defiance of the discipline of the church, was itself an unmistakable sign of 'enthusiasm'. It was all very well for John Berridge's parish to include six counties if only a general diffusion of religion in the middle and lower ranks was intended, and for Rowland Hill to preach wherever people would listen to him though not licensed. It was no way to bring to vital Christian belief and participation in the nation's reform *those who count* and who abhor fanaticism.

A short view of the only Evangelical senator in England when William Wilberforce entered Parliament will make clearer some of the qualities required in the leader of this movement. It must have been believed by more than one of the 'serious' people of the 1780's that they had found a leader when Sir Richard Hill entered public life. Hill was richly endowed. His (Evangelical) biographer, the Reverend Edwin Sidney, points out his great merits with affection and respect, and truthfully. He was 'a layman of birth and fortune', with 'boldness, firmness, integrity and disinterestedness', 'devoted piety and honest patriotism'. 'The amenity and polish of his manners, the benignity of his heart, the uprightness of his intentions, were acknowledged even by his opponents....In all essential points of character, he was a model of a Christian gentleman and an upright Senator.'[1] Those claims are correct, and they were admirable qualifications. But in still other respects the Party could not have wished for a better leader. Hill's family was 'distinguished and ancient' and his country seat Hawkstone in Shropshire was considered one of the handsomest in England.[2] Thus conspicuously of the upper class, Hill also had, and in a spectacular manner, the beaming good humour and happy joyfulness so greatly esteemed by the Evangelicals as testifying that 'religion was falsely accused of

[1] The Reverend Edwin Sidney, A.M., *The Life of Sir Richard Hill, Bart.* (London, 1839), p. vii.

[2] Dr Johnson said it 'should be described by Milton'. There are extensive descriptions of it in Sidney's *Life of Sir Richard Hill* (pp. 4 ff.) and in Pückler-Muskau's *Tour of a German Prince* (London, 1832).

generating moroseness and gloom', that is, that Evangelicals were not 'methodistical'. 'He adopted a style of living suitable to his station in life, and his table had all the characteristics of the most refined and generous hospitality, admirably tempered with the exemplary moderation belonging to his profession of religion.'[1] 'He was one of the very few who had the courage, in the midst of the rank and fashion with which his situation, style of living, and fortune, surrounded him, to declare that he was not ashamed of the gospel of Christ, and of its faithful and despised ministers.'[2]

Furthermore, in his politics Hill struck precisely the right note. His constant care was to show that Christianity is 'the firmest pillar of the state, and the Bible the surest guide to national prosperity, happiness, and order'.[3] With a natural conservatism that was of course an important factor in winning respect, by a simple Evangelical attitude he was always on the right side. Like Wilberforce, he had no politics but always supported the government when he could conscientiously do so, which was on virtually every occasion. The Evangelical Scriptures were clear on the point of obedience to constituted authority, the ministry like the king was in office in accordance with God's will. On parliamentary reform in particular Hill was right in exactly the right way, steadily opposed to significant reform and always in favour of 'moderate reform', which Wilberforce was to call 'very moderate reform', namely that which would 'take the wind out of the radicals' sails' without changing anybody's political status very much.

How well suited this man was, in so many respects, for a leading position in the nation's reform! 'The revivalists of the day hailed his election with the sincerest joy', Sidney says, and it cannot be doubted, 'for they knew that neither the fascinations of courtly society, nor hope of the honours and emoluments of place, nor the notice of the great, would induce him to deviate in the slightest degree, from those principles which the grace of God had rooted in his heart.'[4] 'When with a humble heart and single eye, much fervent prayer for wisdom from above, and a truly Christian walk before God and man, you do all

[1] Sidney, *Life of Sir Richard Hill*, p. 277.
[2] Sidney, *Life of the Rev. Rowland Hill, A.M.* (this was Richard Hill's younger brother) (London, 1834); cited here is the third American edition (New York, 1835), p. 148.   [3] Sidney, *Life of Sir Richard Hill*, p. 331.   [4] *Ibid.* p. 277.

things, what may you not effect for God and your country', Hill's friend Jonathan Scott, a Calvinistic itinerant, wrote. 'I have a hope... that God has in mercy for some such a happy purpose raised you up in our sad day and sinful land, and given you rank, and riches, abilities, and influence, and grace, and put you in Parliament, that you might have the honour of standing in the gap, and by your Christian example, wisdom, and counsel, and fervent prayer, turn away that wrath which is already gone forth...and so be an instrument in His hands of saving a guilty land from ruin.'[1]

That pious expectation was reasonable, though not fulfilled. Sir Richard Hill's merits were so outstanding that it is worth while seeing clearly why he would have made so impossibly bad a leader. 'In the House of Commons, he avowed his motto to be *Pro Christo et Patria*, and always desired to conduct himself...as a Christian senator. No man was ever more thoroughly divested of all fear of the ridicule of the world; and if at times he unnecessarily exposed himself to it, he acted upon an honest principle....This was the cause of his occasionally giving vent to a flow of natural humour, which it would often have been more prudent to have restrained.' He 'was not ashamed to quote in the senate, from what he denominated "a now-a-days obsolete book called the bible", nor ever lost an opportunity of publicly avowing his religious opinions'.[2] In the upper classes of that day 'vital piety', says Sidney, writing in 1831, 'called forth expressions of dislike scarcely credible in this century'.[3] Hill's quotations from the 'obsolete book' were met with jeers and 'prolonged roars of laughter'. A composed and stubborn man, like the older Puritans in more than one respect, Hill went tranquilly along his way, iron-willed and immovable. His first duty as he saw it as a Christian senator was to introduce religious sentiments on all occasions; his second to introduce legislation against vice and infidelity. His maiden speech was in support of a bill for the observance of the Lord's Day. He then tried unsuccessfully to institute a tax on corks, shot, powder, guns and pistols, on prints, printed music and visiting tickets, on theatres, operas, play-houses, masquerades, cards, dice, horse races, magazines, Sunday newspapers and particularly Sunday travel. Actors should be compelled to take

[1] *Ibid.* p. 280.   [2] *Life of Rowland Hill*, p. 148.
[3] *Life of Sir Richard Hill*, p. 80.

out licences and the tax on masquerades such as those popular at Ranelagh and Vauxhall was particularly desirable on moral grounds. It would tend to prevent people who professed to be Christians from 'spending hours, and even whole nights together, in scenes and occupations...where for the most part, the whole of the entertainment consists in seeing and hearing whatever tends to gratify and draw out the evil propensities of the heart.'[1]

Let us say that is true. Where is the 'usefulness' in introducing religious sentiments on every occasion, to make them an object of derision? In larding every speech, no matter what the subject, with scriptural texts, a comic violation of good manners? In obstinately introducing and fighting for measures that have no conceivable chance of success? In selecting as the object of moral legislation sins, vices and worldly enjoyments four out of five of which are those of the upper classes only? Hill's blunt speech and bull-like tactics, his persistent flaunting on all occasions of a tasteless religiosity that only seemed amusing, his unaccommodated Calvinism—all such things that publicly manifested his eccentricity—were unworldly, unrealistic and childlike.

Hill did some good for Evangelicalism in the House. He showed that a truly religious man need not be sour, bigoted and morose, and his lavish hospitality and style of living made it clear that a believing Christian could be a gentleman of wealth and family. Apart from his religious obstinacy he had the manner of the great, and apart from a reforming morality his views were always correct. It was Sir Richard Hill who pointed out during the 'scarcity' of 1800, a period of terrible distress in the lower orders, that it is much better to have a dearth of earthly food than a famine of the word of God.[2] Such things are bound to be noticed. When Hill retired from Parliament in 1806 he had won the respect of many members. But he had only won respect for himself as a courageous Christian gentleman, and to be an upright and courageous Christian senator was not enough. It did not make Evangelicals out of *those who count* or move them to share in the Evangelical reform of England. A great reform movement can be better served than by Sir Richard Hill's uncompromising crudeness.

It was a belief of nearly every Evangelical that even the slightest

[1] Sidney, *Life of Sir Richard Hill*, pp. 283, 295–9, 354–6, 359, 361.
[2] *Ibid.* p. 472.

happenings in the affairs of men are acts of an immanent God protecting
or chastising his people—chance, fortune, luck and accident being
terms of the Gentile world alone. A few Evangelicals believed God's
hand is to be seen only in major happenings, such as concern the fate of
nations. No Evangelical doubted that William Wilberforce had been
redeemed, brought forward, sustained and guided, the obvious leader
of the Party from the moment of his conversion, by explicit act of
Providence. It may seem to some that that view makes the Deity a
perhaps too Evangelical figure, not only rigidly opposed to the High
Church theology, which is probably reasonable in the circumstances,
but acting more than once with a prudence and worldly expediency
not usually thought of as characteristic of divinity. In any case, making
out below the surface the management of this campaign, observing
Wilberforce's patience and judgment, sure tact and deftness, his sensitive and always right estimates of the proper time for any measure and
its chances of success, his resoluteness but at the same time his unparalleled talent for *accommodation*, one may wonder if any other cause
like this had such a commander, perfect through his weaknesses as
through his strength. As this frail, blithe, seraphic little man who moved
ceaselessly about London doing good through more than a third of a
century looked back with his genuine humility over years of incredible
accomplishment, it was impossible for him, at any rate, to doubt that
the divine power had always directed him.

From the time of his second birth to his retirement from Parliament
in 1825, no meeting to establish this moral cause or suppress that
immoral cause was complete unless Wilberforce appeared on the platform to address what the newspapers would call in a day or two the
'noble and respectable gathering'. At the anniversary meetings of the
great Evangelical societies in the London Tavern or Freemasons' Hall,
packed with cheering Evangelicals drunk with the triumphs of their
cause and the increasing possibility that not England alone but all the
world would become truly religious, as his crippled little figure
appeared people would feel their hearts moved simply at the sight of
his face, beaming with tenderness and good will and Christian benevolence. Then the magnificent eloquence, the most moving, winningly
persuasive speech in England, always spontaneous—how could
Wilberforce find time to prepare anything?—lively, witty, bright,

vividly animated by the highest religious principle, brimming with sympathy for those involuntarily destitute of Christianity, and with no word ever of condemnation or even censure, except perhaps, and then in sorrow, for those intractably opposed to the good, such as atheists, blasphemers, infidels, malcontents, radicals and other enemies of Evangelical truth. In private society there was always the warm hand-clasp, the rich vivacious talk, the charm and good humour and good-heartedness, the unaffected playfulness, with genuine love for all people of good will, and always, steadily, the Evangelical morality and the Evangelical piety. When friends saw the frail body worn with un-resting activity it is not surprising that they thought of him as not of this world. As Hannah More said of her more sainted friends, such a one might be on his way to heaven, Wilberforce was there already.

No idea of his activities can be given in a reasonable space. What he could do was incalculable, no one else could do it, and for thirty-eight years he turned tirelessly from one moral and religious project to another, forming, organizing and directing, with gentle persistence and unrelenting pressure. There was the huge task of abolishing the slave trade and after that slavery itself on British soil. In the nearly forty years of his life spent at it there was probably no month, very likely no week, when he was not engaged on other Evangelical matters. There was the Bible Society, the Church Missionary Society and the intro-duction of missionaries into Africa and India and the East and their support there; there was the London Society for the Promotion of Christianity Amongst the Jews, the Proclamation Society Against Vice and Immorality, the School Society, the Sunday School Society, the Climbing Boy Society, the Bettering Society, the Irish societies, the Vice Society. His work on Abolition and in the anti-slavery societies seems the work of a crowded lifetime. He was active in thirty societies for other purposes, or forty, perhaps fifty. Then there was the multitude of topics connected with public philanthropies of all conceivable sorts—provided they somewhere, somehow, had Evangeli-cal 'use': for the manufacturing poor, Blücher's soldiers, French refugees, foreigners in distress, sick strangers, Irish serving-girls and many more. As the Evangelical reform grew to massive proportions there were hospitals, fever institutions, asylums, lying-in homes, in-firmaries, refuges and penitentiaries. There was the publication of religious propaganda and there was Mrs Hannah More's school system in the Cheddar Valley; there was the suppression of irreligious propaganda and the fight against irreligious education, and the prosecution of infidels, blasphemers, atheists and radicals such as Carlile and Mrs Carlile, Hone and Shelley, and the prosecution of brothel-keepers, purveyors of obscene prints and obscene objects, operators of illicit dance-halls and private theatricals, and prostitutes, and Sabbath-breakers. There was the Christian care of orphans, vagrants, juvenile mendicants, youthful sinners and aged saints, distressed widows, poor pious clergymen, poor degraded females, persons imprisoned for small debts, infirm gentlewomen who had seen better days. Let us add to all this that when the Slave Trade Act of 1807 made him the nation's leading Christian philanthropist there was probably no benevolent or reforming project at all that was not brought to his attention, and probably not a week of his life passed without appeals for help from private persons he had never heard of. With a correspondence so burdensome he could seldom catch up with it, to the end of his public life the loss of a single hour seemed a catastrophe.

This life was perhaps unique in dedication and selflessness among people similarly situated during this age. Wilberforce alone of Pitt's young supporters of 1784 received no sinecure, held no office, had no pension and was not raised to the peerage. William Cobbett estimated his fortune at £30,000 a year and in 1797 he married the daughter and heiress of 'an opulent merchant at Birmingham, with whom he obtained a handsome fortune'.[1] But his name is on the subscription lists of some seventy Evangelical societies, his private charities were constant and there are not many biographies of Evangelical clergymen of the day who needed help that do not mention gifts from him. How much he gave beyond that to build churches to which Evangelical clergymen could be presented, to buy advowsons for the introduction of Evangelical clergymen into previously High Church livings, to send young candidates for the Evangelical ministry to Cambridge, to help such projects as Mrs More's schools, will probably never be known. Contributions of that kind are described, or discreetly hinted at, many times in the contemporary Evangelical literature.

[1] So *The Dictionary of the Living Authors*, p. 385. Barbara Ann Spooner's father is usually described as an opulent banker.

One part of the activity of this unresting life was not extempore, the whole complex of things contributing fundamentally to *the best interests* of the English people: the conversion of *those who count* to true religion, furthering the cause in all possible ways in Parliament and through his friendship with the prime minister, placing Evangelicals in key positions in the church, forcing the nomination of Lord Harrowby's brother to the bench of bishops, getting the Duke of Gloucester elected chancellor of the University of Cambridge, helping 'serious' young men and 'serious' clergymen, helping always with the establishment everywhere of more and still more auxiliaries, associations and branches of all kinds of the Bible Society and the Church Missionary Society, the Newfoundland Society and Hibernian Bible Society and dozens more: writing, proselytizing, organizing, uniting, guiding.[1]

IV

The hand of God was clearly evident in his early life, Wilberforce thought, though his home was not truly religious. When his father died in 1768 he lived for a while with an appointed guardian, his uncle William Wilberforce of Wimbledon, who had married a sister of John Thornton of Clapham.[2] Like Thornton, this woman was a follower of

---

[1] In 1811 Louis Simond (*Journal of a Tour and Residence in Great Britain*, Edinburgh, 1817, vol. II, pp. 209–10) saw Wilberforce in the Commons. 'Another little man, as thin as a shadow, and drawing one side of his body after him, as if paralytic, hurried across the floor with a tottering brisk step, and awkward bow, and said in substance, that schools in Ireland were most desirable, and should be organized by all means. These few words were extremely well spoken, with peculiar energy of feeling, and in a manner graceful and impressive. This was Mr Wilberforce. Nothing can surpass the meanness of his appearance, and he seems half blind.'

Wilberforce's eyesight was bad from his youth (his household always included a professional reader), and in later life his head was sunk down on his chest. In 1818 Robert Southey describing him as a domestic man saw 'such a hilarity, sweetness and benignity...that all sense of his grotesque appearance is presently overcome, and you can feel nothing but love and admiration for a creature of so happy and blessed a nature'. Taken with the Wilberforce we see in the cartoons of Gillray, whose likenesses were famous, these descriptions suggest that the familiar portraits of Wilberforce in middle life or later may have been very much idealized.

[2] We come here to the intricate relationship and intermarriage of the Evangelical families, an important factor of their solid unity. John Thornton's son Henry was

George Whitefield.[1] Her Calvinism soon made such an impression on the boy that his mother came to London to rescue him. In Hull he was taken to the theatre 'almost by force'. 'I might almost say, that no pious parent ever laboured more to impress a beloved child with sentiments of piety, than they did to give me a taste for the world and its diversions.' For three years at St John's College, Cambridge, a wealthy man by the death of his grandfather and to all appearances a child of the Gentile world, Wilberforce wasted his time with tutors who encouraged him to do so. In 1780, at twenty-one, he stood as representative of Hull and was elected, at a cost of £8000.

In London he became a close friend of William Pitt, supported him in the House, and set out on the usual life of well-disposed, wealthy young men of the day, dining out, gaming, going to the theatre and opera. His first known connection with true religion after his boyhood came on 7 December 1783 when he heard de Coetlogon at the Lock Chapel. At the hospital and asylum devoted to the help of women

Wilberforce's closest friend after the death of Edward Eliot, M.P., who married William Pitt's sister Harriot. Joseph and Isaac Milner were distantly connected with the Wilberforces. Wilberforce's aunt Judith married John Bird, a brother of Wilberforce's mother Elizabeth Bird Wilberforce; Judith's daughter Hannah Bird married the Reverend Robert Sumner and was the mother of John Bird Sumner, Archbishop of Canterbury, and Charles Richard Sumner, Bishop of Winchester. John Bird was a brother of the wife of Abel Smith, whose sons were Abel, Samuel and Robert (Lord Carrington). Abel Smith's daughter married John Sargent, a favourite disciple of Charles Simeon at Cambridge; their daughters married George Ryder, Henry Edward (Cardinal) Manning, and Wilberforce's son Samuel. Samuel Wilberforce was at one time in the school of the Reverend George Hodson, who was the Reverend Lewis Way's chaplain; Hodson was married to a niece of James Stephen, who married Wilberforce's sister, who had first married the Reverend Thomas Clarke, vicar of Trinity Church in Hull (on whose death Wilberforce canvassed the Corporation and got the vicarage for Joseph Milner; *Wilberforce*, vol. II, pp. 227–8); Wilberforce married a daughter of the Evangelical banker (or merchant) Spooner of Birmingham, Mrs Wilberforce was a cousin of Lord Calthorpe.

[1] When Wilberforce's official biographers, his sons Robert Isaac and Samuel, describe that relationship by saying that Mrs William Wilberforce of Wimbledon 'kept up a friendly connexion with the early methodists' we are given the first of very many uncandid statements in their work, the product of a wish to minimize, or even to conceal so far as they could, their father's adherence to the Evangelical Party, which they thought of as a schismatical and objectionable sect. They could hardly not have known that Mrs Wilberforce was a devout Calvinistic follower of Whitefield.

sufferers from venereal disease, this chapel was especially dear to the Evangelicals. In the same month he dined with Sir Charles Middleton, the naval officer who stopped cursing and blasphemy on his ships and did not allow work on Sundays in the Portsmouth Navy Yard. His name has been noted in the Poor, Pious Clergymen Society. It seemed to Wilberforce later that these were manifest signs of the watchfulness of Providence, even though in February 1784 Mrs Siddons 'sung charmingly' and he danced till half-past four at Lady Howe's ball. In that year, during Pitt's fight with the Coalition, Wilberforce, still only twenty-five, carried a loyal address to the king in Yorkshire against an immense Whig interest, went on to stand for the county and was chosen.

The hand of Providence was still clearer when in 1784 he went on a trip to the continent with Isaac Milner, a younger brother of Joseph. He had not known that Milner was 'evangelical'; if he had known it, he wrote, 'it would have decided me against making him the offer: so true is it that a gracious hand leads us in ways that we know not, and blesses us not only without, but even against, our own plans and inclinations'. 'It was with no small surprise that I found on conversing with my friend on the subject of religion, that his principles and views were the same with those of the clergymen who were called Methodistical.' On a second trip with Isaac Milner in 1785 an acquaintance meeting Wilberforce was surprised to find he thought it wrong to go to the theatre, or travel, on Sunday. 'Milner, though full of levity on all other subjects, never spoke on this but with the utmost seriousness, and all he said, tended to increase my attention to religion.' We find then in the diary for October 1785, 'As soon as I reflected seriously upon these subjects, the deep guilt and black ingratitude of my past life forced itself upon me in the strongest colours, and I condemned myself for having wasted my precious time, and opportunities, and talents.' A period of spiritual agony followed. 'For months I was in a state of the deepest depression, from strong conviction of my guilt. Indeed nothing which I have ever read in the accounts of others, exceeded what I then felt.' He read Pascal and went to hear 'Henry Forster at St Antholin's'.[1] 'My heart is so hard, my blindness so great, that I cannot get a due hatred of sin, though I see I am all corrupt, and blinded

---

[1] This was Henry Foster. Wilberforce often misspelled names and several of them remain uncorrected in the *Life*.

to the perception of spiritual things....' 'I thought seriously this evening of going to converse with Mr Newton', he wrote for 20 November, and on 4 December did go. 'Was much affected in conversing with him.'

As John Thornton attended Foster and had brought Newton to London it is not hard to make out how Wilberforce happened to go to them, and no guessing is needed about the feelings of John Newton the old African blasphemer (as he liked to call himself) at seeing this young man come to him. 'He told me', Wilberforce wrote, 'he always had entertained hopes and confidence that God would some time bring me to him.' 'He now spent several hours daily in earnest study of the Scriptures; he took lodgings in the Adelphi, that he might be within reach of pastoral instructions which simply inculcated its truths; and he began to seek the friendship of those who feared God.'[1] 'You may easier conceive than I can express the satisfaction I had from a few minutes converse with Mr Newton yesterday afternoon', Thornton wrote him from Clapham later in December. 'I am aware of your difficulties, which call for great prudence and caution.' The difficulties were the possible effect of his conversion on his political career. But by the early part of 1786 it was apparent that his career was not to be primarily political. Even earlier, he had begun to notice with pain the lack of religion of his acquaintances. It was in August 1785, in a letter to his friend Lord Muncaster, that he touched on the point at the heart of the Evangelical Movement. 'It is not the confusion of parties, and their quarrelling and battling in the House of Commons, which makes me despair of the republic...but it is the universal corruption and profligacy of the times, which taking its rise among the rich and luxurious has now extended its baneful influence and spread its destructive poison through the whole body of the people. When the mass of blood is corrupt, there is no remedy but amputation.'

In the spring of 1786 he returned to Parliament a new-born man, his conversion from mere nominal Christianity soon a matter of

---

[1] This careful, deviously worded sentence is also a good example of the biographers' attempt to delete Evangelicalism from their father's life. There was nothing of a religious nature *per se* about the Adelphi's situation. It was impossible for the young Wilberforces to say that as there were no 'truly religious' clergy in or near Wimbledon their father took quarters in easy reach of Cecil, Romaine, Newton and Foster in the City.

knowledge among his friends. Before the end of the year that conversion was bearing fruit. 'I hope great usefulness to the public, and in the church of God, will be your present reward', Newton wrote in November. 'To you, as the instrument, we owe the pleasing prospect for an opening for the propagation of the Gospel in the Southern Hemisphere. Who can tell what important consequences may depend on Mr Johnson's going to New Holland? It may seem but a small event at present: so a foundation-stone, when laid, is small compared with the building to be erected upon it; but it is the beginning, and the earnest of the whole.' In October Henry Venn wrote that he had received a letter from 'dear Mr Thornton, saying that he, the last Sunday, introduced Mr Samuel Johnson to two hundred and fifty of his future congregation aboard the Hulk at Woolwich. Through the influence of Mr Wilberforce with Mr Pitt, he is appointed chaplain to Botany Bay.'

In more ways than one it was the beginning and the earnest of the whole. On this foundation stone a great structure was to be built. Looking with new eyes at the moral scene around him, the destructive poison of the universal corruption, seeing its unquestionable source, noting the apathy or worse of the church and the failure of the Methodists, Wilberforce had already seen that 'there was needed some reformer of the nation's morals, who should raise his voice in the high places of the land; and do within the church, and near the throne, what Wesley had accomplished in the meeting, and amongst the multitude'. Some time apparently in the spring of 1787 he entered in his journal 'God has set before me as my object the reformation of manners'.[1]

The same year brought forward a remarkable woman who was to make herself, from a quiet country home, the voice of Evangelicalism. Hannah More was already thought by some to be the leading English woman of letters, in fact had been called by her friend Dr Johnson 'the most powerful versificatrix' in the language, when she turned from fashionable society and literary fame to the cause of virtue and piety. Shocked at the profligacy or indifference to true religion of the London

---

[1] It seems clear that this is the earliest statement of Wilberforce's purpose. Another that is frequently cited appears to be a later entry in his journal (28 October 1787): 'God Almighty has set [it should be 'placed'] before me two great objects, the suppression of the slave trade and the reformation of manners.' A facsimile of it is printed at the end of vol. IV of *Wilberforce*.

scene, she had been declining Sunday engagements and 'withdrawing from the world' even before she had met 'serious people' such as Sir Charles and Lady Middleton. 'I have been into the city to hear good Mr Newton preach', she writes in the spring of 1787; 'and afterwards went and sat an hour with him, and came home with two pockets full of sermons'. She met Wilberforce in the course of the summer. 'It is a singular privilege to have a *consecrated* pen, and to be able and willing to devote our talents to the cause of God and religion', John Newton wrote to Hannah More, in a letter that pointed out the particular merit, of the most obvious sort to be sure, of these wonderful recruits, and at the same time could hardly have stated better the disabling attitude of the Evangelical clergy (of Newton's generation) toward the great. 'There are no persons whom I more compassionate, or of whom I am more afraid, than some of those whom you so well describe, under the character of good sort of people. . . . If I am lawfully called into the company of the profligate, I am too much shocked to be in great danger of being hurt by them. . . . But when I am with your good sort of people. . . the insinuating warmth puts me insensibly off my guard. . . . The circle of politeness, elegance, and taste, unless a higher spirit and principle predominate, is to me an enchanted spot, which I seldom enter without fear, and seldom retire from without loss.'[1]

It was no clearer to Venn, John Thornton and the old slave trader that they had found the leader than it was to Wilberforce that he was consecrated to this work. There is a remarkable passage in his journal, entered in 1797, in which, looking back over the already substantial progress of Evangelical reform and his part in it, he expresses his gratitude that God had not prevented all of it by the simple step of letting him stay under the influence of his aunt Mrs Wilberforce of Wimbledon. It was clear that his mother's tearing him from that Whitefieldian grasp to restore him in Hull to a healthy infidelity was no less than a providential interposition. If he had stayed with his aunt, in all likelihood he would have been a Methodist. Even with the powers of John Wesley, he could not have done more than Wesley had done. He could not have brought the Evangelical truth to the great.

There was one man of the eighteenth century whose simple word would be enough to put that matter beyond controversy, and we were

[1] *More*, vol. II, p. 85.

given it when John Wesley said to a sister of Hannah More, 'Tell her to live in the world, there is the sphere of her usefulness; they will not let us come nigh them.'[1]

'How eventful a life has mine been', Wilberforce wrote, on 14 April 1797, 'and how visibly I can trace the hand of God leading me by ways which I knew not! I think I have never before remarked, that my mother's taking me from my uncle's when about twelve or thirteen and then completely a methodist, has probably been the means of my being connected with political men and becoming useful in life. If I had staid with my uncle I should have probably been a bigoted despised methodist; yet to come to what I am, through so many years of folly as those which elapsed between my last year at school and 1785, is wonderful. Oh the depths of the counsels of God! what cause have I for gratitude and humiliation!'[2]

V

The foundations of the Evangelical strategy had been laid before Wilberforce's conversion. If certain important elements were still to be struck on, nearly all the basic principles were established solidly, correctly and in a way perfectly suited to the undreamed-of expansion to come. For that, England was indebted to the London Russia-merchant John Thornton, who has more claim than any other to be thought of as the founder of the Evangelical Reformation.

A grave, portly, substantial man, Thornton was born in 1720 in Clapham, made himself the wealthiest merchant in Europe after Hope of Amsterdam, it was believed, and died in 1790, humbly sure of salvation through faith in his Redeemer in spite of his total natural depravity and manifold sins, after a life of great piety and of Christian benevolences probably unequalled in his century. In a *Discourse Occasioned by the Death of John Thornton, Esq.* Thomas Scott described his investments in Christian benevolence, which were so great 'that he was rather regarded as a prodigy, which might excite astonishment, than as an example, that other men of equal affluence were in duty bound to imitate...'. His 'simple manner of life left a large surplus out of his income, the chief part of which constantly flowed into the

---

[1] *More*, vol. IV, p. 148.   [2] *Wilberforce*, vol. I, pp. 6–7.

channel of his beneficence...' and to that frugality Thornton added a second principle, to use his large business operations to find means of extending his Christian works. 'Doing good...may more properly be said to have been his occupation, than even his mercantile engagements, which were uniformly considered as subservient to that nobler design. To form and execute plans of usefulness...to form acquaintance, and collect intelligence for this purpose; to select proper agents, and to carry on correspondence, in order to ascertain that his bounties were well applied: these and similar concerns, were the hourly occupations of his life, and the ends of living which he proposed to himself; nor did he think that any part of his time was spent happily, or innocently, if it were not some way instrumental, directly or indirectly, to the furtherance of useful designs.' That practice was carried on so faithfully that Thornton 'not only made the gains of his commerce, in a great degree, a fund for the support of his charity; but his commerce itself was often an introduction to the knowledge of the wants, calamities, and deplorable condition, of mankind in distant regions of the earth; and a medium, through which to communicate to their necessities; and to circulate among them the word of God, and other means of instruction, for the benefit of their immortal souls.'

In this *Discourse* describing how Thornton promoted 'the knowledge and practice of the religion contained in the Bible', we come on some examples of the Evangelical language. Thornton helped to support clergymen by frequent gifts, and to educate pious young men. He used his trade connections to disperse Bibles 'perhaps even in all the four quarters of the globe', and 'with them vast quantities of such books as he thought most suited to awaken the conscience'. Aiming also 'to adorn and recommend, as well as to spread, the religion which he professed, and to shew its genuine tendency in his own conduct toward all men', Scott says, '...he supported and patronized every undertaking, which was suited to supply the wants, to relieve the distresses, or to increase the comforts of any of the human species... provided it properly fell within his sphere of action. Indeed, there was scarcely any publick or private charity, *of evident utility*, to which he was not, at one time or another, in some measure a benefactor.'[1]

We note that the private religious labours of John Thornton antici-

[1] Thomas Scott, *Theological Works*, vol. III, pp. 51–2, 54.

pated the British and Foreign Bible Society and the Religious Tract Society, both founded after his death. In a part of his work hardly more than mentioned by the preacher of this *Funeral Discourse*, we come to perhaps the most important use of his great funds. The extent of his religious benevolence is not ascertainable, but the Evangelicals noted that although he was supposed to be a very rich man (in a period in which the merchant Hope of Amsterdam made a million sterling, Sir Robert Peel something like it in textiles, and Rundell the goldsmith and jeweller still more according to the diarist Charles Greville) Thornton left only £150,000 to his children. It seems possible that he was able to invest a considerable sum in one of the most effective and lasting means of Evangelical reform, the purchase and establishment in trust of church livings, with the object of replacing mere nominal clergymen with clergymen who would preach true religion, which is to say Evangelical religion. In describing that activity of Thornton's, Thomas Scott made its object quite clear. 'In dispensing his bounty it is well known, that he constantly aimed to promote the knowledge and practice of the religion contained in the Bible....For this purpose also he was the general patron of pious, exemplary, and laborious ministers of the gospel; frequently educating young men, whom he found to be religiously disposed; and purchasing many livings, not so much with a view of benefiting the individuals to whom he gave them, as for the sake of planting useful ministers of the gospel in those parts, where he supposed the people to be "perishing for lack of knowledge".'

The Evangelical language had been well established by this time, chiefly by Joseph Milner. 'The religion contained in the Bible' has no reference to High Church religion, 'true Christian principles' are not known to Archbishop John Moore. 'Pious, exemplary, and laborious ministers' are Evangelical ministers, 'young men...religiously disposed' are Evangelical young men, and John Thornton's 'eminence in the religious world' connects him with no fat bulls of Bashan; High Churchmen do not belong to the religious world. 'Doing good', 'to supply the wants', and 'deplorable conditions' have a plain Evangelical meaning, as we shall see, in rich fullness, later on, and of course 'those parts where he supposed the people to be "perishing for lack of knowledge"' are parts where only the Regular clergy are to be heard. Two

of the Evangelical expressions that occur in this basic document introduce vital principles of reform: a proper reform movement will support
and patronize every undertaking suited to supply wants, relieve distresses or increase comforts of any of the human species, *provided it
properly falls within the Evangelical sphere of action*, and any public or
private charity must be supported, among other reasons because to do
so adorns, recommends and manifests true religion, *provided it is concerned with the furtherance of useful designs*—that is to say, *is of evident
utility.* Scott would not have needed to italicize the last three words for
a later Evangelical audience. The peculiar Evangelical motives for
relieving distress and supporting charity were stated plainly, lucidly
and again and again in the many works of Hannah More. No properly
brought up person (that is, reader of Hannah More) would fail to know
what kind of Christian act *properly falls within the Evangelical sphere of
action* and consequently is *of evident utility.*

There must be the adornment and recommendation of true religion,
its open profession by those concerned with the reform of the nation,
together with a Christian conduct that will show the genuine tendency
of true religion to all men. Then, beyond the adornment of religion,
its spread; the Bible and other proper literature must be put into the
hands of all people. Distress must be relieved, charities supported, if
they are Evangelically suitable, that is, useful. Young men who give
promise of 'usefulness' by their 'truly religious' views must be sent to
the universities. 'Pious clergymen' must be given financial support if
they need it (wealthy clergymen who do not need it are already beginning to 'come out from among them', as Rowland Hill, a wealthy
clergyman, expressed the 'happy emergence'). Moral and religious
societies must be established to prosecute the reform of the nation in an
organized, continuous way and to enlist and unite earnest people in its
work. The 'serious clergy' must be got into positions in the church,
not for their benefit but for the good of the cause, and into 'key'
positions when possible, chiefly by the unsparing use of Evangelical
money...which is to become, so employed, a weapon of reform
bitterly referred to by High Church opponents as 'the accursed thing,
the wedge of gold'.

Two of the remaining important elements of the Evangelical strategy
were not consonant with John Thornton's plainness and simplicity:

a conciliatory attitude of respect toward social power, and a civilizing of the Christian religion (which however must remain Christianity, not Wesleyanism) until it can safely be presented as the religion of a gentleman. Like his son Henry, John Thornton was a steadfast Calvinist, an unaccommodated Christian. These people, Evangelically admirable in every other way, lacked suppleness.

CHAPTER 3

DISCIPLES IN CAESAR'S HOUSEHOLD

The close of the eighteenth century witnessed the rise of that spirit that has given birth to all those noble institutions that have been ever since increasing in number, magnitude, and vigour, and are now scattering the seeds of eternal life throughout the world.

THE REVEREND WILLIAM GOODE, JNR., 1828

He attached himself to most of the religious and philanthropic societies of his age, that he might enlist them as associates, more or less declared, in his holy war.

SIR JAMES STEPHEN

One thing must always be taken for granted respecting these people,—that is, wherever they gain a footing, or whatever be the institutions to which they give birth, *proselyting will be their main object;* every thing else is a mere instrument—this is their principal aim. *The Edinburgh Review*, 1808

The Duchess Dowager of Beaufort, with her usual kindness to me said, if I wished it, she would certainly sign; otherwise she thought such an old woman could add no credit to it; but I suggested that her high rank might attract others.

HANNAH MORE, 1799

I trust Lady —— will be a confirmed and exemplary Christian. Her rank, her vast fortune, her fascinating manners, sweet person, and engaging understanding, will serve to recommend religion to those who will not swallow the pill till it is covered with much leaf gold. HANNAH MORE, 1813

I

In the Society to Effect the Enforcement of His Majesty's Proclamation Against Vice and Immorality (1788), known as the Proclamation Society, Wilberforce struck on only a small part of the canonical pattern of the Evangelical moral institutions that in a few years were to cover England. Considered as a tool for national reform this small society was seriously defective. Its scope was slight, its aim diffuse, and a large share in its operations was assigned to people who had signally manifested lack of interest, the bishops. Its leading lay supporters included too large a proportion of persons who had no noticeable allegiance to the good and by its nature it was not suited to expansion, to imitation or to the recruitment of large numbers of people or even of small but meaningful numbers of influential people.

There was no error in two of the principles of the Society's establishment. The first was its tacit policy of confining enforcement of the Proclamation to the vice and immorality of the lower orders. That policy was so obviously demanded by prudence that it is hardly to be thought of as a thing that had to be determined. To prosecute the particular vices of the great would have been an extraordinary way of attracting them. Even in this first Evangelical reforming institution nothing so foolish was attempted as—for instance—the suppression of the fashionable gaming houses. This is consequently the first statement of what became a cardinal, inviolable practice of the Evangelical societies—of none more than the chief of them in this field, the Society for the Suppression of Vice. Such a policy was bound to be misunderstood. In 1792 Gillray's caricature titled *Vices Overlooked in the New Proclamation* pictured Avarice, Drunkenness, Gambling and Debauchery as exemplified in the royal family, namely by the king and queen, the Prince of Wales and the Dukes of York and Clarence, the last shown 'toying with Mrs Jordan'. 'To the Commons of Great Britain this representation of Vices which remain Unforbidden by Proclamation is dedicated, as proper for imitation, and in place of the more dangerous ones of Thinking, Speaking, and Writing, now Forbidden by Authority.'[1] Of course such attacks could be disregarded with rectitude and serenity. Larger designs than Gillray had any means of knowing were in progress.

The form of the Society was sound too in a second respect, pointed out by the Vice Society in the course of a tribute to its predecessor early in the century. 'It may also be observed', an initial *Proposal* says, 'that the members of that Society, though comparatively few in number, from their superior and elevated rank and stations in life, are particularly calculated to be of very extensive use, by the good and eminent example which it is in their power, in their own persons and regulations, to set to all the inferior classes of the community.'[2] The Poor, Pious Clergymen Society, founded in the same year, was clerical with a handful of lay supporters. In the Proclamation Society Wilberforce at once struck upward, to enlist *those who count*, and he did not try to rally the Evangelical clergy. But while his list of subscribers was

---

[1] Thomas Wright, *Works of James Gillray the Caricaturist* (London, n.d.), p. 147.
[2] *Proposal for Establishing a Society for the Suppression of Vice, etc.* (London, 1802).

serviceable for an immediate purpose and their kind correct, the individuals chosen were not correct. The blunder about the Lords Spiritual is particularly striking. The clerical subscribers—there would be few of them, a tiny remnant, in the higher offices of the church from this time on throughout the Evangelical Reformation—were the Bishop of Salisbury (Barrington, not yet at Durham), the Bishop of Chester (Porteus, not yet at London) and seventeen prelates who probably had no interest in any reform and pretty certainly not in Wilberforce's kind. No point was achieved by 'enlisting' such people, a fact made obvious by their open hostility when the Orthodox–Evangelical conflict broke out. No one of the seventeen took any further part in Wilberforce's campaign, and out of the scores of religious, moral or philanthropic institutions that were to be founded or reconstituted during the period none had as many of the bishops as this first society had (barring the National School Society, the Clergy Orphan Society and the Society for Promoting the Enlargement and Building of Churches and Chapels, in which Tomline, Law, Sparke, Dampier and their colleagues were in control *ex officio*).[1] Such men had no active interest in either the avowed object of the Proclamation Society or the more general good it might do. The king himself took alarm at Wilberforce's campaign to abolish the African slave trade, begun in 1788, and his name appears only twice again as gracing any reforming institution. Of the five dukes who signed the Society's prospectus only one (Leeds) is seen again taking part in moral reform.

The Society had a short period of activity under the presidency of Bishop Porteus, during which it 'greatly checked the spread of blasphemous and indecent publications'. 'Many persons were prosecuted and punished for disseminating licentious books; and amongst other acts of beneficial interference, a check was in some measure given to that most pernicious custom of exhibiting publicly indecent prints.' The chief beneficial interference against 'licentious books' was per-

---

[1] The Evangelicals subscribed heavily to those societies too and took as active a part in them as they were allowed. In the Church Building Society the vice-presidents included Lords Hardwicke, Harrowby, Darnley, Brownlow, Sir Robert Peel, Sir Thomas Dyke Acland, Mr Justice Park and Wilberforce; but by the Society's constitution the Archbishop of Canterbury was its president and the vice-presidents included the bench of bishops.

formed in 1795 when the Society successfully prosecuted the publisher of Paine's *Age of Reason*. 'It was necessary to inflict some signal punishment', the bishop's biographer, his chaplain Hodgson, says, 'on the person, who, in violation of all decency, had dared to be the publisher of *The Age of Reason*. The man was a bookseller, of the name of Williams; and against him, though unquestionably only an instrument …a prosecution was set on foot in the Court of King's Bench.' 'Without a moment's hesitation, the Jury found the Defendant guilty; and thus was a stop effectually put to the sale of a publication, which concentrated in itself more impiety, and was calculated to inflict a deeper wound on religion, than any that had ever appeared in this or any other country.'[1]

While this prosecution serves to define some exclusive Evangelical terms for us in the course of expressing a vital principle of Evangelical reform, we see that Wilberforce had not realized the great power he could muster by the organization of such societies. The prosecution of *The Age of Reason* was a step in checking the 'increasing profligacy' of the times. Williams was punished for disseminating a 'licentious book'. As all good morality comes from true religion, the expression 'infidelity and licentiousness' is a tautology; and as long as there is 'licentiousness', that is, irreligion, there will be no morality. This is the universal corruption that has poisoned the whole body of the people. Here the purpose of the Proclamation Society is clearly understood and stated; but apparently there is not yet an understanding of the extended 'use' that this and every Evangelical society will have beyond what the Reverend Thomas Scott is later to call perfectly its 'more immediate purpose'. 'The most effectual way to prevent the greater crimes is by punishing the smaller', Wilberforce wrote to William Hey, 'and by endeavouring to repress that general spirit of licentiousness, which is the parent of every species of vice.'[2] Some voluntary association 'thus

[1] Robert Hodgson, *Life of the Right Reverend Beilby Porteus* (New York, 1811), pp. 103–5, 93–5. Hodgson could have added that although only an instrument, Williams spent two years in prison, that Erskine whom the Bishops of Durham and London employed to lead the prosecution was an unbeliever, and that of course the sale of *The Age of Reason* was not stopped.

[2] Hey was the well-known Evangelical surgeon and mayor of Leeds who worked so zealously at putting His Majesty's Proclamation into effect that he was hanged in effigy by the populace.

becomes to us, like the ancient censorship, the guardian of the religion and morals of the people'.[1] When he goes on to state his regret that the society had an aim 'infinitely inferior' to that of an earlier society in that it did not have the stated design of edifying its members, it seems clear that even he had not seen the peculiar Evangelical efficacy of every such institution. No explicit statement of a design to edify was necessary. How could anyone taking part in such an enterprise fail to be edified, in one degree or another, simply by the act of engaging in it? 'They which minister about sacred things eat of the things of the temple, and they which wait upon the altar have their portion with the altar.'

The 'more immediate' Evangelical value of these early societies lay in their usefulness as proselytizing agencies. Could they serve to collect and unite morally earnest or simply decent and respectable, potentially religious, men and women of influence and social power, strengthen them in piety and give them coherent purpose and activity? The signers of the Proclamation Society's prospectus included in addition to Wilberforce's friend Lord Muncaster, Hannah More's friend Sir Charles Middleton and the Duke of Leeds, whose duchess became one of the leading Evangelical women of the period, other persons of obvious usefulness whose names from this time on appear in society after society concerned in one way or another for the national reform:

Earl Harcourt
Admiral Earl Radnor
Samuel Thornton, M.P., of Clapham Common, eldest son of John Thornton, a governor of the Bank of England
William Morton Pitt, M.P., a cousin of William Pitt

To them we may add the following members of the great or the substantial middle class who appear in the Proclamation Society's lists by 1799, as early members of a socially powerful group that soon takes form as an Evangelical 'directorate', the inner core of the reforming societies:

W. Thornton Astell, M.P., a cousin of the Thorntons, an East India House director
Thomas Bernard, M.P., a relative of Bishop Barrington, a retired conveyancer

[1] *Wilberforce*, vol. I, p. 131.

87

Viscount and Lady Cremorne
Admiral (later Lord) Gambier
Charles Grant, of Clapham Common, later M.P., of the East India Company,
    father of Charles Grant and Robert Grant
Sir Richard Hill, M.P.
Henry Hoare of Mitcham, head of the Fleet Street banking house
William Manning, financier, father of Henry Edward Manning
Sir William Pepperell, barrister, friend and correspondent of Hannah More
Philip Pusey, country gentleman of means, father of Edward Bouverie
    Pusey
Lord Rolle
Henry Thornton, M.P., of Clapham Common, a banker, second son of John
    Thornton[1]

Earlier, in 1796, Wilberforce had joined with Barrington, Pitt's brother-in-law Eliot and Thomas Bernard in establishing the Society for Bettering the Condition and Increasing the Comforts of the Poor, which fortunately came to be known as the Bettering Society. Its officers and committee included (besides the founders and Charles Grant, Henry Hoare, W. Morton Pitt, William Manning and Lord Radnor) still more of the pioneer Evangelicals who constituted the core of the reforming society 'directors':

Earl of Hardwicke[2]
Charles Hoare
Ebenezer and Robert Maitland, of Clapham
Lord Teignmouth, of Clapham, as Sir John Shore Governor-General of
    India
Earl of Winchilsea
Sir Thomas Baring, eldest son of the founder of the great merchant and
    banking house
Lord Calthorpe
Lord de Dunstanville
Lord Dynevor
J. C. Villiers, later Earl of Clarendon, at Cambridge with Wilberforce

---

   [1] *Report of the Committee of the Society for Carrying into Effect His Majesty's Proclamation Against Vice and Immorality for the year 1799* (London, 1800).
   [2] Arthur Young wrote about Lord Hardwicke in 1798: 'I am glad to find a great Lord who is not ashamed of praying to God. May there be many such!' *Autobiography*, p. 339.

Nicholas Vansittart, later Earl Bexley; in 1812 Chancellor of the Exchequer
Robert Peel, M.P., one of the greatest English industrialists, father of Robert
Peel[1]

Apart from Wilberforce's first society there were already in existence
two groups of institutions organized for charitable, moral or religious
purposes. The first consisted of the hospitals, infirmaries, dispensaries
and various medical institutions of London, the second of the British
Naval and Military Bible Society, the Sunday School Society, the
Marine Society and the Philanthropic Society, the last also founded in
1788. It was obviously desirable that such institutions should be
supported and if possible directed and amalgamated with the cause, no
matter how little they had hitherto realized that any benevolence may
be made an instrument of reform. A secondary and important reason
for a heavy support of the medical institutions was that in many cases
they had acquired rights of presentation to church positions. Their
ruling bodies, usually the more substantial subscribers who made up
the governors or life-members, could nominate clergymen to London
chaplaincies or lectureships and in a few cases to livings. But one glance
at the membership lists of these institutions, full of the names of *those
who count*, makes clear the primary reason for supporting them.

No more than a glance too is needed to see that some of these early
institutions were not designed, or suitable, for a heavy Evangelical
exploitation. The Philanthropic Society, for example, had the object of
preventing crime 'by reforming criminal poor children'. It put boys
out as apprentices and girls to service. In 1788 its eight vice-presidents
included Lord Cremorne, Philip Pusey and Lord Bulkeley, and the
original subscribers of 1788 included the Duke and Duchess of Leeds,
Sir Charles and Lady Middleton, Henry Thornton and one seldom
found missing from this time on in any useful society, William
Wilberforce. The following were also subscribers and their names may
be added to the reform 'directorate':

Dudley Ryder, later Earl of Harrowby
John Julius Angerstein, the dominant figure at Lloyd's
Robert Barclay, of Clapham, with his brother Charles, who becomes later a
    prominent Evangelical, head of the brewing company

[1] *Reports of the Society for Bettering the Condition and Increasing the Comforts of the
Poor* (London). These were published at irregular times by Sir Thomas Bernard.

Earl of Egremont
Lady Mary Fitzgerald
Countess of Galway
William Weller Pepys, a barrister, another friend of Hannah More
Thomas (later Sir Thomas) Plumer, Master of the Rolls
Lord and Lady Stormont
Lord Willoughby de Broke
Randle Wilbraham, M.P.
Mrs Boscawen and Mrs Bouverie, Hannah More's friends
Samuel Whitbread, M.P.

New subscribers of 1790 contribute four additional names:

Lord Eardley
John Thornton, of Clapham, son of Samuel Thornton
John Bacon, the sculptor
Sharon Turner, the historian[1]

In itself of course the Philanthropic Society had no interest. It was not an institution in which Wilberforce and his associates could become engrossed for its own sake. The object of preventing crime by reforming juvenile criminals or the children of criminals is praiseworthy, but it has no assured and powerful reference to first causes. At best the Philanthropic Society might help, in a small way, to remove obstacles to Evangelical purposes, but its nature was such that it could reasonably be supported by mere nominal Christians or by radicals or liberals who were not Christians. There were other religious people in it, the dissenters John Coakley Lettsom, Joseph Hardcastle, Daniel Lister of Hackney and Joseph Stonard, and the High Church city magnates Jeremiah Harman and Samuel Bosanquet, heavy contributors to non-Evangelical philanthropic institutions;[2] but it was also supported by the Duke and Duchess of Devonshire who steadily refrained from any

---

[1] *An Account of the Nature and Present State of the Philanthropic Society, etc.* (London, 1804).

[2] The High Church subscribers included also William and Henry Sikes, the group's leading bankers, and Joshua Watson, wine-merchant of Mincing-lane, with Lord Kenyon the lay leader of High Church. That the brothers Sikes were annual subscribers in the amounts of two guineas each, and Watson in the amount of one guinea (and so in nearly all the societies they were in) is not at this far time mentioned in a censorious spirit, but only to point out the significant fact that the contributions of Evangelicals of similar standing were greatly larger.

further recorded support of any such institutions, the Earl of Hertford, a celebrated roué who supported possibly out of mere pagan generosity many societies including some exclusively Evangelical, Thomas Coutts the best-known banker of the age who was probably an infidel rather than a High Churchman, Benjamin Hobhouse the liberal, George Dance the artist, the Reverend Thomas Tyrwhitt the Chaucer scholar, John Gifford the editor of the *Anti-Jacobin Review* and 'Mr Pensioner' Reeves. An institution that can receive such support may be inoffensive and perhaps like the Philanthropic Society do a little good, in a worldly way. But it has no serious purpose. It deals with second causes, it does not attack the evil heart of man.

II

In the meantime Wilberforce was already making all possible use, in the most selfless way the age records, of his unique parliamentary position and his friendship with the prime minister. As he was joined in the House of Commons by Charles Grant, William Manning, Robert Peel, Henry Hoare, Samuel and Henry Thornton, Stephen, Babington, Bernard, Baring and others of the directorate, he found himself the leader of a small coherent group, nearly all Tory but on moral issues virtually always belonging to no party but the Evangelical Party, that had to be respected by the ministry, the more as Wilberforce's moral authority grew into imposing proportions with increasing Evangelical triumphs. This group, 'Wilberforce's neutral party', known as 'the Saints', numbered by 1820 in an average year perhaps twenty-five to thirty members, and in any moral issue through several years of the campaign Wilberforce could count on the support of Thomas Thompson and Joseph Butterworth, Methodists, and his friend William Smith of Norwich (and Clapham), the lay leader of English Unitarianism. In the hands of an astute politician—such as Wilberforce—this 'neutral party' had an extraordinary usefulness noted by many contemporaries.

A close friendship with the prime minister gave Wilberforce up to 1806 a strong claim to whatever favours he could properly ask; and the claim was probably strengthened further by Pitt's knowledge that even though such requests might be made on a personal basis they would never be for Wilberforce himself. It was the tragedy of the age,

Wilberforce believed, that with his great potential usefulness for good Pitt should be held firm in irreligion by Tomline, Bishop of Lincoln, his Cambridge tutor and later his private political secretary. With all Wilberforce's repeated efforts—and there was no one whose conversion to true religion would have meant as much—Pitt remained deeply prejudiced against Evangelicalism and particularly the Evangelical clergy. 'Poor fellow!' Wilberforce wrote to Mrs More in 1797, 'pray that the grace of God may yet visit him. He is the first of natural men, but "he that is the least in the kingdom of heaven is greater than he".'[1] There could be said of him no more than Lady Charlotte Bury said of one known to us only as 'little Lady [——]', that in him 'there would be no fault to be found, were this world all'.[2] Even then, though a bishopric was out of the question, Wilberforce made continual demands on Pitt and others in government, always, probably, with his delicate sensitiveness in judging what would succeed and what would not. All requests of the kind, unless routine or what the minister would think unimportant, had to be made, of course, in what the age considered a decent way, and Wilberforce found no difficulty in that. His sons' *Life* is full of examples that the writers, wholly agreeing with the politic way of accomplishing such matters, saw no reason to suppress. In 1793 Wilberforce was at Wimbledon at Pitt's invitation, expecting a small group that would not waste his time. Instead he found a 'strange mixed party'. 'Going away because Lord Loughborough coming', his diary says, 'but on the whole thought it best to stay, considering that he is about to be made chancellor.'[3] Only to a hasty reader would it seem that there was something not very admirable here, a calculating of personal interest to be advanced by the cultivation of a man respected by no one. The chancellor had the bestowal of numbers of church livings in the Crown gift, and Loughborough was chancellor for the next eight years. There are many references in the contemporary literature of Evangelicalism and in its historians to the usefulness of that circumstance. 'John Graham in 1796 through the influence of Mr Wilberforce was presented to the Chancellor's livings of St Saviour

---

[1] *Correspondence*, vol. I, p. 148.
[2] Lady Charlotte Bury, *Diary of a Lady-in-Waiting* (2 vols, London, 1908), vol. II, p. 202.
[3] *Wilberforce*, vol. II, p. 10.

and St Mary Bishophill Senior, York, which he held till his death in 1844.' 'Tandey was presented by the Chancellor (Loughborough) to the Rectory of St Werburgh's, which he held from 1799 to 1832.' 'William Goode, who succeeded Foster as Romaine's curate at St Andrew Wardrobe, was presented to the living by the Chancellor (Loughborough) on Romaine's death.' In the course of Hannah More's determined and not unpolitic attempts to introduce Evangelical truth in her Somerset neighbourhood, Wilberforce got a living from Loughborough for one of her curates who had been converted from High Church irreligion.

'I am anxious not to let the post go', Pitt wrote on 4 August 1796, 'without telling you that I cannot have a moment's hesitation in assuring you that in case of the Deanery of York becoming vacant, I shall with the utmost pleasure recommend Mr Clarke to succeed to it.'[1] This is a perfect example of the decent way of making requests of the minister. The Reverend Thomas Clarke was not an outstandingly meritorious clergyman who because of marked superiority would be selected over any one of scores of clergymen (or, as Wilberforce must have known, of Evangelical clergymen) for so high a church office. But he had one qualification, and that was the mandatory one. He was correctly provided with 'interest'. He was the only Evangelical that Wilberforce could properly have asked Pitt to name to such an office. In 1796 Pitt would not have named an Evangelical to the deanery of York. He would have named Wilberforce's brother-in-law to it if he had been an Anabaptist.

That sensible acceptance of the manners of the age constituted one of Wilberforce's most special qualifications for the leadership of Evangelical reform and was a major factor of its success. A failure here would have been catastrophic, probably fatal. Perhaps no great public stature has ever been reached but at some cost. The cost that raised Wilberforce to 'a social and political eminence', Sir James Stephen believed, 'never before attained by any man unaided by place, by party, or by the sword' was the forfeiture of the right to act always as a simple Christian man. It was all very well for Joseph Milner to exhort his Evangelical brethren not to attempt to reconcile God and Mammon.

[1] *Private Papers of William Wilberforce* (London, 1897), p. 26. Cited as *Private Papers*.

93

Joseph Milner did not have to lead a giant reform movement the success of which could bring about incalculable good in the most important matter and that could not be led by ingenuous scrupulousness. If Mammon is a proper term for a respectful and conciliatory attitude toward wealth, rank, position, office and social power and a sensible recognition that the things of this world can be moved only by the ways of this world, God and Mammon had to be reconciled by the Evangelical leader if he did not wish his reform to be a pallid continuation of the Wesleyan Revival.

Instances of this obligatory suppleness lie on every hand. When the great Duke of Bedford died, Arthur Young, a devout and peculiarly doctrinaire Evangelical, was stubbornly opposed to voting testimonials to him; the duke was not a religious man but had 'an utter want of religion and piety'.[1] Wilberforce took part in the customary civilities. Of course it was the correct thing to do regardless of the duke's lack of piety. He would also have approved of Young's dining, much against his wish, with the Duke of Grafton. Young thought it wrong to have anything to do with a Unitarian. Wilberforce would not have gone to any trouble to dine with an ordinary Unitarian, but the Duke of Grafton, like Bedford, was a different matter. These were two of the greatest peers. On 28 November 1811 the Bedfordshire Auxiliary Bible Society was established, the Duke of Bedford in the chair making a lengthy and pious address; on 27 May 1813 the Duke of Grafton presided at the foundation of the Northampton Auxiliary Bible Society. Such auxiliaries were being established in these years against the bitterest opposition of the High Church party, that is of nine-tenths of the clergy. In May 1814 John Foster, a prominent Baptist minister and essayist, reviewing for the *Eclectic Review* Wilberforce's published speech on the East India Bill, included a courteous rebuke for his 'exceedingly respectful and deprecating strain of complaisance to his opponents', as for example his saying 'they are actuated no less than himself, by a sincere desire to promote the welfare of their country'. Any language that appears unduly respectful in Wilberforce, Foster hastened to add, 'will unanimously be ascribed to an excess of kindness and candour...'.[2] Not so. For those 'poor creatures', as he used to

[1] Arthur Young, *Autobiography*, p. 368.
[2] *Foster's Essays* (Bohn ed., London, 1860), vol. II, pp. 239–41.

call people who Evangelically disagreed with him (Southey tells us), most particularly for those miserables who opposed sending missionaries to India, Wilberforce had no feeling of kindness. They were wretches manifestly opposed to the will of God. He did not believe for an instant that they were actuated by any goodness and there was neither kindness nor candour in his saying such a thing. In Parliament he had to use the language of Parliament, and beyond that he knew well that nothing is ever gained by abuse and often nothing is gained by plain speaking. The Evangelical leader's duty was to bring about the admission of missionaries into the East, not to rebuke evil senators.

Years later, when the pioneering of Evangelicalism was done and coming to be taken for granted, Sir George Stephen, son of James Stephen, wrote that Wilberforce, 'politically educated in the tone of the last century, felt, perhaps unconsciously, too much deferential regard for rank and power, irrespective, not of the morality, but of the sterling worth of their possessors'.[1] What would have happened to the Evangelical Reformation if anyone who thought about that as Sir George Stephen did had been its leader? How could Wilberforce wait for 'sterling worth' in rank and power? Where did Stephen imagine the new 'sterling worth' in rank and power he saw about him came from?

Wilberforce was not only right about these matters, Young, Stephen and Foster wrong; his motive for acting in such a way, with constant 'moral equivocation' (as William Hazlitt was to point out), was to his mind so clear, his *accommodations* so wholly in the service of God, that it apparently did not once occur to him, a man who practised constant spiritual self-examination, that he was not acting with scrupulous honesty. 'The grand point for imitation, and may we both attend to it', he wrote to his eldest son in 1822, about the old Calvinist Thomas Scott, 'is his *integrity*. He was an Israelite indeed, in whom there was no guile. No consideration of interest, gratification, or credit could make him swerve consciously a hair's breadth from the line of duty.' Wilberforce's journal contains many statements of his weaknesses as he fought to steel himself against praise, admiration, the love of honours and success and the applause of the Christian and no small part of the Gentile world; but there is no single mention that his position and his

[1] *Antislavery Recollections* (1854), p. 79.

task forced him to be an Israelite indeed in whom there was no guile but Evangelical guile.

Against the most obdurate opposition, he got the missionaries into India. Would a John Foster, Arthur Young or George Stephen in the House of Commons have got them in?

Two years after Foster's observations an old episode was brought up against him by an old non-admirer, the *Anti-Jacobin Review*. 'We have ever been disposed to give Mr Wilberforce credit for the goodness of his intentions', they wrote, in 1816, and it may have been so if we except Wilberforce's Evangelical intentions, though it is a little hard to see what we would leave,

but his obstinacy of late has rendered us sceptical on that point, and he is not one of those who would be gratified by a compliment to his candour, at the expense of his understanding. Why, then, will he compel, by his present proceedings,[1] a recurrence to a past transaction which we would fain have consigned to oblivion, as the error of the moment. But when we see the duplicity manifested on that occasion, followed up by the encouragement, at least of duplicity, and even hypocrisy, in his friends, he forces us, in a manner, to remind him of the appointment of the Author of 'The True Churchman'. When a vacancy occurred, in certain benefices at York, application was made to Mr Wilberforce, then Member for the County, by the corporation, to use his interest in procuring the presentation for a clergyman, of whose abilities they had ample experience. Mr W. expressed his concern at his inability to comply with their request, grounded on a resolution of his never to solicit any favour from the government. The corporation, however, intent on the accomplishment of their wishes to serve a very deserving individual, resolved to make a direct application to the Chancellor, in whose gift the livings in question were, when they learned, to their infinite astonishment, that the Chancellor would cheerfully have complied with their request, but that, at the solicitation of Mr Wilberforce himself, he had promised the livings to Mr Overton, the noted champion of schism in the church.[2]

The *Anti-Jacobin's* added statement that this story was not denied when they first published it means nothing. It was Wilberforce's

---

[1] The *Anti-Jacobin* did not like the defence of honest deceit in the Vice Society's operations by the Evangelicals on the Committee—Wilberforce, Stephen, Macaulay, Babington and the Reverend Henry Budd; *Anti-Jacobin*, August 1815 (vol. XLIX), pp. 110–11.

[2] *Anti-Jacobin*, July 1816 (vol. L), pp. 639–40.

practice never to enter into useless controversy, especially with agents of evil. But his biographers' curt statement of their father's 'authorizing denial' 'of the charge...of lying to the York corporation'[1] probably does not mean very much either. While no certainty is possible, Wilberforce did get the livings for Overton from the chancellor, in 1802, and it is extremely likely that the episode happened as described. Not to ask favours for Evangelicalism on every possible occasion would be an inconceivable failure to make use of his parliamentary power and his personal connections. He is on record as asking such favours again and again. To hold that asking the chancellor for the York livings for this obviously High Church clergyman would be asking a favour for himself would be a prime specimen of what opponents were to call 'moral equivocation'. 'That is the kind of request I do not make; and it avoids misunderstandings if I describe my policy simply as "never to solicit any favour from the government".' How could Wilberforce say to the corporation without uselessly risking an injury to Evangelicalism, 'I will not ask Lord Eldon for the livings for your candidate, who is not a truly religious man'?

What good, in a humble way, may not those chancellors have done by giving offices in the church to Evangelical men who held them for thirty and forty years? John Scott, Lord Eldon, one of the age's foremost enemies of true religion, was as nominal a Christian as a Christian can be. His name is missing in the lists of every truly religious, truly moral society and nearly all the rest; he opposed the abolition of the slave trade and of slavery, missionaries for Africa and India, the Bible Society, every cause of morality and piety and virtually every project of humanitarianism. He was chancellor for a quarter of a century. Was Wilberforce wrong in taking pains not to offend him or be offended by him? Lord Eldon, Canon Mozley tells us, gave a good many livings to Evangelicals.[2]

By the end of the century Wilberforce was engaged in the support of religious, moral, educational, charitable, benevolent and philanthropic societies and institutions of all 'useful' kinds in a way that was not equalled or approached by any other person of the age. He was in the

---

[1] *Wilberforce*, vol. III, p. 337.

[2] The Rev. T. Mozley, M.A., *Reminiscences Chiefly of Oriel College and the Oxford Movement* (2 vols., Boston, 1884), vol. I, p. 195.

Bettering and Philanthropic Societies, the Magdalen Hospital and the Foundling Hospital, the Lock Hospital and the Lock Asylum, the Small Debts Society, the Sunday School Society, Marine Society, Naval and Military Bible Society, London Missionary Society and Church Missionary Society, St Bartholomew's Hospital and many others, a governor or life member or on the committee or among the officers. Death was taking its toll, so early in the campaign, of strong servants of the good as already half-beatified saints of the Lord passed on to their fruition: John Thornton in 1790, by the end of the century William Romaine, Cadogan of Reading, Joseph Milner and Henry Venn. The abolition of the slave trade, a project that could not have been more closely allied to the great project, had thus far met with nothing but disappointment and failure. But there had been some encouragement, even some little success. The right principles and strategy were being established, the right people slowly coming forward to Wilberforce's side. It was still clearer to him that he was a man dedicated to a divinely appointed work and that it had to be prosecuted with still greater energy and courage. 'By God's help, I will set vigorously about reform. I believe one cause of my having fallen so short is my having aimed no higher. Lord Bacon says, great changes are easier than small ones. Remember, thy situation abounding in comforts requires thee to be peculiarly on thy guard, lest when thou hast eaten and art full thou forget God.'[1]

III

Not least of the encouragements, an event so felicitous that it was almost equally a manifest sign of the divine concern, was the 'emergence' in 1788, as Wilberforce set out to organize his campaign, of the great propagandist. In that year appeared the formal manifesto of national reform, an anonymous moral essay called *Thoughts on the Importance of the Manners of the Great to General Society*. The first of many religious and moral writings that in the course of twenty-five years made Hannah More the most greatly respected woman of the Christian world, it was followed in 1791 by a companion piece, *An Estimate of the Religion of the Fashionable World*. Both of them were 'universally read', William Cowper wrote, 'by people of that rank to which she addresses them'.

[1] *Wilberforce*, vol. I, p. 139.

Disciples in Caesar's Household

A second edition of the *Thoughts* sold in a few days, a third in hours, a seventh was required in the year of publication. That reception, beyond any fashionable novel's, probably not heard of before in the annals of moral letters, was to mark the publication of every one of Hannah More's formal works and to be far outdone by her informal ones, in a way that is incomprehensible without an understanding of the dimensions of the reform she contributed so much to.

Our fair author, as the *Anti-Jacobin Review* was to call Hannah More with the falsest friendliness, was a woman only recently converted to true religion who saw that those presumed Christians of a 'decenter cast'—henceforth to be known, in her term for them, as 'good sort of people'—were not Christians, and who as a serious woman felt obliged to tell them so. In this her first Evangelical work Miss More stated some underlying Evangelical principles without a single error of tact or taste. It was plain-spoken in a careful way, its religious doctrine diluted to alarm no one and to suit the penetrability of her audience, and it could not be doubted that this call for the religious amendment of *those who count* was made by a respectable as well as respectful person, no radical, dissenter or Methodist. The basic principle was firmly laid down: the reform of the nation depended in an absolute way on the reform of the upper classes. If the spirit of religion would operate on the people 'it must operate on their superiors, it must be received into the heart, and exhibited in the life of the rich and the great'.[1] This manifesto had as motto 'You are the makers of manners', and it was addressed to 'the consideration of those who, filling the higher ranks in life, are naturally regarded as patterns, by which the manners of the rest of the world are to be fashioned'.

The mass of mankind, especially those in circumstances that 'exempt them from the temptation to shameful vice', 'is perhaps chiefly composed of what is commonly called, by the courtesy of the world, good kind of people'. 'Yet...those characters in the New Testament, of whose future condition no very comfortable hope is given, seem to have been taken, not from the profligate...but from that decent class commonly described by the term *good sort of people*.' This essay was therefore about the mischiefs of virtue; it contained nothing about

[1] *Works* (1830), vol. II, p. xvi. This was written by Hannah More for a reprint of *Thoughts on the Manners of the Great* in one of her many collected editions [1809].

people who frequented taverns and gaming-houses or held card assemblies on Sunday, printed Sunday newspapers or operated Sunday stage-coaches and in other ways 'openly insult the laws of the land' as violators of the Sabbath. The Sabbath was a Christian palladium; Christianity stood or fell as it was observed or neglected. 'The city of God will never be wholly taken by the enemy till the observance of that be quite lost.'[1] It was true, however, that good sort of people were as likely to employ hairdressers on the Sabbath as they were to have servants lie about their being 'not at home'; they were prone too to the evils of Sunday concerts and likely to frequent public walks and public gardens on Sunday. Small and apparently harmless things like walks in the country on the Sabbath were in reality dangerous; they were part of the general failure to distinguish sharply between good and evil. Such errors, however, were hardly as harmful as the belief of good sort of people that only gross and actual sins were to be guarded against. Omitted duties 'are the offences against which the Gospel pronounces some of its very alarming denunciations'.

It is clear that *Thoughts on the Manners of the Great* was a preliminary statement, an opening on this great subject to a careless ruling class. If Miss More was no Pascal, a profound agonist would only have alarmed her audience. Her essay was intelligent, sensible, earnest, once in a while witty and sometimes pungent, in the balanced antithetical style of the century. She was careful to emphasize the fact that true religion is not austere and gloomy, nor does it demand that men 'renounce the generous and important duties of active life, for the visionary, cold, and fruitless virtues of an hermitage, or a cloister. No: the mischief arises not from our living in the world, but from the world living in us.' At the end Miss More returned from generalities to speak directly to the constant object of her remarks.

I shall close these loose and immethodical hints with a plain though short address to those who content themselves with a decent profession of the doctrines, and a formal attendance on the offices, instead of a diligent discharge

[1] The necessity of Sabbath observance was a basic Evangelical belief, though not held in Wilberforce's time with the doctrinaire rigour that came later. When the prime minister William Pitt fought a duel with George Tierney in 1798, there seems some reason to believe that the great Evangelical shock and horror was not so much that the duel was fought as that it was fought on a Sunday.

of the duties, of Christianity. Believe, and forgive me—YOU are the people who lower religion in the eyes of its enemies. The openly profane, the avowed enemies to God and goodness, serve to confirm the truths they mean to oppose....But you, like an inadequate and faithless prop, overturn the edifice which you pretend to support....Reformation must begin with the GREAT or it will never be effectual. *Their* example is the fountain whence the vulgar draw their habits, actions, and characters. To expect to reform the poor, while the opulent are corrupt, is to throw odours into the stream while the springs are poisoned.

Hannah More was forty-three in 1788, fourteen years older than Wilberforce. She was born, a daughter of Eve, her biographer Roberts tells us, beginning her course amidst the vanities of the world, in Gloucestershire, the fourth of five sisters, her parents good sort of people, of what the eighteenth century called 'humble origin'. The eldest of the sisters, sent to a Bristol school, taught the others. Eventually they set up a boarding school for young ladies at Bristol, helped by a subscription headed by Dr (later Sir) James Stonhouse and 'some affluent friends', which was so successful that the sisters were able to retire at an early point.

Hannah More's youthful days were filled with signs of marked aptitude for letters and piety, we are told. By the time she was eight her 'thirst for learning became very conspicuous'. 'In her days of infancy, when she could possess herself of a scrap of paper, her delight was to scribble on it some essay or poem, with some well-directed moral.' She was not much older when she set out on her prodigious career in reality by writing at seventeen a work of virtuous tendency suitable for the young. This was a 'pastoral drama' called *The Search after Happiness*, which continued to be printed well into the nineteenth century.

In 1775 we see her in London, greatly admired by Dr Johnson, Burke, Garrick, Sir Joshua Reynolds and the group of learned ladies known as the Bluestockings, as these elderly people were captivated by the wit and intelligence of this gifted young woman and by her sensible flattery. In that year too a new element came into Miss More's life. 'I dined yesterday with Captain and Mrs Middleton.' The captain, later Sir Charles, later Lord Barham, was the first of a long line of Evangelical senior officers and a man of solid merit. At Mrs Boscawen's Hannah More met the Middletons' friend Mrs Bouverie, Lord and Lady

Radnor, the Duchess of Beaufort...still more of the earnest people who were to come to Wilberforce's side. As early as 1777 she refused to listen to music on Sundays. In that year her tragedy *Percy* was produced with hardly equalled success; its first edition, four thousand copies, was sold out in a fortnight, a fantastic thing for a mere play if nothing to the sale of her religious works later on. In 1778 at a dinner at the Middletons' 'the Bishop of Chester and his lady' were present, and though her tragedy *Fatal Falsehood* was produced in 1779 to great applause, the life of belles-lettres, the theatre and society was fading away as we see her steadily in the company of the moral and religious. In 1780 her publisher Cadell in the most comic blunder of the century told her that she was 'too good a Christian for an author'. It was a matter of a few years until no books whatsoever fetched such profits as Evangelical books, including chiefly Hannah More's.

In the same year she wrote to Mrs Boscawen to thank her for *Cardiphonia*. 'I like it prodigiously; it is full of vital, experimental religion.' 'Who is the author?' The author of *Cardiphonia* was the old slave trader John Newton, then moved from Olney to London by the Earl of Dartmouth and John Thornton and at the time within a mile or so of Hannah More. 'I met at dinner the other day, at Mrs Boscawen's, Lady Smith; she is dowager of the pious Lord Chief Baron, really an excellent woman, though a little uncharitable in her opinions about others; she said my friend was the best *natural* woman she had ever known.' Hannah More would understand later what Lady Smythe meant. To be a good natural woman, or the best natural woman, was rapidly coming to be not enough, to her mind and to Mrs Boscawen's too. Still, nothing thus far had appeared in Miss More's letters that could not have been written by an earnest good sort of person. She recorded with elation Dr Johnson's saying of her poem *The Bas Bleu* 'there was no name in poetry that might not be glad to own it' (a wholly incomprehensible judgment), and she was delighted to meet General Oglethorpe, 'one of the three persons still living who were mentioned by Pope'. There was still an enjoyment of unheavenly things, such as Pope. A few years later Hannah More would be quick to see that at this time she was a castaway. In 1784 she wrote about the picturesque scenery of the hills and delicious valleys of Somerset, particularly the cliffs of Cheddar, 'so lofty and stupendous as to impress the

mind with ideas the most solemn and romantic'. Five years later William
Wilberforce, visiting the Mores there, looked at those hills and cliffs
with a different eye, and when next the Misses More viewed them it was
with no thought of enchantment but of shock and horror at the irreligion of their inhabitants.

By 1784 the five Misses More had left Bath, where Hannah More
had lived when not in London, and built themselves a country place in
the Mendips nearby, called Cowslip Green, 'which place, I hope',
Hannah More wrote, 'will favour my escape from the world gradually'.
'I sometimes get an interesting morning visitor', she wrote in May
1786; 'of two or three I have entertained some hope, that they were
beginning to think seriously. Lady B. and I had a long discourse
yesterday; she seems anxious for religious information. I told her much
plain truth.' In this year the publication of her poem *Florio* brought
the first explicit statement of Hannah More's great 'usefulness'. 'You
will make me extremely happy by a sight of any production of yours
calculated for the benefit of *the great and the gay*', Dr Horne wrote. He
was president of Magdalen, soon to be Bishop of Norwich. 'Providence
has led you to associate with them, as it raised Esther of old to the
throne, for this very purpose. We know how skilful an archer you are.
With that bow in your hand, go on and prosper.'[1]

When in 1787 *Percy* was revived with Mrs Siddons the greatest
actress of the age, Hannah More was not present. 'Today (Tuesday)',
she writes, 'I have been into the city to hear good Mr Newton preach;
and afterwards went and sat an hour with him, and came home with
two pockets full of sermons.' On 11 May 1787 Newton wrote to her
in a letter perfect for such an occasion, full of kindliness and friendship
and with no mention of Evangelical religion but enclosing his sermon
on the Fast. Hannah More had happily emerged from her brethren.
Only a year earlier the old African blasphemer had helped with the
conversion of William Wilberforce.

It was at this point that *Thoughts on the Importance of the Manners of
the Great to General Society* came out. 'I was charmed and edified with
it', wrote Bishop Porteus, from this time on one of Miss More's
greatest and, it must be added, least discriminating admirers, 'and am
impatient to see it in the hands of every man and woman of condition

[1] *More*, vol. II, p. 37.

in London and Westminster.' 'Where, now that Soame Jenyns is gone, can we find any one but yourself that can make the "fashionable world" read books of morality and religion, and find improvement when they are only looking for amusement.'[1]

An Estimate of the Religion of the Fashionable World (1791), Hannah More's second introductory statement of the gulf between mere nominal Christianity and true religion, was a longer and more solid work than *Thoughts on the Manners of the Great*, designed to go to the source of the 'visible declension of piety' and consequent profligacy, dissoluteness, depravity and laxness of the upper classes. It has still sharper reference to 'that more decent class' who make a public confession of Christianity and 'are not inattentive to any of its forms' but 'exhibit little of its spirit in their general temper and conduct'. By any test under those simple rules of human duty 'Fear God and keep his commandments' and 'Love the Lord thy God with all thy heart', the fashionable world was far indeed from Christianity; and as much so when judged by 'a third rule, which indeed is not so much the principle as the effect of piety', 'to visit the fatherless and widows in their affliction, and to keep himself *unspotted from the world*'. Hannah More was here striking at a belief commonly held by the fashionable world (who were assured of it by Orthodox spiritual leaders), that by virtue of their station they were exempt from the 'severer' Christian duties, the generosity of their charities and benevolences being an acceptable substitute for true religion. In holding that fatal error up to scrutiny Miss More stated in her open, candid and vigorous way still another basic Evangelical belief. Benevolences and philanthropies are virtuous only because of the Christian love in which they are performed and by no means in the mere act of helping the distressed.

The Age of Elegance is genuinely entitled to be called *The Age of Benevolence*. 'Still it will not be inconsistent with the object of this present design, to enquire whether the diffusion of this branch of charity ...be yet any positive proof of the prevalence of religious principle? and whether it be not the fashion rather to consider benevolence as a substitute for Christianity than as an evidence of it?' All virtue— Hannah More said plainly, in this work and often elsewhere—is a part of the Christian dispensation and of that alone. A charity that is not

[1] *More*, vol. II, pp. 83–4.

a product of Evangelical principle is not a charity. 'The mere casual benevolence of any man can have little claim to solid esteem; nor does any charity deserve the name, which does not...spring from a settled propensity to obey the whole will of God.'

In those passages we are reading one of the basic Evangelical tenets stated in the words of the foremost Evangelical spokesman. This is an unchallengeable authority, an 'incontestable witness'. No one of Miss More's formal Evangelical views, social, moral or doctrinal, was questioned at any time by any Evangelical in any surviving record. Perhaps there seems a possibility of some danger here that in earnest hands the recipients of charity could become tolerably immaterial, the benevolence more important, the motive most important.

Hannah More's deep sincerity at any rate was shortly to be shown on a very large scale. Two years before the publication of her *Estimate of the Religion of the Fashionable World*, in 1789, she had set out on an Evangelical project that came to have national prominence. It was through her establishment of a system of schools for her ignorant and impoverished neighbours down in Somerset that she got the intimate knowledge of the conditions of the lower orders, in rural districts, that made her the spokesman of Evangelicalism to them as well as to the great. In August 1789 on a visit to the five Misses More—'Providence directed Mr Wilberforce and his sister to spend a few days at Cowslip Green'—Wilberforce went one morning for a walk through the wild gorges of the Mendips whose romantic beauty had so enchanted Hannah More five years earlier. At supper that day he said, 'Miss Hannah More, something must be done for Cheddar'. The cliffs were 'very fine, but the poverty and distress of the people was dreadful'. 'The method or possibility of assisting them was discussed till a late hour. It was at length decided in a few words by Mr W.'s exclaiming, "If *you* will be at the trouble, *I* will be at the expense".'[1]

In September 1789 Hannah More and Miss Patty, the youngest of the sisters, established a school at Cheddar, and in the course of ten years, working with tireless devotion, extended it into a system of schools for children, youths and adults. A spectator of this project who knew Miss More's basic principle of charity might have had some misgivings. Were 'the vulgar'—the helpless miners and labourers of the Mendips

[1] *Mendip Annals*, p. 13.

and their families—to be 'objects of bounty'? But the schools were not to be simply a demonstration of Evangelical aims and methods. A larger matter was involved in this encroachment on ecclesiastical precincts held by High Church, namely the whole conflict between Evangelicalism and the defenders of the old order. Hannah More received a spectacular national publicity at the end of the century when her loyalty to church, crown and constitution was challenged by incensed clergymen and laymen of the Orthodox group in the course of a bitter controversy.

IV

In *Thoughts on the Manners of the Great* Hannah More mentioned as a reason for hoping that 'the moral and intellectual scene about us begins to brighten' the 'noble attempt' to abolish the African slave trade. Two letters of the year 1787 describe the beginning of Evangelical interest in a vast project that on the face of it is so at variance with the objects, principles and nature of this reform movement as to be mystifying.

'This most important cause has very much occupied my thoughts this summer', Hannah More wrote; 'the young gentleman who has embarked in it with the zeal of an apostle, has been much with me, and engaged all my little interest, and all my affections in it. It is to be brought before parliament in the Spring.'[1] 'To my feelings, it is the most interesting subject which was ever discussed in the annals of humanity.' 'The other day, just as I was going to dinner, arrived Lady Middleton, saying, I must at all events come away with her immediately to dine with Mr Wilberforce at her house. We had four or five hours of most confidential and instructive conversation, in which we discussed all the great objects of reform which they have in view.'[2]

That account seems to indicate not only the possibility that behind Wilberforce in the reform of the nation stood this intelligent woman but that in some way not immediately apparent the cause of the oppressed Africans was a part of the great cause. For several years it had been evident to humane people that the British slave trade was not defensible. The poet Cowper, his friend John Newton, Bishop Porteus and others had published indignant denunciations. In 1786 Lady

[1] *More*, vol. II, pp. 70–1.   [2] *Ibid.* pp. 106–7.

Middleton suggested that the matter be brought before Parliament. From 1787 when Wilberforce announced he would move in the matter until the final determination forty-five years later no one doubted that the Evangelical commander was the Abolition commander. As he fought on, with his Evangelical lieutenants—Macaulay, Stephen, Henry Thornton, Babington, Gisborne and the rest—introducing the Abolition Act year after year, this became the greatest moral crusade England had known. It enlisted thousands upon thousands of determined men and women throughout the nation. Opposition was grim and enduring, but in 1807 the slave trade was abolished and twenty-six years later Wilberforce heard on his death-bed that the bill to abolish slavery on British soil would pass. One result of this magnificent fight is particularly meaningful for present purposes. Wilberforce's leadership of it made him in thirty years, probably in twenty, 'the most loved and respected man in England', 'the conscience of his country', 'the foremost moral subject of the crown', 'the most powerful man in England who owed nothing to birth or office'.

This achievement has no parallel. To the historian Lecky one of the two or three instances known in history of a national act of such magnitude and unselfishness, Wilberforce's part in it seemed to Sir James Mackintosh to have conferred on the world the greatest benefit that any individual had been able to confer. This is an accomplishment so great that to describe it in a few lines and pass on to other matters seems deeply insensitive. But it is done here in a work that has in part the object of pointing out that, wonderful as that achievement was, Wilberforce did still more; for in estimating its place in his total achievement we come on the extraordinary fact that he did not think of it as his life's work but rather as a part, and not the most important part, of some greater work.

On 23 February 1807, after the second reading of the Act made it evident that the slave trade was ended, there was a jubilant gathering of Evangelical chiefs in Wilberforce's house in Old Palace Yard. 'When the first rush of congratulations was over', Zachary Macaulay's biographer says, 'Mr Wilberforce turned playfully to Henry Thornton and said exultingly, "What shall we abolish next?" The answer fell with characteristic seriousness from the lips of his graver friend: "The lottery, I think"; and may have caused a momentary chill in the assemblage.'[1] Two facts are evident here (beyond the fact that if the assemblage had contained any defender of the old moral order he ought to have felt a momentary chill). When the slave trade had been abolished, we see the Evangelical leaders passing on to the next step within the hour, no final purpose accomplished; and whatever the final purpose was, it was not the abolition of slavery. If that purpose had been in mind no one, least of all Wilberforce, would have asked 'What shall we abolish next?'

But it is further apparent from Wilberforce's own statements that in the larger cause of which Abolition was a part there was another more important part. From the usual view in which he is primarily, or wholly, thought of as 'the liberator of Africa' this is more than a little puzzling. At the end of the session of 1813 he was 'less exhausted', he wrote, 'than at the close of the two or three preceding ones; and this, though I took a very active part in that greatest of all causes, for I really place it before the Abolition, in which blessed be God we gained the victory— that I mean of laying a ground for the communication to our Indian fellow-subjects of Christian light and moral improvement.'[2] The introduction of missionaries into India and the East was more important than the abolition of the slave trade; and that statement Wilberforce made in a still stronger and more explicit way: 'This East India object is assuredly the greatest that ever interested the heart, or engaged the efforts of man. How wonderful that a private man should have such an influence on the temporal and eternal happiness of millions; literally, millions on millions yet unborn!'[3]

But if we accept what seems to be indicated, that the huge Abolition effort was, somehow, no end in itself and not even the most important part of Wilberforce's life work, we are in grave and compounded difficulty. The work of which it was part could hardly be anything other than the great Evangelical cause, the reform of the nation; and in any point of view from which either Evangelicalism or Abolition has thus far been regarded, such a project seems to be in the plainest conflict with the Evangelicals' conception of the Christian man and fundamentally opposed to their whole reforming strategy.

[1] Viscountess Knutsford, *Life and Letters of Zachary Macaulay* (London, 1900), pp. 268–9; *Wilberforce*, vol. III, p. 298.
[2] *Wilberforce*, vol. IV, p. 126.   [3] *Ibid.* p. 115.

Disciples in Caesar's Household

A part of the difficulty can be seen in Hannah More's celebrated poem *The Slave Trade*. We should concede that Miss More's poetry, admired as it was, did not constitute a great service to Evangelicalism, or to art. Her 'effusions' were conventional, badly rhetorical and free of aesthetic value. 'Accept, Boscawen! these unpolish'd lays', her *Sensibility* begins, addressing Mrs Boscawen, not her husband the admiral known as Wry-Neck Dick, and her poem on the slave trade is full of such things: 'Hold, murderers! hold! nor aggravate distress'; 'Barbarians, hold! th'opprobrious commerce spare.' But it has some documentary interest. As we shall see when we come to her writings in defence of English institutions against the subversive doctrines of the French Revolution, Miss More was hardly what is usually thought of as a lover of liberty. With her, libertarianism was an opprobrious commerce. It seems necessary to realize that the word 'liberty' is a large and ambiguous term, like many others used by the Evangelicals, and to assume that Miss More's plea for the Africans demands somehow a discrimination of its meanings.

Her liberty is a sober goddess, not 'the unlicens'd monster of the crowd', but a liberty that respects 'grave Authority and Pow'r'. It is governed by Reason and beauteous order. That understood, she urges Abolition on the grounds that the Africans are sentient human beings, that the slave traffic is not Christian, and that by Abolition England will have

> effac'd the shame
> Inscrib'd by Slavery on the Christian name.

As the passage of the Act shall

> mark our favour'd shore,
> To curb false Freedom and the true restore,

the cherub Mercy can be seen as it

> Restores the lustre of the Christian name,
> And clears the foulest blot that dimm'd its fame.

Among other reasons for following Wilberforce, it would seem, Hannah More had the reason of being a Christian. Even here there is confusion, for if her basic grounds for demanding liberty for the Africans were those of Christianity, there was a substantial theological difficulty in Miss More's position. She was on a firm foundation in the

African business only if she adhered to the unaccommodated Protestantism of the early Evangelicals that insisted strongly on the operations of the Holy Spirit and the stated and quite necessary means of salvation; and one important belief she uttered in *The Slave Trade* would not have been accepted for an instant by Newton, Scott, Milner, Romaine, Venn, Robinson of Leicester or any respected and characteristic Evangelical priest of this early period.

> On Him, who made thee what thou art, depend,

she adjures the unfortunate Africans:

> He, who withholds the means, accepts the end.
> Thy mental night thy Saviour will not blame;
> He died for those who never heard his name.

That is equivalent to saying, John Newton observed (not of Miss More's poem but of the same assurance offered elsewhere), that 'men may be saved without either faith, love, or obedience'. 'I would no more venture my soul upon the scheme which you commend, than I would venture my body for a voyage to the East Indies in a London wherry.'[1] Those couplets from *The Slave Trade* advance a theological view fit for John Wesley, denied flatly time after time by the most vital pronouncements of the New Testament. We may grieve to see the oppressed Africans in a state of helpless condemnation, but we may be assured that they are. The only possible view was stated by Thomas Robinson preaching at the Eighth Anniversary of the Church Missionary Society on 7 June 1808: plainly the heathen cannot be admitted to the felicities of the heavenly world; it is impossible without repentance and holiness, even if they might qualify without a clear apprehension of the appointed way of mercy.[2]

In a few years Hannah More would herself reject that view of a soft, mild and tender Christianity, so like John Wesley's or even that of her own good sort of people. Christianity is a rigorous demanding religion, with 'peculiar' doctrines; in its dispensation the sinner, who is everyone, cannot be saved without 'means', and if the means are withheld so is the salvation. If the Africans without knowing it have a Saviour who

---

[1] *Newton*, vol. VI, pp. 242–3.
[2] Hole, p. 192.

died for those who never heard his name, they are far better off in their oppressed condition than their oppressors are, the activities of the Church Missionary Society are an impertinence, and the demand that the Africans be freed can indeed reasonably be made by libertarians, democrats and Jacobins but hardly by Evangelicals. No Evangelical principle is more unquestioningly held than that all earthly injustices and oppressions mean nothing. There is a future life in which the divine justice is meted out for eternity.

But if Hannah More's or any Evangelical's support of Abolition comes—as one would naturally suppose—from an enlightened conviction that there should be political justice for all people, we are in still more serious difficulty. The Evangelical Christian, as Miss More herself will shortly point out to us, has no immediate concern with politics at all and no Christian duty or right to busy himself with such an organized cause as Abolition. He has a simple political duty: to obey the constituted authorities (who are in their place by the act of God), to have nothing to do with those who are given to change, and to attend to his Christian life. That view is stated again and again throughout the Evangelical campaign, and by weightier minds than Hannah More's.

But beyond that too, the campaign to abolish the slave trade, and then the institution of slavery on British soil, was a frontal attack on the most cherished possession of many of the upper classes, their property. How could Wilberforce, seeing clearly, no one better, that the task of reform God had given him could not be accomplished without the support of the great, deliberately take up a project that laid him open to the charge of radicalism and subversion? When the large majority of the great saw the allies who gathered around him, their claim that Abolition was fanaticism seemed unarguable. Years later the Reverend Charles Simeon of Cambridge, a very gifted Evangelical indeed in practical worldly matters, observed on Sir Samuel Romilly's death that it was now possible for religious people to take up the reform of the legal code. As long as Romilly, a radical and an irreligious man (a Deist), led the fight for it the Evangelicals could not afford to touch it. No one saw such a thing more clearly than Wilberforce. But in his task of bringing the roused opinion of the British public to bear on their representatives he had to have any allies he could get. When he was joined by Charles James Fox, a liberal and an irreligious and dissolute man, by Irishmen some of whom were Roman Catholics, some infidels and few overly respectable, by philosophers, radicals, Methodists and other democrats and not truly religious people—even Tom Paine—he had to accept their help, wholly as he agreed with Hannah More that as they were not Christian men they were not virtuous men. The belief that the reform cause could have been harmed, no doubt was harmed, by Wilberforce's open connection with such people is inescapable. How could a man so realistic not only allow himself to be put in such a position but continue in it through the whole reform period?

The Abolition campaign at once crystallized into enemies two powerful groups who hated Wilberforce from its beginning to the end of his parliamentary life. The first was the reactionary Tories, all those who stood for opposition to any change that could endanger their vested interest. The second was the radicals and liberals, even many who supported Abolition. To their mind there was a vicious contradiction in the Evangelicals' respect for liberty in Africa and disrespect for it in England. 'It was the fear of God', his sons tell us, that armed Wilberforce 'as the champion of the liberty of man.'[1] To someone like William Cobbett such a remark—which in fact could as well have been made about the author of *The Slave Trade*—would seem an astounding effrontery, an inconceivable piece of ecclesiastical impudence. How could anyone so gravely assert what was so manifestly untrue? Wilberforce helped two ministers, Pitt and Liverpool, with a twenty-year interval, to make their repressive acts more repressive. He was steadily opposed to every serious political effort for the help of the oppressed lower orders. 'Is it to be presumed', Cobbett demanded angrily, when his understanding of Wilberforce's motives had forced him, a doctrinaire liberal, one of the great English democrats, to *oppose* the abolition of slavery, 'that Washington, for instance, was not as good and just and humane a man as *Massa Wilby who voted and spoke even for the continuation of the Dungeon-bill, in 1818?*'[2]

[1] *Wilberforce*, vol. I, p. 149.
[2] William Cobbett, *Exposure of the Practices of the Pretended Friends of the Blacks* (extracted from *Cobbett's Register*, 26 June 1830), p. 3.
The often-expressed belief that Wilberforce was a political liberal seems to have come entirely from a natural misunderstanding of his fight for Abolition. As his sons shared his deep political conservatism even their *Life of Wilberforce* contains many statements

The matter was puzzling to William Hazlitt as he saw the Saints fighting to free the slaves. 'What have the SAINTS to do with freedom or reform?' Some believed the whole Abolition campaign was a sham, a sanctimonious mask to cover the Evangelicals' determination to do nothing for the lower orders. How otherwise could alleged philan-thropists and humanitarians be so solicitous for the Africans when such distress was unrelieved at home? 'Oh, that our skins were black!' Daniel O'Connell exclaimed on behalf of the Irish peasantry. Francis Place's bitter denunciation of Wilberforce as 'an ugly epitome of the devil'[1] went with a belief that he had no expectation or intention of succeeding. 'Do you think that the verminous Wilberforce really expected to carry through his Slave Trade Bill?' John Rickman, Lamb's friend, an official of the House of Commons, wrote to Robert Southey in 1804. 'Or that he introduced it so late in the Session that he might augment his odour of sanctity and philanthropy etc., among his devotees, and yet the slaves might still be carried to the W. Indies? You will observe that, had he introduced it directly after Xmas, it might ere now have been law. Oh! Smithfield and fiery faggots for that Holy Man! I would willingly exalt him into a martyr.'[2]

There may be another way of looking at this matter. To take up the cause of the slaves may have been a course of action that Wilberforce believed so greatly valuable, in so certain a way, that it justified in-curring the Gentile enmity that Abolition was sure to rouse.

When he set out on national reform, on the principles laid down by

of it that could hardly be misread. We are told again and again why he defended, and occasionally voted for, 'very moderate reform': it would 'take the wind out of the radicals' sails' (that is, make sure there would be no serious reform) and it might help to decrease bribery and drunkenness at elections. 'I declare my greatest cause of dif-ference with the democrats', he wrote in 1819, 'is their laying, and causing the people to lay, so great a stress on the concerns of this world, as to occupy their whole minds and hearts, and to leave a few scanty and lukewarm thoughts for the heavenly treasure' (*Wilberforce*, vol. v, p. 36). In 1824 in opposing the argument that the prohibition of bull-baiting and the like would rob the poor of their amusements he said, 'I would zealously promote the real comfort of the poor. I love the idea of having comfortable causeway walks for them along the public roads' (*ibid.* p. 214). It would be absurd to take that as the sum of his views on the subject, but with the condition of the poor what it was in 1824 it was a grisly utterance.

[1] Graham Wallas, *The Life of Francis Place* (London, 1898), p. 147.
[2] Orlo Williams, *Life and Letters of John Rickman* (London, 1911), p. 110.

John Thornton with the vital addition of a correct attitude toward wealth and position, the new movement wanted one indispensable thing for great success if such a thing could be found. In his *Early History of the Church Missionary Society* the Reverend Charles Hole, writing in the 1890's, pointed out in a penetrating way precisely what it was. 'What was really wanted...was some grand and weighty public cause, appealing in the plainest and the most direct terms to the activities of every individual who heard the joyful sound, some vigorous undertaking to rouse self-denial, toil and sacrifice. The project of Missions to the Heathen appears to have been the very thing needed, with its grand claims that could never be gainsaid, calculated to arouse the warmest enthusiasm of all who had truly received the doctrine of the Cross.'[1]

The young Evangelical Party needed a great by-end, a subsidiary or instrumental cause that could be made into a crusade, inspiring large numbers of moral and earnest men and women to share in an emotional and spiritual undertaking identified with Evangelical leadership. If it was a cause conspicuously based on principle that would rouse ardour, intensity and continued devotion in merely well-meaning, good-hearted people, even if they had unfortunate Church connections or none, or wrong politics, so much the better; that was its exact purpose. With conspicuous righteousness, it should have a dramatic popular appeal. A prime requisite, consequently, was that it should have all the marks of an end in itself. That was what it was supposed to be taken for. If such a cause could be struck on, to lead vast numbers of people into a spiritually uplifting, nationally unselfish movement, its usefulness for the greater cause could be incalculable.

Hole was right about missions to the heathen. That too—'the greatest object that ever interested the heart or engaged the efforts of man' and like Abolition, it would seem, a part of his God-given purpose—was struck on by Wilberforce before the end of the century. But if it was good to have a cause that would rouse the passionate support of all who had received the doctrine of the Cross, how much better for the Evangelical Reformation to have one that would do that too but at the same time bring into the moral campaign multitudes who had not received the doctrine of the Cross? A truly great instrumental cause,

[1] Hole, p. 33.

perfect for Evangelical use toward the national reform, lay ready to hand in 1787, waiting to be taken up, organized, led and given to the British people. Pending further evidence to the contrary, it will be convenient here to consider Abolition as a by-end of the great cause deliberately conceived as such by a wonderful leader.

If the huge crusade for the Africans was not so thought of, Wilberforce's taking it up was an inexplicable folly that was to turn out as a stroke of inconceivably great good fortune. The Evangelicals might well have thought of it (in either case) as sure evidence of the guiding hand of Divine Providence. A grander instrumental cause could not have been found or imagined.

V

One effect of Abolition was to make it possible before the end of the century for Wilberforce to come before the public with a confession of his religious belief. In 1797 appeared his *Practical View of the Religious System of Professed Christians Contrasted with Real Christianity*, written over several years as he could find the time, and like Hannah More's essays addressed to mere nominal Christians and particularly to the good sort of people among them. He had pondered over the expediency of such a work since 1789. That year was a time of discouragement. There was so much to do, hardly a beginning had been made. 'Alas, with how little profit has my time passed away since I came to town! I have been almost always in company, and they think me like them rather than become like me. I have lived too little like one of God's peculiar people.' 'May I be endeavouring in all things to walk in wisdom to them that are without, redeeming the time; labouring for the spiritual improvement of others.'[1] A memorandum of his thinking for and against publication, written in 1789, is full of interest, among other reasons because the dangers he considers concerned so exclusively the book's effect on national reform that the slave trade is not even mentioned.

The six reasons for publishing:

1. Some careless people alarmed, credit of my name, and general operation.

[1] *Wilberforce*, vol. I, pp. 257, 250.

2. Even to the careless whom I know, I can hardly open myself at least with sufficient plainness, in private.

3. The really well-disposed [would be] taught the difference between being almost and altogether Christians.

4. Things may be said to those in high stations, bishops, &c., which could hardly be personally said to them in private.

5. My way cleared of many difficulties by this explicit avowal of my sentiments; unjust conclusions will no longer be drawn from my cheerfulness, or my not making religion the matter of frequent conversation.

6. Perhaps an association of serious people produced, labouring for the national reform.

The opposed reasoning that kept him from trying to bring out such a book in 1789:

To reasons 1, 2, 3, and 4. I can now speak to my private friends, both of the careless and well-disposed, and even of the bishops.

The dread of an over-righteous man would deter people from co-operating with me for national reform.

My influence with P[itt], Chancellor, present and future, and other great men, even G[eorge] himself, would be lessened: few if any livings obtained; few great men would attend to my recommendations in all the ways wherein I have now influence; few private men, &c. I should be looked on as morose and uncharitable, Bishops would fear me.

To reason 5.—I may effect this without such a publication by private conversations with friends, and by public declarations.

To reason 6.—Such an association would not now do good; the times would not bear it—the courts of law would set their faces against it.

To publish in defence of religion not my particular province.

Were I to express all I think I should be deemed an enthusiast, and were I to withhold I might mislead. Form might be substituted in the place of religion.

My connection with P[itt] and my parliamentary situation put me into the capacity of doing much good in the private walks; I may carry bills of reform, I may get a bishop.[1]

---

[1] *Wilberforce*, vol. II, pp. 399–400.

Disciples in Caesar's Household

The way had been cleared enough by 1797. The Abolition Act had been beaten for ten years and would be beaten for nine more, but over England an army of supporters was forming. Wilberforce was a man set apart, already with a moral eminence that would be greater in a few years than any other living Englishman's. To come forward as a truly religious man would hurt neither his parliamentary situation nor his connection with Pitt—or if it would the chance had to be taken. War had been declared on the Gentile world. The times were worse than in 1789, the state of the church not improved, disaffection in the working classes much greater. There was also an imperative immediate consideration: the conflict in the church between the controlling Orthodox group and the small Evangelical body was becoming unmistakable and open. There were already bitter attacks on the Evangelical clergy, by this time a marked group known as 'the Gospel-preaching ministry' or 'the Methodists in the church'. It was incumbent on the leader to address in their defence a powerful upper class that would not listen to a clergyman. To publish in defence of religion was no more Wilberforce's province than to shepherd the bishops in an attack on vice in 1788, but in such times of spiritual decay and High Church domination it was becoming still more evident that religion is too serious a matter to be left to the clergy.

Wilberforce's judgment in both years was correct, his sense of timing unerring. Though *Practical Christianity* was a direct statement of a religion still close to Calvinism, his deep political conservatism, his earnest moral principle manifested as the Abolition leader, perhaps also his substantial wealth and well-known friendship with the prime minister, had given him so respected a standing that (even with his disreputable Abolition allies) the High Church party received his book for several months with nothing but praise.

Nominal Christians are ignorant of such peculiar doctrines of Christianity obedience to which alone makes the Christian. 'Wherein can be discerned the points of discrimination between them and professed unbelievers?' Such treacherous views as 'It signifies little what a man believes; look to his practice', and 'Sincerity is all in all' are wholly opposed to Christianity; when they are almost universally accepted by the great 'no one can say into what discredit Christianity may hereby grow, at a time when the free and unrestrained intercourse, subsisting between the several ranks and classes of society, so much favours the general diffusion of the sentiments of the higher orders'. Nominal Christians rely 'not so much on the merits of Christ, and on the agency of Divine Grace, as on their own power of fulfilling the moderated requisitions of Divine Justice'. They are 'apt to palliate in themselves what they cannot fully justify, to enhance the merit of what they believe to be their good qualities and commendable actions, to set as it were in an account the good against the bad; and if the result be not very unfavourable, they conceive that they shall be entitled to claim the benefits of our Saviour's sufferings as a thing of course'. They know that vice offends and virtue delights God and that 'without holiness no man shall see the Lord'. 'But the grand distinction, which subsists between the true Christian and all other Religionists (the class of persons in particular whom it is our object to address), is concerning the nature of this holiness, *and the way in which it is to be obtained.*' 'They conceive it is to be *obtained by their own natural unassisted efforts.*' The true Christian '*knows that this holiness is not to* PRECEDE *his reconciliation to God, and be its* CAUSE; *but to* FOLLOW *it, and be its* EFFECT. *That in short it is by* FAITH IN CHRIST *only that he is to be justified in the sight of God.*'

In Wilberforce's fourth chapter, *On the prevailing inadequate Conceptions concerning the Nature and the Strictness of Practical Christianity*, which takes up nearly half of his book and is the core of it, there is a statement of the Christian value of worldly fame and reputation that is an extraordinary self-portrait. In this detailed picture of 'the practical Christian gentleman' we are shown the ideal Evangelical, his object one thing only, to advance 'the state of Religion and Virtue', and in his whole activity as constantly concerned with 'uses' as Hannah More and her exemplary fictional characters. It contains the clearest reference (of course not deliberately) to Wilberforce himself, even to his policy as leader, his unsuccessful predecessors and certain present members of his Party who fall short of a proper attitude of conciliation and accommodation or lack the good manners and gentlemanly culture required of an Evangelical priest. 'The true Christian, in obedience to the lessons of Scripture, no where keeps over himself a more resolute and jealous guard, than where the desire of human estimation and distinction is in question.' But while he endeavours to pay little attention to the favour and applause even of good men, and much less of the world

at large, he is sensible of their worth as means and instruments of usefulness and influence, and in accordance with Scripture's allowance, he is
'glad to possess, observant to acquire, and careful to retain them'.

Acting therefore on these principles, he will studiously and diligently use any
degree of worldly credit he may enjoy, in removing or lessening prejudices;
in conciliating good-will, and thereby making way for the less obstructed
progress of truth; and in providing for its being entertained with candour, and
even with favour, by those who would bar all access against it in any rougher
or more homely form. He will make it his business to set on foot and forward
benevolent and useful schemes; and where they require united efforts, to
obtain and preserve for them this co-operation. He will endeavour to discountenance vice, to bring modest merit into notice; to lend as it were his
light to men of real worth, but of less creditable name, and perhaps of less
conciliating qualities and manners; that they may thus shine with a reflected
lustre, and be useful in their turn, when invested with their just estimation.
But while by these and various other means he strives to render his reputation,
so long as he possesses it, subservient to the great ends of advancing the cause
of Religion and Virtue, and of promoting the happiness and comfort of
mankind, he will not transgress the rule of the Scripture precepts in order to
obtain, or to cultivate, or to preserve it, resolutely disclaiming that dangerous
sophistry of 'doing evil that good may come'. Ready however to relinquish
his reputation when required to do so, he will not throw it away; and so far as
he allowably may, he will cautiously avoid occasions of diminishing it,
instead of studiously seeking, or needlessly multiplying them, as seems sometimes to have been the practice of worthy but imprudent men.

In that passage particularly we seem to hear the voice of a new kind
of Reformation, the last sentence referring to Wilberforce's two great
predecessors in national reform as well as to some of his contemporaries.

There will be no capricious humours, no selfish tempers, no moroseness, no
discourtesy, no affected severity of deportment, no peculiarity of language,
no indolent neglect, no wanton breach, of the ordinary forms or fashions of
society. His reputation is a possession of uses too important to be thus sported
away; if sacrificed at all, it shall be sacrificed at the call of duty. The world
shall be constrained to allow him to be amiable, as well as respectable in other
parts of his character; though in what regards Religion, they may account
him unreasonably precise and strict. In this no less than in other particulars,
he will endeavour to reduce the enemies of Religion to adopt the confession of
the accusers of the Jewish ruler, 'we shall not find any fault or occasion

against this Daniel—except concerning the law of his God': and even there, if he give offence, it will only be where he dares not do otherwise; and if he fall into dis-esteem or disgrace it shall not be chargeable to any conduct which is justly dishonourable, or even to any unnecessary singularities on his part, but to the false standard of estimation of a misjudging world.

At this point, after Wilberforce has taken up the good sort of people from Hannah More's respectful but relentless hands and left them still more ruthlessly exposed, a discussion of the political value of Christianity follows that was not likely to recommend Evangelicalism to the radicals.

In whatever class or order of society Christianity prevails, she sets herself to rectify the particular faults, or if we would speak more distinctly, to counter-act the particular mode of selfishness, to which that class is liable. Affluence she teaches to be liberal and beneficent; authority, to bear its faculties with meek-ness, and to consider the various cares and obligations belonging to its ele-vated station, as being conditions upon which that station is conferred.

That aspect of Christianity seems more striking in its application to the working class.

Thus, softening the glare of wealth, and moderating the insolence of power, she renders the inequalities of the social state less galling to the lower orders, whom also she instructs, in their turn, to be diligent, humble, patient: reminding them that their more lowly path has been allotted to them by the hand of God; that it is their part faithfully to discharge its duties, and con-tentedly to bear its inconveniences; that the present state of things is very short; that the objects, about which worldly men conflict so eagerly, are not worth the contest; that the peace of mind, which Religion offers to all ranks indis-criminately, affords more true satisfaction than all the expensive pleasures which are beyond the poor man's reach; that in this view, however, the poor have the advantage, and that if their superiors enjoy more abundant comforts, they are also exposed to many temptations from which the inferior classes are happily exempted; that 'having food and raiment, they should be therewith content', for that their situation in life, with all its evils, is better than they have deserved at the hands of God; finally, that all human distinctions will soon be done away, and the true followers of Christ will all, as children of the same Father, be alike admitted to the possession of the same heavenly inheri-tance. Such are the blessed effects of Christianity on the temporal well-being of political communities.[1]

[1] *Practical Christianity*, pp. 403–6.

Disciples in Caesar's Household

The most consummate, indeed incomparable, statements of that genuine political belief were not given by Wilberforce but by Hannah More. It was not exclusively Evangelical, however, but likely to be held by any respectable and substantial person.

Politically also the times imperatively demand a revival of vital Christianity. The danger of the nation 'is already such as to require the plainest speaking about its religious state'. Men of authority and influence should by their personal conduct promote the cause of good morals, encourage virtue and discountenance vice, enforce the laws against the grosser infractions of morals, favour and take part in any plans which may be formed for the advancement of morality. True Christians should

consider as devolved on Them the important duty of suspending for a while the fall of their country, and, perhaps, of performing a still more extensive service to Society at large... by that sure and radical benefit of restoring the influence of Religion, and of raising the standard of Morality....

It would be an instance in myself of that very false shame which I have condemned in others, if I were not boldly to avow my firm persuasion, that *to the decline of Religion and morality our national difficulties must both directly and indirectly be chiefly ascribed: and that my only solid hopes for the well-being of my country depend not so much on her fleets and armies, not so much on the wisdom of her rulers, or the spirit of her people, as on the persuasion that she still contains many, who, in a degenerate age, love and obey the Gospel of Christ; on the humble trust that the intercession of these may still be prevalent, that for the sake of these, Heaven may still look upon us with an eye of favour.*[1]

The lack of precision and the diffuse and rambling style of this book necessarily written in the odd moments of a greatly crowded life were more than made up for by eloquence and Christian affection. It was beyond Hannah More's capacities or those of any known clergyman of the age. Wilberforce was not so skilled in the arts of composition as Miss More, but his book was better than any of hers (her matchless moral tales of course excepted) because he was capable of a deeper, more genuine belief. Bishop Porteus was right in thanking Providence that such a book had appeared. Naturally the Evangelical rejoicing was great. 'What a phenomenon', John Newton wrote to Charles Grant, 'has Mr Wilberforce sent abroad! Such a book by such a man, and at

[1] *Ibid.* p. 479.

such a time!' 'I am filled with wonder and with hope. I accept it as a token for good; yea, as the brightest token I can discern in this dark and perilous day. Yea, I trust that the Lord, by raising up such an in-contestable witness to the truth and power of the gospel, has a gracious purpose to honour him as an instrument of reviving and strengthening the sense of real religion where it already is, and of communicating it where it is not.'[1]

'I think you know by this time', he wrote to Wilberforce, 'that I do not much deal in ceremonials and compliments. But I should stifle the feelings of my heart, were I wholly to suppress mentioning the satis-faction, the pleasure, the joy, your publication has given me.' 'I deem it the most valuable and important publication of the present age that I have seen: especially as it is *yours*.' The old African blasphemer—in 1797, two years after William Romaine's death, the Evangelical 'bishop'—was an admirably unworldly man, but he was not so un-worldly as to miss the vital point here. 'There are many persons both in church and state, who, from their situations, are quite inaccessible to us little folks: what we preach they do not hear, what we write they will not read. But your book must and will be read.' 'I rejoice to think what additional weight it will give to all you say or do, as in other places, so especially in the House of Commons.'[2]

[1] *Wilberforce*, vol. II, p. 201.   [2] *Correspondence*, vol. I, pp. 132–4.

CHAPTER 4

CITIZENSHIP IN HEAVEN

Her chief aim was the happiness of her poor neighbours in the next world; but she was also very desirous to promote their present comfort; and indeed the kindness she showed to their bodily wants gave her such an access to their houses and hearts, as made them better disposed to receive religious counsel and instruction.

HANNAH MORE, 1794

How preferable is that bread which endureth to everlasting life, to that which perisheth; and how much more to be dreaded is a famine of the word of truth, than a dearth of earthly food.　　　SIR RICHARD HILL, 1800

I

Before *Practical Christianity* came out in 1797 Hannah More had published a series of incomparable statements of political Christianity in defending her country against the destructions of the French Revolution. This was a signal service to the great cause, and to the nation if her friends were right in considering her the chief agency in checking the flood of philosophy, infidelity and disrespect for inherited privilege that poured fearfully across the Channel from 1790 on.

The honour of raising Mrs More's pen to this task was Bishop Porteus's.[1] In casting about for means of combating that tide of evil he struck on the idea of some cheap literature that would urge piety and subordination in an attractive form suitable to the people. It occurred to him that Hannah More was peculiarly qualified to write such works because of her knowledge of the inferior orders gained in the Somerset schools. Having herself noted the necessity of such literature—the poor could get radical works cheap but had to pay several shillings for the moral tales of Mrs Sarah Trimmer, who furthermore was a High Churchman—Mrs More, after declining the task at first, 'scribbled a little pamphlet called "Village Politics, by Will Chip"'. 'It is as vulgar as heart can wish; but it is only intended for the most vulgar class of readers....Rivington [the publisher] sends me word that "they go off

---

[1] Hannah More did not marry but called herself 'Mrs' in the manner of the day when she became fiftyish.

very greatly, and the purchasers are people of rank".' 'It flew with a rapidity which may appear incredible', her biographer Roberts says, '...into every part of the kingdom. Many thousands were sent by government to Scotland and Ireland. Numerous patriotic persons printed large editions of it at their own expense; and in London only, many hundred thousands were soon circulated.'[1] Roberts was probably right about the circulation. *Village Politics* was caught up avidly and reprinted by the government, by loyal associations and loyal individuals to be sold or given away (neither Mrs More nor her bookseller made anything by it, a bad aspect of reform that turned out later to be unnecessary). Her authorship was soon known. '"Village Politics" is universally extolled', Porteus wrote, 'it has been read and greatly admired at Windsor, and its fame is spreading rapidly over all parts of the kingdom.' 'Mr Cambridge says that Swift could not have done it better. I am perfectly of that opinion. It is a master-piece of its kind.'[2]

This little tract deserves some examination, as the first of a long series that gave Hannah More an audience much greater than she reached in her less vulgar works, fantastically successful as they were, and established her beyond question, and very likely for all time, as the world's leading practitioner in this kind of art. Fortunately they are a matchless statement of the least dissimulating kind, wholly authentic in every part and respect, of Evangelical views on all pertinent moral, social, political and religious topics. It was obvious that to fight off the contamination of the French Revolution two points had to be stressed. The inferior ranks had to be led to see that French philosophy was bad and that English conditions were good. The first was not hard, the poor having little knowledge of such speculation and less interest in it, and it was made easier by a well-established principle. This is the principle that as pitch defiles and evil corrupts, any sensible moral person will avoid all contact with spiritual as well as physical contamination. It is well stated in Mrs More's *History of Mr Fantom the New-Fashioned Philosopher*, in which rash William Wilson the footman is debauched by radical philosophy and dies on the scaffold while prudent Mr Trueman wisely does not read works attacking religion or government. 'I have made it a rule never to cast my eyes on any thing which I know to be of a corrupt tendency; sinful curiosity was the sin of the first woman, and it

[1] *More*, vol. II, p. 346. [2] *Ibid.* p. 348.

is still one of the unhappy effects of that original offence.'[1] Thus Mrs More, having read nothing at all of most of her antagonists' writings, had a telling advantage: she could with perfect sincerity state their doctrines just as she supposed them to be.

On the other hand her arguments that the English working class were well off were pretty much circumscribed by facts that the inferior ranks were closely familiar with. Unfortunately too, severe as times were in the early 1790's, they grew worse. Prices rose, unemployment increased, taxes rose to unheard-of levels and the price of proper food, clothing and fuel to prohibitive levels. An unparalleled series of terrible winters made matters still worse (the point of Wordsworth's *Goody Blake and Harry Gill* of 1798). In the blindness of the great to the causes (humanly speaking) of such things, or their indifference, or equanimity of some sort, we see most clearly the strange callousness to human suffering that is an outstanding characteristic of the age. It is perhaps illustrated in the 'long and placid' life of Lord Sidmouth. As Home Secretary through a good part of the period, he was responsible for the imprisonment for political reasons of scores of his fellow Englishmen and the execution of several, and told his physician Sir Henry Holland 'that no events of the day had ever ruffled his night's sleep'.[2] To many besides the Evangelicals there seemed nothing to be done— the existing order being divinely instituted—but to urge the use of food substitutes (there is a large literature on the subject), stress the compensatory advantages of the British constitution, preach resignation and point out that the rich too were enduring hardships.

Two unhappy circumstances made the situation graver. Thanks to the Evangelicals and dissenters and against the strong opposition of the Regular clergy and laity, many of the poor had been taught to read. In her own schools Mrs More had taken every precaution, but no one had ever struck on a way of teaching the poor to read the Bible without enabling them to read Tom Paine too. A more dangerous difficulty was that possibly because of the inherent fascination of evil to sinful man the atheists seemed more zealous in presenting their case than good people, the inferior ranks more attentive to radical propaganda than to loyal. Worthy Mr Trueman noticed that if he and his friend Mr Fantom

---

[1] Hannah More, *Stories 1818*, vol. I, p. 30.
[2] Sir Henry Holland, Bart., *Recollections of Past Life* (London, 1872), p. 194.

'set out with talking of trade or politics, of private news or public affairs, still Mr Fantom was...sure to end with a pert squib at the Bible, a vapid jest on the clergy, the miseries of superstition, and the blessings of liberty and equality. "Oh!" said Trueman to himself, "when shall I see Christians half so much in earnest? Why is it that almost all zeal is on the wrong side?"'[1]

Village Politics, by Will Chip takes the form of a dialogue between honest Jack Anvil the blacksmith and Tom Hod the mason, not a bad fellow but misled by Tom Paine. A few excerpts will show reason for Bishop Porteus's admiration, though perhaps the cool judgment of times not so immediately vexed by the French Revolution will not insist on Richard Owen Cambridge's comparison with Dean Swift.

Tom Hod wants Liberty and Equality, a new Constitution (*Jack Anvil*: 'Indeed! Why I had thought thou hadst been a desperate healthy fellow. Send for the doctor directly.') and the Rights of Man. But if he wants a reform, he should mend himself, and if he wants a general reform, then every one should mend one. To imitate the French is folly, as they 'began all this mischief at first in order to be just what we are already'. The French are now free...to rob and kill whom they will. They had a poor sort of religion, but bad is better than none. When Tom Hod defends Paine's doctrine that as all men should be free the gaols should be torn down, Jack Anvil counters with the equality before the law of rich and poor in England: 'I may go to law with Sir John at the great castle yonder.' That appears to be satisfactory to Mrs More, and we must believe she had not heard Horne Tooke's remark that the courts were indeed open to rich and poor, like the London Tavern. She makes good use too (together with all other conservative writers of the period) of the hanging of Earl Ferrers for the murder of his steward (of course not the Evangelical Earl Ferrers of Wilberforce's day).

Like Mrs More, Jack Anvil has not read *The Rights of Man*; but also like Mrs More, he knows a good deal about Paine's doctrine. It is so foolish that 'if this nonsensical equality was to take place', he could take away all Tom Hod's property because he is stronger. We come to

[1] *Stories 1818*, vol. I, pp. 10–11. *Fas est et ab hoste doceri*, Mrs More might have said if the *Anti-Jacobin Review and Magazine*, which frequently reminded its readers of such tags, had been in existence then.

some Christian lessons about these matters that quite finish off Tom
Paine with his insistence that there should be no gaols, no taxes, and no
government at all.

Tom. But I say all men are equal. Why should one be above another?

Jack. If that's thy talk, Tom, thou dost quarrel with Providence, and not
with government. For the woman is below her husband, and the children are
below their mother, and the servant is below his master.

Tom. But the subject is not below the king: all kings are 'crowned
ruffians'; [Mrs More's note: a popular phrase at that time] and all govern-
ments are wicked. For my part, I am resolved I'll pay no more taxes to any of
them.

Jack. Tom, Tom, if thou didst go oftener to church, thou wouldst know
where it is said, 'Render unto Caesar the things that are Caesar's'; and also,
'Fear God, honour the king'. *Your* book tells you that we need obey no
government but that of the people; and that we may fashion and alter the
government according to our whimsies; but *mine* tells me, 'Let every one be
subject to the higher powers, for all power is of God; the powers that be are
ordained of God; whosoever therefore resisteth the power, resisteth the
ordinance of God'. Thou sayest, thou wilt pay no taxes to any of them. Dost
thou know who it was that worked a miracle, that he might have money to
pay tribute with, rather than to set you and me an example of disobedience to
government? an example, let me tell thee, worth an hundred precepts, and of
which all the wit of man can never lessen the value. Then there's another
thing worth minding; when Saint Paul was giving all those directions, in the
Epistle to the Romans, for obedience and submission; what sort of king now
dost think they had? Dost think 'twas a *saint* which he ordered them to obey?

Tom. Why, it was a kind, merciful, charitable king, to be sure: one who
put nobody to death or to prison.

Jack. You was never more out in your life. Our parson says he was a
monster—that he robbed the rich, and murdered the poor—set fire to his own
town, as fine a place as London—fiddled to the flames, and then hanged and
burnt the Christians, who were all poor, as if they had burnt the city. Yet
there's not a word about rising.—Duties are fixed, Tom—laws are settled; a
Christian can't pick and choose, whether he will obey or let it alone.

Jack Anvil does not pretend that 'our great folks' are a bit better
than they should be, but 'they'll answer for that in another place'. They
could set us a better example about going to church, but still 'hoard-
ing's not the sin of the age: they don't lock up their *money*—away it

goes, and every body's the better for it'. 'It all comes among the people. Their very extravagance, for which, as I said before, their parsons should be at them, is a fault by which, as poor men, we are benefited; so you cry out just in the wrong place.' The 'private vices, public benefits' argument is one of Mrs More's favourites, under various names and taken in various ways. In *Mr Fantom*, after William the footman has been corrupted by Paine and Godwin, he serves dinner in a very drunken condition. He has often heard Mr Fantom say private vices are public benefits, 'and so I thought that getting drunk was as pleasant a way of doing good to the public as any'.[1] Taken as true or as false this argument was effective in Mrs More's hands.

Without the great and their wealth of course the poor would have nothing.

Their coaches and their furniture, and their buildings and their planting, employ a power of tradesmen and labourers. Now in this village, what should we do without the castle? Though my lady is too ranti-polish, and flies about all summer to hot water and cold water, and fresh water and salt water, when she ought to stay at home with Sir John; yet when she does come down, she brings such a deal of gentry, that I have more horses than I can shoe, and my wife more linen than she can wash. Then all our grown children are servants in the family, and rare wages they have got. Our little boys get something every day by weeding their gardens; and the girls learn to sew and knit at Sir John's expense, who sends them all to school of a Sunday besides.

Furthermore,

when this levelling comes about, there will be no infirmaries, no hospitals, no charity-schools, no Sunday-schools, where so many hundred thousand poor souls learn to read the word of God for nothing. For who is to pay for them? *Equality* can't afford it; and those that may be willing won't be able.

Jack's strongest or at least most typical argument is that although this nonsensical equality 'would not last while one could say Jack Robinson',

suppose it could—suppose, in the general division, our new rulers were to give us half an acre of ground apiece; we could, to be sure, raise potatoes on it for the use of our families; but as every other man would be equally busy in

---

[1] *Stories 1818*, vol. I, p. 45.

raising potatoes for *his* family, why then, you see, if thou wast to break thy spade, I, whose trade it is, should no longer be able to mend it. Neighbour Snip would have no time to make us a suit of clothes, nor the clothier to weave the cloth; for all the world would be gone a digging. And as to boots and shoes, the want of some one to make them for us would be a still greater grievance than the tax on leather. If we should be sick, there would be no doctor's stuff for us; for doctors would be digging too. And if necessity did not compel, and if equality subsisted, we could not get a chimney swept, a lamp lighted, or a load of coal from pit, for love or money.

'I have got the use of my limbs, of my liberty, of the laws, and of my Bible', says Jack Anvil.

The first two I take to be my *natural* rights; the two last my *civil* and *religious* rights: these, I take it, are the *true Rights of Man*, and all the rest is nothing but nonsense, and madness, and wickedness.....Instead of indulging discontent, because another is richer than I in this world (for envy is at the bottom of your equality works), I read my Bible, go to church, and look forward to a treasure in heaven.

Mrs More's authorship of *Village Politics* caused great happiness among her friends, and King George too is said to have been delighted with it. It should be pointed out, however, in justice, that the 'all the world would be gone a digging' argument was not actually hers. She was given it by Sir William Weller Pepys, one of the leading Evangelical philanthropists and a very active supporter of Wilberforce's moral and religious societies.[1] Mrs More was not alone in understanding that pitch defiles.

II

Of course no one knew better than Hannah More that the church 'needed amending as well as attending' or was doing more to amend it, or that the sinecurists, placemen and pensioners were indefensible parasites, the rotten boroughs rotten, the Parliament corruptly constituted and corrupt. Who had blocked every serious effort against fashionable adultery and the slave trade, for taxation on fashionable luxuries and the enforcement of Sabbath observance? It was probably the

[1] *A Later Pepys. The Correspondence of Sir William Weller Pepys, Bart.*, edited by Alice C. C. Gaussen (2 vols., London, 1904), vol. II, pp. 283–4 (letter of Pepys to Hannah More, 5 December 1792).

necessity of disguising such beliefs in exhorting the lower orders that led her always to speak deprecatingly of these works and her friends to refer to them facetiously. They were only intended for the most vulgar classes. But if she did not for an instant believe all she patriotically advanced for the improvement of the discontented inferior ranks she believed a large part of it implicitly, and her belief was shared by Newton and Wilberforce. If none of the Evangelicals of this period who recorded their political views expressed them with such crass candour or in terms so suitable to the vulgar, the number of those who did not agree with Mrs More was tiny. The formal, canonical exposition of Evangelical politics was given by Thomas Scott, rector of Aston Sandford, in several pieces written at the end of the century. Scott had a strength of intellect that took him beyond any other divine of the Party—Wilberforce had great respect for him while regretting his lack of the good manners of the upper classes—and on any Christian matter he spoke for Evangelicalism with grave and judicious authority. In this matter his task was simple, for all essentials of it are clearly stated in the Scriptures. There are three basic principles: all human happenings are God's will; the Christian is not primarily concerned with the things of this world and is instructed to suffer evil; 'we should always prefer suffering to sin'. The supposition that the Bible's commands 'only enjoin subjection to *equitable* laws, absurdly implies that every person is a competent and constituted judge of the equity and reasonableness of all the laws of his country, and may determine for himself whether they are obligatory upon him or not!' 'We are expressly required to pay tribute and custom, for the support of government.' This injunction holds even in the case of iniquitous and oppressive taxes 'collected with most grievous extortion'. 'Christians ought very little to regard such matters; they should be satisfied with their better portion even under persecution; and be very thankful for religious liberty, though hardly dealt with in other things.'

We are commanded '"to be quiet, and to mind our own business," "to be content with such things as we have," "to fear God and honour the king, and not to meddle with those who are given to change", to consider "that we have here no continuing city," for the Christian's "citizenship is in heaven," that "we are strangers and pilgrims on earth;" that "in the world we must have tribulation," let who will govern it;

that we must not love the world, or any of its idolized possessions, distinctions, or enjoyments; and that we must "not mind high things," or "seek them" for ourselves.'

'We profess to seek heavenly treasures and honours', Thomas Scott concludes his statement of Christian politics;

and we should not seem desirous of the perishing distinctions of this world, which commonly ensnare those who obtain them: if we are christians indeed, we are travelling to heaven; and all our earthly prosperity or adversity will soon be swallowed up in the joys of eternity; if we can do any good by the way, we should readily embrace the opportunity; if anything contrary to our consciences be required of us, we should meekly refuse compliance; if we be abridged in our civil privileges, or have hard measure from the world, let us not marvel or murmur, but bear it patiently and cheerfully, as the disciples of a crucified Redeemer.

Though liberty...civil and religious, personal and political, be very desirable, even to the utmost extent that human nature in its present state can bear, and that can consist with God's plan of subordination...and though we should aim, by every peaceable and proper method, to promote it in every land: yet we should shew a decided preference to that liberty which Christ bestows on his redeemed people; for without this, the most celebrated and successful champion for civil liberty must continue for ever the abject slave of sin and Satan.[1]

The old African blasphemer agreed, in every part. 'As Christians', Newton held, 'we have nothing to expect from *this* world but tribulation.'[2] 'As to myself, I am neither whig nor tory, but a friend to both. I am a stranger, and a pilgrim. My politeuma, my charter, my rights, my treasures are, I hope, in heaven, and there my heart ought to be.'[3] It was clear that the providence of God had raised up Mr Pitt—'no man could do what he has done, unless a blessing from on high had been upon his counsels and measures'—and it would be fair to take that statement (the view of all Evangelicals, even Whig Evangelicals) as a sign that Newton was not radically inclined; but his assertion that he had no politics and was not concerned with such a thing was honest. During the troubled days when Mrs More was issuing her antidotes to

[1] Thomas Scott, *Theological Works, Published at Different Times*, vol. III, pp. 539–64.
[2] *Newton*, vol. VI, p. 592.
[3] *Ibid.* p. 593.

French principles he addressed *A Letter on Political Debate, Printed in the Year 1793* to the Reverend D—— W——, apparently a dissenting minister who had tried to engage him in political controversy. 'I hope I am a friend to liberty, both civil and religious, but I fear you will hardly allow it, when I say, I think myself possessed of as much of these blessings at present, as I wish for....I expect no perfection in this state; and, when I consider the Lord's question, "Shall not my soul be avenged on such a nation as this?" I cannot but wonder that such a nation as this should still be favoured with so many privileges, which we still enjoy and still abuse.'[1]

The old slaver consequently urges Mr W—— 'to employ the talents [God] has given you in pointing out *sin* as the great cause and source of every existing evil, and to engage those who love and fear him, instead of losing time in political speculation, for which very few of them are tolerably competent, to sigh and cry for our abounding abominations, and to stand in the breach, by prayer, that, if it may be, wrath may yet be averted, and our national mercies prolonged'. 'The instruments whom the Lord employs in political matters are usually such as are incapable of better employment.' 'His own children...belong to a kingdom which is not of this world; they are strangers and pilgrims upon earth, and a part of their scriptural character is, that they are the "quiet in the land".' The reasoning for a more equal representation in parliament, this able and honest man continues, 'is specious; but, while infidelity and profligacy abound among rich and poor; while there is such a general want of principle and public spirit among all ranks; I apprehend, that, whatever changes might take place in this business, no real benefit will follow'. 'But these', Newton concludes this passage, recalling that he is a Christian, 'are not my concerns.' 'The Christian, however situated, must be free indeed, for the Son of God has made him so.'

An eminent Evangelical worth hearing on this matter is the Reverend Thomas Robinson of Leicester, who would have agreed with Scott and Newton but had an illicit interest in politics, especially practical politics for the poor. 'Strong attachment to government; deference to the powers that be; an high sense of the importance and utility of a dignified hierarchy...were a sort of primary element in his mind.'

[1] *Newton*, vol. VI, pp. 586–9.

He 'regarded the equality system as an object of just loathing and determined opposition'; French levelling and republicanism were 'flagrant and pestilential', 'radically contrary to the plainest declarations of the Scripture'; democracy 'a noxious plant which sprung from the corruptions and deceitfulness of the human heart...'. In enunciating those views Robinson ran into a good deal of trouble with the rabble.

As all Evangelical political philosophers have one and the same unimpeachable and unimprovable source, in passing from one to another of them we naturally meet not only the identical sentiments but the identical language. Robinson pointed out in a sermon of 9 December 1792, designed for the political instruction of the humbler members of his flock, that government is the ordinance of God, subordination his decree. It is not for Christian subjects to 'inquire whether or not the ends of government be answered in the particular proceedings of their existing governors; but to manifest a peaceful deportment under the most trying dispensations, as those who "submit themselves to every ordinance of man for the Lord's sake".' 'Never did any sovereign pervert the ends of government more foully than Nero; yet even to him Paul enjoined submission, tyrannical and oppressive as he was.' It is true that if 'governors impose upon us laws that are plainly contrary to the word of God and good conscience... "we ought to obey God rather than men".' But such conduct of government is not possible in England in the eighteenth century.

Our government is the most favourable to religion of any in the known world.

Much has been said about the rights of man. What! have you a right to insult authority? to subvert all existing establishments? 'Render unto Caesar the things that are Caesar's, and unto God the things that are God's.' The example of Christ shews you what ought to be your conduct....He wrought a miracle to pay tribute to the government, not because they could have demanded it of him, but lest he should offend them.

Would you know what Israel ought to do? Abstain from that malignant spirit which is not afraid to 'speak evil of dignities', and from those writers whose tendency is only to mislead and deceive, and in which there is no solidity of argument. Be thankful that God has placed you where you can get a comfortable subsistence; where there is no persecution, but liberty and toleration. Give diligence to obtain a more perfect knowledge of the counsel and ways of God; exert your influence in your family and neighbourhood to preserve peace and order; explain to your families their duty; inculcate subordination; catechize your young people; teach them to obey the king and all that are in authority under him; to submit themselves to all governors, teachers, spiritual pastors and masters; to order themselves lowly and reverently to all their betters.

Perhaps so that it should not be questioned, some future day, that that was the thinking of a good Evangelical, Robinson's biographer, the Reverend Edward Thomas Vaughan, who had been his curate and went on to become a leading Party divine, after quoting in full that sermon of 9 December 1792 proceeded to point out how admirably it stated the political beliefs of the Evangelical clergy. 'Nearly all, if not all to a man, of that considerable body of the Clergy which coincide with him for the most part in religious sentiment, coincide with him also for the most part, in their views of the authority of government. ...I am the more forward to introduce this remark, because it has been insinuated, that the persons usually designated "evangelical clergymen" are...*democratically inclined*.' Vaughan was writing in 1815 or 1816, when that charge was hardly to be described as 'insinuated', and we see here one strong reason for the Evangelicals' anxiety not to be confused with the Methodists. 'I believe...that few of them held opinions less lofty than those which Mr Robinson avowed...and that few were less decided and energetic than he was, in resisting disloyalty, discontent and jacobinism.'[1] There were some Evangelical clergymen who did no more than coincide 'for the most part' with Robinson in religion, but if there was any one at all of them who did not wholly coincide with him in politics, he did not record his views.

Mrs Hannah More's political doctrine for the lower orders was naturally not full and thorough, necessarily being in a striking dramatic form and enforcing only the simplest elementary concepts; but in proceeding to examine it further we may have the fullest confidence, even apart from the testimony of great and wholly unqualified Evangelical applause, that it will contain nothing that is not sound Evangelicalism.

In 1794 at the continued entreaties of Porteus and many others she

---

[1] Edward Thomas Vaughan, M.A., *Some Account of the Reverend Thomas Robinson, etc.* (London, 1816), pp. 128, 147, 151, 153–9, 162–3.

undertook to write or get friends to write for her three tracts a month, similar to *Village Politics*, for the duration of the crisis. In four years, with the help of Miss Patty and an occasional outside contributor, she turned out a lengthy series of moral, loyal and religious pieces, enough to make three thick little volumes when collected. Old Archbishop Moore headed a committee that bribed hawkers to sell them, for a penny or halfpenny, and worked to get them into display windows in place of radical and atheistic propaganda. Helped by the crisis and the Spirit of the Age, the committee did its work well. In these tracts Mrs More had her greatest audience. Few other people had had one like it.

The high point was reached in 1795. In April, Dr Stonhouse, himself author of *Materials For Talking Familiarly With Children of All Ranks*, wrote with something like awe of the astounding demand. 'After the sale of two hundred and eleven thousand, sixty thousand are now bespoke.' Three months later, 'Seven hundred thousand of Mrs Hannah More's Tracts have been sold, and the demand still so great, that they cannot be printed fast enough. Hazard [one of Mrs More's three publishers] says, a million will have been sold before the end of next month. No such sale has ever been heard of in the annals of England.' They had sold over two millions by the end of the year, 'besides very large numbers in Ireland'.

Mrs More called them the Cheap Repository Tracts, a name soon contracted into Cheap Repository.

These little stories fall into two groups, one designed for the middle ranks, the other for the inferior, both constructed on the fundamental principle that virtue comes only from the Christian religion. In the tales of the second group particularly, which continue to be as vulgar as heart could wish, there is usually a good parish priest or member of the upper classes, worthy and charitable, with a virtuous (and rewarded) member of the inferior ranks, and an impious, dissolute or radical (and punished) member of the inferior ranks. Mrs More's language is simple, vigorous and even racy, with a kind of humour and pungency and what may be called a moral dramatic quality. It would have been beyond flesh and blood for her to keep from preaching, especially as she was accustomed to preach a good deal to her schools, and once in a while it is badly overdone. In *The Two Wealthy Farmers* poor Mr Bragwell receives from good Mr Worthy the most ponderous burden of reproof ever given to any character in fiction. But on the whole the stories deserved their immense reputation. Considered merely as art they were beyond the range of Mrs Trimmer, a respectable but not gifted woman, and in fact beyond the range of anyone else who has appeared in the field. It seems probable that we will not look upon their like again.

Of course subtlety would have been worse than useless. The circumstances were pressing, the artist's method strong and direct. Her good and bad characters are immediately identified in the simplest way by their introduction as good Mr White and bad Mr Black or in some equally understandable fashion. Mrs More as a rule gets quickly to the point and the reader is left in no perplexity as to what is right and what wrong. Mr Bragwell's 'natural disposition was not particularly bad, but prosperity had hardened his heart'. 'Poaching Giles lives on the border of one of those great moors in Somersetshire.' 'Hester Wilmot was born in the parish of Weston, of parents who maintained themselves by their labour; they were both of them ungodly, it is no wonder therefore they were unhappy.' 'John Wilmot was not an ill-natured man, but he had no fixed principle.' 'Mr Johnson on the Saturday evening reached a very small inn, a mile or two distant from the Shepherd's village; for he never travelled on a Sunday without such a reason as he might be able to produce at the day of judgment.' 'William was a lively young servant, who lived in a great but very irregular family.' 'A barrow-woman, blessed be God and our good laws, is as much her own mistress on Sundays as a duchess.' 'But if religious persons will, for the sake of money, choose partners who have no religion, do not let them complain that they are unhappy; they might have known that beforehand.' 'Jolly George, as we used to call him, the ring-leader of all our mirth, who was at the bottom of all the fun and tricks, and wickedness, that are carried on within these walls, Jolly George is just dead of the jail distemper!'

Mrs More writes with vigour and pertinency, and even her longer and more deliberate sentences are nearly always crowded with substantial matter. 'It was the custom in that school, and an excellent custom it is, for the master, who was a good and wise man, to mark down in his pocket-book all the events of the week, that he might turn them to some account in his Sunday evening instructions; such as any useful story in the newspaper, any account of boys being drowned as they were out in a pleasure-boat on Sundays, any sudden death in the parish, or any other remarkable visitation of Providence; insomuch, that many young people in the place, who did not belong to the school, and many parents also, used to drop in for an hour on a Sunday evening, when they were sure to hear something profitable.'[1]

Mrs More's sardonic criticisms of such things as contemporary novels and education in young ladies' seminaries are the work of an intelligent, observant, informed woman. As her friends believed, she knew far more than most the manners of the great and the rural inferior. Her characters are accurately reported and her ideas sensible within the Evangelical framework. With the possible exception of some basic religious, moral and political concepts, which cannot, however, unfortunately, be abstracted from these tales and leave much behind, everything in them is above criticism. Her novice piece *Village Politics* was not only foolish but artless. In the later tales there is less arguing, more conflict, more objective virtue or radicalism. The moral is pointed out in most not by reasoning but by visible results. Black Giles falls while thieving and is killed; honest William Wilson the footman, ruined by Godwinian doctrine, is hanged. Patient Joe the Newcastle coal-miner, who believes all is for the best, steadfastly endures the profligate wit of idle Tim Jenkins, who mocks at the Bible. Joe's lunch is stolen by a dog. Leaving Tim in the pit, laughing and swearing and asking if that too is for the best, Joe hurries off after his lunch, and returns to find the pit fallen in and Tim crushed. In *The Two Shoemakers*, James Stock, honest and pious, rises to affluence, while his fellow apprentice idle Jack Brown sinks lower and lower, haunts evil resorts, plays fives, patronizes jugglers and mountebanks, goes to fairs, and at last is ruined, though helped as much as is prudent by James Stock. It is in *The Two Shoemakers* that Mrs More quotes a stanza of 'that beautiful hymn so deservedly the favourite of all children':

> Not more than others I deserve,
> Yet God hath given me more;
> For I have food while others starve,
> Or beg from door to door.[2]

---

[1] *Stories 1818* ('Black Giles the Poacher'), vol. II, p. 437.
[2] *Ibid.* vol. II, p. 113. We owe this little hymn to Dr Isaac Watts (1674–1748).

Hester Wilmot, in *The Sunday School* and *The History of Hester Wilmot*, refuses to eat cakes and drink ale at the fair, becomes an underteacher in the Sunday school and has prospect of further promotion. Mrs More did not necessarily think that because Hester was virtuous there would be no more cakes and ale, having indeed no objection to either; but she did object to fairs opening on Sunday evenings.[1]

Mrs More is at her best in such a piece as *Black Giles the Poacher: containing some Account of a Family who had rather live by their Wits than their Work*, one of her most spirited tales. It exhibited a knowledge of the life of the poor, in villages and cottages, together with the shifts, wiles, tricks and devices of the lawless poor, that came close to going beyond the knowledge of such things that a respectable member of society could with propriety have. It was this sort of knowledge too that led her friends among the great to refer to Cheap Repository facetiously. Black Giles and Tawney Rachel his wife bring their offspring up to be beggars and pilferers. Their son Dick is 'the best of Giles's bad boys', and when Black Giles and his lads profit by poor widow Brown's absence, at church, to steal all her finest apples it is eventually too much for Dick. Giles plants some of the apples in the home of Samuel Price, a very honest carpenter in the parish, and his son Tom is accused of the theft. Tom Price is the best boy in the school, has once given Dick a piece of his own bread and cheese, and has also saved him from drowning; and when Mr Wilson the worthy clergyman has got Dick into the Sunday evening school, and the master there has shown that the theft of the redstreaks, on a Sunday, has probably broken no fewer than five of the commandments, Dick cannot hold fast to his evil ways.

'If the thief,' the master continues, 'to all his other sins, has added that of accusing the innocent to save himself, if he should break the ninth commandment, *by bearing false witness against a harmless neighbour*, then six commandments are broken for an *apple*! But if it be otherwise, if Tom Price should be found guilty, it is not his good character shall save him. I shall shed tears over him, but punish him I must, and that severely.'—'No, that you sha'n't,' roared out Dick Giles, who sprung from his hiding-place, fell on his knees, and burst out a-crying, 'Tom Price is as good a boy as ever lived; it was father and I who stole the apples!'

[1] *Stories 1818*, vol. II, pp. 307, 331.

Citizenship in Heaven

It would have done your heart good to have seen the joy of the master, the modest blushes of Tom Price, and the satisfaction of every honest boy in the school.[1]

With *A Cure for Melancholy* (*Shewing the Way to Do Much Good with Little Money*) we rise to a more serious doctrinal level. It was written during the 'scarcity' of 1794, one of three extremely severe winters in the first half of the decade. Mrs Jones, a worthy widow, is anxious to do good in the parish, but has no money. It was fortunate for her that the vicar of Weston was a pious man. (Though careful to introduce exemplary clergymen in these tales, Mrs More as we know was not of the opinion that all clergymen in English parishes were exemplary. Though she tried hard to keep views peculiar to Evangelicalism out of these tracts, once in a while something like the pious vicar shows up.) Through him Mrs Jones learns how she can help the poor greatly without money, by benevolent exertions.

Mrs More's statement of good Mrs Jones's activities and aims is the clearest autobiography and the whole story one of the fine pictures of Evangelicalism at work among the humble. 'Her chief aim was the happiness of her poor neighbours in the next world; but she was also very desirous to promote their present comfort: and indeed the kindness she shewed to their bodily wants gave her such an access to their houses and hearts, as made them better disposed to receive religious counsel and instruction.'[2] Apart from the gift of her own moral and religious example and exhortation, Mrs Jones though without funds succeeds in bestowing four considerable benefactions on the parishioners: she gets the blacksmith to inform on Mr Crib the baker whose loaves are light, and succeeds in having sounder views adopted on the necessity and morality of the informer's office;[3] she gets the Squire to fine shopkeepers who keep open on Sundays; she helps in the suppression of superfluous public houses; and she urges and demonstrates the avoidance of expensive foods such as butter, tea, milk and meat, and the use of cheap recipes.

Mrs Jones does other good things too. She 'took care never to walk

[1] *Ibid.* vol. II, pp. 442–3. [2] *Ibid.* vol. I, p. 335.
[3] *Ibid.* pp. 339–41. 'A rash, malicious or passionate informer is a firebrand; but honest and prudent informers are almost as useful members of society as the judges of the land.'

out without a few little good books in her pocket to give away. This, though a cheap, is a most important act of charity; it has various uses; it furnishes the poor with religious knowledge, which they have so few ways of obtaining; it counteracts the wicked designs of those who have taught us at least one lesson, by their zeal in the dispersion of *wicked* books,—I mean the lesson of vigilance and activity; and it is the best introduction for any useful conversation which the giver of the book may wish to introduce.'[1] 'Thus Mrs Jones, by a little exertion and perseverance, added to the temporal comforts of a whole parish, and diminished its immorality and extravagance in the same proportion.'

One could wish, though it is futile at this point, that sometimes Mrs More could have thought of charities without 'uses'. But that would have been opposed to a very basic principle.

Such tracts were devoted chiefly to pointing out the rewards of piety, virtue and orderliness and the punishments of irreligion and profligacy. An important section of Cheap Repository dealt primarily with economic instruction in a way begun by Mrs Jones, that is, told the poor how to get along on their few shillings a week. The destitution of un-skilled labourers in particular, at the end of the century and from then on through the Evangelical campaign, was very severe, as we are told again and again in Mrs More's pages, not only in the children's favourite hymn. In Mrs Jones's parish and elsewhere in Mrs More, fuel was almost unobtainable for the inferior orders and no poor woman could buy milk, 'as the farmers' wives did not care to rob their dairies. This was a great distress, especially when the children were sick.'[2] Mrs Trimmer observed during these years that many of the families of her husband's labourers (at Brentford) were clothed in rags picked up on the roads and sewn together. There were few country labourers' families, according to the testimony of these worthy ladies, that could afford fuel, shoes for the children, or anything but desperate substitutes for good food. It is in 1795, the worst of these years, that rioting advances in Mrs More's stories to the position of the worst sin. Her charitable worthy people, always anxious to share their last penny with the deserving unfortunate, deny their charity to rioters first, passive malcontents second, and profane swearers, drunkards and Sabbath-breakers third. It is also at this time that Mrs More enunciates her

[1] *Stories 1818*, vol. I, p. 337.   [2] *Ibid.* p. 351.

doctrine about honest and prudent informers without malice or bitterness.

Her solution of the evils of extreme indigence, while laying no hand on the political and economic institutions of the land, which are a dispensation of Deity, was twofold and correct in each part. The poor were guilty of too great regard for appearances and of worldly-mindedness, and they had not learned a truth stated long before, in a general way, by an earlier philosopher, that happiness can be attained as easily by decreasing desire as by increasing gratification. It might have occurred to Mrs More that waste and economic folly could reasonably have been expected from 'ignorant' and untaught people, neglected by church and state, but it does not seem to have done so. Hardly anything shocked her so much as the observation that even families living in squalor, clad in filthy rags and without fuel for heat, often had white bread, tea, butter, joints and ale. The less terribly indigent they were, the more waste. When Mrs More and Miss Patty extended their school system to the glass factory at Nailsea they found high wages (ten or eleven shillings a week instead of seven or eight) and 'luxurious' eating and drinking—'the body scarcely covered, but fed with dainties of a shameful description.' 'The high buildings of the glass houses ranged before the door of these cottages', Miss Patty's journal continues, 'the great furnaces roaring—the swearing, eating and drinking of these half-dressed, black-looking human beings, gave it a most infernal and horrible appearance. One, if not two, joints of the finest meat were roasting in each of these little hot kitchens, pots of ale were standing about, and plenty of early delicate-looking vegetables. . . . We were in our usual luck as regards personal civility, which we received even from the worst of these creatures, some welcoming us to "Botany Bay", others to "Little Hell", as they themselves shockingly called it.'[1]

Mrs More had three arguments against such indulgence. First, it shows poor judgment: it would be better to have plainer food and more fuel and clothing. Second, such luxury is worldly-minded, forbidden by the Bible and disrespectful to one's betters (hence the shamefulness of the dainties at the glass factory). Third, there are other dishes equally appetizing and more becoming to one's inferior rank. Her specific reply to the winter of 1795, when sheep froze in the fields and farmers could

[1] *Mendip Annals*, pp. 61–2.

not hire labourers unless they made an effort to make work indoors, was *The Second Part of Tom White the Postboy; or, The Way to Plenty*. This tract, which may be described without a bitterness that would be pointless at this time as one of Mrs More's most terrible works, appeared in Cheap Repository in the middle of the winter. As with so many of these tales, indeed nearly all, the difficulty in describing *The Way To Plenty* (which is done, it is hoped there is no real need of saying, in Mrs More's words) is to determine which sentences must be left unquoted. Through virtue and piety, Tom White has become a respectable farmer. Sober and temperate, he is active and healthy as a natural consequence; industrious and frugal, he has become prosperous. That is not a certain rule, although the ordinary course of Providence, for God is sometimes pleased for wise ends to disappoint the worldly hopes of the most upright men.[1] Tom refuses to sell his corn at a seaport at a high price, knowing it is intended for illicit export; he threshes a small part of it at a time and sells it to the neighbouring poor at less than the market price. He lets his labourers plant potatoes for their own use in his waste bits of ground, and gives up his dogs, which eat food that can be given to the poor (a point stressed by the Evangelical and other philanthropists). He joins in subscriptions for the deserving unfortunate, in the form of selling them rice and coarse bread at reduced prices, naturally wishes his labourers not to go to the public house and is particularly set against the hearty celebration of rural holidays. In pressing a variety of practical counsels on the poor, Tom is abetted by his wife, a very worthy woman, and by the vicar, Dr Shepherd, Mrs More's usual exemplary clergyman. Dr Shepherd is very charitable and condescending; in fact with the exception of Mr Johnson in *The Shepherd of Salisbury Plain* he is Mrs More's most condescending character. He lectures all good poor people tirelessly on their duty to themselves and their betters, and is noteworthy for uttering one of Mrs More's finest things when he tells

---

[1] The companion and more annoying mystery beyond human comprehension was that in those days notorious sinners flourished, lived long and happy lives and died peaceful deaths. Lord Eldon, for instance, lived to be eighty-seven, dominated the English legal scene for some forty years, left almost £700,000 and died serenely, refusing on his death-bed the ministrations of no less than Henry Philpotts, Bishop of Exeter, a misplaced prelate of some iron age whose 'desperate and dreadful face' is described by the diarist Charles Greville. It was Philpotts who excommunicated the Evangelical Archbishop of Canterbury (John Bird Sumner).

the honest wives of the shilling-a-day labourers that their unusual hardships of this winter are particularly valuable as 'prosperity had made most of us careless'.[1]

My good women, I truly feel for you at this time of scarcity; and I am going to show my good will, as much by my advice as my subscription. It is my duty, as your friend and minister, to tell you, that one half of your present hardships is due to bad management. I often meet your children without shoes and stockings, with great luncheons of the very whitest bread, and that three times a day. Half that quantity, and still less if it were coarse, put into a dish of good onion or leek porridge, would make them an excellent breakfast. Many too, of the very poorest of you, eat your bread hot from the oven; this makes a difference of one loaf in five; I assure you 'tis what I cannot afford to do.

Mrs White warmly supports Dr Shepherd in demanding that white bread be given up. Furthermore tea is not only expensive but is slop. It requires a deal of costly sugar and is bad for the stomach. Two pounds of fresh meat cost less than one pound of butter and give five times the nourishment. If the gentry would buy only prime cuts, and not take the cheap, coarse and inferior joints for soups and gravies, the poor could get them instead of good pieces.

Dry peas, to be sure, have been very dear lately; but now they are plenty enough. I am certain then, that if a shilling or two of the seven or eight was laid out for a bit of coarse beef, a sheep's head, or any such thing, it would be well bestowed. I would throw a couple of pounds of this into the pot, with two or three handsful of gray peas, an onion, and a little pepper. Then I would throw in cabbage, or turnip, and carrot, or any garden stuff that was most plenty; let it stew two or three hours, and it will make a dish fit for his majesty. The working men should have the meat; the children won't want it; the soup will be thick and substantial, and requires no bread.

Rice pudding is even cheaper, for anyone who can get skim-milk. Half a pound of rice, Mrs White says, two quarts of skim-milk, and two ounces of brown sugar; cost not above sevenpence. But more than half a day's wage at that, and Mrs More knew well, having frequently pointed it out herself, that no one could get milk except through the kindness of a charitable farmer. There is still another objection. At this

---

[1] *Stories 1818*, vol. II, p. 282.

point in *The Way to Plenty* one of the less worthy poor summons the hardihood to complain that all this leaves the fuel problem unsolved.

Bless your heart, muttered Amy Grumble, who looked as dirty as a cinder-wench, with her face and fingers all daubed with snuff; rice milk indeed! It is very nice to be sure for those who can dress it, but we have not a bit of coal; rice is no use to us without firing. And yet, said the doctor, I see your tea-kettle boiling twice every day, and fresh butter at thirteen pence a pound on your shelf. O dear sir, cried Amy, a few sticks serve to boil the teakettle. And a few more, said the doctor, will boil the rice milk, and give twice the nourishment at a quarter of the expence.

The poor are not allowed to depart with their subscription until Dr Shepherd has warned them that only those who come to church should come for alms. He concludes his exhortation with the one rule from which their benefactors will never depart: 'Those who have been seen aiding or abetting any riot, any attack on butchers, bakers, wheat-mows, mills or millers, we will not relieve; but with the quiet, con-tented, hard-working man I will share my last morsel of bread.'[1] It is clear that that should be taken as the natural exaggeration of a warm-hearted man.

III

No account of these moral writings, and as far as that goes no account of English letters during this period that pretends to any thoroughness, could leave out the work of sustained and unequalled greatness of its kind with which Hannah More crowned Cheap Repository. With *The Shepherd of Salisbury Plain* she rose to a lonely level, for it has no com-petitor. The greatest of Mrs More's tracts and of all tracts, it towers over similar works like another *Agamemnon*, a flawless masterpiece perfect in conception and in execution, likely to remain forever peerless on a height the moral tale will not reach again.

The Shepherd of Salisbury Plain came from Mrs More's pen in 1794. It should be mentioned that the circumstances and character of the Shepherd were taken from a living model. He was discovered by Sir James Stonhouse's curate Stedman when entering on his curacy at Cheverel. His name was David Saunders. He was of the neighbouring

---

[1] *Stories 1818*, vol. II, pp. 271–5, 282.

parish of West Lavington, and he used to keep his Bible, Stedman recorded, in the thatch of his hut on the Plain.[1]

As usual Mrs More gets quickly to the point. Her second sentence introduces her exemplary character of the upper classes, Mr Johnson, riding across the Plain slowly that he might have leisure to admire God in the works of his creation. A 'very worthy charitable gentleman', Mr Johnson is said to have been a portrait of Stonhouse. He meets the Shepherd, a clean, well-looking, poor man about fifty years old. His coat has been patched so often that the original colour cannot be made out, his stockings are entirely covered with darns of different coloured worsted, but have not a hole in them. His shirt, though nearly as coarse as the sails of a ship, is as white as the drifted snow. This is a plain proof of his poverty, but equally of the exceeding neatness, industry and good management of his wife. 'A poor woman who will be lying a-bed, or gossiping with her neighbours when she ought to be fitting out her husband in a cleanly manner, will seldom be found to be very good in other respects.'

Mr Johnson accosts the Shepherd with asking what sort of weather it will be on the morrow. 'It will be such weather as pleases me', answers the Shepherd. Although his tone is mild and civil, Mr Johnson naturally thinks he has mistaken his man. He is soon set right. 'Because', the Shepherd continues, 'it will be such weather as shall please God, and whatever pleases him always pleases me.'

That being quite another thing, Mr Johnson benevolently engages the Shepherd in conversation. 'Your's is a troublesome life, honest friend.' The Shepherd defends his calling in a humble but spirited fashion. His tasks are not nearly so toilsome as those assumed by the Great Master for his sake; he is exposed to cold and heat but not to great temptations. 'Besides, Sir, my employment has been particularly honoured—Moses was a shepherd in the plains of Midian.' Furthermore, it was to shepherds that the angels appeared in Bethlehem. 'Here the shepherd stopped, for he began to feel he had made too free, and had talked too long.' Mr Johnson, however, 'desired him to go on freely, for that it was a pleasure to him to meet with a plain man, who, without any kind of learning but what he had got from the bible, was able to talk so well on a subject in which all men, high and low, rich

[1] Thomas Stedman, *Letters from Job Orton*, pp. 21–2, note.

and poor, are equally concerned'. The Shepherd, reassured, enlarges
on the generosity of the rich in modern times, the privileges of poverty,
and the importance of its place in the Scriptures. 'Sir, I wonder all
working men do not derive as great joy and delight as I do from thinking how God has honoured poverty!'

Turning to his own circumstances, he shows the greatest contentment
and happiness in the face of many difficulties, which are appropriate
enough to his station in life but nevertheless seem to be severe, even in
Mrs More's description.

'I have but little cause to complain, and much to be thankful; but I have had
some little struggles, as I will leave you to judge. I have a wife and eight
children, whom I bred up in that little cottage which you see under the hill
about half a mile off.'—'What, that with the smoke coming out of the
chimney?' said the gentleman. 'O no, Sir,' replied the Shepherd, smiling,
'we have seldom smoke in the evening, for we have little to cook, and firing is
very dear in these parts. 'Tis that cottage which you see on the left hand
of the church, near that little tuft of hawthorns.'

The Shepherd of Salisbury Plain is full of wonderful things perfectly
said, but even so benevolent Mr Johnson's reply has special distinction:

'What, that hovel with only one room above and below, with scarcely any
chimney? how is it possible you can live there with such a family!'

'O! is it very possible and very certain too,' cried the Shepherd. 'How
many better men have been worse lodged! how many good christians have
perished in prisons and dungeons, in comparison of which my cottage is a
palace!'

Mrs More proceeds to a relentless and fearful picture of humble
economy punctuated with condescending admiration. The Shepherd's
wife is sickly, there are no gentry in the parish, and they have no help
except a shilling now and then from the curate. The Shepherd's hovel—
as he calls it later, realizing how he has presumed in calling it a cottage—
costs him fifty shillings a year, his wage is one shilling a day. The three
children under five are no help to him, but before they are six his little
girls are making first a halfpenny and then a penny a day knitting.
The boys keep the birds off the corn, for which the farmers may give
them a penny or even twopence a day, and sometimes a bit of bread and
cheese into the bargain.

While they were in this part of the discourse, a fine plump cherry-cheek little girl ran up out of breath, with a smile on her young happy face, and without taking any notice of the gentleman, cried out with great joy,—'Look here, father, only see how much I have got!' Mr Johnson was much struck with her simplicity, but puzzled to know what was the occasion of this great joy. On looking at her he perceived a small quantity of coarse wool, some of which had found its way through the holes of her clean, but scanty and ragged woolen apron. The father said, 'This has been a successful day indeed, Molly; but don't you see the gentleman?' Molly now made a curtsey down to the very ground; while Mr Johnson inquired into the cause of the mutual satisfaction which both father and daughter had expressed, at the unusual good fortune of the day.

'Sir,' said the Shepherd, 'poverty is a great sharpener of the wits.—My wife and I cannot endure to see our children (poor as they are) without shoes and stockings, not only on account of the pinching cold which cramps their poor little limbs, but because it degrades and debases them; and poor people who have but little regard to appearances, will seldom be found to have any great regard for honesty and goodness; I don't say this is always the case, but I am sure it is so too often. Now shoes and stockings being very dear, we could never afford them without a contrivance. I must shew you how I manage about the shoes when you condescend to call at our cottage, Sir; as to stockings, this is one way we take to help to get them. My young ones, who are too little to do much work, sometimes wander at odd hours over the hills for the chance of finding what little wool the sheep may drop when they rub themselves, as they are apt to do, against the bushes. [Mrs More's note: This piece of frugal industry is not imaginary, but a real fact, as is the character of the Shepherd, and his uncommon knowledge of the Scriptures.] These scattered bits of wool the children pick out of the brambles, which I see have torn sad holes in Molly's apron to-day; they carry this wool home, and when they have got a pretty parcel together, their mother cards it; for she can sit and card in the chimney corner, when she is not able to wash, or work about house. The biggest girl spins it, the little boys knit stockings for themselves while keeping cows or at night, and what the girls and their mother knit is for sale, to help pay the rent.'

Mr Johnson lifted up his eyes in silent astonishment at the shifts which honest poverty can make rather than beg or steal; and was surprised to think how many ways of subsisting there are, which those who live at their ease little suspect. He secretly resolved to be more attentive to his own petty expences than he had hitherto been; and to be more watchful that nothing was wasted in his own family.

Perhaps it is just another of those painful blemishes in the nature of things as they are rather than as they should be that in so far as Mr Johnson and others of his superior station did that, they were rendering null and void Jack Anvil's only remotely admissible argument in favour of the upper classes, in *Village Politics*, that their extravagance benefits all the poor.

Mr Johnson condescends to question the Shepherd further. His wife honest Mary has violent attacks of rheumatism, 'caught by going to work too soon after her lying-in, I fear; for 'tis but a bleak coldish place, as you may see, Sir, in winter, and sometimes the snow lies so long under the hill, that I can hardly make myself a path to get out.... So, as I was saying, the poor soul was very bad indeed, and for several weeks lost the use of all her limbs except her hands; a merciful providence spared her the use of these, so that when she could not turn in her bed, she could contrive to patch a rag or two for her family. She was always saying, had it not been for the great goodness of God, she might have had her hands lame as well as her feet, or the palsy instead of the rheumatism, and then she could have done nothing—but, nobody has had so many mercies as she had.' They have almost no firing and the rain comes through the roof; but if pain is unbearable, the Shepherd explains, it is seldom lasting, and if moderate it can be borne a long time, and when it is taken away ease is the more precious and gratitude is quickened by the remembrance; 'thus in every way and in every case I can always find out a reason for vindicating Providence'.

'"But", said Mr Johnson, "how do you do to support yourself under the pressure of actual want. Is not hunger a great weakener of your faith?" "Sir," replied the Shepherd, "I endeavour to live upon the promises. You who abound in the good things of this world are apt to set too high a value on them." Those who are in white robes "came out of great tribulation.... But, Sir, I beg your pardon for being so talkative. Indeed you great folks can hardly imagine how it raises and cheers a poor man's heart, when such as you condescend to talk familiarly to him on religious subjects. It seems to be a practical comment on that text which says, *the rich and poor meet together, the Lord is the maker of them all*. And so far from creating disrespect, Sir, and that nonsensical wicked notion about equality, it rather prevents it."'

148

Citizenship in Heaven

Promising to come to visit the Shepherd in a few days, Mr Johnson slips a crown into his hands and rides off, more disposed to envy than to pity. 'I have seldom seen, said he, so happy a man. It is a sort of happiness which the world could not give, and which I plainly see, it has not been able to take away.' 'No, my honest Shepherd, I do not pity, but I respect and even honour thee; and I will visit thy poor hovel on my return to Salisbury with as much pleasure as I am now going to the house of my friend.'

'I am willing to hope that my readers will not be sorry to hear some farther particulars of their old acquaintance *the Shepherd of Salisbury Plain*', Mrs More says in beginning Part II of this tale. Benevolent Mr Johnson 'on the Saturday evening reached a very small inn, a mile or two distant from the Shepherd's village; for he never travelled on a Sunday without such a reason as he might be able to produce at the day of judgment'. It is easy to find the hovel, next day, because of the broken chimney. He stays outside for a moment to spy on the Shepherd's family at their Sunday meal. The table is covered with a clean though very coarse cloth, on which stand a large dish of potatoes, a brown pitcher and a piece of a coarse loaf. We meet plump cherry-cheek little Molly again, a picture of glowing health of the pre-vitamin period.

Little fresh-coloured Molly, who had picked the wool from the bushes with so much delight, cried out, 'Father, I wish I was big enough to say grace, I am sure I should say it very heartily to-day, for I was thinking what must *poor* people do who have no salt to their potatoes, and do but look, our dish is quite full.'—'That is the true way of thinking, Molly,' said the father; 'in whatever concerns bodily wants and bodily comforts, it is our duty to compare our own lot with the lot of those who are worse off, and this will keep us thankful: on the other hand, whenever we are tempted to set up our own wisdom or goodness, we must compare ourselves with those who are wiser and better, and that will keep us humble.' Molly was now so hungry, and found the potatoes so good, that she had no time to make any more remarks.[1]

There was no real need for her to do so. She had uttered the supreme remark of the age.

Mr Johnson, discovered, inspects the hovel. There is not the least appearance of dirt or litter. The furniture hardly amounts to bare necessaries, and 'it was pretty clear', Mrs More tells us with her cheery

[1] *Stories 1818*, vol. II, p. 35.

pungency, that the bright spit over the chimney 'was kept rather for ornament than use'. Mr Johnson rebukes the Shepherd, gently, for not having indulged himself, as it was a Sunday, with a morsel of bacon to relish his potatoes, out of that crown. The Shepherd has paid his doctor's bill instead. '"But come", said the good gentleman, "what have we got in this brown mug?"—"As good water", said the Shepherd, "as any in the king's dominions." "When I am tempted to repine that I have no other drink, I call to mind, that it was nothing better than a cup of cold water which the woman at the well of Sichar drew for the greatest guest that ever visited this world."' Mr Johnson offers to send for something better just the same. '"I saw a little public-house just by the church, as I came along. Let that little rosy-cheeked fellow fetch me a mug of beer." So saying, he looked full at the boy who did not offer to stir; but cast an eye at his father to know what he was to do.' The Shepherd, of course, like the little rosy-cheeked fellow, is well above the benevolent gentleman's ruse. Though being seen at a public-house on the Sabbath may seem a small thing, 'in my poor notion', he says, 'I can no more understand how a man can be too cautious, any more than he can be too strong, or too healthy'. The Scripture 'applies to every thing, Sir. When those men who are now disturbing the peace of the world, and trying to destroy the confidence of God's children in their Maker and their Saviour; when those men, I say, came to my poor hovel with their new doctrines and their new books, I would never look into one of them; for I remembered it was the sin of the first pair to lose their innocence for the sake of a little wicked knowledge; besides, *my own Book* told me—*To fear God and honour the king*—*To meddle not with them who are given to change*—*Not to speak evil of dignities*—*To render honour to whom honour is due*. So that I was furnished with a little coat of mail, as I may say, which preserved me, while those who had no such armour fell into the snare.'[1]

IV

Cheap Repository was discontinued in 1798 when the flood of French principles was believed to have fallen off. Before then and long afterward many a conservative and respectable voice was raised in grateful

[1] *Stories 1818*, vol. II, pp. 50–1.

praise. 'The sublime and immortal publication of the "Cheap Repository", I hear of from every quarter of the globe', Bishop Porteus wrote in 1797. 'I am ...determined to eat nothing but Mrs Jones's cheap dishes all this winter.' His playful manner should not be misunderstood; he believed Mrs More's tracts were the chief influence in preventing the spread of revolutionary ideas among the poor. Many were far from facetious about these tracts. There is a story of William Jay, the noted nonconformist divine of Bath, weeping as he read Mrs More's tale of the honest shepherd, and years later William Wilberforce declared that he would rather go up to render his account at the last day carrying with him *The Shepherd of Salisbury Plain* than with all the volumes of Sir Walter Scott's works, 'full as they are of genius'.[1]

It was only a few years after Cheap Repository that Mrs More's home in the Somerset countryside had become a shrine where earnest people came from near and far to meet the celebrated Christian woman. That would not have happened if Mrs More had not spoken the truest, soundest Evangelicalism. Her firm accents were not only inimitable; they were correct. Her statements of true doctrine were necessarily bare, suited to a humble audience. Occasionally they were more strict than prudent. Wilberforce would not have said some things as she did. Neither would he publicly have expressed the view that 'the instruments whom the Lord employs in political matters are usually such as are incapable of better employment'. He had to deal with a realistic and hostile world. Mrs More had too much iron in her soul, admirable for admonishing the poor, not suitable for Wilberforce's task. But the whole corpus of Cheap Repository contains no single thing that Wilberforce would not have agreed with.

The value of Mrs More's utterance is enhanced by its absolute honesty. Her sure knowledge of the truth led her to state it unhesitatingly, without equivocation. In her Mr Trueman, an honest and pious tradesman, simple-hearted and 'of the good old cut', we have the ideal member of the upper lower class. Mr Trueman fears God, follows his business (that is, does not meddle with things above his station), pays his taxes without disputing, reads his Bible without doubting, and sensibly leaves all thought to his betters.[2] Mrs More sincerely believed that he and everyone of inferior station should do so. It is evident to her

[1] *Wilberforce*, vol. v, p. 254.   [2] *Stories 1818*, 'Mr Fantom', vol. I, p. 8.

that her villagers have nothing to do with taxes but to pay them un-complainingly. Poor people should not fly in the face of their betters. For a poor family to have a proper joint is disrespectful to their superiors. It is a noteworthy condescension for her worthy vicar to talk to humble people.[1] Liberty and equality are wicked concepts. The worst thing the lower orders can do is belong to a political club. All property is sacred, 'and as the laws of the land are intended to fence in that property, he who brings up his children to break down any of those fences, brings them up to certain sin and ruin'. If the village women do not send their children to Mrs More's schools and keep them there, it is most likely that both the women and the children will go to hell. It is likely and proper that boys who go boating on Sunday will be drowned, and it is tolerably sure to be Jolly George, the ringleader in the prison at mirth, and jests, and tricks, and wickedness, who will die of the gaol distemper.

Mrs More never loses sight of the great theme in Cheap Repository as in her other writings and her schools. John Newton stated that theme when he urged the Reverend Mr ——— to use the talents God had given him 'in pointing out *sin* as the great cause and source of every existing evil, and to engage those who love and fear him, instead of losing time in political speculation... to sigh and cry out for our abounding abominations'. Sin is the great cause and source of every existing evil; we should always prefer suffering to sin; these are two basic principles of every part of the Evangelical Reformation, and the second injunction does not only mean 'I must prefer my suffering to my sin'; it also means 'I must prefer the suffering of others to their sin'.

There was no need of John Newton to remind Mrs More that that was true, or that 'all truth, honesty, justice, order, and obedience', as her Mr Worthy (of *The Two Wealthy Farmers*) tells us, 'grow out of the Christian religion'.[2] 'Morality is but an empty name, if it be destitute of the principle and power of Christianity.'[3] The vital part of Christianity that enforces moral conduct is its system of rewards and punishments, and

---

[1] 'Dr Shepherd condescended to call on Farmer and Mrs White, to give a few words of advice.' *Stories 1818*, vol. II, p. 240.

[2] *Ibid.* 'The Two Wealthy Farmers', vol. I, p. 136.

[3] *Ibid.* 'Mr Fantom', vol. I, p. 65.

chiefly the punishments. Without them, there would be no moral conduct. 'A rich man, indeed, who throws off religion, may escape the gallows, because want does not drive him to commit those crimes which lead to it; but what shall restrain a needy man, who has been taught that there is no dreadful reckoning? Honesty is but a dream without the awful sanctions of heaven and hell. Virtue is but a shadow, if it be stripped of the terrors and the promises of the Gospel.'[1] The whole sanction of moral conduct is summed up in one short question that 'even a philosopher could not answer': 'Who can dwell with everlasting burnings?'[2] As we have seen, Mrs More was a firm believer in the political and economic structure of England; but for being an anti-Jacobin she had one fundamental reason. We are told it over and again. 'The connection of Jacobinism with impiety is inseparable', says worthy Mr Trueman. 'I generally find in gentlemen of your fraternity an equal abhorrence to Christianity and good government.'[3] This religious basis of all goodness and all liberty becomes a dominating concept as the Evangelical campaign to reform the nation sharpens into clearer focus.

Meanwhile the record is quite clear that the Duchess of Beaufort, Lady Southampton, Henry Hoare of Mitcham, William Wilberforce, even Hannah More, were warm-hearted and compassionate people who fully believed in helping the deserving unfortunate. This was probably true of many Evangelicals apart from those about whom it is unmistakably recorded. Their contributions to benevolences that had only a broad general 'use', and even to some that seem to have had little 'use', were very substantial—much larger than those of any other similar group. Apart from the natural inclination of the heart, it was a Christian duty. It was enjoined on them by a Bible that they took in every part with unqualified seriousness. But there is always the knowledge too that charity and benevolence are good only if done from Christian principle. Their chief good is the good they do the giver. They do not serve *the best interests* of the poor.

In 1811 the young Edward Bickersteth became secretary of the Spitalfields Benevolent Society. 'The objects of the Society', he wrote, 'are, visiting and relieving the poor, chiefly in Spitalfields, and affording them Christian instruction (the last, the chief object), and also for our

[1] *Ibid.*   [2] *Ibid.* vol. I, p. 60.
[3] *Ibid.* vol. I, pp. 30–1.

own improvement.'[1] When in the same year this young man, later a prominent Evangelical priest, became a member of the Widow's Friend Society, can there be much doubt as to the primary nature of the Society's friendly concern for 'the fatherless and widowed'? Bickersteth's statement can be matched by scores, more likely hundreds, from the Evangelical literature of the early century. All benevolences, charities and philanthropies are done by pilgrims on the march, who are leaving *no continuing city*; they are done, in Thomas Scott's perfect phrase, *by the way*. When Mr Trueman brings a box of clothes for Mr Fantom's gardener whose house has burned down, he puts in the box a parcel of good books, 'which indeed always made a part of his charities; as he used to say, there was something cruel in that kindness which was anxious to relieve the bodies of men, but was negligent of their souls'.[2]

A short passage in Mrs More's devotional journal, written in 1794 when she was beginning Cheap Repository, states this fundamental Evangelical principle in a formal and illuminating way. She notes it is then five years since she and Miss Patty, at Wilberforce's suggestion, established their first 'religious institution' at Cheddar (there was no point in calling it a 'school' in a private journal).

O Lord! I desire to bless thy holy name for so many means of doing good, and that when I visit the poor, I am enabled to mitigate some of their miseries. I bless thee, that thou hast called me to this employment, which, in addition to many other advantages, contributes to keep my heart tender. I thank thee also [Mrs More adds], that by thus being enabled to assist the outward wants of the body, I have better means of making myself heard and attended to in speaking to them of their spiritual wants. Let me never separate temporal from spiritual charity, but act in humble imitation of my blessed Lord and his Apostles, whose healing the sick was often made the instrument of bringing them to repentance; yet, while I desire to keep alive a tender compassion for worldly want, I desire also to remember that sin is a greater evil than poverty, and to be still more zealous in touching their souls, than even in administering to their bodies.[3]

---

[1] *Memoir of the Rev. Edward Bickersteth, etc.* By the Rev. T. T. Birks, M.A. (and his wife, Bickersteth's daughter) (2 vols., London, 1851), vol. I, pp. 162, 164. Cited is the second edition (1852).

[2] *Stories 1818*, vol. I, p. 43.   [3] *More*, vol. II, pp. 421-2.

Citizenship in Heaven

Sin is the great cause and source of every existing evil. We should always prefer suffering to sin. Sin is a greater evil than poverty. May I be endeavouring in all things to walk in wisdom to them that are without; labouring for the spiritual improvement of others.

By 1797 William Wilberforce and his fellow-Evangelicals had laid down a set of principles and rule of belief and conduct, for the middle and lower ranks particularly, that if put into practice would have made the great bulk of their country's subjects worthy and exemplary men and women. In the course of that transformation, which did not take place, the Evangelicals would also have created an England in which, until their or some other kind of Reformation had penetrated deep into the ranks of the great, the paradise of privilege, pocket-boroughs, pensions, places, sinecures and pluralities, all the immense profit and vested interest and expropriation of the public domain by the few, could have continued indefinitely, the masses observing a proper subordination as a matter of religious duty and caring in any serious way only for their citizenship in Heaven. That makes one aspect of the attack that broke out on the Evangelicals once the first fury of the French Revolution had subsided particularly unbelievable. That with the content and one would have thought unmistakable purpose of Mrs More's writings, and Wilberforce's unmistakable respectability and Christian conservatism, and the unmistakable respectability and substance of their leading supporters, the High Church party should have been able to persuade a large section of *those who count* that the Evangelicals were subversive radicals bent on the overthrow of church, crown and constitution is truly hard to believe. It was as unfair as absurd that the Evangelicals had to labour for years to convince the great that they were firm believers in the sacredness of rank, position, office and property and profoundly respecters of persons; not radicals, not subversives, not reformers at all except in morals and religion.

CHAPTER 5

SENNACHERIB'S ARMY:
THE RALLY ROUND THE ALTAR

These days of fierce polemical contention (plus quam civilia bella).　　JEBB, 1817

I

The gratitude of the decenter cast of respectable people to Mrs More and Wilberforce was great: among the idol shepherds too, until it began slowly to be impossible to doubt that they were connected with the group of 'Gospel-preaching ministers', 'Methodists in the church', who had been believed for some years to be bent on schism and perhaps worse. For many months this possibility could not be taken seriously even by people who were otherwise well informed about church affairs.

When incredulous and bewildered defenders of the old order could no longer question that the church was being attacked, the morals and manners of the nation deliberately 'gangrened', to use the Reverend Robert Fellowes's term for it, they had been provided with a vigorous medium of warning and exhortation. *The Anti-Jacobin Review and Magazine (and Monthly, Literary and Political Censor)* made its appearance in July 1798 under the editorship of John Gifford, to defend truth, loyalty, virtue, patriotism and conservatism. It did that chiefly by chastising the errors and follies of radical, liberal, Whig, dissenting and all non-High Church publications and anyone who reviewed them favourably. A resolute Tory of some ability, Gifford made the *Anti-Jacobin Review* a strong defender of the right from the point of view of government and a formidable foe of its chosen enemies. It fully deserved its 'very extraordinary encouragement'.[1]

---

[1] Mr G. D. H. Cole in describing Gifford as a 'dull dog' must have had his historical writings in mind. He was far from being a dull editor. The master copy of the first six volumes of the *Anti-Jacobin* with the contributors' names entered is in the British Museum Reading Room (P. P. 3596).

Sennacherib's Army

The High Church party's progress in realizing that this new body of 'schismatics', 'Puritans' or 'fanatics' were not a few scattered and unorganized enthusiasts but potentially a powerful group can be traced in the *Anti-Jacobin*'s pages. It had been known for some time that there were 'Methodists in the church'. The leaders of the Evangelical group at the time of Wilberforce's conversion had never concealed their belief that the religion of the bulk of churchmen was not Christianity. At the end of the century these people were not members of any Methodist connection though their religion seemed very like George Whitefield's; and though they were clergy or laymen of the Established Church their attitude toward their brethren in it was most unbrotherly. Their numbers, however, were tiny and their status not respectable except for a very few of their laymen. If their cause was now being taken up by the most widely published writer of the day, who was known to be a cherished favourite of several of the moral great, it was a serious matter, still more so if it was being taken up by William Wilberforce. If it further appeared that the lay supporters of these clerical radicals already included more than a few people of wealth, rank and political substance, that their numbers were rapidly increasing and that the Bishop of London was closely attached to some of their laymen and openly favouring several of their clergy in his diocese, the matter was more than serious. It was threatening. But could it be possible that such people were coming to the side of these puritanical fanatics? Wilberforce was known to be a wealthy man, conspicuously a close friend of the heaven-sent prime minister, already honoured by many for championing Christianity and justice. Prominent on the committee to circulate Cheap Repository was the king's brother; the archbishop had headed it. At the end of the century the government was still distributing the tracts. Mr Pensioner Reeves's Loyal Association had bought and given out huge numbers of them and Reeves was one of the *Anti-Jacobin*'s contributors. Bishop Porteus was one of the most respected men in the kingdom (except to extremists: the old Duke of Bridgewater used to call him 'that damned Presbyterian'), noted for his moral character, his wealth and his friendship with the king; and he had praised Mrs More's writings in a Charge to his clergy in which he had urged them to read her. How could such people be members of the fanatical group and still worse (as it seemed) leaders of it?

When 'Peter Pindar'—Dr Wolcot, a jocular Whig satirist—published his *Nil Admirari; or, A Smile at a Bishop; Occasioned by an Hyperbolical Eulogy on Miss Hannah More* (namely that Charge) the *Anti-Jacobin* as late as September 1799 launched its solid weight, animated with wrathful righteousness and not for the first or last time, at Peter's head, with warm admiration and high praise for both Mrs More and the bishop. In suggesting that Porteus had helped Mrs More with her works Dr Wolcot's satire was heavy-handed, indelicate, scurrilous and mistaken. The episode was like a 'female race' he had once seen, when

> Ten damsels, nearly all in *naked grace*,
> Rush'd for the precious Prize along the Green.

Sylvia's lover, 'mounted on a goodly Mule, whipped up the damsel on the beast behind him—'

> Then off he gallop'd; passed each panting Maid,
>   Who marked the *cheat* with disappointed eyes;
> Soon brought her in, unblushing at his aid,
>   And for his Favourite boldly claim'd the prize.
>
> Oh say, has nought been *very like* it, here?
>   Did no kind swain his hand to Hannah yield?
> No bishop's hand to help a heavy *rear*,
>   And bear the nymph triumphant o'er the field?

Porteus would have been among the first to point out that his writings were not on Mrs More's level. But obviously the whole tone of *Nil Admirari* was grossly objectionable (it was different for Mrs More herself to refer humorously to her physical proportions and apparently those of all the sisters, in some such way, writing to commission Sir William Weller Pepys to buy them a carriage). To the mind of the *Anti-Jacobin* all parts of the work were equally outrageous. 'If Peter had ranged over the whole kingdom in search of two objects of public derision, one of either sex', John Gifford wrote, 'he could, with difficulty, have selected two that would have answered his purpose better, than the BISHOP OF LONDON and Mrs H. MORE; for he could not have found two characters of more unimpeached integrity, of more spotless purity in private life; two of more amiable and more benevolent dispositions; nor two whose zeal was more ardent, whose efforts were more laudable to meliorate the hearts and minds, and to better the condition, of their fellow creatures.'[1]

In May of the same year, in a review of the Reverend Richard Polwhele's poem *The Unsexed Females*, an attack on Mary Wollstonecraft and other ladies who were tainted with French ideas, Gifford printed a note from the poem containing an equally fervid tribute to Mrs More. 'To the great natural endowments of Miss Wollstonecraft Miss More has added the learning of lady Jane Gray, without the pedantry; and the Christian graces of Mrs Rowe, without the enthusiasm. Her "Percy," her "sacred dramas," her "Essays," and her "Thoughts on the Manners of the Great," will be read as long as sensibility and good taste shall exist among us.'[2]

The *Anti-Jacobin* was soon to change its mind about Hannah More, and it had already begun its savage and long-continued attack on 'the gospel-preaching ministry', Sunday schools and other manifestations of subversion in the church. In October 1798 the Reverend Samuel Henshall sounded a solemn warning and a call to arms. A sect was rising in the church that was hostile to its principles and even to its existence. Against these new malignants the bishops must take instant and vigorous action. It was indeed high time 'to arm and to act'

when *schismatics* are embraced in the bosom of our church; when *treasurers* of *Calvinistic Charity Schools* have educated their sons for pastors of the Church of England; when rich *societies* of dissenters have been formed, and have purchased *livings*, and built episcopal *chapels* for *fanatics*; when the most *opulent rector* of our church petitions for the *repeal* of those *statutes* which secure our establishment; when more than half of the lecturers in London have learnt their divinity as *tradesmen*, or are *semi-methodists*; when *Bishops patronize and promote* such *deluding enthusiasts*; when Diocesans discourage their clergy that exclude such *deceivers* from their pulpits; and when the Chancellor of one of our *Universities* attends the *Unitarian Conventicle of Lindsey*. These are *facts*; we can prove them, and will not shrink from the investigation.... If our Bishops *will not*, or *dare not*, enforce such power in them vested, we may consider them as *cowards* when they should discharge their duty to God; *betrayers* of that established religion which they are bound

[1] *Anti-Jacobin*, September 1799, p. 322.
[2] *Ibid.* May 1799, p. 33.

to maintain; and as divines patient-suffering an act of suicide on our church. But, fortunately, we have every reason to entertain a very different opinion of them.[1]

The list of evils threatening the church was not directed against the Evangelicals only; the opulent rector was Paley, the Unitarian chancellor (of Cambridge) the Duke of Grafton. But the societies of 'dissenters' who were purchasing livings and building chapels for 'fanatics', the semi-methodist lecturers and the lecturers who had no formal theological training and were defended by the 'Bishops' (which probably meant Porteus only) were all members of what they themselves and their enemies were shortly to be calling 'the school of Mr Wilberforce'.

When in the following month, November 1798, the *Anti-Jacobin* printed a lengthy and favourable review by Henshall of Wilberforce's book, it is clear enough that these frightened and angry defenders of the ecclesiastical *status quo* had not yet realized that the 'gospel-preaching ministry' really were of that school. A blunder of the next issue, for December, perhaps shows why it was so hard for them to grasp. This was a favourable review of a volume of sermons by the Reverend Richard de Courcy of Shrewsbury, a veteran pre-Evangelical, the review written by none other than Sir Richard Hill. This was probably Hill's only appearance as a contributor in the *Anti-Jacobin*'s pages (he later appeared many times as a victim). Until the evidence was overwhelming it was impossible to believe that a wealthy man in all ways substantial and respectable, furthermore a baronet, and not one by any mere service or accomplishment but by birth, could be a 'Methodist in the church'.

The apprehensions of the *Anti-Jacobin* were stated again in September in a review of a pamphlet of Thomas Scott. This included 'some Account of a Society of Clergymen, in London, who have agreed to preach, in Rotation, Weekly Lectures, in each other's Churches and Chapels'. It was not clear to the reviewer, the Reverend Jonathan Boucher, that the bishop had allowed this unusual and unnecessary

---

[1] *Anti-Jacobin*, October 1798, pp. 399–400, 402. Henshall appears to have been that Samuel Henshall, M.A., Fellow of 'Brazen-Nose College', Oxford, whose historical and antiquarian works were so favourably received by the *Anti-Jacobin Review and Magazine*.

procedure. In any case, 'if...they merely are evangelical preachers, of that class, whom we of the establishment, perhaps, too indiscriminately, call methodists, but who take no common pains to be regarded as still, according to their own phraseology, *in the connection of the Church of England*, it proves to us, what we have long surmised, that their pretensions are neither so humble, nor their views so limited, as many good men are willing to believe'. The Society of Clergymen (and the *Anti-Jacobin*'s public) were reminded 'that fanaticism has its points of danger, as well as profligacy; and, finally, that if our constitution be destroyed, it will be but a poor consolation to us to reflect, that, as in the last century in this country, it has been destroyed by saints, rather than, as is now the case in France, by profligate sinners'.[1]

Boucher's review of Mrs More's *Strictures on the Modern System of Female Education* in October, as favourable and friendly as Henshall on Wilberforce, marks an advance in the *Anti-Jacobin*'s slow process of recognition. Mrs More is rebuked, lightly, for giving 'a novel turn to the Epistle of Saint Paul' by advocating—mistakenly, as Archdeacon Daubeny had already pointed out—'one of the favourite, though ill-founded, tenets of some particularly zealous and respectable Christians of our times; who, by this and some other similar misconceptions, seem to many, as well as to ourselves, to threaten hardly less danger to our national church, than it has to apprehend from avowed separatists'. The reviewer supposes that Mrs More 'took up this notion...from the school of Mr Wilberforce (since it is by that title that the Christians in question are said now to distinguish themselves)'.[2] In November 1799 the issue is stated in a less tentative though still contingent way. In a review of Archdeacon Daubeny's *Letter to Mrs Hannah More, on some Part of her Late Publication, entitled Strictures on Female Education*, Boucher noted again that Daubeny had pointed out to 'our fair author'...'an error of great moment' in her interpretation of *Romans*.

The position here objected to is, that faith is naturally and necessarily productive of the fruits of Christianity. This position is the child of enthusiasm; and the parent of many dangerous errors. Faith without works, and faith necessarily productive of works, appear to us to stand on the same footing of mischievous delusion; alike destructive of Christian purity in faith and practice. ...If Mrs More be really of Mr Wilberforce's school, her faith, like his, is

---

[1] *Ibid.* September 1799, pp. 34, 35.   [2] *Ibid.* October 1799, pp. 195–6.

Calvinism in disguise; and her attachment to the Church of England, of a very questionable kind....We shall lose no slight portion of that sincere respect which we feel for this distinguished writer, if she does not receive the friendly admonition, contained in this Letter, with unfeigned gratitude.[1]

It is a chastening thought that religious reformers so devoted to their country's good, so desperately concerned, as a matter of fundamental importance, not to be taken for Methodists, dissenters, political radicals, liberals, or any kind of people disliked by the great, should have been violently charged with just such corruptions through the most crucial decades of their campaign. With a loyalty to all respectable English institutions that was as unquestionable as the *Anti-Jacobin*'s, the Evangelicals held precisely the views of Gifford, Henshall, Polwhele and Boucher apart from certain aspects of their theology and their deeply puritanical morality. Both parties were attached with equal devotion to the prime minister and all sound conservative principles. But no thoughtful member of the High Church party had forgotten what the word 'Calvinist' had meant in the seventeenth century. Archbishop Laud had been executed, in defiance of justice and even of established legal procedure; and no one had forgotten either that Laud was an Arminian, that he had loathed Calvinism and done his best to stamp it out, and that there were many Calvinists in the parliament that kept him in the Tower for years without a trial and sent him to his death. When now there appeared a group of 'dissenters' in the church who were assuming the aspect of Calvinistic sectaries, with the language and habits of the Puritans who had been actual revolutionaries, it was natural in days of ferment and alarm that the loyal party should raise the old cry 'The Church in danger'.

There were striking similarities between the old Puritans and the new. For some years, when one came to think of it, the clergy of the school of Mr Wilberforce had called themselves the 'gospel-preaching ministry'. So had the Puritan ministers two hundred years earlier. They were already accusing the Orthodox clergy of being merely 'nominal Christians'. That too was an early seventeenth-century expression. The modern Puritans had begun their penetration into London pulpits (and had already made good progress) by acquiring—that is, by buying up, or by heavy subscriptions to the proper societies, or by securing the

[1] *Anti-Jacobin*, November 1799, pp. 254-5.

election of suitable persons—the chaplaincies and lectureships in London churches and charitable institutions. Laud had taken drastic steps to suppress the lectureships and private chaplaincies of the early seventeenth century as a notorious abuse, as notorious as the wandering preachers who corresponded ominously to the 'itinerant' preachers of Wesley, Whitefield and Lady Huntingdon and to not a few of the early Evangelicals. The moral aspects of the Evangelicals' religion were even more specifically puritanical. Their rigorous observance of the Sabbath, especially their antagonism to sports, games and pastimes on the Sabbath, recalled one of the most distinguishing and controversial aspects of the old Puritans. Hardly anything, it was held, did more to inflame the fanatics of their day than Laud's efforts to preserve a humane and reasonable attitude about Sunday recreation.[1]

And this was the school of Mr Wilberforce. A young man, only thirty-five when Cheap Repository appeared, brilliant, wealthy, already marked for high standing in the Commons—how could Mr Wilberforce be a sectary, Puritan, Calvinist, subversive, of the same blood and bone as the abhorrent fanatics of the last century? But if these people were correctly referred to as of that school, and Hannah More too was one of them, then other things must be believed: perhaps Bishop Porteus himself was not acting unwittingly in refusing to stop the encroachments of the fanatics in his diocese, giving some of them livings, instituting them as lecturers, making one of them his chaplain. The alarm of the Orthodox was particularly intensified as it became more and more unmistakable that these 'schismatics' so greatly antagonistic to High Church were having a considerable success in buying their way into church positions. As early as 1795 the Bampton lecturer, Dr Croft, had pointed out that that encroachment was well advanced: 'Hull affords one unfortunate instance of their success, for all the churches there are occupied by these pretended favourites of heaven.'[2]

While the truth was being slowly realized, one of the *Anti-Jacobin's* most vigorous writers, Samuel Henshall, spoke his mind plainly, pungently and with detailed information. His attack was more resolute than violent and thus not characteristic of him, as he was one of the

[1] *A Complete History of England* (London, 1706), vol. III, pp. 66–73.
[2] The Rev. George Croft, *Thoughts Concerning the Methodists and the Established Clergy*, p. 29. Quoted in Balleine, p. 78.

11-2

most offensive critics of the day. It has, however, unique value as a description of High Church–Evangelical relationships at the end of the century and deserves extensive quotation. The occasion was a review of Richard Cecil's *Discourses of the Hon. and Rev. William Bromley Cadogan*. This pioneer Evangelical, who died in 1797, held the living of St Luke's, Chelsea, was vicar of St Giles's in Reading and chaplain to his relative Lord Cadogan. Richard Cecil was attended at St John's Chapel, Bedford-row, by Wilberforce and most of the Evangelical leaders in London.

Some ministers in this kingdom have, for many years, arrogated to themselves the peculiar title of GOSPEL PREACHERS, as characteristic of the amazing efficacy of their doctrines to procure salvation for their followers. These teachers pride themselves as being the only true members of the Church of England. . . . To prove these assertions, we extract the subsequent passage from this publication, relative to the late Rev. WILLIAM ROMAINE, Rector of St Andrew, Wardrobe, and St Ann, Blackfriars:—

'When he first began, the numbers of those who PREACHED THE GOSPEL, and CHURCHES open to them, were few indeed; it might consist of UNITS, it increased afterwards to tens, and then to hundreds, and, before he died, he had a list of above FIVE HUNDRED BRETHREN AT ONCE [Henshall's note: Blasphemy, since alluding to the witnesses of our Saviour's Resurrection], for whom he could pray as FELLOW LABOURERS with himself, in the word and in doctrine. He constantly remembered them in his prayers, and set apart one day in the week, which he called his Litany-day . . . when he mentioned them every one by name before the throne of grace. The CHURCH OF ENGLAND, *then*, has lost a great FRIEND, a steady and a praying friend, in Mr Romaine; and you will do well to try your best to make amends for his loss, and to follow his faith in this particular. The prayer of faith availeth, and, waiting, as well as praying, faith did wonders for this excellent man; he lived to see MANY DOORS [Henshall's note: Church doors.] OPENED to him, which were SHUT against him; and was not only himself stablished, strengthened, settled, after he had suffered for a while, but placed in a most respectable situation, as Rector of this parish, in which he has discharged his duty with great fidelity and usefulness, and, his work being ended, is gone out of the world with as much credit as ever man left it, to give an account of himself unto God.'

This charge is *precise, decisive, and clear*. It is made by the leaders of these schismatics. It was written by Mr Cadogan, delivered by him before the society, and is now printed under the sanction of Mr *Cecil's* name, and with his concurrence. It is unequivocally stated, that the general body of the Clergy do *not preach the gospel*, and that they are not *true members of the Church of England*. We have long been acquainted with these circumstances, and have often heard similar assertions, and continual insinuations, to this purport, from the pulpits where *Cecil, Newton, Forster, Gunn* and *Goode*, have *spoken*. But now, 'Litera scripta manet,' they have publicly brought forward this *heinous accusation*, and every preacher in the established church must ask his own conscience whether he does *not preach* the gospel. ...

But let us examine what these schismatics mean by THEIR *Church of England*. Over this church Mr Romaine was *Overseer*, 'WILLIAM ROMAINE was the RIGHT REVEREND FATHER IN CHRIST;' 'he had that RULE over the church to which his great age and long experience in the things of GOD so justly entitled him'; he is 'ranked (by these sectaries) among those of whom the apostle may be supposed to speak.' 'Remember them which had the rule over you, who have spoken to you the word of God, whose faith follow, considering the end of their conversation. ... In Mr Romaine we had a leading man, whom we might consult in private, and hear in public, with profit and pleasure. His congregation, on Tuesday morning, was, generally, a choice company of ministers and people.'

He had 'five hundred ministers in his list' of gospel preachers, who spoke 'in the churches of the saints,' and many of whom, probably, had the implicit faith of Mr Cadogan, who states, that 'I could not but observe, the last time I heard him, a light upon his countenance, which appeared like the dawn, or a faint resemblance of glory.' We ask whether such ministers have not separated themselves from their diocesan—whether they are not members of a *church* within a *church*—whether such teachers who, in the language of Mr Cecil, are reported 'like Mr Cadogan, to have *happily emerged* from their brethren,' are not guilty of the sin of SCHISM, and whether their separation from the church government of this realm 'may not rise in judgement against them?' For these seceders from our episcopal church are numerous, active, united, and supported by opulent patrons. The Rev. John Newton, Rector of St Mary, Wolnoth, may, perhaps, be their present director and head, for Mr Cadogan addresses him as a 'father,' when he was but a 'little child and a young man.'

This fraternity, under the auspices of a gentleman, whose name we would never mention without that respect which is due to fervent piety, virtuous intentions, and an irreproachable character, Mr *Wilberforce*; of the *Thorntons, Oldham*, &c. &c. has purchased many livings in different counties of the kingdom, has erected numerous chapels in populous towns, and has even engrossed, we understand, a majority of the lectureships in LONDON. The agents of these separatists are indefatigable, and if they once obtain a majority in a corporate body, they never lose it. Thus, in the Weavers Company, where the nomination of two evening lecturers is vested in the court of assistants, no person is now admitted a member of such court until he has given a promise to vote for Mr Cecil and Mr Forster alternately. In populous districts, as the whole society's strength is exerted in favour of the methodistical candidate, they have frequently carried the election, and, if the Rector should refuse his pulpit, (where he has the power, for in the new churches he has not the power,) he incurs all the odium of this measure, while his diocesan is applauded for his liberality, candour, and toleration. For there is one 'living prelate of exalted character,' whom Mr Cecil does 'not name, from motives of delicacy,' who certainly does *not persecute* these *vital preachers of Evangelism.*

But, as these enlightened and spiritualizing divines pretend to preach, exclusively, the *whole counsel* of God, in opposition to the general body of the Clergy; as they affect to understand the articles of our church with greater precision, and to comprehend them more systematically, than any other Clergymen, let us investigate the fundamental principles on which they pretend to ground their superiority over their *nominal* brethren.

These teachers of the gospel of Jesus, who enforce damnation by abrogating redemption from the *non-elect*, the non-justified by their *vital knowledge* and *experience* of their *feeling* salvation (for their doctrines or language are not 'fully understood, but by those who have felt'), affect extraordinary superiority over priests in general. They despise the language of the schools and universities, and assert that 'a person may pass through most of our public seminaries, and our two *famous* Universities also, and never *once* have put into his hands, as the book for study and meditation, the SCRIPTURE GIVEN BY INSPIRATION OF GOD.'...These Gospel-ministers, as their followers are instructed to call them, upbraid the Clergy of our Church with not preaching the whole counsel of God. We boldly reply to such charge, that the sound and orthodox divines, of whom there are thousands in England, firmly believe, and frequently preach, as pure and true doctrines, those contained in the 9th, 10th, 11th, 12th, and 13th articles of our faith, on which these separatists continually dwell, and almost exclusively.... 'If these conscientious Ministers of the church,' who preach the 'renunciation of righteousness,'—'evangelical religion,' and the '*sufficiency of Christian grace*,' to the *elect*, the *called*, the *saints*, will deliberately weigh the probable consequences resulting from such doctrines propagated amongst the poor and illiterate, they cannot but admit that there is considerable danger, lest, while divine grace is continually exalted, and the merits of Christ perpetually dwelt upon, that some auditors may pervert such doctrines, as convenient to their sinful course of life, as indulgent to their immorality and profligacy....But sound members of the church preach doctrines that cannot be so misunderstood...they ascribe our salvation solely to [Christ's] merits...but they also preach the necessity of good works, as grateful to God, and acceptable to Christ.

There was no really irreconcilable conflict between Orthodoxy and Evangelicalism over the place of good works in the consummation of the Christian life. One difference, however, was vital. 'But there are other *principles* which these sectaries teach not, omit, or misrepresent', Henshall continued,

one of which is '*the doctrines of baptism.*' The church of England catechism states, 'I heartily thank my heavenly Father, that he hath called me to this state of salvation,' by BAPTISM; the necessary consequence educible from this is, that our church supposes all those who are baptized to be in a state of salvation. But what do these seceders inculcate? That no one knows Christ, is a true Christian, until he can specify the *precise time* and *hour* of his *conversion*, until he can speak of his experience; though their leader, and Bishop, Romaine, almost at the close of his life, 'saw much before him to be learnt and experienced.' Thus Mrs Littlehales, who had been regularly educated and baptized, in conformity to the canons of the church, is represented by Mr Cadogan, at the age of fifty-nine, as having 'only been a follower of the Lord thirty years;' *ergo*, we are not followers of the Lord by baptism. Indeed, these schismatics, either deficient in the power of discrimination, or perversely blind, represent the inhabitants of England as heathens in the age of the Apostles; and those, whom they affect to have converted, are said to have 'turned from *idols* and *vanities.*'

In one further objection of Henshall's to this work of Cadogan and Cecil any sensible, practical Evangelical (such as William Wilberforce) would have concurred in the heartiest way.

But we cannot conclude our comments on this publication, by *an honourable gentleman*, without noticing a proof of want of *charity*, which it is impossible to account for, except by a supposition that he wished to ingratiate himself with the lower orders at the expence of the superior ranks. 'The gospel, which proclaims this grace' [he goes on to cite from Cadogan] 'brings down and levels with the dust all sorts and conditions of men: it teaches the WISE, the MIGHTY, the NOBLE, (IF ANY SUCH ARE CALLED,) to share its blessings in common with the poor; whose privilege it is to be "evangelized," and "chosen rich in faith, and heirs of the kingdom, which God hath promised to them that love him."'

Surely, such false insinuations manifest not the *fruits* of a Christian spirit, but the 'leaven of malice:' and, surely, the loyalty of these men, and their attachment to our established government, must be strongly questioned, when we find them adopting the following language: 'To the poor we look for reformation.'

'It is to be lamented' [Henshall further quotes these unworldly Evangelical priests] 'that persons, placed in superior stations, and qualified to do the most good by their rank or wealth, are the least disposed to do it by their habits or inclinations. They want all their money and their time for their pleasures; and, living in a constant round of dissipation, they know nothing of misery but by the name. So great are their calls for the sports of the country, and the diversions of the town, that they have nothing left for the relief of the poor.'

The *world* can bear witness, that this is a *misrepresentation*, (for British liberality, generosity, and charity, are themes of praise in every clime,) not spoken from the *candour* and *truth* that is by Jesus Christ.[1]

So Mr Henshall, in April 1799. In the last matter, while it is clear that he was wholly ignorant of the Christian doctrine of charity and actually believed that liberality and generosity are Christian virtues, he could not have made a more telling point (without knowing he was doing it). His statement of the attitude of such Evangelicals as Cadogan and Cecil toward the wealthy and the powerful was correct, and from the point of view of anyone who wanted the Evangelical Reformation to succeed no attitude could have been more harmful.

II

In 1799 and 1800 the *Anti-Jacobin* increased the violence and dimensions of its attack on one of the most cherished Evangelical reform agencies, the Sunday schools. The education of the poor was not favoured by the *Anti-Jacobin*. 'That the practice of virtue is promoted, among the lower orders, by the distribution even of the most approved books, is a point which we consider as problematical', Polwhele wrote in June 1799. 'In the humbler walks of life, those who are acquainted with the plain and practical parts of their Bible, possess knowledge "sufficient unto salvation". To such persons more extensive acquirements have often proved pernicious.' 'We are no friends to Sunday-schools', Gifford added in a footnote, 'which we are convinced, have been the nurseries of

---

[1] *Anti-Jacobin*, vol. II, pp. 361–71.

fanaticism.'[1] In the same issue, in a review of still another article attacking Sunday schools, Gifford printed a lengthy defence of his journal's antagonism to them that contained, for the first time in this conflict, an explicit warning to the High Church party on the necessity of a faithful and constant attention to their duty.

At no period, since the aera of the reformation, has so strong and urgent a necessity existed for the exertion of uncommon vigilance, circumspection, and energy, on the part of our Clergy, as at this moment, when wolves are, indeed, prowling about in sheep's clothing; and the most insidious manoeuvres are employed, even by those who profess to be members of the established church, (with a view to impose on the credulity, and to quiet the consciences of many of their most scrupulous auditors,) for subverting the establishment. Under such circumstances we cannot too strongly impress, on the minds of the parochial clergy, a sense of the immense advantages that must accrue from *residence* in their respective parishes.

Though we give the fullest credit to the worthy characters who originally instituted, and encouraged the extension of SUNDAY SCHOOLS, yet we ever entertained very strong doubts, arising partly from permanent, partly from temporary, causes, of the policy, the expediency, and the utility, of such institutions....We knew perfectly well that *Sunday schools* had, in many instances, been rendered channels for the diffusion of bad principles, religious and political.[2]

It was not only that the Sunday schools fostered Methodism. The High Church group (in general) saw them also as agencies for the spread of political radicalism. 'The descendants of the puritans are still found among us, in great numbers; they retain the same principles which in England and America have produced so much disturbance; they take care, by their offspring and their seminaries, to transmit those principles to their posterity; and they have, with few exceptions, admired, extolled, nay, even encouraged and promoted, to the utmost of their power, the French Revolution, because it was founded upon their own principles.'[3]

The author of that passage, John Bowles, was of course referring to the dissenters, who up to 1800 probably had as much to do with Sunday schools as the Evangelicals. After 1800 when the Evangelicals had taken over the Sunday School Society and other such institutions it

[1] *Ibid.* vol. III, p. 180.   [2] *Ibid.* pp. 319–21.   [3] *Ibid.* October 1800, p. 87.

was an easy matter to transfer to them, most unjustly, the dissenters' sympathy for at least some aspects of the French Revolution.

From July 1798 for many years hardly an issue of the *Anti-Jacobin* appeared without articles, reviews or communications pointing out the danger to the church and the nation from the progress of 'puritanical fanaticism'. These alarmed and unremitting notices varied from attacks on Hawker, Romaine, Haweis, Cecil, Gunn, Cadogan, Rowland Hill and other Evangelicals or semi-Evangelicals to expositions of the harmful effects of Evangelical preaching, the laxity of the episcopal bench in taking no action, the evils of Sunday schools and particularly the Evangelical purchases over the nation of next presentations and advowsons and the rapid inroads of Evangelical lecturers in London. 'Lectureships, in many particulars, are great and increasing evils.... They are often nurseries of schism, and introduce a motley compound of Dissenters, Methodists, and Republicans, into the Church of England, sometimes, in opposition to the Rector, the proper proprietor of the church.' This anonymous correspondent of the *Anti-Jacobin* had especially in mind lecturers chosen by vote of the seat-holders. 'The means of obtaining these marks of popular favour are often scandalous in the extreme.' 'Very lately, in a populous parish in the west part of the town, public-houses were opened for more than two months before the election, to treat the pious and worthy voters. The violent and scandalous conduct, at another election, must not soon be forgotten, when the electors came to the church, hallowing and hooting, in coaches; some not the most sober, and one party bore these words chalked on their carriages—"F—— and Jesus Christ for ever."'[1]

The pages of the *Anti-Jacobin* were thus substantially occupied with a resolute resistance to Evangelicalism when the Calvinistic Controversy of 1798–1812 broke out. Throughout it probably every book and pamphlet that appeared was reviewed, often at great length—its review of Overton's *True Churchman Ascertained*, for example, running through six numbers in perhaps thirty thousand words, as if to give the impression of matching the work reviewed in length as well as in intemperance. The formal issue at debate in this Controversy and the debate itself were equally profitless. Were the Articles of the church

[1] *Anti-Jacobin*, vol. III (June 1799), p. 178. That description of the election of the Reverend Henry Foster is given (in the same way) in several places.

Calvinistic? At the outset it was pointed out by several sober persons that 'at the time of the reformation, some of the compilers of the articles were Calvinists, others were Arminians; with much temper and judgment they so framed the articles as to embrace both, well knowing that a national church ought to stand on a broad foundation'.[1] If the Articles were Calvinistic, the Regular clergy were false to the doctrine of their church, for they were opposed to Calvinism to a man. So also were many of the Evangelicals even by the end of the century. But there were enough articulate, stubborn and tactless Calvinists in the ranks, in particular old Dr Hawker and old Sir Richard Hill, to give the impression that the whole iron doctrine was held by all the 'school of Mr Wilberforce', including to his distress Wilberforce himself, little tainted with Calvinism at this time and not at all later on.

If there was no vital issue in the formal terms of the Calvinistic Controversy there was much at issue in the Evangelical assault on the Orthodox clergy that the controversy was part of. The real point of this struggle was not whether the Articles of the church were Calvinistic; it was whether the 'idol shepherds' were scribes and Pharisees, unconverted clergymen, fat bulls of Bashan. In the larger struggle the magnitude and bitterness of this skirmish over Calvinism points to substantial Evangelical growth and the Orthodox recognition that their attack was already formidable. 'Within the writer's remembrance', Thomas Scott wrote in 1811, 'the Calvinists, especially the evangelical clergy, were so inconsiderable and neglected a company, that, except in a declamation now and then in a visitation-sermon, little publick notice was taken of them. But now, it seems, they are become so numerous and successful, that, unless more decided measures be adopted, there is danger lest "all the world should go after them." And "in this I do rejoice, yes, and will rejoice."'[2] Wilberforce rejoiced too, in the growth of the Evangelical clergy, but it was no source of happiness to him that the grim spectre of a religion so uncompromising, so little suited to his purpose, should have been revivified in this way. Needless to say, he and Mrs More took no part in this engagement, Mrs More among other things being painfully engaged during the first years of it

[1] The Reverend William Agutter, *Anti-Jacobin*, vol. v (January 1800), p. 47.
[2] *Remarks on the Refutation of Calvinism by The Lord Bishop of Lincoln* (London, 1811), vol. I, pp. iii–iv.

in a controversy of her own. John Newton had still another reason for taking no part. He was a fully believing, quite unaccommodated Calvinist, knowing that if God had not arbitrarily saved him with a high hand, in defiance of himself, with no slightest act of merit on his part, he must have been lost.[1] He knew also that all controversy is bad and that this one was peculiarly likely to produce nothing but ill will. But Newton, it may be remembered, was the possibly unique Calvinist to whom it made no difference whether a man called himself a Calvinist or not provided he was manifestly making his way to the Cross. It was natural that he should view this Controversy sadly from the sidelines. 'How pleased is Satan when he can prevail to set those at variance who are in so many respects united!'

The Controversy may be said to have begun (though a few pamphlets that did not attract attention had appeared earlier) with the publication in 1798 of Archdeacon Daubeny's *Guide to the Church*, addressed to Wilberforce and intended to correct the errors of his *Practical Christianity*. It set forth in nearly five hundred pages, with the motto 'There should be no Schism in the Body', the Arminian doctrine that to Daubeny's mind was that of the whole church. Sir Richard Hill, who had been a doughty contender in this arena years before, when he had met face to face a champion greater than Archdeacon Daubeny, namely John Wesley, replied to it in the same year with his *Apology for Brotherly Love*, in two hundred pages, with the motto 'Love as Brethren', title and motto hardly indicating the sternness of Sir Richard's love for those brethren who did not agree with him. Daubeny replied with his *Appendix to the Guide to the Church* in more than six hundred pages, Hill returned with *Reformation Truth Restored* and *Daubenism Confuted*, the Archdeacon came into the lists again in 1803 with *Vindiciae Ecclesiae Anglicanae*. Earlier, in 1797, the Reverend George Croft (of University College, Oxford) had come forward against the Puritans and in the same year appeared Thomas Ludlam's *Four Essays*, which attacked Evangelicalism generally and in particular Scott, Newton, Milner, Venn and Robinson. The wrath of the Reverend Mr Ludlam was at least in part a product of human frailty. He had been a supporter and friend of Thomas Robinson of Leicester until, on one unfortunate occasion, anti-Arminian doctrine caused Robinson to utter permanently offensive words.

[1] *Newton*, vol. v, p. 207.

Mr R. I am going to Cambridge, sir! Will you lend me your cloak?

Mr L. O yes, not my cloak only, but my head if you like.

Mr R. Your head! I should like some things in it very well.

Mr L. Nay take it all; take it all; it is as God made it.

Mr R. Excuse me, sir! not as God made it, but as you have corrupted it.[1]

'Note after note, explanation after explanation, followed these words', says Robinson's biographer, the Reverend E. T. Vaughan. 'But all in vain.' Mr L. was offended deeply, and in time his enmity, 'now working secretly and privately for many years', broke out into four metaphysical essays. They were followed in 1798 by *Six Essays upon Theological (to which are added two upon moral) Subjects,* and in 1807 Thomas Ludlam and his brother William Ludlam, both Cambridge men and greatly opposed to the alarming progress being made in the University by Evangelicalism, published a reissue entitled *Essays, Scriptural, Moral and Logical,* directed chiefly against Robinson, Newton, Milner and a new Evangelical controversialist, Overton, which with appendices now constituted a pamphlet of one thousand and eight pages. Mr Thomas Ludlam, Robinson's biographer tells us, could not take a joke, though he was himself in a general habit of jesting and raillery of a profuse and intemperate sort, but Mr Vaughan was assured 'that the last year or two of his life was peaceful, and that his irritation on religious subjects had almost wholly subsided, before he died'.[2]

The Controversy was fairly under way with the engagement of Sir Richard Hill and Archdeacon Daubeny, and it was joined year after year by a large number of combatants. It may be thought of for present purposes as ending with Bishop Tomline's *Refutation of Calvinism* of 1811 and Thomas Scott's two-volume *Remarks on the Refutation of Calvinism by the Lord Bishop of Lincoln* of the same year. In this duel between the leading Evangelical Calvinist (John Newton having died in 1807) and his bishop, a wily, supple and shallow man came to grips with a broodingly thoughtful and solidly informed man who knew greatly more about Calvinism. When Tomline cited a passage 'by modern Calvinistic writers' as an example of wrong thinking on the matter, Scott pointed out to him that it came from the Book of Homilies.

[1] Vaughan, *Some Account of the Rev. Thomas Robinson,* p. 207.
[2] *Ibid.* pp. 217, 220.

His Lordship has here inadvertently made a concession of so great importance as, if carried to its full consequence, determines the question, Whether the church of England be Calvinistick in doctrine or not? The passage, inclosed by double inverted commas, is adduced as the words of 'modern Calvinistick writers;' but are indeed a quotation from the Homilies of our church! Ergo, the compilers of our homilies were Calvinistick writers. The same persons formed our articles and liturgy: (for the homily, whence it is taken, is one of those set forth in Queen Elizabeth's reign, 1562:) Ergo, they who formed our articles and liturgy were Calvinistick writers....I shall only add, my sincere desire and prayer, that all our bishops, priests, and deacons, may become so familiarly acquainted with the language of the homilies, as to be effectually secured from falling into such mistakes in future.[1]

Tomline removed the citation, without comment, from his next edition, and may have recalled the warning of a man of greater stature, Bishop Horsley, that particularly as Calvinism was chiefly drawn from Augustine, one of the great figures of the Church Universal, it was a good idea before one entered into controversy about it to find out what it was.

III

Beyond pointing out the growing strength of the 'school of Mr Wilberforce' and the resentment and fear of the Regular clergy and their supporters, the Calvinistic Controversy has the value of bringing out the unquestioning belief of the Orthodox that they were fighting against a morose and harmful puritanism.

Invective and offensive language in the Controversy was not used only by the *Anti-Jacobin* and the High Church writers. In the Evangelical John Overton's *Four Letters to the Editor of the Christian Observer* (1805) he complained that his opponents' attacks were notoriously characterized by violence, dishonesty and unqualified calumny. Daubeny he believed had been guilty of glaring polemical dishonesty, garbling and misquoting. (The Archdeacon in fact set a high standard, for this Controversy, in good manners and avoidance of misrepresentation.) The reasoning of another of Overton's opponents, Dean Kipling of St John's College, Cambridge, was 'debased by the intermixture of

[1] *Remarks on the Refutation of Calvinism etc.*, vol. I, pp. 105–6.

the very grossest scurrility and calumny'; 'may God forgive every Dignitary of a Christian Church, who can so far forget what becomes his character and his station, and so outrageously violate his duty towards his neighbour'.[1] Still harsher language was used in the course of the Controversy, much of it coming from Sir Richard Hill, a veteran of theological dispute in the good old days of Toplady, Berridge and Grimshawe when it was customary to utter religious truths in the plainest speech. 'I must shelter myself under the wings of an Elijah', Hill said, '...when addressing the prophets of Baal.'[2] The title-page of his *Apology for Brotherly Love* contained the charge that Daubeny had made a false quotation from an early pamphlet of his, and in the text he charged the Archdeacon with poor trite cavils and unfair representations; had he been a less respectable figure he would have been treated with silent pity and contempt. James Lackington the Methodist bookseller, who had made the same misquotation, 'often raises his head out of the dunghill of filth, falsehood, and ridicule of sacred truths...'. 'I trust I shall never say par nobile fratrum.'[3]

In *Reformation Truth Restored* Sir Richard Hill concerned himself still less with courtesies. Daubeny had so increased the number of dissenters in his own parish 'that the grass grows at the Church door', his style was felt to be pompous and stilted, it was believed he published only to attract notice, his quotations were false and scurrilous, his account of Martin Luther indecent, abusive and a foul slander. Daubeny was now, as a result of Hill's pamphlets, flat on his back; 'but as some animals defend themselves best in such a position, you will do well to avail yourself of it for that purpose'. He had cruelly, disdainfully and despitefully cast foul aspersions and insinuations and was opprobrious, abusive and sneering. It should be said for Hill that he meant no harm by such language, or at least said so repeatedly, and it should be said for Daubeny that Hill's charges were unfounded. The Archdeacon though

[1] *Four Letters*, p. 30.
[2] *Apology for Brotherly Love*, p. vii.
[3] *Ibid.* p. 109. An interesting feature of this Controversy was the decent spicing of writers' pages with Latin tags attesting a gentlemanly and cultured background: 'principiis obsta', 'fas est et ab hoste doceri', 'ex uno disce omnes', 'quem deus vult perdere prius dementat', 'amicus Plato, amicus Socrates, sed magis amica Veritas', etc., etc.

pained was always scrupulous, and one of Hill's expressions about his works, 'a mingle-mangle of trickery, misstatement and dishonesty', applies much better to his own writings.

Such language may be described as not well designed to make for harmony, and it was common in most of the pamphlets. In particular three contributions of the Reverend Robert Fellowes, the admired correspondent of the Swan of Lichfield Miss Anna Seward, abounded in violent language. Fellowes was a very young man, a Whig, a reader of William Godwin and a pupil and follower of Dr Samuel Parr.[1] But tainted with liberalism, even radicalism, as he was, the ingenuous rhetoric of his abusiveness made him an interesting contributor to the Controversy and the general nature of his assaults brings out two note-worthy features of it.

Though the present increasing luxury in one part of the community, with the increased and increasing distress in another, do greatly favour the corruption of public morals, I think that another very vigorous and active cause of the declension of virtue and the increase of vice will be found in those polluted, unreasonable, and absurd representations of the Christian religion, which have, of late years, been with too little consideration patronised by the great, and with too much facility listened to by the populace. [Most people, following the easy path,] are pre-disposed to lend a willing ear to the instructions of any religious juggler who endeavours to persuade them, that faith without holiness, grace without exertion, or righteousness by imputation will supersede the necessity of personal goodness, and exempt the favoured convert from the painful toils of practical morality. Such admonitions, coloured over with a great deal of cant, in order to disguise the rottenness of the ingredients and the unwholesomeness of the mixture, have been called 'Evangelical Preaching'; and, at other times, emphatically 'Preaching the Gospel'; and the great and everlasting principles of moral duty have been shamelessly libelled, and most industriously lowered in the public estimation, by men professing to teach the holy doctrine of the holy Jesus.

The attempts which have been made, of late years, to bring what has been

---

[1] His tutor's influence on Fellowes is noticeable. Dr Parr, he wrote, was 'one, who is equally distinguished by the vigor of his intellect and the fervor of his benevolence; who is a philosopher without dogmatism, a critic without bitterness, and a priest without intolerance and without guile'. This assertion, the last three statements of which are grossly incorrect, is exactly what Parr thought expressed exactly as Parr would have said it.

too contemptuously termed '*moral preaching*', into disrepute, are too notorious to be forgotten, and too destructive of national virtue not to be mentioned with abhorrence.[1]

A more precise statement of that belief in Fellowes's *Religion Without Cant* shows how right the Evangelicals were in avoiding, in every way they could manage, the possibility of connecting them with the Methodists. Here we see the cause of their insistence on a Christian cheerfulness, good humour and even jocularity that in many cases (for example Sir Richard Hill) really seems to have been carried too far. Hence too Wilberforce's frequently expressed regret that some of the Party clergy, notably Legh Richmond and Scott, lacked the manners of the cultivated gentleman, and his courteously masked but recognizable uneasiness at being among dissenters. What Fellowes described as the appearance and practice of 'Evangelical preaching' was absurd as a description of even Scott, Newton and Romaine, the most dissenter-like of the Party clergy, though no more absurd than to describe Wilberforce as a Jacobin. This substitution of a wraith of the Puritan 'vessels' of the seventeenth century, or of some of the extremer contemporary Methodists, for the real form of the leading Evangelicals was precisely the chief dread of the Party strategists. Nothing could have damaged their cause more. 'In whatever village the Fanatics get a footing, drunkenness and swearing,—sins, which being more exposed to the eyes of the world, would be ruinous to their great pretence to superior sanctity, will, perhaps, be found to decline; but I am convinced, from personal observation, that lying and dishonesty, that every species of fraud and falsehood,—sins, which are not so readily detected, but which seem more closely connected with worldly advantage, will be found, invariably to increase.'[2] The hearers of the 'whining, unintelligible cant' of the Evangelical preachers often have 'bodies covered with rags, incrusted with filth, or wasting with disease;—a state of misery and indigence to which they are too often reduced by neglecting their proper calling, and the reasonable worship of their forefathers, to listen to the pernicious jargon of some juggling fiend'.[3]

In his *Picture of Christian Philosophy* (1798) Fellowes had attacked Wilberforce hotly for his Puritanism, and in *Religion Without Cant* and

[1] *Religion Without Cant*, pp. xiii–xiv.
[2] *Ibid.* pp. 28–9.   [3] *Ibid.* p. 31.

also in *The Anti-Calvinist* he returned still more vehemently to the attack with a baleful picture of the stubborn ignorance or perfidious wickedness of the 'horde of fanatics', their miserable, whining, drivelling cant, their 'gangrened sperm and abortions of hypocrisy', their 'fanaticism, whose absurdity is always surpassed by its malignancy', their funereal aspect, 'the roaring torrent of their fierce and merciless imprecations', their acrimonious severity, 'made more hideous and loathsome by desponding shrugs, doleful sighs and hollow-sounding groans', and the 'scorching fires of their intolerance'.[1] In particular, 'the Fanatics are very industrious in establishing Sunday schools, in order to gangrene the principles of the country; and to give an unkind, unsocial Calvinistic complexion to the manners of the people'.[2]

Fellowes's *Picture of Christian Philosophy* is adequate evidence that he knew the difference between Wilberforce's Evangelicals and the debased characters of the passages cited, that he had no proper notion of the true principles of benevolence, and that his own Christianity, deeply contaminated by his reading of William Godwin and as far removed from proper High Church doctrine as it was from Evangelicalism, was of so mild, sweet and gentle a nature as hardly to be considered a religion at all.

I shall here say a few words on the fashionable (shall I call it orthodox?) practice of stigmatizing many sincere believers by the cant appellation of 'Nominal Christians,'—a mode of phraseology very usual with Mr Wilberforce and the Christians of his school. They call every man a 'Nominal Christian,' who will not yield an unconditional assent to their unscriptural decrees, or who cannot ascend to the height of their visionary raptures.'...
'Mr Wilberforce...seems to suppose, that a steady and undoubting conviction of the inborn and radical corruption of the human heart, is the foundation-stone of righteousness....Can any man, in his senses, and the exercise of whose understanding is not palsied by the dwarfish cowardice of superstition, acquiesce in the notion of inbred and inalienable guilt? Does sin consist, not in sinning, but in passing our mother's womb?

Our mere descent from Adam, does not make us sinful; nor, *till we have sinned in our own persons*, can we be worthy objects of divine punishment...'.
'The pretended Evangelical preachers, who have found a patron and disciple in Mr Wilberforce, endeavour to lay what they imagine the foundation stone of righteousness, by convincing their followers of their universal, inbred and

---

[1] *Anti-Calvinist*, pp. iv, v, vi.   [2] *Religion Without Cant*, p. 31, note.

radical corruption....As [they] affect to preach nothing but Jesus, it is strange they should so rarely recommend to the imitation and practice of their followers, the striking lineaments of his character, and the most prominent features of his doctrine! In a cant unmeaning jargon, they talk much of vital faith; but they say little of vital benevolence, without which faith can be but a sound....Mr Wilberforce would have acted more wisely, if he had made religion to consist, as Jesus Christ evidently did, in those benevolent sympathies which invariably lead to benevolent actions. Here there is no room for hypocrisy or delusion. Religion is appreciated by a rule of which we cannot mistake the application.

Whoever 'is wanting in that spirit of benevolence', Fellowes concludes, 'which, more than anything else, designates the true Christian, deserves the opprobrious name of "Nominal Christian"'.[1]

That soft, feeble and fearfully wrong view of Christianity had already been crushed by the sledge-hammer of Calvin (to name no others), and in the hands of the old African blasphemer or the old Lincolnshire shepherd the Reverend Mr Fellowes would not have lasted a minute. Mrs More had equally demolished his curious Godwinian–Christian view of 'general benevolence' as the essence of Christ's teachings. But his beliefs were so remote from those of the correct Orthodox section of his church that (as he was also a Whig) it is no wonder he remained curate of Harbury all his life.

IV

In the Preface to volume II of the *Anti-Jacobin* (1799) John Gifford uttered a warning graver and more emphatic than any yet given. It contained again a clear-sighted exhortation to the kind of conduct demanded of the Regular clergy by their critical situation. The Puritan encroachment was no longer a threatening possibility, Gifford believed; it was a present danger. 'It only remains to offer a serious admonition to the Clergy of the Established Church; to exhort them to unusual vigilance in performing the duties of their stations, and in keeping intruders out of their folds; to recall to their minds the salutary adage —Principiis obsta—leaving its application to their own sense and penetration; to warn them that their enemies are indefatigable in their

---

[1] *A Picture of Christian Philosophy*, pp. xix–xx, 109–113, 114, 132, 152–8.

exertions to undermine the establishment, and that the defeat of every effort for this purpose, from whatever quarter it may proceed, depends essentially, if not solely, on themselves. On *our* unwearied support and assistance they may repose the fullest reliance.'[1]

The *Anti-Jacobin*'s fear that the school of Wilberforce were scheming to bring George III and old Archbishop Moore to the block was probably assumed, though it was the belief of the Reverend Edward Crosse, one of their contributors, that the 'fanatics' were 'a faction, equally puritanic, and perhaps equally sanguinary with that, which has already dragged degraded monarchy from its throne, and forced insulted prelacy into exile'. Gifford's repeated warnings about the strength and activity of Evangelicalism were justified. A warning as urgent as his and better informed was given to the public two years later by a really formidable anti-Evangelical, William Cobbett. It was brought out by an episode of the conflict known as the Blagdon Controversy, the heroine of which was Hannah More. There had been a time when Cobbett was delighted with Cheap Repository—he had circulated it in America—and in a letter of April 1800 he had called Peter Pindar's lampoon an attempt 'to ridicule the incomparable Mrs H. More'. But that was in earlier days. His maturer views were stated in an eloquent denunciation of Mrs More and the 'schismatics' that appeared in the first issue of his *Political Register* in February 1802. It took the form of a letter on religious conditions in England to a Philadelphia correspondent.

'The public matter here, which seems to have most particularly engaged your attention, is, that which has been lately agitated in the west of England, and which, as you justly fear, has *discovered*, but not *made*, an alarming schism in the Church of England.'

Affecting to regard Mrs More, 'who has laboured so zealously in the cause of virtue and religion', as a well-meaning woman, loyal to church and crown but deceived by subversive fanatics—a tactical disingenuousness that the Orthodox party gave up in the course of the year—Cobbett went on to draw a picture of aggressive Evangelicalism that was true and penetrating in point after point. Even with some old error and some new, it takes place with Henshall's article of April 1799 as the most acute and striking statement about the membership, aims

[1] *Anti-Jacobin*, vol. II, p. iv.

and methods of the Evangelical Party made by their adversaries during the early reform period.

The sect, Sir, who have engendred all this disturbance, mischief, and disgrace, are not, as you seem to imagine, mere misguided fanatics, newly born, and destined soon to die. They are cool, of consummate cunning, of great industry, and perseverance, and supported by men of no little wealth; and, they possess all the influence, which coolness, cunning, industry, perseverance, and wealth united, can give. They are of long standing, and, I greatly fear, will not...soon be converted from the error of their ways.

They are the offspring, but not the open imitators, of the methodists. They discovered, that, to accomplish their ambitious objects, it was necessary to dissent from that wild rant, and that beggarly itinerancy, which, though they serve to extort pious groans from the lowest of the ignorant, finally expose the operators to general derision and contempt. Profiting from this discovery, the chosen vessels of the sect assumed a more placid appearance, a deportment less austere, and a language less vulgar and insolent. They no longer thundered out their impious anathemas on the Clergy of the Church, whom, on the contrary, they affected to regard as labourers in the same vineyard, claiming for themselves the precedence in piety alone. That the world is very apt to take professions upon trust, especially when garbed in the veil of worldly humility, did not wait for a proof in the success of this sect, who having, little by little, worked themselves into countenance and favour, have, at last, succeeded in scaling the walls of the Church, which is now tolerably well stocked with Gospel-Ministers, an appellation which the vessels of the sect have exclusively assumed.

The mention of Gospel-Ministers will certainly recall to your mind the 'Gospel-Preaching-Ministry,' so loudly clamoured for by the apprentices and chimney-sweepers of London in their petitions to the regicide Parliament; and, my dear Sir, painful as is the acknowledgement of the fact, I am fully persuaded, that the puritans of the present day are very little better than those of the disgraceful era, to which I have alluded. Those of that day were destitute of many of the specious pretexts, and many of the other advantages, which their more fortunate successors enjoy. Legislative solicitude for bettering the conditions of Negro slaves had not then made an opening for the intrusion of their hypocritical compassion, nor had the philanthropic title of citizen of the world sanctioned indifference to country, and broken the more sacred bonds of allegiance.

In one point, and that too of more importance than is generally attached to it, the puritans of the two epochs bear a critical resemblance, namely, their hostility to rural and athletic sports; to those sports which string the nerves and strengthen the frame, which excite an emulation in deeds of hardihood and valour, and which imperceptibly instill honour, generosity, and a love of glory, into the mind of the clown. Men thus formed are pupils unfit for the puritanical school; therefore it is, that the sect are incessantly labouring to eradicate, fibre by fibre, the last poor remains of English manners. And, sorry I am to tell you, that they meet with but too many abettors, where they ought to meet with resolute foes.[1]

Returning to Mrs More's controversy over her school system with Thomas Bere the Orthodox curate of the parish of Blagdon, Cobbett ended with the charge that she was secretly receiving powerful and highly placed support that should have been defending church and crown against her subversive practices. 'I think it right to mention to you, that my reason for discontinuing to send the British Critic is, that that work has, in its criticisms on the pamphlets, relative to the Blagdon Controversy, abandoned the Church for the defence of which it was originally established. I well know what influence produced this shameful abandonment, and, though it will give me great pain to trace it to its lofty origin, and expose it to the world, yet the cause of the injured and oppressed Mr Bere, the cause of truth, the cause of the Church and true religion, demand this exposure from some one, and from no one more loudly than me.'[1]

The Blagdon Controversy had been before the public for more than a year when Cobbett's letter was written. It was at first simply a dispute between a country parson and Mrs Hannah More over the alleged 'Methodism' of the teacher of one of her schools. Taken up by the London journals, it roused national interest when the Orthodox party saw it correctly as a symbol of Evangelical aggression. In the end it concerned not only Mrs More and the Reverend Mr Bere, with their Somerset aides and supporters, but Wilberforce and other contributors to the maintenance of the schools, Cobbett, Gifford and his writers, the *British Critic*, the *Christian Observer* and other journals, and at least five prelates of the church. Thirty or so pamphlets and perhaps some hundreds of reviews, articles and letters were published in two or three years, most of them angry and abusive. The resentment and alarm of High Church were heightened when they came to the belief

[1] *Cobbett's Annual* [later *Political*] *Register*, 20–27 February 1802.

hinted at by Cobbett at the end of his letter that 'puritanical fanaticism' was being secretly supported by Beilby Porteus, Bishop of London.

A picture in little of the whole gathering struggle over England's morals and religion, the Blagdon Controversy is crowded with striking examples of reforming and counter-reforming tactics, and very opulent in a merely dramatic way with issues and personalities of the conflict. Its story has never been told with any understanding of its relationship to the great controversy, or with anything but the blindest partiality to its heroine. The rally of her local friends early in 1800, the marshalling of powers in the church and in the countryside, the undercover intrigue of her resolute and powerful allies in London, the threats veiled and unveiled of the High Church party, the incredible charges brought against Mrs More and her own womanly retaliations, the vehement backing of the curate of Blagdon by Cobbett and the *Anti-Jacobin*, the unmeasured violence of clerical invective and the suave workings of episcopal diplomacy, make it a truly 'useful' episode. It is particularly valuable for its slowly but unerringly drawn portrait of Mrs More. The Orthodox first learned in the Blagdon Controversy of a prominent characteristic of their 'enemies' that from this time on with their usual bluntness they called 'the Evangelical cunning'.

PART II
LABOURING FOR THE SPIRITUAL IMPROVEMENT OF OTHERS

CHAPTER 6

GANGRENING THE PRINCIPLES OF THE COUNTRY

It is a fearful thing to think of, that this woman had under her tuition the children of a large portion of England.   WILLIAM COBBETT, 1802

Every parish may be convulsed, and *every* Clergyman may be oppressed, if the cunning of Mrs More can thus combine such discordant principles together, can thus conjure up even good spirits, even the very angels of the church, to do her work of mischief for her.   *The Anti-Jacobin Review*, 1801

No one has condemned, more strongly than ourselves, the personal invective and degrading acrimony, which have unhappily marked, in too many instances, this lengthened controversy. Such weapons we have uniformly rejected, and invariably deprecated.   *The Anti-Jacobin Review*, 1802

This man's malice is inflamed by the Anti-Jacobin Magazine, which is spreading more mischief over the land than almost any other book, because it is doing it under the mask of loyalty. It is representing all serious men as hostile to government.
                                                            HANNAH MORE, 1800

It is a most mischievous publication, which, by dint of assuming a tone of the highest loyalty and attachment to our establishment in church and state, secures a prejudice in its favour, and has declared war against what I think the most respectable and most useful of all orders of men—the serious clergy of the Church of England.... Its opposition to the evangelical clergy is carried on in so venomous a way, and with so much impudence, and so little regard to truth, that the mischief it does is very great indeed. It accuses them in the plainest terms, and sometimes by name, as being disaffected both to church and state.   WILBERFORCE, 1800

I

After retiring from their young ladies' seminary the five Misses More settled eventually at a country place, Cowslip Green, 'about ten miles from Bristol on the Exeter Road'. It was in August 1789 on a visit to the Mores that Wilberforce took the walk in the Mendip Hills nearby from which he returned silent and distressed: the cliffs were very fine but the poverty of the people was dreadful; if the Mores would do something about it he would put up the money. With the help of her

187

younger sister Martha—Miss (later Mrs) Patty—Hannah More established a school at Cheddar, in 1789, and in a few years had added several others in the neighbourhood. 'We were not long in discovering a sufficient number of wretched, ignorant parishes', Miss Patty wrote, the people 'brutal in their natures, and ferocious in their manners.' Even in such places, religion had penetrated in spite of Orthodox clergymen. At Shipham the rector 'had claimed the tithes for fifty years, but had never catechized a child or preached a sermon for forty';[1] the vicar of Axbridge was civil but the black shades of his character, Miss Patty had to write later, were too melancholy to be sketched;[2] and when the first school was opened at Cheddar the non-resident incumbent made what Patty called ironically a 'discourse upon good Tory principles'.[3] But there was a curate in the district who had become Evangelical by his own efforts, and a dairy-maid who had established a small Sunday school and was to be heard of later over the Christian world under the name Hester Wilmot.

In 1795 Mrs More and Miss Patty, having by then moved in on several districts, opened schools, on the curate Thomas Bere's invitation, at Blagdon, a parish which 'excelled in wickedness, if possible, any we had hitherto taken in hand'. By 1800, when the Blagdon Controversy broke out, two parishes had been given up and nine were still being served, with thirteen or fourteen hundred children under instruction and perhaps as many more adults in the evening meetings, the schools of industry and instruction, and the benefit clubs. The sisters had converted two of their curates (though not Mr Bere) to religious views and got the living of Brockley for one of them and the living of Shipham for the Evangelical curate already there.[4] In the beginning, the other Orthodox clergy whose parishes were being benefited were unsuspecting. But Mrs More's success was mixed from the beginning— the wealthy farmers and some of the gentry were greatly opposed to educating the poor even on her 'extremely limited' scale—and toward the

---

[1] *Mendip Annals*, pp. 27, 29.   [2] *Ibid.* p. 41.

[3] Nobody had better Tory principles than Miss Patty. It would be just an Orthodox clergyman who would fail to see that he should have discoursed on good religious principles.

[4] One of them was in the Crown gift and is another instance of the usefulness of Lord Loughborough.

end of the century the Regular clergy began uneasily taking stock of the situation. Mrs More had built up a large organization inside the church. Suspicion was growing that her teachers were not really responsible to the clergymen in charge of the parishes but to Hannah More. It was true that her religious character, if tinged with strictness, was of the utmost respectability. Or was it true? Was it the case rather that there was a schismatical group, bent on undermining church and state, known as 'the school of Mr Wilberforce', and could Mrs More be of that school?

As she told John Newton, Hannah More drew from her own experience in writing her tales for the lower ranks. That helps us to give a straightforward answer (which could have been given anyway) to the question that the local clergy came to believe was the crux of the argument. What was the object of Mrs More's schools? The answer is explicitly stated in Cheap Repository, for in *The Sunday School* and *The History of Hester Wilmot* we have an instantly recognizable description of her own educational experiences in the Mendip Hills.[1] Thus no pains are required to discover that to educate her children, youths and adults was far from Hannah More's aim. Some time before these days the word 'school' had come to mean a place where people's minds are trained, and when Mrs More tells us, also in Cheap Repository, that Betty Brown the St Giles's orange girl 'came into the world before so many good gentlemen and ladies began to concern themselves so kindly that the poor might have a little learning', it sounds for an instant as if it meant that to Mrs More. But her usual candid statements can be put in evidence in profusion. Mrs Jones's charity girls will all be wives of the poor or servants of the rich, nothing could be more useless than to teach them anything fancy. 'I do not in general approve of teaching charity children to write', Mrs Jones says. It would be useless knowledge for them in their humble station. 'I confine within very strict limits my plan of educating the poor. A thorough knowledge of

---

[1] 'The reader who is conversant with the Cheap Repository Tracts of Mrs Hannah More will see, from a perusal of the ensuing journal, that the tracts of that series which bear the title of "The Sunday-school" and "Hester Wilmot" were written *experimentally*, and founded upon fact.' *Mendip Annals*, Introduction, p. 10. These are the words of Patty More's editor Roberts, son of Mrs More's official biographer, father and son of course Evangelical.

religion, and of some of those coarser arts of life by which the community may be best benefited, includes the whole stock of instruction, which, unless in very extraordinary cases, I would wish to bestow.'[1]

Of course Mrs More meant by 'thorough knowledge of religion' a knowledge of simple religious duties to be performed without question, and if a 'very extraordinary case' that ought to be taught to write turned up in her schools it was sent elsewhere. Mrs More took pains to teach her scholars to read as little as it is humanly possible to do and did not teach anybody to write. 'Now, the whole extent of learning which we intend to give the poor', Mrs Jones says, 'is only to enable them to read the Bible.' So far as 'learning' is concerned, that is, anything apart from the coarser arts of life, there is no other statement of purpose from Hannah More. 'My grand principle is', she wrote some time before 1802 to Miss Wickham of Frome, the niece of one of her neighbours, Dr Sedgwick Whalley, 'to infuse into the minds of the young people as much Scriptural knowledge as possible.' 'I am extremely limited in my ideas of instructing the poor.... To teach them to read, without giving them principles, seems dangerous; and I do not teach them to write, even in my weekly schools [the evening schools for youths and adults].'[2]

The Sunday School also describes a further purpose of the schools that eventually becomes unmistakable as their primary purpose. Mrs Jones is in course 'confirmed in a plan she had before some thought of putting into practice'.

This was, after her school had been established a few months [this is her children's Sunday school], to invite all the well-disposed grown-up youth of the parish to meet her at the school an hour or two on a Sunday evening, after the necessary business of the dairy, and of serving the cattle was over. Both Mrs Jones and her agent had the talent of making this time pass so agreeably, by their manner of explaining scripture, and of impressing the heart by serious and affectionate discourse, that in a short time the evening school was nearly filled with a second company, after the younger ones were dismissed. In time, not only the servants, but the sons and daughters of the most substantial people in the parish attended. At length many of the parents, pleased with the

[1] *Stories 1818* ('A Cure for Melancholy'), vol. I, pp. 355–6.
[2] *Journals and Correspondence of Thomas Sedgwick Whalley, D.D.*, by the Rev. Hill Wickham, London, 1863, vol. II, p. 142. Cited as *Whalley*.

improvement so visible in the young people, got a habit of dropping in, that they might learn how to instruct their own families. [Mrs More's note, in 1818: This experiment was successfully made, and the practice has been continued for nearly thirty years by the writer of these tales.] And it was observed, that as the school filled, not only the fives-court and public house were thinned, but even Sunday gossiping and tea-visiting declined.[1]

It could hardly be clearer that all these are *ipsissima verba*. But there is no need to belabour the point that the primary reason for the establishment of these schools was that Hannah More could only in that way introduce Evangelical religion and morals into parishes where the incumbent and his curate, the regularly licensed priests of the church, were greatly opposed to them. There was no question in anyone's mind about the purpose of the schools until Mrs More's biographers of a much later period assumed they were places of education where young people's intellects were exercised. Neither Wilberforce nor Mrs More ever thought of them as anything but 'religious institutions', and the inscription under the first stone of the school built at Nailsea said simply that the little building was to benefit the parish in its most important interest, that of educating children in the knowledge and practice of the Christian religion.[2]

The Sunday School also tells us Mrs More's method (and manner) of opening one of her campaigns.

Mrs Jones, in the following week, got together as many of the mothers as she could, and spoke to them as follows:

Mrs Jones's Exhortation

My good women, on Sunday next I propose to open a school for the instruction of your children. Those among you, who know what it is to be able to read your Bible, will, I doubt not, rejoice that the same blessing is held out to your children. You who are *not* able yourselves to read what your Saviour has done and suffered for you, ought to be doubly anxious that your children should reap a blessing which you have lost. Would not that mother be thought an unnatural monster who should stand by and snatch out of her child's mouth the bread which a kind friend had just put into it? But such a mother would be merciful, compared with her who should rob her children of the opportunity of learning to read the word of God when it is held out to

---

[1] *Stories 1818*, vol. I, pp. 387–8.   [2] *Mendip Annals*, p. 43.

them. Remember, that if you slight the present offer, or if, after having sent your children a few times, you should afterwards keep them at home under vain pretences, you will have to answer for it at the day of judgment. Let not your poor children, *then*, have cause to say, 'My fond mother was my worst enemy. I might have been bred up in the fear of the Lord, and she opposed it for the sake of giving me a little paltry pleasure.—For an idle holiday, I am now brought to the gates of hell!' My dear women, which of you could bear to see your darling child condemned to everlasting destruction?...Is there any mother here present, who will venture to say—'I will doom the child I bore to sin and hell, rather than put them or myself to a little more present pain, by curtailing their evil inclinations!'...If there are any such here present, let that mother who values her child's pleasure more than his soul, now walk away, while I set down in my list the names of all those who wish to bring their young ones up in the way that leads to eternal life, instead of indulging them in the pleasures of sin, which are but for a moment.

When Mrs Jones had done speaking, most of the women thanked her for her good advice, and hoped that God would give them grace to follow it; promising to send their children constantly. Others, who were not so well-disposed, were yet afraid to refuse, after the sin of doing so had been so plainly set before them.

After it has been made clear by Mrs Jones that she will not receive the younger children of any family that does not send the older ones (as she does not intend to be used as a baby-sitter), 'Mrs Jones told them not to bring any excuses to her which they could not bring to the day of judgment.'[1] Perhaps in less stringent circumstances it would have occurred to Mrs Jones that she was not authorized to threaten poor village women with the day of judgment. She had no cure of souls, was not the Established Church incumbent of the parish or an ordained priest of any kind, and had assumed moral and spiritual authority by self-bestowed credentials of good intent and superior merit. Perhaps the recollection that she was a miserable sinner like the objects of bounty might have led Mrs Jones—and of course then Hannah More and her lieutenant-general Miss Patty—to hesitate at certain points.

This is what the Blagdon Controversy was about, and it could not have been contested very evenly, in spite of Evangelical skill in evading the real issue, if the Regular clergy round Cowslip Green had read Cheap Repository carefully. Accounts of the Controversy written by

[1] *Stories 1818*, vol. I, pp. 369–73.

admirers who have taken Mrs More's word for it that her adversaries were obscurantists opposed to education have wholly missed the point. It is clear enough as we see her in *The Sunday School* (and elsewhere) threatening with eternal torture children who should be kept away from a kind of religious training that their duly appointed pastors were strongly opposed to. 'Whenever I open a school', she wrote, in December 1800, in the course of the Controversy, 'I always say to the mothers, who are always present, and before the clergyman: "Remember, I do not go to this expense merely to take in your little brats to relieve you from the trouble of nursing them: if you will not send your big children, we shall not take your little ones; we do not keep a nursery, but a school." This has been converted...into a strong insinuation that the school was only a pretence, and that the Conventicle, as Mr Bere is pleased to call it, was the real object.'[1] 'Conventicle' may not have been the word Bere should have used, but the charge was correct. Anything in the nature of a school as the word is usually understood was never intended. If this Somerset project had not been a part of the Evangelical Reformation, and symbolically an important one, Mrs More would not have prosecuted her infiltration into the Orthodox parishes around her with such obdurate high-handedness, nor would the Blagdon Controversy have become a matter of national religious interest.

II

One difficulty in particular that Mrs More was called on to meet was not only harassing but insurmountable, and it was this that set off the Controversy. With the best will in the world she could not get teachers who had the tact and adroitness to introduce Evangelicalism without the High Church clergyman's knowledge. The more devoutly Evangelical any available teachers were, the harder it was to keep them from 'fanatical' practices and even open disrespect to the Orthodox clergy—the more so as their Evangelical superiors did not set them a very good example. After a sermon of Mr Boake's Mrs More entered in her journal 'I congratulated him on the hatred his new doctrines were beginning to draw on him',[2] and when Mrs Baber their Cheddar schoolmistress died, Boake preaching the funeral sermon 'said, with an

---

[1] *Whalley*, vol. II, p. 165.   [2] *Mendip Annals*, p. 117.

emphasis in his voice, and a firmness in his look, "This eminent Christian first taught *salvation* in Cheddar"', 'though Mr ——, the vicar, was there, and he himself was curate'.[1] Such things were not likely to endear Boake or Hannah More to Mr —— or to have the best effect on the manners of less educated people. But still worse, it was at once apparent that Mrs More could not get Evangelicals as teachers in all her schools. At the outset Wilberforce advised her, in a letter that Cobbett or the *Anti-Jacobin* would have been happy to have in 1801 and 1802, to get Methodists. Though nothing could be done in 'the regular way', he wrote, 'these poor people must not, therefore, be suffered to continue in their present lamentable state of darkness. You know you told me they never saw the sun but one day in the year, and even the moon appeared but once a week for an hour or two. The gravitation to Wells was too strong to be resisted. My advice is then, send for a comet—Whiston had them at command, and John Wesley is not unprovided.'[2] Mrs More had to follow that advice, it seems in several cases, certainly in the case of the Cheddar mistress. 'I hope Miss W[ilberforce] will not be frightened,' she wrote in 1789, 'but I am afraid she must be called a methodist.'[3] A special interest of those letters would lie in her supporters' repeated denials that she had hired Methodists, when that became an important issue of the Controversy.

Sooner or later one of the High Church incumbents chancing to be in his parish was bound to see what was going on. Extempore prayers were offered, sermons read that he did not compose or select, in every case by people he had not appointed who were zealously teaching a 'schismatical' Christianity he was much opposed to. The trouble to come had still another factor. Mrs More had suffered all her life from the adulation and flattery of her sisters and many other admirers. She was the foremost woman writer of the day, a welcome visitor in any civilized circle of the great, used to the affectionate friendship of half a dozen prelates and the admiring esteem of as many more. Of course

[1] *Mendip Annals*, p. 123.

[2] *Wilberforce*, vol. I, p. 247. The sun is the rector or vicar, the moon the curate, the gravitation to the cathedral and the bishop's palace, the comet the Methodist irregular. The inclusion of this letter in the *Life of Wilberforce* was a thoughtless error on the part of his sons.

[3] *More*, vol. II, p. 208; *Mendip Annals*, p. 18.

she laboured, as Wilberforce did constantly, to keep in mind the worth-lessness of the world's applause to a pilgrim on the march. 'Had a little serious talk with the Duchess of Gloucester, Lady Amherst, and the Duchess of Beaufort. Lord, let me be no mean respecter of persons, but make me valiant for thy truth.' 'This week has been too much spent in receiving visits from the great.' 'Oh! let me feel more and more that I am a miserable sinner.'[1] But there are signs that in Mrs More some sinful human vanity was still active. In an affair of this kind she was likely to think of her enemies as miserable sinners and not likely to be ingratiating to an obscure curate.

In September 1798, establishing another school in the large parish of Wedmore, she met more than the usual opposition from the leading residents, with the usual argument that God has ordained the poor to be not only poor but ignorant. That belief is cited with pity, or amuse-ment, by most of Mrs More's biographers. No one could have held it more unquestioningly than Mrs More did, or any Evangelical of this period. But she at least believed the poor should be taught to read the Catechism, and the landowners of Wedmore did not. Their antagonism was bitter. At the same time a 'violent opposition took place', Patty's journal says, 'among the great folks at Axbridge against our evening reading. It was proceeding too successfully for the great enemy of souls not to raise an alarm among the worldlings.'[2] In Congresbury the celebrated T. T. Biddulph, for many years the best-known Evangelical clergyman in the West, preached at the anniversary meeting of the schools, which served the parish of Yatton too. The children of both parishes went to hear him, the Orthodox incumbent of Yatton was greatly annoyed. In Rowberrow the rector 'decoyed away' the larger boys in the school to sing in his choir—'a wicked action', Patty wrote, 'and he will find he must account for it at the day of judgment'.[3]

Mrs More brought the Wedmore situation to the attention of her diocesan, Bishop Moss of Bath and Wells, who was to have thrust upon him a large and painful part in the Controversy. 'His reception of me was highly cordial, and even affectionate.' From the chancellor of the diocese—he was the bishop's son, after the fashion of the day—she learned what charges had been brought against her Wedmore school-

---

[1] *More*, vol. III, pp. 58, 59. This is in 1798.
[2] *Mendip Annals*, p. 214.   [3] *Ibid.* p. 217.

master. He had called the bishops dumb dogs, had said that everybody who went to church but did not come to hear him would go to hell, and had distributed a Guide to Methodism.[1] 'But the mischief lies deeper', Mrs More wrote to Wilberforce. 'A clergyman in my own neighbourhood, where we have a flourishing school, has turned Socinian, and is now enraged at the doctrines *we* teach; and is doing all possible injury to us and our schemes. This cause too, *has a cause*—and this man's malice is inflamed by the Anti-Jacobin Magazine, which is spreading more mischief over the land than almost any other book, because it is doing it under the mask of loyalty. It is representing all serious men as hostile to government;[2] and our enemies here whisper that we are abetted by you, and such as you, to hurt the establishment. This is only an episode, for I must talk to you more at large, and see if no means can be employed to stop this spreading poison.' It is probable that the 'means' Mrs More had in mind are named in her next sentence. 'I hear that the author [of the *Anti-Jacobin* attacks] is ——, who, having been refused some favour by the Bishop of London, exercises his malignity towards him in common with those whom he calls Methodists.'[3]

These occurrences were plainly pointing to serious trouble, which broke out shortly in Mrs More's own parish of Blagdon. In April 1800 the curate Thomas Bere, offended by irregularities of the adult school teacher, one Younge, irately accused him of Methodistical practices and called on Mrs More to remove him. She declined to do so unless charges were publicly brought and proved, but suggested that the matter be referred for mediation to Sir Abraham Elton, a wealthy clergyman and mine-owner of the neighbourhood. It occurred to Bere that as Elton was well known as the leading Evangelical of the district next to Mrs More he might possibly not make the fairest mediator.[4] If Mrs More had been a humbler woman she might have taken the simple step of transferring Younge to some other sphere of Evangelical usefulness. He had already got into trouble in the parish of Nailsea—

[1] *More*, vol. III, pp. 101–2.

[2] Of course Mrs More meant all 'serious', that is, Evangelical, Christians.

[3] *More*, vol. III, p. 102.

[4] Sir Abraham had been Robinson of Leicester's curate for some months, round 1783 when he first went into Orders. Vaughan, *The Rev. Thomas Robinson*, pp. 176–7.

'pride, and a consciousness of really tolerable abilities, seem to be the besetting sins of Mr Younge', Patty wrote.[1] But behind Mrs More stood William Wilberforce, Henry Hoare of Mitcham and Henry Thornton, the powerful figure of the Bishop of London and the magnificent figure of the Bishop of Durham, and Mrs More stood firm.

Bere stood firm himself. The leading men of the parish, opposed to the dangerous education of their labourers and no doubt with a much exaggerated idea of the education they were getting, stood with him. As the affair became a local scandal, with feeling bitter and language angry, Bere began to hint that Mrs More's loyalty to the church was questionable and that knowing her teacher was methodistical she was secretly abetting fanatical practices. When Mrs More still refused to take Younge away, he collected thirteen depositions charging him with ecclesiastical offences and sent them to his rector.

Dr Crossman the rector of Blagdon, absentee and timid, sent the depositions to his diocesan. The Bishop of Bath and Wells was aged, weary and indisposed to have trouble. His business seems to have been transacted entirely by his son Dr Moss, the chancellor. Son and father were friendly, suave and as non-committal as it was possible for them to be. They knew Mrs More well, they were not unmindful of her great church influence, but were inclined to feel that Younge ought to be removed if it could be done without bad feeling. The bad feeling being already of the heartiest, the conflict intensified. At an anniversary of the Shipham schools, Sir Abraham Elton preached a strong, or violent, sermon defending Mrs More and attacking Bere with animosity. 'A truly admirable discourse in every point of view', Miss Patty wrote. It could hardly have been so in the curate's. 'Mr Bere had threatened us with penal statutes; Sir A. returned the compliment to him, by explaining what provision the law makes against clergyman of the Church of England who openly deny the Trinity, which Bere has repeatedly done.'[2] 'Sir A.'s talents and rank in life', Miss Patty added, were influential in turning the tide against Bere in the neighbourhood, at least for the moment, and in July 1800 Mrs More carried the fight forward with determination. Without notifying either Bere or his rector she sent a series of accusations against him to the bishop and chancellor. Dr Moss and his father forwarded them to Dr Crossman the rector,

---

[1] *Mendip Annals*, pp. 128, 169.　　　　[2] *Ibid.* p. 229.

Dr Crossman sent them back to the chancellor and bishop. In September the two of them committed the gravest ecclesiastical blunder: they decided that Younge must be dismissed. Mrs More rallied Sir Abraham, who wrote to Bere urging that it was impossible not to allow an accused person to confront his accusers. It is doubtful if Sir Abraham Elton knew at this point that Mrs More had herself brought secret charges against Bere, who was never able to confront his accuser through the whole Controversy. In a letter to Elton Bere declined to go further into the matter, which would be 'presumptuous in him' after the bishop and chancellor had decided it, and ended his letter with a sincere and hearty forgiveness of all his enemies. There can hardly have been a controversy in which more sincere and hearty forgiveness was accompanied by more vindictive retaliation, and in that Mrs More was even forwarder than Mr Bere.

Elton reaffirmed that every man had a right to a public hearing. Appealed to again, Crossman and Dr Moss decided that Bere should make his evidence public. On 12 November 1800 he did so, in a dramatic and wily fashion. He called a meeting of neighbouring gentlemen and clergy at the George Inn at Blagdon, to act as a judicial body before which he could present his depositions and witnesses. In selecting these referees Bere rather more than gave Mrs More tit for tat respecting her proposal of Elton as arbitrator. The five clergymen were selected from the Orthodox group, the laymen were no more likely to vote fanatically, and in the chair was a prominent obscurantist of the district, Colonel Francis Whalley, a neighbour of Mrs More's notorious for his abhorrence of Methodism, Evangelicalism and education. To these judges Bere presented his evidence to the effect that Younge the schoolmaster had referred to himself as a Calvinist, allowed extempore prayer, himself prayed extempore, said he could save souls and explain the Scriptures better than Bere and that church ministers were false teachers. It could not have surprised anybody that the meeting unanimously recommended Younge's dismissal. And Mrs More committed her third blunder, hard to account for on any other ground than plain pique. She closed the parish schools.

The schools were closed on 16 November 1800. Dr Crossman wrote congratulating Bere and regretting that Mrs More had seen fit to take such a step, which would be hard on the children. Not profoundly intelligent or even up on his facts, Dr Crossman in the course of the Controversy succeeded in misunderstanding everything. At this advanced point of the struggle and with the charges against Younge in his hands, he seems not to have realized that neither Mrs More nor his curate had any primary interest in the children and that it was the adult schools that were causing the trouble.

For the moment the combat was deadlocked. Thanks chiefly to Sir Abraham Elton the leading people of the district had rallied round Mrs More, with the exception of Colonel Whalley, Mr Hiley Addington (this caused anxiety; he was the brother of the coming prime minister), and one or two other Gentiles. While Elton was an open Evangelical, he was one of the largest of the Mendip mine-owners, and in such a man, as in Sir Richard Hill, a good deal of fanaticism could be overlooked. In spite of Sir Abraham, however, Bere had carried everything so far as the church was concerned. His rector Dr Crossman, the chancellor Dr Moss, and old Bishop Moss himself, in so far as he had been absolutely forced to give an opinion and in spite of his friendship and respect for Mrs More, were all on his side. But if the church was against Mrs More in Somerset, in London it was not. Toward the end of the year the powerful and secret influence that William Cobbett spoke of began to work strongly on Bishop and Chancellor Moss. They were in town in December. While they were there, Mrs More's episcopal allies and the Evangelical commander, it is quite impossible to doubt, found means to impress them with a different view either of the points at issue or more important points. In addition to their position in the church and their wealth both Barrington and Porteus had as easy access to Windsor as Wilberforce had to the prime minister. There is no need to bring in any element of personal advantage to the Mosses, but if there were it would be enough to point out that while Bishop Moss was at the end of a long life, Chancellor Moss was not. In some way bishop and chancellor on their return to Somerset had reason to see Mrs More's schools, or Mrs More, in a greatly changed light. 'A strange, and unexpected alteration, took place', Bere wrote later, 'THE CAUSE OF WHICH, I may conjecture; but dare not presume, to account for.'[1]

---

[1] Thomas Bere, *The Controversy Between Mrs Hannah More and the Curate of Blagdon, relative to the conduct of her Teacher of the Sunday School in that parish* (London, 1801).

Events came rapidly. In January 1801 Dr Crossman wrote his curate a severe letter. He had had additional information from Mrs More and Elton; Dr Moss was by no means satisfied; would Bere send his composition for the tithes by bearer. On January 16 Crossman wrote that Dr Moss had information proving Bere anti-Trinitarian and otherwise unorthodox and that it would be wise for him to resign; on January 23 he demanded his resignation and on February 2 formally notified him that he was no longer curate. Bere declined to resign or be put out and again appealed to the bishop. Hearing from Dr Moss that Crossman's instructions would not be changed, he published early in 1801 a pamphlet in which he printed the entire correspondence in his hands.[1] It pointed out that he had never been confronted with his accusers or seen the charges against him, charged that Mrs More and her supporters were methodistical Puritans, and hinted that a powerful influence in London was supporting Mrs More against the interests of the church.

III

While all that was going on, with Sir Abraham manfully championing the Mores in their grave need—'Paddock', said Bere's second pamphlet, 'never appears at the call of the Weird Sisters but in the last extremity' —another champion had been brought into the field. Mrs More was not wholly satisfied with Sir Abraham, admirable in rank and wealth but a man of some timidity who had to be whipped on. The new champion was an odd one: he was that Thomas Sedgwick Whalley whom the Bishop of Ely presented to the unhealthy Lincolnshire living when he went down from Cambridge with the stipulation that he should never reside. An Orthodox clergyman and brother of Colonel Francis Whalley, he was a literary dilettante, a collector of jewellery and paintings and a correspondent of Miss Anna Seward the Swan of Lichfield, in the Evangelical view no more a Christian than Bere or the Bishop of Lincoln and altogether as unlikely a person as could have been found when Paddock failed. If Dr Sedgwick Whalley was anything but helpful to Mrs More, as it turned out, he was most helpful to the historian, for it is entirely due to his entrance into the Controversy that it is possible to write a realistic account of it. In a biography of him

[1] Thomas Bere, *op. cit.*

published in 1863 his nephew the Reverend Hill Wickham printed a series of letters, chiefly from Mrs More, that reveal in detail the Cowslip Green faction's secret machinations from November 1800. Prefacing the letters with a list of thirty-four actors of the drama, eleven of whom achieved in the Controversy what Whalley's friend the Swan called 'authorism', Wickham printed them with complete detachment and little or no comment.[1]

The Evangelical forces had already with astuteness and dexterity succeeded in shifting the issue from Younge's religious practice, on which they had no case, to Bere's religious and political practice and personal qualities. In Mrs More's account he was anti-Trinitarian and a liberal and either he or his supporters had been guilty of wild and violent slanders. 'Such horrid reports are abroad', Patty wrote to Whalley, 'that some strong measures must be taken, and that immediately. The emissaries of Satan are spreading strange things in London; even the Bishop writes in great agitation and alarm, as if dreadful things had reached his ears.' Bere and 'his emissaries', Mrs More wrote, had sent lying accounts of the circumstances to several of the bishops. 'One report says that I have been tried and found guilty of sedition, another that I have actually been taken up. These things the bishops themselves write me with the strongest expressions of affection to me, and of contempt and abhorrence of the author of these calumnies. The calumnies, however, are of too dreadful a nature to be borne, except from the full conviction that it is the will of God, who is pleased thus to exercise me for my purification.'[2] We should probably allow here for Mrs More's writing in great agitation herself. It is hardly possible to believe that Bere and his friends would make such fantastic allegations to members of the bishops' bench about matters of fact.

By December Whalley, defending his old friend and neighbour out of the merest chivalry, had composed an immense letter denouncing Bere and sent it off to the chancellor. Throughout Wickham's series of letters concerning the Controversy Mrs More is seen as the field commander of her forces, planning, scheming and directing, leading Whalley along with intelligent flattery, instructing him in the smallest details and it seems even if necessary revising his compositions. In a

[1] *Journals and Correspondence of Thomas Sedgwick Whalley, D.D.* Cited as *Whalley*.
[2] *Whalley*, vol. II, pp. 147, 148.

second piece, apparently a letter Whalley was writing, she had marked for change the words 'request' and 'requested', she wrote in January: '...they are the only words which do not make you look like a complete volunteer'.[1] No statement either for the chancellor or the public would do the least good, she wrote again and again, if it merely praised her. It had to attack Bere. 'Nothing short of unmasking him will open the judicially-blinded eyes of those with whom we have to do.' 'I do not want myself to be praised, but Bere exposed. Suppose you were to say that, as Bere has coupled my name with that of sedition, I am advised to bring an action against him, but that both my temper and declining health prevent me. Should not his democratic speeches at Simmons' Club, two years ago, be glanced at?'[2]

By the turn of the year Dr Moss the chancellor had made up his mind which side it was better to be on, and was getting on it with the happiest combination of celerity and dignity he could manage. In December he wrote Mrs More that he had known nothing about the George Inn meeting, and lamented that her delicacy toward a man who had shown her none (Mrs More's wording) should have kept him in ignorance of Bere's real character. 'I am astonished and shocked at the disclosure which your letter makes of the duplicity, hypocrisy, and impudence of Mr Bere', he wrote to Whalley (December 29).[3] After recovering from his initial blunder, the chancellor acted throughout with consummate policy, and no doubt well deserved the reward he was shortly to get. All doubts and difficulties were disregarded as decisive action was at last taken. 'The Dr', Mrs More wrote (this is Crossman), 'has sent him word he is not his curate after 25th March, but is to have a guinea a Sunday until Midsummer, if his house cannot be ready sooner.' The house was one Bere was assumed to be building at Butcombe, a tiny parish of which he was rector and to which it was assumed he would remove. 'The Dr is timid and unwilling to inflame him. Bere is resolved to make another attempt on the Bishop.' But by the middle of January 1801 it seemed that the Blagdon Controversy was at an end, as Mrs More's efforts, and Whalley's efforts, and perhaps not least the secret efforts in London, had had their effect. On January 19, Mrs More wrote that the affair was drawing to a close.

---

[1] *Whalley*, vol. II, p. 172.   [2] *Ibid.* p. 152.
[3] *Ibid.* p. 167.

Bishop Porteus had counselled her to make sure that not only Crossman but the chancellor wished the schools reopened, and Dr Moss did so wish. Mrs More was jubilant. The event was set for January 25, although Bere still showed no signs of leaving the parish. 'I should gladly have delayed the restoration of the school till the removal of Bere had taken place', Mrs More wrote, 'but Descury tells me the Methodists, who are always on the watch, are disposed to take advantage of the disunion between the minister and his parishioners'—a matchless description of the Blagdon Controversy—'and will seize the moment to slip in.'[1] She was most anxious, however, to have no public rejoicing. 'It would give me the severest pain. May it please God to make this disgrace which they have brought on themselves, an instrument of bringing them to a better way of thinking! They have my constant prayers.'[2] Whalley, not a Christian perhaps but a gentleman, had qualms at re-establishing the schools with Bere still in the parish and wrote that he would not be present. Mrs More agreed. 'I would not for the world have any outward appearance of joy. God forbid there should be any indecent triumph! As a fallen man, I pity him.'[3]

Mrs More was to find her triumph far removed, her previous sufferings little to those to come. In the face of his rector, his chancellor and his bishop, Bere refused to resign or to leave and stood his ground. It was at this point that he made his final appeal and was curtly refused further consideration. He set out for London with his pamphlet, to seek help in the ranks of those who did not like the school of Mr Wilberforce. By 1801 they were not hard to find.

IV

On 30 December 1800 Mrs Piozzi, rounding out her long life at Bath in a jolly way—not an Evangelical, she gave a large ball to celebrate her eightieth birthday, which shocked Mrs More very much—wrote to Whalley lamenting Bere's 'vile detractions'; and on 13 January 1801 Mrs Siddons hoped Whalley had 'completely crushed the head of the venomous serpent who has thus malignantly aimed its sting against, I verily believe, one of the best women in the world'. On February 21 a dissenting letter was addressed to Whalley that questioned Mrs More's

---

[1] *Ibid.* p. 177.   [2] *Ibid.* p. 180.   [3] *Ibid.* p. 178.

good faith and innocence in decided terms. It introduced an episode that is additionally illuminating about Evangelical practice. The writer was Anna Seward, one of Whalley's oldest friends and most esteemed correspondents. Miss Seward was an admired writer of polite verse, a voluminous, pompous and affected letter-writer and a warm-hearted and occasionally very shrewd literary lady. A friend and correspondent also of the Reverend Robert Fellowes, she thought Mrs More the foremost woman of the day in the field of letters, and she abhorred Evangelicalism.

You must not, dear friend, from what I am going to say, think me the least inclined to vindicate a man whom you denounce, because I recall to your recollection what passed on my introduction to your excellent Mr Inman, the day we dined with him. It was in his own parlour, before morning service, that he told you a request the preceding night from Miss H. More had made him very uneasy and dissatisfied with himself, for having granted it against his judgment, viz. to suffer a friend of hers to preach from his pulpit that morning. 'You know,' said he, 'how this country is infested (that was his strong word) with Methodists. We all believe that this lady means excellently, but we also know that of late years her judgment has been warped into an adoption of some of their tenets, and into encouraging their propagation from the pulpit. If this friend of hers should preach them from mine, I shall not easily forgive myself for the weakness of an assent given against my consciousness that I ought to refuse it, since it puts in the power of a stranger to counteract my endeavours, hitherto successful, to preserve my own parishioners from the infection of those tenets.'

Miss M.'s friend proved to be Newton, the comfortless conscience-keeper to poor Cowper, and to whom the Bishop of Peterborough, Cowper's relation and friend, I hear, attributes the long misery and final overthrow of that noble mind. Mr Newton's doctrine that morning, you will surely recollect, was highly Methodistic. Mr Inman, who came into the pew during the sermon, displayed in his countenance the utmost marks of uneasy disapprobation; but Miss More and her sisters looked not at him, conscious, probably, how he would look. They kept their eyes fixed on the ground, as in humble assenting edification. They did not come to Mr Inman's after church—and you will remember how strongly he repeated his self-censure for the given opportunity of disseminating principles he so warmly disapproved. With equal warmth you joined in that disapprobation, and blamed Miss H. More extremely on the occasion....

It is hardly to be supposed possible that Miss H. More's teacher would not inculcate those doctrines, whose diffusion from Mr Inman's pulpit she took such an extraordinary step to procure. Mr Inman did not think them the bread of life, neither do I.[1]

Miss Seward's *Correspondence* was published in 1811, shortly after her death, and a later letter to Whalley on this same episode was included in it. And writing to Lady Olivia Bernard Sparrow in 1812, Mrs More, referring to that letter, hotly denied the charge of having introduced the old African blasphemer into Inman's pulpit. Good taste revolted at Miss Seward's letters, in Mrs More's opinion, and 'truth and candour abhor them'.[2] 'I know not to what passage of Miss Seward you allude', she wrote to Lady Olivia, 'as she so frequently does me the honour of designating me by the appellation of the *gloomy Calvinist.*' Mrs More was wrong there. She is never so called in the six volumes, though that expression or something like it is frequently used of Evangelicals generally. 'Did I tell you of one egregious falsehood repecting me? She speaks of Mr Newton preaching strange doctrine in a Mr Inman's Church and that I flattered him to the Skies, and Mr Inman said afterwards "now this man has done more harm in my church in one sermon than I can repair in many months." What will you think of the Lady's veracity, when I tell you that Mr Newton never saw Mr Inman nor ever preached in his Church. Many such things might be adduced.'[3]

Ten months after he had received Miss Seward's first letter, Whalley found time to answer it. She wrote in reply the letter that was printed in her posthumous *Correspondence* and roused Mrs More's indignation.

Indeed, I have every honour for Mrs H. More's talents and virtues. It was entirely owing to my recollection how much she had, in the year 1791, when I was your guest, distressed the feelings of that dear saint, that genuine Christian, Mr Inman, by introducing into his pulpit the rank Methodist, Mr Newton, which induced me to believe, that her endeavours to promote Methodist principles were continued in her neighbourhood. Mrs H. More expressed to me, at her own house, admiration of the despicable rant we had heard, the preceding Sunday, from Newton; of which Mr Inman, yourself, and all our party, had expressed our horror. That good man imputed to

---

[1] *Whalley*, vol. II, pp. 183–5.   [2] *More*, vol. III, p. 357.
[3] British Museum, Eg. 1965, ff. 3, 4. This letter is not in Mrs More's official biography.

Mrs More the increase of those pernicious principles in your county. I have read nothing of the late controversy on that subject, except from your statement. Notwithstanding your acquittal of the lady, I own I thought it not likely, that she, whom Mr Inman had heretofore so deeply blamed on that subject, should be wholly blameless in the similar arraignment brought against her 'by a gownman of a different make.'

The misery, the despair, which the gloomy Calvinistic tenets have produced, makes me abhor them; they are not Christianity; they are not common sense.[1]

It is easy to see how Mrs More could be annoyed at Miss Seward's letter, even when published as late as 1811. On the face of things and in the absence of further evidence, the honours seem to be the High Church lady's here. The Swan revelled in such episodes and cherished them with an exceptional memory. Her account of what happened is concrete and full of factual details of the most realistic kind. Eighteen months later, in a letter to William Hayley, she told the same story in the same terms,[2] and she mentioned it again to Whalley six years after that, still in the same terms, in the last letter she wrote him.[3] The known facts all tend to corroborate her story. Inman was the incumbent of Whalley's parish, as Miss Seward noted in 1791; it would naturally be his church she would be taken to.[4] John Newton paid the Mores a visit in August 1791 and the week he was there coincided with Miss Seward's visit to Langford Cottage.[5] It is also evident that Whalley did not deny any of the story but simply tried to make out a case for Mrs More as a woman of talent and virtue. While Mrs More's denial, it is noticeable, was narrowly worded—Newton never saw Inman and never preached

---

[1] *Letters of Anna Seward*, vol. v, pp. 411–12.

[2] 'I once heard Mr Newton preach a violently methodistical, and consequently absurd and dangerous sermon. Miss H. More and her sisters had requested for him the pulpit of the late pious and excellent Mr Inman, their neighbour; Mr and Mrs Whalley were his parishioners, and I was their guest in 1791. When church was over Mr Inman expressed deep regret for having, however reluctantly, granted Miss More's request. Now, said he, has this man, in one hour perhaps, rendered fruitless my labour of many years to keep my parishioners free from those wild, deceiving principles, which have turned the heads of half the poor ignorant people in this country.' *Ibid.* vol. vi, p. 65.

[3] *Whalley*, vol. ii, p. 328. The letter was written on 25 January 1809, two months before Miss Seward's death.

[4] *Letters of Anna Seward*, vol. iii, p. 100.

[5] *More*, vol. ii, pp. 266, 270; *Letters of Anna Seward*, vol. iii, pp. 93–103.

in his church—it does not seem that Miss Seward had the wrong clergy-man and pulpit even; it would not be like her to make such a mistake and if it had been a mistake Whalley would probably have said so.

It can at least be noted that Mrs More's statement to Lady Olivia Sparrow was not pointless. Lady Olivia, a daughter and heiress of the Earl of Gosford, 'vastly wealthy', was in process of conversion.[1]

The episode illustrates a cherished practice of the Evangelicals, to introduce a serious clergyman into an Orthodox pulpit whenever and wherever it could be done. Whatever the facts about her alleged obtaining of Inman's pulpit for John Newton, Mrs More would not have hesitated an instant to do it, or Newton to preach knowing well that Inman did not approve of his doctrine. Of course that would have been the reason for doing it. It would be remarkable if, having as her guest the most celebrated Evangelical divine of the day next to Romaine, Mrs More had not tried to get him into someone's pulpit.

The literature of Evangelicalism contains several stories of the intro-duction, or attempted introduction, of a serious clergyman into an idol-shepherd pulpit. When Charles Simeon visited Arthur Young around 1805 Young tried to get a local pulpit for him but failed. 'Oh! for the dumb dogs of our clergy who will neither preach the Gospel themselves nor let others do it.'[2] This practice began at an early period. When Romaine visited Shrewsbury in 1769 Sir Richard Hill got him per-mission to preach at St Chad's. 'Mr Romaine did not lose that oppor-tunity of declaring the gospel of Christ without reserve', says Hill's biographer, 'which excited, as it did at that time all over the kingdom, the bitterest hostility against him. Dr Adams, the incumbent of the parish, followed him into the vestry and said in a very angry tone, "Sir, my congregation is not used to such doctrine, and I hope will never hear such again". Mr Romaine, although thus addressed in the presence of a good many people, received the rebuke with meekness, and merely replied, "Sir, this surely is neither a proper time nor place for disputes". A fortnight after, Dr Adams delivered a violent sermon in reply.'[3]

[1] In 1858 Patty More's *Mendip Annals* was dedicated by its editor Arthur Roberts to Lady Olivia Sparrow, by then eminent among the Evangelical ladies for nearly half a century.

[2] Arthur Young, *Autobiography*, p. 400.

[3] Sidney, *Life of Sir Richard Hill*, pp. 156–7.

Adams published his sermon and of course Sir Richard Hill published a reply to it.

It may be observed incidentally that Anna Seward's picture of good Mr Inman, which is the only description we have of any of Mrs More's clerical neighbours not drawn by a participant in the Controversy, seems to indicate that the blackness of character of some of them may have been a little exaggerated.

V

It would have been a good thing for Mrs More, and everybody else, if Miss Seward had spoken correctly, in November 1801, of the 'late controversy'. The whole affair should have been as dead as Marley. The authorities had dismissed a curate, the Blagdon schools were in operation again and if the bishops were not all genuinely on Mrs More's side none of them was openly against her. But Bere stood firm, no doubt much strengthened by his visit to London. As the manner of his dismissal had been grossly improper, there was a solid charge of injustice that could be brought against the Cowslip Green party when the pamphlets began to come out. Viewing the matter on the lowest level only, it must be felt Mrs More had committed a grave blunder, surprising in a woman of her intelligence and realism, in getting Bere dismissed as she had done.

His first pamphlet was promptly answered by Sir Abraham Elton; Bere replied with a second, Elton answered that too; Thomas Sedgwick Whalley came forward, so did Mrs More's two young Evangelical curates Boake and Drewitt, and so did Bere's friends among the local clergy, as well as interested persons, clerical and lay, in Bath and other friends and foes from near and far including several who remain anonymous. It would be useless to go into the welter of charge and counter-charge, statement and misstatement, invective and counter-invective, of these works. None enriched the polemical literature of England, most were guilty of gross misrepresentation. Bere's after his first were extremely abusive, Elton's worse, and Whalley's was equalled by none except Shaw's burlesque *Life of Hannah More*, a rollicking, ferocious and vulgar *jeu d'esprit*. That a Christian priest could have written either of the last two in particular is a sign of the bitterness of the whole Orthodox–Evangelical conflict. The Mores were immensely pleased with Whalley's, or told him so. Some odd points turned up. It appeared that though Bere's immediate forebears were humble people he was proud of an ancient Welsh lineage, and Mrs More's side, chiefly Whalley, had a good deal of sport with him on both counts. It appeared further that the Blagdon faction disliked Cheap Repository and were actually liberals. That, as one would think might have been foreseen, was enough in itself to cost them the support of most of the respectable, and when it became known did so at once.

The first year of the pamphleteering saw some important events of the Controversy. The public belief that Bere did not receive fair play, the scandalous situation created by his continuing to officiate though dismissed by everybody, were too much. In September 1801 he was 'reinstated'; and Mrs More again dissolved her schools, in accordance, she wrote, with her constant practice of never doing anything against the wishes of the resident clergyman of the parish. Younge was sent off to Ireland where (or somewhere) he should have been sent a year earlier, and where he gave great satisfaction, Mrs More wrote, 'to the opulent and very respectable family of the Latouches, near Dublin'. It seems unusually unnecessary to mention that that opulent and respectable family were Evangelical.

Bere's victory was so severe a blow that for a time the whole school system appeared to be in danger. A most felicitous event that occurred on 13 April 1802 possibly saved Mrs More from disaster: old Bishop Moss died, full of years and gold, at his house in Grosvenor Square, and was succeeded by Dr Richard Beadon, more active, more intelligent and very well disposed toward Mrs More. She immediately wrote him a long letter stating her case and asking his pleasure, and received the polite reply that it was not necessary for Mrs Hannah More to vindicate her principles against malicious and groundless attacks. The side of the heaviest artillery had long been apparent, in the ecclesiastical world, and Bishop Beadon though not an Evangelical was not an imbecile.[1]

---

[1] Bishop Moss died at the age of ninety-one, leaving a fortune of £140,000, nearly all of which went to his son, whom he had made Archdeacon of Carmarthen and given the sub-deanery of Wells, the precentorship and three prebendal stalls as well as the chancellorship. Beadon had been tutor of the Duke of Gloucester. *The Dictionary of National Biography* says of him that 'he did not neglect the opportunity which his

All would thus have been well if it had not been for the truculent non-ecclesiastical aid that Bere had won in London. When he went there he seems first to have tried to get the support of the Bishop of Lincoln. Pretyman-Tomline was a bitter enemy of the Evangelical cause, noted for acting as severely as he could against Evangelicals in his diocese, and at the very time of Bere's approach was covertly attempting an attack on the Party by parliamentary action that took all Wilberforce's influence with Pitt to fight off. Two factors kept Bere from making headway with him. In spite of the general High Church antagonism to Sunday schools Tomline favoured them and had established them in his diocese. The second factor was probably the decisive one. With his boundless influence over the prime minister and with Dr John Moore in a feeble old age, the throne of Canterbury was almost in Tomline's grasp. So astute and wily a man was hardly likely to offend any powerful figure in the support of a country curate.[1] From William Cobbett and John Gifford, Bere met a different reception. Neither wished to be archbishop, both were convinced that Sunday schools were instruments of fanaticism and sedition and that subversive Puritans were making alarming progress in the church and in the nation. They must have listened to Bere's account of affairs in the parish of Blagdon with quite unmixed feelings.

In June 1801 the *Anti-Jacobin* printed a letter signed 'E.S.', attacking Mrs More and the *British Critic*'s review of Bere's first pamphlet. The letter, purporting to come 'from a clergyman resident in one of the parishes where Mrs More has a school established', asserted that the schools had increased Methodism and that the church had no control whatever over them. The *Anti-Jacobin* contributed an introduction. It had forborne to make any statements on the Controversy until it had 'all the pamphlets' before it; it was willing however to print correspondence without taking responsibility for its accuracy.[2] That policy

bishopric offered him of forwarding the interests of his family'. His making his son chancellor when he got to Wells should not have surprised his clergy. Both of the bishops are said by the *D.N.B.* to have been kindly, urbane and thoroughly inoffensive men. It also says, however, that Moss warmly supported Mrs More in the promotion of Christian education in the Cheddar Valley. Mrs More certainly did not think so.

[1] If that was Tomline's thinking it was probably correct. George III was friendly with both Porteus and Barrington and it was he who kept Tomline from the archbishopric when Moore died in 1805.   [2] *Anti-Jacobin*, June 1801, p. 201.

was abandoned with the greatest possible celerity, for in the succeeding number, for July 1801, there appeared a twenty-page review, of eight to ten thousand words, of Bere's and Elton's first pamphlets and Bere's reply. 'At length the whole of this controversy is fairly before the Public.'

The *Anti-Jacobin Review* was not roused in this piece to the heights of denunciation and invective that it reached later, but it was tolerably outspoken. It was also at this stage right in all particulars. The review cannot be objected to except for the harshness of its language, for Mrs More's conduct throughout the Controversy had left her badly vulnerable. It was a gross impropriety in her, the reviewer believed, not to have dismissed Younge at once, or sent him to another school, and still worse to have brought secret accusations against Bere; and Dr Crossman was to blame for not having notified Bere of the accusations. There was no justification for Mrs More's closing the schools. 'Were the interests of morality, virtue, and religion to be abandoned, because Mr Younge was to be discharged? The public, we fear, judging with ourselves from the documents here presented to their inspection,[1] will be apt to descry in this conduct, little of that calmness of investigation, soberness of discussion, soundness of judgment, and rectitude of thought, which so strongly mark most of the writings of this lady; but much of that spleen, peevishness, and disappointment which are too frequently allowed to regulate the actions of inferior minds, untempered by reflection, unimproved by study, and unenriched with knowledge.'[2]

The *Anti-Jacobin* repeated its solemn protest against religious instruction of adults by laymen, and against Sunday and evening schools for adults. 'We have long had our apprehension that in our laudable anxiety to avoid the *Scylla of licentiousness* we run some risk of falling into the *Charybdis of Puritanism*. Both should be avoided, with almost equal care.' To be avoided too was conduct like Elton's, for it was marked by paltry equivocation, mean shuffling and gross prevarication. In fact unfortunate Sir Abraham was the epitome of all that was bad in religious controversy.

[1] The *Anti-Jacobin*'s pretence of knowing nothing about the Controversy except from these documents was given up later.

[2] *Anti-Jacobin*, July 1801, p. 286.

14-2

His adulation of Mrs More is gross, fulsome, and offensive...we are bold to say, it disgraces alike the object of it, and the person by whom it is lavished.

We think as highly of, and, we trust, we appreciate as justly, the general exertions of Mrs More, in behalf of religion, morality, and social order, as the warmest of her friends; but...when we are told that even to be exposed by her would be 'some trophy' (even for a clergyman) 'to boast of'; that she is a female *Scipio*; that to accuse her of tolerating methodistical practices is 'an innuendo so atrocious' as to make his 'hand tremble'; that her 'reputation is *so sacred*;' when we read this, and much more of the same *stuff*, the imagination sickens, the judgment revolts, and patience is exhausted. Sir Abraham Elton may, if he pleases, fall prostrate before the shrine of the idol which he has raised up to himself; and lavish his incence with senseless profusion; but let not his temerity condemn those whose sober reason resists such idolatry; and who think they see, in such glaring *enthusiasm*, fair grounds for believing in the existence of a mind more ready to censure by words, than to reject, by actions, the bold and fanatical vagaries of Methodism.[1]

The *Anti-Jacobin* wished particularly to say that it had judged the Controversy solely on the facts. It had known, however, that

Sir ABRAHAM ELTON, Mrs More's champion, was himself refused ordination, on his first application to the Bishop, on the ground of his known attachment to the tenets and practices of methodism; and that he actually preached in a Tabernacle before he was admitted into the pale of the Church!!!

To have to say such things was painful.

But we think that those are not her friends who have endeavoured to persuade her that she has no concern in this controversy; an idea so preposterous as, in our apprehension, to be referable only to infatuation or imbecility! unquestionably she is concerned in it; and that most deeply....In our opinion, too, it is a subject on which she ought not to have employed a champion, but to have manfully fought her own battle. We have now discharged our duty, which, however painful it may prove, we shall always endeavour to discharge, sincerely and resolutely....*Amicus Plato, Amicus Socrates sed magis Amica Veritas.*[2]

[1] *Anti-Jacobin*, July 1801, pp. 286, 291.
[2] *Ibid.* p. 295.

VI

That opening review stressed an element of the Blagdon Controversy in which the *Anti-Jacobin* was at least as much interested as in anything going on down in Somerset. It was incredible, to its mind, that without some concealed cause

the Bishop and Chancellor should have condemned and *punished* a clergy-man of the established Church unheard, and without even informing him of the precise charges on which they proceeded to pronounce judgment.... Upon the whole we cannot but refer the conclusion of this strange business to the exertion of some secret but powerful influence, which it would be less difficult perhaps to confine than to controul. The exertion of such influence, we most earnestly deprecate as hostile to the true interests of the established Church; but should it continue to be exerted, in the way in which it appears to us to have been exerted in the present instance, we shall feel it a duty incumbent upon us, whose ardent and inviolate attachment, to the religious establishments of the country, is warped by no prejudice, and biased by no fears, to explore its devious course, and to unfold its private recesses to the public eye.[1]

The private recesses were those of Beilby Porteus, closely attached to Mrs More for many years. There is probably no reason to doubt that he did secretly exert his influence for Mrs More against Bere, certainly no doubt that the *Anti-Jacobin* believed so. It continued to take Bere's part with increasing violence. In August 1801 two more pamphlets against Mrs More were reviewed. The author of *The Blagdon Controversy etc. by 'A Layman'* it seems was a naval officer, or as the *Anti-Jacobin* put it, a veteran of the deck. He reasserted the unjustness of Bere's dismissal and reaffirmed that in spite of the denial of her friends it was Mrs More who had procured the dismissal. The *Anti-Jacobin* highly approved of the veteran's contribution, which in fact was only too solidly informed whoever he may have been. 'The *cunning* of Mrs More has never been professedly exposed. Yet it is apparent in all this transaction.' If that may be thought of as a correct way to describe a certain aspect of Mrs More's actions, there were far more instances of it than the *Anti-Jacobin* had any way of knowing about. Her first bad tactical blunder, however, was only too obvious—the really not very ingenuous proposal that Sir Abraham should be employed as arbitrator.

[1] *Ibid.* p. 289.

This single stroke marks her character strongly, and we, therefore, dwell upon it. In the progress of the business she pushes Sir Abraham forward, without one blush of shame on her cheek, for having mentioned him as a common friend and a fair referee before, to be her pleading, her writing advocate, her very strenuous champion, her very zealous advocate. Comparing the proceedings, we see the dishonourableness, we had almost said the dishonesty, of the proposal completely.

One point remained the important point, and, gathering courage, the *Anti-Jacobin* was still more outspoken about that.

And when we collate all the facts together...we cannot but unite the cause with the effect, and be sure that the hand, which produced and concealed the charges, did, in the same concealed manner, produce the punishment also. Only, another hand was induced to act, and a *Bishop* was engaged to lift a brother Bishop's arm for striking the blow. Mr Bere, and the Bath clergy, all know a little the medium of management. And we, who know more of this than they do, shall be strongly inclined, (if justice is not immediately done to Mr Bere) to lay all before the publick.[1]

The first pamphlet of William Shaw, rector of Chelvey, Bere's chief of staff, also reviewed in the issue of August 1801, made the same charge in a more diplomatic and more offensive way. 'I cannot say more, it is impossible to say less, than, that by some agency yet invisible to the public'—though visible, the *Anti-Jacobin* interpolated in its quotation, 'to ourselves and some others'—'the Bishop and his son, whose object is always to do right, have been grossly imposed upon'. The editor of the *Anti-Jacobin* was not, like Shaw, in the Mosses' diocese. 'We cannot speak so tenderly as Mr Shaw speaks. We blame severely all the parties hostile to Mr Bere. Dr Crossman, indeed, has proved himself too low for our very reprobation, by his shuffling, contradictory, and mean spirit.' He could hardly, the *Anti-Jacobin* had thought, sink himself lower in its estimation, but he had done so: 'the reptile has crept deeper into the mud, and buried himself completely in it'.[2] It was a shocking thing to say of the poor rector, whose sole wish through the whole Controversy was to be offensive to no one. The conduct of Bishop Moss, the *Anti-Jacobin* continued, was 'contradictory, violent and cruel'. But 'the principal blame must rest upon the head of the Chancellor,

[1] *Anti-Jacobin*, August 1801, p. 393. [2] *Ibid.* p. 394.

who appears to have been acting, throughout the whole, just as he was prompted by another Bishop, who again became prompter to the venerable infirmities of his father's mind, and who has thus involved himself with Dr Crossman, with both the Bishops, in a conduct that is the disgrace of all. We say this, in a lively reverence for the Clergy, and in the liveliest reverence for the Bishops.' For it was imperatively called on to do so. '*Every* parish may be convulsed, and *every* Clergyman may be oppressed, if the cunning of Mrs More can thus combine such discordant principles together, can thus conjure up even good spirits, even the very angels of the church, to do her work of mischief for her, and standing, as she does, in all the glory of a good angel, yet beginning to feel the taint of a bad one, can thus be able to "Ride in the whirlwind, and direct the storm", upon the head of opposing worthiness itself.'[1]

Reviews and letters in the same vein followed. On Bere's 'reinstatement' the *Anti-Jacobin* printed an article that in general went beyond anything it had previously done. Smug, self-righteous, arrogant and dishonest, it was in the absolute manner of the Reverend Samuel Henshall or the Reverend Richard Polwhele. In February 1802, after a short respite, the *Anti-Jacobin* took up the Controversy again in a review of 'Josiah Hard's' pamphlet. 'In our next number, we shall unfold some of the secret manoeuvres of the false friends of the Church, which, hitherto, from conciliatory motives, we have withholden from the public.'[2] That was the last threat uttered by the *Anti-Jacobin Review* against Porteus. Its March number had nothing about the Controversy. In April it was resumed, with sincere regret that it continued, and still more that it was degenerating into 'personal invective, and degrading ribaldry'. In this article of April 1802 it is apparent for the first time that the secret and powerful influence, its work with Chancellor Moss completed, had been brought to bear on the *Anti-Jacobin*. Gifford continued to condemn Crossman, Moss and even Mrs More (though always with a hearty reiteration of his constant respect for her apart from the Controversy), but it is clear he had received a quiet word to give up his attack on Porteus.[3]

[1] *Ibid.* p. 394.   [2] *Ibid.* February 1802, p. 194.
[3] There seem to be other indications too that Gifford was subsidized by the Government.

We are more particularly anxious for the concurrence of one of those, for whose spirit, for whose talents, and for whose conduct, we have a peculiar veneration; but who appears to us to have been induced in the present instance to deviate from his general correctness of opinion, by his very zeal for religion, by his esteem for a writer in defence of religion, whom every friend to religion must esteem, and by that cunning in the writer which too plainly marks her character, which, we should have thought, could not *always* have concealed from *his* eye the Calvinism which it has betrayed to ours, but which now appears to be grasping at *power*, in order to promote disunion, as well as Calvinism, among us.[1]

The *Anti-Jacobin* had not yet realized what it would have inferred at once from the known character of Porteus but for its hatred of Evangelicalism, that Mrs More's loyalties were identical with its own. For the time, without further reference to Porteus, Gifford and his reviewers stuck to their guns, in the same issue of April 1802 even going aggressively on to the charge that Mrs More had attended the dissenter William Jay's chapel in Bath and had received the Sacrament from him. In their opinion, that was decisive on the issue of her loyalty to the church. 'Gifford now possesses undeniable proof', Cobbett wrote to William Windham, '*juridical* proof, that Mrs Hannah More has several times received the sacrament from the hands of a layman. This decides the controversy....It is a fearful thing to think of, that this woman had under her tuition the children of a large portion of England.'[2] In the same issue a letter of 'Honestus' attacked Mrs More and her friends savagely. 'Petulant hosts of mercenary and anonymous scribblers' were now engaged in the Controversy and using the most virulent invective and the coarsest of personal allusions; Honestus exhorted Bere to 'leave the low arts of malignant slander and personal jeering' to Hannah More and her 'envious swarm of myriads of skulking minions'. In particular the *Animadversions* on Bere's three pamphlets (by Sedgwick Whalley) was 'one of the grossest compounds of vulgar abuse and personal insult that ever disgraced the aera of Christianity, liberality, and good manners'. Later, Honestus might point out some truths respecting 'the mean author of the mean pamphlet entitled "Animadversions, etc."'

[1] *Anti-Jacobin*, April 1802, p. 424.
[2] British Museum, Add. MS. 37853 f. 38. Quoted in *Letters from William Cobbett to Edward Thornton*, ed. G. D. H. Cole, London 1937, pp. 11–12.

Gangrening the Principles of the Country

Honestus's letter was unusually abusive even for this controversy, and when in the issue of May 1802 the *Anti-Jacobin* printed an intelligent and civilized letter from 'Honestior' protesting against the use of such language about Mrs More, it seized the opportunity of agreeing with him heartily. 'No one has condemned, more strongly than ourselves, the personal invective and degrading acrimony, which have unhappily marked, in too many instances, this lengthened controversy. Such weapons we have uniformly rejected, and invariably deprecated.'[1] That statement takes ranking place as the blandest and most unconscionable falsehood uttered during the entire Controversy, even with full appreciation of the many bland and unconscionable falsehoods uttered by Mrs More's side.

The *Anti-Jacobin* had hoped to conclude its account of the Blagdon Controversy in its May issue, but the pamphlets were still coming out. Spencer's, in its judgment, and it was a good judge, was perhaps the most offensive of any yet issued, with its use of such terms as vulpine craft, vile calumnies, malevolent falsehood, dirtiest servility and most despicable duplicity. In the June issue there was nothing about the Controversy and in July it had sunk to the 'Miscellanies'. Seven pamphlets were reviewed briefly there, including Sedgwick Whalley's *Animadversions*. The *Anti-Jacobin* fell savagely on that and mangled it. It was violently and sneeringly abusive of Bere, chiefly on the grounds of his low birth, 'replete with the most low, vulgar, and scurrilous abuse of Mr Bere and his friends, and with the most fulsome adulation of Mrs More'. To level a blow at her eminent piety 'is to level one at religion', Whalley had written; 'impudent blasphemy!' the *Anti-Jacobin* rejoined. 'If all the stores of Grub-street had been rifled, they could not have produced...matter more disgusting, more disgraceful, or more stupid.'[2] They congratulated Mrs More on so honourable an advocate.

The sisters had urged Whalley on again and again to attack Bere unsparingly in *Animadversions* and thought highly of it. It is odd that, strangely unwarned, he had responded particularly by ridiculing Bere for his parentage, a point on which the Mores were themselves vulnerable if it is to be thought of in that way.

[1] *Anti-Jacobin*, May 1802, p. 106.   [2] *Ibid.* July 1802, pp. 306-7.

VII

The *Anti-Jacobin Review* had committed three bad tactical blunders
in its handling of the Blagdon Controversy. The third was corrected
when it was made to realize it was not up to exposing the Bishop
of London. The first was common to most of the Orthodox: the
misconception that Evangelicals were political malcontents. The second
was tacitly to have accepted Bere, Shaw and their associates as loyalists
of their kind. The appearance of the Reverend William Shaw's *Life
of Hannah More, with a critical view of her writings*, by 'the Rev. Sir
Archibald MacSarcasm, bart.', a burlesque lampoon, made it clear
that not all High Church clergymen were Tories. In August the
Anti-Jacobin clutched at the opportunity to demonstrate its fairness and
impartiality.

The *Life of Hannah More* was the only serious blunder made throughout the Controversy by the emissaries of Satan down in Somerset, but it
was of a kind that made one blunder enough. A sympathizer with some
of the French doctrines and one who deplored the persecution of
Dr Priestley, Shaw charged that Cheap Repository had helped make the
French War popular, or, as he put it, Mrs More's 'bloody piety' caused
her to 'exalt her vulture's croak' to engage the nations in war. 'If
virtue and religion were in a mean habit', he held further, 'she would
deny both.' There were some penetrating observations in Shaw, though
not worded in a courtly way. The famous recipe of the rice milk, in
The Second Part of Tom White the Post-Boy; or, The Way To Plenty,
which Mrs More said would feed eight men well for sevenpence,
Shaw declared 'would not be too much for one man'. 'None but such
a stomach as can digest the copious dose of Jacobinism administered in
this book', the reviewer replied, 'could possibly receive the mess here
asserted not to be "too much for one man".' The *Life of Hannah More*
in fact contained many assertions any one of which was enough for the
Anti-Jacobin. If the author had not himself said he was an ecclesiastic
it would have called such a statement attached to so shameful a work
a libel on the church.

Even then Gifford took pains to extract from Shaw's work every
allegation or innuendo of the slightest plausibility about Mrs More that
could conceivably be damaging to her. One of them was very much so,

to Mrs More's mind. On the subject of her parentage her good biographers are vague, her other biographers make statements that cannot be shown to be true. The letters and other writings of the sisters seldom refer to the matter and never give any precise information about it. Shaw said explicitly that their father was a domestic servant of Norborne Berkeley Esq., of Stoke House, Gloucester, who had married a fellow servant. He was appointed teacher, by Berkeley's interest, of a small charity school, where thirty poor children were taught. Her sisters were helped to set up their young ladies' seminary by a subscription in which Sir James Stonhouse was influential. In view of Whalley's savage attack on Bere for his 'low birth', the *Anti-Jacobin*'s comment on Shaw's account must be admitted to have a degree of felicity. 'The same observations which suggested themselves to our minds on the imputed low extraction of Mr Bere', the reviewer remarked, 'will equally apply to that of Mrs More.... They may both congratulate themselves on having, by their own personal exertions and merits, raised themselves to a higher situation in life than that in which, by their birth, they seemed destined to move.'[1] The *Anti-Jacobin* never phrased an honest judgment with more skilful malice or uttered fairer words so carefully designed to wound.

Shaw did not forget the affair of Mr Turner of Belmont. Some time before Mrs More went up to town to make her fortune Turner proposed marriage to her and was accepted. He then changed his mind, for reasons now unknown. It seems fanciful to think he might have foreseen *The Shepherd of Salisbury Plain*. Mrs More's friends came to her defence and caused him to make a settlement.[2] Shaw called that 'purchasing an annuity of £200 a year for her life, at a very easy rate'. Turner also entered her for a sum in his will. The *Anti-Jacobin* observed that 'there was nothing in any of the circumstances attending the transaction, in the smallest degree injurious to her reputation', and after devoting two pages to the affair ended with the judgment that 'such loose imputations disgrace the biographer'. To refer throughout the review to this vicious caricature as a biography was the very height of false friendship. It is true there were one or two malignant little items

[1] *Anti-Jacobin*, August 1802, p. 429.
[2] So all the biographers, following Roberts; it has some resemblance to the conduct of her friends Elton and Whalley in the Blagdon Controversy.

they did not extract, such as the implicit statement that Mrs More was coincidently the mistress of an actor and two officers.

The *Anti-Jacobin* was convinced that Bere would read the *Life of Hannah More* with indignation.[1]

It was this review that Mrs More wrote about, on September 10, to Wilberforce. 'It is from no kindness to *me* that the Anti-Jacobin has changed its note; but they are frightened for themselves, now that the world has found out what are the real principles, religious and political, of the party they have so zealously espoused; but even jacobins and infidels are to be upheld, if by doing so, Methodism, (or what they call so) may be crushed. Peace be with them ! Their repentance comes too late to do me any good.'[2]

There were a few more reviews and a good many more letters about the Blagdon Controversy in the *Anti-Jacobin*. In October its conductors heartily wished the whole affair at an end. There was no doubt they had attached more importance to the matter than many. 'But we have considered it as materially connected with the growth of schism *into* the church and sectarianism out of it, which daily increases in rapidity and extent.' The Act of Toleration should be revised; enthusiastic persons could then be prevented from becoming ministers of the church. Even at this time, it seems, the *Anti-Jacobin* had not heard of Bishop Tomline's part in the Blagdon Controversy.

Letters kept on appearing, for and against Mrs More, and the Controversy dragged on, in a desultory if unpleasant fashion, to its end. As late as December 1803 the *Anti-Jacobin* printed a long unsigned letter agreeably describing an anniversary meeting at one of Mrs More's parishes. Written by a very observant eye-witness, this is the only impartial account of such a meeting that has been preserved.

On Wednesday the 22nd I was in a shop in Bristol; when a party of ladies came in for blue ribbons, who, from their animated expressions of hope for fine weather on the ensuing day, and the blue knots ordered, I was induced to inquire where they were going, and learnt to Miss More's Shipham club. I instantly determined to make one, and observe the proceedings of the day, and to gather all I could, and judge for myself. In the morning I went to Shipham, but found all the party I had seen were gone, with many others, to

[1] *Anti-Jacobin*, August 1802, p. 444.
[2] *More*, vol. III, p. 208. The letter is erroneously dated 1804.

breakfast at Miss More's house. About twelve they began to arrive; the church bells struck out, and on the wild hills of Shipham, and surrounded by Mendip, the ladies made a very gay and beautiful appearance: they soon sat down to dinner; there were several tables, and plenty of beef, lamb, ham, and chicken; and soon very true English enthusiasm was displayed, both by clergy and laity: the bottle went round very moderately, for in less than an hour the company were summoned to arrange themselves for church, when I saw at the least two hundred poor women, respectable and neatly dressed, most of whom I learnt, prior to this institution, had scarcely a gown, all with blue knots, and very happy countenances; and a great number of poor children, all ranged in couples, and a band of country music: the clergy then followed the poor, and the ladies them to church, round Shipham hills.[1]

Mr Jones, the rector, read prayers; Mr Boak preached; then I expected ebullitions of enthusiasm and flattery. The text was—'Mary has chosen the good part'; he pointed out the one thing needful in so plain and practical a way, that I said well here is no enthusiasm. I then waited to hear if he guarded the poor from supposing if they think they have chosen that one thing needful they may be lazy and immoral, with all the deductions of that sort, that methodists leave their poor infatuated followers to draw: but truth obliges me to say, I never heard the moral duties more fully, clearly, and on higher motives enforced.... Well, I said, here is no methodism; here is no faith without works; here is not what is as much to be disliked as either, any Calvinism; they returned in the same order, and two Miss More's, one of whom I learnt was Miss H. More, appeared more prominent.

I now felt some certainty of seeing what I had all day been looking for in vain; but here was no methodism. The poor children were called forward, and their master gave out a psalm, and then I became an enthusiast myself; their little voices employed in praise of their Creator, instead of the sad reverse; their shining faces all directed one way, to the six large baskets of cakes, as their reward, operated on the countenances of most present; and I felt strongly, as all must have done who were prejudiced against the whole of Miss More's institutions, such temporal benefits bestowed (as nearly every child had some clothing on provided by the charity), such kindness and exertion conferred, merited not the obloquy Miss H— M— had received.

Tea was then made in five rooms for all the poor women, by the ladies; four or five hundred drank tea in the whole, with much glee; they then went out again to the open place where the children had received their cakes, and the vicar produced the accounts of what the club was worth, and many ladies present gave handsomely towards the fund: when Miss Martha More spoke

---

[1] Paragraphing by the present writer.

to them of their gratitude due to the company, to God, their superiority to the French poor, who never saw so many guineas in all their lives; no Sunday schools; no gentry taking care of the poor there; money not like ours, most all gold, but *tinsel*. Miss H. More then said, good women, here will be more taxes, remember you have nothing to do with them but to pay them, not to talk about them, that is not our business, but to pay them. God save the king was then played and sung; with huzzas three times three, in which I found myself so heartily joining, that any of my acquaintances, had they seen me, might have exclaimed, 'Is Saul among the prophets?'[1]

VIII

So the Blagdon Controversy ended, with the principals in it much the same as they had been in November 1800, and not very much done except the intensifying of misunderstanding, dislike, suspicion, resentment and rancour. Down in Somerset there was no school and no benefit club for the parish of Blagdon, and no extempore prayer from Mr Younge. Thomas Bere remained Rector of Butcombe and apparently curate of Blagdon until his death, Mrs More still conducted her schools in eight parishes, with the approval of her diocesan, and Beilby Porteus was still Bishop of London. On the whole the honours, if any, rested with Bere; but there were few of the contestants who could look back on this engagement with satisfaction. Mrs More's agents and defenders (with the exception of her two young curates), Bere's 'emissaries' and aides, the go-betweens, intriguers, arbitrators and referees of all descriptions, in particular the princes of the church with their dignified adherence to the theological principle of the benefit of the closest friends, certainly Mrs More's two leading local champions Dr Sedgwick Whalley and the Reverend Sir Abraham, and Dr Crossman too, whom nobody had a good word for, played unhappy parts.

Crossman was the hero of an episode that does not appear in any of what may be called the 'official' accounts of the Controversy. Some time during the summer of 1801 the Blagdon party stooped, as it would appear, to a really low piece of buffoonery. 'What is the meaning of Hannah More's marriage being thus gravely announced in every newspaper, and resounding here in N. Wales from every mouth, while you

[1] *Anti-Jacobin*, Appendix following the issue of December 1803, vol. XVI, pp. 531-2.

say not one word on the subject?' Mrs Piozzi demanded of her constant correspondent Mrs Pennington, a cousin of Mrs Whalley.[1] Some exhilarated person had gone to the trouble of inserting it seems in many papers an announcement of Mrs More's marriage to Crossman, a bit of malignant clowning that sounds like Dr Shaw the jocular rector of Chelvey. No word is said about this hideous affront, apparently too gross to be mentioned at all, in the preserved correspondence of any of the principals in the Blagdon affair.

The part played by Wilberforce in the Blagdon Controversy proper is impossible to describe, as thanks to the peculiar method of his biographers it has thus far remained concealed. In the middle of the Controversy he played a part of incalculable importance to Evangelicalism when his resoluteness and friendship with Pitt turned back a dangerous assault. It had been evident for some time that Tomline, probably the most powerful High Church prelate, was an enemy. As he was an arrogant man little noted for the charity and humility proper to one who (if he had remembered) was a transgressor from the womb, it was always surprising he had been silent through the Controversy, except indeed to utter a cordial approval of Mrs More and a hearty if premature congratulation of Bishop Porteus on her 'victory'. He was in fact playing a very hostile part from beginning to end.

The issue was the proposed introduction by Pitt of Tomline's measure disingenuously described in the *Life of Wilberforce* as 'aimed at Methodists and dissenters' through a restriction of the Toleration Act. 'I dread lest God have given our government over to a spirit of delusion', Wilberforce's diary says for 16 March 1800; '—that they should think of attacking the Dissenters and Methodists! I fear the worst....Pitt I am convinced has no trust in me on any religious

---

[1] *The Intimate Letters of Hester Piozzi and Penelope Pennington* (London, 1914), pp. 228, 230. Mrs More's unknown libeller may have remembered that in 1789 the newspapers published a report of her marriage to Dr Priestley (*More*, vol. II, pp. 185–6). Lest it should appear nothing in the romantic line ever happened to Hannah More beyond the episodes of Turner, Priestley and Crossman, it should in fairness be recorded that in her early London days she received a proposal of marriage from Lord Monboddo, a 'learned and acute' man, says the *New Universal Biography* (1838, p. 126; *More*, vol. I, p. 253), but who 'exposed himself to much and merited ridicule' by asserting certain absurdities, 'particularly his whimsical speculations relative to a supposed affinity between the human race and the monkey tribe'.

subject. To see this measure drawn out in a bill! Never so moved by any public measure.'[1] Something is clearly wrong here, for there is nothing in the bill as so described to give him deep personal distress. He was not fond of either Methodists or dissenters. An earlier reference in his journal (11 April 1799) to 'the more serious clergy' gives a clue. The measure was also aimed at the Evangelicals. For the Bishop of Lincoln to have professed the warmest sympathy for Mrs More was a polished suavity of a high order.

Having some trace of political suppleness himself, Wilberforce would not have been deceived; but he had been aware for some time of trouble in the prime minister's quarter. On 8 April 1799 he wrote to William Hey that the government was about to bring forward repressive measures against the radicals. 'So far, I think, no man instructed by experience can object. Indeed I see nothing in all this contrary to the genuine principles of political and social liberty. But...some check is wished to be imposed on the indiscriminate right of preaching.' The measure apparently provided that magistrates could withhold licences, but beyond that would have 'regulated' the teaching—all religious instruction except duly authorized services—of both ministers and clergymen. 'I told Mr Pitt', Wilberforce wrote to Hey on September 7, when this emergency had apparently been met successfully for the time being, 'that I was ready to assent to one restriction, namely, that no one should exercise the office of a teacher without having received a testimonial from the sect to which he should belong.' 'I fear the Bishop of Lincoln (this is whispered in your private ear in the strictest confidence) will renew his attempt next year. If such a bill as was lately in contemplation should pass, it would be the most fatal blow both to church and state, which has been struck since the Restoration.'

In the sentence that follows we see the vital importance to the Evangelical Reformation of his relationship to Pitt. 'I believe I told you before...that I place more dependence on Mr Pitt's moderation and fairness of mind, (though less in this instance than in any other,) than either on the House of Lords or Commons. In short, so utterly ignorant in all religious matters is the gay world, and the busy, and the high, and the political, that any measure government should propose would be easily carried.'[2]

[1] *Wilberforce*, vol. II, p. 360.   [2] *Ibid.* pp. 360–2.

To have kept Pitt from passing this measure may have been one of Wilberforce's chief political services. His account of the outcome was given years later and was most discreet even then.

The intelligence that some such measure was about to be proposed to parliament, reached the ears of some of the dissenting ministers, from one of whom I believe it was that I received the first intimation of the design. I lost no time in conferring with Mr Pitt on the subject, but he had been strongly biassed in favour of the measure by Bishop Pretyman,[1] on whom I urged in vain the serious consequences that must infallibly ensue....The Bishop, however, would not assent to my view of the case, and finding Mr Pitt intended to bring the measure forward, I begged I might have a full confidential discussion of the subject. Accordingly we spent some hours together at a tete-a-tete supper, and I confess I never till then knew how deep a prejudice his mind had conceived against the class of clergy to whom he knew me to be attached.[2]

That statement alone is enough to show that the measure went beyond the regulation of Methodist and dissenting ministers. Such people were not included in 'the class of clergy to whom he knew me to be attached'. They were not clergy and Wilberforce was not attached to them. The point is put beyond question by the sentence that follows in his narrative. 'It was in vain that I mentioned to him Mr Robinson of Leicester, Mr Richardson of York, Mr Milner of Hull, Mr Atkinson of Leeds, and others of similar principles; his language was such as to imply that he thought ill of their moral character, and it clearly appeared that the prejudice arose out of the confidence he reposed in the Bishop of Lincoln.' No more need be observed than that Thomas Robinson, William Richardson, Joseph Milner and Miles Atkinson were not Methodists or dissenting ministers but Evangelical clergymen of the Established Church. The only 'others of similar principles' were other Evangelicals.

'All I could obtain from Mr Pitt was an assurance that the measure should not be actually introduced without his giving me another opportunity of talking the matter over with him. Happily that opportunity never occurred; of course I was in no hurry to press for it; and the attempt never was resumed.'[3] 'I had several discussions, and, in par-

---

[1] This is Tomline, who changed his name on receiving an inheritance.
[2] *Wilberforce*, vol. II, pp. 363-4.   [3] *Ibid.* vol. II, p. 365.

ticular, one long tete-a-tete (at supper in Downing Street)', Wilberforce wrote to Lord Sidmouth ten years later when another measure of the same kind was brought in; '...and though the bill was actually drawn, and though it was strongly pressed, in defiance of all its consequences, by one person who, with reason, had great influence over his mind, I at length prevailed with him to pause; and that ended in his not carrying on the measure.'[1]

It can be taken for granted that apart from this episode Wilberforce played a leading part in the Blagdon Controversy. He was one of Hannah More's closest friends, the originator of the schools, the head of the Evangelical Party. Long before its end the Controversy was an accepted symbol, among informed people, of the whole conflict. There is no conceivable doubt that he was in the closest touch throughout it, at Fulham Palace and in Somerset so far as Mrs More saw fit to keep him informed. In his sons' biography there is no explicit understandable reference to the Controversy at all except the letter advising Mrs More to get a Methodist as teacher, which was. printed with deletions. It would probably be rash to maintain that he played no part in the Mosses' about-face, or the abrupt ending of the *Anti-Jacobin*'s exposure of Bishop Porteus.

The part played by the heroine herself—some of the secret history of the Controversy being known thanks to Hill Wickham—can hardly be thought of as showing her in a very good light. Apart from the incident of Newton, Inman and Anna Seward, which fortunately for Mrs More the *Anti-Jacobin* did not know about during the Controversy, there were many happenings that gave substance to its most personal charges against her. To mention no others, the lengthy and detailed letter Mrs More wrote in about April 1802 to the new Bishop of Bath and Wells contained statement after statement of the most unfortunate sort. We may let one of them stand for all the rest. 'Your Lordship's enlightened mind will give me credit for studiously abstaining from what would, with ordinary judges, have best served my cause; I mean a resentful retaliation on the conduct and motives of my adversaries.'[2]

---

[1] Dean Pellew, *Life of Sidmouth*, vol. III, p. 61.
[2] The letter, misdated 1801, is printed in *More*, vol. III, pp. 123–39. Roberts, who almost certainly did not have access to the More–Whalley correspondence, says 'Through all these attacks she preserved the dignity of silence' (*ibid.* vol. III, p. 121).

Gangrening the Principles of the Country

The fiction that Mrs More took no part in the Controversy was repeated many times, by her friends and by Hannah More. 'I resolve not to defend myself, let them bring what charges they will', she wrote to Wilberforce, who must have known nothing (it seems from that statement) about her detailed, explicit, continued direction of Sir Abraham's and Whalley's activities.

By a later period she had convinced herself, perhaps, that she had taken no part in her defence. It was asserted so often, and so gravely, at any rate, that the *Anti-Jacobin* was deceived at the time and many others later. At a Cheddar Anniversary meeting at the height of the Controversy, Mrs More's 'Charge' to the lower orders present included the prayer that 'every rebellious motion may be subdued that exalts itself against peace, and patience, and gentleness, and meekness of spirit'. On the same day, at the same anniversary, at Mrs More's instance, the Reverend Sir Abraham launched another attack against Bere. 'I prevailed on him to preach again at our second club at Cheddar, a few days ago, in order to follow up the blow, lest the first sermon might be construed into a sudden ebullition of zeal.'[1] Patience Mrs More had a reasonable amount of, but her good qualities did not include gentleness and meekness of spirit.

'I cannot sufficiently acknowledge that restraining grace', she wrote

There are indications (such as his printing the letter to Bishop Beadon) that Roberts did not know very much about the Blagdon Controversy; but if he had done, his great reverence for his subject, and his conception of his art, would have made him superior to any difficulty. 'The biographer, in carrying her through this stormy period, has only to fling around her a mantle taken from the rich fabrics of her own wardrobe' (vol. III, p. 117). That mantle has served every biographer of Mrs More since. Her steadfast refusal to retaliate was, however, accepted, in learned works, at an early point, before Roberts. 'A sharp controversy was carried on by a neighbouring clergyman against the schools, and several others in their favour; but, to the honour of the founder herself, she took no part in the strife, leaving the fruits to justify both her motives and her conduct' (*Dictionary of the Living Authors*, 1816, p. 241). That notice seems to have been copied by *Biographie Etrangère* (Paris, 1819, Supplément), p. 444. 'Il s'ensuivit une guerre de plume à laquelle miss More ne prit aucune part, se contentant de répondre à ses injustes détracteurs par d'heureux résultats'.

Could Bishop Beadon perhaps have known enough about the Blagdon Controversy to appreciate Mrs More's attributing 'in great part this long and unmitigated persecution...to the defenceless state of our sex'? (*More*, vol. III, p. 123.)

[1] *Mendip Annals*, pp. 231, 238.

in 1805 to her friend Mrs Kennicot, 'which has preserved me, not only from attacking others, but from defending myself, and that I was enabled to commit my cause to him who judgeth righteously.'[1]

Mrs More's final statement on the Blagdon Controversy is contained in a letter written three years after that to her old friend William Weller Pepys, the Evangelical barrister and philanthropist, a strong figure in the reforming societies, who had suggested the 'all the world would be gone a digging' argument in *Village Politics* sixteen years earlier. Two 'Jacobin and infidel curates, poor and ambitious,' she wrote, 'formed the design of attracting notice, and getting preferment, by attacking some charity schools...as seminaries of vice, sedition, and disaffection'. 'My declared resolution not to defend myself, certainly encouraged them to go on. How thankful am I that I kept that resolution; though the grief and astonishment excited by this combination nearly cost me my life. I can now look back, not only without emotion, to this attack, but it has even been matter of *thankfulness* to me; it helped to break my too strong attachment to the world, it showed me the vanity of human applause, and has led me, I hope, to be *more* anxious about the motives of my actions, and *less* anxious about their consequences.

'I am happy in the esteem of my neighbours', Mrs More added, 'and my schools flourish.'[2]

In 1808 the Blagdon Controversy had long been forgotten, by the general religious public. Bere died in October 1814[3]—'called away', Hannah More might have said of him as she did of another of her adversaries—'to answer at the bar of God, for a life spent in opposition to the light of knowledge and education'. Chancellor Moss became Bishop of Oxford in 1807.

---

[1] *More*, vol. III, p. 221. When 'Charlotte Elizabeth' met Mrs More fifteen years later this story was long-accepted fact: 'She had...triumphed over all, by meekly committing her cause to him who judgeth righteously' (Charlotte Elizabeth, *Personal Recollections*, 4th ed., 1854, p. 225).

[2] *More*, vol. III, pp. 253–5.

[3] *Dictionary of the Living Authors*, p. 414.

IX

A good deal of light is cast on various aspects of Evangelicalism by the Blagdon Controversy. Particularly illuminating is that passage at the end of the *Anti-Jacobin*'s unsigned letter of December 1803 where in two superbly reported sentences we hear the voices of Mrs Hannah and Miss Patty addressing their parishioners in the very accents of Dr Shepherd, Mrs Jones and Mr Johnson. In her schools Mrs More was simply practising on some three thousand people in the Mendip Hills, to great Evangelical applause, the religious and social truths she had demonstrated in the words of Mr Worthy, Mr Trueman and her honest Shepherd.

She was particularly not likely to forget that one of the primary objects of an Evangelical leader is to attract 'useful' people to participation in Evangelical enterprises and through them to serious religion. No finer illustration of her whole-hearted subordination to that basic principle could be wished for than the Shipham meeting described by the *Anti-Jacobin*'s anonymous but invaluable correspondent. The substantial and cheerful viands were not given to the poor but to the ladies and gentlemen who were looking on, having breakfasted a short time earlier, no doubt cheerfully and substantially, at Mrs More's home. It was those ladies and gentlemen who displayed true English enthusiasm as the bottle went moderately round. The poor women drank tea, the poor boys had six baskets of cakes. That practice, in its extended aspects a chief cause of the Evangelical success, was not adopted in any thoughtless way. 'We entertained about seventy of the gentry at dinner', Mrs More wrote about another anniversary, '—acting like the rest of the world, giving a dinner to those who did not want it, and only tea to many, many hundreds who had no dinner at home.'[1] By reversing that entertainment of the great and the little, Mrs More knew well, she would not have accomplished a single useful thing. She might have offended important people, she would have done nothing for the *best interests* of the poor.

It seems to have become a 'received' opinion that in spite of their insistence on subordination the Evangelicals were well aware of the unjustifiable degradation of the poor and had a strong determination

[1] *Mendip Annals*, pp. 231-2.

to do something about it—any view to the contrary being a matter of our misunderstanding the Evangelical way of speaking. That view is so desirable that it is a pity it is so untenable. The record could hardly have been written more clear. This is not to say that Mrs More and Patty did not do some secondary, worldly, good for their poor neighbours. On the contrary, one of the unhappiest aspects of the schools is that with conditions of existence such as they were for the Mendip people the Mores' charities must have played a large part in their lives. These particular objects of bounty lived in a state of bare survival, with comforts unheard-of and necessaries scarce, sometimes on the verge of starvation and with few pleasures except illegal or immoral ones. Into lives like that, well reported in Patty's journal as in the Cheap Repository tales, any benevolences, no matter what terms they were offered on, must have brought much. There is no reason to think Patty exaggerated the help given the poor country women and their children or the gratitude of many of them for what 'the ladies' were doing. This huge task was also Evangelical in the best sense. It took courage and devotion to penetrate into those 'savage, proud parishes' where knowledge of Christ was like that in the heart of Africa and civilization much the same, and into some of which no constable cared to go. The Mores went into them Sunday after Sunday for many years, on horseback when they had to, for ten miles or sometimes twenty miles, over 'dreadful roads', in spite of weather and illness and always in the face of steady discouragements even before the local incumbents rallied against them.

Miss Patty could well feel 'it seems to require an unusual stock of patience to endure such mistaken folly and ignorance', and not only from the misguided rich farmers. The poor women sent their children to shops on Sundays and the girls indulged in dangerous frivolities particularly during the winters. On the cliffs on Sundays and in the paper mill at Cheddar and the Nailsea glassworks, places of 'dreadful sin and wickedness', there were scenes that Miss Patty did not care to do more than hint at. But there was steady progress; some of the scholars more steadily 'escaped the snare'; in one parish 'near twenty young women saved from the destructions of the winter'.[1] As the ladies of Cowslip Green slowly penetrated into district after district where English

[1] *Mendip Annals*, pp. 112–14.

subjects lived in conditions hardly better than the Climbing Boys', they did more than bring some rudiments of the Evangelical religion where before there had not been even rudiments of the High Church religion. They brought in a little civilization, probably raised many of their destitute neighbours to some kind of good conduct, helped them to have a decency they had no way of having before. In bad times they even gave financial help, when no one in the parish could, to people for whom an illness or lay-off of the wage earner was a desperate catastrophe. Simply to show these colliery and farm labourers and their families that the gentry had concern about them must have done something to raise their social and moral tone. In addition, Mrs More was forced by the immutable nature of things to confer on these children and youths and a few of their parents an inestimable gift; in teaching them to read the Bible she had to teach them how to read. Beyond that, it stands to reason (as in the nature of things too) that Hannah More, and rather more certainly Wilberforce, felt some useless love for their fellow human beings in distress.

But those facts should not blind us to basic facts. Useless love is a mere natural feeling. It can be felt by a pagan or lower animal, even an infidel or atheist. It is not Evangelicalism. A mere contributing to the worldly good of suffering people does nothing for their *best interests* and is not true charity and benevolence. Tea and cakes are better than starvation no matter how instrumentally and incidentally they are offered; but those offering them must not forget that such an act is done *by the way*. Its true object is pointed out by good Mrs Jones: the kindness she showed to their bodily wants gave her such an access to their houses and hearts, as made them better disposed to receive religious counsel and instruction.

Worldly good is nothing to eternal good. Indigence, suffering and degradation are appointed by the Deity for His wise purposes. The 'scarcities' are afflictive dispensations. They are to teach the poor submissive obedience. The rich suffer hardships too. Sin is the great cause and source of all evil. Suffering is always better than sin. Sin is a greater evil than poverty. Miss Patty's *Mendip Annals* gives us another statement of basic Evangelicalism that is the absolute foundation of all Evangelical activity without exception. Mrs More's 'Charge' of 1800 to the Cheddar Anniversary expresses in a simple way the lesson to be drawn by religious people from the Sunday schools and the meetings of the older people. Their success should 'impress us with a full determination of making every scheme subservient to religious purposes'.[1] The true object of benevolent people who are actuated by religious principle is to give Evangelical instruction, with sound views of order and subordination, to the poor, to improve and discipline in Evangelical activity and devotion those people engaged in the benevolence, and to engage substantial people in the reform of the nation.

The Blagdon Controversy unsettled no Evangelical principle of thought or action. Its chief effect, as it revealed in Evangelicalism a strength, subtlety—or 'cunning'—and an obdurateness that had only been suspected, was to increase the alarm and determination of the Orthodox. Mrs More saw that her quarrel with Bere had roused a more bitter and resolute enmity, and she saw too that it had enlisted against Evangelicalism more than the Regular clergy and laity and more than people of only religious motivation. 'Alas! it is not me individually', she wrote to Wilberforce in 1802; 'I am only a petty victim. Could such a man as B[ere], with principles equally hostile to the church and state, be supported by men professing themselves warm friends to both, if...a general hostility to serious religion were not a common rallying point to two descriptions of men opposite enough in all other respects?'[2]

That division of those opposing the establishment of the kingdom of Christ so well constituted by the *Anti-Jacobin Review* was far from giving up when Shaw's *Life of Hannah More* forced the abandonment of the curate of Blagdon. Gifford and his staff kept up the assault, month after month, on all Evangelical activities and leading clerical figures, on Sunday schools, Calvinism and the Abolition cause, with special emphasis on the Party's resolute acquisition of footholds in the church and their rise into a compelling position in the life of the nation. In the early 1800's they were given choice new targets in the larger Evangelical societies, whose undreamed-of success remains the surest sign that it was not High Church that was in harmony with the religious and moral Spirit of the Age.

At the end of the eighteenth century the Evangelical policy had been established with its methods and principles, the great propaganda begun,

[1] *Mendip Annals*, p. 232. [2] *More*, vol. III, p. 174.

the society organization started off, those people collected and united who were known to the Evangelical leaders to be well disposed, and the penetration into the church and the great clearly under way. The Evangelical Reformation had not yet, so far as its leaders, or anyone, knew, struck into the body of the English people except in so far as something very close to it had been accomplished by Wilberforce's huge campaign for the Africans. The institution that was to penetrate first and unmistakably into the life of the mass of Englishmen, revealing a great strength of religious principle waiting only for a cause and a leader, was the British and Foreign Bible Society.

CHAPTER 7

MISSIONARIES TO ENGLAND

These once formidable enemies have, like the army of Sennacherib, melted away. We went to sleep, as it were, surrounded with these inveterate foes, and...when we 'arose in the morning, they were dead men'.   THE CHRISTIAN OBSERVER, 1816

It will perhaps be found, that the most active friends to missions, are also the most diligent in promoting christianity at home.   THOMAS SCOTT, 1801

By inviting [the humbler orders] to subscribe their smaller sums...you present to them a noble stimulus for their endeavours, you promote a higher tone of general morals, you raise them to a participation in all the good that is now on foot in the nation.   DANIEL WILSON, 1813

The British and Foreign Bible Society have had the honour of commencing a new era in the Christian world.   THE SOUTH CAROLINA BIBLE SOCIETY, 1815

The public mind is gradually undergoing a great moral revolution. Christians are acquiring enlarged views of the nature of their religion, and the obligation to impart it....Incalculable is the national good which is daily springing up from such exertions. It now appears capable of demonstration, that the moral wilderness will eventually blossom as the rose, through the blessing of God on Bible and Missionary institutions. The opposition of error and prejudice seems to languish and decay; while the triumphant career of sacred benevolence conveys life, light, peace, and love.
     LEGH RICHMOND, c. 1814

I

The years between the establishment of the Proclamation Society and the end of Mrs More's controversy were critical for Wilberforce. Almost at the beginning of his campaign England was at war with France and the long domestic quiet of the eighteenth century was shattered by unrest and disorder. A period could hardly be more hostile to such a reform movement. Even if Evangelicalism had won over many more influential supporters than the records show, its survival through those fifteen years would probably have to be thought of as due chiefly to the spiritual reinforcement of Abolition.

The early years of the century were still crucial. The Blagdon and Calvinistic Controversies may have helped to strengthen individuals in Reformation Christianity but they were not likely to recommend

234

Evangelicalism to the great. Through the months between Pitt's return to Downing Street in May 1804 and his death there was the extreme menace of Bishop Tomline's possible nomination to the see of Canterbury. He could have done great harm as primate. The king's personally naming his friend Manners Sutton (unsympathetic but not actively vicious) to the office was one of the spectacular 'providential interpositions' of the age, if hardly from Tomline's point of view. There had been some progress. Wilberforce's book was widely read and fruitful, Mrs More's Evangelical writings more so, Porteus and Barrington remained steadfast friends. The Proclamation Society and the Bettering Society had enlisted several more of the great who are found at Wilberforce's side from this time on and the records of the Philanthropic Society show a growing Evangelical control, by the end of the reform period probably complete. Its president in 1814 was the Duke of York. This prince, unlike his brothers Kent and Sussex, was mere decoration, with no recorded moral inclinations. But the vice-presidents in that year included Pusey, Lord Bulkeley, Lord Hardwicke and

Earl Grosvenor

and on the committee were

W. Morton Pitt and
Benjamin Harrison, of Clapham Common, the 'Czar' of Guy's Hospital

New subscribers included:

Lord Balgony, later Earl of Leven and Melville, John Thornton's son-in-law
Thomas Bainbridge, of Clapham
The Reverend Thomas Gisborne, clergyman of means, at Cambridge with
    Wilberforce, one of the most esteemed, kindly and dull of Evangelical
    writers
General Hervey
J. S. Harford of Bristol, later a biographer of Wilberforce (his country seat
    Blaise Castle was one of the Evangelical show pieces)
William Mellish, financier
George Wolff, of Clapham: this man, the Danish consul, was a (true) convert
John Broadley Wilson, of Clapham: this man probably made heavier contri-
    butions and subscriptions to moral and reforming societies of the day than
    any other person with the possible exception of Wilberforce

John, later Sir John, Simeon, a Master in Chancery
George Scholey, of Clapham, a London alderman
The Hon. Bartholomew Bouverie
Countess Fortescue
Lady Maria and Lady Harriet Finch
Alexander Gordon, financier
Lord Lilford
Lady Elizabeth Perceval
Lady Caroline Murray
John Pearson of Golden-square, the famous Evangelical surgeon, a son-in-law
    of William Hey of Leeds
Lord Robert Seymour

In 1816 Henry Hoare of Mitcham and Benjamin Harrison are on the committee of the Philanthropic Society, in 1821 Sir Thomas Plumer is a vice-president. Among new life members appear

The Duke of Gloucester
The Earl of Bristol
Lord Carrington, Wilberforce's cousin Robert Smith
Hannah More
Bishop Barrington
Samuel Hoare jun., of the Lombard-street and Hampstead Heath Hoares, one
    of the many Quakers who became Evangelical

New subscribers to the Philanthropic Society include

Matthew Wood, London alderman
Lady Olivia Bernard Sparrow (the Lady —— of p. 83 above), Hannah
    More's friend and convert, daughter of the Earl of Gosford; and her
    daughter
Lady Millicent Sparrow, later Viscountess Mandeville, later Duchess of
    Manchester

In 1823 the vice-presidents included Wilberforce. The president of the Society was then the Duke of Leeds, the remaining vice-presidents were the Earl of Hardwicke, Earl Grosvenor, the Earl of Harrowby, Viscount Middleton, Bishop Barrington, Philip Pusey, Jeremiah Harman, three others and

Earl Spencer[1]

---

[1] *An Account of the Nature and Present State of the Philanthropic Society, etc.* (London, 1804, 1814, 1816, 1818, etc.). In addition to George Scholey of Clapham the Society

A similar benevolent institution was the Marine Society, founded in 1756 with the object of rescuing poor boys by training them and fitting them out for the sea. This vocation seems to have been thought of as the last resort, though probably not by seafaring people. The historian of the Church Missionary Society tells us that 1814 was a sorrowful year in Legh Richmond's family; their son Nugent had so greatly failed his Evangelical training that 'no other course remained but to send him to sea'.[1] Here again, an activity of a merely worldly nature and the same obvious 'use'. In 1819 the vice-presidents of this Society were Samuel Thornton, Admiral Sir John Colpoys, Earl Spencer, Lord Gambier and two others, with Thornton the treasurer. The subscribers included some strong new Evangelicals:

Thomas Fowell Buxton, M.P., of the brewing firm; Wilberforce's parliamentary successor in 1825
Osgood and Sampson Hanbury, of the brewing firm, Buxton's uncles
Lord Darnley
Charles Elliott, of Clapham, London manufacturer, father of Charlotte Elliott
Sir George Grey
Lord Henniker
Sir Evan Nepean
Admiral Earl Nugent
Alexander Riddell, banker
Admiral (later Lord) Saumarez
Abel Smith and Samuel Smith, Wilberforce's cousins
Sir Robert Wigram, M.P.[2]

Admiral Viscount Exmouth, another solid Evangelical, was added to the vice-presidents in 1831. Thornton Astell was treasurer of the Marine Society then, the Duke of Gloucester patron.

In 1801 came the reorganization of one of the most interesting of these small early institutions, the Benevolent, or Strangers' Friend

included several Evangelical City men, merchants, importers, etc. who were not of the large financial stature of the Hoares, Barclays, Angerstein, Thorntons, Elliott and the other Evangelical magnates, but who played a steady and substantial part in the support of the societies: John Blades, Sylvanus and David Bevan, John Capel, Jesse Curling, John Wells, John Whitmore, George Bridges, Robert Marsden, Thomas Oldham Oldham, Sir Charles Price.

[1] Hole, p. 565.   [2] *General State of the Marine Society, etc.* (London, 1819, etc.).

Society, founded in 1785 by the Methodists for the purpose, as its full name tells us, 'of Visiting and Relieving Sick and Distressed Strangers, and Other Poor, at their respective Habitations in London and its Vicinity'. There is no better example of the Evangelical capture of a society of the kind[1] and the extension of its original purpose to truly religious 'use'. 'The committee and visitors can with the utmost sincerity affirm', the first *Report* published after the reorganization says, 'that their desire is only to communicate religious instruction consistent with the New Testament, the liturgy and articles of the Church of England.' In a small but promising beginning after the reorganization, the Society made nearly eight thousand visits in 1802, giving relief, of one kind or another, to nearly two thousand families. In 1803 they relieved 2683 families in 10,632 visits. There was already an Evangelical flavour merely in the addition to the original object of 'religious instruction', and larger concepts were now to prevail. 'The great object of the Society', says the *Report for 1806*, 'is first to seek out and relieve those who, from sickness, want of employment, or unforeseen and unexpected calamity, are experiencing the greatest distress, or literally perishing of want; and secondly, to endeavour, by such means as appear best calculated for the purpose, to cause the voice of Providence to be heard in the afflictive dispensation.'[2] The voice of Hannah More and many a true associate sounds in those words as the strangers drop from sight in the visitors' interest and the second object stated above gradually displaces the first. By 1806 the Evangelicals, led by Wilberforce, Bernard, Barrington and others who have been noted in the Philanthropic, Proclamation and Marine Societies are making their way in the Strangers' Friend Society in London and no doubt into its provincial branches.

It is worth while to see what could be done with such a small institution and still more what it could lead to. By 1817 the Society had made over a hundred thousand visits. Its primary purpose at that time, the

---

[1] It is to be seen also in the London Fever Hospital, London Jew Society, Religious Tract Society, Infirmary for Asthma, Consumption and Other Diseases of the Lungs, Refuge for the Destitute, Asylum for the Deaf and Dumb Children of the Poor, Society for the Suppression of Vice and others.

[2] *The Nature, Design and Rules etc. of the Benevolent, or Strangers' Friend Society* (London, 1803, 1806, etc.), 1806, p. 7.

accomplishment of religious and moral reform through benevolence, is clearly stated in its literature. The Society, says the *Report for 1818*,

is the secret but powerful auxiliary of several other most valuable institutions, having the same general subjects—the alleviation of human suffering, and the moral improvement of the lower orders of society.

It would be impossible to estimate the benefits resulting to the families themselves and to society at large, from the weekly intercourse of upwards of Three Hundred Visitors from this Charity with the poor in every part of this great City; who, while they convey to them the bounty of the rich, use every possible means to improve their moral condition, by inculcating the fear of God—respect and gratitude to their superiors and benefactors—a quiet and orderly conduct—and an attentive observance of all other moral and religious duties.

The Visitors of the *Strangers Friend Society*, are pious men, zealously and conscientiously attached to their king, their country, and its constitution; taking the bible as the guide of their lives, and the rule of their conduct, in their intercourse with the poor, they constantly enjoin upon them, in its authoritative language, the duty of submitting to every ordinance of man for the Lord's sake; that honour is to be rendered to whom honour is due, and tribute to whom tribute; that to fear God and honour the King, is the imperative command of Holy Scripture; and to avoid all meddling or association with those who are given to change, one of its most salutary cautions. They inculcate upon men as powerfully as they can, the duty of submission to the will of Providence; and with that, and a spirit of subordination to the constituted authorities, connect their hope of comfort here and happiness hereafter. Carefully guarding against unkind and envious feelings toward the rich and noble, the Visitors assure them that such persons are touched with tenderness and compassion towards them in their afflictions, and that it is owing to their bounty, they are visited and relieved by the Strangers' Friend Society. And as the poor especially in this world suffer depression, they set before them the excellency of that religion, which can sweeten every lot in life, and without which, even the most elevated cannot be happy; and attaining unto this, they will be contented with such things as they have, and feel constantly that godliness with contentment is great gain.[1]

The *Report for 1818* proceeds to a statement of the charity's effectiveness, which there is probably no reason to doubt, after expressing so

[1] *The Nature, Design and Rules etc. of the Benevolent...Society* (London, 1803, etc.), 1819.

candidly those undisguised sentiments of men who are perfectly assured no respectable person would disagree with them. Hannah More was particularly interested in the Benevolent, or Strangers' Friend Society. If that *Report* was not in her very words, it was written by someone who had read Mrs More's source and Mrs More herself often and well.

This Society had the honour of originating, at any rate for this age, the 'district visiting' method of religious reform, and of teaching it to the British and Foreign Bible Society and many another. This technique for the enforcement of morality and piety among people who are obliged to accept the help of benevolent persons was put to prodigious use during the 1830's and 1840's. Even earlier, the labours of the three hundred visitors of the Society are dwarfed by the astronomical swarm of annual hundreds of thousands of religious visits, the larger societies making use of purely amateur volunteers, chiefly the idle women of Evangelicalism, in a way far exceeding the activity of the Strangers' Friend Society's semi-professional agents.

There was never any confusion about the object of district visiting. At Wheler Chapel, Spitalfields, Edward Bickersteth rallied his communicants to the work of Evangelical reform in 1829. 'Amongst them he looked to find Sunday School teachers, and visitors for the Benevolent and District Societies.' 'He told them that the strength of Ministers was quite unequal to the work of Christianizing London; that their people must be their fellow-helpers, and that for this purpose, District Visiting had been planned.' 'Thus, while his own time for personal intercourse with the people of the district was very limited, he strove to gather round him, and train for service, a body of faithful fellow-labourers, through whom he might reach the wretched wanderers in every street and alley round his chapel, and bring them, if possible, within the sound of the Gospel.'[1]

That is some distance from the work of a society originally planned and organized by the Methodists to help sick transients. We see again, here, that there is a considerable difference between doing good to people and doing good to them for edification, and that the Methodists did not have the requisite imaginative resourcefulness for national reform.

---

[1] *Memoir of Bickersteth*, vol. I, pp. 435–7. What limited Bickersteth's time for work in his chapel district (later in his parish) was his constant travelling for the Evangelical societies.

Missionaries to England

In 1828 all such groups as Bickersteth's at Wheler Chapel were gathered into an apparently monstrous General Society for Promoting District Visiting. It was founded on the fear, libellous to the remodelled Benevolent, or Strangers' Friend Society, surely, that the smaller institutions, which by then had spread over the nation, were not 'of an aggressive character'. To supply that deficiency, the *District Visitors' Record* continues, '*a regular system of domiciliary visitation* was thought to be necessary, by which *every poor family might be visited at their habitations, from house to house and from room to room, and their temporal and spiritual condition* diligently yet tenderly examined into, and appropriate treatment applied'.[1] There is no doubt the diligence was great, if possibly the tenderness may have lost something in Christian love as it became more professional. In 1831 London was divided into 866 sections where the 573 visitors 'regularly employed' by the twenty-five local District Visiting Societies made that year 163,695 visits.

It was this activity of the Evangelicals, not in the hands of the clergy or selected persons but necessarily entrusted either to employed agents or volunteers from the ranks, that confirmed castaways most resented. Dickens's Mrs Pardiggle, brisk, hard and apparently not instructed about the tenderness, is a district visitor and one who would have hailed with grim ardour those fearful words just cited from the *District Visitors' Record*. 'I am a School lady, I am a Visiting lady, I am a Reading lady, I am a Distributing lady; I am on the local Linen Box Committee, and many general Committees'; 'I do not understand what it is to be tired; you cannot tire me if you try!' 'That gives me a great advantage when I am making my rounds. If I find a person unwilling to hear what I have to say, I tell that person directly, "I am incapable of fatigue, my good friend, I am never tired, and I mean to go on till I have done".'

The *Fiftieth Annual Report* of the Benevolent, or Strangers' Friend Society for the year 1834 informs us that Lord Calthorpe, then a veteran Evangelical, was its president. The list of subscribers and donors up to that year includes for so small a society a magnificent roll of Evangelicals of William Wilberforce's day.[2]

---

[1] *District Visitors' Record for 1832* (London, n.d.).
[2] The institutions named to receive subscriptions are Butterworth and Sons (this is the Methodist lay-leader, a law publisher), the Evangelical publisher Hatchard and Son,

The progress achieved by 1800 or so was good and helpful. If such societies even introduced to the work of religious benevolence potentially useful people who did not advance beyond the stage of 'associates,

(*footnote, cont.*) and three Evangelical bankers: Hoare, Williams Deacon, and Labouchere. The subscribers include:

Duchess of Beaufort	Truman, Hanbury,	Zachary Macaulay
Duchess of Buccleuch	Buxton and Co.	William Manning
Lord Bexley	Charles Grant	William Marriott
Lord Barham	Sir George Grey	W. T. Money
Robert Barclay	W. A. Garratt	Samuel Mills
Thomas Bainbridge	Alexander Gordon	John Mortlock
Sir Thomas Baring	Lord Henley	Hon. Charles Noel
Sylvanus Bevan	Lady Henley	Marchioness of Ormond
R. C. L. Bevan	Thomas Hankey	and Ossory
Marquis of Cholmondeley	Henry Merrick Hoare	Earl of Onslow
Marchioness of	Henry Hoare	Earl of Pembroke
Cholmondeley	Henry Hoare jun.	Lady Emily Pelham
Earl of Clarendon	Charles Hoare	Lady Elizabeth Perceval
Countess of Carysfort	Samuel Hoare	Mr Justice Park
Lord Calthorpe	Henry Hugh Hoare	Sir William Weller Pepys
Earl of Carhampton	Sir Robert Inglis	Lady Plumer
Earl of Chichester	Sir John Kennaway	Hon. Philip Pusey
Jesse Curling	Lord Lilford	Lady Emily Pusey
Bishop Barrington	John Labouchere	John Pearson
Lord de Dunstanville	Legacies from:	Earl Radnor
Lord Dynevor	Bishop of Durham	Earl of Rocksavage
Henry Drummond	Joseph Butterworth	Lady Rolle
Earl of Egmont	Earl of Crawford and	Lord Rivers
Dowager Marchioness of	Lindsay	Lord Sandon
Exeter	Mrs Hannah More	Lord Robert Seymour
Lord Eardley	Countess Macartney	Lady Robert Seymour
Lord Ebrington	Countess Manvers	Lord Sherborne
Earl Ferrers	Viscountess Mandeville	Lord Sondes
H. P. Sperling	Viscountess Middleton	Lady Olivia Sparrow
Dowager Countess	Lord Milton	Randle Wilbraham
Mordaunt	Lady Robert Manners	John Broadley Wilson
Duke of Gloucester	Lady Vernon	Trust Money of the late
Lord Gambier	Lord Vernon	Mrs Stephen, by W.
James Stephen	Miss Vansittart	Wilberforce and James
James Stephen jun.	Edward Bootle	Stephen
Henry Thornton	Wilbraham	William Wilberforce
Samuel Thornton	Henry Charles Hoare	

more or less declared, in the holy war', that too was valuable. Many of the charitable societies that mere moral Gentiles were induced to support and help direct were actively religious, particularly the hospitals, asylums, penitentiary refuges and lying-in homes for unmarried women where suffering could naturally be given the form of an 'afflictive dispensation'. That such institutions could lead to reforming activities well beyond their ordinary (un-Evangelical) scope could hardly be better shown than by the Benevolent, or Strangers' Friend Society. They were a 'useful' means of forming in the church an Evangelical Party that by 1800 included a small but rapidly growing body of the clergy, perhaps some two to three hundred substantial and influential people, and scattered over England unorganized and unknown groups of truly religious people.

All that was plainly not enough, and it was not likely that the Sunday School Society, Philanthropic Society or Bettering Society, admirable as their objects were and though each of them had branches in the counties—the Sunday School Society many branches—could be made into anything of really first-rate Evangelical use. They were not the kind of agency for reform that would rouse the passionate devotion of good men and women wherever the Evangelical message could reach; and that agency had to be struck on if Wilberforce's reform of the nation was to surpass John Wesley's or even equal it. The Abolition campaign, which by 1800 had penetrated into the remotest parts of the land, had laid the foundation of a true crusade that would be as powerfully emotional and have a more explicit Christian righteousness. A cause of such a kind could rouse, inspire, organize and put into action religious zeal where none had been actively manifested, and it could carry the Evangelical campaign proper far beyond Wesley's. It could draw into the Evangelical Reformation under Evangelical leadership every truly believing Methodist and dissenter...and beyond them the thousands upon thousands of men and women of social power whom John Wesley could not touch. That crusade was the accomplishment of the British and Foreign Bible Society.

II

Canonically, the distinction of proposing the chief religious means of labouring for the spiritual improvement of others belongs to the dissenters. When the committee of the Religious Tract Society was appealed to for Bibles for Wales in December 1802 it was the Reverend Joseph Hughes, a Baptist, who asked 'Why not for the world?' and it was Hughes who struck on the name of the institution that was to spread the Scripture over the face of the earth. But at a public meeting held in the London Tavern, on 7 March 1804, a Clapham Evangelical, Granville Sharp, was in the chair and it was Bishop Porteus's Evangelical chaplain John Owen who rose, deeply affected, to move the resolutions establishing the Society. The scene before Owen 'carried him back in the spirit to the zeal and charity of the apostolic age'. An Anglican clergyman, he found himself listening that day to a Methodist, a Baptist and a German Lutheran, in an 'audience containing many Quakers'. Such a union in this new society seemed to him to 'indicate the dawn of a new era in Christendom; and to portend something like the return of those auspicious days, when "the multitude of them that believed were of one heart and of one soul"'.[1]

It could portend it only to someone who was able to overlook the great majority of the Established Church. The auspicious days that may be courteously conceded to the apostolic age were far off, in 1804, the early days of the Bible Society quite unmarked by Orthodox charity. It was apparent at once that there was almost no High Churchman at all so of one heart as to join, or tolerate, a society that admitted Quakers, Unitarians and Roman Catholics. A chorus of violent condemnation rose at once and was long continued. More than half the bishops publicly attacked the new society and enjoined their clergy to have nothing to do with it.

People remembered later that at that London Tavern meeting 'no royal prince, no nobleman, no bishop, no member of parliament was present'. Those words of the historian probably give in effect a wrong idea of the Bible Society's origin. In the canonical account, no project of the sort had been even thought of before the Religious Tract Society's committee meeting of December 1802. At least one member of parlia-

[1] William Canton, *The Story of the Bible Society* (London, 1904), pp. 11, etc.

ment had been concerned about it for some time. By these years no one who was contemplating such a society and was in his right mind would have failed to call on Wilberforce; but his own interest in a widespread distribution of the Scriptures had been publicly expressed at least as early as 1797 and there is some indication that it was Wilberforce who called on others.

'Let him urge the fond wish he gladly would encourage', the closing sentence of *Practical Christianity* says, in defending its author against the charge of 'presumption for taking upon him the office of a teacher', 'that, while, in so large a part of Europe...Infidelity has lifted up her head without shame, and walked abroad boldly and in the face of day; while the practical consequences are such as might be expected, and licentiousness and vice prevail without restraint: here at least there might be a sanctuary, a land of Religion and piety, where...mankind might be able to see what is, in truth, the Religion of Jesus, and what are its blessed effects; and whence, if the mercy of God should so ordain it, the means of religious instruction and consolation might be again extended to surrounding countries and to the world at large'.[1] A single entry in Wilberforce's diary (its inclusion in the *Life* perhaps a careless oversight on his biographers' part), taken with that fervent wish, gives grounds enough to believe that he was probably the actual originator of the Society. In January 1802 Hughes dined with him, and Wilberforce did not often have dissenters at his table. In September 1802—three months before the meeting of the Religious Tract Society committee—'Mr Hardcastle with me', the diary says, '—going to France to inquire, &c. with a view to the diffusion of the Bible.'[2] On 5 April 1803 'Hughes, Reyner and Grant breakfasted with me on Bible Society formation'; and a short time later 'a few of us met together at Mr Hardcastle's counting-house, at a later hour than suited city habits, out of a regard to my convenience, and yet on so dark a morning that we discussed by candle-light, while we resolved upon the establishment of the Bible Society'.[3]

[1] *Practical Christianity*, pp. 490–1.
[2] *Wilberforce*, vol. III, p. 69.
[3] *Ibid.* p. 91. Hardcastle and Reyner were business partners, Reyner a Baptist, Hardcastle a Methodist of the kind that attended Romaine, Foster, Conyers and Newton.

Wilberforce may have been kept from the London Tavern meeting by the press of affairs. Always fantastically busy at a multitude of private parliamentary and Evangelical projects, he was unusually occupied at this time with Abolition, with an attempt to do away with Sunday military drills, with preparations against Napoleon's army of invasion, and with the organization of the Climbing Boy Society and the Society for the Suppression of Vice. It is still so odd he was not at the founding meeting that it seems probable he was afraid to risk the loss of his moral influence by a premature support. He did take a vice-presidency and went on the committee. Lord Teignmouth, suggested by Porteus, accepted the presidency of the Society in May 1804, Charles Grant, Babington and Zachary Macaulay took office and Porteus himself came forward, followed shortly by Shute Barrington. The adherence of those two prelates was the most important thing that happened to the Bible Society for some years, perhaps decisive for its success, and there is no better sign of their closeness to Evangelicalism.

Who else would come forward? The dissenters and Methodists of course. Beyond them, the issue was greatly doubtful. It was unquestionable from the first that the Society would be bitterly opposed in the church, very questionable that it would be supported by *those who count*. For four years, the fortunes of the Bible Society hung in the balance, maintained on the church side only by Wilberforce's closest Evangelical friends such as Teignmouth, Grant, Macaulay and Babington and by those persons he had recruited for the early moral societies. Then, in its fifth year, as much to the astonishment as the exultation of the Party, there began to stream in to the side of the Evangelical leaders, in great numbers, from all parts of Britain and from all British classes and professions except that class and profession known as High Church, the new recruits who were to make the Bible Society the greatest single agency of moral reform under the Christian dispensation that the world has seen.

In 1809, 'suddenly, and with a strange spontaneity', auxiliary and branch societies began to be formed in the counties: on March 23 Reading, on March 25 Nottingham, in a few days eight more, in seven years five hundred and forty-one in the United Kingdom. From 1809 on the new auxiliary societies to support the parent Society, and the associations to support them, and the branches to support both, pour in in an inconceivable way. Eighteen hundred people attend the Seventh Anniversary meeting of the Bible Society on 1 May 1811, and it is already evident that Freemasons' Hall, Queen-street, Lincoln's Inn Fields, the largest in England, is not adequate to hold these Evangelical anniversaries. At the founding of the Bedfordshire Auxiliary the Duke of Bedford is in the chair, no Evangelical but a particularly substantial associate in the holy war; Viscount Hinchingbrooke is in the chair at the founding of the Huntingdon Auxiliary (the president, the Duke of Manchester, a talk of earnest piety given by Earl Carysfort). In August, the first ladies' auxiliary, in Westminster; in November the first association, at High Wycombe. The Colchester Auxiliary was founded against the opposition of the Bishop of London (Randolph; Porteus died in 1809). Viscount Anson was president of the Staffordshire Auxiliary and vice-president of the Norwich Auxiliary, at the establishment of which, in September, the Bishop of Norwich (Bathurst) made the first public appearance of an English bishop for the Society. In January 1812 came the Buckingham Auxiliary, in the chair the Marquis of Buckingham, another associate in the holy war, who made a religious talk. In Bath, Sir Horace Mann Bart. in the chair, the Earl of Leven and Melville a vice-president; Admiral Harvey (court-martialled some years earlier for calling his commander Admiral Lord Gambier a Methodist) in the chair to establish the South-West Essex Auxiliary (Lord Henniker president, Sir Robert Wigram a vice-president). On August 7 the City of London Auxiliary was established at a public meeting in the Mansion House, the Lord Mayor, 'a zealous member of the Church of England', in the chair; seven members of parliament (and nine residents of Clapham) took part in founding this auxiliary, Wilberforce not included; he was not a City man and it was not possible for him to belong to every branch of every Evangelical society.

He was naturally a member of the Auxiliary Bible Society of Clapham and vicinity, founded at a meeting in Kennington in 1812 (the president, Samuel Thornton). In February, an auxiliary was formed at Blackheath, in the chair John Julius Angerstein, 'a gentleman long distinguished for his zeal and activity in the promotion of every benevolent and patriotic undertaking' (and many Evangelical undertakings). The first resolutions were moved by Major-General Burn (Royal Marines) and Dr Olinthus Gregory the encyclopaedist. Ten Bible associations were at work in the Blackheath district in support of this auxiliary. On May 29 the Northampton Auxiliary was formed, the Duke of Grafton in the chair. At the formation of the Bloomsbury and St Pancras Auxiliary, 25 February 1813, with Charles Grant in the chair, Sir Digby Mackworth the principal speaker, the 1200 persons present included 'seven or eight hundred' women, the first time in the history of the Reformation that women appeared at a public meeting except for the ladies' associations. On March 1 the St George's (Southwark) Association, not an auxiliary but a mere society to support an auxiliary, was established with about one thousand persons present. On March 16 twelve to fourteen hundred persons, about one-half women, attended the formation of the North-east London Auxiliary Bible Society, in the chair the royal Duke of Kent, supporting him the Earl of Darnley, Lord Gambier and Lord Holland (which is the first and last heard of Lord Holland as an Evangelical associate). The officers included Gambier, Wilberforce's cousin Lord Carrington, Henry Thornton, Samuel Hoare jun., William Mellish, Thomas Fowell Buxton, his uncle Sampson Hanbury, Samuel Whitbread,[1] and Wilberforce.

That participation by the immediate royal family in an Evangelical undertaking strongly opposed by the entire strength of High Church was repeated two days later when the Duke of Sussex took the chair at the establishment of the North-west London Auxiliary, supported by Lord Robert Seymour, the Earl of Bessborough (a vice-president too of the Auxiliary Bible Society of Clapham and vicinity), the Evangelical sculptor John Bacon, Sir Thomas Bernard, the Bishop of Cloyne and many other noble or respectable persons; the Bishop of Durham was president, the vice-presidents a long list of peers.

While the Bible Society's auxiliaries came into existence, in every English county before the end of 1814, the associations, juvenile associations and ladies' associations budded off from them, more prolific still and penetrating even more deeply into English life in both town and country. It was the wise policy of the Society not to give away its Bibles and Testaments but to sell them unless 'circumstances of utter

---

[1] Whitbread's participation in this and other Evangelical societies and his taking office in them together with the nature of his recorded talks at their meetings make it apparent that he was at least an associate in spite of his strong antagonism to Wilberforce's politics.

destitution' made it impossible. In the first five years of its life the Society distributed some 150,000 Bibles, in the second five over 800,000. 'The secret of this striking vitality was the rapid growth of the Bible Associations, which sprang up outside the Auxiliaries in dozens, in scores, in hundreds.' The Evangelicals were not sure of the propriety of women coming forward publicly even in such a cause, and the Evangelical ladies were not allowed to attend an anniversary meeting of the Society until 1831. But by 1824 there were five hundred ladies' associations. In 1825, five hundred ladies were 'actively engaged' in Glasgow, and in Liverpool the Ladies Branch Association is described as a 'brilliant example'; 'under the patronage of the Countess of Derby, over six hundred ladies were engaged in a methodical investigation and supply of 341 districts'.

It was only twelve years after the London Tavern meeting that the *Christian Observer*, official organ of the Party, reviewing John Owen's *History of the Bible Society*, could soberly make the extraordinary statement that perhaps 'no historian has been suffered to collect and display the annals, either of so great or so successful a cause'. It was impossible, 'even for the friends of the society, to contemplate its almost instantaneous and gigantic growth without something of "awe". It has all the effect of a vast harvest, springing up the instant we have cast in the seed; or of an enormous mansion, covering the plain as soon as we have dug the foundation. Those who know all the labours of the Society . . . are as much compelled, as the mere by-stander, unacquainted with them all, to admit, that there is something more than natural in the progress of the institution.'[1]

There was at least one simple natural thing about it. It was the single supreme testimony, out of all the Evangelical testimony, that there were very large numbers of English men and women, in all parts of the nation and all walks of life, who were sick at heart at the spiritual barrenness and manifold corruptions of the Church of England as controlled by the Regular clergy and who did not care to be Methodists or dissenters. They were hungry for the religious life and grateful for a project that offered active service in the Christian cause. These were the men and women who came forward, in the Established Church, to the Evangelical front, by thousands upon thousands, from the penny-

[1] *Christian Observer*, November 1816, p. 720.

subscribers to the peers. When Wilberforce retired from parliament in 1825, neither archbishop had joined the Bible Society and no more than five English bishops had been members of it at any one time. But it had spent £1,165,000, issued 4,252,000 Bibles, and promoted the translation, printing or distribution of the Bible or parts of it in one hundred and forty languages and dialects including fifty-five in which it had never before been printed. There were 859 auxiliaries in England and about 2000 associations including the 500 ladies' associations. The Bible Society's vast accomplishments in later years are not part of this story. Even by 1825 its operations extended throughout the British Dominions in every quarter of the globe, and in many other countries it had fostered and supported unbelievable associate operations. Reading the voluminous publications of the Society, with their sixty and eighty page lists, printed on crowded pages over and again during this period, of donors, life members, benefactors, legators, subscribers, patrons and other officers, agents, auxiliaries, branches, associations, ladies' branches—even without the thousands of accounts preserved in scores of volumes of devoted labours in foreign parts— it is hard to realize that all this was still a small part of the whole Evangelical effort.

III

With the Bible's Evangelical usefulness for stating a social conduct and politics suitable to the inferior orders, it could be expected there would be some characteristic claims made for the Bible Society. 'There are no statistics by which we may gauge the pressure it brought to bear on the social questions of the time; the share it took in abolishing barbarous and oppressive laws and securing conditions of a more prosperous existence; the impulse it gave to education; the effect it had in checking the spread of atheism and infidelity, and in keeping men sane and orderly in dark years of distress, labour troubles, and political excitement.' Here again is the anachronistic distortion that has so much plagued later viewers of the Evangelical Reformation: as just and enlightened people we are for education, more prosperous existences and the abolition of oppressive laws; Wilberforce and Hannah More, just and enlightened people, must have been for them too. During the Age of Wilberforce the Bible Society took no single step, direct or indirect, to abolish oppressive laws, to secure more prosperous existences (in this world) or to promote education (except as Mrs More did in her schools). In the field of 'labour troubles' the historian is on solid ground. Distress prevailed in all parts of the kingdom. Were the nearly 600,000 copies of the Scriptures circulated in 1831, for instance, by the 2614 organizations of the Society 'but so much waste paper'? 'Or was the Bible Society in truth a living and far-reaching power among the moral, social, and political forces of the period?' It was the historian's belief that 'when distress was acute...and the nation was distracted by Corn Law agitation, clamour of infidels and socialists, outbreaks of Chartism—the ever increasing number of auxiliaries and associations, the hundreds of meetings held annually throughout the country, the work of the district secretaries and local agents, the hundreds of thousands of Bibles and Testaments which had been distributed, restrained the passions of multitudes of men, and guided them into the paths of moderation and constitutional reform.'[1]

Evangelical voices of the period stated that view in a more Evangelical way. The well-known clergyman Stowell believed, Canton says, that the defeat of Chartism was due 'not to the promptitude of the magistracy, not to the wise and timely measures of the Government—these, he believed, would have been insufficient to keep the people, under the pressure of their sore distress, calm, tranquil, submissive: "it was the Bible that had done it".' Mrs Hannah More struck that keynote truly. Another testimony cited by the *Christian Observer* was very likely the source of some of her information. Her tract of 1817 called *The Delegate* dealt with the distresses of the Spitalfields weavers and the influence of the Bible in assuring the subordination of the poor. Those distresses were not fanciful, particularly during 1816 and 1817. 'The Rev. Josiah Pratt, who officiates in a church in Spitalfields, and has exerted himself most laudably in diminishing the pressure of distress, remarked, that there was a resignation to Divine providence apparent among the poor in Spitalfields. Religion had taken deep root among them, and had taught them to bear their sufferings with submission to the will of Him who knew their wants. This arose out of their growing knowledge of the holy Scriptures. Out of 15,000 homes, 10,000 were idle, and 45,000 persons were wholly unemployed....It was

[1] W. Canton, *The Story of the Bible Society*, pp. 102–5.

evident that Providence designed to try, by the present dispensation, the benevolence of the rich, and the patience of the suffering poor.'[1] That somewhat unilateral test at least would appeal to Mrs More.

There is no questioning the sincerity of all such claims, but they do very little justice to the Bible Society. Its Bibles in a peculiarly obvious way were not distributed only to the English inferior ranks, and it can be assumed the Evangelicals had no particular reason for translating their defence of subordination into Eloo and Tagalog. One of the Society's finest attributes was that on its highest level it came close to being pure, that is, 'useless'. With its cognate and almost equally valuable and immense project of distributing missionaries, it was the most devoutly pursued of all that Thomas Scott (again perfectly) called 'more immediate objects'. The chief reason was simple, and good. We are dealing here with no mere values of this world but with the sole enduring value. The Bible is the revealed word of God directly communicated to man, wholly inspired and equally inspired in every word of every part. It and it alone is the infallible guide to righteousness and eternal life. But that being so, to place the Bible in the hands of every man and woman in the world would be to make the world truly religious. This was the reason that the whole mass and complex of everything Wilberforce had brought into action, in the church and out of it, Evangelicalism and its associates and allies *in toto*, gave itself without limit to the work of this Society.

The Evangelical belief in that immense truth became firmer and more exalted as it became evident that not all the High Church reactionaries in England could stop the Bible Society's giant progress. The dimensions reached even during Wilberforce's parliamentary life made it wholly reasonable to believe that its benefits were not for England alone but for the world. It was astounding, unbelievable, but true—so true, if so astounding, that time and again the conviction was expressed that the Millennium was at hand. How could anyone have dreamed that those meetings of a handful of people at Wilberforce's breakfast table and in Mr Hardcastle's counting-house at Old Swan Stairs would in twenty years have brought about nearly three hundred Bible Societies in Russia and nearly four hundred in the United States? Of all the Society's achievements perhaps nothing compared with the establish-

[1] *Christian Observer*, November 1816, p. 762.

ment of the Bible Society in St Petersburg. John Owen's account of the two dauntless agents Paterson and Pinkerton conferring in Moscow in early September 1812, of Paterson's trip to Petersburg ('along a road, crowded with fugitives, prisoners, and recruits') when it became apparent that matters were unsettled in Moscow, and of the founding of the Russian Bible Society at a meeting of 'noble and respectable persons' in the palace of Prince Galitzin on 23 January 1813, is full of dramatic interest. No Evangelical heart could fail to beat high at such an accomplishment less than ten years after the London Tavern meeting. How could it be expected that those who were at the heart of this great force could fail to think of it with boundless confidence?

'For ourselves we are free to own', the *Christian Observer* said in November 1816,

that *we regard the institution of the British and Foreign Bible Society as one of the grand epochs in the history of religion.* We are persuaded that no ten years, with the exception of the apostolic era, have done more than the ten first years of this society towards the promotion of true religion....To the extent of the benefits likely to be conferred by the institution of Bible societies, we can conceive no possible limits. In countries where Christianity is already introduced...it is sowing the seeds, and diffusing the principles, of reform, which will gradually, by the resistless energy of truth, subdue all opposition, and convert apparent into real reformation....It is upon these grounds, then, that we do not hesitate to consider the institution of the Bible Society as marking one of the most important 'epochs' in the history of religion. *It is the first time that a fair hope has been held out to us that the written will of God should be made known to the whole world.*[1]

Looking with pride at 'the delightful harmony, union, and love, which everywhere prevailed within the circle of the Society's operation', and at many a sign presenting 'a just ground of gladness and thanksgiving', the Evangelical leaders spoke with still greater joy and assurance after 1813 and 1814 when the Church Missionary Society had duplicated the Bible Society's triumphs. That the Society's work was received with gratitude by 'so many who have long borne the name of Christ, but have seldom, if ever, had the word of Christ', that the Protestant Bible was being received by so many Roman Catholics (in Ireland, France, Germany, South America) and by the Greek and

[1] *Christian Observer*, November 1816, pp. 730–1.

Armenian Churches, that the New Testament translated into their own language was being read by 'the Jewish nation'—all such things were 'circumstances greatly calculated to give birth to the purest and most lively joy'.[1] 'The British and Foreign Bible Society have had the honour of commencing a new era in the Christian world. They have roused the torpor of other religious institutions; they have thrown down the barriers which separated man from his brother, and united in one body all the energies of the pious and the wise.'[2] It was evident to the Earl of Bristol speaking at the Fifth Anniversary of the Suffolk Auxiliary, 4 October 1815 (at which time it was still necessary for him to declare that there was no man 'more warmly attached to the Established Church') that 'in an age when the most tremendous revolution ever known had desolated the fairest portion of the world, and shaken to its foundations the whole fabric of civil society; mankind, roused by the awful vicissitudes of the scene, had risen superior to the paltry objects of worldly anxiety, and taken refuge in the consolations of Christianity. The immense number of religious institutions which the last few years had raised up, were a proof of this opinion.' Lord Bristol 'hailed, then, the day which gave birth to the Bible Society, as one of the most auspicious in the annals of Christianity'.[3]

Perhaps in this undoubting high belief of the Evangelical chiefs—in the conversion of Russia, for instance, to Reformation Christianity—there is something like the saddest vein of the purest comedy, as in the exploits of the great knight errant of Spain just two hundred years earlier. All error was to disappear before the Society's irresistible truth. In a backward glance over twelve years of its operations, the *Christian Observer*, reviewing Owen's *History*, saw the Bible diffusing almost instantaneously over the world. Nations once discordant are assisting one another, religious feuds have disappeared in its presence, universal love has 'scattered its seed in all countries'.

Prejudice, selfishness, indolence, covetousness, the spirit of nationality, of monopoly...had, up to this point, proved to be principles of a tough, unbending, unaccommodating texture—principles, which have a thousand

[1] *Twenty-third Report of the Bible Society* (1827), p. lxxxiii.
[2] Quoted in the *Christian Observer*, November 1816, p. 539, from the publications of the South Carolina Bible Society.
[3] *Ibid.* p. 760.

times turned back, blunted and dishonoured, every weapon which truth and beneficence could aim at them. But now, except in a committee room or two, or in the shady purlieu of a professor's solitary study, or in the chilling corners of a few quadrangles, where the spirit of Popery is not cast out, these once formidable enemies have, like the army of Sennacherib, melted away. We went to sleep, as it were, surrounded with these inveterate foes, and...when we 'arose in the morning, they were dead men'.[1]

These were Evangelicalism's most triumphant days. Little wonder if they led to the blindest confidence, an assurance and 'highmindedness' so great that no one correctly estimated the strength still enduring in Sennacherib's army both abroad and at home. That army seems to melt away less easily in modern times. Manifest and even open enemies of the truth—Tomline, Cobbett, Bishop Herbert Marsh—lived on, relentless and obdurate, and still more and worse were to come. They cast no shadow in these days. It was an astonishing thing, the *Christian Observer* continued, that the zeal of the Bible Society was deeper, fuller, stronger in its twelfth year than in its first, and astonishing that it should have spread among all ranks of the community. 'High and low, rich and poor, have "met together", as the servants of that God who "is no respecter of persons", to discharge their part in this great work.' 'But we are still more astonished at one fact...that, notwithstanding all these circumstances—of so convincing, do we say?—of so overwhelming a nature, there should be still found enlightened, benevolent, and even religious men, inhabitants of this happy country, and members of our most charitable church, who continue to oppose this Society, and almost to call down fire from heaven upon some of its supporters. When we think of this, we remember, with the deepest awe, the well-known sentiment of an ancient—"Quos Jupiter vult perdere prius dementat"— and we tremble to think what may be the effect of such an "infatuation".' Such people, 'running counter to the general voice and feeling of mankind', since they cannot hope to 'arrest the movements of this vast machine' should 'retire to a happy becoming distance' and 'forbear to oppose its progress', in contemplating 'both the vastness and the beneficial tendency of the Society, and the corresponding depth of the delusion under which they appear to labour.'[2]

Of course it was not only that such people could be found. Even

[1] *Ibid.* p. 760   [2] *Ibid.* pp. 727-9.

when the success of the Bible Society had shown 'the general voice and feeling of mankind' they still constituted the great majority of members of the church. In 1827, after nearly a quarter-century, neither archbishop had joined the Society and four English bishops only were in its list of officers (Barrington having died without replacement). But it was clear by then that the Society had no need of the rest. The episcopal die-hards were hurting themselves alone. Numerous and stubborn as they might be, all enemies of the Bible Society and the Evangelical cause, at the time the *Christian Observer* spoke, were 'running counter to the general voice and feeling'. Even when, on sober reflection, some doubt began to rise about the world's conversion to true religion, there was no stopping the magnificent course of the Bible Society at home. In 1813 Isaac Milner despaired of an auxiliary in Carlisle; but in 1813 the one hundred and seventy-nine Bible Society auxiliaries alone, excluding the parent society and the associations and all other branches, had as patrons and presidents:

The five English bishops then supporting the Society: Durham (Barrington), Norwich (Bathurst), St David's (Burgess), Bristol (Mansell), Salisbury (Fisher); the Lord Primate, the Archbishop of Dublin, the Bishop of Cork, the Bishop of Derry, and the Bishop of Sodor and Man

Sir R. Eden, Bart., Sir W. W. Wynn, Bart., Sir R. Wilmot, Bart., Sir A. Lauder, Bart., the Reverend Sir T. Horton, Bart., Sir George Robinson, Bart., Sir F. L. Wood, Bart., General Henniker, the Reverend Sir C. Anderson, Bart., Sir J. Doyle, Bart., Sir Henry Etherington, Bart., Sir W. Geary, Bart., Sir Robert Peel, Bart., Sir J. Murray, Bart., Sir W. Clayton, Bart.

Lords Braybrooke, Falmouth, Barnard, Vernon, Grenville, Gray, Boringdon, Milton, Cathcart, Henniker, Bolton, Grimston, Anson, Leveson-Gower, Bulkeley, Foley, Middleton, Gambier

The Earls of Uxbridge, Northesk, Dudley and Ward, Dartmouth, Liverpool, Stamford and Warrington, Mexborough, Fitzwilliam, Hardwicke, Coventry, Moray, Grosvenor, Glasgow, Romney, Darnley, Moira, Derby, Dunmore, Onslow, Spencer, Rothes

The Marquises of Huntly, Camden, Tavistock, Buckingham, Northampton, Downshire, Lothian, Wellington

The Dukes of Norfolk, Bedford, Beaufort, Atholl, Grafton, Marlborough, Buccleuch and Queensberry, Manchester

Their Royal Highnesses the Dukes of Kent, Sussex, Cambridge, Cumberland, Gloucester and the Princess Caroline

That not every person named in that list was a devout Evangelical is beside the point. They had come forward to support a society for religious purposes that neither archbishop would support and that was opposed by four-fifths of the bench and nine-tenths of the clergy. From this time on it was an absurdity to claim that Evangelicals were Methodists or subversive fanatics. One part of the Evangelical strategy that could not have been more important, struck on at the outset by a consummate leader not likely to repeat John Wesley's blunder, had succeeded.

IV

That success points equally to an important reason for opposing the Bible Society (and all Evangelical societies) that the eloquent reviewer for the *Christian Observer* may not have understood. Regardless of its stated purpose or its 'more immediate object', every Evangelical society always had 'use'; it was serving the cause simply by enlisting people in whatever work it was doing. In that respect, how could the Bible Society's prodigious 'use' have been more open, public and spectacularly visible? It was pointed out triumphantly by the Society itself every time it published a list of its supporters. How could anyone have missed it? No mentally competent person could fail to see how the Bible Society was carrying the Evangelical morality and the Evangelical religion into every hamlet in the land and how it was enlisting the great in an Evangelical enterprise. At the least helpful, that gave the Party the finest conceivable seal of respectability. At the most, it made Evangelicalism supported and respected by *those who count*; and there was hardly a better way of leading them to embrace truly religious views. If the object of those so fantastically ill-assorted enemies of the Evangelical Reformation—Radicals, atheists, philosophers, infidels, utilitarians, liberals, High Churchmen and all immoral and irreligious persons, defenders of the old order, pagan citizens of the Gentile world—was to keep Evangelicalism from becoming the morality and religion of the country, how could they fail to see a clear and pressing danger in those published membership lists studded with the names of the rich, the influential and the powerful? Cobbett was not inconsistent in hating the Evangelicals when he was an Orthodox churchman and hating them still when he had become an anti-clerical Radical. We remember

Mrs More's pointing out to Wilberforce at the end of the Blagdon Controversy that such Evangelical enemies as Bere, with principles 'equally hostile to church and state', could not be supported by the *Anti-Jacobin Review* 'if a general hostility to serious religion were not a common rallying point to two descriptions of men opposite enough in all other respects'.

But the British and Foreign Bible Society had a use that went beyond that use, great as it was. Its sole object, stated categorically and continuously in its literature, many hundreds of times during this period, was to print and distribute the Bible or parts of it without comment, that is, without the particular formularies of any church or sect: 'The object of the...Society is, exclusively, to promote the circulation of the Holy Scriptures.' That statement was also made, hundreds upon hundreds of times, outside the Society's literature. 'How it should have happened, that our steadiness and perseverance in the simple distribution of the Bible, should have exposed any of us to the charge of being "fiery zealots", or "determined partisans", exceeds my comprehension' (Isaac Milner to the Second Anniversary Meeting of the Cambridge Auxiliary, 1813); 'With all my respect for the motives which induced you to take up your pen in defence of the Bible Society... I cannot help thinking, that the greater share of ingenuity belongs to those who have discovered...that any arguments could be urged against a Society of which the plain and simple object was to extend the circulation of the Holy Scriptures' (Lord Hardwicke to Isaac Milner, 1813).[1] But we would very much underestimate the Society, as the most cursory examination of its operations shows at once, if we assumed that the expression 'to promote the circulation' or 'the simple distribution' meant simply to make the Bible available to those who applied for it. In 1812 the Southwark Auxiliary had twelve supporting associations 'with 650 agents working among a population of 150,000'. 'The Tyndale Ward Auxiliary reported that twenty-four Associations, at work in a population of 29,605 among the Northumbrian moors, were gathering subscriptions and donations at the rate of £1603 per annum.' We have noted the ten associations at work in the Blackheath district; the five hundred ladies 'actively engaged' in Glasgow, the six hundred ladies 'engaged in a methodical investigation' of 341 districts in Liver-

[1] *Isaac Milner*, pp. 586, 587.

pool. What were those thousands upon thousands of Bible Society 'agents' 'at work at', 'actively engaged' in, 'methodically investigating'? They 'came into closer contact than even the Auxiliaries', the historian tells us, 'with the masses of the people; they searched out the spiritual destitution of the country, and provided the means of relieving it.' In plain words, they were instituting on a really useful scale the 'district visiting' invented by the Benevolent, or Strangers' Friend Society—the most formidable means of moral reform the Evangelicals struck on. Going into tens of thousands of English homes, they were persuading, exhorting and when necessary and possible (if the satirists are to be trusted) coercing English men, women and children to accept the Bible and conduct themselves according to its teaching as 'evangelically' understood. It was not a matter of serving people who wanted Bibles but people who had to be made to see that they wanted them.

It was natural that the historians of the Bible Society should dwell almost entirely on its extraordinary success in spreading the Scriptures over the earth to its remotest parts. That approach happens however to be the canonical way of missing its vital achievement for the Evangelical Reformation and the English people; and that achievement in England became more unquestionable as doubts began slowly to rise about any real achievement abroad. After the Age of Wilberforce, when later Evangelicals were taking the Society's true accomplishment for granted, it was easy to mistake this matter. Sometimes the mistake was stated by scrupulous Evangelical or at least earnest observers to whom it caused the deepest pain. Bewildered men noticed that a profoundly unhappy thing had to be faced. It was so clear, in 1816, that everywhere, to an unbounded extent, error was to disappear before the resistless energy of truth! But alas, the nations of the world, deluged with Bibles and Testaments, in scores upon scores of languages and editions 'beyond reckoning', were remaining much the same as before. Somehow, the religion of the Jewish world and of the Russias did not seem greatly improved, or the face of either the heathen or the Catholic world much changed.

'To Lord Teignmouth, and to the other founders of the Bible Society', Sir James Stephen, son of James Stephen, wrote in 1844, 'an amount of gratitude is due, which might, perhaps, have been more freely rendered, if it had been a little less grandiloquently claimed by the periodic eloquence of their followers. Her annual outbursts of self-applause are not quite justified by any success which this great Protestant *propaganda* has hitherto achieved over her antagonists. Rome still maintains and multiplies her hostile positions—heathen and Mahomedan temples are as numerous and crowded as before—ignorance and sin continue to scatter the fertile seeds of sorrow through a groaning world—and it is no longer doubtful that the aspect of human affairs may remain as dark as ever, though the earth be traversed by countless millions of copies of the Holy Text.'[1]

Could there be a statement of that blindness that would more wholly miss the Bible Society's immense Evangelical achievement? Sir James Stephen's father would not have forgotten that this Society was more than a Protestant propaganda and had antagonists who were not alien religionists. The character of the English public scene had changed so greatly by the time of Wilberforce's death in 1833 that it was easy, even for the later Evangelicals, to forget what it had been like. Taking as a matter of course the thousands upon thousands of 'serious' English men and women, a great and fearfully active moral bloc animated by true religion and efficiently organized to do good (for edification) to their fellow-creatures and themselves in the Evangelical way (or in the way of a High Church that had been forced to be serious), Sir James Stephen did not remember that fifty years earlier not one sizeable moral organization supporting true religion was in existence. In the 1840's the Bible Society had its hundreds upon hundreds of active branches over Britain, the Church Missionary Society had years before stopped printing its lists of subscribers because it could not spare so great a space in its Reports and truly vigorous Evangelicals were likely to belong to twenty, or to thirty, other societies of the same moral kind; but fifty years earlier there were Lord Dartmouth, Baron and Lady Smythe, Sir Charles and Lady Middleton, Sir Richard Hill, the Thorntons, Wilberforce and so few more that the name of every known one of them in England could be printed on this page. In Borrioboola-gha little progress, perhaps. What had happened in England to the religious and

[1] *Essays in Ecclesiastical Biography* (London, 1844; 4th ed. 1866), p. 565. We might note that Stephen, though brought up in the Evangelical inner circle, did not know that Lord Teignmouth was not a founder of the Bible Society.

moral point of view so well represented by the Regent, the Dukes of Cumberland, Marquises of Hertford and Earls of Barrymore, the bucks, bloods, rips, rakes and faro queens, the gaming houses and the monks of Medmenham Abbey, the time-serving court-sycophant prelates and episcopal despots who put down the Evangelicals in their dioceses, the swarms of fox-hunting three-bottle absentee parsons and their galloping curates, and sly leering clerical authors like Laurence Sterne? In the aspect of the Bible Society that was vital to the Evangelical Reformation, the creation of a serious moral and religious public in England, its failure abroad, if it was a failure, has no meaning. It is not because of restrictions of space or sympathy for the reader that there are no accounts in these pages of prodigious labours in Borrioboola-gha and all other foreign parts. If every one of the 4,252,000 Bibles issued by 1825 had been printed in the language of the Esquimaux and piled up on the frozen tundra the Bible Society would still have been next to Abolition the most powerful agency of Evangelical reform. Sir James Stephen might have noticed a distinguished exception to his assertion that no nation seemed to have profited very much by the distribution of the Bible, namely the nation that was doing the distributing.

V

In 1813 Wilberforce turned for a moment from Abolition to work in an intensified way at another superb Evangelical by-end. His biographers record without comment his astonishing statement that to further the Christianizing of India was a more important mission than to bring liberty to African slaves.[1] The chief implement to effect this additional Evangelical purpose, apart from Wilberforce himself, his group of 'Saints' in parliament and his fellow-Evangelicals among the East India Company directors, was the Church Missionary Society (1799). As early as 1801 the *Proceedings* of its First Anniversary Meeting contain an interesting statement of the common 'use' of all Evangelical societies.

The politic leaders probably would not be found pointing out publicly that every Evangelical society enlisting English men and women in its work was enlisting them on one level or another in the

[1] *Wilberforce*, vol. IV, pp. 115, 126.

Evangelical reform of England. The preacher of the first Anniversary Sermon[1] of the Church Missionary Society was Thomas Scott, not a politic but a forthright man. The unworldly Evangelicalism of the early part of this period had no more authentic voice. In John Newton's church that Tuesday in Whitsun week, 26 May 1801, Scott took time to answer the charge, often made through the period (and far later), that the 'benevolence' and the passion for 'liberty' expended by the Evangelicals on Africans and East Indians, Newfoundland fishermen, Irish serving-girls, North American Indians, on everybody everywhere except in England, would be better expended at home. It is not possible to bring against William Wilberforce a charge based on a more fundamental misunderstanding of his object and method. The old Lincolnshire shepherd's reply was simple and correct.

It would perhaps be found that the most active supporters of moral reform outside England 'are also the most diligent in promoting christianity at home'; and as for the fear that by sending missionaries abroad we will deprive our country of christian instruction, 'Alas! there is little reason to apprehend, that any considerable number of such men, as would be likely to do effectual service at home, will engage in the work of missions: a far more zealous and courageous spirit must prevail among christians than we have hitherto witnessed, before there could be any danger on that side'. If, however, such a number of men should appear for reform abroad, the effect would be exactly the opposite of that feared. 'So far from diminishing our measure of scriptural instruction, it would exceedingly increase it: for nothing can be imagined so likely to stir up all ministers to zeal and activity; to turn the thoughts and inclinations of pious christians to the work of the ministry; to enlarge the acquaintance of multitudes with the holy Scriptures; and to excite a very general attention to the Gospel.'

'I cannot doubt', Thomas Scott continued,

but that well conducted and successful plans for evangelizing the heathen, would prove most powerful means of more fully evangelizing Britain; and on this ground, as well as on all others, the thought and desire have for years been prominent in my mind....Indeed it is no small advantage, no inconsiderable success, arising from the zeal which has lately been shewn for missions; that it has excited a great attention to the revival of christianity in this

---

[1] Because of 'unsettled conditions' there was no Anniversary Meeting in 1800.

land: and though every thing that man does must be found defective; yet I would indulge a hope, that both in that respect, and in the more immediate object in view, these efforts shall at length be crowned with indisputable and permanent success.... The timid defensive state, in which christians have long been contented to stand, in respect of the gentile world, has tended greatly to extinguish the spirit of zeal for the conversion of sinners at home; at least it has greatly languished and lain dormant; but if once the servants of God should become, generally and thoroughly engaged in scriptural efforts for the conversion of the heathen, and should declare offensive war against the kingdom of the devil; depend upon it, zeal for pure christianity in our own country and in our own hearts, will revive in proportion.... As therefore, the revival of pure christianity would exceedingly promote the cause of missions; so, wise and holy zeal for missions would reciprocally promote the revival of pure christianity.[1]

The Church Missionary Society had declared such a war in 1799, but it was not able to mount anything resembling a real offensive for even longer than the Bible Society. That it was still more grimly opposed, though it had no dealings with dissenters beyond accepting their money, was due to various factors. For one thing it could hardly have been more obvious that the Society's missionaries were not likely to spread any Christianity but the Christianity of the school of Mr Wilberforce. A serious difficulty met at the outset was that as suitable agents were not to be found at home, nearly all the early missionaries were aliens, and to some Englishmen it seemed a ludicrous thing to have an un-English name. Sydney Smith's mirth at the name Ringeltaube ('Mr Ringletub')[2] is in point, and if he had known more about the missionary world he could have made merry over Messrs Janz, Saas, Vos, Seidenfaden and Supper (secretary of the Java Auxiliary Bible Society), no one of whom had a good English name, like Smith. It was not exactly their fault they had been born German, Dutch or Danish, but it was unfortunate. On the whole, however, the antagonism of High Church and respectable people probably shows that if financial passion is less powerful than religious passion it speaks more masterfully than mere ecclesiastical animus. The circulation of the Bible without the Prayer

[1] Thomas Scott, *Theological Works* (1807), vol. III, pp. 205-8.
[2] *Essays of Sydney Smith* (London, Routledge, n.d.), p. 148 (*Edinburgh Review*, April 1809).

Book was not really likely to destroy church, crown and constitution. To force Christianity on the reluctant Indians was held more than likely to endanger a huge British stake in a golden province.

It took principle and courage to come forward for the Church Missionary Society. In thirteen years it won no public support from any single ranking figure of the church. So robust an Evangelical as Isaac Milner was not even a member for that time.[1] Before the appearance of Henry Ryder, Dean of Wells, at the Anniversary Meeting of 4 May 1813 (Lord Gambier in the chair, supporting him Viscount Galway), the Society had never been attended by 'any Church dignitary whatever'.[1] In the same year Burgess, Bishop of St David's and a close friend of both Wilberforce and Hannah More, was asked to become a vice-president. He replied that he could do so only if one of the older bishops, such as Barrington, would do so. When Barrington declined, the Reverend Josiah Pratt, secretary of the Society, urged Wilberforce to 'press the point', and Wilberforce refused.[1] Through the Society's first decade even Porteus would not join; it had no bishop until 1813 and then only Bathurst; it had no other bishop until Ryder's elevation to the bench in 1815 and no strong episcopal support at all during its first thirty years. More than forty years elapsed before the archbishops came in (bringing in with them the fourteen prelates who had not yet joined).[2]

Nevertheless the Church Missionary Society was to do as much for its country, in the Evangelical way of labouring for the spiritual improvement of others, as the Bible Society. Fortunately Charles Hole's account of its early years recognized, if not in a complete way, at least in a unique one, what the Society was doing for the reform of England. Of his six hundred pages, covering only the first fourteen years of its existence, nearly four hundred describe its penetration into English life in the two years 1813 and 1814. In 1790 this cause was powerfully advanced by the return to England of Charles Grant of the East India House; he was one, Hole properly notes, who could associate on behalf of missions (and many other Evangelical projects) 'with men of position, business, and wealth'. In 1792 Wilberforce called on Sir John Shore, just selected by Pitt as Governor-General of India, later

[1] Hole, pp. 240, 266, 272.
[2] T. T. Birks, *Memoir of the Rev. Edward Bickersteth*, vol. II, pp. 172-3.

as Lord Teignmouth president of the Bible Society for many years. In 1793 Wilberforce's amendment to the East India Company's charter providing for the 'religious and moral improvement' of the natives in British India was defeated. In 1799, on March 18, the Eclectic Society meeting in Richard Cecil's St John's Chapel vestry agreed that a missionary society should be instituted at once and that it should be 'founded upon the *Church principle*, not the *High Church* principle'. 'It must be kept in evangelical hands.'[1]

It was a penetrating judgment of Charles Hole's that the Party needed 'some grand and weighty public cause, appealing in the plainest and the most direct terms to the activities of every individual who heard the joyful sound, some vigorous undertaking to rouse self-denial, toil, and sacrifice. The project of Missions to the Heathen appears to have been the very thing needed, with its grand claims that could never be gainsaid, calculated to arouse the warmest enthusiasm of all who had truly received the doctrine of the Cross.'[2] Considering only the Society's 'more immediate object' and without regard to its greater 'use', its simple and lofty Christian purpose and its establishment as a society of churchmen only were bound eventually to make the opposition of Christians of the Established Church ridiculous or worse; and the Evangelical 'use', of an obvious nature, was stated by Thomas Scott in his direct way: 'Probably we shall engage a set of men, and draw most of our resources, from quarters which are out of the reach of other societies' (that is, already existing missionary societies of various dissenting groups that had no access to the great).

With Charles Elliott of Clapham Common, Samuel Thornton of Clapham Common and Charles Grant of Clapham Common taking leading parts, the Society was founded on 12 April 1799. Wilberforce was proposed as president. By the second General Meeting, in 1799, Vice-Admiral Gambier had come forward. Wilberforce, deputed to wait on the Archbishop, wrote to John Venn, Rector of Clapham, that Dr Moore 'regretted that he could not with propriety at once express his full concurrence'; he had, however, 'expressed himself concerning your society in as favourable a way as could be expected'. Wilberforce's use of the words 'your society', his declining the office of president and appearing at no public meeting of the Society for ten years, taken with

[1] *Eclectic Notes*, pp. 98, 99.   [2] Hole, p. 33.

his manifested interest in its object and unquestionable belief that no object could be more important, indicates plainly that (for that length of time) he did not care to risk his position in the moral world for an unsupported cause that was certain to be strongly opposed.

That moral eminence was already one of the major assets of Evangelical reform. It was greater in twenty more years, or in ten more years; but even before the Bible and Missionary Societies had begun to gather their huge strength it was perhaps greater than that of any other Englishman of Wilberforce's lifetime after the death of Wesley. Who stood near him as a moral leader? The king was lapsing into insanity and no other member of the royal family was respected; no ecclesiastic was even outstanding, the great following of Pitt, Fox, Wellington, Scott and Byron did not come from moral attainments. It has been noted that Evangelicalism already had a cause as grand as missions to the heathen and in the larger view much weightier, calculated to rouse the passionate support not only of religious people but of very many others who might become religious. One milestone in the unparalleled achievement of an English commoner neither in Holy Orders nor in office was reached on the night of 23 February 1807. The second reading of the Act for the Abolition of the Slave Trade, already carried in the Lords, was carried in the House of Commons by a majority that assured the passage of the Act. After the vote came an extraordinary scene testifying to the more than Evangelical stature of the Evangelical leader. 'The spontaneous expression of enthusiastic sympathy, as the whole House cheered Wilberforce in his hour of success, was an unprecedented tribute.' As a climax of that scene, when Sir Samuel Romilly, no Evangelical, a mere liberal reformer, 'entreated the young members of parliament to let this day's event be a lesson to them, how much the rewards of virtue exceeded those of ambition; and then contrasted the feelings of the Emperor of the French in all his greatness with those of that honorable individual, who would this day lay his head upon his pillow and remember that the Slave Trade was no more; the whole House...burst forth into acclamations of applause "such as was scarcely ever before given", says Bishop Porteus, "to any man sitting in his place in either House of Parliament"'.

Wilberforce was so overcome by Romilly's tribute that he did not even notice the cheers of the House. 'The House was on its feet, giving

Wilberforce an ovation such as it had given to no other living man. Round after round, they cheered him, till the tumult echoed in the ancient roof that had looked down on every scene of Wilberforce's parliamentary career, but never on such a scene as this. It was the supreme moment of Wilberforce's life, but Wilberforce himself was scarcely conscious of it. In the middle of Romilly's noble tribute, when he spoke of his happy welcome home that night, his emotions overwhelmed him. Insensible, as he afterwards confessed, to all that was passing around him, he sat bent in his seat, his head in his hands, and the tears streaming down his face.'[1]

'You have the power to do more good at present', Sir John Cox Hippesley (not an Evangelical) wrote, 'than any other man in the kingdom', and Sydney Smith (not an Evangelical), hoping Wilberforce would now take up the cause of the oppressed Irish, believed there was 'no man in England who...could do it so effectually.'[2] In 1807 Wilberforce received a letter from Sir James Mackintosh that is a perfect statement, from a more general point of view, of his accomplishment and his position in the moral world. Mackintosh was an able man, one of England's leading jurists and not an Evangelical.

To speak of fame and glory to Mr Wilberforce, would be to use a language far beneath him; but he will surely consider the effect of his triumph on the fruitfulness of his example. Who knows whether the greater part of the benefit that he has conferred on the world, (the greatest that any individual has had the means of conferring,) may not be the encouraging example that the exertions of virtue may be crowned by such splendid success?...Benevolence has hitherto been too often disheartened by frequent failures; hundreds and thousands will be animated by Mr Wilberforce's example, by his success, and (let me use the word only in the moral sense of preserving his example) by a renown that can only perish with the world, to attack all the forms of corruption and cruelty that scourge mankind. Oh, what twenty years in the life of one man those were, which abolished the Slave Trade!...How noble and sacred is human nature, made capable of achieving such truly great exploits![3]

From the early years of the century, such tributes of admiration, esteem and reverence—greatly disturbing to a man who knew the applause of the world is vanity and laboured steadily to consolidate

[1] R. Coupland, *Wilberforce* (Oxford, 1923), p. 341.
[2] *Wilberforce*, vol. III, p. 309.   [3] *Ibid.* pp. 302–3.

himself in Christian humility—poured in on Wilberforce. If addressed
to any other man since the death of George Washington they would
have been preposterous. To the end of his life this chorus swelled, as
men and women of good will over England and over the world saw in
this frail dedicated little man the spiritual leader of his country and the
world's foremost moral citizen. The weight of his opinion, great as it
was in parliament, was greater still with the public—'far greater',
Robert Southey thought, 'than of any other individual'. At a public
meeting in March 1814 to raise funds for the relief of German victims
of the war, Madame de Staël noted that 'l'homme le plus aimé, et le
plus consideré de toute l'Angleterre, M. Wilberforce, put à peine se
faire entendre, tant les applaudissements couvraient sa voix'.[1] Like the
others cited, these witnesses were not Evangelical and except for
Mackintosh, a steady associate in the holy war, were far from it. 'We
have seen much of Wilberforce', Henry Thornton wrote to Mrs More,
'and heard his letters from many of the renowned of the earth, all seem-
ing to pay homage to him.... The name of Wilberforce has attained
new celebrity, and his character and general opinions a degree of weight
which perhaps no private individual not invested with office ever
possessed.'[2]

Let us pass over for the moment a profound error in some of those
expressions of esteem, for instance in the assertion that thousands might
be animated by Wilberforce's example to 'attack all the forms of corruption and cruelty that scourge mankind'. To do more than observe that
this towering reputation of the commander had some effect on the
Evangelical Reformation would be disrespectful to the reader. Even
before the passage of the Act he was becoming the acknowledged leader
of the great majority of morally right-thinking people in England who
stood for virtue and religion and were respectable and substantial or
valued such attributes. 'What a familiar little clique it was that ran the
British Empire!' Mr P. W. Wilson says. 'Pitt himself, Grenville,
Chatham, Temple, Wilberforce, Auckland, Stanhope.' The statement
was made of a time several years before the abolition of the slave trade.
Wilberforce alone of that group owed nothing to connections of birth
or marriage; he was in it because, 'a man who asked nothing for him-

---

[1] Quoted in *Wilberforce*, vol. IV, p. 158, from her *Considerations sur la Révolution Française.* [2] *Wilberforce*, vol. IV, pp. 221–2, 373.

self, he had become the very incarnation of the national conscience'.[1]
In 1825 Harriette Wilson, wishing for her scandalous chronicle such
a symbol of moral rectitude, thinks of no one else: there is 'a method-
istical-looking servant' 'whom one might have taken for Wilberforce
himself'.[2]

This was the standing and authority that Wilberforce could not
jeopardize by the premature support of a society that was certain to be
denounced as a threat to property and in other ways a methodistical
fanaticism; but while he had no open connection with the Church
Missionary Society, except mere affiliation, through its first decade it
probably can be taken for granted that no one had more to do with its
establishment.

As late as 1809 there were 'only a few members' present at the
Anniversary Meeting and the Society's small operations were still
directed only by the close inner circle of Evangelicalism minus Wilberforce: Grant, Babington, Macaulay, Charles Elliott, George Wolff, all
of Clapham; Sir Richard Hill and Nicholas Vansittart; the banker
Thomas Bainbridge of Clapham and the banker Richard Stainforth of
Clapham. In April and May 1804 collections had been received from
thirteen English counties. In 1805 the (highly prominent and respectable) house of the Rt Hon. David La Touche and Co. were appointed
the Society's Dublin bankers. The Reverend Robert Shaw writes in
from Ireland, however, that 'Jerusalem is building in troublous times'.
At the Fifth Anniversary, in 1805, Basil Woodd sent in £245, most of
which was collected after one sermon at his Chapel in Paddington Road.
In October after a sermon of Woodd's at Storry's church in Colchester
'bank notes amounting to £600 were put into the plates by General Sir
James Pulteney and his lady the Countess of Bath'. So far, very slowly;
but at the Eleventh Anniversary, on 4 June 1811, Wilberforce was in
the chair. A master of sensitive timing no less than prudence and steadfast
patience had pronounced the time ripe, and he was not mistaken.

In August 1811 a donation was received from the Earl of Crawford
and Lindsay (very prominent in Evangelical affairs for many years) and
ladies appeared for the first time at an open meeting of the committee.

[1] P. W. Wilson, M.P., *William Pitt, the Younger* (New York, London, 1930),
pp. 302, 330.
[2] *Harriette Wilson's Memoirs* (New York, 1929), p. 121.

In 1812 Vice-Admiral Lord Gambier was named president of the Society, the vice-presidents then including Lord Barham, Sir William Pepperell, Earl Ferrers, Lord Teignmouth, Charles Noel Noel later Earl of Gainsborough, and Nicholas Vansittart who became Chancellor of the Exchequer on June 9. Sir Thomas Baring of the great merchant house had come forward, one of the most active, intelligent and able of the Evangelical chiefs. On the Twelfth Anniversary Lord Calthorpe, Baring and T. R. Kemp, M.P., were added to the vice-presidents, then numbering five peers and nine members of the House. At the end of the year the establishment of local branches had begun: Bristol in October, in December the London Church Missionary Society Association (treasurer William Henry Hoare of Clapham, secretary John Poynder of Clapham), and in the same month the Ladies Association of London. It was evident that such associations should spread over the nation and that London alone would need greatly more than one association and one ladies' association.

VI

The historian of English manners and morals in the years 1813 and 1814 should find the work of this Society very useful to him. The first remarkable phase of its activity is the spread of the associations, branch associations, ladies' associations, juvenile associations and penny associations through nearly all parts of the land. The second is Wilberforce's masterful leadership of his Saints to compel a reactionary government (Liverpool, Eldon, Sidmouth and Castlereagh) to open British India to the missionaries while at the same time he yielded nothing on Abolition.[1] The third is the devoted, tireless and greatly fruitful opera-

---

[1] One part of Wilberforce's tactics was to flood Parliament with missionary petitions, 'a greater number than were ever known', his diary says (*Wilberforce*, vol. IV, pp. 124–5). They 'carried our question instrumentally, the good providence of God really'. We would not be badly wrong in thinking that his 'neutral party' in Parliament was an important factor. He was usually able to carry most of them to the side of the ministry in urgent matters. Hardly anything shows his great moral authority so clearly as his ability to support Sidmouth and Castlereagh in their suppression of the lower orders without alienating the liberal members who were supporting the fight to enforce the Slave Trade Act. This was a tricky matter requiring great delicacy and one he was always concerned about. In 1817 a sudden illness kept him from going to the House to vote for the Repressive Acts (which he had helped in committee to make

tions of the Evangelical missionaries who went out, wave after wave, against the Gentile world in England: Pratt, Wilson, Woodd, Scott, Budd, Burn, Goode, Horne, Dikes, Richmond, Cunningham, Dealtry, Sargent, Way, Marsh, Saunders, Maddock, Stewart, Jowett, Edwards, Hoare, Noel and the others. The fourth is the Society's discovery, in place after place, of groups of 'truly religious' people, and in many places 'truly religious' clergy, whom the Evangelical leadership in London had known nothing about. The fifth is the success with which the Society's missionaries carried the Evangelical gospel beyond the limits of their Party into the hearts of the dissenters and, without disguising its antagonism to nominal Christianity, of the good sort of people in the church.

The first provincial association in support of the parent Society was in Warwickshire; in March 1813 came Professor Farish's near Cambridge, and the first association in Wales. The Leeds Association was set in progress by William Hey. In Bristol, extraordinary steps were taken as the soil (after long preparation) proved receptive beyond anyone's imagination. Five clergymen of the parent society, Pratt, Scott, Woodd, Budd and Burn, helped in the foundation of this association, the leading

more thorough). 'Perhaps', the diary says, '... my not being able to attend the House, was kindly intended by Providence to prevent my needlessly differing from some who are friendly to my object of West Indian reform' (*Wilberforce*, vol. IV, pp. 316–17)—a deeply Evangelical supposition that may be soberly described as worthy of the Reverend Charles Simeon himself (all in all, Evangelicalism's most shining vessel).

Looking back from mid-century Sir George Stephen commented on the great increase of the religious world 'in power and influence, as well as in numbers, since the days when the little compact body of "saints" counted their twenty or thirty votes: perhaps a third part of the House are, at the present time, more or less men of avowed religious principles' (*Antislavery Recollections*, pp. 230–1). When Wilberforce was converted the Saints were Sir Richard Hill and himself. The new House of Commons in 1818 included Lord Nugent, Francis H. Ommaney, W. Thornton Astell, General Finch, General Manners, John Maitland, Sir James Graham, Lord Rocksavage, Sir George Henry Rose, Sir W. W. Wynn, Edward Bootle Wilbraham, R. W. Newman, Nicholas Vansittart, John Gladstone, Lord Robert Manners, Sir Robert Wigram, C. W. Sibthorp, Matthew Wood, William Manning, William Mellish, Samuel Smith, William Smith, R. H. Gurney, Sir Gerard Noel Noel, Sir Robert Peel, E. F. Maitland, Thomas Fowell Buxton, Lord Spencer, W. T. Money, Sir Thomas Baring, Robert Grant, Charles Grant jun., Robert La Touche, J. La Touche, Viscount Jocelyn and Viscount Bernard.

local clergymen Biddulph and Vaughan were very active, and the leading layman of the district (after Mrs More of course), John S. Harford, 'who two years later succeeded to his father's beautiful property of Blaise Castle'. Missionary sermons were preached in seven Bristol churches and 'there were at least two more pulpits in which, had there been need, sermons would have been welcome'.[1] That circumstance, correctly stressed by the Evangelical historian, unique outside London as bishop after bishop charged his clergy to refuse their pulpits to the 'itinerants', was made possible by the subtle non-resistance of Dr Mansell, whose conduct was as amicably cautious yet discreetly friendly *qua* Bishop of Bristol as it was *qua* Master of Trinity. Hardly any sign of the times, out of such great numbers, is more eloquent than this Bristol outburst of Evangelical (or Evangelical-supporting) fervour so hearteningly joined, on 25 March 1813, by people of good will. In the chair at the founding meeting was the mayor of Bristol; thirty gentlemen, 'many of them leading Bristol men', accepted position on the committee; the vice-presidents were the mayor and both city Members of Parliament; a leading merchant was treasurer, and—a splendid triumph—the president of the Association was the great magnate of the district, the Duke of Beaufort...what price Mrs Hannah More's long and assiduous interest in the dowager and the duchess? This, a bare two decades after Wilberforce had set out, and in support of a religious society for which in thirteen years and in all England not one clergyman above the rank of a parish incumbent had come forward.

It would be pointless even if possible to list these branch institutions. There could be no doubt of 'a *missionary spirit* spreading in all directions, and prayer for the conversion of the heathen everywhere remembered among religious people, in individual devotions, in social meetings, in family worship, in secluded villages, in humble cottages, and even from children'.[2] Who could question what good, of the Evangelical sort, this fraction (but vital fraction) of the total Evangelical effort was accomplishing, in England in the year 1813? 'Our little auxiliary is daily gathering strength', Richard Blacow writes in from Liverpool on June 15. Their society had been established the month before, under 'very unfavourable circumstances'. 'I already begin to see in this institution the seeds of much good, not merely from pecuniary

[1] Hole, p. 258.   [2] *Ibid.* p. 269.

contributions, but from the favourable bias it gives to those engaged in it. A door of *religious* access is also opened by it to some minds... which would have repelled any direct communication on spiritual topics.'[1] The Reverend Mr Blacow could not have struck more absolutely to the heart of the matter; and what was happening in the unfertile soil of Liverpool, sprinkled with African gore, happened over England as association followed association. 'The whole Christian world', Charles Simeon wrote exultantly, in his high-spirited way, 'seems stirred up almost as you would expect it to be in the Millennium', and we are reminded once more that to the best (or most characteristic) Evangelical way of thinking the antagonistic bishops and the Regular clergy and their lost followers—all those who stubbornly set themselves against the truth—were not members of the Christian world.[2]

On 21 July 1813 the Reverend Basil Woodd, whose Bentinck Chapel Wilberforce used to attend when Dr Robert Hawker, who was on too intimate terms with God, was at the Lock Chapel, set out toward Leeds, to preach for the Church Missionary Society twice a day, or three times if possible, wherever friends of the Society and the cause could find him a pulpit. From that time on, bishops or no bishops, Bonaparte or no Bonaparte, the missionaries to England streamed out, year after year, in a campaign whose issue, Claudius Buchanan believed, was 'far more interesting to thousands than that of Lord Wellington'. In this assault of the Evangelical clergy launched by the lay directors of the Society at the Gentile world, the Party achieved a tactical triumph of major proportions, one of the greatest and most fruitful of the Reformation. The Methodist 'itineration' had been condemned by all respectable people. Wesley's wandering preachers who 'held forth' anywhere had included some who were unqualified, untrained, uneducated and even unauthorized, their only sanction their conviction that the Holy Ghost had given them power. The magistrates could not refuse the application for a licence to preach of any person who could pay a sixpenny fee. No qualifications were needed, not even evidence of good character. Wilberforce mentions William Jay's telling him of the 'raw, ignorant lads' at Bath who used to go out on 'preaching parties'. This was religion in a superstitious and debased form. The Evangelical itineration was a different matter. These missionaries were in Holy

[1] *Ibid.* p. 281.   [2] *Simeon*, p. 364.

Orders, all or nearly all of them beneficed clergymen, and they preached in churches only, and only when invited by incumbents. There were already, in 1813, enough Evangelical churches to enable them to travel far and wide without violating Established Church procedures. On that first sortie beginning in July 1813, on which Basil Woodd helped to 'promote' twenty-eight auxiliaries and took over £1000 in church collections—an amount that one of Mrs More's honest rural labourers could not earn in a long lifetime—he preached in forty-three pulpits in Yorkshire and Derbyshire only (besides 'addressing' various groups in other places 'on the object of the Society'). Some years before Edward Bickersteth's long services for the Society were ended he had preached, his daughter and son-in-law say, in between eight and nine hundred churches.[1]

It would take a resolute hostile bishop to keep such legitimate visiting preachers out of his diocese. The Society had made itineration ecclesiastically respectable; and in doing so, in its evangelizing of Britain, the Church Missionary Society had gone beyond and added greatly to the triumphs of the Bible Society. At this point begins the active, dramatic, vital usefulness of the Evangelical clergy, and at this point they have an importance in the Evangelical Reformation that they had not had before. From these days on, what Bickersteth called 'the bustle of the religious world', already begun in the direction, management and operation of the societies, rapidly assumes the status of an extraordinary religious phenomenon. It is no longer confined to the growing May anniversary meetings of the great societies, Mrs More's 'week of the saints', the 'sainte Semaine'. Nothing on the High Church side compares with it.

As the Evangelical missionaries went out in pairs, the junior 'taking the villages' while the senior 'stormed the towns', Evangelicals in outlying districts 'were equally energetic with the secretary in London', Hole says, 'and every pulpit within reach...was being anxiously engaged, large collections being not the only inducement. The spread of a missionary spirit among the people and the clergy, that was a great concern never out of view'. How could these men implant and foster that spirit? Only by 'unfolding in a host of provincial pulpits the Gospel of the grace of God according to their apprehension of it'. In

[1] T. T. Birks, *Memoir of the Rev. Edward Bickersteth*, vol. II, p. 63.

that apprehension the necessity of Evangelical Christianity, the failure of the Orthodox clergy, was strongly emphasized. The prominent features of Legh Richmond's usefulness in his many tours were 'the establishment of missionary principles' and 'the close connection of the missionary cause with the advancement of personal piety'. That cause could hardly be advocated by Evangelicals without their pointing out plainly that the Orthodox clergy and laity had done next to nothing and were not likely to do more. No Christian good was to be consummated by unconverted clergymen and the blind led by them. While Richmond 'spoke of the souls of the Heathen or Jews, he faithfully reminded his hearers of their own; admonished them...that nominal Christianity was, after all, little better than Heathen ignorance; while it involved greater guilt, and a more tremendous responsibility'.[1]

A new East India Company Charter Bill with provisions giving the missionaries access to the Indian heathen had received the royal assent on July 21. In view of the alarm of the defeated opponents who saw nothing accomplished but the possible loss of a great political and financial stake it was wise, Nicholas Vansittart believed, not to strike into India until the passions of parliamentary debate were forgotten. There was no slackening of the mission to England. Noting the unbelievable 'readiness of large numbers, clergy and laity alike, to accept the Society on its own principles where ever it appeared before them', noting the swelling income, the new subscribers pouring in from everywhere, the rise of the associations one on the heels of another, Hole noted too 'that by this ramification into every quarter of the kingdom the Society to a very large extent created its own constituency, and greatly extended within the Church of England that new public opinion which was to be, humanly speaking, its main and its growing resource'.[2] It was standing side by side with the Bible Society in creating a great new constituency of Evangelical reform.

Its recruits were coming too from outside any previous Evangelical body and from outside the church. When Haldane Stewart preached at Havant Church in Portsmouth, the dissenting minister shut up his meeting and came with all his people. In many places where Woodd preached, the dissenters closed their chapels to hear him. 'An immense

---

[1] T. S. Grimshawe, *Memoir of Legh Richmond* (1827), p. 252.
[2] Hole, p. 252.

18-2

congregation in the great church of Kettering...all the Dissenters attending, their own chapels being closed on purpose, and the Rev. Andrew Fuller holding a plate.'[1] The good sort of people too heard the message of the English missionaries. 'We plainly see in this gentleman', Hole says of a Yorkshire churchwarden who forwarded a collection of Woodd's to the Society, 'an example of many Church people of exemplary lives, not particularly interested in religious matters generally...who yet could be aroused to a very genuine interest in the cause of spreading the religion of Christ among the heathen....These messengers of the missionary cause were improving the religion of the people at large, and for this reason many an earnest pastor welcomed them to his pulpit without being always ready to endorse...the evangelical foundations on which the preachers mainly relied in discharging their great errand.'[2]

When many an earnest pastor also barred them from his pulpit, the Missionary Society demonstrated, as the Bible Society had done, that opposition was setting itself up against the moral Spirit of the Age. 'Mr Basil Woodd preached in the three pulpits opened to him, the parish church being refused.' Sometimes such refusals came from the incumbent's own antagonism, often because of the explicit charge of his bishop. In Liverpool Mr Blacow despaired 'of seeing anything done ...beyond the limited means already adopted, until the cause is *openly* sanctioned by the highest dignitaries of the Church'.[3] In Exeter, five pulpits were closed to Woodd, Bishop Pelham objecting. The four Shrewsbury clergymen applied to declined their pulpits 'in the briefest terms'. At Grantham, the pulpit was obtained for Saunders 'by a chain of providential circumstances'; the Bishop of Ely was Dampier, who came so close to suppressing Simeon's evening religious meetings. In Manchester, little hope at present. 'Our diocesan has done you no very friendly turn by a charge he lately delivered among us, in which he cautioned the clergy against admitting into their pulpits advocates of the Bible Society, the Jewish Society, and of all such institutions as yours.'[4] Unfortunately the diocese of the Bishop of Chester (Law, a brother of Lord Ellenborough) included Lancashire and Westmorland. In Kirkby Lonsdale, William Carus Wilson could have got two pulpits

---

[1] Hole, p. 327.   [2] *Ibid.* pp. 321–2.
[3] *Ibid.* p. 307.   [4] *Ibid.* p. 543.

for Isaac Saunders if it had not been for Law's charge. In Edinburgh, the bishop refused his sanction and in Ireland there was no success with the primate and consequently none with any of his bishops.

But in Yorkshire, preaching tirelessly, day after day, Basil Woodd was met by Claudius Buchanan, Thomas Kilvington, William Richardson, warm Evangelicals; by John Overton and John Graham, each indebted to Wilberforce (and to the Lord Chancellor) for his living; by Thomas Fry, by William Gray the 'veteran supporter of Mr Richardson's ministry and of all spiritual work at York'. When Goode, Burn, Daniel Wilson and Haldane Stewart set out from London they met men who were 'warm, cordial, and active', 'warm promoters of religion among their people', curates who were 'pious, active, and intelligent', 'warm friends', intimate friends everywhere 'of Mr Simeon' (or Mr Gisborne, or Mr Wilberforce, or Mr Grant, etc., etc.). 'Where I have been', Goode writes in September 1813, 'every attention has been paid, every exertion made; the clergy appear most ready to promote the cause, and the people have been liberal to the full extent and beyond expectation; and the aspect, as to the general influence of the cause itself is very encouraging and gratifying.'[1] 'Nothing could exceed the attention we have both received at the different places', Burn writes, and this is in Law's diocese; 'both from the clergy and the principal inhabitants.'[2]

As heartening as the support of the 'principal inhabitants' (so often referred to in the records of these missionaries, or of any Evangelical society) was the discovery that wholly unknown to the London leaders there were many places in the country where Evangelicalism was already firmly established. At Knaresborough, Woodd found 'a home-mission of remarkable promise', where for ten years two Evangelical ladies 'had been labouring, without stint, attracting various ranks of the people, and not the poor only nor yet the young only, to their room, which was a large hay-loft over the vicarage stables. This is yet another instance of Evangelical ground in the north undiscovered by the Society previous to the Association period.' In November, Melville Horne reported 'I have the pleasure to say that religion begins to flourish in Shropshire, and the number of serious clergy is greatly increased', and in Ireland, Daniel Wilson noted 'a considerable revival

[1] *Ibid.* p. 332.　　　　　[2] *Ibid.* p. 334.

of piety among many of the clergy around Armagh'. 'There is a whole family in this vicinity, two of them clergymen', a clergyman wrote in from Devon, 'who have within a short time become completely changed.' 'I have met with many pious clergymen before unknown', Basil Woodd wrote on one of his journeys.[1]

Throughout these militant operations old Thomas Scott's wise prophecy of 1801 was voiced again and again. By 1813 it had become clear to many that the benefits of the Society's work were not all for Africa and the East. There was also great benefit 'done by this Society to the Church of England at large by propagating itself as it did through the length and breadth of the land. For most unquestionably the religion of the people of all ranks was warmed and animated, and stirred to its depths, by the missionary addresses.' At the establishment of the Suffolk and Ipswich Association in November, Daniel Wilson's address 'was one more instance of the fathers of this institution seeking to make their cause a blessing to England itself'. Wilson's theme was that the Society's noble purpose should not be restricted to any one part of the people and in particular should include 'the humbler orders'. 'By inviting them...to subscribe their smaller sums to this association you present to them a noble stimulus for their endeavours, you promote a higher tone of general morals, you raise them to a participation in all the good that is now on foot in the nation.'[2]

On September 29 the Norwich Association was formed, with Vice-Admiral Murray and Lord Calthorpe as vice-presidents and the Bishop of Norwich as president. There were many doubts about Henry Bathurst, but it was possible to hold that at this point any bishop was better than no bishop. At the meeting '...the clergyman of the largest and most fashionable church in Norwich offered me his pulpit', Daniel Wilson reported to London, properly emphasizing Evangelically vital aspects of this work in a way that would not have occurred to Wesley or John Fletcher of Madeley. Fifteen hundred people heard him there— 'all the principal families in Norwich, mayors old and new, mayors' wives, aldermen, members of Parliament, merchants, lawyers, gentlemen'. 'In the afternoon I preached at St Lawrence's, a small church in comparison.... People pressed to church half an hour before the service

[1] Hole, pp. 317, 388, 507, 528, 580, etc.
[2] *Ibid.* pp. 380–1.

began. I imagine there must have been 1,000 people....I am informed that all the most wealthy and influential persons were present.'[1]

Major-General Neville (father-in-law of the Reverend William Carus Wilson) had tried unsuccessfully to enlist the royal dukes of Kent, Sussex and Gloucester—a strong evidence of the Society's disrepute, for all three were in many Evangelical societies. 'How curious that none of the Bishops join', Claudius Buchanan remarked in October 1813. 'What are they afraid of?' The bishops were afraid of Claudius Buchanan, of Simeon, Pratt, Woodd and Wilberforce and the increasing danger to the old order that they stood for. When Tomline, asked to be patron of the association in his diocese—a formality could not be purer—politely declined on the ground that proper men could not be found to go abroad, it seems possible this astute man saw clearly that the really proper men had no intention of going abroad. Archbishop Manners Sutton who did not even approve of the Bible Society was hardly likely to be a friend; the Archbishop of York (Harcourt) was not wholly unfriendly but disapproved of preaching on week-days and his archdeacon wholly disapproved of all aspects of the Society. When Burgess and Barrington, after Porteus's death the bishops who were closest to Evangelicalism, had declined to take office, no other bishop (except Norwich) was likely to do so. But it made no difference to the English people. When on December 13 the Southwark Association was established with Henry Thornton in the chair 'many hundreds of people' could not get into the Spiritual Court, St Saviour's. 'It appears that Providence is not only increasing the means of our Society,' the president, Lord Gambier, wrote on December 1, 'but is also opening the way to its operations for the extension of the kingdom of Christ upon earth.' Lord Gambier had in mind particularly 'the friendly attitude of the India House', and it had bearing on that attitude that at the India House were Charles Grant, Edward Parry, Thornton Astell, Sir John Kennaway and for a time Robert Thornton. At the end of the year the officers of the parent Society included seven members of the House of Lords and seventeen of the Commons, with the Chancellor of the Exchequer. In November a general committee of the Society was able to make the hardly credible recommendation that 'the office of Patron should be reserved for members of the Royal

[1] *Ibid.* p. 350.

279

Family' and that the vice-patrons should be 'confined to peers, spiritual and temporal'. Lord Gambier is recorded as rejoicing again (December 13) 'at the increase for importance and prosperity of the Society', and on the same day Wilberforce as delighted to witness 'the annual, nay, almost daily, growth of good designs and institutions'.[1]

VII

In 1814 the Church Missionary Society went on to still greater triumphs. In England the new branch societies swarmed in; in Ireland already great Evangelical progress had prepared the way for fantastic missionary achievements. At Clifton, Lord and Lady Lifford were waited on by Vaughan and Hensman (soon to be a biographer of Hannah More) and Lord Lifford readily promised to be a vice-patron for both Ireland and England. 'Lady Lifford manifested the warmest interest in the extension of the Society to Ireland, and gave a list of nobility and gentry deemed more or less attainable.' 'Our Sunday School Society and Bible Society was attended last week at the annual meeting', the Reverend Robert Shaw, who had found Jerusalem building in troublous times, wrote from Dublin, 'by thousands of ladies and gentlemen, the largest public room in the city so filled that the people were pressed —bishops, noblemen, &c. &c.—and so glorious a sight never was seen in this nation before'.[2] But would such support extend to the Church Missionary Society? Lady Lifford wrote on May 2 that Lord Lifford thought the Archbishop might not be hostile; he was 'liberal to the Hibernian Bible Society'. Lady Lifford had founded a Dublin Ladies Association of the Missionary Society before the arrival of the Evangelical missionaries Wilson, Pratt and Jowett; her vice-presidents included Lady Norton and Lady Lucy Barry, sister of Viscount Valentia and daughter of Lord Mountnorris.[3] 'It was the promptitude and energy of this Viscountess at a critical moment,' says Hole, 'seconded by a few great Dublin dames, that really took possession of Ireland for the Church Missionary Society.' The moment was truly critical, the sanction of the Primate or any bishop rather more than doubtful.

[1] Hole, p. 361.   [2] *Ibid.* p. 453.
[3] Lady Farnham when her husband succeeded to the title; both strong Evangelicals from this time on; she died in 1833, Lord Farnham in 1839.

But devoted people rallied; in came Mr Thomas Parnell, 'a gentleman moving in the first Dublin society', a subscriber to the London Jew Society and a 'life member of the Hibernian Auxiliary' from 1815 to 1869, hopeful that the Society would 'make the few serious clergy better known to each other, more united, more attached to the Church and to England'. Prospects were soon bright. 'I doubt not we shall be able to form a grand Society', Wilson wrote on June 15. 'Without us no society would have been formed; whereas now in a few years Ireland will be covered with societies.'

Lord Lifford believed the clergy would support a private meeting but not a public meeting without the Archbishop's approval. One was held nevertheless, with the Lord Mayor of Dublin in the chair and twenty-one speeches. Lord Lorton was patron and president of the Association, the vice-patrons the Earl of Westmeath, Earl Desart, the Earl of Gosford and Viscounts De Vesci, Valentia and Northland. The vice-presidents included the Lord Mayor, Lord Lifford's eldest son the Honourable James Hewitt, and David and Peter La Touche. The Evangelical clergymen had already visited 'the extensive Bellevue demesne' of Mr and Mrs Peter La Touche, and we remember where Mr Younge was at last sent off to in the course of the Blagdon Controversy. David La Touche was treasurer; the committee of twenty-four gentlemen included Arthur and Benjamin Guinness. 'Here were some of the most influential and respected men in Dublin and all Ireland', says Hole; furthermore it is pleasant to add the Guinnesses to Whitbread, Buxton, the Hanburys, Barclays, Hoares and Perkinses; only Meux lacking, and Meux and Co. subscribed to several of the Evangelical societies.

The general meeting to establish the Church Missionary Society in Ireland was attended by five hundred men and women; later Josiah Pratt preached to twelve hundred. When Daniel Wilson went on to Armagh the Hon. James Hewitt had 'prepared everything'; there was an Armagh Association, the Earl of Gosford president, the vice-presidents the Earl of Caledon, Lord Lifford, Count de Salis, Sir Capel Molyneux, the Dean of Cloyne and the county members. 'Our journey has wonderfully prospered', Wilson wrote back to London. He knew of no clergyman or gentleman in the neighbourhood 'who withheld his support'. On 2 June 1814 the secretary of the Hibernian

Auxiliary of the Bible Society transmitted six hundred pounds, 'their first fruits', and reported that at the annual meeting the chair was filled by the Earl of Westmeath.

At home, the associations multiplied everywhere. As Kemp and Saunders went through Wakefield to Leeds, to Durham, to Northumberland, Basil Woodd was in the West. At Bridport, Lyme Regis, Exeter, Okehampton, Launceston, Bodmin; at St Austell (preached to 600); at Megavissey, 'a very poor pilchard port', the small church 'crowded by an immense congregation of about 800, and the church-wardens had to break the windows for air'. At Truro, in the church of the celebrated pioneer Evangelical Samuel Walker, Woodd preached to nine hundred, at Falmouth in the evening to about twelve hundred, at St Paul to a thousand, at Redruth, where the incumbent belonged to the family of Lord de Dunstanville, patron of the living, to thirteen hundred. At Padstow next, and at Plymouth Rock, where the president of the association was Sir Thomas Dyke Acland, with Major-General Nepean a vice-president—like de Dunstanville firm Evangelicals and strong workers in the societies.[1]

At Manchester the situation was bad, the bishop antagonistic, the soil 'very unfavourable to the cultivation and growth of any religious institution whatever.... The Golden image is the grand idol of adoration here, pleasure next.' 'Had the friends of 1799 in St John's Vestry resolved to take no action until they had gained over the fathers of the Church', Josiah Pratt wrote back to the 'fainting brother' who made that report, 'where would have been the Church Missionary Society in 1814?' The soil of Manchester was hardly less favourable than any soil in England had been only a few years earlier. 'The public advocacy of the Church Missionary Society at Manchester might prove a powerful means of raising the tone of its citizens...to a higher level.'

Kemp and Saunders arrived at Netherby Hall where they were welcomed by Sir James Graham, and at Casterton Hall where they were welcomed by the Reverend William Carus Wilson (a few years later, in the account given by a daughter of the Reverend Patrick Brontë, formerly of St John's College, Cambridge and now the Evangelical incumbent of Haworth, 'Jane Eyre' will be at Lowood School, otherwise the Evangelical Clergy Daughters' School, a few

[1] Hole, pp. 511–26.

miles from Casterton Hall, where Carus Wilson presided as 'Mr Robert Brocklehurst'). In Lancaster Mr Housman's church is open to them, for Mr Housman is 'a convert of Simeon's'.

On 4 September 1814, a powerful worker set out on his first Church Missionary Society itineration. Legh Richmond was already beginning to be well known as the author of Evangelical tracts that later reached a prodigious circulation, and he carried his message to large audiences. At a sermon at Sheffield his congregation was 'computed at 3500; many hundreds unable to get in'. 'The collection was said to be the largest ever made in this church on any occasion. It is not easy to describe or conceive the effect of such a congregation as this at Sheffield.' 'The Bishop of Chester is levelling his charge against Bible Societies and clerical itineration; but I think he is eventually doing us more good than harm. However, for the present, he shuts up cold pulpits here and there.' Richmond preached three sermons on September 25 at Leeds, 'the congregations overflowing'; thirteen local clergymen spoke at their anniversary meeting. At Bradford Church, where the vicar was 'the venerable, apostolic, blind' John Crosse, Richmond preached three times on October 2, to 'a fine congregation, a still larger congregation, an overflowing congregation'; 'I never saw anything like it'. 'The morning, afternoon, and evening congregations were estimated at two thousand, three thousand, four thousand respectively.'[1]

On 31 December 1814 the Reverend Robert Shaw wrote again from Kilkenny. 'We have got a new bishop [this was Fowler], who is more determinately hostile to every society, and declares to us quite openly that he looks on them as dangerous to the State and Establishment. But our private subscriptions and penny societies go on quietly, and when we find an opportunity we shall take an auxiliary form....In spite of our enemies truth is prevailing, and enquiry exciting on every side.'

'The opposition of error and prejudice seems to languish and decay' before 'the triumphant career of sacred benevolence.' How could these people fail to believe so, seeing directly about them the huge accomplishments of the two great Evangelical societies alone? It was clear to them too that they were helping to bring about great things beyond any 'more immediate object'. None of them could doubt that 'the improved tone of moral feeling...which is now so perceptible through-

[1] *Ibid.* p. 574.

out the kingdom, may, to a considerable extent, be traced to the influence of these, and similar missionary excursions.' So the Reverend T. S. Grimshawe, writing his *Memoirs of Legh Richmond* in 1827. Long before his death in that year Richmond could see a remarkable increase of 'missionary principles.' In 'the earlier days of these institutions' he noted that 'the public mind is gradually undergoing a great moral revolution. Christians are acquiring more enlarged views of the nature of their religion, and the obligation to impart it. In communicating it to others, they are increasingly impressed with its importance to themselves.' 'Incalculable is the national good which is daily springing up from such exertions. It now appears capable of demonstration, that the moral wilderness will eventually blossom as the rose, through the blessing of God on Bible and Missionary institutions.'[1]

Sir James Stephen could have pointed out the failure of the Church Missionary Society as he did the Bible Society's. He would again have been wrong, in the same way. Those concerned with the progress of Reformation Christianity and Evangelical morals might think the great missionaries of this age were not Carey, Martyn, Buchanan and Ringeltaube, who gave their lives to the heathen in far parts, but Woodd, Pratt, Wilson, Richmond and the other clerical servants of this society and its associated societies who carried the Evangelical gospel into nearly every town and district of their country.

[1] Grimshawe, *Memoir of Richmond* (4th ed., London, 1828), pp. 253–4.

CHAPTER 8

THE CRISIS AT CAMBRIDGE

I

The titled members of the Bible Society's auxiliaries were not actually unnumbered, neither were the editions of the Bible though many, and the bishops did not keep coming in one by one. Beyond those understandable inaccuracies of the Society's historian the establishment of the auxiliary at Cambridge points to another. It could be described in many ways, but not as spontaneous and unpremeditated. Probably many, and perhaps most, of the Society's branches in small communities were begun in the face of the kind of active hostility met at Cambridge in 1811. This valuable episode, set off by some rashly zealous Evangelical juniors, lacks the violence and unbridled hatred of the Blagdon Controversy, but it has passion, intrigue and a general richness of its own. If unfortunately its cast has no tragic-comic character of the stature of Hannah More, in taking us to the second capital of Evangelicalism it introduces some noteworthy new 'emissaries' and new champions, strong figures of the larger struggle that the University of Cambridge contributed to the Puritan cause as it had done in the sixteenth and seventeenth centuries.

Earlier in the year, Wilberforce shared in repulsing a second parliamentary attack on Evangelicalism, the details of which as given in his sons' *Life* are more puzzling than those of Tomline's attack of 1798–1800. Henry Addington, Lord Sidmouth, had not so far taken an open part in the fight against the truth, though down in Somerset his step-half-brother Hiley Addington, Mrs More's neighbour, was opposed to it in the Blagdon Controversy, and Sidmouth's Orthodox adherence was known. Not at the moment in office, he was an important political figure by virtue of his premiership from 1801 to 1804, his narrow, tenacious and wholly closed mind and his unreserved devotion to vested interest. Early in 1811 he moved a bill to regulate the licensing of dissenting ministers and teachers, and in May moved the second reading.

The whole story of the Protestant Dissenting Ministers' Bill seems not yet to have been revealed. By his own account Sidmouth expected the support of persons who heartily opposed him at the crucial time, and in the end he seems to have given up his bill in bewilderment. On the face of it, it was not objectionable. Sidmouth had consulted the archbishop, the bishops of London, Durham, Ely, Carlisle and Salisbury and Lords Eldon, Redesdale, Ellenborough and Erskine. One clause of the bill, he claimed, was suggested to him by Wilberforce's friend William Smith the Unitarian and as late as April 1811 he believed he had the support of both Dr Coke the Methodist moderator and Dr Adam Clarke the group's leading preacher of this period. But by the second reading a sensational opposition had broken out. Some five hundred petitions were presented, including, it was said, many signatures of churchmen. Neither Liverpool nor Eldon supported the bill and even Archbishop Manners Sutton pointed out that there seemed to be an error in Sidmouth's claim that the dissenters favoured it. Erskine was joined in speaking against it by Holland, Grey and Stanhope, no one except Sidmouth spoke for it, and it was lost without a division.[1]

The dissenters opposed the bill because they were afraid of further measures such as the enforcement of the Conventicle Act, which had never been repealed. The Methodists could not have themselves certified as dissenters.[2] The ministry had no interest in a measure that profitlessly offended so powerful a body of Englishmen. The liberals were defending civil rights. Why was Wilberforce concerned, who was not a dissenter, Methodist, member of the government or liberal? 'He disliked the whole measure', his sons' *Life* says, 'but feared especially lest, whilst aimed at others, it should cripple the pastoral instructions of the clergy.'[3] That polished half-truth is one of the most deft of the delicate disguises in which the *Life of Wilberforce* is so rich. The word 'Evangelical' inserted before the word 'clergy' makes it correct. On March 26, Wilberforce had gone to the prime minister, Perceval; '...opened to him about...the clergy, and the operation of the Conventicle Act; with the benefit derived from religious societies conducted

[1] *Cobbett's Parliamentary Debates*, vol. xx, pp. 233–55.
[2] Dean Pellew, *Life of Sidmouth*, vol. ii, p. 53.
[3] *Wilberforce*, vol. iii, pp. 507–8.

with caution by the minister himself. I told Perceval these effects in Richardson's case and others, and stated to him Richmond's diligence and its effects.'[1] At the end of April, Sidmouth having refused Perceval's request to give up the bill, Wilberforce went to see him. 'I was chiefly afraid lest he should stop the private religious meetings of the clergy; and I urged the danger of all who should come under serious impressions, going off in that case to the Methodists, and described the excellence of their discipline.'[2]

If the bill was directed only against dissenters and Methodists, Wilberforce's citing William Richardson and Legh Richmond to Perceval (as he had cited Richardson, Atkinson, Robinson and Milner to Pitt) would have been as pertinent as pointing out to him that Wellington was doing well in the Peninsula. It is not possible to repel attacks on dissenters by urging in rebuttal the excellences of people who are not dissenters. Neither is it true that Wilberforce was afraid the measure would 'cripple the pastoral instructions of the clergy'. Sidmouth had consulted six bishops and four celebrated lawyers. It would be strange if Wilberforce alone saw the measure as a possible danger to the Established Church. He was not concerned about nine-tenths of the clergy. 'What I strongly enforced on [Sidmouth] was, that he must provide that members of the Church of England might meet together for devotional exercises, without being [required] to declare themselves Dissenters. I own, I fear, if he does not admit some such provision, numbers will be forced into the ranks of the Methodists.'[2] That points only to the Evangelicals, as High Churchmen did not meet together for 'devotional exercises', such meeting being one of the distinguishing features of Evangelicalism that they constantly denounced. What Wilberforce saw in the bill was that it could be interpreted to put an end to Evangelical evening or week-day religious meetings or to schools. Simple meetings of friends in a private dwelling for religious purposes were already illegal unless fewer than twenty people were present. Once in a while Wilberforce had to count carefully before he could have family prayers. The unauthorized lectures, Sunday schools, and the like played so large a part in Evangelical 'pastoral instructions' that in this same year a very eminent clergyman of the Party, Charles Simeon, described them as constituting two-thirds of his ministry.[3]

[1] *Ibid.*   [2] *Ibid.* pp. 509-10.   [3] *Simeon*, p. 331.

There was no danger of High Churchmen being forced into the ranks of the Methodists by any provisions of Sidmouth's bill, as there was nothing in it that concerned them; nor was there any danger of Evangelicals being forced to go off to the Methodists. As they pointed out to Lord Sidmouth (it is odd Wilberforce did not notice) the Methodists were not dissenters and could no more take out licences than clergymen could. But if the bill had forced numbers of the Evangelicals to take out licences as dissenters, the cause would have received a crippling blow.

It was in 1811 too that a not wholly detached event took place in Evangelical surroundings when a young lady of one of the several female seminaries in Clapham, Harriet Westbrook, eloped to contract an unhappy marriage with an ardent young man she had been meeting through the summer for clandestine lovers' walks on the Common. He had had a small connection with Evangelicalism, which is described in a single letter, from Mrs De Quincey to her son Thomas. 'A curious little Boy is just arrived with a Note in his hand from Hannah More, begging us to receive him for a couple of days (Barley Wood overflowing with company).' Mrs De Quincey had settled close to Wrington to be near Mrs More. 'This Boy is the son of Mr Macaulay, Editor of the *Christian Observer*; he is now sufficiently pleased by himself among the Books.' Tom Macaulay, aged eleven, occupied a place in the postscript too, but had to be removed, in part, to make room for a more important item of news. 'I have scratched out much of our Baby genius to tell you that a Baronet's Son has written what he calls the "Necessity of Atheism." He has sent it with a Letter to Hannah More, requesting, "if she finds the proof satisfactory, that she will not hinder the circulation of the Book by her intolerant Religion!"'[1] Probably in the written annals of mankind there have been many works whose loss posterity should mourn, but few are more to be lamented than Hannah More's reply to Percy Bysshe Shelley, if any. His only other known connection with the Evangelical Reformation came in 1822 when the Society for the Suppression of Vice successfully prosecuted the sale of *Queen Mab*.

[1] *De Quincey Memorials*, vol. II, pp. 92, 95.

II

On 9 October 1782 Henry Venn, then incumbent of Yelling near Cambridge, a shining light of early Evangelicalism, wrote that a young undergraduate named Charles Simeon had been six times to see him. 'He is calculated for great usefulness, and is full of faith and love.... Oh, to flame, as he does, with zeal, and yet be beautiful with meekness!' Four years later Venn wrote, to the Reverend Rowland Hill, 'Indeed there is a pleasant prospect at Cambridge. Mr Simeon's character shines brightly. He grows in humility, is fervent in spirit, and very bountiful and loving. Isaac Milner kept an act in the schools... on justification by faith *only*.... The pit could not contain the masters of arts, and a greater number there was of students than has been seen there for years.' 'Jonathan Edwards's works are now called for; and what is remarkable indeed, the professor of law (Dr Jowett) and the three first mathematicians in the university confessedly, Milner, Coulthurst, and Farish, are all on the side of the truth.' 'Mr Simeon's light shines brighter and brighter', he wrote two months later, again to Rowland Hill. 'He is highly esteemed, and exceedingly despised; almost adored by some; by others abhorred. O what numbers, if the Lord will, shall come out of Cambridge in a few years, to proclaim the glad tidings!'[1]

'Such news as this', Rowland Hill's biographer Sidney says, 'would deeply affect him to whom it came.' It was Hill whose older sister Jane, a convert of Lady Glenorchy, had warned him about the fat bulls of Bashan when he was first coming up to St John's. 'The gospel he preached in the university... now influencing the lives, opinions, and characters of the first men in Cambridge!' Evangelical truth was upheld at both universities, in the early days, almost entirely by undergraduates like Hill and Simeon. At Oxford, 'the Common Room had never forgiven Wesley'. At Cambridge the frail Evangelical ramparts were held at first by one resolute man, helped by a strong Protestant tradition, a quiet early infiltration at Magdalene,[2] the pioneer Evangelicals Berridge and Venn nearby, and a High Church blunder of the most fruitful kind. Isaac Milner, a Yorkshire weaver's son, had been an usher in a grammar school conducted by his older brother Joseph.

[1] *Venn*, p. 263; Sidney, *Life of Rowland Hill*, pp. 157, 158.
[2] J. D. Walsh in *Church Quarterly Review*, Oct.–Dec. 1958, pp. 499–509.

At Cambridge he was Senior Wrangler, marked 'Incomparabilis' by the examiners. He entered Holy Orders in 1775, was elected a tutor of his college, Queens', in 1777 and in 1783 Jacksonian Professor of Natural and Experimental Philosophy. The trips to the Continent that led to Wilberforce's conversion were in 1784 and 1785. Three years later Milner was elected President of Queens' College.

'This place has obtained more evangelical means since I was here last', Joseph Milner wrote in 1794 to James Stillingfleet, a 'tower of Evangelical strength' in the North for many years. 'There is now Simeon; and it is to be regretted that his congregation is not so large as were to be wished. Of those, however, who do attend, there are a number of solid Christians; and whether God may please again to make this place a nursery for the Gospel, as doubtless it was in a very high degree at the time of the Reformation, we know not.'[1] Milner modestly left out the chief cause at that period of the improvement of Evangelical means at Cambridge. 'Queen's College, under the government of Isaac Milner, became remarkable for the number of religious young men who studied there, and of whom many are still, in various places, serving God and their generation, as able and faithful clergymen of the establishment, or in other influential stations.'[2] So, in 1842, Isaac Milner's biographer, his niece Mary Milner. She describes, somewhat obliquely, how that was brought about. Her biography includes an episode called 'Misunderstandings between the President and Fellows of Queen's College', in the six pages of which it is impossible to discover the nature, cause or consequences of the misunderstanding. It would be easy to prove that 'throughout these occurrences Dr Milner acted with a determined view to the real good of the society which he governed'. He 'completely outlived the prejudices which, in the minds of certain members of his college, had once operated to his disadvantage, and died in the possession of their hearty esteem and reverence'.[3] Miss Milner qualifies as a good member of the Evangelical school of biography with those assertions, for a letter in her own book, printed some pages before her account of the 'misunderstanding', shows they are hardly candid. One trouble, at least, was over the election of tutors of the college. 'At Queen's, we happened unfortunately to have several

[1] *Isaac Milner*, p. 100.   [2] *Ibid.* p. 46.
[3] *Ibid.* pp. 265–70.

clever Fellows, some time ago', Milner wrote to Wilberforce, in March 1801, 'who should have filled our offices of trust, as tutors, &c., but were disqualified on account of their principles.' We may read that last clause 'but were [arbitrarily] disqualified [by Dr Milner] on account of [his dislike of] their [anti-Evangelical] principles'. 'I was positively determined to have nothing to do with Jacobins or infidels, and custom has placed in my power the appointment of the tutors, provided they be Fellows of our own College. Our own being very unfit, we went out of college sorely against the wish of several; however, by determining to make no jobs of such things, but to take the very best men I could find, I carried the matter through, in no less than three instances;—Thomason, Barnes, Sowerby.'[1]

It is not surprising that Thomason, Barnes and Sowerby turn out to be Evangelicals. What happened at Queens' College is more straightforwardly described by Balleine (though even his account has a few touches in the true manner of Mrs More).

The religious traditions of Queens' were strongly latitudinarian, but the new President, like his brother, was a keen Evangelical, and he determined to make his college a sort of School of the Prophets, the stronghold of Evangelicalism in Cambridge. Of course there was much opposition, but Milner was not by any means an easy man to crush; the tutors who opposed him had to resign or retire to country livings, and as the appointment of their successors rested with the President alone [Milner's letter to Wilberforce shows that it did not, except under a condition that the men he was bringing in did not meet], soon, as a contemporary wrote, 'he acquired such entire ascendancy over the Fellows that after a few years no one thought of offering the slightest opposition to his will'. Under his benevolent despotism the college prospered mightily. Evangelical parents sent their sons, young Evangelicals seeking ordination came from all parts of the country, and before long, instead of being one of the smallest colleges, Queens' became one of the largest in the whole University.[2]

Balleine brings up the point that in December 1791 Isaac Milner's difficult task of acquiring ascendancy (in the simplest known way) was made much easier by his appointment as Dean of Carlisle. This extraordinary good luck (or 'providential interposition') is a striking example of the unsuspecting innocence of High Church in the Party's

[1] *Ibid.* p. 243.   [2] Balleine, pp. 127–8.

early days. Milner was their first man to hold high church office and the only one for twenty-one years. 'For this preferment', his biographer tells us, he was 'chiefly indebted to the active kindness of his friend, Dr Pretyman, Bishop of Lincoln.' The deanery was a prime minister's appointment, and this is that same Pretyman-Tomline who was Pitt's secretary. 'The bishop espoused my cause with such a glow of friendship as is never to be forgotten', Milner wrote to Wilberforce. 'In short he said "he should never rest till he saw me settled in a comfortable income."'[1] There was some fear Paley might be chagrined at Milner's appointment (he had been archdeacon and chancellor of the diocese for some years), but he was friendly. 'Preferment is reckoned a wholesome thing; and I hope you will find it so', he wrote with his distinguished quiet humour.[2] Two factors Milner may not have known about could have been important. 'Travelled all day—calling at Bishop of Lincoln's—talked about Milner', Wilberforce's diary records for 10 June 1790 when he was engaged in the general election.[3] The non-Evangelical Cambridge historian Gunning observes that Paley's friends 'entertained (which was doubtless a well-founded suspicion) that he had been so far misrepresented to Wilberforce as to place an effectual bar to his obtaining any preferment from the Crown'.[4]

In Cambridge's eminence throughout the period in the support of Evangelical truth, the decisive element as the years went by was not Isaac Milner but the man who all in all must be taken as the very Israelite of very Israelites, beyond Wilberforce and beyond Mrs More the finest flower of Evangelicalism. It is simplest to say of Charles Simeon that he had all the superior Evangelical virtues, and all the superior Evangelical faults, in an exalted and unparalleled degree. Very intelligent, wealthy, with equal spiritual and physical power, he laboured unrestingly and irrepressibly to advance Evangelical righteousness from his second birth in 1779 at the age of nineteen to his death in 1836. In the most conspicuous way, Charles Simeon's every act was the product of an elevated, unintermittent and entirely acceptable righteousness that he was intensely and unintermittently aware of. Probably few

---

[1] *Isaac Milner*, p. 71.   [2] *Ibid.* p. 75.
[3] *Wilberforce*, vol. I, p. 271.
[4] Gunning, *Reminiscences of Cambridge*, vol. II, p. 266. The evidence does not seem to indicate that Wilberforce had such influence with Pitt in church appointments.

men have so completely succeeded in achieving their most rigorous conception of what they ought to do. One result that was most happy for the Party was that in prosecuting their aims in his high-spirited, high-handed, supremely right way Simeon was serenely superior to any suspicion that he could be wrong: in what may have been his most eminent service (out of many) to the Reformation, the collection of Evangelical gold to buy places in the church, he regarded without a moment's questioning as wholly admirable a practice that if it had been the High Church party's he would at once have seen as unscrupulous and unchristian.

This was no ordinary man. In the 1780's Henry Venn, announcing to Rowland Hill this light shining bright and more bright and correctly looking forward to the numbers that were to come out of Cambridge to proclaim the glad tidings, noted at the beginning of Simeon's career that he was adored and esteemed, abhorred and despised. That was true all his life. An Evangelically exuberant and indomitable man, by long odds the most vitally robust of a Party that had many other powerful vessels, he seems to have been too vitally robust for the entire liking of even some of them. Wilberforce's letters to him never have the playful affection, or unreserved Evangelical love, that is seen in his letters to his own kind of Evangelical. They are courteous and respectful, sometimes friendly, but always guarded. Simeon was the perfect bridge between eighteenth- and nineteenth-century Evangelicalism. We go with him from John Thornton to William Carus Wilson, and in doing so we do not take William Wilberforce along with us. He could not be at ease with the 'vessels' who were on close and friendly terms with the Deity.

Even among people so assured and manifestly happy, Charles Simeon was outstanding in the esteemed Evangelical qualities of high good spirits, jocular mirth and a beaming, dynamic, always manifested and to some witnesses intolerably offensive Evangelical joy. The sable hue of mind and soul attributed by ill-wishers to some of his disciples was not acquired from him, and he was finely Evangelical too in his distaste for asceticism. The 'evangelical poverty' we hear of, elsewhere and in other times, was not characteristic of any of the Evangelical leaders, and Simeon had no use for it at all. It was remarked by competent observers that in his large financial dealings he was extraordinarily astute; but he was also fond of living in a strikingly handsome style, with 'princely hospitality', very well turned-out and costly servants, coach and horses, and a costume that surprised many by its elegance and richness. This luxuriousness was within divinely sanctioned limits. 'To this hour do I reap the benefit of these habits [of early economy],' he wrote; 'for though my income is now very large, I never indulge in any extravagance. I have, it is true, my establishment on rather a high scale in comparison of others; but I never throw away my money in foolish indulgences, nor spend more of my income upon myself than I believe God himself approves.'[1]

That manner of thinking might seem to tend slightly toward spiritual presumption, or arrogance, in an ordinary man; but not in Charles Simeon, for no one then living who left any pertinent record of himself had so certain an understanding of the ways and intent of the Almighty. In particular Simeon was matchless, even among the later Evangelicals, for his unqualified assurance, amounting to perfect knowledge, of his salvation, and naturally the damnation of those who vitally disagreed with him. He had been a Christian, he told Arthur Young round 1804, for some twenty-five years, 'during all which time', Young says, 'he has never doubted of his future salvation'. 'I mentioned Fry's calculation of three millions of Christians; but he very properly thought it very erroneous. He thinks Cambridge a fair average, and in 10,000 people knows but of 110 certainly vital Christians.'[2] The humility observed with joy by Henry Venn was one of the proudest humilities on record.

'Mr Simeon evidently assumes among them a character somewhat Apostolical,' the Reverend Lewis Way (the High Church, not Evangelical, Lewis Way) wrote in 1817, 'not only in [deference] paid to his age and experience, but he possesses a kind of Spiritual Authority.'[3] There was every reason for that, and indeed Simeon was known by the Evangelicals as 'the Old Apostle' many years before the end of his fifty-three years' ministry at Holy Trinity Church. In the last third of his life his Sunday evenings are said to have had an average attendance of two hundred and fifty undergraduates, and Bishop Wordsworth,

[1] *Simeon*, p. 17.
[2] Arthur Young, *Autobiography*, pp. 400, 398.
[3] Herbert W. L. Way, *History of the Way Family* (privately printed, 1914), p. 116.

no Evangelical, thought he 'had a much larger following of young men than Newman, and for a much longer time'.[1] 'There are, I am rejoiced to hear it,' Arthur Young added to his account of Simeon in 1804, 'many very pious young men in the colleges'; and we may with untroubled confidence rest assured that those young men included all of, and none but, the current generation of the Old Apostle's spiritual sons, the 'Simeonites', who for nearly half a century went out from King's, Queens', St John's, even Trinity, to spread the Evangelical gospel at its most characteristic over England and exert their influence on the morals of the English people. That influence of Simeon's 'very firstfruits of Achaia' was not slight. They went out in large numbers, and they were in a position of peculiar authority, for Simeon was almost (though not quite) as certain of their salvation as of his own: 'Respecting his transition to glory,' he wrote of the Reverend Thomas Lloyd on his death in 1828, 'I have no more doubt than of the Apostle Paul's.'[2]

The Cambridge Evangelicals thus had a solid position even in the earliest years of the century. They were thought of with hostility or contempt by the liberals, infidels and High Churchmen; only one head of a house stood outright for Reformation Christianity; but they were resolute, assured, militant and entrenched. At Queens' the 'benevolent despot' Isaac Milner, huge, boisterous and overpowering (a large-framed man and hearty eater and drinker, he is said to have weighed twenty stone), was arbitrarily forcing the retirement of High Church fellows and illegally appointing religious tutors. In their quieter way Farish and Jowett were helping such serious young men as came under them, and Charles Simeon was growing in strength yearly. It was in those circumstances that in November 1811 'about two hundred undergraduates', says Isaac Milner's biographer, 'resolved to take measures for the establishment of an Auxiliary Bible Society at Cambridge'.

III

When the undergraduates set out on the establishment of the auxiliary they 'very properly', Dean Milner's niece says, 'applied to their seniors and superiors for advice and direction'. Like so many statements of the later Evangelicals who wrote the biographies, that statement has a

[1] Quoted in Hole, *Manual of English Church History*, p. 385.   [2] *Simeon*, p. 619.

touch of the deliberately misleading. The problem was not so simple. It was not a matter of applying to seniors but to the right seniors. An application to the Regius Professor of Divinity, for instance, if he could be found,[1] or to Lady Margaret's Professor of Divinity, Dr Herbert Marsh, would at once have put a sharp end to the establishment of any such thing as a Bible Society auxiliary. That being common knowledge, the undergraduates sensibly applied to the one avowedly, boldly Evangelical head of a college, Dr Isaac Milner. The state of the times so far as these matters are concerned is strikingly shown by the perturbation and indecision of this domineering man and his conclusion that he could not take a public part in the affair. There was no question of his devotion to the Bible Society—he was a vice-president of it, one of the few English clergymen of rank who would take office—and no question either of his courage; he had come forward time after time when a timid man would have held back. It was a matter of policy and expediency. How far was it wise to go in supporting a small body of greatly disliked, presumptuous undergraduates who knew well that nearly all their seniors and superiors were opposed to any such step? The thing was charged with danger.

At the public meeting at which the Cambridge Auxiliary would be established no other head of a house would be present. Dr Mansell, Bishop of Bristol and Master of Trinity College, was favourable, in a cautious way; he was even president of the Bristol Auxiliary. But the meeting would be held in the diocese of the Bishop of Ely, Dr Dampier, who was not favourable. Dr Mansell would be kept by delicacy from appearing for the Society in Dr Dampier's territory, and Dr Mansell had himself to be treated with great delicacy: he had been tutor of the new prime minister Perceval and raised to the bench by him; no pressure or importunity could be exerted in so important a quarter. Henry Bathurst, Bishop of Norwich, might appear. As he was an open Whig, liberal and supporter of Protestant nonconformist and Catholic emancipation, it was always a question whether his opposition was not more beneficial than his support; and furthermore he was a noted *enfant terrible*

---

[1] The Regius Professor was that Dr Richard Watson who was also Bishop of Llandaff but enjoyed the agricultural life more than the academic or ecclesiastical, apart from their financial aspects, and was not often to be seen either in his diocese or in Cambridge.

and one motive for his presence, perhaps the chief, would be to annoy Dr Dampier. If he came it would be still less decorous for the Dean of Carlisle to appear.

Whatever the desirability of the auxiliary, he was the only Evangelical in high church position; it was folly for the Dean of Carlisle to risk his power of helping Evangelicalism in such a notoriously opposed, insubordinately begun operation. The senior Cambridge Evangelicals decided therefore—so Milner thought—to suspend the business and take it up next term 'if circumstances should be found sufficiently favourable'. That decided, the Dean of Carlisle went on a short trip to London, to discover while there that a public meeting to establish the auxiliary had been called by Farish and Simeon in his absence.

It was most unwise; nothing could be more awkward; it would appear as if the undergraduates had forced the issue. Their 'absolute declaration should have been obtained', Milner wrote in agitation, 'that they had dissolved their meetings, their committees, and, in short, their whole apparatus'. 'The undergraduates are the real movers in this matter; there is no dissembling that.' Indeed, the Dean wrote, in a passage about which it is impossible not to feel that it is almost worthy of Hannah More, dissembling would not help—it would be seen through at once. Even if the undergraduates should now announce they had dissolved their whole apparatus, 'such a step would be represented as a piece of finesse, and would be open to the imputation of insincerity and political management'.[1] With the admitted intelligence of the High Church group at Cambridge, it obviously would have been so represented, particularly, perhaps, as it would have been nothing else. Dr Milner's perplexity and anxiety were great.

It is very plain to me, that I should be calumniated as being the only Head of a College who had stepped forward to countenance a multitude of undergraduates who had been holding meetings...and...I believe, that the effects of the slander would be both mischievous and permanent. It would spread in the world through the means of unprincipled writers in newspapers, &c., &c., and my usefulness in giving a little help, sometimes, to the oppressed evangelical clergy, would be very much cramped, and lessened....Ecclesiastical questions, and politico-ecclesiastical questions, of great magnitude, are ripen-

[1] *Isaac Milner*, p. 468.

ing fast for public discussion: and it requires no great acuteness to see, that it must tend to annihilate any little weight which I might hope to add to the scale, to be pointed at as the only Governor in the University, who had thought proper to join turbulent pupils, (as they would be called,) in these delicate seasons.... Observe, with the character, or even the mere clamour against me, of having supported turbulent undergraduates, it would have been absolutely impossible for me to have helped Mr S—— last spring against the Bishop of Ely.[1]

Milner was right, about helping Mr Simeon and about the fast ripening politico-ecclesiastical questions. The malign influence of Tomline was still great; he was translated to Winchester in 1820 by the Earl of Liverpool, who resisted conversion throughout his long premiership, though helpful in the Bible Society; Sidmouth was Home Secretary from 1812 to 1821; the Archbishop of Canterbury was strongly antagonistic. No doubt one of the events that Milner had in mind, of great magnitude, was the elevation of Lord Harrowby's brother Henry Ryder, Dean of Wells, to the bench, which was truly the matter of a delicate season. The prime minister Spencer Perceval was possibly on the very verge of becoming truly religious, even thought of by some as already Evangelical (and so referred to by the Reverend Sydney Smith, no Evangelical, in 'Peter Plymley's' *Letters*). He was counted on with intense earnestness to give the Party its first bishop, but it would be against the grimmest opposition. The times were ticklish, the fight at Cambridge a mere skirmish in a great campaign. By these days no intelligent High Churchman doubted that his party was facing aggressive opponents burning with zeal, greatly practical, supported by large wealth and influence and in all ways formidable, and no prudent Evangelicals doubted (the Bible Society's great days not yet reached) that they still had a difficult road ahead.

There were circumstances to give added perturbation to Isaac Milner. Even apart from the helpless infidels of Queens' the growth of Evangelicalism at Cambridge had not been brought about in an amicable way. It was not in the nature of Charles Simeon to be unnoticed or of High Church not to fight back. From the beginning Simeon's mission had been carried forward against bitter antagonism. It was still active in the early years of the Bible Society. In 1805 Dr Marsh, Lady

[1] *Isaac Milner*, pp. 467, 469.

Margaret's Professor of Divinity, preached a body of sermons professedly, Simeon wrote, 'in opposition to the peculiar doctrines maintained by me and my friends'. Simeon replied in a sermon preached before the University that brought an answer from Dr Pearson the Christian Advocate. A part of Simeon's sermon, he believed, had 'the evident design of supporting the unfounded notions, entertained by *Evangelical* or *Calvinistic* divines of the total corruption of human nature, and of justification or salvation by faith only as opposed to *obedience*....I cannot conceive, that it is calculated to answer any purpose either of truth or utility; unless indeed it be to expose the weakness of the cause, which is attempted to be so defended.' Simeon did not agree; his work, he wrote to John Venn, Rector of Clapham, 'seems to have made more stir and impression than any of my Sermons'. In November 1809 he preached in the University Church a sermon published under the title *Evangelical and Pharisaical Righteousness Compared*, the nature of which it would be hard to imagine erroneously. It too brought forth a reply from the Christian Advocate. Simeon's object, it now seemed to Dr Pearson, was to shut out 'those from salvation, whom he had previously determined to condemn', and among those persons 'who have a disapprobation of real piety lurking in their hearts' were apparently many of his brethren in the Church of England. 'What are we to think of such a passage as this in a sermon, preached at an University Church, and printed at an University Press? If Mr Simeon can point out any other interpretation of this passage, which the passage itself will fairly bear, I shall be happy to attend and receive it. At present, I can consider it in no other light than as a *libel*.'[1] A reply drew still another pamphlet from Pearson, which Simeon refrained from answering. 'Thus amicably terminated a controversy, which for some months caused considerable excitement in the University', the Reverend Mr Carus remarks. 'Would that all discussions on religious topics, between earnest and serious men, were conducted in the same spirit of candour, and brought with the like courtesy and Christian feeling to a conclusion!'[2] In what sense it is a manifestation of such feeling to call one's opponents Pharisees and libellers was not fully brought out by Mr Carus, and of course no conclusion had been reached.

In 1808 Bishop Yorke of Ely, kindly and perhaps even sympathetic,

---

[1] *Simeon*, p. 280.   [2] *Ibid.* p. 291.

who had been Simeon's diocesan through his entire ministry, died and was succeeded by Thomas Dampier, a prelate of a different stamp. 'Little sympathy or respect was felt by Bishop Dampier for the Minister of Trinity Church.' His first Charge contained an attack on the Evangelicals and later on in the year he called on the Vice-Chancellor of the University 'to convene the Heads of Houses,' Simeon wrote, 'and to enquire, whether they approved of the young men coming to my evening lectures (there being no doubt what answer would be given to an enquiry so made), that so he might put down the lectures, and cast the odium on them'.[1] In this assault on the unauthorized religious services of the Evangelicals there came to Simeon's rescue one of those juxtapositions of events that seemed to truly religious men (when benefiting them or harming High Churchmen, infidels or other sinners) the most manifest intervention of the Deity. Such things, known at first as 'providential interpositions', came to be called 'providences'. Some splendid examples are recorded, this one not the least. 'The Heads were convened', Simeon's account continues, 'ostensibly to consult respecting the restoration of Mr D., of —— College, to his degree….' 'They were all met; and, without one syllable of the *ostensible* business being mentioned, the Bishop's letter was produced, and a written answer of disapprobation was produced with it, and they all rose up to sign it. It happened that one Head of a House, a friend of mine, who scarcely ever attends such meetings, was there—was there, I had almost said, by miracle.' Isaac Milner, of course 'the friend', was able to prevent action. At a second meeting, 'the same friend being there, not one word of *my* business was brought forward…and thus the cloud which had threatened my ministry (two-thirds of which would have been curtailed) was dispersed….'. 'My friend had long been engaged to be 300 miles off', Simeon's autobiographical fragment of 1813 continues,

and would actually have been there, but for the following astonishing combination of circumstances. The Duke of Grafton our Chancellor died. The Duke of Gloucester was a candidate to succeed him. The Duke of Gloucester succeeded; and his Installation was to be at the Commencement. The Duke of Gloucester wishing to have as great an attendance of respectable friends there as possible, personally requested Mr Wilberforce to come down. Mr W. not

----

[1] *Simeon*, p. 329–30.

having any other person in Cambridge, at whose house he could so properly, or so comfortably be, as at my friend's, wrote to request him to delay his departure till after the Installation. This detained my friend in Cambridge, and prevented his going for about three weeks; *towards the close of which time* the Convocation before mentioned was called; so that the Duke of Grafton's death—the Duke of Gloucester's success—his personal application to Mr Wilberforce, and Mr W.'s request to my friend, were all so many links in the chain of Providence to protect me from the impending storm; and after all, my preservation had not been accomplished, if my friend had not protracted his stay nearly three weeks beyond the time that had been required, and *accidentally*, as we say, attended a Meeting which he was not accustomed to attend. The want of any one of these links had ruined me beyond recovery. If I do not bless and magnify my God, the very stones will cry out against me.[1]

Appointed select preacher at Great St Mary's, Simeon delivered in November 1811 a course of sermons on *The Excellence of the Liturgy*. On November 25, before Isaac Milner's return from London, Lady Margaret's Professor of Divinity, resolutely resisting the Evangelical encroachment, published a pamphlet called *An Address to the Members of the Senate, Occasioned by the Proposal to Introduce into Cambridge an Auxiliary Bible Society*.

'Now opposition became very formidable', Simeon wrote to his disciple Thomason. 'Dr Marsh published a paper against the plan, and with incredible industry put it into the hands of all the great men in the County, and all the leading members of the University, so that we could not get a person, except a few pious characters, to join us.'[2]

It was at this stage of the proposed establishment that Isaac Milner, staying at Wilberforce's house in Kensington Gore, learned of the public meeting. 'I beg you to be discreet and cautious', he wrote on December 7 to Jowett, and on the same day sent off another letter. 'Mr Wilberforce has been with the Chancellor this morning, and has used all his influence to induce him either to go to Cambridge, or, in some way, to make his approbation of the thing known—and all without effect.'[3] It is not to be thought that in a crisis of this nature, at a place occupying the position of Cambridge in the Evangelical Reformation, the commander-in-chief would not be found playing a part. Earlier in the year he had already been doing so, in connection with

[1] *Ibid.* pp. 331.   [2] *Ibid.* p. 309.   [3] *Isaac Milner*, p. 469.

what seems on the face of it an amiable pleasantry, the election of the Duke of Gloucester as Chancellor of the University. The diary for February 1811 notes that he dined at Gloucester House. 'The Duke talked to me about accepting the chancellorship of the University.' The peculiar circumstances of this accomplishment, one of Wilberforce's most inspired and brilliant political strokes, seem to make it quite obvious that we should read that entry 'I talked to the duke....'. It would be a characteristic way for Wilberforce to describe the matter, which far from being a pleasantry was of great importance.

At the moment a prior, realistic problem was more pressing, the duke's election as Chancellor in the poll on March 26. On the 16th Wilberforce wrote a strange letter to Simeon. 'The Duke of Gloucester has been [un]commonly active in promoting institutions of a benevolent kind, and more especially he has been incessant in his attentions to the interests of the African Institution, and to all which has tended to the benefit of the African race. I therefore must feel warmly interested for him.'[1] A similar letter apparently went to Milner. There are odd circumstances here. Wilberforce had no more need to tell those two what the Duke of Gloucester had been doing for Evangelicalism than to tell them who he was. The mere statement that he was a candidate would secure the support of every Cambridge Evangelical and the vote of every elector they could influence. William Frederick Duke of Gloucester was at the time president of the African Institution and a supporter of many other Evangelical operations 'of a benevolent kind'. The cause was in steady need of the backing of the respectable and the great, and there was no promising Evangelical prospect in England who was more so. His possible great 'usefulness' had long been noted— in his early youth Wilberforce and Hannah More particularly were engaging his mother the Dowager Duchess, his sister, William Frederick himself, later his duchess, in tactful and fitting discussions of serious religion—and it seems unlikely that his candidacy was any less premeditated than all other parts of Evangelical reform.

Dean Milner, his biographer says, received numerous requests for his interest from supporters of both candidates, but 'many reasons determined him to give his support to the Duke of Gloucester'. It would be interesting to know what reasons beyond the only reason

[1] *Wilberforce*, vol. III, p. 502.

Miss Milner had in mind. Two events after the duke's victory point to the extreme importance of this tactical move. When he was installed, at Commencement, June–July 1811, the Dean of Carlisle absented himself from a cathedral chapter to attend him. 'Considering my situation here, and the part which I had taken in the election of our new Chancellor, as well as some other important circumstances,' he wrote to his Bishop, 'I at last found, that it would be almost impossible for me to be absent without giving great offence.'[1] To be absent from the chapter, Milner was forced to get a royal dispensation for non-residence. Simeon's description of him as staying in Cambridge for Wilberforce's convenience was peculiarly dishonest. And Wilberforce, at a time when he had never been more pressingly engaged,[2] took an entire week off, with the House of Commons sitting, to be present at the duke's installation, an additional and weighty indication that it was he who had persuaded the duke to be a candidate.

The immediate vital problem, to persuade him to attend the public meeting at Cambridge or at least to indicate publicly his approval of the Auxiliary, is introduced in Wilberforce's *Life* with one of Robert Isaac and Samuel Wilberforce's most guileful sentences. 'A few extracts from [his] letters written at this time to Mr Simeon exhibit some of those secret links by which all through his long public life he was connected with the efforts of religious men in every quarter.'[3] In Milner's second letter to Jowett he was underestimating Wilberforce's unyielding persistence and persuasive power and perhaps the Duke of Gloucester's gratitude for the support he had received at the installation. 'My dear Sir,' Wilberforce replied on December 6 to Simeon's plea for help, '...I believe the Dean would attend, if you could name to him almost any respectable people who would be present. Cannot you do this? Would not the Earl of Bristol attend?...The Dean would be quite decided if the Bishop of Bristol would attend....I am sorry the Duke of

[1] *Isaac Milner*, p. 456.
[2] *Wilberforce*, vol. III, pp. 513–18, etc., etc. 'Wasted twenty or twenty-five most precious morning minutes' (diary, April 27); 'my Sundays are so precious to me in these weeks of bustle' (May 19). When on July 13, Gloucester installed, he set out to join his family at Brighton, he 'could not be easy, and so returned to London on the 15th, and was in the House till near three o'clock'.
[3] *Ibid.* p. 559.

Gloucester is out of town. As nothing can be done—rebus sic stantibus—you should desire Lord Hardwicke to prevail on some other grandees to be present.'[1]

On the following day he wrote again. He had seen the Duke and 'was with him some time; but I am sorry to say, that not only is his going down out of the question, but that I fear he will not even write a letter approving of the scheme, for which I pressed, when I found no more could be obtained.......[2] I shall however continue to do my best; but alas, that best is very little; however, "it is in my heart".' But persistence, friendliness, encouragement, the use of all possible means of persuasion and influence, and no doubt that sense of past favours that Mrs More and Miss Patty urged so strongly on their villagers, at last won. On Tuesday December 10, two days before the meeting, Wilberforce was able to send great news. 'When all my prospects were dark and gloomy, behold the light suddenly breaks forth', he wrote to Simeon. 'Who should be announced to me this morning, but the Duke of Gloucester, who with a cheerful countenance accosted me by saying, that he had come himself to let me know that though on the whole he still thought it would not be proper for him to attend in person, he had written to desire that it might be stated to the meeting that he highly approved of it, and took a lively interest in the Society's success; that he desired to be put down as a subscriber of 50 guineas; and that if there should be a request made to him to become President or Patron of the Society, he should not decline the situation.'[3]

Even then, with a support from the Chancellor of the University as hearty as he dared give, the meeting nearly failed to come off. The discouragement of the Cambridge Evangelicals, with one exception, was very great. Until the morning of the meeting they did not know what support they would have. The Earl of Hardwicke would take the chair, Lord Francis Osborne would support him; but Lady Margaret's Professor's assiduous circulation of his *Address* among all the noble and respectable in the University and county had done great harm, and there was still a question of who would support Lord Hardwicke and

---

[1] *Wilberforce*, vol. III, pp. 560–1.

[2] Deletion by Wilberforce's biographers (?matter of Evangelical reference so palpable that it could not be misunderstood).

[3] *Wilberforce*, vol. III, pp. 561–2.

Lord Francis Osborne. Even earlier, the decision to issue the handbills announcing the meeting had required a dauntless courage that came not from Simeon, as one might expect, but from perhaps the mildest and gentlest of all known Evangelicals, William Farish. When he heard of the decision of the Committee meeting in his absence to postpone *sine die* the meeting to establish, '*he* positively refused to be bound by it. He said that *he* had personally obtained the grant of the Town Hall from the Mayor, and *he would himself hold the Meeting*, and so give due sanction to the proceedings, even though every other Senior in the University should refuse to attend. He then succeeded in convincing Mr Simeon of the remarkably critical position in which the affair was standing.'[1]

So, on the appointed day, the public meeting was held in the Town Hall under Senior auspices, with great excitement, the Earl of Hardwicke well supported in the chair and over a thousand people present. Isaac Milner came down from London the night before, his doubts and fears resolved. 'Our great and admirable friend, the Dean of Carlisle... exercised his extraordinary powers to the credit of himself and the furtherance of this most important cause, which I have the happiness to say was well planted, and is likely to be most thriving', the Bishop of Bristol wrote to Wilberforce from Trinity Lodge. His own inability to attend was 'for reasons I will explain when we meet'.[2]

Simeon's account written a few days later is full of interest.

The meeting was called for Thursday. I would at that time have given a large sum that we had not stirred at all; and so would all my colleagues, *and if it had been possible to have recalled the letters and notices, we should have done it.* But it was not possible; and we all trembled, lest Lord Hardwicke, when he came to take the chair, should complain that he had been deceived by us. On Tuesday however we heard with joy, that Lord F. Osborne would come and support Lord H. Still, however, we were in a very painful predicament. *Who* must speak on the occasion? None but ourselves.... At last however we had joyful tidings from different quarters. The Duke of Gloucester was willing to be President: and now we felt that we had firm standing. We sent off a deputation to Lord Hardwicke, and another to Lord F. Osborne, to inform them, and to give them the Resolutions that were prepared. And then at last the day arrived. But how? Truly God shewed that he reigns in the earth. The Earl of Bristol, to whom we had sent an express at Bury, gave us his name. Dr Milner

---

[1] *Simeon*, p. 317, note.   [2] *Wilberforce*, vol. III, pp. 562-3.

had come down during the night. The Dukes of Bedford and of Rutland gave us their names. The Bishop of Bristol permitted us to use his also. And, to crown the whole, Mr Nicholas Vansittart sent down a printed letter to Dr Marsh in answer to his. (N.B. Mr V. is of the Privy Council.)

In this letter to Thomason, one of the out-of-College tutors whom Dean Milner had found it necessary to bring into Queens', Simeon proceeds to describe 'some circumstances, which will not appear before the public'. 'Dear Mr Steinkopff, the moment he rose, was applauded for a great length of time, and all that he said was most affecting and well received.' Steinkopff, a Secretary of the parent Society, was a dissenter, and his reception probably shows the truth of the High Church claim that many, or most, of the supporters of such a meeting (at Cambridge, in 1811, after Dr Marsh's indictment) would be 'Methodists'. 'Mr Owen was brilliant beyond measure, and more chastised than usual.' 'Professor Farish, with all his placidity, was animated and bold as a lion: but owing to the weakness of his voice he could not be heard.' 'Dr Clarke, the Professor of Mineralogy, was extremely eloquent. He was aware, that by taking an active part he was likely to cut himself off from all hopes of the Mastership of Jesus College; but avowed his determination to disregard all hints of whatever kind, and from whatever quarter, and to do what he thought most acceptable to God.'

The Reverend Dr Clarke of Jesus College was a recruit who seems to have played no part in Evangelicalism at Cambridge until this meeting. On its announcement he came forward with unexpected zeal, 'under a great degree of excitement', his biographer the Reverend William Otter says, which '...having been roused to a high degree of enthusiasm by the sympathies of a crowded assembly, burst out at last in a flood of eloquence which was declared by the friends of the Society, to have been the finest the subject had given birth'.

I trust I have seen the greatest and brightest day of all my life [Clarke wrote]. The opposition to the Bible Society was so great, that they not only could not get a single Clergyman of known adherence to the Church of England, to support them; but even such men as —— and —— took the general panic. That great cry, '*the Church is in danger*,' pervaded every heart.... This memorable morning came—never shall I forget it—nor, I trust, will our adversaries. ...All the avenues to the Town Hall were then crowded—no sooner did the doors open than it was quite full. A deputation of four of us went to the Rose for Lord Hardwicke, and we regained our seats with him, upon the rostrum, about twelve o'clock.

Could I but now describe the grandeur, and solemnity of this meeting. The most surprizing and overwhelming sight to me was that the faces of all that vast assembly, even of the young gownsmen, were seen streaming with tears of rapture. Of course this was not neglected by one of our speakers... who with almost inspired energy called it, '*a contribution, every drop whereof was treasured in the phials of Heaven!*' Well! Lord Francis Osborne moved the resolutions, and I rose (God help me! thinks I) to second them. It is impossible to describe the animating shouts, with which I was encouraged—every sentence was cheered. M—— said the effect was such, he expected they should all have their windows broken. Letters with gratulations have poured in upon me from every quarter.[1]

'Dr Milner', Simeon's account continues, 'spoke nobly and manfully, and took shame to himself for being so long in making up his mind. Lord Francis also spoke well, though short. The unanimity was like that of the day of Pentecost.... I consider our beloved and honoured friend, Mr Wilberforce, as very eminently instrumental in this great and wonderful work, by speaking to the Duke of Gloucester for us: for though he did not succeed at first, I believe we owe it chiefly to his exertions, that both the Duke and Dr M. were brought to take the part they did.'[2] 'The bitter Sermons preached at the Commencement by a Dr —— and Dr —— both against all spiritual religion', Simeon added a few days later to his account of affairs at Cambridge, 'were generally disapproved, even by those who hate religion. They were thought to be out of place and unseasonable, not to mention vehement and uncharitable.'[3]

IV

The vehemence and lack of charity of such as the Reverend Drs —— and —— were not diminished by the establishment of the Cambridge Auxiliary on 12 December 1811. In their elation the Evangelicals per-

[1] *The Life of Edward Daniel Clarke* (London, 1824), vol. II, pp. 260–3. Clarke died in 1822 without college advancement. His biographer Otter became Bishop of Chichester in 1836, by which time his stand on party adherence in the church was so diplomatic that he was described as not fish, flesh or fowl.

[2] *Simeon*, pp. 308–13.   [3] *Ibid.* p. 320.

haps did not realize even the immediate consequence of their victory. 'After more than forty years' residence in this University, and, of course, after having attended a variety of public meetings,' Isaac Milner said at the First Anniversary Meeting of the Auxiliary, with Lord Francis Osborne in the chair, 'I can honestly declare, that there is not one on which I reflect with so much sincere and solid satisfaction, as on that meeting which took place in this room last December.' In his characteristic way Charles Simeon expressed an even stronger satisfaction. 'I do not conceive that many such days have been seen since the day of Pentecost. Many, many tears were shed on the occasion; and God himself was manifestly present.'[1] An adverse consequence of the meeting nevertheless was that it brought still more to the front of the battle a High Churchman who was to displace Bishop Tomline as the most dangerous enemy Evangelicalism had. It is probably fair to assume with respect to Simeon's 'God himself was manifestly present' that there were many in Cambridge who did not believe so, namely all the High Churchmen, and perhaps one of them with less assurance may have had more knowledge. At any rate he had concerned himself about the matter in an intellectual way that was close to unique in England.

If the Evangelicals were not already, as Isaac Milner was to point out to the Archbishop, 'supported by such a mass of property, and such a number of respectable characters', it would have been an extreme misfortune for them to have run head on at this point into Dr Herbert Marsh. The age had no more learned, acute and combative controversialist, and incessant practice kept Dr Marsh's weapons always sharp. He was one of the several characters contributed to the Orthodox-Evangelical drama by St John's College[2] and had studied at Göttingen. Between 1791 and 1801 he published in four volumes his translation of Michaelis's *Introduction to the New Testament* with notes of his own. In the third volume appeared a *Dissertation on the Origin and Composition of the Three First Gospels* in which Marsh stated his hypothesis that

---

[1] *Simeon*, pp. 311–12.
[2] They included also Wilberforce, Rowland Hill, Thomas Gisborne, Bishop Beadon, Bishop Ryder, the Earl of Harrowby, Charles James Hoare, Thomas Clarkson, John William Cunningham, the Rev. Samuel Butler, Patrick Brontë and (later) John William Colenso.

Matthew and Luke had made use of an earlier record in Greek of the sayings of Jesus. Simply from its nature as a critical work this was deeply shocking to many religious persons; it was 'derogating from the character of the sacred books', Bishop Randolph of London said, 'and injurious to Christianity as fostering a spirit of scepticism'. Marsh replied to his adversaries, among them Dealtry, who succeeded John Venn as rector of Clapham in 1813, in what Randolph called 'a coarse strain of low abuse'. In religious controversy he was outstanding even in this age as a bad-tempered and sarcastic writer. In his controversy over the composition of the New Testament, at least, his opponents' total incompetence was some excuse.

In June 1811 Marsh published a sermon entitled *The National Religion the Foundation of National Education*, attacking the British and Foreign School Society, founded by the Quakers with heavy Evangelical support. He was concerned only with the churchmen in the Society, who had no right, he believed, to help educate the poor except in the principles of the Established Church; to join with dissenters in a merely Christian education neglected the Liturgy and tended to weaken the church. In 1812 appeared 'one of his most powerful and stinging pamphlets', called *An Inquiry into the Consequences of Neglecting to give the Prayer-Book with the Bible, interspersed with Remarks on Some Late Speeches at Cambridge, and Other Important Matter Relative to the British and Foreign Bible Society*. This was in part a reply to pamphlets against his *Address* by Farish, Clarke, Vansittart, Dealtry, Otter and still others. In his discussion of these attacks Marsh maintained on the whole a sweet if not unvigorous reasonableness while protesting at the kind of language used by some of his adversaries. 'Circulated as the New Testament has been described to be, without tract or comment', one anonymous work declared, 'they who oppose [the Bible Society's auxiliaries] oppose the circulation of the word of God, as originally delivered forth, and would have probably opposed *our Saviour himself*, had they lived in his time.' 'On such language and conduct', Marsh replied, 'it is unnecessary to make an observation.' Vansittart's *Letter* was 'written in all the amiable spirit of a sincere and benevolent Christian. Let other Advocates of this Society take a lesson from Mr Vansittart.' They could have taken a lesson from Farish, who in 1810 had warned Simeon against the use of ridicule in religious controversy. Simeon had more than a little tendency toward the manner of Sir Richard Hill in theological disputes.

This particular controversy came to an end in 1813. Dr Marsh, invincible in argument, had the misfortune to be opposing the moral Spirit of the Age. Bishop of Llandaff in 1816 on the death of Watson, he was translated in 1819 to Peterborough, where his anti-Evangelical fervour was so active that it attracted national notice. It is a sign of the long drawn-out death of the old century that so intellectually honest and able a man gave his twenty-four year old son the 'lucrative' rectory of Barnack and in the following year a prebendal stall in his cathedral, and kept his professorship and the house that went with it, though he was only twice again in Cambridge, until his death in 1839.[1] It is also noteworthy that the *Dictionary of the Living Authors*, which states, not censoriously but as a matter of information, what patronage led to the elevation of every other bishop then living who had achieved 'authorism', has nothing to say under that head about Herbert Marsh. He was related to no noble patron, had tutored none and was indebted to none. In continuing relentless warfare on the Evangelicals his chief weapon was a famous series of eighty-seven questions designed with learned and subtle malice to detect Evangelical candidates for ordination. It was known, by a popular rather than accurate name, as Marsh's 'Trap to Catch Calvinists'. The Calvinism as such was not very troublesome in those days, but one matter could not be 'accommodated', the Evangelical position on Baptismal Regeneration. In Marsh's diocese no candidate for Orders who held the necessity of a personal rebirth could be ordained, and even clergymen in orders remained unlicensed if they declined to answer the Eighty-seven Questions or failed to answer them to Marsh's satisfaction. At this point, though he defended his policy in the House of Lords, it was widely felt to be harmful to the Church.

Even during the controversy of 1812 the Evangelicals were convinced that Marsh was helping them more than harming them, and they may have been right. 'Of all the men in Britain that have done

---

[1] *Dictionary of National Biography*. The Duke of Sussex writing to Dr Parr in 1823 spoke against Marsh's 'determination that all should believe as he did' (Parr, *Works*, vol. VII, p. 5). In that respect Marsh could hardly have gone beyond his Evangelical adversaries.

good to the Bible Society, there is scarcely one, except the Secretaries, that can vie with Dr Marsh', Simeon wrote in August 1813. 'In doing all that man can do against it, he has advanced it a thousand times more than if he had written in its favour.'[1] Marsh's strong language offended some, his criticism of the New Testament many. By and large the High Church party were as greatly shocked as the Evangelicals at his attempts to read the Bible intelligently, and it may well have been that his enmity was helpful. When it is considered that Tomline's *Elements of Christian Theology* held the field as the standard manual of the church until well past the reform period, it is understandable that Marsh's views should have been horrifying. The first volume of the *Elements*, reprinted as *An Introduction to the Study of the Bible* (19th ed., 1849), contained few statements of conjecture, in any important matter, and still fewer of fact, that a thinking member of the church would accept today.[2]

V

Perhaps after Marsh, Simeon, Wilberforce and Isaac Milner the most interesting Cambridge figure in the establishment of the Auxiliary Bible Society was the man who was so conspicuously absent from the Town Hall meeting, the Chancellor of the University. It is natural that his Royal Highness Prince William Frederick, Duke of Gloucester, should be a very particular prize of the Evangelicals. He was the son of William Henry, the old duke who helped in the distribution of Cheap Repository, consequently a great-grandson of George II, a first cousin of the Regent, and having married Mary, fourth daughter of George III, the king's son-in-law as well as nephew. There is a respectability here that does not need emphasis, and no explanation is needed of the

---

[1] *Simeon*, p. 373.

[2] 'It appears from Deuteronomy, that the...whole Pentateuch, written by the hand of Moses, was...deposited in the tabernacle, not long before his death.' 'After the temple was rebuilt, Ezra...made a collection of the sacred writings...and as Ezra was himself inspired, we may rest assured, that whatever received his sanction, was authentic.' 'The great length to which human life was extended in the patriarchal ages, rendered it very practicable for the Jews, in the time of Moses, to trace their lineal descent as far as the Flood, nay even to Adam.' Methuselah, Noah's grandfather, 'was 243 years contemporary with Adam, and 600 with Noah'. *Elements of Christian Theology* (1820; 13th ed. of vol. I), vol. I, pp. 5, 9–10, 64–5.

interest the two great proselytizers, Wilberforce and Hannah More, had shown in him for years. 'I paid my visit to Gloucester House yesterday', Mrs More wrote to Wilberforce in 1795. 'Lady Waldegrave presented me to the Duchess. We had two hours of solid, rational, religious conversation. It would be too little to say, that the Duchess's behaviour is gracious in the extreme. She behaved to me with the affectionate familiarity of an equal; and though I took the opportunity of saying stronger things of a religious kind than perhaps she had ever heard, she bore it better than any great person I ever conversed with, and seemed not offended at the strictness of the gospel.... The Duchess presented me to Princess Sophia, and Prince William. The manners of these two young personages were very agreeable. They found many kind things to say to me, and conversed with the greatest sweetness and familiarity.... The Duchess quoted "The Shepherd of Salisbury Plain" two or three times.'[1]

Sixteen years later the Duke of Gloucester seems to have been a genuinely well-meaning man, desiring within the limits of his mind and training to be on the side of good. Lady Charlotte Bury speaks of his 'solid basis of religion and virtue'. Lady Charlotte was a virtuous and Christian woman herself (to the extent that a non-Evangelical could be), and a good observer. It is true she also speaks of the Duke and Princess Caroline making 'a joke on the conveniences attached to the private boxes' at the theatre.[2] 'I well remember the installation of the Duke of Gloucester as Chancellor of the University of Cambridge', the Reverend J. Richardson wrote in his *Recollections*, published in 1856. He had come up to Cambridge in 1809 or 1810. 'I and scores of other people were, on that occasion, introduced to his Royal Highness. He was then in the prime of life [the duke was thirty-five in 1811], and his appearance, without betokening a man of princely rank, was that of a gentleman. His countenance was not unpleasing, but partook, in some degree, of that vacuity of expression which, coupled with his mode of observation, procured him the soubriquet of "Silly Billy" from the scoffers of rank and royalty. He appeared to have one form of interrogatory and remark for every person to whom he addressed himself. "To what College do you belong?" "How long have you been here?" "Charming weather." "Very pretty breakfast" (alluding to

[1] *More*, vol. II, pp. 434–5.
[2] *Diary of a Lady-in-Waiting*, vol. I, pp. 112–13.

the public dejeuner provided), and with these words, repeated several hundred times, he got through the business of the day very well.'[1]

The Reverend Mr Richardson's strange book, abounding in trashy anecdotes and fantastic yarns offered as true, is far from trustworthy. But it was right about the Duke of Gloucester. He was universally known (except to the Evangelicals) as Silly Billy, and it seems evident he was not normally intelligent. In 1832 the Reverend Thomas Shore, a nephew of Lord Teignmouth, was explaining to his twelve-year-old daughter what a university is. 'The Chancellor is commonly a nobleman', her journal says. 'The Chancellor of Oxford is now Lord Grenville; that of Cambridge, the Duke of Gloucester. He is a very silly man. Papa told us that one day, as he was riding out, he complained that the flies would get into his mouth, and he could not keep them out. The servant replied, "Perhaps your Royal Highness had better shut your mouth", for he was in the habit of riding with his mouth open. Another time he bid his servant fetch his handkerchief from his room, but hesitated, and said, "I am pretty sure I locked the door, but I cannot remember whether I left the key on the inside." These anecdotes made us laugh heartily.'[2] When the satirical journal *Figaro in London* was established toward the end of the duke's life it ran for over a year a weekly series of *Gloucesteriana*. 'It is remarkable that the Duke of Gloucester is of an exceedingly cheerful disposition, though the *very little piece* of mind his Royal Highness possesses is proverbial.' 'The Duke of Gloucester is said to have remarked with great simplicity on hearing of the intended abolition of corporal punishment in the army, that "he certainly should give the project his support, as he had always thought it hard military flogging should be made to fall only on the Corporals".' 'His Royal Highness of Gloucester asked how boats were moved, and he was told by an attendant, that it was by means of men who put their *sculls* into the water. "Bless my soul," was the single-minded duke's reply, "I have put my skull into my wash-hand basin at least a hundred times, and I have never moved an inch."'

For its one hundredth issue *Figaro* announced a benefit for the duke.

This extraordinary resolution has been come to after a most mature deliberation upon his Royal Highnesses claims, and it has been decided, that the Duke

[1] The Rev. J. Richardson, *Recollections of the Last Half Century* (2 vols., London, 1856), vol. I, pp. 189–90.　　　[2] *Journal of Emily Shore* (London, 1891), p. 27.

having from nearly the commencement of this publication shed the lustre of his wit in *Gloucesteriana* through its pages, he has a full right to expect from the subscribers, (which may be said now to be synonymous with the nation,) a slight mark of gratitude. When it is considered that the Duke's pocket-money is small, and that Higgins [Colonel Higgins the aide] stands him in at least five shillings a-week, we are convinced every thing will be done by the public on the occasion of his benefit. Full particulars will be duly announced. In the mean time tickets may be had, and half-yearly parts secured on application to the Duke, Gloucester House, Piccadilly, or of Colonel Higgins's mother at the apple-stall opposite.[1]

Figaro was a radical reform journal and a distinguished scoffer of rank and royalty, and many (if not all) of its anecdotes of the Duke of Gloucester are patently manufactured. A mass of evidence elsewhere indicates that the duke did not reflect much credit upon his and Dr Marsh's Alma Mater or his tutor Bishop Beadon. One of the Silly Billy stories preserved by G. W. E. Russell is primarily about the 'racy vigour of conversation' of the Duke of Cumberland. He was once walking 'along Piccadilly when the Duke of Gloucester (first cousin to Cumberland, and familiarly known as "Silly Billy") came out of Gloucester House. "Duke of Gloucester, Duke of Gloucester, stop a minute. I want to speak to you", roared the Duke of Cumberland. Poor Silly Billy, whom nobody ever noticed, was delighted to find himself thus accosted, and ambled up smiling. "Who's your tailor?" shouted Cumberland. "Stultz", replied Gloucester. "Thank you. I only wanted to know, because, whoever he is, he ought to be avoided like the pestilence." Exit Silly Billy.'

It should be recorded that some of the stories about the Evangelically installed Chancellor of the University of Cambridge show a definite trace of the reasoning faculty. 'Of this inoffensive but not brilliant prince,' Russell says, '...it is related that once at a levée he noticed a naval friend with a much tanned face. "How do, Admiral? Glad to see you again. It's a long time since you have been at a levée." "Yes, sir. Since I last saw your Royal Highness I have been nearly to the North Pole." "By G——, you look more as if you had been to the South Pole."'[2]

[1] *Figaro in London*, 14 September 1833, p. 147.
[2] *Collections and Recollections* (1904), p. 196.

'Prominent, meaningless eyes; without being actually ugly, a very unpleasant face, with an animal expression; large and stout, but with weak, helpless legs.' So Baron Stockmar described the Duke of Gloucester.[1] Charles Greville pictured him breakfasting with members of the royal family in 1830; '...the Duke of Gloucester bowing to the company while nobody was taking any notice of him or thinking about him. Nature must have been merry when she made this Prince, and in the sort of mood that certain great artists used to exhibit in their comical caricatures; I never saw a countenance which that line in Dryden's M'Flecknoe would so well describe—

And lambent dulness plays around his face.'[2]

There was good intent in this prince so unkindly treated by nature and art. He was not an exemplary Evangelical. Good Evangelicals did not swear, did not go to the theatre, and if they had gone would not have made jokes about the conveniences. But he supported the cause in a way that took courage, in a shy and awkward man, and was probably as good an Evangelical as his peculiar kind of fallen nature allowed. The protracted and persistent labours of Wilberforce and Hannah More were not thrown away.

Silly Billy was a military man and rose to the rank of field marshal. The one notable saying recorded to his credit is evidence enough that *Figaro's* picture of him was not realistic. When his cousin William IV signed the Reform Bill, the Duke of Gloucester, as strongly opposed to Reform as any good Evangelical, remarked 'Who's Silly Billy now?'

VI

The crisis at Cambridge—and the whole fantastic opposition to the Bible Society—seems to present some difficulty. How is it possible that the union of churchmen with dissenters in so simple a Christian act could bring about such fears and anxieties, the tumult, violence and hostility and all the passionate contrivings? How can we understand the discreet correspondence (which so greatly helped the Evangelical

---

[1] Quoted in Lewis Melville, *The First Gentleman of Europe*, vol. II, p. 158.
[2] Greville, *A Journal of the Reigns of King George IV and King William IV*, vol. II, p. 8.

biographers), the secret manœuvres, the desperate rallyings of noble and respectable support? How can we explain the manipulated election of a simpleton as chancellor of one of the world's great universities? the incredible pains taken by Wilberforce and Milner to attend his installation? the bitter sermons preached by Drs —— and —— against all spiritual religion? That there should be opposition at all, on the part of Christians, to such a society, would on the face of it seem bewildering. That conduct so beyond measure and reason as that at Cambridge could have been set in action, at a Christian institution, by the simple proposal to form a branch of a society that existed only to distribute the Bible is hardly believable.

Is it, in fact, believable at all? Can it even be possible that the admission of dissenters and consequent distribution of the Bible without the Prayer Book was not actually the issue at Cambridge and that in some basic sense these were not primarily theological antagonists? Perhaps the view is worth considering that this seemingly fantastic clash is not really to be understood in terms of the stated object of the Bible Society or its apparent mode of operation. As late as the end of the century the state of Evangelical affairs at Oxford (for instance) was greatly discouraging. Even there, in the home of lost causes, where no Milner had worked and no Simeon, the Oxford and Oxfordshire Auxiliary of the Bible Society was established a few months after the affair at Cambridge with greatly less opposition and greatly more support from *those who count*. 'In point of effect, the Meeting was very, very far below that of Cambridge', Charles Simeon wrote, and it must be assumed that for some reason although Simeon was present God was manifestly not; 'but upon paper it is far, very far above us: for even at the first, they had six Masters [of Houses] and four Professors to countenance them, and several of the nobility; and now they have the Duke of Marlborough (Lord Lieutenant) and Lord Grenville (the Chancellor), with a host of others.'[1] If the Bible Society did not exist only to carry out the 'more immediate object' of distributing the Scriptures, then the whole action at Cambridge can be quite simply understood as part of a strategical accomplishment that to the casual observer could appear merely incidental, a thing done 'by the way', but that was in fact, designed or accidental, an Evangelical triumph.

[1] *Simeon*, p. 370.

CHAPTER 9

TEN THOUSAND COMPASSIONS
AND CHARITIES

Ours is the age of societies. For the redress of every oppression that is done under the sun, there is a public meeting. For the cure of every sorrow by which our land or our race can be visited, there are patrons, vice-presidents and secretaries. For the diffusion of every blessing of which mankind can partake in common, there is a committee. That confederacy which, when pent up within the narrow limits of Clapham, jocose men invidiously called a 'Sect', is now spreading through the habitable globe.

SIR JAMES STEPHEN

What soldier ever serveth at his own charge? who planteth a vineyard, and eateth not the fruit thereof? or who feedeth a flock, and eateth not of the milk of the flock?... Even so did the Lord ordain that they which proclaim the gospel should live of the gospel.

I CORINTHIANS

I

The dimensions of the Bible and Missionary Societies were not reached again by any religious or benevolent society of this age. But from beginning to end of it moral, religious, educational, charitable and bene- volent institutions sprang up in an unheard-of way, many of them branching out through the provinces, all of them 'useful' in one degree or another and many spectacularly so. It seemed to some observers watching them with amusement or wonder, perhaps also uneasiness, that they left no field of social activity untouched. 'This is the age of societies', the young Thomas Babington Macaulay wrote in 1823. 'There is scarcely one Englishman in ten who has not belonged to some association for distributing books, or for prosecuting them; for sending invalids to the hospital, or beggars to the treadmill; for giving plate to the rich, or blankets to the poor.' Even at twenty-three the greatly admired youthful friend of the More sisters, Mrs De Quincey's 'Baby genius', son of one of Wilberforce's right-hand men, nephew of another, could have given a less patronizing and perfunctory picture of this huge activity, its scope, power and reforming value far greater than his trivial examples indicate. He could have added that as each

317

new society was launched at a 'numerously attended' public meeting of 'noble and respectable persons' it was unusual if William Wilberforce was not on the platform, supported by his Evangelical lieutenants. It is unusual too if the names of the commander and some or many of his Evangelical 'directorate' do not appear in each new society's surviving lists of heavy subscribers (governors, life members), or on the committee, or among the officers. By the middle of the period, as England seems to become a network of thousands upon thousands of local branches of these societies, the few hundreds of those Evangelical men and women who constituted the chief support of the parent (London) societies, the names of many appearing in twenty or thirty or more, begin to take on the look of a moral directorate that is not figurative but literal.

By the 1820's these societies had become so common a feature of English life that they were hardly noticed (and have hardly been noticed since). In fact our chief idea of them comes from their parodists. The novelists especially, most of them heartily anti-Evangelical like Dickens, Thackeray and Wilkie Collins, enjoyed diverting their readers and themselves with comic accounts of this kind of reform. Those accounts are always amusing and never show any knowledge of the nature of the societies, or of course of any object they might contribute to beyond their more immediate object. The constantly expressed view that the conductors of such institutions were motivated by a sanctimonious hypocrisy on the one hand or a Godwinian 'general benevolence' toward all the world on the other was a particularly serious misunderstanding.

In *Bleak House* (1853) Mrs Jellyby, devoted to Africa, educates and provides with pocket-handkerchiefs the natives of Borrioboola-gha, leaving her family 'in a devil of a state'. She 'received so many letters that Richard. . .saw four envelopes in the gravy at once', and according to Mr Quale had 'as many as one hundred and fifty to two hundred letters respecting Africa in a single day'. Mrs Jellyby's neglect of her family is not characteristic of her friend Mrs Pardiggle the School lady, Visiting lady, Reading lady, Distributing lady, whose offspring are morally regimented in a thorough way:

'Egbert, my eldest (twelve), is the boy who sent out his pocket-money, to the amount of five-and-threepence, to the Tockahoopo Indians. Oswald, my second (ten-and-a-half), is the child who contributed two-and-ninepence to the Great National Smithers Testimonial. Francis, my third (nine), one-and-sixpence-half-penny; Felix, my fourth (seven), eightpence to the Super-annuated Widows; Alfred, my youngest (five), has voluntarily enrolled himself in the Infant Bonds of Joy, and is pledged never, through life, to use tobacco in any form.'

We had never seen such dissatisfied children. It was not merely that they were weazened and shrivelled—though they were certainly that too—but they looked absolutely ferocious with discontent. At the mention of the Tockahoopo Indians, I could really have supposed Egbert to be one of the most baleful members of that tribe, he gave me such a savage frown. The face of each child, as the amount of his contribution was mentioned, darkened in a peculiarly vindictive manner, but his was by far the worst. I must except, however, the little recruit into the Infant Bonds of Joy, who was stolidly and evenly miserable.[1]

The children are also allowed to contribute to Mrs Jellyby's African project, and to take part in such activities in general in a liberal way.

'My young family [Mrs Pardiggle continues] are not frivolous; they expend the entire amount of their allowance, in subscriptions, under my direction; and they have attended as many public meetings, and listened to as many lectures, orations and discussions, as generally fall to the lot of few grown people. Alfred (five), who, as I mentioned, has of his own election joined the Infant Bonds of Joy, was one of the very few children who manifested con-sciousness on that occasion, after a fervid address of two hours from the chairman of the evening.'

Alfred glowered at us as if he never could, or would, forgive the injury of that night.

The Reverend Mr Chadband in *Bleak House*, 'a large yellow man, with a fat smile, and a general appearance of having a good deal of train oil in his system', was 'attached to no particular denomination'. Dickens seems to have been careful about hurting the feelings of large numbers of readers. Even Mrs Jellyby and Mrs Pardiggle have no specific religious affiliation, or even religion, apparently, but are 'philanthropists' who have a 'Brotherhood of Humanity'.

A novel of 1845 called *Hawkstone*, attributed to one Elizabeth Sewell, comes a good deal closer (in a patronizing High Church way) to what

[1] *Bleak House* (London, 1853), pp. 71–2.

the Evangelical society activities were like in a provincial centre. Miss Mabel Brook, 'a warm Conservative at heart, and whose errors were only overflowings of real benevolence and piety ill instructed', is secretary of the Hawkstone Dorcas or Benevolent Lying-in Union Society, and of a good many others.

And to-day there was the Grey School committee, and the National School to be visited. And Mr Bentley's new plans for the Sunday School to be talked over with four or five other ladies, and the last private meeting with three or four others to originate a new ladies' association for the discouragement of drunkenness, and the accounts of the Tract Society to be audited, and the reports of the Ladies' District Visiting Club to be drawn up; and, greatest of all, the first meeting of the Ladies' Society for the Conversion of the Irish, which was to be held in the great ball-room at the Bell, and where Mr Bentley and Mr Bryant would each make a speech, and perhaps pay a compliment to her 'laborious and energetic offices as secretary', amidst cries of 'hear!' and 'hear!' and the amiable congratulations of female friends to cover her natural confusion. The day was filled up to the brim.

In fact Miss Brook was a leading worker in every female society of the town.

It was Miss Mabel who undertook the management of the national schools; Miss Mabel who was secretary and chief mover, not only of the Dorcas Society, but of all the ladies' societies which flourished with a mushroom growth at Hawkstone; the Ladies' Branch Bible Society, the Ladies' Anti-Cruelty-to-Animals Society, the Ladies' Book Society, the Ladies' Association for the Conversion of the Jews, the Ladies' District-Visiting Society, the Ladies' Penitentiary, the Ladies' Female Orphan, and Deaf and Dumb, and Pastoral Aid, and General-Religious-Purpose Society. None could flourish, and few had originated, without Miss Mabel; her whole soul was in doing good. And if there mixed with this ardour of sincere benevolence some little bustle and over-zeal, and no little ignorance as to the right mode of doing good, it was the fault not so much of Miss Mabel herself, as of the age in which she was born.[1]

In Wilkie Collins's *The Moonstone*, Miss Drusilla Clack (who is also one of the finest of all tract-distributors) is prominent on the Select Committee of such institutions as the Mothers'-Small-Clothes-Conversion Society. 'The object of this excellent charity is—as all serious

[1] *Hawkstone*, Bentley's Standard Novels, vol. XLVI (London, 1845), pp. 46, 14.

people know—to rescue unredeemed fathers' trowsers from the pawn-broker, and to prevent their resumption, on the part of the irreclaimable parent, by abridging them immediately to suit the proportions of the innocent son.' Mr Godfrey Ablewhite is the perfect chairman of this benevolence, as indeed of Ladies' Committees and Evangelical meetings generally.

He stood over six feet high; he had a beautiful red and white colour; a smooth round face, shaved as bare as your hand; and a head of lovely long flaxen hair, falling negligently to the poll of his neck.... Female benevolence and female destitution could do nothing without him. Maternal societies for confining poor women; Magdalen societies for rescuing poor women; strong-minded societies for putting poor women into poor men's places, and leaving the men to shift for themselves—he was vice-president, manager, referee to them all. Wherever there was a table with a committee of ladies sitting round it in council, there was Mr Godfrey at the bottom of the board, keeping the temper of the committee, and leading the dear creatures along the thorny ways of business, hat in hand. I do suppose this was the most accomplished philanthropist (on a small independence) that England ever produced. As a speaker at charitable meetings the like of him for drawing your tears and your money was not easy to find.... And with all this the sweetest-tempered per-son...the simplest and pleasantest and easiest to please—you ever met with. He loved everybody. And every body loved *him*.[1]

It is true the young daughter of the Mr Betteredge who is the narrator of that passage does not love Mr Godfrey Ablewhite but on the contrary thinks he is a 'nasty, sly fellow'. Miss Clack does not think so. 'My gifted friend made her one of the most truly evangelical answers I ever heard in my life. "I hope, Rachel, I take up the cause of all oppressed people rather warmly", he said.'[2] Miss Clack as she puts it has 'learned Perseverance in the School of Adversity', and later on manages very well, in the Evangelical way, when Mr Betteredge's daughter turns out to be right and Mr Godfrey turns out to have been all along a dishonest rogue and what Miss Clack admirably calls a 'con-firmed castaway'.

The year before Wilberforce's death a charge of interested motive in the Evangelicals' support of their societies was made by *Figaro in London*. It cited the *Nottingham Review*'s estimate that the income of

---

[1] *The Moonstone* (New York, 1873), p. 69.   [2] *Ibid.* p. 226.

the leading religious societies of England for the year would be over £300,000.

The above is a...rather curious document, showing how liberal the rich people of England can be in their contributions for the spiritual good of the poor, while they leave their bodily care so entirely to other hands, that want and starvation are almost as plentiful as bibles.... We should be the last to find fault with the system of giving religious instruction to the poor, but when twenty times as much money is devoted to the purpose as would clothe and feed some thousands of starving families, it becomes a matter of consideration what can be the source of so much exclusive liberality in the cause of piety. The fact is, that too many of the contributors to Bible funds are actuated by the most interested motives; and taking in the literal sense the words 'He that *giveth* to the poor *lendeth* to the Lord', there are thousands who put down so much per annum in this manner, and look to their heavenly Father as they would do to the bank for the interest....Charity is in many cases a mere matter of merchandize, and whoever sports most, often does so with a view of turning it to a good account hereafter. If the charity be of a religious cast, it is considered to be killing two birds with one stone, and hence the prosperity of the Bible and Missionary Societies.[1]

We hear there the Gentile voice of one unacquainted with the true principles of Christian benevolence as stated years earlier by Hannah More, or with the true motives, both immediate and unimmediate, of the men and women who were directing these societies. No doubt the ranks of what Mrs More's successor Mrs Sherwood customarily referred to as 'the elect' were spotted here and there with pious rogues and no doubt some who were not rogues had an idea that such benevolences would not harm their future standing. By and large the Evangelical motives were uncompromisingly righteous. If they were to do any harm to their country in the nineteenth century it would come from Evangelical virtues rather than pagan vices.

It would be a mistake to take the comic accounts of the societies as gross parody, mere clowning and buffoonery with no relation to reality. In fact in basic respects they were nearly always short of what they were designed to exaggerate. Miss Clack is not morally of the Evangelical fibre, but her religious language and mannerisms have a clear sound ring of the lower Evangelical speech of the period following

[1] *Figaro in London*, 8 September 1832, p. 158.

Wilberforce. Her declaration that there can be 'no very assured hopes', as Mrs More worded it, for Lady Verinder, and her edifying exclamations, are not exaggerated. 'Sorrow and sympathy! Oh, what Pagan emotions to expect from a Christian Englishwoman anchored firmly on her faith!'[1] And when Miss Clack informs the old solicitor Mr Bruff[2] that she is to witness Lady Verinder's will and is told she is an acceptable witness—'You have not the slightest pecuniary interest in Lady Verinder's will'—her consolatory reflections during a period of meditative silence have a striking resemblance to the recorded thoughts of the young Edward Bickersteth on learning that Mr Carus Wilson's aged relative whom he had cared for had similarly left him nothing. 'Not the slightest pecuniary interest in Lady Verinder's will. Oh, how thankful I felt when I heard that! If my aunt, possessed of thousands, had remembered poor Me, to whom five pounds is an object—if my name had appeared in the Will, with a little comforting legacy attached to it—my enemies might have doubted.... Not the cruelest scoffer of them all could doubt now. Much better as it was! Oh, surely, surely much better as it was!'[3]

It seems to indicate a penetration into English life so deep as to make these societies taken for granted and not much attended to that in aspects more important than easily ridiculed mannerisms, and even in some very simple respects, their parodists' knowledge was wholly inadequate. The number and variety of Miss Mabel Brook's memberships are far short of those of any leading female of the Party in the great period, just as the satirical accounts of the Evangelical tracts are likewise much short of reality, in their invented titles, in their nature (it is not possible to parody *The Shepherd of Salisbury Plain*) and in the numbers of their editions. So too with the names of the fictional societies. The truth was hardly to be parodied there either. There was no actual Infant Bonds of Joy, but there was a Forlorn Females Fund of Mercy. There was an Institution for the Protection of Young Country Girls, and a Maritime Female Penitent Refuge for Poor, Degraded Females.

[1] *The Moonstone*, p. 235.
[2] 'A man, I grieve to say, grown old and grizzled in the service of the world. A man who, in his hours of business, was the chosen prophet of Law and Mammon; and who, in his hours of leisure, was equally capable of reading a novel and of tearing up a tract.'   [3] *Ibid.* p. 237.

There was a Friendly Female Society for the Relief of Poor, Infirm, Aged Widows, and Single Women, of Good Character, Who Have Seen Better Days. There was an Aged Pilgrims Friend Society, and a Ladies Association for the Benefit of Gentlewomen of Good Family, Reduced in Fortune Below the State of Comfort To Which They Have Been Accustomed. Above all, perhaps, there was a Society for Returning Young Women To Their Friends in the Country.

It is noticeable too that while those who made merry with the societies recognized they were in some way 'evangelical', great error persisted in important matters. The leading conductors of these reforming institutions were not precisely to be described as 'philanthropists', they did not love everybody and they were not interested in taking up warmly the cause of all oppressed people. Another error is noteworthy in the mid-Victorian satirists. Even when they are allegedly writing of a time early in the century they are not describing the Evangelicalism of Henry Hoare of Mitcham, Lord Gambier, Henry Thornton, the Duchess of Beaufort, Sir Thomas Baring or even Hannah More but a later and quite different kind preserved for us in such works as George Eliot's *Scenes of Clerical Life* and Samuel Butler's *Way of All Flesh*. In Charlotte Brontë's *Jane Eyre*, for example, published in 1847, the action opens round 1807, at the time of the abolition of the slave trade, when the Reverend William Carus Wilson, who appears in the story as the conductor of 'Lowood School', was in fact only a promising youth not yet even sitting at the feet of Charles Simeon at Cambridge. The real Evangelical school Brontë was describing was opened sixteen years later, in 1823. This distortion is seen most clearly in the references in all mid-century pictures of the Evangelicals, even when statedly taking place earlier, to District Visiting and temperance societies. There were no organized District Visiting societies, by that name, while Wilberforce was in parliament and no temperance societies until 1831, two years before his death. It should also be pointed out, with reference to Master Pardiggle of the Infant Bonds of Joy, that there was no organized attack on the evil of tobacco until the Age of Wilberforce was being unhappily succeeded by what J. L. and Barbara Hammond fitly call the Bleak Age.

As there were marked differences between the two Evangelicalisms, of Charles Grant, the Duchess of Gordon, Lady Olivia Sparrow and

Wilberforce on the one hand and Mrs Pardiggle, Mrs Jellyby, Miss Clack and William Carus Wilson on the other, injustice is often done to the Evangelicalism of the great period. There is an instance of it in *A Christmas Carol*. The Second Spirit denies, with some heat, Scrooge's charge that he and his 'family' are trying to enforce a peculiarly discriminatory kind of Sabbath observance.

'Spirit,' said Scrooge, after a moment's thought, 'I wonder you, of all the beings in the many worlds about us, should desire to cramp these people's opportunities of innocent enjoyment.'

'I!' cried the Spirit.

'You would deprive them of their means of dining every seventh day, often the only day on which they can be said to dine at all', said Scrooge. 'Wouldn't you?'

'I!' cried the Spirit.

'You seek to close those places on the Seventh Day', said Scrooge. 'And it comes to the same thing.'

'I seek!' exclaimed the Spirit.

'Forgive me if I am wrong. It has been done in your name, or at least in that of your family.'

'There are some upon this earth of yours', returned the Spirit, 'who lay claim to know us, and who do their deeds of passion, pride, ill-will, hatred, envy, bigotry, and selfishness in our name who are as strange to us and all our kith and kin, as if they had never lived. Remember that, and charge their doings on themselves, not us.'

As a happy contrast to the attempts of some of the Saints after Wilberforce's retirement to close cook-shops on Sundays, Dickens presents to us 'two portly gentlemen, pleasant to behold' who ask Scrooge to contribute to a 'fund to buy the Poor some meat and drink, and means of warmth', which after his reclamation he handsomely does. Dickens did not know it, but if he had been thinking of *A Christmas Carol* as taking place in 1810 or in 1820 the chances are good that his sabbatarian Puritans and his two benevolent gentlemen were equally Evangelical if perhaps of different generations. In Wilberforce's day no other persons, whatever their motive, raised funds so tirelessly to give the poor meat, drink and coals as well as to give them Bibles, and that is probably true also of the later Evangelicals who laboured to keep the poor from dining out on Sundays and other worldly enjoyments.

The typical Evangelical of the early period was certainly portly and pleasant to behold. That seems to have been particularly true of the clergy. Scott, Robinson, Henry Venn, Newton and others appear to have been corpulent and even rubicund, and Romaine, the gravest and most sombre of them all, described with dignified humour how his pulpit grew smaller year by year until he could hardly get into it. This fashion was set, so to speak, by the comfortable proportions of John Thornton the Russia-merchant, admirably kept up by Isaac Milner and Sir Thomas Fowell Buxton, noted eaters and drinkers, and even lasted into the post-Wilberforce period in spite of the increasingly typical fleshly severity of such as the Reverend Carus Wilson. Sir Robert Harry Inglis, the last of the great Clapham Evangelicals, was the visible embodiment of good humour, cheerfulness and benevolence; Daniel O'Connell said he had the sleekest, fattest and happiest countenance he ever saw. Dickens's old Fezziwig himself, with his comfortable, oily, rich, fat, jovial voice, could well have been a fine Evangelical merchant if it had not been for the wicked dancing on Christmas Eve. Nothing could have been more essentially typical of Evangelical standing than to be a beamingly prosperous man of affairs.

II

The range of 'more immediate objects' of the moral, benevolent and religious societies existing, and most of them founded, during the early years of the century is remarkable, and not less so the great size and power reached by several of them, their manifest 'use' in enlisting men and women of good will and their equally manifest 'use' in achieving the basic Evangelical aim, pointed out by Mrs More so wisely and often, of bringing influential people to live of the gospel by proclaiming the gospel. Between 1787 and the establishment of the Young Men's Christian Association in 1844—with which the list that follows is arbitrarily ended—there came into existence what may soberly be described as a large number of moral institutions with a considerable range of stated objects. There were societies for publishing religious tracts and propagating Evangelical knowledge, and societies for suppressing irreligious tracts and obliterating un-Evangelical knowledge. There were societies for publishing religious tracts of particular churches, and homilies, and Prayer Books. There were societies for preventing the sale of indecent books and encouraging the sale of pious books, for getting seditious and atheistic literature out of the hands of hawkers and loyal literature into their hands. There were societies for preventing the sale of obscene objects and for encouraging the sale of clothing to the poor at reduced prices; for urging the poor not to eat white bread and teaching them to eat potato bread; for opening chapels and closing bawdy-houses, for protecting fighting dogs, bulls and bears (but not, as the Reverend Sydney Smith pointed out, for protecting the deer, the fox, the fish and the pheasant).

There were societies for putting down gin-mills and Sunday fairs and closing cook-shops on Sundays, for sending Bibles, homilies and Prayer Books everywhere and for keeping country girls at home. There were societies for educating infants, and adults, and juveniles, and orphans, and female orphans, and adult orphans, and nearly everybody else, either according to the formularies of the Established Church or not according to them but always according to some religious formularies. There were societies for the deaf and dumb, for the insane, for the blind, for the ruptured, for the scrofulous, for the club-footed, for the penitent syphilitic and for the impenitent syphilitic; for legitimate children and illegitimate children, for chimney sweepers' apprentices and against Tom Paine and Shelley; in aid of juvenile prostitutes and against juvenile mendicants; for distressed respectable widows, for poor pious clergymen in the country, for poor females in the maritime districts, for distressed foreigners, for small debtors, for prisoners, for female émigrées, for the deserving poor, for respectable married women and disreputable unmarried women, for sick people in hospitals and sick people out of hospitals, and for simple ordinary sick strangers.

There were societies for gentlewomen of good family, for penitent females, juvenile penitent females, and poor, deserted, friendless females; for orphan females and widowed females and young females the settlements of whose parents could not be found, and for infirm, and faithful, and respectable, and destitute, and forlorn, and degraded females. There were societies of friends of children, of labouring men, of animals, of aliens, of females, of aged pilgrims, of the poor, of the Hebrew Nation, of sick men, of orphan boys to be sent to sea, of peace; there were societies for the Irish Roman Catholics, young men in London, governesses, teachers and female servants; for the gypsies, for the Africans, for seamen and clergymen and the destitute and deserving relatives of seamen and clergymen; for Irish charity schools, for the West Indian Negroes, for sick travellers, for sick children, for the North American Indians; for the London Irish and the London Scottish, for the Jews, for fishermen, for ministers' daughters, for the Moravians, for the Continent, for the Irish poor and the Irish Sunday Schools and the Irish female peasantry and the Irish clergy; for the poor of Australia and the poor of Newfoundland and for poor destitute boys, for infant poor, for poor friendless deserted girls and for aborigines; there were societies against fire, and opium, and alcohol, and intemperance, and tobacco, and Sabbath-breaking, and accident, and shipwreck, and suspension of animation.

There were societies to improve, to enforce, to reform, to benefit, to prevent, to relieve, to educate, to reclaim, to encourage, to propagate, to maintain, to promote, to provide for, to support, to effect, to better, to instruct, to protect, to supersede, to employ, to civilize, to visit, to preserve, to convert, to mitigate, to abolish, to investigate, to publish, to aid, to extinguish. Above all there were societies to suppress.

The police magistrate and reformer Patrick Colquhoun lists as existing in London in 1795 (eliminating Friendly Societies, alms-houses, sickness benefit clubs and public companies making appropriations for charity) sixty-seven institutions devoted to public morals and benevolence, a large number of which were for the unfortunate of particular trades and professions and very few of which had local branches. Of all the societies whose date of establishment Colquhoun gives, only nineteen were founded in the last half of the eighteenth century and only five in the last quarter. The 'mushroom growth' came after the French Revolution when Wilberforce and his associates set to work. The list of moral and benevolent societies of the period that follows probably indicates that in London alone this activity could reasonably be described as having a mushroom growth. It probably includes all large or important societies of the Age of Wilberforce. It lists organizations founded before 1785 if they were active during the period, it omits all alms-houses and Friendly Societies, all small trade or professional societies of local activity, all auxiliaries, associations, ladies' auxiliaries or branches of any kind except for a few with specific functions such as the Merchant Seamen's Auxiliary Bible Society,[1] all small endowed institutions such as the French and Welsh Hospitals for decayed nationals, all merely local societies in the provinces,[2] and all societies that were exclusively or chiefly dissenting in control (although the Evangelicals contributed heavily to many of them such as the London Missionary Society). It lists first hospitals, dispensaries, infirmaries and other medical institutions, and second societies of a primarily religious, moral, educational or 'philanthropic' purpose. It is impossible to be exactly categorical here, as many of the medical institutions, where suffering could be labelled an 'afflictive dispensation', had explicit moral objectives.

I. HOSPITALS, INFIRMARIES, DISPENSARIES AND OTHER MEDICAL CHARITIES

1539   St Bartholomew's Hospital, for afflicted and diseased persons[3]
1553   St Thomas's Hospital, for the sick and lame, especially sailors
        Bethlem Hospital, for lunaticks
1719   Westminster Infirmary, for sick and diseased persons

[1] The inclusion of such branch societies would make this list into a volume. To add to the branches of the Bible Society, Church Missionary Society and Religious Tract Society those of the Jew Society, Prayer Book and Homily Society, Sunday School Society, Hibernian Bible Society and other Irish societies, the Book Society, the penitential, vagrancy, tract and other missionary societies, would be to amass a staggering and useless roll of reforming institutions.

[2] Of which there were probably many hundreds, such as:
The Southampton Society for the Reformation of the Gypsies (1829)
The Manchester Ladies Society, for Employing the Female Poor (1808)
The Plymouth Asylum for Penitent Prostitutes (1808)
The Lincoln Lying-in Charity (1805)
The Warwick Asylum for Juvenile Offenders (1822)
The Bath Penitentiary and Lock Hospital (1816)
The Ladies Association for the Benefit of Gentlewomen of Good Family, Reduced in Fortune Below the State of Comfort to Which They Have Been Accustomed (1815; founded by Lady Eleanor King, a friend of Mrs More's, near Bristol)
The Lincolnshire Medical Benevolent Society (1803)
The Bristol Penitentiary (1800)
The Chester Institution for the Instruction of Poor Girls (1816)
The Lincoln Dorcas Society (1816)
[3] The descriptions are Colquhoun's.

1721 Guy's Hospital, for sick and impotent persons, and lunaticks
1733 St George's Hospital, for the sick and lame
1740 London Hospital, for persons meeting with accidents
1745 Middlesex Hospital, for the sick and lame, and pregnant women
1746 The Lock Hospital, for persons afflicted with the venereal disease
     The Small-pox Hospital, for inoculation of poor persons
1749 The British Lying-in Hospital (Brownlow-street) for poor *married* women
1750 The City of London Lying-in Hospital, for poor *married* women
1751 St Luke's Hospital for lunatics
1752 The Bayswater General Hospital
     Queen Charlotte's Lying-in Hospital (Lisson Green)[1]
1757 The Lying-in Charity, for delivering pregnant women in their own homes
1765 The Westminster Lying-in Hospital
1767 The Lying-in Hospital (Tottenham Court-road), for poor pregnant women *generally*
1770 The Royal General Dispensary
1772 The Dispensary for Infant Poor
1774 The Hospital Misericordia, for venereal diseases
     The Westminster Dispensary (Gerrard-street)
     The Humane Society for the recovery of drowned and suffocated persons
1777 The London Dispensary (Primrose-street)
     The Surrey Dispensary (Borough)
1778 The General Lying-in Dispensary (Charlotte-street)
1779 The Metropolitan Dispensary
1781 The Finsbury Dispensary
1782 The Public Dispensary (Cary-street)
     The Eastern Dispensary (Whitechapel)
1784 The Society Known as the Sick Man's Friend
1785 The Mary-le-bone Dispensary (Wells-street)
1786 The New Finsbury Dispensary[2]
     The National Truss Society for the Relief of the Ruptured Poor
1787 The Benevolent Medical Society
1788 The City Dispensary Society[3]

[1] The existence of a 'Queen Charlotte's' hospital several years before there was a Queen Charlotte indicates the re-naming of an earlier institution.
[2] Probably a reorganization of the earlier society.
[3] Probably an auxiliary of an earlier institution.

1789 The Western Dispensary
1792 The Universal Medical Institution
      The Tower Hamlets Dispensary
      The Bayswater General Lying-in Hospital
1796 The Royal Infirmary for Sun Bathing
1799 [reorganization of] The Benevolent Medical Society
      The Vaccine Pock Institution
1800 The Society for Promoting Vaccine Inoculation
1801 The Bloomsbury Dispensary (Great Russell-street)
      The London House of Recovery (which became
1802 The Institution for the Cure and Prevention of Contagious Fever in the
      Metropolis and was later known as The London Fever Hospital)
1803 The Royal Jennerian Society
1804 The Royal Infirmary for Disorders of the Eyes
      The New Rupture Society
      The London Ophthalmic Infirmary (Finsbury)
1806 The London Vaccine Institution
1807 The City of London Truss Society
1810 The Northern Dispensary (Tavistock-square)
1812 The Chelsea, Brompton and Belgrave Dispensary
1814 The Infirmary for Asthma, Consumption and other Diseases of the
      Lungs
1815 The New Bethlem Hospital (St George's-fields)
1816 The Royal Universal Infirmary for Children
      The Royal Westminster Ophthalmic Hospital
      The Dispensary for Diseases of the Ear
1817 St George's and St James's General Dispensary
1818 The Charing Cross Hospital
1819 The London and Westminster Infirmary for the Treatment of
      Cutaneous Diseases
1820 The Metropolitan Infirmary for Sick Children
      The Royal Institution for the Cure of Diseases of the Poor
1821 The Seaman's Hospital Society
      The Islington Dispensary
      The South London Dispensary
1822 The Asylum for the Cure of Scrofulous and Cancerous Diseases
1824 The Queen Adelaide Lying-in Hospital[1]

[1] This is probably the institution that was reorganized in 1829. The existence of a
Queen Adelaide Hospital six years before there was a Queen Adelaide indicates the
re-naming of an earlier institution.

[*c.* 1824] The National Institution for the Preservation of Life from Shipwreck

1828 The Free Hospital for the Destitute Sick
      The Farringdon Dispensary (Bartlett's-buildings)

1829 The Queen Adelaide and British Ladies Lying-in Institution

1830 The Western City Dispensary[1]
      The Western General Dispensary[1]

1831 The Pimlico Dispensary
      [William Wilberforce died in 1833]

1834 The Metropolitan Infirmary for Diseases of the Eye and Ear
      The St Marylebone Provident Dispensary

1836 The Metropolitan Free Hospital

1837 The St Pancras General Dispensary

1838 The Paddington Provident Dispensary
      The Orthopaedic Institution or Infirmary for the Cure of Club Feet and other Contractions

1842 The Society for Improving the Condition of the Insane

Undated Institutions[2]

The Lying-in Hospital (Surrey-road)
The Lying-in Hospital (Bayswater Hall)
The Middlesex Dispensary (Great Ailiff-street)
St James's Dispensary (Berwick-street)
The Ossulton Dispensary (Bow-street)
Royal Universal Dispensary (Holborn)
The Parkinean Institution
The Charitable Fund and Dispensary (near Goldsmiths' Hall)
The London Infirmary for Disorders of the Eye
The London Electrical Dispensary
The Lying-in Institution (Little Night Rider-street)

II. RELIGIOUS, MORAL, EDUCATIONAL AND PHILANTHROPIC INSTITUTIONS AND SOCIETIES

1552 Christ's Hospital[3]
1553 The Bridewell Hospital for Dissolute Apprentices
1665 The Scots Corporation
1670 Chelsea Hospital, for worn-out and disabled soldiers

[1] Probably the same institution.
[2] Some of these may be duplicates of a dated institution.
[3] The 'hospitals' of this list are homes, asylums or refuges.

1678 The Sons of the Clergy
1694 The Greenwich Hospital, for worn-out and disabled sailors
1698 The Grey-Coat Hospital
1699 The Society for Promoting Christian Knowledge
1701 The Society for the Propagation of the Gospel in Foreign Parts
1702 The Ladies Charitable School of St Sepulchre
1709 St Anne's Society
1714 The Society of Ancient Britons
1739 The Foundling Hospital, for Deserted Infants
1747 The Society for the Relief of Sick and Maimed Seamen in the
        Merchants' Service
1749 The Society for Cloathing, Maintaining and Educating Poor Orphans
        of Clergymen
1750 The Book Society for Promoting Religious Knowledge Among the
        Poor
1756 The Marine Society, for Educating Poor Destitute Boys to the Sea
1758 The Magdalen Hospital for the Reception of Penitent Prostitutes
        (incorporated in 1769)
        The Asylum, for Poor, Friendless, Deserted Girls under Twelve Years
        of Age
1768 The Society for the Relief of Poor Widows and Children of Clergymen
1771 The Naval Charitable Society
1772 The Society for the Discharge and Relief of Persons Imprisoned for
        Small Debts
1776 The Society for Preventing Crimes by Prosecuting Swindlers, Sharpers,
        and Cheats
1780 The Naval and Military Bible Society
        The Society of Clergymen for the Education of Poor Pious Young
        Men for the Ministry in the Established Church
1784 The Benevolent Society of St Patrick
1785 The Society for the Support and Encouragement of Sunday Schools
        The Benevolent, or Strangers' Friend Society
1786 The Society of Universal Good Will
1787 The Lock Asylum for the Reception of Penitent Females
        The Society for the Abolition of the Slave Trade
1788 The Philanthropic Society Founded for the Prevention of Crime
        The Society for the Relief of Poor, Pious Clergymen, of the Estab-
        lished Church, Residing in the Country
        The Society for Carrying into Effect his Majesty's Proclamation
        Against Vice and Immorality

333

1790　The Incorporated Society for the Management and Distribution of the Literary Fund

1791　The Samaritan Society

1792　The British Society for the Encouragement of Servants
[*c.* 1792] The Society for Promoting Charity Schools in Ireland
The Asylum for the Support and Encouragement of the Deaf and Dumb Children of the Poor

1793　The Society for Religious Instruction to the Negroes in the West Indies
The United Society for the Relief of Widows and Children of Seamen, Soldiers, Marines, and Militiamen
The Society for the Relief of Poor Widows and Orphans of the Clergy

1794　The Society for Maintaining and Educating the Poor Orphans of the Clergy[1]

1795　[reorganization of] The Charity Schools of St Anne's Society
[*c.* 1795] The Society for Promoting the Knowledge of the Scriptures
The Charity for the Relief of Female Emigrants
[The London Missionary Society]

1796　The Society for Bettering the Condition and Increasing the Comforts of the Poor

1799　The Institution for the Relief of the Poor of the City of London and Parts Adjacent
The School for the Indigent Blind
The Church Missionary Society
The Religious Tract Society

1800　The Society for Promoting the Religious Instruction of Youth
The Society for the Relief of the Industrious Poor
The British National Endeavour for the Orphans of Soldiers and Sailors
The African Education Society
The Naval Asylum for the Support of the Orphans and Children of British Sailors and Marines
The Asylum or House of Refuge, for the Reception of Orphan Girls the Settlements of Whose Parents Cannot be Found

1801　[reorganization of] The Benevolent, or Strangers' Friend Society
The Institution for the Protection of Young Country Girls

1802　The Society for the Suppression of Vice
The Friendly Female Society, for the Relief of Poor, Infirm, Aged Widows, and Single Women, of Good Character, Who Have Seen Better Days

[1] Possibly duplicates the preceding entry.

1803   The Sunday School Union
        The Society for Superseding the Necessity of Climbing Boys
1804   The British and Foreign Bible Society
        The Ladies Society for the Education and Employment of the Female
            Poor
        The Refuge for the Destitute
1805   The African Institution
1806   The City of London School of Instruction and Industry
        The Society for Promoting the Civilization and Improvement of the
            North-American Indians
        [or earlier] The Charity for the Relief of Clergymen and the Widows
            and Children of Clergymen[1]
        The London Hibernian Society
1807   The Society of Friends of Foreigners in Distress
        The London Female Penitentiary (Pentonville)
        The Aged Pilgrim's Friend Society
1808   The British and Foreign School Society
        The London Society for Promoting Christianity Amongst the Jews
        The Society for the Diffusion of Knowledge upon the Punishment of
            Death, and the Improvement of Prison Discipline
        The Society for the Suppression of Juvenile Vagrancy
1809   [reorganization of] The Clergy Orphan Society
        The Society for Promoting the Observance of the Christian Sabbath
        The Christian Tract Society
1810   The London Peace Society
        The Society for Promoting the External Observance of the Lord's
            Day, and for the Suppression of Public Lewdness[1]
1811   The National Society for Promoting the Education of the Poor in the
            Principles of the Established Church
        The Benevolent Society for Visiting and Relieving Cases of Great
            Distress
        The Church of England Tract Society
1812   The Ladies Royal Benevolent Society
        The Prayer Book and Homily Society
        The Guardian Society, for the Preservation of Public Morals by Pro-
            viding Temporary Asylums for Prostitutes
        The Forlorn Female's Fund of Mercy
        The Hawkers' Tract Distribution Society
        The National Benevolent Institution[1]

                    [1] May be a duplication.

                            335

1812 The Society of Young Ladies to Sell Clothes at Reduced Prices

The London Society for the Encouragement of Faithful Female Servants

1813 The London Clerical Education Society

The City of London National Schools

The London Orphan Asylum, for the Reception and Education of Destitute Orphans, Particularly those Descended from Respectable Parents

The Caledonian Asylum

1814 The General Benevolent Institution for the Relief of Decayed Artists of the United Kingdom

The Irish Evangelical Society

1815 The Loan Society

The Downs Society of Fishermen's Friends

The New Caledonian Asylum (Islington)

The City of London Society for the Instruction of Adults

1816 The Society for the Promotion of Permanent and Universal Peace

The School for the Education of Ministers' Daughters

The Irish Society

The London Association for the Relief and Benefit of the Manufacturing and Labouring Poor

[c. 1816] The London Association in Aid of the Moravian Mission

The Juvenile Benevolent Society for Furnishing the Poor with Clothing

The Auxiliary Association of the London Female Penitentiary

1817 The British and Foreign Philanthropic Society

1818 The Merchant Seamen's Bible Society

The Society for the Suppression of Mendicity

The Society for the Improvement of Prison Discipline and for the Reformation of Juvenile Offenders

The Incorporated Society for Promoting the Enlargement, Building, and Repairing of Churches and Chapels (incorporated 1826)

The Protestant Union Society

The Provisional Protection Society for Females

The Continental Society

The Scripture Admonition Society

The Port of London Society for Promoting Religion Among British and Foreign Seamen

1819 The Association for the Refutation of Infidel Publications

The Houseless Poor Asylum
The Home Missionary Society
The British and Foreign Bethel Seamen's Union
1820 The Incorporated Society for the Conversion and Religious Instruction and Education of the Negro Slaves in the British West India Islands
The Adult Orphan Institution
The Religious Tract and Book Society for Ireland
The Cloathing Society for the Benefit of Poor Pious Clergymen of the Established Church and their Families
1821 The Westminster Asylum
The British Society of Ladies for Promoting the Reformation of Female Prisoners
[in Paris: La Société de la Morale Chrétienne]
1822 The Royal Asylum for Destitute Females
The Royal Female Philanthropic Society
The London Society for Educating Native Irish in their Own Tongue
The Irish Society for the Relief and Employment of the Poor of Ireland
The British and Irish Ladies Society for Improving the Condition and Promoting the Industry and Welfare of the Female Peasantry in Ireland
The Institution for the Cure of Various Diseases by Bandages and Compression
1823 The Gospel Tract Society
The British Newfoundland and North America Society for Educating the Poor
The Society for the Mitigation and Gradual Abolition of Slavery
The Society for the Relief of Distressed Widows
The Ladies Hibernian Female School Society
The Society for Educating Clergymen's Daughters
1824 The Village Sermon Society
The Society for the Prevention of Cruelty to Animals
The Infant School Society
1825 The School of Discipline
The Royal Union Association
The Invalid Asylum for Respectable Females
The House of Reform for Female Children
The Episcopal Floating Chapel

1825　The Society for Promoting Christian Instruction in London and its Vicinity

The British and Foreign Seamen's and Soldiers' Friend Society [which shortly had four subsidiary societies]

The Sea and River Tract Society

The Sailors' Home and Royal Brunswick Maritime Establishment

The Destitute Sailors' Asylum

The Sailors' Orphan Establishment

1826　The Philo-Judaean Society

The Philo-Judaean Ladies Association

1827　The British Society for Promoting the Religious Principles of the Reformation

The Society for the Investigation of Prophecy

The British Orphan Asylum (Kingsland; Clapham)

The Infant Orphan Asylum

1828　The General Society for Promoting District Visiting

The Continental Society, for the Diffusion of Religious Knowledge over the Continent of Europe

The Episcopal Floating Church Society

'A Real Society of Honest People'

1829　The Metropolitan Female Asylum

The Maritime Female Penitent Refuge, for Poor, Degraded, Females

The Friends of the Hebrew Nation

1830　The Children's Friend Society (a reorganization of The Society for the Suppression of Juvenile Vagrancy)

The British Open-Air Preaching Society

1831　The Association for Promoting Rational Humanity Towards the Animal Creation[1]

The Society for Promoting the Observance of the Lord's-Day[1]

The Labourers Friend Society

The Trinitarian Bible Society

The British and Foreign Temperance Society

1832　The Church Reformation Society

The Sacred Harmonic Society

The Animals' Friend Society[1]

The British and Foreign Sailors Society

1833　[or earlier] The Society for the Suppression of Sunday Trading

[or earlier] The Sunday School Society for Ireland

[or earlier] The Irish Scripture Readers' Society

[1] Not a duplication of any previously named society.

338

The London Christian Young Men's Society
[or earlier] The Infant School Teachers' Society
[William Wilberforce died in this year]

1834 The Established Church Society
1835 The Protestant Association
The Australian Church Missionary Society
The London City Mission
The Metropolitan Young Men's Society
The New British and Foreign Temperance Society[1]
The European Missionary Society
The London Society for the Protection of Young Females
1836 The Clergy Daughters School (St Mary's)
The London Female Mission
The Society for the Protection of Life from Fire
The Home and Colonial Infant School Society
The Church Pastoral Aid Society
1837 The Monthly Tract Society
The Town Missionary and Scripture Readers Society
The Aborigine Protection Society
The Clergy Aid Society
1838 The Rosse Institution for the Daughters of the Irish Clergy
1839 The Shipwrecked Fishermen and Mariners' Benevolent Society
The British and Foreign Anti-Slavery Society
1840 The Parker Society
[c. 1840] The Accident Relief Society
[c. 1840] The London Young Men's Church Missionary Society
The Foreign Aid Society
The Society for the Extinction of the Slave Trade and the Civilization of Africa
The Working Men's Religious Tract Society and Library
1841 The Governesses Benevolent Institution
1842 The Society for Irish Church Missions to Roman Catholics
[c. 1842] The Colonial Church and School Society
1843 The Society for Improving the Condition of the Labouring Classes
The Associate Institution for Improving and Enforcing the Laws for the Protection of Women
1844 The North London Church of England Young Men's Society for Aiding Missions at Home and Abroad
The Young Men's Christian Association

[1] Not a duplication of any previously named society.

Undated Institutions

The British Female Penitent Refuge[1]
The South London Penitentiary
The House of Occupation
The New Bridewell Hospital
The Millbank Penitentiary (Westminster)
The Royal Victoria Asylum
The London Society for the Prevention of Juvenile Prostitution
The London Society for Bettering the Condition of the Poor[1]
The Society for Returning Young Women to their Friends in the Country
The Friends of the Poor
The Society for the Reformation of Manners[1]
The Metropolitan Society
The Society for the Relief of Clergymen's Widows[1]
The Laudable Society for the Relief of Widows[1]
The Society for the Relief of Officers, their Widows, Children, Mothers, and Sisters
The London Maritime Institution
The Philological Society for Educating Orphan Boys[2]
The Hibernian Society for Promoting Schools in Ireland[3]
The Society for Educating the Children of Debtors
The Society for Reclaiming Prostitutes[1]
The Society for Propagating Christianity in the Highlands of Scotland
The Institution Association for the Relief of Destitute Seamen
The Trinitarian Society for Ireland
The Christian Instruction Society
The Female Mission
The Widows Friendly Society
The School of Reform
The Metropolitan Female Association
The Sabbath School for Ireland

[1] These entries are probably duplications.
[2] This oddly named society was more interested in boys than philology and was quite active.
[3] Probably one of the Irish societies already named.

Many of those societies, which ranged from the tiny and trivial to great size and usefulness, are still active, a few are now only a name mentioned in the periodical literature of the day or in the lists of institutions they worked with. The London Society for the Prevention of Juvenile Prostitution, the London Society for the Protection of Young Females, most unfortunately the Society for Returning Young Women to Their Friends in the Country, a few others of a moral nature and several of the medical societies seem to have no surviving records. The few odd reports, or the single report, left by a society occasionally give vital information such as a list of subscribers or the names of officers and committee. The larger societies and many of the smaller left voluminous records, with yearly reports listing their officers and entire membership (of a parent society), sometimes with elaborate and in several cases periodical literature, quarterly or monthly. They were not all Evangelical and their names are not a sure indication of their use for reform or lack of it. The Climbing Boy Society, for example, was one of the most useful. Its attempt to rescue chimney sweepers' apprentices from barbarous treatment attracted the heavy support of benevolent Christian people as well as infidels of good will, the circumstances of the climbing boys so far as their *best interests* were concerned being hardly different from the Africans'. The property involved here was trivial and in the hands of callous people of no influence or interest, and there was a clear religious issue. In the Climbing Boy Society the truly religious and the religious, led by Wilberforce, joined hands with liberals, radicals and philosophers, as a later Evangelical leader the Earl of Shaftesbury was still doing after fifty years to achieve the Society's stated aim.

The Royal Humane Society, which modestly restricted its helpful services to 'persons in a state of suspended animation', shows equally the Evangelical good will and the organized proportions that could be reached even in such a cause. This Society was compoundedly un-Evangelical. It had no moral or religious purpose and the objects of its bounty were not poor, not penitent and not cases of 'afflictive dispensation' but mere selections of pure chance. It had led, however, to the establishment of nearly fifty provincial societies in Britain by the time of Wilberforce's retirement, with others in foreign parts, and it received a decent Evangelical support. The vice-presidents in 1827 included Earl Brownlow, Earl Spencer, Lord Henniker, Philip Pusey, Mr Justice Park, Sir Richard Carr Glyn, Sir Charles Price, Robert and Charles Barclay and William Mellish, and John Blades and John Capel were on the committee. The Society was doubly distinguished by the support of Lord Eldon, not noted as a sacrificial giver, and the non-support of Wilberforce.[1]

The eight great Evangelical societies for what may be called for purposes of classification 'purely religious' objects were the following:

The Church Missionary Society (1799). First called The Society for Missions
   to Africa and the East
The Religious Tract Society (1799). Dissenting in origin
The British and Foreign Bible Society (1804)
The London Society for Promoting Christianity Amongst the Jews (1808)
   Dissenting in origin; the control acquired by the Evangelicals and member-
   ship restricted to churchmen in 1815
The Prayer Book and Homily Society (1812)
The British Newfoundland and North America Society for Educating the
   Poor (1823). Restricted to members of the Established Church
The General Society for Promoting District Visiting (1828)
The Church Pastoral Aid Society (1836)

Beyond those societies there were many that had Evangelical usefulness. Apart from the 'purely religious' societies there is no doubt about the Society for the Abolition of the Slave Trade and the many other Aboli-

---

[1] Persons in a state of suspended animation were sufferers from drowning, asphyxiation, lightning stroke or other mode of unconsciousness. *The Fifty-Third Annual Report of the Royal Humane Society, etc.* (1827), pp. 1, 2, 81–115. Evangelical subscribers included in addition the Duchess of Buccleuch, Lord Bexley, Sylvanus Bevan, the Earl of Crawford and Lindsay, Jesse Curling, Bishop Barrington, William Dealtry of Clapham, Henry Drummond, Sir Charles Flower, the Duke of Gloucester, Thomas Gisborne, the Earl of Harrowby, Sir Claudius Stephen Hunter, Benjamin Harrison of Clapham Common, the Earl of Leven and Melville, the Bishop of Lichfield and Coventry (Ryder), William Manning, Ebenezer Maitland of Clapham, Christopher Smith, Samuel Thornton, Admiral Sir John Orde, Lord Robert Seymour, Lady Olivia Sparrow, Sir James Shaw, Admiral Sir James Saumarez, George Scholey of Clapham, John Broadley Wilson of Clapham Common, Daniel Wilson and Matthew Wood. There were also the High Church Haldimands and Harmans and the Quaker Gurneys, Trittons and Overends.

tion societies, the Benevolent, or Strangers' Friend Society small as it was, the Refuge for the Destitute, the Magdalen Hospital, the Lock Hospital and Asylum, the Mendicity Society, the Naval and Military Bible Society, the Sunday School Society,[1] the Asylum, the Foundling Hospital, the Asylum for Deaf and Dumb Children of the Poor, the School for the Indigent Blind, the Marine Society, the Climbing Boy Society, the British and Foreign School Society, the Bettering and Philanthropic Societies and a good many others, particularly the later societies designed to rescue the Irish from Roman Catholicism, a project that became an Evangelical passion.

Enough of the literature of these associations is preserved to make it evident that all of them of any importance were controlled and directed by a few hundred people interested in reform or philanthropy and able to contribute heavily. It is not likely that the more resplendent names among the officers of several of the societies, even when they appear repeatedly, represented any genuine interest. In the Royal Jennerian Society for example there were one hundred and fifty-five officers of the rank of vice-president and above, with the entire royal family as patrons and patronesses. The Dukes of Kent and Sussex possibly had some kind of sincere interest in religious or benevolent causes, and that can be said too of the Duchess of Gloucester and Princess Sophia of Gloucester (two more objects of Mrs More's proselytizing activities). The Duke of Gloucester can be thought of as a kind of royal Evangelical. Nothing of the sort can be said of the Prince Regent or the Duke of York, whose names were given to many institutions, or of the Queen and the Duke of Cumberland, the first celebrated for thrift and the second (it was said) for vice. In the matter of such adornment the Society of Friends of Foreigners in Distress was still more impressive:

[1] On 6 May 1812 three thousand people attended the Fifth Anniversary of the Sunday School Society; many hundreds were unable to get in Freemasons' Hall, Lincoln's Inn Fields, the largest hall in England, including Lord Hardwicke and several members of parliament; Lord Teignmouth in the chair, supporting him Lord Calthorpe, Sir Thomas Baring, Lord Gambier, Charles Grant, the Chancellor of the Exchequer. In this year the president of the Society (controlled at first by dissenters) was Lord Barham, the thirteen vice-presidents included Baring, Grant, William Henry Hoare, John Maitland, Sir Thomas Plumer, Pusey, Thomas Raikes, Samuel Thornton, and Wilberforce, the treasurer was Henry Thornton. By 1812 the Society was helping to support 3370 schools with over 300,000 scholars.

its Protectors, Patrons and Patronesses included two reigning emperors, three kings, twenty-two princes, nine princesses, and the president of the United States, who were supported by some forty noble or respectable vice-presidents. The president himself of these two societies (in the 1820's) was probably not greatly interested in their work. He happened to be the Duke of Wellington, even less of an ardent philanthropist than Lord Eldon.

It was still necessary for any serious institution to have some earnest and responsible officers. In the Friends of Foreigners in Distress, after the long list of dignitaries mentioned, ending with John Quincy Adams, the list of vice-presidents includes the names of Earl Radnor, Lord de Dunstanville, Bishop Barrington, the Earl of Crawford and Lindsay, Lord Eardley, Lord Calthorpe, Lord Bexley, Lord Robert Seymour, Sir Thomas Plumer, Sir William Grant, Sir Thomas Dyke Acland, J. C. Villiers, Philip Pusey, William Manning, and Wilberforce. Even in a society such as this, the working officers included the Evangelical leader and more than a dozen of his chief Evangelical lieutenants. Those fifteen men held nearly five hundred memberships in moral societies and nearly half as many offices.

The names of the age that remain best known are not found playing a large part in this work. Its leading literary figures took next to no part at all. The names of Wordsworth, Coleridge, Keats, Shelley, Blake, Southey, Walter Scott, Hazlitt, Leigh Hunt, Godwin, Fanny Burney, Jane Austen, Mrs Inchbald, Thomas Holcroft, Moore and Landor do not occur in the surviving subscription lists. Shelley's father Sir Timothy Shelley gave a guinea a year to the Clergy Orphan Society, Southey's brother Herbert subscribed to the Middlesex Hospital, and Wordsworth's brother Dr Christopher Wordsworth to the Society for the Conversion and Religious Instruction of the West Indian Negroes. The single recorded subscriptions of Lord Byron, Maria Edgeworth and George Crabbe were to the British and Foreign School Society. J. P. Morier subscribed to the London Female Penitentiary, Captain Marryat to the Marine Society. Mrs Marcet, writer of school texts, subscribed to the British and Foreign School Society and the School for the Indigent Blind, Mrs Barbauld to the Refuge for the Destitute, Mrs Opie and Mrs Trimmer to the Society for Bettering the Condition of the Poor. Mrs Trimmer subscribed also to the Slavery Abolition

Society and the Society for the Suppression of Vice, and the Countess of Blessington to the Society for the Improvement of Prison Discipline.

Charles Lamb was a steward and vice-president of St Luke's Hospital for Lunaticks, the only literary figure of the age to hold office in any society, and John Lamb subscribed to the Seamen's Hospital Society. John Gifford subscribed to the Clergy Orphan Society and the Asylum, Henry Hallam to the Mendicity Society, Matthew Gregory Lewis to the Naval Charitable Society and the Lock Asylum; Robert Nares to the Clergy Orphan Society, Thomas James Mathias to the Bettering Society, the British and Foreign School Society and the Society for the Relief of Seamen. William Gifford subscribed to the Philanthropic Society and the Refuge for the Destitute, also supported by Samuel Rogers and Henry Crabb Robinson. There were occasional subscriptions by noted persons in other arts: George Dance to the Philanthropic Society, John Flaxman to the Refuge for the Destitute, Mrs Siddons to the Climbing Boy Society, and Mme Catalini to the Middlesex Hospital. Another distinguished person who subscribed to that hospital was the banker Henry Fauntleroy, who was distinguished by being the last person in England to be hanged for forgery.

With some mistakes, the support of the literary people was given to societies that had no apparent religious or moral reforming purpose. The philosophic radicals and utilitarians, the Benthamite and quondam-Godwinian groups, and the more liberal members of parliament, belonged to such societies only and as a rule to few of them. Francis Place and James Mill subscribed to the British and Foreign School Society only. Bentham also subscribed only to it unless he is the Jeremiah Bentham included in 1822 among the subscribers to the Peace Society, which was almost entirely Quaker. Francis Horner subscribed to the School Society and the Scots Corporation. Joseph Hume's name occurs from time to time in similar institutions. Robert Owen, Basil Montagu and Sir Samuel Romilly subscribed to several of the societies not avowedly connected with religious or moral reform. Sir James Mackintosh, once so reputed for political and philosophical abilities, subscribed though a poor man to as many societies, probably, as anyone not affiliated with a church party except David Ricardo, and Patrick Colquhoun and the Whig Earl of Dudley and Ward were in several societies. The genial and debauched Marquis of Hertford and his genial and debauched son and successor, one or the other the original of Thackeray's Lord Steyne, contributed steadily, as a rule to societies not religious or moral, though like the Regent, his brother York and some other noted performers in the amorous history of the age they seemed to feel a claim on them of the institutions caring for prostitutes, women with venereal disease, and seduced, pregnant or otherwise unhappy unmarried young women, whether from town or country. Sir Francis Burdett subscribed to seven societies, his father-in-law Thomas Coutts the banker to ten. Coutts was a vice-president, like Burdett, of the London Truss Society and a governor of the Magdalen Hospital. The leader of this group was the economist Ricardo, a wealthy stockbroker. He subscribed to fifteen societies, was on the committee of the British and Foreign School Society and a vice-president of the Asthma Infirmary.[1]

The British and Foreign School Society, established by the Quakers and conducted by the Quaker Joseph Lancaster on a basis of non-sectarian religious training, had the largest number of names still known: Byron, Romilly, Henry Grattan, Francis Horner, James Mill, Mackintosh, Ricardo, Bentham, Basil Montagu, Francis Place, John Thelwall, Maria Edgeworth, Robert Owen, Malthus, Mrs Marcet, Dr Butler, George Crabbe, Mathias, John Bowles, Thomas Bowdler, Spencer Perceval, Baden Powell, Dr Keate of Eton, John Gifford. It is easy to see why Wilberforce could not be persuaded to be an officer of this Society (but in any case he was not fond of dissent or of non-sectarian religious training). The Society for the Suppression of Mendicity ranks next with the following subscribers (the symbol '£' indicates 'only known subscription'): Colquhoun, Ricardo, George Canning, Henry Hallam, Basil Montagu, Sir George Beaumont (£), Burdett, Huskisson,

---

[1] Ricardo subscribed to the following societies:

The Mendicity Society	The Benevolent, or Strangers' Friend
The Diseased Artists' Society	Society
The Unitarian Society	The British and Foreign School Society
The Lying-in Charity	The Infirmary for Asthma and other
The Marine Society	Diseases of the Lungs
The London Hospital	The Society for the Improvement of
The Middlesex Hospital	Prison Discipline
The Refuge for the Destitute	The London Vaccine Infirmary
The London Orphan Society	The Christian Tract Society

Dr Maltby (Tomline's nephew, eventually Bishop of Durham), Thomas Bowdler, Lady Byron, Dudley and Ward, John Rickman (£), Lord Sidmouth, Benjamin and John Cam Hobhouse, Henry Holland, Lord John Russell. The Clergy Orphan Society had Lord Kenyon, Joshua Watson, Baden Powell, John Bowdler the Elder, John Gifford and Robert Nares (all leading High Churchmen), Lord Castlereagh, Lord Sidmouth, Lord Eldon, Lord Ellenborough, Hertford, Lord Henry Petty and the Reverend Thomas Tyrwhitt the editor of Chaucer.

Thomas Bowdler also subscribed to the Bettering Society and the Society for the Conversion of Negro Slaves in the West Indies, the Proclamation Society and the Vice Society; Sir Anthony Carlisle, Capel Lloft, Dr Parr, Maltby, Montagu, Robert Owen and Sir Richard Phillips to the Society for the Diffusion of Knowledge upon the Punishment of Death; Mackintosh, Brougham, and Thomas Babington Macaulay to the Slavery Abolition Society; John Galt (£) to the British and Foreign Philanthropic Society, the Reverend Archdeacon Paley (£) to the Bettering Society (Paley died early in the period); George Canning also to the Merchant Seamen's Auxiliary Bible Society, Lady Noel Byron also to the Westminster Asylum and the Children's Friend Society; Sheridan Knowles to the Society for the Protection of Life from Fire. John Horne Tooke subscribed to the Middlesex Hospital and the Asylum or House of Refuge, William Pitt (£) (who also died early in the period) to the London Hospital, the Marquis of Cornwallis to the Middlesex Hospital, Michael Faraday to the London Fever Hospital. Subscribers to the Magdalen Hospital for Penitent Prostitutes included the Duke of York, Lord Hertford and Lord Deerhurst, three celebrated impenitents, and the Ladies Charitable School of St Sepulchre had, somehow, the name of Sir John Lade, of Brighton, Bart., one of the least attractive of the hellfire rakes.

Such men as Burdett, Coutts, Romilly, Montagu and Ricardo had no part in the direction of these institutions generally or of more than one or two of them individually, were not as a rule heavy contributors or office-holders and have no claim to membership in the moral society directorate of the age. Their interest in the Society for the Diffusion of Knowledge upon the Punishment of Death, which they controlled, the Juvenile Delinquency Society and the Mendicity and Prison Discipline Societies is enough to show their concern for a social amelioration without larger usefulness. The slightest examination of such institutions makes clear their disqualification as agencies of national reform. The Committee for Investigating the Causes of the Alarming Increase of Juvenile Delinquency in the Metropolis was constituted in 1815 by a few individuals who investigated 'the cases of several boys, who had been convicted of capital offences'. Finding an 'alarming prevalence of organized juvenile delinquency', they got together a list of one hundred and ninety delinquent boys who were friends of inmates of Newgate Prison and later, from Newgate prisoners only, collected the names of seventeen hundred such boys. The committee came to the belief that probably some thousands of boys under seventeen were daily engaged in the commission of crimes and frequented houses 'of the most infamous description', associating with 'professed mature thieves, and with girls who lived by prostitution'. The causes of that condition were the improper conduct of parents, want of education, want of suitable employment, violation of the Sabbath and habits of gambling in the public streets. So far there is at least some kind of connection with the evil heart of man, but the Committee's Report goes on to find powerful 'auxiliary causes': the defective state of the police, the existing system of prison discipline and the severity of the criminal code. Their programme included education, the enforcement of laws prohibiting gambling on the streets and on Sundays, abolition of the system of rewards for the capture of criminals, which led officers of the law to overlook petty offenders and encourage thieves' haunts ('flash houses'), and above all the reform of the criminal code 'which inflicts the punishment of death on upwards of 200 offences'.[1]

The conductors of this Society are well removed from 'serious', 'truly religious' interests, methods and policies, and even their object, as implemented, was not one that Wilberforce and his associates could be Evangelically interested in. With the exception of the Sabbath violation—and that objected to on a wrong basis—there was nothing of value here for national reform and much that Evangelicalism could not afford to take part in. The directors of this Society had not learned that the great source of evil is infidelity. Not only did their institution fail to strike at the root of the matter; its support could jeopardize the

[1] *Report of the Committee for Investigating the Causes of the Alarming Increase of Juvenile Delinquency in the Metropolis* (London, 1816), p. 21.

enlistment of the great in reform. The suspicion of liberalism could not be incurred for the sake of bettering the worldly condition of a few thousand delinquent boys. Of the same nature was the Society for the Diffusion of Knowledge upon the Punishment of Death, and the Improvement of Prison Discipline, established in 1808, which also attracted many of the liberals and few of the Evangelicals. The fact that these two societies had no officers and got along without the support of the great is in itself an indication of slight 'usefulness'. Such causes could be supported at all, by thoughtful Evangelicals, only if they were strongly enlisting the great, or perhaps as a courteous co-operation with people who were helping with Abolition. They were dominated by men of mere worldly enlightenment—Basil Montagu, James Mill and David Ricardo.[1]

In the Society for the Discharge and Relief of Persons Imprisoned for Small Debts we have an example of an institution in which an originally marked Evangelical interest became perfunctory as it failed to meet rigorous standards of value. It was established in 1772 with the Earl of Romney as president and John Thornton as a vice-president. This Earl of Romney was a truly religious man, and as late as 1799 the vice-presidents all told were Philip Pusey, Earl Radnor, Sir Charles Middleton and the Marquis of Hertford. Beyond that strong sign of Party approval the Small Debts Society was approvingly mentioned by Hannah More in one of her most esteemed works and in the early days it had the names of many who took place beside Wilberforce in the societies of the Nineties. Mrs Bouverie and Mrs Boscawen were members, Lord Bulkeley and Lord Balgony, Lord de Dunstanville and Lord Eardley, Lady Charlotte Finch and Lady Mary Fitzgerald, the Earl of Hardwicke, Henry Hoare, Plumer, Pepperell, Pepys, Lord Sondes and Lord Suffield, Samuel, Henry and Robert Thornton, Miss Vansittart, Lord Willoughby de Broke, and Wilberforce himself. By 1808 a few more Evangelical names appear: Bootle, Cremorne, Admiral Colpoys, Benjamin Harrison, Lord Gambier, Morton Pitt, Lord Rolle, Admiral Saumarez, the Earl of Stamford and Warrington, a lone Evangelical clergyman the Reverend Sir Harry Trelawney, and Cowper's friend Mrs Unwin.

[1] *An Account of the Origin and Object of the Society for the Diffusion of Knowledge upon the Punishment of Death, and the Improvement of Prison Discipline* (London, 1812).

The Small Debts Society had discharged and relieved over twenty-four thousand debtors, by 1808—with their families, over seventy-nine thousand persons—at a cost of £66,000. Many of those rescued 'appeared to be worthy and useful members of society'; some 'were confined for their *fees* only'. This was a genuinely philanthropic institution, its object both good-hearted and sensible; and the names of its subscribers cited above are those of firm, active Evangelicals. But at best this institution had no real claim on anyone except in so far as he was interested in helping the distressed. As a service done in the Lord's name *by the way*, it deserved a decent Evangelical support and got it; but it remained a mere amelioration, attacking second causes, going to the root of no evil. In 1808 the president was a later Earl of Romney, no Evangelical, and the Society's moving spirit James Neild was palpably not an Evangelical but a mere philanthropist who devoted his life to this cause. The originators of the Society besides Neild were an Orthodox clergyman and a Quaker physician, and its literature, while not without religious reference, to Heaven and the blessings of Providence, spoke the language of mere nominal Christianity. Worse still, the successive reports of Neild, an able man who visited nearly all the prisons of the kingdom, strongly condemned their operating conditions, all current systems of prison management and the laws of civil imprisonment. This was the kind of society that should have been supported by such a good-hearted, non-serious man as the Reverend Sydney Smith, as it was. In its lists of legators there is no known Evangelical name.[1]

[1] *An Account of the Rise, Progress and Present State of the Society for the Discharge and Relief of Persons Imprisoned for Small Debts* (London, 1799, 1808, etc.). This Society served to illustrate one of Hannah More's most interesting theological beliefs, in the matter of the Problem of Evil—a doctrinal view that possibly makes the Evangelical Reformation the final cause of African slavery. Good Mr Trueman, who is a subscriber to the Society, has helped to rescue Tom Saunders, a very honest brother tradesman. 'Suppose now, Tom Saunders had not been put in prison, you and I could not have shown our kindness in getting him out; nor would poor Saunders himself have had an opportunity of exercising his own patience and submission under want and imprisonment. So you see one reason why God permits misery, is, that good men may have an opportunity of lessening it.' *Stories 1818* ('History of Mr Fantom'), vol. 1, p. 53.

IV

The large, active and substantial body of supporters whose names appear in society after society, including those directly concerned (in varying ways) with the evil heart of man—in the lists of legators, life members, governors, committees and officers—can be divided into four groups: the Quakers, other dissenters, Orthodox churchmen, and the Evangelicals.

So many of the Society of Friends became Evangelical members of the church during this period that categorical certainty about their religious adherence is not always easy to arrive at; but in any case so many known Quakers were outstanding society supporters that their great reforming strength is unquestionable. One noticeable weakness is indicated by the fact that the two prominent Evangelicals on the Juvenile Delinquency Committee were Samuel Hoare jun. and Thomas Fowell Buxton, and the four in the Prison Discipline Society were Hoare, Buxton, and Charles and Robert Barclay—all of Quaker origin and all still tinged with the addiction to useless philanthropy that the sect was susceptible to. Even in such a matter as Abolition it is likely that their motive cannot be thought of as having the purity of Wilberforce's. Still, the record is clear. In the work of the societies they were second only to the Evangelicals. Their leader was the chemical manufacturer William Allen of Plough-court; other leading figures were Joseph Fox, Robert Alsop, Joseph John Gurney, Robert and Josiah Forster, Samuel Gurney, Samuel Gurney jun., Samuel Hoare of Stoke Newington, Samuel Hoare the Elder of Hampstead, and the Frys, Rowntrees, Cadburys, Trittons and Overends. Sir Thomas Fowell Buxton's sister-in-law Elizabeth Fry remains the best known of the Quaker reformers, but there were few societies of the day to which dissenters were admitted that were not heavily supported by their wealthy members in trade, finance and industry.

Apart from them there were twenty or so dissenters of various sects who took a greater part in the work of the societies than any non-religious supporters and all but a handful of High Churchmen. They were London merchants, manufacturers, brokers, importers or financiers. The chief were:

Joseph Butterworth, M.P., of 43 Fleet Street. A Methodist. He was a law bookseller and publisher. He subscribed to 29 societies, was vice-president

351

of five, treasurer of one, governor of four and on the committee of two. This is the leading Methodist layman.

Thomas Wilson, of Highbury. An Independent. He appears to have been the treasurer and a chief supporter of the dissenters' college at Hackney, was a silk-manufacturer and probably related to William Wilson, silk-manufacturer of Milk-street, Cheapside, and so to the Reverend Daniel Wilson. 24 societies, vice-president 4, treasurer 1, governor 2, committee 2.

Benjamin Shaw, M.P. A Baptist. He was a director of the Union (Insurance) Society and of various mining and railway companies. 28 societies, vice-president 2, treasurer 1, governor 4, committee 1.

Joseph Reyner, of Old Swan-stairs, London-bridge. A Baptist. A cotton importer and shipper. 19 societies, treasurer 1, governor 2, committee 4.

Thomas Breme Oldfield, of Jamaica Coffee-house. Ship owner. 18 societies, governor 1, committee 2. There seems a possibility that this man was a Churchman, in which case he was Evangelical.

Joseph Hardcastle, of Old Swan-stairs. A Methodist, business partner of Reyner. 17 societies, governor 6, committee 1.

Joseph Stonard. A deputy chairman of the Union Society. 17 societies, governor 2, committee 2.

James Meyer. A Roman Catholic. 14 societies, vice-president 1, governor 2.[1]

The contributions of this group were steady and substantial.

The third group supporting and directing these societies is the High Church party. Lord Kenyon, the first of two leaders in this work, son of the Lord Chief Justice noted for his severity in cases of fashionable adultery, may be described in a greatly flattering way as the Wilberforce of the group. He was president and treasurer of the Infant Orphan Asylum, a governor of the Magdalen Hospital, vice-president of the Clergy Orphan Society, the Children's Friend Society, the Labourers' Friend Society and St Luke's Asylum, subscribing in all to a dozen societies. His contributions except to the Clergy Orphans were

[1] These figures of memberships and offices are offered as meaningful and accurate enough to give a correct comparative idea of the extent of interest in the societies of the people listed. Some of the records preserved in the Reading Room of the British Museum are incomplete, some fragmentary, some consist of a single report. To compile accurate figures if possible at all would be a labour out of proportion to any use. These figures indicate that in the course of the whole period the name of Joseph Butterworth, identified as M.P. or of 43 Fleet-street, is found in the lists of twenty-nine different societies and as a holder of the offices named, and so with the others.

moderate. The lay leader of the so-called 'Clapton Sect' and generally with Kenyon of the Orthodox Party, the retired wine-merchant Joshua Watson, was treasurer of the Clergy Orphan Society, a governor of the London Fever Hospital and subscribed in all to fourteen societies. Neither of the two took part in Evangelical or Evangelically dominated institutions. The High Church bankers Sikes were in several of the non-Evangelical societies and medical institutions but do not appear to have held office. Their support was slight in comparison with that of any one of scores of Evangelical financiers. The leading men of affairs in the High Church connection were Joseph Cotton, Beeston Long, Jeremiah Harman, William Haldimand and Samuel Bosanquet, industrialists, company directors and philanthropic capitalists, apparently of considerable wealth. Their names are not found in the Evangelical society lists. Their support of the institutions they patronized, and comparatively (as there were many fewer societies they could patronize) the number of their institutions, were equal to all but the highest circle of the Evangelicals.

The fourth group is the Evangelical Party. The following list is restricted to those whose names are found as subscribers to more than fifteen societies. A few names put in square brackets are doubtful and possibly should be listed as associates in the holy war rather than Evangelicals. These subscribers are included in each case because of their continued support of societies that did not admit dissenters to membership and were openly attacked by High Church, such as the Church Missionary Society and the London Jew Society; or, if their support was given to institutions admitting dissenters, when there is evidence that they were Churchmen and not supporters of exclusively High Church societies.[1]

---

[1] In some cases categorical certainty is perhaps impossible. The Earl of Egremont, for example, described by Arthur Young as not 'religious', may be taken as indicating that the merest citizen of the Gentile world could be a heavy supporter of societies that were thoroughly Evangelical in aim and operation. It seems likely that he was as much Evangelical as High Church, which is probably to say neither. The case of Philip Pusey may even be evidence that a (very unusual) High Churchman could support societies spectacularly opposed by High Church generally. Lady Emily Pusey his wife was Evangelical and their son Edward Bouverie Pusey was brought up 'with strong Evangelical impressions'. Pusey himself is described as a High Churchman. If so he was an extraordinary associate in the holy war, subscribing to forty-nine societies and

The Earl of Stamford and Warrington. 17 societies, patron 1, president 1, vice-president 2, governor (or life member, and so through the list) 3.

The Earl of Winchilsea. 17 societies, president 1, vice-president 4, committee 2, governor 2.

H. G. Key. 17 societies, committee 4, governor 1. Alderman.

William Marriott, of Hoxton-square. 18 societies, treasurer 1, committee 1, governor 2.

[Lord Arden. 18 societies, vice-president 2, governor 4.]

Admiral Lord Radstock. 18 societies, president 1, vice-president 4, committee 2, governor 3.

Henry Curwen Christian. 19 societies, vice-president 3, committee 4, governor 1. Banker, company director.

John Hatchard, of Clapham Common. 19 societies, vice-president 1, committee 2. Publisher.

[Sir John W. Lubbock. 19 societies, vice-president 2, committee 2, governor 5. Banker, company director.]

Earl Spencer. 19 societies, patron 1, vice-president 8, governor 2, committee 1.

W. Thornton Astell, M.P., of Clapham Common. 19 societies, president 1, vice-president 2, treasurer 1, committee 5. Banker and company director.

Earl of Darnley. 19 societies, president 3, vice-president 7, governor 2.

Samuel Mills. 20 societies, committee 2, governor 6.

Sir James Shaw, Bart., M.P. 20 societies, president 1, vice-president 9, governor 6, committee 1. Alderman, Lord Mayor, company director.[1]

The Hon. Bartholomew Bouverie, M.P. 20 societies, vice-president 2, governor 4.

Thomas Babington, M.P. 20 societies, vice-president 11.

The Reverend Thomas Gisborne. 20 societies, vice-president 1, committee 1, governor 6.

Earl Henley. 20 societies, patron 2, vice-president 11, governor 2.

W. T. Money, M.P. 20 societies, vice-president 9, patron 1, committee 2.

Admiral Lord Saumarez. 20 societies, president 3, vice-president 9, patron 2.

Alexander Riddell. 21 societies, committee 1, governor 6. London merchant.

holding a total of twenty-one offices, in several societies definitely Evangelical and others clearly controlled by the Evangelicals. There is a possibility of confusion too in the case of dissenters, particularly those who attended Evangelical clergymen. Societies that 'did not admit' dissenters were sometimes not above accepting their money. Joseph Butterworth was a subscriber to the Newfoundland Society. (The Evangelicals subscribed heavily to the London Missionary Society and other dissenting societies.)

[1] A vice-president of the Bible Society, City of London Auxiliary, 1812; not a dissenter.

[Sir Matthew Wood. 21 societies, vice-president 10, governor 3. Alderman, Lord Mayor.][1]

Benjamin Harrison, of Clapham Common. 21 societies, vice-president 2, governor 6, committee 2. Treasurer and 'czar' of Guy's Hospital.

George Wolff, of America-square and Balham Hill (near Clapham). 22 societies, vice-president 1, governor 3, committee 1. The Danish consul-general (Hole); attended Clapham Church.

Lord Barham. 22 societies, president 1, patron 1, vice-president 4, committee 1, governor 3. First Lord of the Admiralty. This is Sir Charles Middleton, father-in-law of the succeeding Lord Barham.

John Bacon the Younger. 22 societies, vice-president 3, governor 6.

Earl Hardwicke. 22 societies, patron 2, vice-president 11, governor 2.

Lt.-Gen. Lord Lorton. 22 societies, president 3, patron 2, vice-president 10.

John Mortlock. 22 societies, committee 6, treasurer 1, governor 2. London merchant.

Joseph Wilson, of Clapham. 22 societies, president 1, committee 5, governor 6.

Marquis of Cholmondeley. 23 societies, president 4, patron 2, vice-president 8.

Zachary Macaulay, of Clapham Common. 23 societies, committee 9.

Lord Barham. 24 societies, president 1, vice-president 11. Brother of the Reverend Baptist Noel and the Reverend Gerard T. Noel.

Sir Charles Flower. 24 societies, vice-president 9, governor 5. Alderman, company director.

John P. Anderdon. 24 societies, governor 2. Merchant and company director.

Earl of Crawford and Lindsay. 24 societies, patron 1, vice-president 4, committee 1, governor 3. 'Charles Crawford, then claiming those titles...' (Hole).

Earl Grosvenor. 24 societies, patron 2, president 4, vice-president 10.

Sir Thomas Plumer. 24 societies, vice-president 6, committee 1, governor 5. Master of the Rolls.

Sir George Rose. 24 societies, vice-president 10, committee 2, governor 2. Ambassador to Berlin.

Lord Teignmouth, of Clapham Common. 24 societies, patron 4, president 1, vice-president 4, committee 1. Retired Governor-General of India.

Thomas Bainbridge, of Clapham. 24 societies, treasurer 1, committee 3, governor 8. London banker.

Henry Piper Sperling. 24 societies, vice-president 1, treasurer 1, committee 1, governor 3. Insurance company director.

[1] He continued membership in the London Jew Society after 1815 when it did not admit dissenters.

[Henry Drummond. 25 societies, vice-president 3, treasurer 2, governor 2. Banker.]

Earl of Harrowby. 25 societies, patron 1, president 1, vice-president 9, governor 2. Lord President of the Council.

William Morton Pitt, M.P. 25 societies, vice-president 2, committee 5, governor 4. Financier, cousin of William Pitt.

Earl Radnor. 26 societies, president 4, vice-president 4, committee 1.

Samuel Whitbread, M.P. 26 societies, vice-president 4, committee 2, governor 6.

Sir Thomas Bernard. 26 societies, vice-president 7, committee 2, governor 4. Retired conveyancer.

Sir Claudius Stephen Hunter. 27 societies, vice-president 9, governor 5, committee 1. Alderman, Lord Mayor, financier.

Earl of Clarendon (J. C. Villiers). 27 societies, patron 1, vice-president 6, governor 5, committee 2.

Jesse Curling. 27 societies, president 1, vice-president 1, governor 5, committee 2.

[Earl of Liverpool. Not an Evangelical, Lord Liverpool, no doubt because of his position and perhaps with some genuine good-heartedness, was a powerful associate in the holy war, even taking part in the work of the Bible Society. 28 societies, president 2, patron 3, vice-president 19, governor 2, committee 2.]

John Capel, M.P. 29 societies, president 2, vice-president 6, governor 7, committee 2. Broker.

Sir Thomas Dyke Acland, M.P. 29 societies, president 2, vice-president 11, governor 4.

[Earl of Egremont. 29 societies, president 1, vice-president 5, governor 5, committee 1. It is not likely that he was more than an associate.]

John Deacon, of Clapham Common. 30 societies, treasurer 8, governor 6. Banker.

John Labouchere, of Clapham Common. 30 societies, president 1, patron 1, vice-president 2, treasurer 8, governor 3, committee 3. Banker.

The Duke of Gloucester. 31 societies, president 3, patron 14, vice-president 3. This is Silly Billy.

Sir William Weller Pepys. 31 societies, vice-president 2, committee 1, governor 4. This is the Evangelical barrister who helped Mrs More with *Village Politics*.

John Blades, of 5 Ludgate-hill. 31 societies, vice-president 2, governor 11, committee 2. Merchant.

Lord Eardley. 32 societies, vice-president 5, committee 1, governor 7.

John Julius Angerstein. 32 societies, president 1, vice-president 6, governor 4.

William Mellish. 33 societies, president 2, vice-president 13, governor 3. Banker, company director.

Alexander Gordon. 33 societies, vice-president 2, treasurer 2, committee 1, governor 8. Merchant.

Thomas Roberts, Charterhouse-square. 33 societies, committee 1, governor 10.

Thomas Hankey, of Clapham. 34 societies, treasurer 1, committee 1, governor 9. Banker.

Sir Robert Harry Inglis, M.P., of Clapham Common; Sir Hugh Inglis. Over 30 societies, president 2, vice-president 9, treasurer 1, governor 1, committee 2.

Sir Thomas Fowell Buxton, M.P. 35 societies, president 1, vice-president 6, treasurer 2, committee 5.

John Broadley Wilson, of Clapham. 36 societies, vice-president 1, committee 3, governor 10.

Sir Robert Wigram, M.P. With his family, 69 subscriptions; he was a vice-president of 4 societies, committee 1, governor 12. Banker and company director.

Admiral Lord Gambier. 39 societies, president 3, patron 3, vice-president 11, governor 3, committee 2.

William Manning. 40 societies, vice-president 10, governor 9, committee 3. Banker. Father of Cardinal Manning.

Charles and Robert Barclay. 86 subscriptions; president 1, vice-president 12, committee 13. Brewers.

Sir Thomas Baring. 47 societies, president 1, vice-president 22, committee 4, governor 6.

Lord Calthorpe. 46 societies, president 3, patron 1, vice-president 24, governor 4.

The Bishop of Durham. 47 societies, president 5, patron 2, vice-president 12, governor 6.

Lord Bexley (Vansittart). 47 societies, president 2, vice-president 23, patron 2, committee 2.

William Wilberforce. 69 societies, patron 1, vice-president 29, treasurer 1, governor 5, committee 5.

From three leading Evangelical families:

Charles Grant, Charles Grant jun. (Lord Glenelg) and Robert Grant. 51 subscriptions, president 1, vice-president 14, governors 7, committee 3.
Henry Hoare of Mitcham, Henry Merrick Hoare, Charles Hoare, Henry

Hugh Hoare; Samuel Hoare, Samuel Hoare jun. 220 subscriptions; vice-president 12, treasurer 8, governor 31, committee 13.

Henry, Samuel, Robert and John Thornton (the Younger). 173 subscriptions; president 2, vice-president 20, treasurer 14, governor 40, committee 9.

From the Evangelical ladies:

Duchess of Buccleuch. 23 societies, president 4, patroness 4, governor 3.

Duchess of Beaufort. 23 societies, president 6, patroness 2.

Lady Calthorpe. 16 societies, president 1, patroness 2.

Duchess of Gloucester. 14 societies, patroness 8.

Dowager Countess Harcourt. 19 societies, president 2, patroness 1, governor 3, committee 1.

Duchess of Leeds. 13 societies, president 2, committee 1.

[Duchess of Kent. 18 societies, patroness 15, governor 2.]

Mrs Vansittart. 22 societies, governor 2.

Lady Olivia Bernard Sparrow. 29 societies, president 1, patroness 2, vice-president 2, governor 4.

Miss Sophia Vansittart. 33 societies, patroness 2, vice-president 3, governor 7, committee 1.

That record of activity in the societies, which far exceeds any other group's and does not include any of the thousands upon thousands of auxiliaries, associations and other branch societies, still leaves out the names of many powerful Evangelical workers in the field. The Reverend Lewis Way was virtually in control of the London Society for Promoting Christianity amongst the Jews, as Benjamin Harrison was of Guy's Hospital and Sir Thomas Bernard was of the Bettering Society and the Foundling Hospital. No comprehensive account would omit (for instance) Lord Bulkeley, Earl Brownlow, the Earl of Bristol, Lord Willoughby de Broke, Alderman John Bridges, Dr Charles Parr Burney, Charles Elliott of Clapham Common, Lord Farnham, Lord de Dunstanville, Lord Dynevor, Sir George Grey and Hudson Gurney, M.P., who made altogether 169 subscriptions, include three presidents of societies and held 59 other offices. A total of 336 subscriptions are recorded for the Earl of Rocksavage, the Earl of Roden, Lord Rolle, Lord Robert Seymour, Alderman George Scholey of Clapham, James Stephen, the Hon. George Vernon, John Wells, M.P., Edward Bootle Wilbraham, Randle Wilbraham, John Whitmore, Thomas Allan,

Alexander Black, Sir Richard Hill, Lord Henniker. the Earl of Lilford, Admiral Viscount Exmouth, Sir James Graham, the Earl of Gosford, Henry Goulburn, M.P., Sir Digby Mackworth, Ebenezer and John Maitland of Clapham, Sir Oswald Mosley, Sir Evan Nepean, Admiral Earl Nugent, Edward Parry of Clapham Common, John Pearson of Golden-square and Sir Robert Peel. Of that group Rocksavage, Scholey, Vernon, Exmouth, Peel and Mosley were presidents (or joint-presidents) of seven societies. The group held 154 additional offices.

Beyond them should be mentioned the Earl of Chichester (president of the Home and Colonial School Society), the Earl of Galloway, Viscount Galway, John Gladstone, Lord Mandeville, the Earl of Mount-norris, the Earl of Mount Sandford, General Macaulay, General Neville, General Calvert, Admiral Sir John Orde, Sir William Pepperell, George Agar Ellis, M.P., Captain Edward Pelham Brenton, R.N. (president of the Maritime Female Penitent Refuge, for Poor, Degraded Females; succeeded on his death by his brother Admiral Sir Jahleel Brenton, R.N.), Abel Smith, M.P., of Clapham, Admiral Earl Torrington, Granville Sharp, William Wilson, Carus Wilson, Daniel Wilson; and among the Evangelical women Countess Carysfort, the Marchioness of Chol-mondeley, Countess Darnley, the Countess of Dartmouth, Lady Mary Fitzgerald, Lady Galway, Lady Farnham, the Duchess of Gordon, the Countess of Leven and Melville, Lady Mandeville later Duchess of Manchester, Dowager Countess Manvers, Countess Rosse, the Countess of Southampton, Lady Sherborne, Lady Macartney, Lady Eleanor King.

There remains a considerable number of Evangelical Londoners, all apparently men of business or finance, not so substantial as the Grants, Hoares, Thorntons, Manning, Angerstein and the like, who served steadily, with substantial contributions, in smaller capacities, usually on the committee of society after society: Samuel Luck Kent, Edward, Henry and Thomas Kemble, J. G. Lockett, William Pearson, John and Thomas Poynder of Clapham, Samuel, Francis and John Paynter, Samuel Robinson, W. W. Terrington, William Jenney and others.

Other Evangelical presidents (or joint-presidents) of societies:

Earl Radnor: Magdalen Hospital, Friends of Foreigners.
Bishop Barrington: School for the Indigent Blind, Society for Bettering the Condition of the Poor, Climbing Boy Society.

Duke of Gloucester: (includes office of patron) Society for Bettering the Condition of the Poor, Society for the Gradual Abolition of Slavery, Tropical Free Labour Company, African Institution, London Hospital.

Duchess of Leeds: London Orphan Asylum, Infant Orphan Asylum.

Duchess of Beaufort: Infant Orphan Asylum, British and Irish Ladies Society, City of London Ladies Association of the Newfoundland Society.

Marquis of Cholmondeley: Society for the Relief of Distressed Widows, Friendly Female Society, Naval and Military Bible Society, General District Visiting Society, Society for the Protection of Life from Fire, Vaccine Pock Society.

Lord Radstock: Naval Charitable Society.

Lord Barham: London Jew Society.

Sir Thomas Baring: London Jew Society.

Lord Barham (the Younger): Sunday School Society.

Earl of Dartmouth: The Lock Asylum, Society for the Suppression of Vice.

Lord Gambier: Church Missionary Society, Downs Society of Fishermen's Friends.

Lt.-Gen. Lord Lorton: Religious Tract and Book Society for Ireland.

Lady Olivia Sparrow: Westminster Asylum.

Sir Thomas Dyke Acland: The Royal Union Association.

Lord Calthorpe: Infant Orphan Asylum.

Earl Grosvenor: Children's Friend Society.

Sir Thomas Fowell Buxton: Aborigines Protection Society.

Lord Darnley: Infirmary for Asthma and Consumption.

Lord Bexley: London Orphan Asylum, British and Foreign Bible Society.

[Earl of Egremont: Royal Jennerian Society.]

Sir Robert Harry Inglis: National Truss Society.

William Mellish: London Infirmary for Diseases of the Eye.

Lord Teignmouth: British and Foreign Bible Society.

Earl Henley: Infant Orphan Asylum.

John Capel: City of London Auxiliary Schools.

Sir James Shaw: St Bartholomew's Hospital.

Even more than the unbelievably huge written propaganda of the Evangelicals and their penetration into the upper classes and the church —two vital factors of their Reformation that have had to be omitted almost entirely from this study—the immense 'usefulness' of the Evangelical societies is impossible to describe in a few pages.

PART III
ENGLAND IN DANGER

CHAPTER 10

SABLE SUBJECTS,
SOULS IN DARKNESS

It is the dread of the predominance of this faction, who are making rapid strides toward ascendancy in the state, that renders it an imperious duty to open the eyes of the public to their real motives and views, as developed by their actions.

The Anti-Jacobin Review, 1816

Pride, Satan's grand instrument. PATTY MORE

I

The old cry 'The Church in Danger' became 'England in Danger' early in the new century. While the anti-fanatic pamphlets, articles, reviews, letters, clerical lectures and bishops' or archdeacons' charges came out, in large numbers, with new attacks on the Bible, Religious Tract, Church Missionary and Vice Societies, on the prostitution and penitential societies, on the abolition of slavery, the missionaries and the prodigious Evangelical activity for benighted foreigners, a compounded case against the Evangelicals was repeatedly stated by the Reverend Sydney Smith, whose request to Wilberforce in 1807 to take up the cause of the oppressed Irish now he had done with the Negroes showed such an ingenuous misunderstanding of the Evangelical purpose. Smith perhaps stood for the utmost opposition to the truly religious character that an intelligent and virtuous clergyman could attain. A liberal and hater of injustice, pedantry and humbug, after Paley's death in 1805 he was possibly the best exponent in England of a religion of good-hearted common sense in which the 'peculiar doctrines' of Christianity were wholly wanting. He was one of the great English wits, very skilful in exposing ludicrous pretentiousness or falsity and, with some shallowness and smugness, on the side of the angels if they are non-Evangelical angels. His four articles in the *Edinburgh Review* in 1808 and 1809 were widely read and considered damaging.[1]

The first of them was in some respects the most detailed and offen-

[1] Their effect was noticeable in the House of Commons; Wilberforce 'saw that we are likely to be more run at' (*Wilberforce*, vol. III, p. 364).

sive. In Robert Ingram's *Causes of the Increase of Methodism and Dissension* too much had been assumed as generally known, Smith believed, of the spirit and object of the people dealt with. To remedy that, he proposed to present the reader 'with a near view of those sectaries, who are at present at work upon the destruction of the orthodox churches, and are destined hereafter, perhaps, to act as conspicuous a part in public affairs, as the children of Sion did in the time of Cromwell.' 'We shall use the general term of Methodism, to designate these three classes of fanatics [that is, Arminian and Calvinistic Methodists and 'the *evangelical* clergymen of the Church of England'], not troubling ourselves to point out the finer shades and nicer discriminations of lunacy, but treating them all as in one general conspiracy against common sense, and rational orthodox Christianity.'[1]

Taking up first the peculiar belief of the 'Methodists' in providential interpositions in what the profane would call trivial matters, he cites such methodistical phenomena as a 'change effected by the power of the Holy Spirit' on a sinful person whose heart had been 'devoted to music, dancing, and theatrical amusements'; a clergyman who, spending an evening at cards, dropped down dead when it was his turn to deal ('the third character in the neighbourhood which had been summoned from the card table to the bar of God'); a young man uttering the most dreadful oaths and imprecations who is stung by a bee 'upon the tip of that unruly member (his tongue)'; ('thus can the Lord engage one of the meanest of his creatures in reproving the bold transgressor who dares to take his name in vain'); Mr David Wright who was simultaneously cured of infidelity and scrofula by one sermon; and Captain Scott who was divinely warned not to preach in Mr Romaine's chapel by a violent storm of thunder and lightning. There is also the innkeeper who boasted he would have a greater congregation at his cock-fight than the Methodist parson. 'But what is man! how insignificant his designs, how impotent his strength, how ill-fated his plans, when opposed to that Being who is infinite in wisdom.' The evil innkeeper's corpse was carried by the meeting-house 'on the day, and exactly at the time, the deceased had fixed for the cock-fight'.[2]

[1] *Essays by Sydney Smith, Reprinted from the Edinburgh Review* (London and New York, George Routledge and Sons, n.d., p. 92); *Edinburgh Review*, January 1808.
[2] *Essays*, p. 94.

We should be slow to assume that these 'methodistical' episodes and characters are not consonant with good Evangelicalism, less so in the Age of Wilberforce, greatly more in the generation after it.

A young man of the name of S—— C——, Smith continues, in great agony of mind endured a horror that 'brought on all the symptoms of raging madness'; the apothecary 'as soon as he entered the house, and heard his dreadful howlings...inquired if he had not been bitten by a mad dog'. 'He then acknowledged that...he had gone to a fair in the neighbourhood, in company with a number of wicked young men; that they drank at a public-house together till he was in a measure intoxicated; and that from thence they went into other company, where he was criminally connected with a harlot....He survived this interview but a few days.' (This is 'one of the most shocking histories we ever read. God only knows how many such scenes take place in the gloomy annals of Methodism.')[1]

The conversion of people who are already Christian communicants is next noted, and the establishment of 'religious newspapers'.

Nothing can evince more strongly the influence which Methodism now exercises upon common life, and the fast hold it has got of the people, than the advertisements which are circulated every month in these very singular publications. On the cover of a single number, for example, we have the following:—

'Wanted, by Mr Turner, shoemaker, a steady apprentice; he will have the privilege of attending the ministry of the gospel; a premium expected.— Wanted, a serious young woman as servant of all work.—Wanted a man of serious character, who can shave.—Wanted, a serious woman to assist in a shop.—A young person in the millinery line wishes to be in a serious family.— Wants a place, a young man who has brewed in a serious family.—Ditto, a young woman of evangelical principles.—Wanted, an active serious shop-man.—To be sold, an eligible residence, with 60 acres of land; gospel preached in three places within half a mile.—A single gentleman may be accommo-dated with lodging in a small serious family.—To let, a genteel first floor in an airy situation near the Tabernacle.—Wanted, a governess, of evangelical principles and corresponding character.'

'The Princess of Wales Yacht,' another advertisement says, 'J. Chap-man, W. Bourn, master, by divine permission, will leave Ralph's Quay every Friday.'[2]

[1] *Ibid.* pp. 95–6.   [2] *Ibid.* pp. 98–9.

Smith notices the rapid spread of these 'Methodistical' principles in the army and navy, the immense spread of the missions and the home missions and the phenomenal activity of the tract distributors. Since the year 1799 'upwards of *Four Millions* of Religious Tracts have been issued under the auspices of the [Religious Tract] Society; and...considerably more than one fourth of that number have been sold during the last year.'[1]

'We must remember, in addition to these trifling specimens of their active disposition, that the Methodists have found a powerful party in the House of Commons, who, by the neutrality which they affect, and partly adhere to, are courted both by ministers and opposition; that they have gained complete possession of the India House; and under the pretext, or perhaps with the serious intention, of educating young people for India, will take care to introduce (as much as they dare without provoking attention) their own particular tenets. In fact, one thing must always be taken for granted respecting these people', Smith continues in one of the most acute judgments expressed about the Evangelicals during the period, '—that, wherever they gain a footing, or whatever be the institutions to which they give birth, *proselytism will be their main object*; everything else is a mere instrument—this is their principal aim.'[2] We see in this passage that to refer as 'Methodists' to what is obviously Wilberforce's 'neutral party' in the House is as confusing, and misleading, as to call 'Evangelical' all anti-Orthodox religious activities of the period.

To what degree will Methodism extend in this country?—This question is not easy to answer. That it has rapidly increased within these few years, we have no manner of doubt; and we confess we cannot see what is likely to impede its progress. The party which it has formed in the Legislature and the artful neutrality with which they give respectability to their small number,—the talents of some of this party, and the unimpeached excellence of their characters, all make it probable that fanaticism will increase rather than diminish. The Methodists have made an alarming inroad into the Church, and they are attacking the army and navy. The principality of Wales, and the East-India Company, they have already acquired. All mines and subterranean

---

[1] It was a tiny part of the Evangelical religious and moral propaganda, or even of the Party's tractarian activity alone—a subject that restrictions of space do not allow to be included in this study.   [2] *Essays by Sidney Smith*, p. 100.

places belong to them; they creep into hospitals and small schools, and so work their way upwards. It is the custom of the religious neutrals to beg all the little livings, particularly in the north of England, from the minister for the time being.[1]

In 1808 and 1809 two articles attacked the progress of missions to India. It is an easy matter for Smith to show that the leading missionaries (who had actually gone out, none of them Evangelical)— Brother Carey, Brother Ringeltaube, Brother Cran and so on—are fanatics and enthusiasts. Why risk an empire to spread the religion taught by such people?

The duties of conversion appear to be of less importance, when it is impossible to procure proper persons to undertake them, and when such religious embassies, in consequence, devolve upon the lowest of the people....Who wishes to see scrofula and atheism cured by a single sermon in Bengal? Who wishes to see the religious hoy riding at anchor in the Hoogly river? This madness is disgusting and dangerous enough at home:—Why are we to send out little detachments of maniacs to spread over the fine regions of the world the most unjust and contemptible opinion of the gospel?...The instruments employed for those purposes are calculated to bring ridicule and disgrace upon the gospel; and in the direction of those at home, whom we consider their patrons, we have not the smallest reliance; but, on the contrary, we are convinced they would behold the loss of our Indian empire, not with the humility of men convinced of erroneous views and projects, but with the pride, the exultation, and the alacrity of martyrs.[2]

A pointed little passage ending this article shows that Smith not only had a sensible and well-informed opinion about the obdurate fight to force Christianity on India but knew well what he was doing in so jumbling Methodist, dissenter and Evangelical. John Owen, whose work he is reviewing, had said the position of any opponent amounted to establishing an 'alternative to which Providence is...reduced, of either giving up that country to everlasting superstition, or of working some miracle in order to accomplish its conversion'. The idea of Providence being placed in such a dilemma, 'by a motion at the India House, carried by ballot!' strikes Sydney Smith as worse than the religious yacht, the card-playing clergyman and the evangelical newspapers.

[1] *Ibid.* p. 104.
[2] *Ibid.* (*Edinburgh Review*, April 1808), p. 124.

Providence reduced to an alternative!!!!! Let it be remembered, this phrase comes from a member of a pious party, who are loud in their complaints of being confounded with enthusiasts and fanatics.

We cannot conclude without the most pointed reprobation of the low mischief of the Christian Observer; a publication which appears to have no method of discussing a question fairly open to discussion, than that of accusing their antagonists of infidelity. No art can be more unmanly, or, if its consequences are foreseen, more wicked.—If this publication had been the work of a single individual, we might have passed it over in silent disgust; but as it is looked upon as the organ of a great political religious party in this country, we think it right to notice the very unworthy manner in which they are attempting to extend their influence....The baseness and malignity of fanaticism shall never prevent us from attacking its arrogance, its ignorance, and its activity.[1]

In 1808 also Sydney Smith's *Letters on the Subject of the Catholics*, by 'Peter Plymley', had as its hero 'the sepulchral Spencer Perceval', the Evangelical, perhaps about-to-be Evangelical prime minister. The Party were not primarily concerned but come in for mention from time to time and it is in this work they were first called, in a widely circulated piece, the 'Clapham' group.

As for the dangers of the Church...I have not yet entirely lost my confidence in the power of common sense, and I believe the Church to be in no danger at all; but if it is, that danger is not from the Catholics, but from the Methodists, and from that patent Christianity which has been for some time manufacturing at Clapham, to the prejudice of the old and admirable article prepared by the Church. I would counsel my lords the Bishops to keep their eyes upon that holy village, and its hallowed vicinity: they will find there a zeal in making converts far superior to any thing which exists among the Catholics; a contempt for the great mass of English clergy, much more rooted and profound; and a regular fund to purchase livings for those groaning and garrulous gentlemen, whom they designate (by a standing sarcasm against the regular Church) Gospel preachers, and vital clergymen.[2]

In general Sydney Smith's observations were informed and acute. One matter in particular of the utmost importance he saw clearly. He undoubtedly knew that John Venn was the rector of Clapham and who

[1] *Essays by Sidney Smith*, pp. 124–5.
[2] *Works of Sydney Smith* (New York, 1871) ('Letters on the Subject of the Catholics, by Peter Plymley', Letter v), p. 463.

the Evangelical clergymen were who had most to do with the Party's missionary effort; but he also knew that the 'principal encouragers' of the Church Missionary Society were not the Reverend Messrs Venn, Simeon, Scott and Newton but 'Messrs Wilberforce, Grant, Parry, and Thorntons'.[1] He knew too that the head of the 'Evangelical church' was not Newton, Scott or Simeon. The Pope has no such 'power over the minds of the Irish', he wrote in 1808, 'as Mr Wilberforce has over the mind of a young Methodist converted the preceding quarter';[2] and 'How many Protestant Dissenters are there', he asked in 1827, 'who pay a double allegiance to the King, and to the head of their Church, who is not the King? Is not Mr William Smith, member for Norwich, the head of the Unitarian Church? Is not Mr Wilberforce the head of the Clapham Church?'[3]

The alarm and dread of the *Anti-Jacobin Review* at the Evangelical corruption of manners and morals into puritanism was not lessened during the first and second decades of the century. As it viewed the Bible, Church Missionary and other successful Evangelical societies its early fears about 'the school of Mr Wilberforce' were comparatively slight. It kept stubbornly at the task of combating this danger, encouraging all loyal people to join it and calling on ecclesiastical and other dignitaries to take steps against 'the fanatical exertions of those spurious philanthropists, who are labouring to *puritanize*...the public mind, and, consequently, to destroy the best energies, and the best feelings, of Englishmen'.[4]

The extent of the *Anti-Jacobin*'s alarm is indicated by its publication of a letter attacking two of the royal princes for their support of dissenting and Evangelical activities, which in fact was much greater than the writer or the *Anti-Jacobin* realized. There was an incidental attack in it on Sir Claudius Stephen Hunter, the Evangelical Lord Mayor, who was also secretary at this time of the Proclamation Society, for his activity in the London Society for Promoting Christianity Amongst the Jews (which the Dukes of Kent and Sussex were prominent in). The editors added to the letter a 'respectful but earnest' (and threatening)

---

[1] *Ibid.* ('Indian Missions', *Edinburgh Review*, April 1808), p. 49, note.
[2] *Ibid.* ('Plymley's Letters', Letter x), p. 478.
[3] *Ibid.* ('Catholics', *Edinburgh Review*, March 1827), p. 261.
[4] *Anti-Jacobin*, vol. L (July 1816), p. 637.

note recommending greater care to the royal dukes. 'Should these hints be neglected, we shall take an opportunity of addressing their Royal Highnesses, in more plain and direct terms. Meanwhile, we shall conclude our brief admonition, with the expression of a fervent wish— THAT THE HOUSE OF BRUNSWICK MAY NEVER FORGET THE PRINCIPLES WHICH SEATED THEIR FAMILY ON THE THRONE OF THESE REALMS.—Edr.'[1]

Before 1807 the *Anti-Jacobin* had been doubtful of the wisdom of abolishing the slave trade; after 1807 it was violently opposed to the Evangelical attempts to enforce Abolition and later to abolish the institution of slavery on British soil. In these crucial years its pages were crowded with attacks on the hypocrisy and duplicity of the Abolitionists, 'ignorant fanatics, speaking the true cant of the tabernacle.' 'The Members of the African Institution [by which the reviewer meant the noble and respectable officers of the Institution, a majority of whom— it was impossible to realize even by these years—were Evangelical] should be ashamed to give encouragement to such fanatics.'[2] Beginning in March 1816 the *Anti-Jacobin* gave some new pamphlets a ninety-page review continuing through several numbers. The miserable cant of the Evangelicals, their semi-methodism, their spurious philanthropy, their fanatical exertions, their attempts to 'puritanize', were pointed out with the *Anti-Jacobin*'s usual vigour and many instances. This journal was the chief organ of the repeated charge of actual financial gain by the Party through pretended philanthropy. Stephen, the *Review* said, had completed his 'philanthropic harvest' by acquiring the lucrative situation of Master in Chancery and law adviser to the Colonial Department. 'And Mr Macaulay has driven a still more lucrative trade, by his traffic in philanthropy, which has, at once, filled his coffers, and introduced him to respectable society. But for Sierra Leone, and the African Institution, poor Zachary Macaulay might have been a negro-driver, instead of a negro-patron. His traffic, however, has been lately discovered to be too good a thing for the monopoly of a single saint; another of the fraternity, of the name of Babington, has, therefore, been taken into partnership. So much for the disinterested efforts of these noisy philanthropists.'[3]

[1] *Anti-Jacobin*, vol. XLIX, pp. 618–22.   [2] *Ibid.* vol. L, p. 117.
[3] *Ibid.* p. 640.

Sable Subjects, Souls in Darkness

The mistaken charge that Zachary Macaulay had made a fortune out of his philanthropy was repeated many times—'all acquired, too, without the aid of money, solely, by the employment of smooth words, and oily professions, the whine and cant of the tabernacle, which has filled many an hungry stomach, and many an empty pocket, among the saints'.[1] The confusion of Evangelical and less substantial religionist, probably at this point deliberate on the part of the *Anti-Jacobin* too, is very offensive here. The whine and cant, if such terms are ever Evangelically appropriate, are of a post-Wilberforce era, not of these years. The rest of the charge is still worse, as it was an especial characteristic of Evangelicalism in general that its leading figures, in large numbers, had pocket and stomach pleasantly filled.

The *Anti-Jacobin* went on to two strong statements of the increasing power of the 'fanatics' and the imperative necessity of an immediate and general resistance.

With how much greater truth and justice [than Burke had had in exclaiming against the increasing influence of an Indian party] might any one now express his apprehensions of the growing influence of an African faction, who are grasping at every thing; who are, at present, sufficiently numerous in the House, to carry great weight with them; who have already friends sufficient to purchase livings in the church, for the introduction of fanatics into her bosom; and who, from the immense profits which accrue from their trade of philanthropy, may be enabled to buy boroughs and so to acquire a preponderance in the senate, that may restore the times of the usurpation! It is the dread of the predominance of this faction, who are making rapid strides toward ascendancy in the state, that renders it an imperious duty to open the eyes of the public to their real motives and views, as developed by their actions.[2]

With puritans in the senate, and in the army; with the spread of schism over the land; and with encouragement to its diffusion in quarters whence effectual remedies might have been expected; the man who does not discover, in the signs of the times, sufficient ground for apprehension; must be either stoically indifferent, or wilfully blind. Let churchmen stand firm at their post—let them rally round the altar—let them 'cry aloud and spare not,' or we may be destined to witness a second *usurpation* without the chance of a second restoration.[3]

[1] *Ibid.* p. 654.   [2] *Ibid.* p. 645.
[3] *Ibid.* p. 640.

II

England was in danger; but the danger was not what the *Anti-Jacobin* believed or affected to believe. No sovereign would be led out to the scaffold, no church and constitution be destroyed, no rank, property, respectability and decency go down in subversive violence. The danger was merely spiritual. It was intangible, subtle, seen by only a handful of close and acute observers. Except for a few manifestations in spectacularly offensive activities such as those of the Society for the Suppression of Vice it was so huge and slowly pervasive as to be missed by almost everybody.

Neither would it be the danger of power coming into the hands of dishonest pseudo-philanthropists. That charge too was wrong. But there were possibilities of grave danger if the Evangelicals should get social and spiritual authority, and to do that they would not have to have 'ascendancy in the state'. One major source of harm could be that whatever reforms their puritanical nature led to would be urged and enforced with a religious fervour so single-minded that it made every scheme subservient to religious purposes. Even beyond the confusion of Evangelical and Methodist, the failure to see that the Evangelical Reformation was religious in every part is the chief source of failure to understand it. The *Anti-Jacobin*'s assumption from the Abolition movement that the Evangelicals were 'philanthropists' (either real or spurious) was thus more gravely wrong than their quite mistaken charges against Stephen, Macaulay, the young Babington and other Evangelical Abolitionists; for of all the happenings of the Reformation the campaign to free the Africans shows most clearly that the term 'philanthropists' must be left to the liberals, romantics, benevolent pagans and such good-hearted religionists as the Quakers who were ignorant of 'uses'.

In 1814, with Napoleon defeated, Wilberforce, working with all his strength to make sure the treaty of peace with France did not allow a return to the full practice of slaving, demanded that 'the Slave Trade should not be revived where it had been actually suppressed'. He stated his case in a letter to Talleyrand and urged on his continental correspondents, von Humbolt, Madame de Staël, Sismondi. Mme de Staël and the Duchesse de Broglie translated parts of his *Letter* to his

Yorkshire constituents. On 15 November 1814 he 'heard from the Duke of Wellington [Ambassador to Paris] that the French had actually issued an order, prohibiting all French subjects from slaving to the North of Cape Formosa. A grand business....' 'Soyez sure que votre nom et votre persévérance ont tout fait', Madame de Staël wrote, in her glowing way. 'D'ordinaire les idées triomphent par elles mêmes et par les tems, mais cette fois c'est vous qui avez devancé les siècles.... Vous avez écrit une lettre à Sismondi qui est pour lui comme une couronne civique, ma petite fille tient de vous une plume d'or qui sera sa dot dans le ciel. Enfin vous avez donné du mouvement pour la vertu à une génération qui sembloit morte pour elle. Jouissez de votre ouvrage, car jamais gloire plus pure n'a été donnée à un homme.'[1]

Such sentiments were deeply embarrassing, for Madame de Staël, so brilliant, so famous, so little endowed with English reserve and in other respects too so unlike Mrs More, was not Wilberforce's ideal; to his mind, astonished as she would have been to learn it, she was not a truly religious person. Even that letter, breathing an ardour of homage, contained one thing no serious Christian could have written. It was not objectionable to say that Wilberforce had conferred a distinguished civic honour on Sismondi simply by addressing a public letter to him. But to say the gold pen he had given the Duchesse de Broglie would be her heavenly dower.... Serious people did not so lightly use the great terms of their religion.

One result of the standing that Abolition gave Wilberforce was still more embarrassing. Coming from a profound misunderstanding of what he was trying to do, it built up, eventually, what may be thought of as the Wilberforce enigma. From early in the century, there was no worthy scheme for the reform of any abuse that was not brought confidently to his attention. The great philanthropist, humanitarian, libertarian, the recognized champion of the oppressed, he must be ready and anxious to take up all matters of conspicuous injustice. 'I hope, now you have done with Africa', Sydney Smith wrote, 'you will do something for Ireland. There is no man in England, who, from activity, understanding, character, and neutrality, could do it so effectively as Mr Wilberforce....I hope you will stir in this matter.'[2]

[1] *Wilberforce*, vol. IV, pp. 216–17.
[2] *Ibid.* vol. III, p. 309.

It was clear to many, both friends and enemies of Abolition, that there was no need for Wilberforce to turn his attention to foreign parts. Among others the *Anti-Jacobin* pointed that out in its usual manner. 'The abortive attempts made by the Sierra Leone Company and the African Institution, prove the futility of our best endeavours, when directed to remote objects....If Mr Wilberforce really means to do good, let him apply his attention to objects within his view...then his confidence cannot be abused, nor his judgment misled. We, therefore, seriously advise him to exert his humanity, in the first instance, on behalf of those who have the strongest claim to its exercise, his own countrymen.'[1]

This view was expressed more often and strongly as it was noticed that in the swarm of new societies to aid Indians, and North American Indians, and Newfoundland fishermen, and Irish Protestants, and to translate the Bible into unknown languages and send missionaries to unknown places, Wilberforce was always on the platform at the noble and respectable meetings to establish them and his name always in the subscription lists and the rosters of officers. As early as 1799 an anonymous pamphlet had earnestly called on him, as the champion of the unfortunate, the mistreated and the oppressed, to take up the cause of the London prostitute. 'The pious, benevolent, enthusiastic Wilberforce, though frequently baffled and deluded in the Senate, returns again and again to the charge of humanity, and reiterates, in vain, his incontestable arguments in favour of the wretched negroes. But are there no instances of extreme misery that ask for the interposition of piety and humanity within our own hemisphere, our own quarter of the globe, our own island, that we extend our views to the West Indies and to Africa? What are the sorrows of the enslaved negro from which the outcast prostitute of London is exempted?'[2] In 1819 the reformer Major John Cartwright, after quoting from the *Edinburgh Review* a passage describing the entanglement and delay of the Court of Chancery, exclaimed 'We feel for climbing boys as much as any body can do; but what is a climbing boy in a chimney, to a full grown suitor in the master's office? And whence comes it, in the midst of ten thousand

[1] *Anti-Jacobin*, March 1815, p. 255.
[2] *Thoughts on Means of Alleviating the Miseries Attendant upon Common Prostitution* (London, 1799), pp. 26–7.

compassions and charities, that no Wilberforce, Bennett, or Sister Fry, has started up for the suitors in Chancery?'[1]

In 1816 Wilberforce was called on in indignant language to stop traversing the world in search of objects of philanthropy and turn his attention to still another cause in England. 'Whilst you, Sir, and other philanthropists ranged the earth, in order to break the fetters off the slave, you disregarded with singular inconsistency, the ill treatment which the British seaman, the guardian of your independence, has been obliged to endure.' Such indifference combined with ostentatious sensibility toward the Africans must, if continued, cause Wilberforce's sincerity to be questioned. 'To the condition of the lower classes in this and every other country, hardships are attached, which demand as much sympathy as the case of the Africans.'[2] In a review of this pamphlet the *Anti-Jacobin* fully agreed. 'Indeed, we heartily wish our philanthropists would attend more to the homely adage—"Charity begins at home;" they will find, among the Irish peasantry, much more wretchedness, suffering, and misery, than either now does, or ever did, prevail among the slaves in our colonies. Yet strange to say, not one word is uttered, even by way of compassion, for those sufferers, the relief of whose sufferings would be productive of injury to no one.'[3]

Madame de Staël may have been right in saying that Wilberforce was the most loved and respected man in all England; but it is certainly true that he was one of the most detested men in all England. The simple and bewildering fact is that of all those projects so compellingly brought to his attention, and there were many more than those cited, this recognized champion of the oppressed did not stir in the matter (as Sydney Smith expressed it) of a single one; and many of them he was well aware of without those earnest informants. When it became clear that he was not stirring in any such matters, but on the contrary went on steadfastly opposing all measures for the social, political and economic betterment of the lower orders, and supporting all measures for the suppression of democratic activities, the Cobbetts, Whitbreads, Hunts and Hazlitts believed more and more strongly that he was a pious rogue.

[1] *The Black Dwarf*, 10 March 1819, p. 147.
[2] Thomas Urquhart, *Letter to William Wilberforce* (London, 1816), p. 22.
[3] *Anti-Jacobin*, March 1816, p. 278.

In 1825 William Hazlitt included Wilberforce in a group of sketches of notable contemporaries called *The Spirit of the Age*. Throughout his superb portrait runs one simple error, of such a kind that it is not outrageous to say Hazlitt would have been absolutely right if he had not been absolutely wrong. A noble preacher in this cause, an incontestable witness himself, naturally taking Wilberforce as a reformer like Sir Samuel Romilly, Hazlitt described him as a man in whom a genuine wish to do good fought a losing battle with self-interest. That charge was sincere, and anyone who thinks Wilberforce was a reformer like Romilly—interested, as Sir James Mackintosh also assumed he was, in attacking 'all the forms of corruption and cruelty'—has no choice but to agree with it, for on that basis Hazlitt was dead right.

He carefully chooses his ground to fight the battles of loyalty, religion, and humanity, and it is such as is always safe and advantageous to himself! This is perhaps hardly fair, and it is of dangerous or doubtful tendency. Lord Eldon, for instance, is known to be a thorough-paced ministerialist: his opinion is only that of his party. But Mr Wilberforce is not a party-man. He is the more looked up to on this account, but not with sufficient reason.... He has all the air of the most perfect independence, and gains a character for impartiality and candour, when he is only striking a balance in his mind between the *éclat* of differing from a Minister on some 'vantage ground,' and the risk or odium that may attend it. He carries all the weight of his artificial popularity over to the Government on vital points and hard-run questions; while they, in return, lend him a little of the gilding of court-favour to set off his disinterested philanthropy and tramontane enthusiasm.... By virtue of religious sympathy, he has brought the Saints over to the side of the abolition of Negro slavery. This his adversaries think hard and stealing a march upon them. What have the SAINTS to do with freedom or reform of any kind?

That question is a powerful statement of the Wilberforce enigma, for as asked it is unanswerable in any way creditable to Wilberforce. With freedom or reform of the kind Hazlitt meant the Evangelicals had nothing to do. They were steadily opposed.

He acts from mixed motives. He would willingly serve two masters, God and Mammon. He is a person of many excellent and admirable qualifications, but he has made a mistake in wishing to reconcile those that are incompatible. He has a most winning eloquence, specious, persuasive, familiar, silvery-tongued, is amiable, charitable, conscientious, pious, loyal, humane, tractable to power, accessible to popularity, honouring the king, and no less charmed with the homage of his fellow-citizens....

We can readily believe that Mr Wilberforce's first object and principle of action is to do what he thinks right; his next (and that we fear is of almost equal weight with the first) is to do what will be thought so by other people....He does not seem greatly to dread the denunciation in Scripture, but rather to court it—'Woe unto you, when all men shall speak well of you!'...His ears are not strongly enough tuned to drink in the execrations of the spoiler and the oppressor as the sweetest music....He must give no offence. Mr Wilberforce's humanity will go all lengths that it can with safety and discretion: but it is not to be supposed that it should lose him his seat for Yorkshire, the smile of Majesty, or the countenance of the loyal and pious. He is anxious to do all the good he can without hurting himself or his fair fame. His conscience and his character compound matters very amicably. His patriotism, his philanthropy are not so ill-bred, as to quarrel with his loyalty or to banish him from the first circles. He preaches vital Christianity to untutored savages; and tolerates its worst abuses in civilized states. He thus shows his respect for religion without offending the clergy, or circumscribing the sphere of his influence. There is in all this an appearance of a good deal of cant and tricking....

Mr Wilberforce has the pride of being familiar with the great; the vanity of being popular....He is coy in his approaches to power: his public spirit is, in a manner, *under the rose*....Mr Wilberforce is far from being a hypocrite; but he is, we think, as fine a specimen of *moral equivocation* as can well be conceived. A hypocrite is one who is the very reverse of, or who despises the character he pretends to be: Mr Wilberforce would be all that he pretends to be, and he is it in fact, as far as words, plausible theories, good inclinations, and easy services go, but not in heart and soul, or so as to give up the appearance of any one of his pretensions to preserve the reality of any other.[1]

In that portrait the feeling that with all his cultivating of respectability and power Wilberforce was still on the side of virtue, the recollection that after all he was 'the liberator of Africa', struggle with Hazlitt's sorrow and anger that in the contest for the rights of the little

---

[1] *The Spirit of the Age* (2nd ed., London, 1825), pp. 328, 324-7. 'After all', Hazlitt ends his sketch, 'the best as well as most amusing comment on the character just described was that made by Sheridan, who being picked up in no very creditable plight by the watch, and asked rather roughly who he was, made answer—"I am Mr Wilberforce!" The guardians of the night conducted him home with all the honours due to Grace and Nature.'

Wilberforce was, alas, only too much on the side of the great. From Hazlitt's point of view and natural assumption, how faultless a description! Close, detailed and penetrating in observation, relentless and sound in judgment, it is wholly admirable. But in one basic respect Hazlitt's point of view and natural assumption were wrong. He did not know who Wilberforce was.

One simple change in that text makes every statement it contains unchallengeable: for 'self-interest', read 'Evangelical interest'. Wilberforce did act from mixed motives and would willingly serve God and Mammon, did wish and constantly attempt to reconcile incompatible qualifications; but not for himself. It is true he was tractable to power and charmed with the homage of his fellow-citizens, when the cause was to be helped by them. Of course he wished to be thought right by other people who might be Evangelically useful. It would have been a serious blow to Evangelicalism if he had lost his seat for Yorkshire or the countenance of the loyal and pious. His conscience and his character did compound matters amicably, when it was necessary for religious reform. How could he afford to circumscribe the sphere of his usefulness? That was the whole point of his being the kind of man he was. Familiarity with the great was vital to him and nothing could have been more damaging to the Evangelical Reformation than for him to be banished from the first circles. And Hazlitt was right, in his wrong way, on another point, for it is true Wilberforce was a supreme specimen of moral equivocation. How could he be otherwise and succeed? Politics and Christian principle are incompatible by their nature. They can be reconciled in one way only. Wilberforce's whole deft and supple management of his Saints, the 'neutral party' that both Sydney Smith and Hazlitt (with many others) tell us about, was only possible by a perfection of moral equivocation.

Hazlitt had not learned who Wilberforce was. It seemed to him that the simplest consistency obliged the man who had fought against African slavery to fight against analogous oppression in England. If he did not, his failure had to be explained in terms of moral weakness. How otherwise could an intelligent, honest Englishman, brought up with a passion for fair play and justice reinforced by a deep devotion to the teachings of Christ, work so indomitably to strike the fetters from the Africans and resist steadily every effort to strike them from his oppressed fellow-countrymen? On the canonical assumption that Abolition was to put an end to a shameful inhumanity as the reasonable man would understand it, Hazlitt was irrefutably right. But there is one way to answer this question that he could not answer. That is, by pointing out that the canonical assumption was wrong and that there was no oppression in England analogous to African slavery.

There is an uncanonical explanation of this interest in the Africans. Before that question Hazlitt could not answer there is a necessary preliminary question. Why should the Evangelicals engage in the matter at all? By their own principles they appear to have had no legitimate interest in any crusade of the kind. The ardent interest of Charles James Fox or William Cowper causes no difficulty. They were true libertarians and lifelong foes of the Tory die-hards. No difficulty is caused either by the interest of the Quakers and other dissenters, the Irish, radicals and philosophic radicals. They were concerned with political freedom. When Hannah More, however, concerns herself with liberty for Afric we are in real trouble; and the difficulty goes deeper still. It is more than the difficulty presented by the political conservatism of the Evangelicals. It is the puzzling circumstance that they were interested so deeply in any political activity whatever—for on a basis of Christian consistency to Christian principle as they understood it they had no right to be.

Calvin had told them, Thomas Scott had told them, John Newton, the Bible itself, that Christians have no true concern with political affairs. Their *best interests* do not appear in the matter. It is no part of their citizenship in heaven. No doubt the African natives are deprived of natural rights, refused law and justice, cruelly oppressed. So were the Christian subjects of Nero. These are worldly matters. They have no permanent importance. The African natives should hold to a clear course. They should realize that they inhabit *no continuing city*, that no act man can perform against them affects their best interests, that this life is short and inconsequential and that at the bottom of the account of their oppressors in the trade of blood has been written already 'Paid in full'. By their oppressors' names in the Book of Life stand the grimmest words of the Christian dispensation: they have had their reward. The Africans should be submissive and contented, endure their unfortunate lot and live, like the Shepherd of Salisbury Plain, upon the promises. Mrs More pointed all this out to the Mendip miners

379

and the Spitalfields weavers. No Evangelical principle is more clearly established than that suffering is better than discontent. In how much more comforting a position eternally speaking are the Africans than their oppressors ! The slavers, the merchants of Bristol and Liverpool, their parliamentary agents, the West Indian investors and the High Church bishops and all reactionaries who fought on this issue against William Wilberforce *have had their reward.*—Those statements in the abstract are all Evangelically true and made time and again by all articulate Evangelicals of the period. How then can the Evangelicals take up this political matter?

Because it is not a political matter. Because those statements cannot be made to the Africans. Because eternally speaking the Africans do not inhabit *no continuing city.* They inhabit a continuing city, the city of unbelief and everlasting death. They are not like the Christian subjects of Nero. They are not and they cannot be candidates for salvation. They are forced by slavery not to be Christians. They have no chance of life eternal. The sable subjects of the most horrible oppression the modern world has seen must be and must remain souls in darkness. They are 'perishing for lack of knowledge'.

'What have the SAINTS to do with freedom or reform of any kind?'

With the kind of freedom or reform that you mean—Wilberforce could have replied to Hazlitt—the Saints have nothing to do. *Neither has the Evangelical campaign to abolish the slave trade and the institution of slavery on British soil.* Our interest in the Africans is a religious interest. It is not inconsistent for a truly religious man to concern himself with Abolition knowing well that political affairs do not serve his *best interests*—for Abolition is not a political affair. You did not know that with us all purposes are subservient to religious purposes. There is a greatly more important kind of freedom and reform than you know, and it is with that, and almost exclusively with that, that we are concerned.

The failure to understand that Wilberforce's interest even in the abolition of the slave trade was religious, his interest in Emancipation so in a far more exalted way, leaves him defenceless against charges that with that understood do not bear an instant's examination. To Cobbett's indignant assertion that George Washington who owned slaves was as just and humane as 'Massa Wilby' Wilberforce could have pointed out that his magnificent labours for the Africans were not primarily in the categories of justice and humanity, any more than they were concerned with the relief of suffering, wretchedness and misery as Cobbett would have understood those words. He could have pointed out to those other critics cited that there is no hardship attached to the condition of the lower orders in any Christian country that demands as much sympathy as the Africans' hardship, for the enslaved Negro has a source of wretchedness that the outcast prostitute of London, the British seaman, the Irish peasant and the Chancery suitor have not got. The 'liberator of Africa' was not correctly described as a 'philanthropist' and a 'friend of humanity'. It is not likely that Wilberforce would have thought of that night of 23 February 1807 as 'the supreme moment of his life'. He could have explained to Sir James Mackintosh, a good man (were this world all) but not an Evangelical, that if thousands were animated by his example and success 'to attack all the forms of corruption and cruelty' they would be doing something he had declined over and again to do and had no motive to do or intention of doing.

Even in the early days, the belief in his hypocrisy was so prevalent among his enemies that it was frequently charged he did not really wish to end the slave trade and was 'growing weary' of a cause he had been carrying on for personal advancement. 'In truth', he wrote, in 1790, 'the principles upon which I act in this business being those of religion...can know no remission, and yield to no delay.'[1] With that understood he stands unassailable by the charges made against him and in particular the charge of helping the Africans at the expense of the British.—I have done everything for the British, Wilberforce could have said, that I have done for the Africans and far more. I have done everything I could do to see that the word of God is brought to them. My purpose has always been to bring the Evangelical truth to all people, the British first. From the beginning, my campaign for the Africans was basically, not incidentally, a part of that purpose. By means of it alone I have done immense things for the *best interests* of my fellow-countrymen. I have done more for them than any other man of the age. I have prevented the Africans from being forced to remain heathen; I have made it possible to bring true religion to those souls in darkness, so they may receive the Christian faith that alone provides man's only

[1] *Wilberforce*, vol. II, p. 21.

triumph over suffering; but at the same time I have taken away the necessity of sin from the slavers and the slave owners and their supporters; I have removed a shameful blot, a foul corruption, from the moral and religious fabric of my country; and I have enlisted in that religious task a vast number of people who cannot fail to have been made more moral and more religious by taking part in it. Many have come through it to serious religion, many have been led by it to take part in the whole great cause of the religious reform of England and the world.—Let them rejoice in their work, for never has a glory more pure been given to a people.

The duty of doing what one can for suffering human beings is an imperative Christian duty, the debasing inhumanity of the slave trade is opposed to the will of God. A large part of Wilberforce's priceless time and a large part of his wealth were spent in relieving mere worldly distress. But such benevolent acts are small in value when compared with the incalculable value of bringing a fellow human being into the way of salvation. How small in that comparison? Wilberforce has told us. In 1811 his terrible burden of work and always poor health made him think for a while of resigning the representation of Yorkshire for an easier parliamentary place. But 'I shrink with awe', he wrote to Stephen, 'from the idea of at once giving up for life all the efficiency for religious and humane purposes, (the former weigh with me ninety-nine parts in a hundred,) which would arise from my continuing in the House of Commons'.[1]

On 2 September 1814 Wilberforce wrote to his wife in the country that he was kept in London. 'The work to be done is far too important to be neglected, or not to be done where it can be done best. The interests at stake are so prodigious that even the probability of advancing them constitutes an object of vast amount [? moment].' What were these prodigious interests? The freedom of the Africans? At this time, in 1814, after twenty-seven years spent in the cause of Abolition, Wilberforce had not once so far as any record shows thought of emancipation. The removal of England's shameful sin? That too is not what he meant. 'What a comfort it is that my absence from you and our dear children is...in the work of mercy and love; a work which may truly be said to breathe the same spirit as that of Him whose coming

[1] *Wilberforce*, vol. III, pp. 538–9.

was announced as "peace on earth, and good-will toward men"! Aye, and surely we need not leave out the most honourable part of the service, "Glory to God in the highest". For I am occupied, I trust, in preparing an entrance into Africa for the gospel of Christ. I must say that I account it one of the greatest of the many great mercies and favours of the Almighty, (oh how many and how great!) that His providence connected me with this good cause. I might have been occupied as honestly, but in ways, political ways for instance, in which the right path was doubtful.'[1] The way of Abolition was not a political way.

'I greatly fear', Wilberforce wrote to Stephen at this time, 'if Hayti grants to France a colonial monopoly in return for the recognition of its independence, that all commerce with us will be excluded, and with it our best hopes of introducing true religion into the island. Now I will frankly own to you, that to introduce religion appears to me the greatest of all benefits.... God grant we may not hinder the gospel of Christ. O remember that the salvation of one soul is of more worth than the mere temporal happiness of thousands or even millions. In this I well know you agree with me entirely.'[2]

A glory more pure than the glory of abolishing the slave trade, Mme de Staël believed, had never been given to a man. Wilberforce would not have thought so. Sir James Mackintosh believed that the abolition of the slave trade was the greatest benefit that any man had been able to confer on the world. Wilberforce would not have agreed. The brilliant Frenchwoman and the distinguished jurist, good as they were were this world all, did not know that to pilgrims on the march only best interests matter. Emancipation itself was not an end. It might lead to the wonderful accomplishment of introducing the Gospel. If it should not do so it would still have value. It would have one part of value out of one hundred parts. The opening of Africa and the East to the missionaries was the thing itself.

III

Years later, Robert Isaac and Samuel Wilberforce in writing their father's *Life* stressed the unaffected and deep humility with which he looked back over his career. 'That which was of all things most worthy

[1] *Ibid.* vol. IV, pp. 205–6. [2] *Ibid.* p. 206.

of remark in his review of his past life, was his unfeigned humility. He observed in many different directions, the improvement that had taken place since he first came upon the stage, but he never seemed aware of the degree in which he was himself its cause....Notwithstanding the many clouds which he thought gathering over the political horizon [these are ominous clouds of liberal reform, in 1832], he noticed "with delight the improvement in the middle and rather higher ranks of society"; and in "the despondency which various circumstances" caused, he was "always revived and comforted by contemplating the vast improvement in the character and conduct of our clergy"; but that he had been a great instrument in this happy change never seemed to occur to him.'[1]

In one way those are extraordinary statements, for in the best part of five volumes that precede them the biographers have hardly since their account of the establishment of the Proclamation Society in 1788 recorded a single explicit fact or made an explicit statement to show their father as an instrument or cause, or interested in being one, of any national advance in virtue. But it is surprising if we think of Wilberforce as a worldly man that he retired from Parliament looking back on forty-four years filled with unparalleled successes with painful regret for how little he had done. In 1825 friends urged him to accept a peerage and retire 'to the calmer atmosphere of the upper House'. 'I will not deny that there have been periods in my life', he replied, 'when on worldly principles the attainment of a permanent, easy, and quiet seat in the legislature, would have been a pretty strong temptation to me. But, I thank God, I was strengthened against yielding to it. For...as I had done nothing to make it naturally come to me, I must have endeavoured to go to it; and this would have been carving for myself, if I may use the expression, much more than a Christian ought to do.'[2]...'I am but too conscious of numerous and great sins of omission, many opportunities of doing good either not at all or very inadequately improved....When I consider that my public life is nearly expired, and when I review the many years I have been in it, I am filled with the deepest compunction, from the consciousness of my having made so poor a use of the talents committed to my stewardship.'[3]

'To himself he appeared "a sadly unprofitable servant,"' his sons

[1] *Wilberforce*, vol. v, pp. 344–5.   [2] *Ibid.* p. 229.   [3] *Ibid.* pp. 230–1.

also say, 'and needed constantly "the soothing consideration that we serve a gracious Master, who will take the will for the deed. Thou *didst* well (even the phraseology is indicative) that it was in thy heart."'[1]

That view of Wilberforce, created from 'conversational memoranda' and his sons' constructed misrepresentations, is one of the gravest injustices done him by their biographical method. As it did not allow them to describe him as an Evangelical they had to assume he was simply a distinguished Christian senator; and if we accept that view the passages cited attribute a very bad pseudo-humility to him. It is absurd to think he did not know what he had done as a political man. He was one of the foremost members of the House for years, his power and his successes very great, and everyone knew it. But his humility was genuine and came from a true understanding of what he was. He did not look back on forty years of parliamentary activity but on forty years as the Evangelical commander. The task he had been set was not that of a legislator but a spiritual leader, in a position so exalted in its relationship to the best interests of the English people, so responsible, so crowded with opportunities for unlimited good, that no human being could have held it without at the end of his time being conscious of unprofitable service. It was not that Wilberforce might humbly suspect he had not done as much as could have been done. He knew he had not. No man could have done. But not even an Evangelical Deity would be likely to receive him with the words 'Thou didst well that it was in thy heart'.

The sole purpose of Evangelicalism as led by Wilberforce from 1787 to 1825 was to reform the manners and morals of the English people by combating the infidelity that is the cause of vice and sin. Its sole aim was to bring true religion to them and where necessary enforce it among them for edification. The huge campaign for the Africans, as led by Wilberforce, was from beginning to end the outstanding practical application of the basic Evangelical principle of action—in Hannah More's words, to make every scheme subservient to religious purposes. England being what it was, the Evangelical object clearly could not be accomplished without an unsparing use of the means of the world. Without the steady attraction of the great, the relentless use of Evangelical wealth, the deft and determined employment of Wilberforce's

[1] *Ibid.* p. 345.

'neutral party', the advancement of the cause in every practical way, the Evangelical Reformation would be Wesley, Whitefield and Lady Huntingdon all over again. There is a simple question that focuses all elements of danger. Can the agents of the good, employing the means of the world in the promotion of virtue and true religion, escape the world's insidious, perilous contaminations, so celebrated and even canonical?

There is no Evangelical who left records of his thinking but pointed out again and again, to others and to himself, the next-to-irresistible enchantments of the world and the fatality of succumbing to them. Attitudes toward this matter varied from carelessness, contempt and over-confidence to the gravest consciousness of pressing danger.

> I quit the world's fantastic joys,
> Her honours are but empty toys,

says one of Mrs More's poems:

> Let fools for riches strive and toil,
> Let greedy minds divide the spoil;...
> I look with pity and disdain
> On all the pleasures of the vain...

and some expressions from life seem to be rather in the same manner. 'Through grace, I trust, we [the writer, his wife and children] are proof against all the pollutions which are in the world. We stand on an eminence above its votaries, and contemplate their short-lived pleasures, and vanities, and lusts, with pity as to them, and with indifference as to ourselves.'[1] That anonymous Evangelical correspondent of the *Christian Guardian* was not much removed from Mrs More in some of her aspects. 'I have now entered a new scene of life', she wrote in her journal on taking up residence in Bath. 'O Lord! fit me for the duties and keep me from all the temptations of it. I thank thee that the vain and unprofitable company with which this place abounds, is a burden to me.... And do thou remove those prejudices which obstruct the growth of some of my friends in divine things.'[2]

[1] *Christian Guardian*, August 1811, p. 276.
[2] *More*, vol. II, p. 423.

In Wilberforce's position the incurring of these dangers was an Evangelical necessity. It had to be seen clearly that he could not avoid them (and remain the Evangelical leader) and that they could not be forgotten or underestimated. 'My worldly connections certainly draw me into temptations great and innumerable, yet I dare not withdraw from a station in which God has placed me.' 'Christ says, through His apostle, "Be not conformed to this world." Do thou teach me, Lord, the true limits of conformity.'[1]

The problem becomes more severe as the campaign moves on, for while mediocrity or failure is safe, great success is dangerous in itself. 'La rivière ne grossit pas', the French tell us, 'sans être troublée.' Satan retreats leaving hidden traps behind him. His grand instrument, Mrs Patty More (with many others) believed, is pride. Years before Wilberforce was reborn and dedicated, the wise old African blasphemer redeemed from the bondage had pointed out, in one of his most eloquent passages, that pride in its blackest reaches can be attained only by Christian professors. They alone can be proud of merits they know are not their own. There were assured vessels in Charles Simeon's quarter. Could that inveterate enemy of all that is good and true, the *Anti-Jacobin*, have been correct in its tersest description of the Evangelicals—'elated with an overweening and arrogant conceit of their own superior spiritual attainments'?[2] If so even in a moderate degree there could be danger indeed, for from the years when the auxiliaries and associations of the Bible and Church Missionary Societies began to spread over the land they had great social power; by the time of Wilberforce's retirement they were in a position—if there is harm in spiritual pride—to leave a pervasive and perilous heritage to the Victorian Age.

The Evangelical views, aims and principles being what they were, Satan with his grand instrument ('the subtlest serpent with the loftiest crest') would have only one task to accomplish: to inspire the school of Mr Wilberforce with the simple conviction that they were not as other men.

In 1808 Edward Bickersteth believed he saw in the clergy besides mere nominal Christians and good Christians a third group, 'those who

---

[1] *Wilberforce*, vol. i, pp. 328, 326.
[2] *Anti-Jacobin*, March 1815, p. 217.

partake in some measure of enthusiasm, and I fear, encourage pride in their hearers, as if they were a people set apart and all others were reprobates'.[1] In the same year, on the threshold of Evangelicalism's great flourishing, when the Bible and Missionary Societies were on the verge of bringing all the world to true religion, Isaac Milner pointed out that his own religious party might be in some such peril. Wilberforce's diary notes Milner's suggestion of 'a danger in living together at Clapham—danger of conceit and spiritual pride, and a cold critical spirit. He imputes this less to me than to some others—but the danger great.'[2]

There were others who believed they noticed such a thing. The Reverend Lewis Way of the London Jew Society had a cousin in Orders, also the Reverend Lewis Way, who was not an Evangelical. He was anxious to think of his cousin's associates with Christian charity, but he saw certain characteristics in them that did not seem good.

In my visit to Colchester I saw more of that party in the Church who are denominated Evangelical, than on any former occasion, and I formed a very favourable opinion of their sincerity, their zeal, and their devotion, and I may add their brotherly love as far as our own party are concerned. But I could not help observing a good deal of spiritual pride, and apparently a desire of human praise: there seemed to be a jealousy and unwillingness to allow any merit to those who differ from them in regard to certain points of doctrine and a great proneness to flatter each other in their speeches. Mr Simeon evidently assumes among them a character somewhat Apostolical, not only in [deference] paid to his age and experience, but he possesses a kind of Spiritual Authority.

Upon the whole they appear to me chiefly deficient in Christian Charity, and humility. But I speak of the party at large, and in their public conduct, for those defects if I may so call them appeared much less in private than in public.[3]

[1] Birks, *Memoir of Bickersteth*, vol. I, p. 43, note.

[2] *Wilberforce*, vol. III, p. 387. As it was not possible for Wilberforce's sons to point out what people were 'living together at Clapham', and why they were more in danger of spiritual pride than those who were living together at Marlow, Richmond or Islington, this is another of the references that are meaningless to the unbriefed reader, like the spiritually advantageous situation of the Adelphi (p. 75).

[3] *History of the Way Family*, p. 116 (8 August 1817).

Sable Subjects, Souls in Darkness

Wilberforce left Clapham in 1808 and by 1812 several of his closest Evangelical friends, such as Grant and the Thorntons, had moved into town. But many Evangelicals stayed there.[1]

[1] The Evangelical strength in and near Clapham seems to have been much underestimated. In 1919 a tablet was placed in the south wall of Clapham Parish Church bearing the names of ten members of the Party. 'Let us thank God', the inscription says, 'for the memory and example of all the faithful departed who have worshipped in this Church, and especially for the undernamed Servants of Christ sometime called "The Clapham Sect" who in the latter part of the XVIIIth and early part of the XIXth Centuries laboured so abundantly for the increase of National Righteousness and the Conversion of the Heathen and rested not until the curse of slavery was swept away from all parts of the British Dominions.' The men named are

Charles Grant	Henry Thornton
Zachary Macaulay	John Thornton
Granville Sharp	Henry Venn
John Shore Lord Teignmouth	John Venn
James Stephen	William Wilberforce

It is possible that this tablet is the chief source of the belief that the men named were 'the Clapham Sect', a belief apparently held by many who have written about them. Of the ten, Stephen did not live at Clapham (though he may well have worshipped occasionally at the Parish Church), John Thornton was dead in 1790, Henry Venn in 1797 and only Macaulay lived to see the end of slavery. John Venn, Teignmouth and even Granville Sharp were of no such importance in the reform campaign as numbers of Clapham residents between 1800 and 1830 who took prominent parts in the societies. A glance through a few membership lists selected at random, for the period after Wilberforce had gone, gives the following names (limited to those playing notable Evangelical parts):

Robert Barclay, Clapham	John Broadley Wilson, Clapham
Robert Barclay, Clapham Common	John Gladstone, Clapham Rise
Benjamin Harrison, Clapham	Sir Robert Harry Inglis, Battersea
William Smith,	Rise
Joseph Bradney,	Joseph Blades, Clapham
Joseph Bradney jun., of Clapham	George Scholey, Clapham Common
Common, and	John Deacon, Bloomfield House,
William Esdaile, Clapham, all	Clapham Common (this is Wilber-
Dissenters	force's house)
Ebenezer Maitland, Clapham	Joseph Wilson, Clapham
Robert Maitland, Clapham	Charles Elliott, Clapham
Thomas Poynder, Clapham Common	Thomas Poynder jun., Clapham
John Poynder, Clapham Common	Common

Those names are taken from lists of the Philanthropic Society, the Lying-in Hospital,

'The honey of a crowded hive, Defended by a thousand stings....'
William Cowper like his friend Newton well knew the subtle insidious-
ness of the world's seductions, slowly, imperceptibly, turning the souls
of even the firmest professors, unless steadfastly on guard, from God
toward far this side Jordan. There is a canonical view that the Christian
should not stay withdrawn in foolish dread of lions in the street; but
some streets are full of lions. Isaac Milner believed, it seems, that
spiritual conceit and pride can lead to great peril. William Wilberforce
believed so. But if pride can be powerfully corrupting in any notably
advanced religious character, the Evangelicals could be in peculiar
danger. Those who stand on an eminence above the world's votaries
are likely to be especial objects of Satan's interest. By 1815 and still
more by 1825 the Evangelicals, carrying on a greatly extended religious
enterprise, were in a sharply exposed position. There could be unusual possibilities of harm to those who were dramatically engaged in
'the bustle of the religious world'. Some men who cannot be lured
from the way of righteousness by commodities such as wealth and
titles can be bought by consideration, prominence, respect, importance
and applause. 'Charlotte Elizabeth', of all the great Evangelical propa-
gandists the most learned in the ways of the Satan, would probably
agree that one of his craftiest wiles is to lead his victims to ask themselves
the wrong questions in their spiritual exercises, those questions only
that are likely to leave the Christian professor—if John Newton was
right—with a hard doctrinaire thinking, a tasteless pedantry of devotion,
little penetrating self-criticism, little humour, little humility.

In so far as Evangelicals approached the perfection of the Evangelical
character they were governed by four convictions, two of them
perfectly stated by Hannah More, the others by everybody. (1) Nothing
that belongs to God but belongs to the Bible.[1] (2) All schemes must

the Seamen's Hospital, the Labourers' Friend Society and St Luke's Hospital for
Lunatics. Others who lived in Clapham or nearby after Wilberforce's time are the
bankers John Labouchere, Richard Stainforth, Thomas Hankey, Thomas Bainbridge;
Edward Parry of the East India House, Abel Smith, M.P., Robert Marsden, J. H. Key,
William Henry Hoare, W. Thornton Astell, the publisher John Hatchard, the brewer
Charles Barclay, John Maitland, M.P., and the 'universal secretaries' Nadir Baxter and
Miss Sophia Neave.

[1] *Mendip Annals*, p. 110 (the Shipham Anniversary *Charge*, 1794).

be made subservient to religious purposes. (3) There are the elect, a peculiar people, children of God, already half-beatified saints of the Lord, a people set apart, and there are the unconverted, the blind and their blind leaders. (4) It is the obligatory duty as Christians of those of the second birth to make the others good for edification. From the first of those basic working principles comes a rigid puritanical morality. From the second comes a fervour of working for the spiritual improvement of others. From the third and fourth could come, under the circumstances feared by Newton, Milner and so many more, a conviction that the converted are allowed and even commanded to employ ways and means, when in their judgment necessary, that are not virtuous in ordinary people.

How are the extraordinary people, of so great spiritual stature, known? They are known by themselves; and they know themselves by the sharp, vivid, certain clarity of their own convictions.[1]

A contributing factor of basic importance here is that such Evangelical beliefs were held with integrity of heart and mind by conspicuously good men and women. It is not only in the assured vessels, in whom it is most evident, that there appears the spiritual arrogance of people who know the truth that sets them apart from all others. Wilberforce's term for those differing from him in religious opinion is 'poor creatures', Henry Venn, advising his son John entering on his ministry, reminds him, in a letter described by an Evangelical writer as breathing 'the spirit of the Evangelical Revival', that 'savages are not more ignorant of His glory and love than are nominal Christians'.[2] In the beginning of the campaign everyone, not only Mrs More who gave them their name but Newton, Milner, Wilberforce and many others, pointed out that it is the good sort of people who are dangerous. The openly vicious do little harm to the virtuous. But if the good sort are dangerous, clearly the best sort are more so. The truly religious have

---

[1] 'He has experienced a real change in his affections and tempers. Surely, he must be allowed to be a competent judge of what he has felt; he may preach too by his life the truth and power of the Gospel to others; and, as he will find his evidence increase more and more, he may be more and more happy, from the consciousness of God within him now, and the prospect of perfect bliss hereafter' (Joseph Milner; *Joseph Milner*, vol. VIII, p. 88).

[2] John Telford, *A Sect that Moved the World*, p. 82.

a fortiori a capacity for great and peculiar harmfulness. The disingenuousness of disingenuous people (for instance) is not harmful in any large or interesting way. The disingenuousness of people who are truly religious and whose lives are of unimpeached excellence can be harmful in the extreme. If evil people practise guile, no one is taken off guard. When Hannah More (or a successor) practises her 'sort of righteous cunning', as her biographer Roberts calls it, it is a different matter. A practice of righteous cunning—pious fraud, honest deceit, justifiable moral equivocation—handed down, an Evangelical legacy, to the Victorian age, with the sanction of eminently respectable and genuinely devout people, could result in incalculable damage.

Out of a truly large number of episodes that could be taken as justifying in some degree the constant claims of such as the *Anti-Jacobin Review*, a simple little one of a later period, cited innocently by a historian of the nineteenth-century prostitution societies, is a good example of what enemies meant by the 'Evangelical cunning'. One W. W. Thomas, who with his wife founded the London Female Preventive and Reformatory Institution, was converted round 1844 by Baptist Noel. He had brought to him the case of a young woman with a bastard child. 'The legal evidence of paternity was by no means strong, but the man was nevertheless written to for an interview. He came to 200 Euston Road, and on stating who he was, Mr Thomas said, "I want to see you about the child of...." In astonishment the man replied, "Do you mean to say that that is something to my advantage?" "Certainly," was the answer; "it is always to a man's advantage to be put in the way of doing his duty." The paternity was admitted, and very soon arrangements were made for the proper maintenance of the child.'[1] Mr Thomas's ruse is a good specimen, but our author's ruse in omitting a direct statement of it is a better one.

Here we approach the Palladium of the moral world. To paraphrase Mrs More further, if there is disingenuousness, expediency and opportunism beyond Jordan we have lost one of our strongest arguments for a future life. If in the long run our universe is a scene of divine justice, we have here below, this side Jordan, rather more than enough of trickery and virtuous cunning. If God is in his heaven, all must be right with it, if not with the world.

[1] William J. Taylor, *The Story of the Homes* (London, 1907), p. 84.

CHAPTER 11

SATAN'S GRAND INSTRUMENT

They are wise in their own eyes; their notions, which the pride of their hearts tells them are so bright and clear, serve them for a righteousness, and they trust in themselves and despise others.

JOHN NEWTON

To the question, 'What have the Evangelicals to fear?' I reply, 'Themselves'.

LORD SHAFTESBURY

I

For every Evangelical during those great years of the Bible and Church Missionary Societies there was a sure indication of the divine approbation, for nothing else could have made possible the advance of the nation in virtue and piety that was clearly visible around them. Years before, John Newton had expressed the solemn view, never questioned by any Evangelical, that the execution of the divine vengeance on a sinful land was kept off only for the sake of 'the few who lov'd the Saviour's name'.

> Lord, still increase thy praying few!
> Were Olney left without a Lot,
>   Ruin like Sodom's would ensue....
>
> See the commission'd angel frown!
>   That vial in his hand,
> Fill'd with fierce wrath, is pouring down
>   Upon our guilty land!
>
> Ye saints, unite in wrestling pray'r,
>   If yet there may be hope;
> Who knows but mercy yet may spare,
>   And bid the angel stop?[1]

'So the inhabitants of Sodom were weary of Lot, though the destruction of their city was only retarded by his continuance in it', Newton wrote to Mrs More in December 1798, 'and the very day when he was

[1] *Olney Hymns*, Book II, LXIX, LXIV.

removed they all perished.'[1] But even from 1798, there was much reason for hope; the praying few, Mrs More's 'already half-beatified saints of the Lord', were increasing, and in ten years increasing greatly; writing time and again of the religious improvement of the nation, she could justly feel that an extraordinary mercy had been extended. In 1801, to Wilberforce: 'I have some good things to tell you as to the increase of religious clergymen among us'; in 1811, 'It is delightful to witness the many accessions to the cause of Christian piety in the higher ranks of life'; in 1813, to Lady Olivia Bernard Sparrow: 'My heart rejoices at the progress of religious society—wide, and more wide the blessed circle spreads in the elevated walks of life'; in the same year, 'I have...the satisfaction of finding a great increase of piety, especially in the higher classes'.[2] No one attentive to the religious state of the country could have disagreed with her.

'Few things, in the present day, so pregnant with wonderful events', says the Committee of the Merchant Seamen's Auxiliary Bible Society,

and with revolutions of the most extraordinary character and the most extensive influence, are more calculated to fix the attention of the contemplative mind, than the general and simultaneous movement, which, for some years past, has been taking place in the moral world...as brighter day seems to dawn upon us. And when we regard the growing zeal for the education of the poor,—the associations formed on all sides for carrying the glad tidings of salvation even to the ends of the earth,—the Scriptures, translated into all languages and travelling forth, the harbingers of mercy, into all lands,—all the divisions of the christian world, forgetting their grounds of distrust and separation and uniting, in the work of evangelizing mankind;—while the kings, and princes, and nobles, lay their honours at the feet of the King of kings, or rather communicate to them a higher lustre, by giving their powerful patronage to this best of causes;—what can we do but prostrate ourselves, in thankful adoration, before Him by whom this mighty change has been produced? This is the Lord's doing, and it is marvellous in our eyes.[3]

In particular Mrs More rejoiced at the 'prosperous state of all these blessed institutions' as the great Evangelical societies signalized their moral triumphs in the anniversary meetings crowded into the first few

---

[1] *More*, vol. III, pp. 46–7.   [2] *Ibid.* pp. 145, 401.
[3] *Third Annual Report of the Committee of the Merchant Seamen's Auxiliary Bible Society* (London, 1821).

days of May—the 'sainte semaine', 'Saints' Festival', 'Saints' Jubilee'. In fact the dreadful state of the country, Mrs More believed, was caused by the Bible and Church Missionary Societies: 'Satan could not bear their triumphant prosperity.'[1]

Mrs More was an unparalleled instance of triumphant prosperity herself for that matter. Her *Strictures on Female Education*, published in 1799, patronizingly reviewed by Jonathan Boucher and 'animadverted on' by Archdeacon Daubeny, was in a sixth edition in the same year and a ninth in 1801. The first edition of her *Practical Piety* in 1811 was sold out before publication and in a seventh edition the year after, her *Christian Morals* of 1813 was sold out before publication and her *Essay on the Character and Practical Writings of St Paul* fell off very little: it was sold out on the day of publication. After a 'mortal illness' of nearly two years she went indomitably on; apparently dying in August 1820 she survived her 'twenty-first death-bed'; soon she could say the only remarkable thing about her as an author was that she had written eleven volumes after the age of sixty. It was not the only remarkable thing. In 1819 her *Moral Sketches of Prevailing Opinions and Manners* sold out on the day of publication; the times were bad for the book trade but there was a seventh 'large edition' in the middle of 1820; 'it is on every table', Daniel Wilson wrote (he was soon to be Bishop of Calcutta, named, it was charged, by Charles Simeon). *The Spirit of Prayer* (1824), a compilation of passages from earlier works, was sold out when first announced, a fourth edition appearing within a year. In April 1826 came the fourteenth edition of *Practical Piety* and the sixteenth of *Coelebs in Search of a Wife*.[2] Most of these were two-volume works, pious, solid, heavy, and sold at a published price that brought publisher and author handsome returns.

The claims of Mrs More's friends that her writings were a permanent part of English religious literature seem to have been wrong; but the

---

[1] *More*, vol. IV, p. 64.

[2] This anonymous work, a long and to modern taste excessively tedious fictional account of an Evangelical young man's attempts to mate suitably, appears to have had more editions, and to have brought in more profits, during the Age of Wilberforce, than *Waverley*. 'Ce roman, qui a eu dix éditions dans une année, est essentiellement moral et religieux, et peu animé par les incidens.' *Biographie Étrangère* (Paris, 1819), Tome Second, p. 444.

Evangelicals' belief that in her field she was peerless, England's foremost religious and moral writer for the people, was sound. Her scores upon scores of editions point to a serious reading public extending beyond Evangelical into 'evangelical' ranks and increasing greatly up to and beyond the time of her death. How can we doubt that they helped to create that public? From the first years of the century Mrs More looms high and more high, a towering figure of the moral world. More than thirty years before her death we see the Reverend Sir Abraham Elton and Dr Sedgwick Whalley celebrating her position of immense respect, indeed of a devotion and reverence given to no other writer of the age, in a way amusing to Sydney Smith and to the mind of the *Anti-Jacobin Review* shockingly blasphemous. As early as 1810 she was finding her work seriously interrupted by the vanguard of the crowds of visitors, increasing to the end of her long life, who made their way from all parts of England, from Ireland, continental Europe, North America,[1] to her home in Somerset, to pay homage to the celebrated Christian woman.

A point comes up here that is important in judging the virtue and piety of the few who lov'd the Saviour's name. We have noted that there was an 'Evangelical language' and that sometimes it is in need of translation if we are to understand it. Anyone who came unsuspecting on such Evangelical words as 'serious' and 'truly religious', or even 'religious', and naturally took them in their usual meaning would be greatly deceived—a circumstance that was very helpful to Wilberforce's sons in composing their uniquely strange biography. Mrs More has shown us what is Evangelically meant by 'charity', 'liberty', 'ignorance', and 'education'. Indeed when we read that Mrs More laboured ceaselessly to educate the poor people of Mendip, Wilberforce spent his life to win liberty for the enslaved Africans and the Reverend William Carus Wilson had a deep Christian love for the young ladies of the Clergy Daughters' School that he supervised, it is a necessary conclusion that words are being used in some special sense. This is

[1] The subject of the Evangelical impact on the United States of America, which was great, must be brought up and dismissed with the statement that Hannah More's *Coelebs* and other works, Wilberforce's *Practical Christianity*, Scott's *Bible Commentary* and no doubt still more had much larger sales there than in England. In 1816 Mrs More wrote to Wilberforce that she had 'many visitors from America, where religion appears to be rapidly advancing' (*More*, vol. III, p. 441).

perhaps likely to be true of any large ambiguous term used by a peculiar people holding that all schemes must have use and all virtue comes from a specific source. Of course Mrs More's schools in the Mendips, for instance, were a product of Christian love and benevolence. But those manifestations of charity and loving-kindness were of a particular sort; they have to be distinguished from the acts of compassion and benevolence that a High Churchman, or an admitted infidel, might do out of the weakness of our common humanity from natural goodness.

In Mr E. M. Forster's recent valuable book about his great-aunt Marianne Thornton there are some fine examples of the Evangelical language, particularly useful because they are spoken by so intelligent and little doctrinaire an Evangelical. This daughter of Henry Thornton was justly respected. Her religion was neither bigoted nor unctuous and her opinions of some Evangelicals of her acquaintance (and fortunately, of ours) were direct and sharp. She was not much concerned over differences between High Church and Evangelicalism and to her great credit she described Mrs More's biographer Roberts as an oaf. If anyone among the true Evangelicals of the period seems to speak the language of our century it is this civilized woman. On a visit to the Mores she went with them to their 'school'. This seems not to have been one of the children's classes but some kind of adult meeting or perhaps one of the anniversaries. 'Now Bell and Lancaster were unknown then, and to read their Bible was the highest summit of knowledge to which they aspired. I chiefly recollect Mrs Hannah's or Mrs Patty's eloquent exhortations made to the whole school in the most familiar homely language, full of anecdotes of the people round them, as well as of the good people who lived in old times, and full of practical piety brought down to such minute details one never hears now.'[1]

Still more pleasant are Marianne Thornton's recollections of Hannah More's and all the sisters' kindness to their young guest, Mrs More's sympathy, warmth and charm, her vivacity and fondness of fun, her cheerfulness in her constant illnesses, and all the delights of the hospitable Barley Wood household. 'Surely there never was such a house, so full of intellect and piety and active benevolence.' We can understand how Marianne's parents 'loved them all'.

[1] E. M. Forster, *Marianne Thornton, a Domestic Biography* (London, 1956), p. 40.

Bell and Lancaster were well known, to someone like Hannah More, when Marianne Thornton was a child, if Bell and Lancaster were needed to instruct anyone that poor children could be taught more than a little reading. But to use Dean Milner's expression we may let that hare sit. We happen to possess the finest conceivable accounts of the methods, object and whole point of view of the Mores' 'reforming operations', in Hannah More's addresses (or Patty's, and it does not make any difference) to the anniversary meetings of the schools; that is, the exact evidence on which Marianne Thornton was forming her opinion of Mrs More's benevolence and piety, as opposed to her charm, vivacity and fondness of fun. The complete texts of five of the ladies' 'Charges', as their friends humorously called them, were preserved by Miss Patty herself in her journal of the Cheddar Valley project and printed as verbatim records by its editor. No one could read those Charges without seeing that charity has no purpose at all unless it is 'subservient to religious purposes'. By means of the schools Evangelical morality and religion are enforced with that union of material and spiritual aid of which Hannah More was the classic master of the age. The poor women are exhorted to keep their children away from the riot and disorder of lewd plays and licentious dancing matches—dancing in the midst of religious institutions is particularly indecent and abominable—and from other shocking scenes of vice.[1] The abominable custom of sending children to shops on Sundays is a wickedness in every view and the poor women who get their bit of tea and sugar in that way eat in sin and will have to account for it at the day of judgment. It is the prayer of the Cowslip Green ladies that no affliction may take place unless accompanied by a conviction of sin and the substantial sin of ingratitude is constantly and vigorously attacked, as Mrs Hannah or Patty impresses on 'their poor dark minds' that 'shewing a respectful sense of past favours' is 'a propriety, not to say decency, always to be observed'.[2] 'They have so little common sense', Patty wrote in her forthright way, '...that we are obliged to beat into their heads continually the good we are doing them; and endeavouring to press upon them, with all our might, the advantages they derive from us.'[3] ('I must once in a month recount what thou hast

[1] *Mendip Annals*, p. 112. [2] *Ibid.* p. 163.
[3] *Ibid.* p. 67.

398

been, which thou forget'st.') 'It is hard sometimes to go on doing them good against their will.'

'This last winter, we flatter ourselves, the club has been particularly acceptable, the scarcity having added much to your trials; and I trust you did not forget that the distress was sent by a merciful Father, who does not afflict willingly.... In suffering by the scarcity, you have but shared in the common lot, with the pleasure of knowing the advantage you have had over many other villages, in your having suffered no *scarcity* of *religious* instruction.'[1] All such chastisements are blessings. Because of the scarcity the religious husbandman will 'more deeply feel the alternate blessing of shower and sunshine than he did before, and a more immediate sense of the Divine presence will lighten every labour; and it is a vast consolation to know, that every hard-working parent in this parish, when he returns from the fatigues of the day, and partakes, with his family, of his humble meal, can find a child who can bring the additional refreshment of reading to him a few verses of Scripture'.[2] This Charge ends with thanks offered as from the inferior ranks present for the religious instruction and the seasonable provision and with Mrs More's prayer that the affluent will be grateful for being enabled to give and the poor thankful for the mercy of receiving.

Naturally it is pointed out that the bounty of the affluent will be given only to those who are Evangelically religious and proper in conduct (Mrs More's heart, Roberts tells us, was 'warm toward those whose hearts were warm in the cause of righteousness and truth'),[3] and it is stated plainly and often that the poor have no right to this benevolence, a point stressed as much as their good fortune in being able to contemplate the greater suffering of others ('For I have food while others starve, Or beg from door to door'). The Charge of 1801 to the women of Shipham was emphatic about that. The 'scarcity' of this year was as bad as that of 1800. 'Let me remind you that probably that very scarcity has been permitted by an all-wise and gracious Providence, to *unite* all ranks of people *together*, and to shew the *poor* how immediately they are dependent upon the *rich*, and to shew both *rich* and *poor* that they are all dependent on *Himself*.'[4] There is some vagueness as to how that lesson is brought home to the rich by such means—we see even in

[1] *Ibid.* p. 235. [2] *Ibid.* pp. 236.
[3] *More*, vol. III, p. 440. [4] *Mendip Annals*, p. 243.

Cheap Repository that the scarcities had little meaning to them unless they happened to be concerned over the suffering of the unfortunate—but it would be unfair to single out Mrs More among all the Evangelicals to bring that against.

'It has also enabled you to see more clearly the advantages you derive from the government and constitution of this country—to observe the benefits flowing from the distinction of rank and fortune, which has enabled the *high* so liberally to assist the *low*; for I leave you to judge what would have been the state of the poor of this country...had it not been for their superiors....We trust the poor in general, especially those that are well instructed, have received what has been done for them as a matter of *favour*, not of *right*—if so, the same kindness will, I doubt not, always be extended to them, whenever it shall please God so to afflict the land.'[1]

But in spite of the Evangelical language or with due allowance for it, the evidence is clear that sharing with Hannah More in the extraordinary increase of religion and virtue were some (and no doubt there were many) who did not wholly share Mrs More's views, who were more concerned with what they took to be good Christian conduct and less with points of view of any kind, who led lives of simple piety and Christian charity. Probably there were many such among those Evangelicals whose names appear again and again in the lists of the societies, as subscribers, on the committee or among the officers. Those societies furnish full evidence of the Evangelical superiority to the serene spectators of suffering, destitution, vice and helpless degradation who seem so numerous during the Age of Elegance. There was not one of them that was devoted to the relief of distress and left surviving records —hospitals, infirmaries, dispensaries, lying-in homes, refuges, asylums, penitentiaries and all other institutions to help the unfortunate—in which the Evangelicals did not play a prominent part, in many, perhaps most, a dominant part, except small specialized or local societies and they were in many of them. Not only in peculiarly Evangelical institutions such as the Naval and Military Bible Society, the Newfoundland Society, the North American Indian Society, the London Jew Society and the many Irish societies but in the Foundling Hospital, the Asylum, the Societies for the Blind and for the Deaf and Dumb Children of the

[1] *Mendip Annals*, pp. 243–4.

Poor, the Magdalen Hospital, the Vaccine Pock Institution, the City of London Truss Society for the Relief of the Ruptured Poor Throughout the Kingdom, the New Rupture Society and many more, the several hundred Evangelical leaders in this field played so large a part that only a score or so of others approached them.

In some of those Evangelicals, perhaps many, we probably see men and women of simple goodheartedness and unostentatious piety, people who like Wilberforce would not be very happy among assured vessels, jargon-peddlers full of pious phraseology and 'professors' abounding in pious ejaculations, and they would not have been deeply addicted to morbid introspection, to long drawn-out deathbeds (for example), with delightful scenes of triumphant deaths, or to terrifying little children with tales of a vengeful burning God. Such a one is preserved for us in an unexpected testimony, *The Letters of Private Wheeler*, edited by Captain Liddell Hart in 1951. The writer, a soldier in an element bound for Portugal to reinforce Wellington, embarks in January 1811 on one of his majesty's men-of-war, apparently the *Revenge*.

The Captain goes by the name of 'Father.' Cursing and swearing is not allowed. The good feeling existing between the captain and sailors was fully displayed last Sunday morning, when the ship's company assembled for the Captain's inspection. It was truly pleasing to see the good old man, their 'Father' as the men have justly named him, walking through the ranks of sailors, who all appeared as clean as possible, with health and contentment glowing on their faces. As he past the men he seemed to impart to each a portion of his own good nature.

After the sailors, our inspection came on. The good old man accompanied the Colonel through our ranks, his affectionate looks and smiles gained all our hearts. After inspection all hands were piped to church....This day the spirit of the fourth Commandment was put into force far beyond anything I could have expected, nothing was done but what was absolutely necessary, the sailors neat and clean employing themselves agreeable to the bent of their own inclinations. In one place might be seen a sailor sitting on a gun reading to his shipmates, others reading to themselves...while others less careless would assemble in some sequestered spot, offering up prayers and singing Hymns of praise to their Creator and Redeemer.

That portrait of a captain of the Royal Navy needs no comment, and we are probably safe in taking him for one of the many Evangelical officers to be found by 1811 in both services, even though while some sailors 'whose souls are more refined are singing praises to the GOD of battles', on the two evenings each week devoted to amusement on his ship, some may be seen 'dancing to a fiddle, others to a fife.... We could not part from the crew without feelings of sorrow at the thought of parting with men who had deprived themselves of many comforts to add to ours; there was one pleasing prospect, we were leaving them under the fostering care of their good old "Father," not a man had been flogged during the time we were on board.'[1]

No doubt after the great period, the Age of Wilberforce, there were many such religiously unassuming and unpedantic men and women in the Evangelical ranks, and decent non-unctuous families, successors to the Babingtons and Gisbornes and William Grays of York, who had an interest in the arts and sciences, such as Zachary Macaulay tried to advance in the *Christian Observer* with its reports of the proceedings of learned societies. In such families it would not have been felt necessary to turn the pictures face to the wall on Sundays as Ruskin's mother did and to make a seventh of the week intolerable by Sabbatarian rigour. In particular the Evangelical clergy (of the early period) are impressive in many ways. George Eliot's Reverend Mr Archibald Duke, 'a very dyspeptic and evangelical man, who takes the gloomiest view of mankind and their prospects' and strikingly laments the immense sale of *The Pickwick Papers* (another proof of Original Sin, however), would not be much like them. The 'unimpeached excellence' of the Evangelical character admitted by Sydney Smith was as true of the clergy as of the prominent laymen he had in mind. It is even a little extraordinary that only one charge of 'personal immorality' (in a vulgar physical sense) against an Evangelical clergyman is recorded in the course of an angry and prolonged struggle when such a charge probably could have been brought against more than one non-Evangelical clergyman. The accusation was made against the Reverend Samuel Frey of the London Jew Society, who (at the worst) was at least not a native Evangelical but a Jewish convert. Probably no attention need be paid to Mrs Frances Trollope's novel *The Vicar of Wrexhill*, in which, drawing in her 'Rev. Mr Jacob Cartwright' an apparently

[1] *The Letters of Private Wheeler*, edited by B. H. Liddell Hart (London, 1951), pp. 46, 47, 49.

recognizable portrait of the well-known Evangelical clergyman John William Cunningham, 'Mother Trollope', as *Figaro in London* used to call her ('this wretched libeller') went so far as to have him seduce one of his parishioners.[1] Under a pious and suave exterior the blackness of Mr Cartwright's character has turned his daughter into an atheist, and his unscrupulous greed and cunning are such that he is barely circumvented by the mere nominal Christians of the parish. It was rather neat of Mother Trollope, just the same, to tell us that in purifying the vicarage of all Evangelical taint they even replaced 'the serious servants' with 'honest ones'.[2]

A story of piety and single-minded devotion is told by all the biographies of the Evangelical clergy. There are more of them than of the laymen of the Party and few indeed of the High Church clergy. The biographers were naturally Evangelicals, except in extraordinary cases, usually the subject's son, daughter, wife, niece or son-in-law, curate or chosen disciple: Cadogan on Romaine, Cecil on Cadogan, Pratt on Cecil, Cecil on Newton, Pratt on Pratt, Vaughan on Robinson, Grimshawe on Richmond, Goode on Goode, Wilks on Wilks, Wilkinson on Wilkinson, Shore on Shore, Scott on Scott, Venn on Venn, Venn on Venn on Venn, Carus on Simeon, Sidney on Richard Hill and Rowland Hill, the Wilberforces on Wilberforce; the life of Bickersteth by his son-in-law and daughter, of Cecil by his wife, Richmond by his wife, Milner by his niece, Bernard by his nephew (who was not Evangelical), Macaulay by his granddaughter, Lord Gambier by his niece, Buxton by his son, the Clapham group by the son of James Stephen. There is no known one of the clerical biographies but was reprinted, and some of them many times. They too were a part of the great propaganda. They described men of zeal and unresting industry. To the spread of true religion everything else was subordinated or for it everything else was given up, as Hannah More renounced the drama and polite letters. Henry Venn, a fine athlete, gave up cricket—'I wished never to hear it said, "Well struck, parson!"'—Richard Cecil destroyed his

---

[1] The Vicar of Wrexhill was meant 'for the Vicar of Harrow on the Hill, Mr Cunningham. It is a most abominable personal attack' (Samuel Wilberforce; *Life of Bishop Wilberforce*, vol. i, p. 114).

[2] Mrs Frances Trollope, *The Vicar of Wrexhill* (London, 1837; new ed. revised, Bentley's Standard Novels, 1840), p. 346.

violin.[1] Many a one of them, in thoughtless days a reader of the classics or belles-lettres, like Cecil and Hannah More gave up all reading except the Bible and was proud to describe himself as *homo unius libri*. 'Life how short, eternity how long!' was their constant cry. It was not to be said of them, as Carus Wilson said of infidels, that indolence nailed them to the bed in drowsy stupidity.

To lead a normal life it perhaps is not absolutely necessary to read Lord Byron or even Walter Scott, play cards on Sundays and go to the theatre, particularly the English theatre as it was in the 1830's and 1840's when concern for a happy life would plainly lead any sensitive person to stay away ('The Drama has fallen now so low', even *Figaro*, an addicted theatre-goer and no Evangelical, observed in 1832, 'that we do not consider its redemption possible').[2] In many families like the Grays it is probable that the puritanical severities of the more typical Evangelicals were mitigated and mellowed. Sir Gilbert Scott's recollections of his childhood include an anecdote of his grandfather Thomas Scott, a grave figure in rusty black who, grown deaf, would have to ask what the bursts of laughter at the dinner table were about, his invariable comment when told being 'Pshaw'. That has value as indicating that at the dinner table of even the most solid Evangelical family there were bursts of laughter. No doubt there were strongholds of true religion and strict morality where children laughed and played, some where they could dance. On Clapham Common the children rebelled until they were allowed to have dances even at Christmas.

Among the Evangelicals of Wilberforce's generation there was always a less bigoted Puritanism than developed at the end of the reform period and was a notable mark of the Bleak Age. In one or two aspects it was even moderate, at least in comparison with some modern reforming efforts. In the field of the immoral consumption of drink it also had some similarity to them. Temperance and total abstinence societies sprang up only after 1830. In 1831 the British and Foreign Temperance Society, founded in that year, already had fifty-six auxiliaries. It probably is not worthy of comment that such societies, which pledged

---

[1] It was a communicant of his, Mrs Sarah Hawkes, who was eventually strong enough to stop 'the singing of songs', the last part of worldly conformity she was able to give up (Catherine Cecil, *Memoir of Mrs Hawkes*, London, 1837, p. 18, note).

[2] *Figaro in London*, 1 December 1832, p. 208.

their members to abstain from distilled spirits, were heavily supported by the Evangelical brewers and the total abstinence and anti-tobacco societies by the Quakers and Evangelicals of Quaker origin who made biscuits and chocolate confections, the Rowntrees, Cadburys, Frys and Messrs Huntley and Palmer. As those societies were not supported by the Evangelical brewers there was a slight rift in the solid reforming front. There was strong Party support of both kinds, however, on purer grounds.[1] These early institutions led to such as the British League of Juvenile Abstainers (1847), which pledged its youthful members to refrain from alcoholic liquors, tobacco and opium, and the British Anti-Tobacco Society (1853), in which Messrs Gurney, Barclay, Bevan, Cadbury and Huntley and Palmer were especially active. The Cadburys also gave up dealing in tobacco, which was slave-produced in addition to being inherently evil. The first *Report* of this Society records one interesting occurrence: 'A boy, ten years of age, said that he would be the best smoking boy in Cheltenham, and one morning he bought Tobacco and smoked two pipes full. His mother wished to send him on an errand, but he said he could not go. He then laid his hand on his temple and said, "Murder! Mother! Murder, Mother! I am going to die. God bless you!" and fell at her feet to rise no more.'[2]

In the early period no one had learned there was anything wrong in drinking alcoholic beverages, though it was felt that spirits were not suitable to a gentleman and opprobrium attached to Tom Paine and Richard Brinsley Sheridan who drank brandy. So far as is known, all Evangelical ladies and gentlemen took wine. Southey described Sir William Scott's once reminding Wilberforce that it was he who introduced Hermitage into England.[3] When the Reverend Lewis Way turned Stansted Park over to Wilberforce for a few days he was careful to leave him 'a case of port, and an order for half a buck'. Buxton and his friend and brother-in-law Samuel Hoare jun. not only brewed but drank their rival brews, and almost the complete roll of English and Irish brewers were in the Evangelical front. Even Hannah More was not opposed to the use of malt liquors, even by the poor, of course in a way suitable to their station, and drew at least one idyllic picture of its

[1] *Report of the British and Foreign Temperance Society* (London, 1832), p. 5, etc.
[2] *Report of the British Anti-Tobacco Society*, 1853, p. 8.
[3] *Wilberforce*, vol. IV, p. 322.

happy consumption. After a fray has taken place at the Chequers and it is put down as a nuisance, in *A Cure For Melancholy: Shewing the Way to Do Much Good With Little Money*, 'Mrs Jones, in her evening walks, had the pleasure to see many an honest man drinking his wholesome cup of beer by his own fire-side, his rosy children playing about his knees, his clean chearful wife singing her youngest baby to sleep, rocking the cradle with her foot, while with her hands she was making a dumpling for her kind husband's supper'.[1]

There were other indulgences too. Sir Thomas Fowell Buxton and Samuel Hoare not only brewed and drank but shot, and Wilberforce and Simeon were not above accepting some of their bag, though Simeon was upset once when Buxton went shooting instead of attending a meeting of his Jew Society, one of the many auxiliaries of the London Society for Promoting Christianity Amongst the Jews (which several of the Party leaders did not seem to care much about). Buxton was a big, powerful, full-blooded man, scrupulously honest in the English sense of the word, above trickery and accommodation and worth a dozen Simeons, though of course not Evangelically. Wilberforce named him as his parliamentary successor in the fight on slavery. To indicate his extreme peripheral position in the Party ranks, it is enough to add that he preserved game, bred dogs and horses, was an outstanding sportsman and the only Evangelical of the day who could have said about Wilberforce (whom he greatly admired) 'I think it odd that we should suit so well, having hardly one quality in common'.[2] Lord Teignmouth took snuff but was a little ashamed of doing it and urged his sons not to take it. In the early period it had never occurred to anybody that tobacco was evil. When John Newton left his pipe at the Mores' (on that visit in 1791) it was deposited in the blackcurrant bush and there was a good deal of epistolary humour about it. Wilberforce and Isaac Milner took opium in large quantities, on a doctor's prescription, and William Cowper drank gin, apparently with open enjoyment.

If many Evangelicals had been like Cowper, the Victorian Age might have been different. But no Evangelical was like him in many respects, few were like him in any, and between him and the great or

---

[1] *Stories 1818*, vol. I, p. 350.
[2] Charles Buxton, *Memoirs of Sir Thomas Fowell Buxton* (2nd ed., London, 1849), p. 135.

typical Evangelicals there is a chasm of opposition. He has always been taken as one of them; but to do so we accept an accidental, pitifully unfortunate association with John Newton and reject almost every other known thing about him. It seems not only simpler and more satisfactory but even more sensible not to do it.

The view that Newton drove Cowper insane by his gloomy Calvinism—we have heard it from Anna Seward—is untenable in that form. Cowper was a Calvinist and had had attacks of insanity before he met Newton, who furthermore was the least gloomy Calvinist known. He was still responsible for the tragic unhappiness of Cowper's life, and without any sin on his part except the sin of ignorance. He came into an Orthodox clergyman's parish, a characteristic thing for an Evangelical to do, to pay a call of Christian helpfulness on a bereaved family whom Cowper happened to be staying with—a dire 'counter-providence', for of all the good-hearted men of the age Newton was one of the last who should have turned up to bring spiritual encouragement to a timid, desperately insecure man. Since his conversion John Newton had never been sick in body or soul a single day. In the spiritual combat of the Christian life he was a serene, powerful champion. Doing everything, with the greatest love, that he knew to do, blind to the fearful danger such an exposure could be to a soul not so iron as his own, he brought Cowper out into the fierce glare of the religion of John Calvin that he himself found wholly comforting. He might as well have pushed him into the squared ring with John Jackson. If, in the mysterious workings of the Deity he wrote about, this shy, gentle man with the exquisite sense of humour, so gifted at seeing and describing the beautiful things of everyday life, had to be allotted one of the Evangelical shepherds, it is a pity he could not have drawn one less triumphant than the old African blasphemer.

Cowper enjoyed the world below, this side Jordan, much more than a pilgrim on the march should do. In his soul there was no place for subterfuge or accommodation, propitiation or conciliation, anything resembling the 'Evangelical duplicity'. To be ingratiating to the socially powerful or to force others to hold his views for their good to edification would never have entered his mind. The Society for the Suppression of Vice opposed cruelty to animals because it morally harmed the lower orders; Cowper opposed it because it physically harmed the animals. The Society was not opposed to the ruling class's cruelty to animals; Cowper denounced it indignantly again and again. He was a liberal because he loved liberty and hated the oppression of the little, he opposed Negro slavery because he hated cruelty and believed in social justice. Mr Gilbert Thomas tells us of his respect for the poor and constant great courtesy to them. He was not an idolater of royalty and believed that if kings are unjust they should be condemned severely. He wrote about 'the rights of man', the oppressor grinding down the poor, 'some royal mastiff' panting at the people's heels. What Evangelical of the age can those statements be made about?

One group of the Evangelicals Cowper would have enjoyed, in a personal way, and it is a pity he did not know them. It is a chief gap in the Party history that we have no sober factual account of the Cambridge Evangelicals omitting Charles Simeon and his disciples. Here and there, chiefly in non-Evangelical literature, there are glimpses of Milner, Farish and one or two others showing a happy eccentricity and a humanity not easy to find elsewhere in the Party. It is seen in Fowell Buxton too, who was not a man to force other people to think as he did. With good classic Evangelical qualities these Cambridge men had a simplicity, humour and warmth that is pleasantly worldly. Their interest in boxing did not have any 'muscular Christianity' about it but admirably to the contrary was just an interest in boxing. Milner, a huge burly man, would have delighted Cowper with his Yorkshire humour, his great indolence, his gormandizing and his perpetual hypochondria. He did card tricks, liked to expose professional charlatans and used to walk naked in the rain in the Master's garden, forgetting or not caring that he could be seen from neighbouring windows. His dinners were noted for large amounts of food and drink. When a puzzled visitor wondered how a man who believed himself so ailing could take so many different kinds of both, Milner pointed out to him that when his weak stomach had digested all it could of one kind he thereby enabled it to turn to another. Jowett used to have music parties in his apartment and Farish, whose colloquial Latin alone would put him in a special Evangelical class if a preserved sample is typical, the direction to a lecture-room student 'verte canem ex', was once caught reading *Tristram Shandy*.[1]

[1] J. D. Walsh in *The Church Quarterly Review*, Oct.–Dec. 1958, p. 508.

II

Isaac Milner and William Wilberforce believed that even a virtuous people set apart can incur grave risks. Before the moral campaign had begun, the old slaver redeemed from the bondage had held before all 'vital professors' a warning as solemn as John Gifford's to the idol shepherds. Newton was writing on this occasion on *Causes, Symptoms and Effects of a Decline in the Spiritual Life*. One cause is spiritual pride and complacency, one error in basic Christian belief, the third 'an inordinate desire and attachment to the things of the present world'.

Even under that third head, evident as it is that in his present relationships the Christian's first commandment is 'Be ye not conformed to this world', there was grave danger to the Evangelicals, and it was of the simplest kind. It had long been recognized that the Church of Christ in modern times can hardly turn its back on men and women of wealth. The ineligibility of such people for salvation is as obsolete as the sinfulness of taking interest for money. That aspect of Christianity nevertheless remains an accommodation and one that should not be disguised. Thus one would think that those fortunate Evangelical members of the upper classes who combined so acceptably an unworldly religion and a life of affluent comfort, living up to 'what is expected' (in the Evangelical literature it is likely to be 'what is required') of their rank or 'position in society', might have had the sense of humour not to describe themselves in early Christian terms suitable to humbler members of simpler communities—such for instance as 'giving their all to the Lord'. Indeed in the Evangelical apportionment of one's wealth between the requirements of true devotion and the obligation to live in a correct way in this world, the claims of religion, even among the firmest members of the Party, seem often to have come off second best.

There were at least three Evangelicals of Wilberforce's time who saw this problem clearly. One was Wilberforce, who lived far below 'what his station and fortune entitled him to' and regretted that many Evangelicals did not live less comfortably and give more to the cause. So much of his large fortune went into religious and charitable works that the loss of an investment in a dairy-farming operation for his eldest son, which could hardly have been a huge amount, was a shattering blow. Another was Henry Thornton, who is said to have given four-fifths of his income to religion when unmarried and one-half when he had a large family, even while avoiding austerity. His children looked askance at their uncle Samuel Thornton who seemed to them to live in an unduly handsome manner and to have a fondness for the society of the rich. That did not keep Samuel Thornton, incidentally, from playing a very prominent part, both personally and with his money, in a large number of Evangelical reforming institutions or from bringing up his son John to do the same, and perhaps his view of the matter was Evangelically sounder than Henry's.

A third was Buxton, who saw that his devotion to some aspects of costly worldliness kept him from being the best kind of serious Christian and had some compunction about it, though not enough to give it up. 'The world, and the spirit of the world', he wrote to a young clergyman in 1826,

are very insidious, and the older we grow the more inclined we are to think as others think, and act as others act; and more than once I have seen a person, who, as a youth, was single-eyed and single-hearted...in maturer age become, if not a lover of the vices of the world, at least a tolerator of its vanities. I speak here feelingly, for the world has worn away much of the little zeal I ever had. 'What is the harm,' you will say, 'of a convenient house; what is the harm of a convenient house being elegant; of an elegant house being suitably furnished?' The same personage who insinuated this to you, said to me, 'Where is the harm of having a few dogs,—those few very good; you preserve game—do it well—do it better than other people;' and so he stole away my heart from better things. I have more game, and better horses and dogs than other people, but the same energy, disposed of in a different way, might have spread Bible and Missionary Societies over the Hundred of North Erpingham....

Now every word of this sermon is inconsistent with my own practice; but never mind that; truth is truth, whoever speaks it.[1]

Perhaps it is peculiarly necessary that the Christian professor in a group of people extensively making use of the means of the world for a Christian purpose should see precisely what he is doing, and perhaps too in hardly any other matter are there so many subtle shades of

---

[1] Charles Buxton, *Memoir of Sir Thomas Fowell Buxton*, pp. 188-9.

insidious and barely perceptible variation between rectitude and compliance. That there is a fine line here somewhere between an outmoded apostolic poverty and a complete though virtuous service to Mammon is unquestionable, but so is it that as they gathered power the Evangelicals by and large are to be found noticeably to the right of centre. Their attitude is probably well expressed in good Legh Richmond's happy exclamation as he contemplated his beloved leader: 'How beautiful a sight is riches united with godliness.' ('Yet who that has the latter is not truly possessed of the former.')[1]

The formal position of Evangelicalism in the matter was never in doubt. Sir Richard Hill in his youth started out as a lay preacher, but 'was prevailed on to relinquish that work, and seek other modes of usefulness derivable from his fortune and station'.[2] There is a simple and pleasant statement of the principle written by Mrs Henry Thornton before her marriage (she declined Thornton's first proposal as it forced her to write to him on a Sunday). 'Mr T. tells me we must do good both to the bodies and souls of men,' she writes to her mother, 'and to gain an influence over the minds of our equals is perhaps most necessary, which cannot be done if we are not equally free from austerity and ostentation. Laying this down as a general rule, I am going this morning about my clothes. Moderation and modesty is to be the order of the day, but yet my dress is to be elegant and fashionable.'[3]

Of course all Evangelical leaders held possession and position as stewardship, their wealth wholly from the Almighty and wholly at his service. In William Carus Wilson's often-repeated demand 'Give all to God!' they would have joined unhesitatingly. There is only the difficulty of determining how far the part can reasonably stand for the whole. It is noticeable, and was pointed out frequently by Gentiles, that the Evangelicals were over-careful to avoid fanaticism here; and it was not merely that in these men of political or financial affairs there was a natural element of prudence. As we hear throughout the Evangelical literature of the proper religious person's 'duty' to live up to his 'station in life' or his 'rank and position in society' we begin to get a picture of an Evangelical Deity as greatly concerned about these things

[1] Grimshawe, *Memoir of Richmond*, p. 65.
[2] Sidney, *Life of Rowland Hill*, p. 61.
[3] *Marianne Thornton*, pp. 17–18.

as his earthly servants. This appears even in Hannah More's worthy and exemplary members of the middle class in her moral fictions. Her Mr Trueman would give up his acquaintance with Mr Fantom, who he knows is a wicked man, except that Fantom owes him some money that he hopes to collect.

In short, even among dedicated Evangelicals of unquestionable religious principle, such as Sir Richard Hill, Babington, Gisborne and dozens more, there was a marked feeling of primary responsibility to the social duties of an English gentleman that was unhesitatingly approved by the Party (Wilberforce's expression of regret at the extent to which the feeling was sometimes carried being the only one recorded). It is perfectly expressed in Viscountess Knutsford's *Life and Letters* of her grandfather Zachary Macaulay. She is describing the young Macaulay's introduction to Evangelical society within the 'ancient walls' of Rothley Temple, the beautiful Leicestershire seat of Thomas Babington, one of the most honest and unaccommodatable of the Party, who was married to Macaulay's sister. 'He now found himself living in intimate association with men in whose daily life he beheld every pure Christian principle brought into action, and whose motives and habits bore un-flinchingly the closest scrutiny. Instead of the systematic indulgence and selfishness of those with whom he had spent his youth, he saw his present companions voluntarily renouncing that ease and enjoyment to which their wealth and position entitled them', Lady Knutsford con-tinues, 'in order to labour unceasingly for the welfare of their fellow-creatures, to whose necessities they devoted all the money they could spare from the duties of hospitality.'[1]

It would be hard to find a better example of how to live in the world and yet not be of the world, to employ in a Christian way all the money that can be spared from correctly filling one's allotted place in society, than that provided by the 'sustained splendour of the stately life' of the great Evangelical of the North, the Duchess of Gordon. This eminently pious woman was converted to true religion chiefly by Lady Leven, John Thornton's daughter, and by Mrs Hannah More's Lady Olivia Sparrow. Her life is the canonical illustration of the working of Evangelicalism among the great and by them on the great, the middle and the inferior. In 1833 an American journalist, Nathaniel Parker

[1] *Life and Letters of Zachary Macaulay* (London, 1900), pp. 15–16.

Willis, came along who repaid a kindly welcome to Gordon Castle by publishing an extensive account of its magnificence, which was annoying to the duchess perhaps for more than one reason. Willis was a correspondent of the New York *Mirror* and probably did not under-colour his picture. But the parts of it quoted by the duchess's evangelical biographer Moody Stewart, a minister of Scotch Presbyterian persuasion, omitted the inaccurate portions, and presumably what is left was merely tinted with the natural reverence a young and little-travelled American would have for scenes of a social loftiness not remotely approached in his own country.

The immense iron gate surmounted by the Gordon arms, the handsome and spacious stone lodges on either side, the canonically fat porter in white stockings and gay livery lifting his hat as he swung open the massive portal, all bespoke the entrance to a noble residence. The road within was edged with velvet sward, and rolled to the smoothness of a terrace walk; the winding avenue lengthened away before, with trees of every variety of foliage; light carriages passed me, driven by ladies or gentlemen bound on their afternoon airing; keepers with hounds and terriers, gentlemen on foot idling along the walks, and servants in different liveries hurrying to and fro, betokened a scene of busy gayety before me. I had hardly noted these various circumstances before a sudden curve in the road brought the castle into view, a vast stone pile with castellated wings; and in another moment I was at the door, where a dozen powdered footmen were waiting on a party of ladies and gentlemen to their various carriages. I passed the time till the sunset looking out on the Park. Hill and valley lay between my eye and the horizon; sheep fed in picturesque flocks, and small fallow-deer grazed near them; the trees were planted, and the distant forests shaped by the hand of taste; and broad and plentiful as was the expanse taken in by the eye, it was evidently one princely possession. A mile from the castle wall, the shaven sward extended in a carpet of velvet softness as bright as emerald, studded by clumps of shrubbery like flowers wrought elegantly on tapestry, and across it bounded occasionally a hare, and the pheasants fed undisturbed near the thickets. This little world of enjoyment, luxury, and beauty lay in the hand of one man, and was created by his wealth in these northern wilds of Scotland. I never realized so forcibly the splendid results of wealth and primogeniture. . . .

Dinner was announced immediately, and the difficult question of precedence being sooner settled than I had ever seen it before in so large a party, we passed through files of servants to the dining-room. It was a large and very lofty hall, supported at the end by marble columns. The walls were lined with full length family pictures, from old knights in armor to the modern dukes in kilt of the Gordon plaid; and on the sideboard stood services of gold plate, the most gorgeously massive and the most beautiful in workmanship I have ever seen. There were among the vases several large coursing cups, won by the Duke's hounds, of exquisite shape and ornament.[1]

While the duchess is said to have been vexed at Willis's account 'in various respects', her biographer, though he thought it 'highly colored throughout', does not seem really displeased about it but rather to dwell with innocent happiness on the worldly circumstances of this famous Evangelical. Willis's worst fault, it appears, was his naïveté. 'When most faithful, it is the account of a foreigner detailing nothing that was peculiar to Gordon Castle, but only what he would have found in the mansions of other noblemen and gentlemen.'

After the Duke of Gordon died in 1836 (this is that Marquis of Huntly who according to his mother Jane Duchess of Gordon would soon be above his trade) it was clear that the duchess should go on living in her accustomed manner. Moody Stewart's statement of that determination is perfect (this is the Presbyterian pastor who referred to Jane's conversation as 'unchastened but exuberant'). To have reduced greatly that establishment described by Willis 'would have saved her many temptations, spared her much trouble, and given her a magnificent opportunity of directly furthering the cause of the gospel, relieving much distress, and promoting many schemes for the good of mankind. But to use her own words, she saw that "position is stewardship"; and she wisely resolved not to cast it away, but to devote it to the Lord and his service. The precept, "Let every man abide in the same calling wherein he was called", she took as the guide of her path; and having been numbered by the Lord in the rank of the "not many noble that are called," she determined therein to abide with God.' 'The circumstances in which I have been placed in England,' the duchess wrote, 'not only by my rank, but by the friendship and esteem of my Queen [this was Adelaide], forbid me to place myself now in such a position as might mar my future usefulness, if it be the will of God to give me grace, wisdom, strength and opportunity.'[2]

[1] Moody Stewart, *The Last Duchess of Gordon* (New York, 1868), pp. 127–9.
[2] *Ibid.* pp. 220–1.

Of course that choice was Evangelically correct, though more so in 1800 than after Wilberforce.

It is impossible to calculate the good she was enabled to accomplish by thus retaining and adorning the position that belonged to her. The light that shines through the cottage window in the low valley will cheer and guide the midnight wanderer, who chances to pass within its narrow range; but the lamp on the lofty lighthouse is seen far and near, and directs thousands to the sheltering harbour. Her burning lamp was placed on such an elevation; her pure and loving and heavenly life told the world whence its light was kindled, and guided some of its children to the hope within the veil, where they, also, might cast their anchor and be forever safe; while her steadfast and holy walk was a lofty pattern in the Church, an epistle known and read of all men, which provoked many in their humbler spheres to walk as she did on an elevation so peculiarly trying. Compared with this wide influence, the benefit must have been little that would have been produced by the additional means to be placed at her disposal by descending into a lower path of life.[1]

For nearly thirty years the Christian light of this widowed duchess shone clear, bright and very visible, from a passionate Evangelical conviction that was changed in no respect except formal adherence when in 1846 she became a member of the Free Church of Scotland. Huntly Lodge, where she lived when the Castle went to other heirs, 'was marked by simplicity, regulated with strict economy, and conducted with remarkable quietness', 'while wanting nothing that became her position', and it does not appear that the duchess had any regrets at being called on by Providence to adorn so exalted a station. In one or two passages Moody Stewart's account is worthy of a more famous pen. 'To some of her friends, it seemed that her own taste would have led her to prefer the retired life of a simple gentlewoman, without the establishment associated with her rank. But the preference of the Duchess was certainly rather for a measure of the state to which she had been so long accustomed.' 'Her daily life at Huntly Lodge was a testimony against those doctrines which level all earthly distinctions; a constant witness to the scriptural institution and the attractive beauty of a regulated order in the world.'[2] On that sentence let us confer a supreme commendation: It could have been written by Hannah More.

Any such tinge of the world did not prevent one of the most striking

---

[1] *Ibid.* pp. 221–2.   [2] *Ibid.* pp. 219, 218.

of all Evangelical testimonies. At Huntly Lodge, Sunday was 'a day of holy rest to the servants'; all work possible was done on Saturday evening, no fires were lighted in the drawing room, both to save unnecessary work and 'to present no inducement for visitors to meet together for idle conversation'. No letters were received or posted and no visitors arrived or departed. At times of religious service, the doors of the Lodge were locked and only one servant or at most two left at home. 'But there was no slave-like bondage on the holy day, no want of sunny cheerfulness, no restraint from admiring and rejoicing in all the works of the Lord', though probably the duchess would have agreed with Hannah More that walks in the country on Sunday are indefensible. Other Evangelical duties were as scrupulously performed. From an early time the duchess had built and supported 'infant schools', and that work was redoubled. She built chapels and struggled earnestly to supply them with good clergymen. Death reigned in mere nominal Christian parishes, the duchess believed, and nothing could induce her to look upon 'a minister lacking the great essentials for his office' except as 'a cumberer of holy ground'.[1] These views were earnestly communicated to others in her walk of life as well as to the poor. The Duchess of Gordon's gold vase for a chapel in Morayshire led, we are told, to 'the consecration of the Duchess of Beaufort's diamond earrings for a chapel in Wales', and it was believed that the duke himself as well as his sister the Duchess of Bedford was led to serious views.

The duchess was accustomed year after year to relieve the wants of between two and three hundred poor families. 'Her regular disbursement for the poor in meat, clothing, and money was very large.' In this as in her attitude toward the performance of all religious duties done for others, for their good to edification, a basic Evangelical principle was not overlooked. 'She did not forget', in her charities for the poor, 'the Lord's command to "make friends of the mammon of unrighteousness", but took care to provide spiritual counsel for those who shared her temporal bounty.'[2] In this too the duchess was following in the approved way the precept and practice of Hannah More, who gave us the finest statements and the finest examples of the principle of making the dependency of poor people, in illness or in want, 'useful' for the inculcation of Evangelical truth.

[1] *The Last Duchess of Gordon*, p. 280.   [2] *Ibid.* p. 230.

III

In Newton's *Causes, Symptoms and Effects of a Decline in the Spiritual Life* the second head is 'spiritual pride and self-complacence', and here, in one of his finest passages, he is speaking with great directness to many an Evangelical professor. As with attachment to the world, 'unless this evil be mortified in the root, it will in time prevail over the most splendid profession.'

'I am afraid there are no people more fully answer the character, and live in the spirit of the pharisees of old,' Newton had said earlier, in 1780, speaking about 'wise-headed Calvinists' but addressing any vessel 'elated with a sense of his own superior spiritual merits', 'than some professed sticklers for free grace. They are wise in their own eyes; their notions, which the pride of their hearts tells them are so bright and clear, serve them for a righteousness, and they trust in themselves and despise others.'[1]

If our attainments in knowledge and gifts, and even in grace, seduce us into a good opinion of ourselves, as if we were wise and good, we are already ensnared....For God, who giveth more grace to the humble, resisteth the proud; he beholds them with abhorrence, in proportion to the degree in which they admire themselves. It is the invariable law of his kingdom, that every one who exalteth himself shall be abased. True Christians, through the remaining evil of their hearts, and the subtle temptations of their enemy, are liable, not only to the workings of that pride which is common to our fallen nature, but to a certain kind of pride, which, though the most absurd and intolerable of any, can only be found among those who make profession of the Gospel. We have nothing but what we have received, and therefore to be proud of titles, wealth, or any temporary advantage, by which the providence of God has distinguished us, is sinful; but for those who profess themselves to be sinners, and therefore deserving of nothing but misery and wrath, to be proud of the peculiar blessings which are derived from the Gospel of his grace, is a wickedness of which even the fallen angels are not capable....

Ministers who are honoured with singular abilities and success, have great need of watchfulness and prayer on this account.[2]

An exalted certainty that Evangelicals are right, all others wrong, is to be seen in the unquestioning conviction that the truly religious, but no others, are in an immediate, personal, way the constant object of concern to God. Inside the Established Church, it was a touchstone of

[1] *Newton*, vol. VI, p. 197.   [2] *Ibid.* pp. 407-9.

'truly religious' adherence to hold that the Deity, watching steadily over the well-being of his elect in this present world, frequently interposes for their benefit even in apparently trivial affairs.

No Christian would deny that God's hand is to be seen in great events —even Sydney Smith pointed out[1]—such as the exaltation or destruction of nations. Thus it would appear reasonable to the High Church group, granting the necessary premise of Wilberforce's divine commission to reform the country, for him to hold his friends' coming to his support in the costly election of 1807 as a direct act of God. 'You will not conceive that I am less grateful to them because I trace it to a still higher source, and look with humble and I hope thankful wonder at the Divine goodness, which so influenced in my favour the affections of men.'[2] Probably the High Churchmen of Cambridge would not have conceded such magnitude to Milner's rescue of Charles Simeon at the Cambridge Senate of 1811. It seemed greatly important to Simeon, and of course it showed in the clearest way the existence of a God constantly solicitous for the success of Charles Simeon's ministry. 'And now, my soul, say whether there be not a God that ruleth in the earth?' he wrote; '—say whether there be not One who "doeth according to His will in the armies of heaven and among the inhabitants of the earth, whose counsel shall stand, and who will do all His will?" Yes; I see it on this occasion as clearly, as if I had seen the sun stand still on Gibeon, or the shadow go back on the sun-dial of Ahaz.'[3] In the year of Wilberforce's election a divine intervention brought about a still more spectacular happening. In August 1807 Wilberforce notes 'awful suspense whilst doubting what we shall hear from Admiral Gambier'. Gambier was in command of the expedition sent to seize the neutral Danish fleet, on the pretext that it was about to be used against the Allies. The 'awful suspense'—with Wilberforce thinking about matters as he did—must have been caused by his doubts of the justice of the act. On the day following the Danish surrender the good Evangelical admiral wrote him that Providence had favoured them in the most remarkable manner in all particulars.[4]

---

[1] *Essays of Sydney Smith, op. cit.* p. 93.

[2] *Wilberforce*, vol. III, p. 343. It was this election in which the friends referred to raised a fund of £64,455 of which £28,600 was spent (*ibid.* vol. III, pp. 334–5).

[3] *Simeon*, pp. 329–30. [4] *Wilberforce*, p. 347.

Even in the most minute happenings, apparently inconsequential or commonplace, God's work is always to be seen. Meeting a group of the Evangelical clergy at a 'religious party', Arthur Young noted approvingly that 'they made every possible event, the most trivial, providential'.[1] The lives of those who were devoted to God in the Evangelical way, and perhaps more significantly those who in the course of time would come to be devoted to Him, were directed sometimes in tiny detail. As unquestioningly held is the belief that God's hand is similarly to be seen in the punishment of sinners in this present world. Both beliefs were recorded in a multitude of episodes all of which a High Churchman or infidel would ascribe to chance or accident. There are not many Evangelical biographies, and still fewer autobiographies, that do not list instances of escape from imminent danger or less spectacular but remarkable instances of the watchful guarding of Evangelicals; many also contain collateral instances of the divine discomfiture or punishment of scoffers, blasphemers, infidels, Evangelical persecutors or other enemies. There are few human activities in which such interpositions are not recorded. 'I would adore the providence of God which tenderly preserved you, in your danger by the little Welsh horse', Joseph Milner wrote in 1792 to James Stillingfleet. 'Pray ride the ill-natured beast no more. We are not sufficiently thankful for such interpositions. I had one myself, of another kind. While I was at Carlisle, some wanton fellows, with more boldness than wit, brake into my school one night; and though a desk with my history, sermons, &c., happened to be there, unlocked, they did no harm to them.'[2] It was evident to Milner and all Evangelicals that such a happening was a specific interposition of the Deity for his servant Joseph Milner.

'Setting aside the incidental obliquities which appear in many particular cases,' Milner says, 'every reader of history, every observer of public and private life, may see, that there is a moral government of God carrying on in the world, in which rewards and punishments are regularly dispensed, as the certain attendants of the proceedings with which they are respectively and infallibly connected. Prudence, industry, fidelity, fortitude, humanity, want not on the one side their rewards in the constant course of things; no more do rashness, sloth,

[1] *Autobiography*, p. 392.   [2] *Isaac Milner*, p. 78.

deceit, meanness, and cruelty, want their punishments on the other.... Then add to all this, that the history of ages will furnish us with a large collection of experiments, for ascertaining a very considerable display and exertion of providence in particular cases, which seem to call more immediately for them.'

Milner explains what he means in a footnote. 'The well-known case of the woman, who at Devizes, about fifty years ago, dropped down dead in the market-place immediately after having uttered a notorious falsity, affords one instance of the species of facts to which I here refer. This woman had publicly and positively averred, that what she said was true, and had expressed a wish that if it were not so, she might then suddenly drop down dead. To deny the providential interference of Almighty God in punishing such daring wickedness, seems little better than Atheism itself. A well-authenticated collection of similar cases might prove very useful in restraining that disposition, which seems to increase among us, the disposition to exclude the Divine agency from ever interposing in the affairs of the world.'[1]

The ways of God must have seemed mysterious indeed to these people if they contemplated the torrent of 'horrid blasphemies', vice, sin and assorted iniquity that as so many witnesses testify they could see on London streets any time, or even the Sunday boating parties that were not drowned (if there were any, which it is true seems unlikely from the Evangelical literature).

In his memoir of his brother Joseph, Isaac Milner points out an excellent providential interposition. 'How inscrutable and how wonderful are the ways of Providence! Certain it is that Mr Milner was a great favourite with his Patrons, the Mayor and Aldermen of Hull, and with the leading gentlemen of the town, for the space of three years from the time of his election; and it is equally certain, that about that time a most important revolution in his sentiments and conduct took place; which revolution', Isaac Milner goes on to say—the 'revolution' being of course his brother's conversion from mere nominal Christianity—'if it had happened before he was elected to the school and lectureship, would, in all probability, have prevented his having a single vote for either of those situations.' Isaac Milner tells us what might have happened then. 'His aged mother might have died in want: His

[1] *Joseph Milner*, vol. VIII, p. 457.

nephew and niece might have remained destitute orphans, and un-educated; and his brother Isaac, instead of being employed in writing these pages in the Master's Lodge of Queen's College, or in the Deanery of Carlisle, might at this moment have been labouring with his hands in the manufactories of Yorkshire.—But all these are poor insignificant trifles, compared with what remains to be mentioned.—The populous Town of Hull might have continued in the dark, irreligious, state in which he found it: Thousands might have died without ever hearing the glad tidings of the Gospel properly stated; and the succession of truly worthy and evangelical preachers, who have been his pupils or contemporaries, might never have taken place.'[1]

In the matter of the proper timing of his conversion so that it would do no worldly harm Wilberforce was helped even more signally. His election as member for Yorkshire was a conspicuous manifestation of a 'gracious Providence' in coming when it did. 'Had the change in my religious principles taken place a year sooner, humanly speaking I could never have become member for Yorkshire. The means I took, and the exertions I made, in pursuing that object, were such as I could not have used after my religious change; I should not have thought it right to carve for myself so freely, if I may use the phrase...nor should I have adopted the methods by which I ingratiated myself in the good-will of some of my chief supporters; neither after my having adopted the principles I now hold, could I have conformed to the practices by which alone any man would be elected for any of the places in which I had any natural influence or connexion.'[2]

Wilberforce never doubted that the hand of Deity was constantly guiding and shielding him in all matters. 'I believe there is not any-one, who has at all observed the dealings of Providence in his own instance with any thing like a due measure of attention', he wrote in 1830, 'who will not have seen many, many particulars in which he has been deeply indebted to the preventing or directing grace of God.'[3] Before the trip to the continent on which the seeds of conversion were planted in him by Isaac Milner, the required 'seriousness' was given to

---

[1] *Ibid.* vol. VI, pp. xvi–xvii. 'It will always be our true wisdom to observe, with grateful and reverent attention, what God has actually done, and to trace his directing hand in the causes and connexions of events.'

[2] *Wilberforce*, vol. I, p. 383. [3] *Ibid.* vol. V, p. 320.

Milner by a providential severe illness. The Lord Chancellor's offering his son Robert Isaac a living, although he had not heard of Wilberforce's financial losses, was 'an indication of the favour of God'.[1] A large number of the many recorded interpositions of Deity in his life, and in others', were performed on a lower level, many in connection with the hazards of transportation. In 1818 he was travelling to 'Mr J.'s' near Liverpool ('How gratifying that we have some Christian merchants!'). 'When we got upon the paved roads, our linch-pin twice came out, and our spring-straps broke. A kind Providence favoured us, that no accident. Praise the Lord, O my soul.'[2] He was saved several other times from coaching accidents. On one occasion he had been reading on the bank of the Avon when it occurred to him that his 'portable seat' was not safe. He had barely moved it to a distance from the bank when it broke and he fell to the ground—'a most providential escape'.[3] Years later he remembered the anniversary of that interposition. Once he narrowly escaped breaking his leg ('Deo gratias—how we are always in His hands!'),[4] and again when playing cricket with his son William and Babington.[5] Bishop Barrington was also saved by interposition in a coach accident and Mrs More was providentially saved when a coach turned over and twice when thrown by a horse. When her clothes caught on fire at Barley Wood it was providential that a quick-witted friend happened to be there. As a child the Reverend Richard Cecil fell through the ice on a pond and was rescued by workers who 'accidentally' noticed him. He once caught his coat in a mill-wheel and would have been crushed if he had not stopped the horse that was turning the wheel. In adult life Cecil was thrown, when his horse fell on the icy road, in front of a loaded cart, and once in Sussex he was held up by highwaymen who spared his life.[6] Wilberforce recorded a 'singular interference' in the life of Henry Venn: '... when all gloomy for want of means to pay the butcher, a £50 note came; from whom he never found out.'[7]

In the life of the Reverend A. R. C. Dallas the constant immanence

[1] *Wilberforce*, vol. v, p. 331.　　[2] *Ibid.* vol. IV, p. 385.
[3] *Ibid.* vol. III, p. 132.　　[4] *Ibid.* p. 316.
[5] *Ibid.* pp. 446–7.
[6] *Memoir of the Rev. Richard Cecil* (London, 1810), pp. 4, 5, 6, 12, etc.
[7] *Wilberforce*, vol. III, p. 69.

and attentiveness of God was very striking. 'The hand of the Lord has been over me at all times.' 'If you have eyes to see spiritually, you may trace the links of the chain of Providence folded together, hanging upon some very trifling event, afar off in time, which, if it had not happened, the great event at the end would not have been.' 'I may now add one or two of those striking preservations, with which it has pleased God to mark the current of my life.' A wolf he met in the road did not attack him and he was able to frighten off a herd of wild horses by shouting at them. Once in his youth he stopped by divine guidance to talk to a servant girl who was picking cherries; that led to his meeting her mistress, through whom he met people who became important in his life. Fifty years after Waterloo, he went back to the scene and by interposition met the woman at whose house he had stayed immediately after the battle. It was providential, in a general way, that he was in the chapel at Fulham on the morning of his ordination instead of a lock-up house. The most striking of all such things in Dallas's life was his providential escape from going on a tour with a relative of his, Lord Byron.[1]

The life of the great propagandist 'Charlotte Elizabeth' as a young bride in Nova Scotia, where her husband Captain Phelan was in the military, was virtually one continuous divine intervention. She was provided with an Arabian mare, 'wilful, intractable and wild'. 'Upon her I was daily mounted; and surely the Lord watched over me then indeed!...I threw myself entirely on the fond attachment of the noble creature...and never for a moment did she endanger me. This was little short of a daily miracle, when we consider the nature of the country, her character, and my unskilfulness. It can only be accounted for on the ground of that wondrous power which having willed me to work for a time in the vineyard of the Lord, rendered me immortal until the work should be done.'[2] In addition to that 'continuous preservation on horseback', Charlotte Elizabeth experienced 'the same interposing providence' when violently upset in a gig. There was only one clear spot on either side of a rocky road, for miles, and at that spot she was thrown, 'where a carpet of the softest grass overspread a perfect level of about twelve feet in length, and nearly the same in

---

[1] *Incidents in the Life and Ministry of the Rev. Alex. R. C. Dallas* (London, 1871), pp. 18, 20, 21, 60, 65, etc.

[2] *Personal Recollections* (4th ed., London, 1854), pp. 92–3.

width'.[1] On her first trip to Ireland she was providentially saved from falling overboard, and jumped out of a runaway coach without harm. During all this time she was an infidel, 'living without God in the world'[2] (that is to say, she was a good Orthodox member of the Established Church of which her father was a clergyman).

A 'most signal' escape occurred when in ignorance of the Nova Scotian winter Charlotte Elizabeth froze her fingers and then tried to warm them at a fire. The signalness of the providential interposition lay in the fact that the soldier who stopped her from doing so was a Catholic. 'Had he, poor fellow, known how busy those fingers would one day be against his religion—for he was a French Romanist—he might have been tempted to sheath his bayonet and give me free access to the tempting fire, the immense faggots of which would have sufficed to roast a heretic.'[3]

The Reverend William Hunt writing for the *Dictionary of National Biography* tells us that Edward Bickersteth, eminent servant of the Church Missionary Society, was once thrown out of his carriage and run over, 'the cart which passed over him, oddly enough, being engaged in hauling materials for the erection of a Roman Catholic church'. Probably Charlotte Elizabeth would not have thought there was anything odd about it.

Certain circumstances that a non-Evangelical would have considered accidental cut short Bickersteth's classical education, 'the peculiar work for which the providence of God intended him requiring a different training'. A still more special interposition occurred to him in 1812. 'At the request of his friends at Casterton Hall'—Bickersteth was born in Kirkby Lonsdale, had been helped by William Wilson Carus Wilson and was a close friend of his son William Carus Wilson—'he had frequently visited an aged relative of theirs—had led him to attend a Gospel ministry, and had been made a great spiritual blessing to him. He attended his dying bed. "I hope", he wrote, "I was made an instrument of some good;—he seemed to accept my help with gratitude,

---

[1] *Personal Recollections*, pp. 95–6. The stern, 'high-minded', excessively Evangelical lady who wrote under that name was Charlotte Elizabeth Browne, later Phelan, later Tonna (1790–1846); she published immensely and was apparently read so, her chief themes the Satan and the Roman Catholic Church, which she equally viewed with virulent hatred and abhorrence.   [2] *Ibid.* p. 103.   [3] *Ibid.* pp. 97–8.

and I prayed with him daily. He was in much composure of mind the night before he died." Then, mentioning that the relatives were in town, and that all seemed satisfied with the will, he added, to his parents' (his 'earthly parents', the Evangelical biographers call them elsewhere), '"And here, I may tell you, I feel grateful on another account, that Mr Carus did not make a second will, in which I believe he purposed to have left me a legacy: this would have given a tinge and aspect to my attentions, which would have distressed me exceedingly. O my parents, what continual reasons I have for gratitude to that heavenly Master I serve, who ordereth all things for me!" Such', the biographers continue, 'were his own feelings, but his liberal friends would not let the matter drop here. Influenced either by a knowledge of their aged relative's intention, or by their own grateful sense of the attention he had paid him in his last hours, as well as of the assistance he had rendered in some legal business, they placed in his hands a draft for £200.' This was a circumstance that 'afforded him fresh proof of the watchful care with which his heavenly Father provided for all his wants'.[1]

Phenomena of that sort, referred to in the earlier Evangelical literature as 'providential interpositions', became familiarly known as 'providences'. It must be said they took some strange forms, not least one described in the Reverend Watts Wilkinson's *Memoir* of his father the Reverend Watts Wilkinson. An unnamed Evangelical owed his rectory to the 'chance' that a bishop to whom he was unknown was taken ill in the little town where he was curate and detained at the inn overnight. Having nothing to do, the bishop thought the local curate might amuse him by reading to him. He had the curate in, liked him, promised him preferment, and got it for him—'a striking proof', says the younger Wilkinson, 'that the most accidental circumstances are under the direction of that providence that overrules and governs all things'.[2] If it is a proof it is truly a striking one, and the Deity can hardly ever have moved in a more mysterious way, for the bishop was that Earl of Bristol, Bishop of Derry, described as a madman and a determined infidel.[3]

---

[1] Birks, *Memoir of Bickersteth*, vol. I, pp. 201–2, 192.
[2] *Memoir of the Rev. Watts Wilkinson* (London, 1842), p. 7.
[3] Childe-Pemberton, *The Earl-Bishop*, passim.

A providence that even the Evangelicals might have looked on as extraordinary occurred in the life of the Reverend Lewis Way, the director of the London Society for Promoting Christianity Amongst the Jews. While reading law before entering the ministry he met a John Raymond Way, not related to him, who had made a large fortune. John Raymond Way, who was childless, had decided to leave his money to a son of his first cousin named Thomas Way. At dinner one evening with this heir he brought out a bottle of port and found that his corkscrew had been misplaced. His cousin Thomas produced one. After the two had had an enjoyable dinner and drunk the wine, it occurred to John Raymond Way that 'any man who went about with a corkscrew in his pocket was not likely to make a good use of wealth'. He left a little of his fortune to Thomas's wife and children but nothing to him, and to Lewis Way, whom he had been taken with because of his name, he left £300,000.[1] The money was to be devoted to the uses of God. A 'chance' meeting with an eccentric advocate of the conversion of the Jews decided which uses, and a large part of John Raymond Way's money was poured into the London Jew Society and other Evangelical Jewish projects. John Raymond Way also left £10,000 to the Reverend Basil Woodd, whom he occasionally attended at Bentinck Chapel, which Woodd appears to have put to the good Evangelical use of buying the chapel for himself.

It seems one of the clearest signs of the religious 'highmindedness' of the Evangelicals, as visible in the mildest and gentlest as in the Simeons, that they were able to overlook several aspects of these occurrences. The first is that so many were bewilderingly incomprehensible. One such took place during the Hundred Days. In 1814 it was possible for England to refuse any peace settlement that did not pledge France to discontinue the slave trade. Castlereagh came back from Vienna with a provision that it might be done away with in five years. Heartsick, Wilberforce and his lieutenants kept on with the fight through the most discouraging period of the Abolition struggle. In 1815,

---

[1] A. M. W. Stirling, *The Ways of Yesterday* (1930), p. 95. The *Memoirs of Joseph Wolff* puts the amount at £380,000. These recollections of a powerful and preposterous Evangelical (he is described as having among other unusual characteristics a passionate abhorrence of soap and water (Stirling, *The Ways of Yesterday*, p. 207)) were hastily dictated at odd moments, and probably the smaller amount is more trustworthy.

returned to Paris, Napoleon abolished the French slave trade 'with a stroke of his pen'. No comment of Wilberforce's has been preserved. He had always thought of Napoleon as the instrument of God's punishment for England's sins. 'Never surely was the hand of the Almighty more strikingly manifest', he wrote to William Hey on Napoleon's abdication.

A second characteristic of these providences that might have occasioned some doubt is that in many of them benefit to Evangelicals involved serious harm to other people. The Copenhagen providence is an instance, and Augustus Toplady was favoured by one of the kind: he had barely moved out of a vicarage when it was destroyed by fire. A third aspect is their constant occurrence for the benefit of non-Evangelicals and indeed of castaways, or in a way damaging to Evangelicals. Felicitous happenings that they would have thought of as chance no doubt occurred to Hume, Gibbon, Voltaire and Rousseau and probably a search would turn them up in the lives of such manifest rogues as the Earl of Sandwich, the Marquis of Hertford, Harriette Wilson and John Wilkes. Samuel Wilberforce was killed by a fall from a horse, also Lord Suffield who supported Abolition, and the Duke of Wellington, a noted sinner, rode all his life to the age of eighty-three. The Sunday boaters were drowned but the Forsters, admirable leaders in moral reform, were lost in the wreck of the *Rothesay Castle*. Tom Paine was saved from slaughter during the Terror by the blunder of an executioner's helper who chalked the death mark on the inside of his cell door (momentarily standing open) instead of the outside, beyond which a providence can hardly (humanly speaking) go.

If it became necessary to postulate the existence of counter-providences, Charlotte Elizabeth for one, of all writers of the age the most aware of the dreadful activity of the Satan, would not have been unwilling, and some of the enemies of Evangelicalism may be thought of as affecting a belief in them. 'Mr Poynder moved for the appointment of three new bishops for India, where four have died within the last few years, and at short periods after their arrival', *Figaro in London*, anticlerical as well as radical and wholly of the Gentile world, quoted in 1831 from the daily press. 'We cannot but admire the justice of providence in not giving to any one country more than its share of those evils to which humanity is deservedly subject. It has dealt out to each its curses and its blessings with an equal hand, and while we are free from crocodiles, jackals and other ravenous animals by which India is infested, that country, as if to counter-balance the misery it is subject to from the disgusting brutes above mentioned, possesses in its climate an effectual preservative against *bishops*.'[1]

IV

The Society for the Suppression of Vice, established on 1 April 1802, began its operations by detecting and informing against certain Italian gentlemen who were selling obscene prints in young ladies' boarding schools; it crowned the first two decades of a turbulent and detested career by suppressing the poems of Percy Bysshe Shelley.[2] This Society has a peculiar interest beyond the fact that its activities, methods and motives were more violently attacked than any other Evangelical society's. To simple people there was something excessively flagrant about its calculated blindness to gilded vice, and it had still other dubious aspects. But its special claim to attention over and above its callous disregard of the open vices of the great and its curious use of honest fraud is that it was one of Wilberforce's favourite institutions. As its objects were ostensibly moral and not religious and it had High Church members and did not have dissenting members, it was suitable to be mentioned from time to time in the young Wilberforces' greatly guarded biography. In fact anyone getting his knowledge of Wilberforce's activities from their pages only would think he gave more of his time to it than to any other society.

This peculiarly Evangelical activity has still another point of interest as indicating that some Evangelicals, perhaps many, did not approve of it. *Queen Mab* was bad enough, the editors of the *Christian Pocket Magazine* thought, in December 1822, but such prosecutions were wrong, and earlier these Evangelicals had said so in a more vigorous way: 'We cannot but regret the adoption of this Roman Catholic mode of convincing people of their errors.'[3] Perhaps it was that point of view

[1] *Figaro in London*, December 1831, p. 15.

[2] On 21 October 1822 the Society obtained a verdict in Queen's Bench 'against one Clarke for selling Queen Mab, a publication of an infidel character' (*Christian Pocket Magazine*, November 1822, p. 259). [3] *Ibid.* September 1822, p. 151.

that made this the only known Evangelical society of any significance during the period of which the parent (London) society lost members. Its first list of subscribers, in 1802, had some two hundred names. In 1803 there were over eight hundred subscribers, in 1804 'upwards of 1200 members, among whom are to be found persons of the first rank and consequence in the country',[1] and in 1825, two hundred and thirty-six. Furthermore from incomplete but not scanty surviving records there appear to have been some prominent Evangelicals who were not at any time members: notably Samuel, Henry, Robert and John Thornton, Sir Thomas Fowell Buxton, and other Evangelicals of Quaker origin such as the Barclays, Bevans, Gurneys and Samuel Hoares. On the other hand those who did believe in the Society's mode of convincing people of their errors represent the Party at its most Evangelical (Henry Hoare, Sir James Graham, Hannah More, Lords Calthorpe, Gambier, Radstock, Teignmouth and Cremorne, the clergymen Simeon, Cunningham, Budd, Pratt, Woodd and Bishops Burgess and Barrington, and of the Clapham group Elliott, Grant, Hatchard, John Broadley Wilson, John Poynder and Joseph Wilson), and very likely at its most intelligent, for through the whole period or most of it Macaulay, Babington, Gisborne, James Stephen (according to the *Anti-Jacobin Review*) and Wilberforce served actively on its committee, and this is the only Evangelical society of which that can be said.

What, to the mind of this Society, constituted 'Vice'? In 1817 the object of the Society was described to the police committee of the House of Commons as the suppression of (1) Sabbath-breaking; (2) blasphemous and licentious books, prints, drawings, toys and snuff-boxes; and (3) private theatricals, fairs, brothels, dram-shops, gaming-houses, illegal lotteries and fortune-tellers. By their nature the targets of the third group, though the Society worked at them when the chance offered, were not possible to do much with. The only course of action, on receiving information of a legal offence, was to send an agent to get evidence and to lay an action before a magistrate. As the Society's principles prohibited the employment of an immoral person (they had also learned it did not pay to bring witnesses of bad character before juries), and their agents were forbidden to use deceit, it was not

[1] *Statement of the Proceedings of the Society for the Suppression of Vice, etc.* (London, 1804), p. 20.

possible to do anything against brothels and several other evil institutions except as 'disorderly houses'. The operators of such places could only be presented as rogues and vagabonds. Still, on a third conviction they were liable to transportation. The Society was able generally to put an end to 'such public dancing as is not authorized by Act of Parliament' and had occasional successes against dram-shops that sold only gin (no publican could legally sell spirits unless he was also licensed to sell beer). But the results achieved were not encouraging, and within a few years the Society had pretty well settled down to warning, threatening and bringing actions against Sabbath-breakers, dealers in obscene devices, and 'infidel and blasphemous' publications.

In enforcing Sabbath observance the Vice Society was able to put an end to 'the shameful practice of Rowing Matches and Boat Races on Sundays' on the river above Westminster Bridge and fought actively but without much success against the Sunday drilling of the volunteers during the French War (one of Wilberforce's special interests).[1] In connection with the obscene devices some interesting aspects of the Society become visible. The devices were prints, drawings, toys and snuff-boxes (with false lids hiding obscene paintings or engravings), the prints and snuff-boxes openly exhibited in shop windows but marketed chiefly in girls' schools, by a company of six hundred principals and agents, all Italians. The toys were French, manufactured except in peace-time by prisoners of war.[2] It is in this connection that the Vice Society's principle of honest deceit came to be established. Their agents, who were not used to find offenders but to confirm information received from respectable sources and to provide evidence, were not allowed to use falsehood or make use of 'alluring to sale by the offer of a price'. But as the respectable source who originally acted as informer, and more certainly the agent in buying for example an obscene object, could hardly have avoided some mode of dissembling, it might appear to an ill-disposed person that any distinction between the Society's practice and simple dishonesty would perhaps be fine-drawn.

At this point a determination by Lord Ellenborough (Chief Justice) was helpful. The first person convicted by the Society's efforts was an Italian named, the *Report* says, Gainer, who was given six months'

---

[1] *Statement of the Proceedings of the Society for the Suppression of Vice, etc.* (1804), pp. 8–10.　　[2] *Report of the Society, etc.* (1825), p. 41.

imprisonment for the sale of immoral prints. He 'admitted that he was at the village where the offence is stated to have been committed, and that the person employed by the Society had there offered him the prints, for the sale of which he was prosecuted'. Perhaps even Charlotte Elizabeth, Holy Church's foremost Evangelical foe of the age, might have conceded that for the Society to sell to an evil person the obscene prints for the resale of which he was sentenced to imprisonment was rather more than a Roman Catholic method of convincing people of their errors. Ellenborough's justification of this mode of promoting virtue—that a wily old offender like Gainer was hard to catch—was stated during the trial of one Baptista Bertazzi, detected selling obscene articles by the same method. There is a valid distinction between provoking an innocent person to crime and an evil person. 'If a person induces another, who is innocent, to commit a crime, that inducement is a crime of the highest enormity; but if a person be in *a habitual course* of committing crime, and it be *difficult* to detect him... then to produce a declaration of that which may lead to his detection ...*is no crime but a beneficial service to the community*. I thought it necessary only to say so much to prevent any misconception.'[1]

There was internal dissension over this matter. In 1805 Wilberforce attended a meeting where the Society's managers were debating the subject of 'artifice'. He was shocked at 'the extremes to which the justifiers of artifice hurried', and spoke for 'nearly an hour'. There was a 'private meeting' then a little later, 'on the use of fraud, when came to a compromise by their agreeing not to practise falsehood'.[2] It would be valuable if the Society had recorded a clear statement of the unfalse fraud, or unfraudulent falsehood, that was determined on. Of course the defenders of plain straightforward trickery were the High Churchmen still sharing in 1805 in the Society's direction.

The least unobjectionable part of these labours on the whole was the prosecution of 'infidel and blasphemous' literature such as Paine's *The Age of Reason*. The *Report for 1825* states that since 1817 fourteen authors or publishers of such works had been punished. But the activity that roused greatest public indignation was the Society's attempts to put an end to amusements and pastimes of the lower orders while remaining suavely oblivious to quite similar pastimes of the

[1] *Ibid.* p. 47.   [2] *Wilberforce*, vol. III, p. 236.

great, and it was this activity that brought out Sydney Smith's strongest attack. As the pieces his article in the *Edinburgh* (in 1809) was ostensibly reviewing were published five years earlier it seems likely he had something in mind beyond a notice of contemporary letters.

The power of such an institution against small individuals was far too great, Smith believed. 'The very influence of names must have a considerable weight with the jury. Lord Dartmouth, Lord Radstock and the Bishop of Durham, *versus* a Whitechapel butcher or a publican! Is this a fair contest before a jury? It is not so even in London; and what must it be in the country, where a society for the suppression of vice may consist of all the principal persons in the neighbourhood? These societies are now established in York, in Reading, and in many other large towns.'

Such a society fails to achieve its object. 'There is something in the self-erection of a voluntary magistracy which creates so much disgust, that it almost renders vice popular, and puts the offence at a premium.' 'The greatest delicacy is required in the application of violence to moral and religious sentiment. We forget, that the object is, not to produce the outward compliance, but to raise up the inward feeling which secures the outward compliance.' We have here a simple statement of an anti-Evangelical view of reform, wholly opposed to Wilberforce's. His object from the beginning, with the establishment of the Proclamation Society in 1788, and throughout the Evangelical Reformation was to accomplish an outward compliance. The inward feeling, he believed, would follow.

'You may drag men into church by main force', Smith goes on, 'and prosecute them for buying a pot of beer,—and cut them off from the enjoyment of a leg of mutton; and you may do all this, till you make the common people hate Sunday, and the clergy, and religion, and every thing which relates to such subjects.... We have no great opinion of the possibility of indicting men into piety, or of calling in the Quarter Sessions to the aid of religion. You may produce outward conformity by these means; but you are so far from producing (the only thing worth producing) the inward feeling, that you incur a great risk of giving birth to a totally opposite sentiment.'[1]

In his gravest charge against the conductors of the Vice Society, directed, he believed, against a policy of great unfairness if not dis-

[1] *Essays by Sydney Smith*, pp. 137, 139. (*Edinburgh Review*, January 1809.)

honesty and one that showed strongly the 'cant and hypocrisy' of these reformers, Smith was hitting between wind and water.

Nothing has disgusted us so much in the proceedings of this Society, as the control which they exercise over the amusements of the poor. One of the specious titles under which this legal meanness is gratified is, *Prevention of Cruelty to Animals.*

Of cruelty to animals, let the reader take the following specimens:—

Running an iron hook in the intestines of an animal; presenting this first animal to another as his food; and then pulling this second creature up and suspending him by the barb in his stomach.

Riding a horse till he drops, in order to see an innocent animal torn to pieces by dogs.

Keeping a poor animal upright for many weeks, to communicate a peculiar hardness to his flesh.

Making deep incisions in the flesh of another animal while living, in order to make the muscles more firm.

Immersing another animal, while living, in hot water.

Now we do fairly admit, that such abominable cruelties as these are worthy the interference of the law: and that the Society should have punished them, cannot be a matter of surprise to any feeling mind.—But stop, gentle reader! these cruelties are the cruelties of the Suppressing Committee, not of the poor. You must not think of punishing these.—The first of these cruelties passes under the pretty name of *angling*:—and therefore there can be no harm in it— the more particularly as the President himself has one of the best preserved trout streams in England.—The next is *hunting*;—and as many of the Vice-presidents and of the Committee hunt, it is not possible there can be any cruelty in hunting. [Smith's note: 'How reasonable creatures (says the Society) can enjoy a pastime which is the cause of such sufferings of brute animals, or how they can consider themselves entitled, for their own amusement, to stimulate those animals, by means of the antipathies which Providence has thought proper to place between them, to worry and tear, and often to destroy each other, it is difficult to conceive. So inhuman a practice, by a retribution peculiarly just, tends obviously to render the human character brutal and ferocious,' &c. &c. (*Address*, pp. 71, 72). We take it for granted, that the reader sees clearly that no part of this description can possibly apply to the case of *hunting*.] The next is, a process for making *brawn*—a dish never tasted by the poor, and therefore not to be disturbed by indictment. The fourth is the mode of *crimping* cod; and the fifth, of boiling lobsters; all high-life cruelties, with which a justice of the peace has no business to meddle.

Any cruelty may be practised to gorge the stomachs of the rich,—none to enliven the holidays of the poor....Heaven-born pity, now-a-days, calls for the income tax, and the court guide; and ascertains the rank and fortune of the tormentor before she weeps for the pain of the sufferer....The trespass, however, which calls forth all the energies of a suppressor, is the sound of a fiddle. That the common people are really enjoying themselves, is now beyond all doubt: and away rush Secretary, President, and Committee, to clap the cotillon into the Compter, and to bring back the life of the poor to its regular standard of decorous gloom. The gambling houses of St James's remain untouched.

It is not true, as urged by the Society, that the vices of the poor are carried on in houses of public resort, and those of the rich in their own houses. The Society cannot be ignorant of the innumerable gambling-houses resorted to by men of fashion. Is there one they have suppressed, or attempted to suppress? Can anything be more despicable than such distinctions as these? Those who make them seem to have for other persons' vices all the rigour of the ancient Puritans—without a particle of their honesty or their courage. To suppose that any society will ever attack the vices of people of fashion, is wholly out of the question....What gentleman so fond of suppressing, as to interfere with the vices of good company, and inform against persons who were really genteel? He knows very well that the consequence of such interference would be a complete exclusion from elegant society....We see at the head of this Society the names of several noblemen, and of other persons moving in the fashionable world. Is it possible they can be ignorant of the innumerable offences against the law and morality which are committed by their own acquaintances and connexions? Is there one single instance where they have directed the attention of the Society to this higher species of suppression, and sacrificed men of consideration to that zeal for virtue which watches so acutely over the vices of the poor?[1]

At the end of the Vice Society's *Address to the Public* of 1803 there was an earnest plea for the reform of the vicious great, a clear sign that at that time the Society was in the hands of Orthodox churchmen. Wiser counsel prevailed as the Evangelicals came into control. It would have been a simple answer to Sydney Smith to point out to him that the last man in England who had gone vigorously about an attack on the vices of the great, no respecter of persons, was Archbishop Laud and that in the year 1645 Archbishop Laud was beheaded. Of course it was not

[1] Sydney Smith, *Works*, pp. 140–2.

possible for the conductors of the Vice Society to be ignorant of the vices of fashionable life, and of course there was no single instance of their concerning themselves with any 'higher species of suppression'. In 1815 on the occasion of a notorious 'gaming transaction in high life, in which an immense sum of money was said to have been lost', an unknown person, ironic or most ingenuous, wrote in to the Society offering to provide the 'needful evidence' if they would institute a prosecution. He was given the polite answer that the Society attacked only 'public gaming-houses', their object being 'to check those violations of public decency and decorum, which are scandalous, open, and obtrusive'. Mr Pritchard the Secretary could have thought up a better answer than that scandalous and open dishonesty, the fantastic gaming of the West End clubs being far more notorious and harmful than anything that took place in Saffron Hill. But for Wilberforce to have done anything else would have been an inconceivable folly. It would have violated the fundamental practical principle of the Evangelical Reformation.

The Society for the Suppression of Vice must by its very nature be unpopular, the *Occasional Report No. VI* (June 1812) says. That is an argument for it rather than against it. 'The union of the truly virtuous, small as their number comparatively may be, would be fully adequate to check the confederacy of the wicked against the Laws expressly passed for the protection of the public morals.'[1] It is a simple matter. The truly virtuous are engaged in a righteous war on the confederacy of the wicked, those who are not for the Vice Society are against it, and any act whatever that is done by the truly virtuous for a virtuous end is wholly justifiable. Echoes of the voices of Hannah More, Charles Simeon, William Carus Wilson, and, alas, William Wilberforce are heard many times in the Vice Society's literature.

In London there is determined opposition to the Society, and some lack of agreement among its members. In twenty years the parent Society, never large, has lost four-fifths of its supporters. It probably should be thought of as one of Wilberforce's two failures. But the union of the truly virtuous is proceeding in a gigantically successful way in general, and out in the provinces is making a good deal of progress even in this Society. Of course the amount of good the Society

[1] *Occasional Report No. VI* of the Society (1812), p. 5.

28-2

could do had no relationship to its numbers. There is a Vice Society at Bristol and one at Gloucester; at York, Hull, Chatham, Rochester, Reading, at Liverpool, Stowmarket, Newcastle upon Tyne. It is hoped that such societies, 'multiplying in the kingdom', will 'eventually produce an important effect on public morals'.[1]

All the rigours of the ancient Puritans, without a particle of their honesty or their courage.—Sydney Smith was partly wrong there, as wrong as Hazlitt and for the same reason. It is strange that seeing as much as he did he missed the vital fact about the Vice Society. The Wilberforce who was at its head was the same Wilberforce who Smith knew was the head of the 'Clapham church'.

He was right that there was a close likeness to the ancient Puritans in that 'church', and it held for nearly every quality except the seventeenth-century sturdiness against the prerogative and hatred of 'legitimacy' (a sensible respect for social power was not unknown to the older vessels). To the Evangelicals the evils most grossly opposed to spirituality are those most obviously of the flesh; sexual offences are the most abhorrent of all common sins. Nothing is so worldly as fornication, and the physical relationship of the sexes naturally must only be referred to in the abstract or *en masse* as seduction or prostitution. The basic principle of action of the Party in this field is shown by their intense horror at the scandal of the Duke of York and Mrs Clarke in 1809 and the still more spectacularly offensive trial of the queen in 1820 for adultery. The shocking aspect of such affairs was not the immorality revealed but the example set the nation by people so conspicuously at the head of those who established the rules of national manners and morals. It was a triumph, of a sort, for Evangelicalism that in its early stages the trial of Queen Caroline, apart from political jockeying, was dominated by Wilberforce. Turned to by both parties because of his moral leadership and sensitiveness to correct policy, he

[1] *Part the First (Second) of an Address to the Public from the Society for the Suppression of Vice* (London, 1803 (1804)); *Statement of the Proceedings of the Society, etc.* (London, 1804); *Occasional Report, etc.* (June, 1812); *ibid.* (1816); *Reports of the Society, etc.* (London, 1825); *Anti-Jacobin Review*, February, March, 1803, pp. 199, 294, 287–8; *Christian Guardian*, March 1822, pp. 215–16; *Christian Pocket Magazine*, September–December 1822, pp. 150–1, 259, 308–9; *Wilberforce*, vol. III, pp. 186, 236; vol. v, p. 39. British Museum, Eg. 1964, fos. 99–102.

struck at once at the Evangelical crux of the matter. With no attempt to get at the facts he carried a compromise course that would have got the offensive spectacle out of sight if Caroline had been sensible.

The Evangelical practicalness is nowhere clearer than in the multitude of asylums, refuges and hospitals they founded or supported to combat prostitution, where the constant aim was to get the offending women out of the theatres and off the streets. The magnitude and true offensiveness of the evil is not so much the thing itself as the incalculable harm such a spectacle does to still virtuous people at large. Arthur Young mentions another practical evil resulting from prostitution. Wherever he travelled in England he found attractive unmarried girls. 'The fornication of men with the abandoned of the sex robs thousands of such virtuous and good girls of husbands.'[1]

The flesh being in itself evil, it and its attributes, manifestations and operations must be concealed and in no way, or only in the most oblique way, referred to. Of the kinds of flesh the female is admittedly more evil than the male. The point of feminine modesty, particularly in dress, is consequently one of importance well beyond the mere matter of worldly vanity. Any degree of female decoration was held to approach the meretricious, particularly by the moral theorists of the post-Wilberforce generation. Young girls should be taught from early days to dress with a decent plainness. Adornment was viewed with suspicion, even the least garish. It could never exceed the simplest kind of display. The Evangelicals as a rule frowned on the use of jewellery. Lewis Way did not allow his daughters to wear it, Mrs More wore no such adornment and condemned its use, and the Reverend William Carus Wilson was very severe about it. There is some evidence that this prohibition, and others of the sort, was not easy to enforce. Mrs More, however, is described, even toward the end of her days, as wearing the not unrich costume, of course of a seemly design, of the century of her birth, and there was not so much severity in general among those of Wilberforce's generation as later. In the older Evangelicals there was a general feeling that true religion did not call on them to eschew the standards set by the good breeding and good taste of the upper classes.

In the 1830's and 1840's complaints from the stricter members of

[1] *Autobiography*, p. 336.

the Party on this theme are plentiful. Dr Judson, missionary to Burmah, one of Mrs More's favourites, deplored the worldly vanity, the love of dress and display, 'which has, in every age, and in all countries, been a ruling passion of the fair sex'. Even the missionary sisters who came out from England were too likely to be 'dressed and adorned in that manner, which is too prevalent in our beloved native land'. In Dr Judson's own native church (after he had been absent for a year) he beheld 'appalling profusion of ornaments, and saw that the demon of vanity was laying waste the female department'. When he visited 'the Karens, a wild people', he found that the same enemy 'had reigned with a peculiar sway, from time immemorial'. On one Karen woman he was able to count between twelve and fifteen necklaces.

I saw that I was brought into a situation that precluded all retreat. For a few nights I spent some sleepless hours....I asked myself, 'Can I baptize a Karen woman in her present attire? No.'

Again, I considered that the question concerned not the Karen only, but the whole Christian world; that its decision would involve a train of uncommon consequences; that a single step would lead me into a long and perilous way....I repeatedly offered myself to Christ, and prayed for strength to go forward in the path of duty, come life or death, come praise or reproach; supported or deserted, successful or defeated, in the ultimate issue.[1]

The feminine love of fine clothes apart, there was no question but that there must be an adequate amount and number of clothes at the same time. The female 'person' had to be concealed as much as possible and not only was it indecent to reveal, even in outline or general form, any of the more objectionable parts of it, where we approach the absolute essence of worldliness, but they could not be referred to and the garments clothing them could be referred to only with rhetorical help. This holds for men's garments too. It led to those interesting euphemisms coined or brought into use by an early nineteenth century undergoing puritanical reform. Some of them may have had a comic use in the beginning. 'Inexpressibles', for drawers, later for trousers, was first used in 1790, according to the Oxford English Dictionary. 'Unmentionables' for trousers, which was in wide use, came in in 1830, 'shorts' for short drawers in 1826, and the expression 'the naked' for

[1] *The Friendly Visitor*, vol. xx, pp. 194-6.

the nude in art is said not to have been in use after 1815. 'Nightgown', apparently for 'bed gown', 'a long, loose, light garment worn by women or children in bed', appears first in 1822; 'toilet' for bathroom or lavatory first in 1819. The primary purpose of skirts on chairs, we are told, was not so much to conceal the legs of the chairs as to ensure that no gentleman or lady was led into pronouncing the word 'legs' in mixed company. There were other euphemisms. Lady Charlotte Bury's *Diary* has an entry for 31 May 1813 about the Princess Caroline's going to the opera 'the other night'. 'Mr Whitbread had written her a letter, begging that she would be very careful about *her dress*—in short explaining that she ought to cover *her neck*. . . . She absolutely wept some tears of mortification and anger, when she received this letter from Mr Whitbread.' This Lady Charlotte called 'a bold *act of friendship*'.[1]

The hardly credible extent to which the language of propriety was developed in the United States, by the 1840's a very Evangelical country indeed, can be seen in H. L. Mencken's *The American Language*.

Mrs More, Mr Gisborne of Needwood Forest in his *Duties of the Female Sex*, and all Evangelical writers concerning themselves with the female department, had a great deal to say on the subject of womanly modesty. There is a once-celebrated passage in Mrs More's *Coelebs in Search of a Wife* in which a practical point is stressed. Women should realize, Mrs More points out, that modesty makes them much more attractive to men than brazenness, let their motive for being attractive be what it will. 'Oh! if women in general knew what was their real interest! if they could guess with what a charm even the *appearance* of modesty invests its possessor, they would dress decorously from mere self-love, if not from principle. The designing would assume modesty as an artifice; the coquet would adopt it as an allurement, the pure as her appropriate attraction, and the voluptuous as the most infallible art of seduction.'[2]

'If there is any truth in this picture', the Reverend Sydney Smith observed, 'nudity becomes a virtue; and no decent woman, for the future, can be seen in garments.'[3]

For a clergyman to refer in public print to a woman seen without garments was particularly shocking. On one occasion the nineteen-

[1] *Diary of a Lady-in-Waiting*, vol. I, p. 152.   [2] *Coelebs*, vol. I, p. 189.
[3] *Essays of Sydney Smith*, p. 153 (*Edinburgh Review*, April 1809).

year-old Drusilla Way, daughter of the Reverend Lewis Way and sharer for many years of his labours for the Jews, was brought face to face with the Venus de' Medici. 'As to the Venus she looks like what she *is*, and ought to be', she wrote privately. '*A naked woman thoroughly ashamed of herself! Perfect nudity* I never saw before, and how ladies can stand *looking* and *staring* and *admiring* with gentlemen at it, I cannot conceive and hope I never shall.'[1]

The matter was given still more importance by the extremeness of women's fashions during parts of this period, particularly during and after the break in the French War when the *monde* flocked to Paris, to the horror of most of the Evangelicals. There are many references in the early years of the century to the lavish exposure of the feminine person. Arthur Young noted on one occasion that Mrs M.'s dress was horrid; she managed to make her prominent bust more prominent still, and was thinly clad. In Young's opinion, these fashions were purposely contrived. Around 1814 an anonymous writer in Bath complained eloquently about such things. It was not merely that young women ran about alone or in groups from one end of the town to the other, 'without any servant or steady friend to accompany them; talking and laughing at the corners of streets, and walking sometimes with young men only'. Far more shocking were the ladies' evening costumes. 'To behold a row of ladies at an evening assembly, fills the mind with the most fearful apprehensions of an approaching complete dissolution of manners—approaching did I say? it is upon us, it has taken possession.' Gentlemen were disgusted, if not more deeply affected, by such attire. 'The dress which appears as if it must drop, by the accidental failure of one tight ligature, really fills one with terror and apprehension.... I know a gentleman of distinguished talents, elegant literary taste, and fine feeling, who was twice so disgusted, as to be unable to continue his seat: once by a lady of fashion, of some age, who had descended from her room half-dressed, and seated herself by him: he actually, as he said, shuddered—arose, and removed himself to another part of the room. On another occasion, he was seated at a dinner-table, when the appearance of a lady so discomfitted him, that he begged a gentleman to change seats with him, as he could not have eaten his dinner, he said, in view of so revolting an appearance.'

[1] A. M. W. Stirling, *The Ways of Yesterday*, p. 238.

It was worse to see the old so: '...a grandmother [with her] large person fashionably bared....Oh! the charm, the grace of a sober head-dress—a dark satin, a black velvet, a kerchief neatly folded across the breast!'[1]

The scrupulous observance of the Sabbath is one of the most immediate, and most important, marks of the emerged person; failure to observe the Sabbath is a manifest mark of the infidel or mere nominal Christian. Wilberforce would not travel on Sundays or even write letters, important as his correspondence was to the cause and overwhelmed with it as he always was. But Wilberforce, lax in other respects too, did not urge the pedantic Sabbatarianism of the later period.

As Mrs More pointed out at the beginning of the campaign, Sunday observance is the Christian Palladium; when it is lost, everything is lost. The Evangelical attack on violations of the Sabbath was thus an important part of the campaign. The Party kept up a constant pressure of propaganda and wherever possible regulation and even legal enactment, until the Sunday was at least externally observed in England with propriety so far as pressure could make it so. Persuasion and exhortation were not neglected. After Wilberforce's retirement, particularly in the 1830's, some of the Saints kept up a vigorous attempt at Sabbath observance enforcement. In that Sir Andrew Agnew and the younger Spencer Perceval were prominent. A leading Evangelical antagonist here was *Figaro in London*, which was particularly annoyed by Agnew and Perceval's efforts to shut up cook shops on Sundays, the activity that provoked the passage quoted from *A Christmas Carol*. In *The Bleak Age*, J. L. and Barbara Hammond have described the English Sunday of the 1830's and 1840's. 'For the mass of the working classes there was only one day on which they were free from the discipline of mill and workshop. On that day they were refused recreation for mind or body, music or games, beauty of art or of nature.' Those who were dependent on public institutions were of course equally refused it if they were not working men. Chadwick, the Hammonds point out, cites 'an engineer who had been abroad' and who describes the difference of continental life. At Mulhausen after services the workmen 'spent the rest of the day in the country playing games, whereas

[1] *Bath, a Sketch* (2nd ed., 1814), pp. 6–16.

in England "a man can do nothing but go to a public house on Sunday, and when there you can do nothing but drink"'. Even public gardens were closed on Sundays, at Leeds, Manchester, Liverpool and no doubt at many other places or all other places. 'The observance of the Sunday in England is rigorously enforced by church and state. There is only one exception: the dram shop. All shops must be closed, all places of innocent amusement or instruction, such as Botanical Gardens or Museums, must be rigorously shut, but the folding doors of the gin palace may open to any man who pushes his foot against them.' Attempts were repeatedly made against this, but 'Sabbatarian prejudice was too strong, and the English people were left to gloom and drink'. 'The Methodists did with the English Sunday what they did with the English theatre'—a conclusion that perhaps would have astonished Joseph Butterworth and Dr Coke as much as William Wilberforce and Hannah More.[1]

Many amusements or entertainments and some arts condemned by the Evangelicals were to the Orthodox way of thinking harmless or even valuable . Chief among them were fairs and rural sports, dancing and the theatre. When it was possible on a clear evening to see the sun sparkling on the helmets of Napoleon's army of invasion at Boulogne it was obvious to practical irreligious men that manly sports of all kinds should be encouraged to keep alive the 'hard bulldog strain' in the lower orders. The Evangelicals did not agree. 'More especially', the *Christian Guardian* said in an account of the murder of Weare by Thurtell, Hunt and Probert, 24 October 1823, 'we must notice the entangling nature and the brutalizing effect of some of those recreations, amusements, and exhibitions which prevail among us'. 'We are not exactly informed of the conduct and character of this criminal in earlier life [Thurtell, who did the actual murder and was executed]. He is, however, understood to have been a frequent attendant at boxing-matches, horse races, the gaming table, &c. Now all these amusements appear to us to have a direct tendency to brutalize the mind and harden the heart; they are productive of pure, of unmingled evil; the end of these things is death.' One course, furthermore, 'even if not evil in itself, leads on to worse; the transition to evil is very easy'.[2]

[1] *The Bleak Age* (1947 edition), pp. 127–9.
[2] *Christian Guardian*, February 1824, pp. 75–6.

Satan's Grand Instrument

The Evangelicals objected to all dancing, not merely to new inventions of foreigners, and on much more basic grounds than the *Anti-Jacobin* had done. The *Christian Guardian* urged that children be not taught to dance at all. 'That it is neither carnal nor sensual I most readily allow [this passage is not referring to waltzing]. But it does not follow from hence, that it is according to godliness. Most evidently does it appear to be of the world.' 'Of two young ladies whose hostess was not opposed to dancing a correspondent says, 'Fiddlers and dancing Masters are, to them, a kind of fatality',[1] and it is pointed out that on this subject Mrs More, in her character Lady Aston in *Coelebs*, is very lax. Wilberforce was equally so, to the mind of the Evangelicals who followed him. He was not opposed to private (family) dancing but to the 'whole tone' of a public assembly. Dancing wastes time, the *Christian Guardian* believed, gives opportunity for familiarities, is no improvement to the mind, needlessly endangers health and limbs, puts the body often in not the most modest positions, and is a favourite amusement with the world.[2] Card-playing of course, even apart from gaming, is wholly indefensible. It is irreligious in itself and leads to the neglect of religion.[3] In card-playing at best you shut yourself out from 'that continual waiting on the Lord'.[4]

In January 1825 the *Christian Guardian* published a typical letter opposing Christmas celebrations. It was all right to have cheerful and innocent amusements, which could be provided, their correspondent thought, by introducing 'entertaining and instructive books' and encouraging 'philosophical and scientific recreations'. The home should not be made dull, gloomy and disagreeable. On the other hand such 'destructive amusements' as the theatre, evening parties, large suppers and the like, above all dancing, are utterly inexcusable.[5]

This attitude was opposed to what may be thought of as a typical Orthodox view and was vigorously denounced many times. Total abstinence from music, cards, dancing, and public spectacles could not be proved necessary for salvation, in High Church opinion, nor could it be shown that such things inevitably lead to danger. It was reported in the (Orthodox) *Christian Remembrancer* that an Evangelical clergy-

---

[1] *Ibid.* August 1811, pp. 274–5.   [2] *Ibid.* March 1817, p. 88.
[3] *Ibid.* February 1824, pp. 75–6.   [4] *Ibid.* August 1825, p. 292.
[5] *Ibid.* July 1825, p. 21.

man had refused a ticket for confirmation to a candidate not willing to give a solemn promise that she would never be present at a ball or a play. This Evangelical clergyman was William Marsh, a favourite disciple of Simeon's. Such an act was a 'usurpation of spiritual authority'. 'It is to be perceived, what would be the effect of such principles were they permitted to reign without control.'[1] Indeed the *Christian Remembrancer* feared their effect was already (1819) beginning to be shown in some force.

In 1827 a note appears in the *Christian Guardian* about the happily unflourishing circumstances of an institution to which every Evangelical without exception was staunchly opposed, the theatre. The editors would be happy, a correspondent is told, to insert a paper on the impropriety of clergymen's attending plays or in any way encouraging such pernicious and immoral amusements, if they had the least idea that such clergymen would either read or pay any attention to it. Attendance at stage plays is indefensible. 'Every theatre is found practically to introduce poverty, vice, and wickedness into its immediate vicinity. Those who know from personal investigation the vicinity of Covent Garden and Drury Lane have a more convincing proof of this painful fact than ten thousand arguments. We understand, however, that theatrical property is everywhere in this country a losing concern: and hope that this indicates an improving state of public morals.'[2] It indicates at least a state of morals, and it seems likely that the Evangelical abhorrence of the stage, spreading over England as the literature, the missionaries and the branch societies spread, contributed as greatly to the dreariness of the English theatre after Goldsmith and Sheridan and through the nineteenth century as it did to the circumspections of English fiction.

On 17 March 1800 the Eclectic Society discussed the question 'On what grounds should a Christian discountenance theatrical amusements?' In this discussion by John Newton, Basil Woodd, John Venn, George Pattrick, William Abdy, Henry Foster, Josiah Pratt, Richard Cecil and Thomas Scott, nine of the leading Evangelical clergymen of the day, there was no disagreement. The theatre is totally evil; at its very best, no good can be said of it. It is 'the great support of the Devil's Kingdom' and Satan no doubt 'has a prime motive to regulate

[1] *Christian Remembrancer*, July 1819, vol. 1, pp. 432–7.
[2] *Christian Guardian*, February 1827, p. 80.

444

the play' (Venn); 'the theatre is the very last of all places to which I would allow a child of mine to go' (Newton); 'The matter is so plain to me, that I wonder at Christians questioning it, as much as I should if they questioned the sin of swearing'. 'Frequenting plays affords a proof of the depravity of human nature beyond most other things' (Foster); 'a sermon is the essence of dulness after a play: this shews the evil of the play-house' (Pratt); 'the taste generated in the play-house is as opposed as possible to the taste of Jesus Christ' (Cecil, himself an old—regenerated—playgoer). The most devastating observation of the evening on the evils of the theatre, of all those expressed by these eminent, grave and severe Evangelical priests, came from Basil Woodd. 'Mrs More's sacred dramas have done injury. They have associated the idea of innocence with the drama. I know of two young men now on the stage, in consequence of being taught to act Mrs M.'s sacred dramas.'[1]

V

Four classical Evangelical portraits may be introduced, for whatever value they may be held to have in the matter of what William Wilberforce's accomplishment led to. Of course nothing useful would be gained by bringing forward manifest caricatures such as Wilkie Collins's Miss Clack in *The Moonstone*, whom Swinburne called 'the Evangelical hag', works of anti-Evangelical violence such as Mother Trollope's *The Vicar of Wrexhill* and Sheridan Le Fanu's *Uncle Silas*, or on the other hand Dickens's amusing but not seriously intended characters such as that Mr Chadband who seemed to have so much train oil in his system. As a rule the Evangelical of the 1840's or so was likely to impress his castaway contemporaries as having a systemic need of train oil.

In Samuel Butler's *The Way of All Flesh*, Ernest Pontifex falls in at Cambridge with some 'earnest' young men (they were 'serious', in Wilberforce's day), the spiritual descendants of the original Simeonites and still, in 1858, known by the Old Apostle's (abbreviated) name. Butler's well-known chapter begins with the gravest inadvertence. 'The Evangelical movement, with the exception to which I shall revert presently, had become almost a matter of ancient history.' Disregarding

[1] *Eclectic Society Notes*, pp. 159–63.

445

the incalculable influence of Evangelical 'seriousness' on English life that statement could have been made of a time twenty years earlier, or ten years earlier. For 1858 it was thoughtless. Butler had forgotten that the prime minister was Palmerston, that his ecclesiastical patronage was being exercised for him by his wife's son-in-law the Earl of Shaftesbury, the Evangelical leader, and that Shaftesbury was naming to the bench of bishops as many solid Evangelicals as he dared and no one liked by High Church.

There were still a good many Simeonites, or as they were more briefly called 'Sims,' in Ernest's time. Every college contained some of them, but their headquarters were...among the sizars of St John's. Behind the then chapel of this last-named college, there was a 'labyrinth' (this was the name it bore) of dingy, tumble-down rooms, tenanted exclusively by the poorest undergraduates, who were dependent upon sizarships and scholarships for the means of taking their degrees....In the labyrinth there dwelt men of all ages, from mere lads to grey-haired old men who had entered late in life. They were rarely seen except in hall or chapel, or at lecture, where their manners of feeding, praying and studying, were considered alike objectionable; no one knew whence they came, whither they went, nor what they did, for they never showed at cricket or the boats; they were a gloomy, seedy-looking confrérie, who had as little to glory in in clothes and manners as in the flesh itself....Unprepossessing, then, in features, gait and manners, unkempt and ill-dressed beyond what can be easily described, these poor fellows formed a class apart, whose thoughts and ways were not as the thoughts and ways of Ernest and his friends, and it was among them that Simeonism chiefly flourished. Destined most of them for the Church...the Simeonites held themselves to have received a very loud call to the ministry, and were ready to pinch themselves for years so as to prepare for it by the necessary theological courses. To most of them the fact of becoming clergymen would be the entrée into a social position from which they were at present kept out by barriers they well knew to be impassable; ordination, therefore, opened fields for ambition which made it the central point in their thoughts.

Placing themselves under the guidance of a few well-known tutors they would teach in Sunday Schools, and be instant, in season and out of season, in imparting spiritual instruction to all whom they could persuade to listen to them. But the soil of the more prosperous undergraduates was not suitable for the seed they tried to sow. The small pieties with which they larded their discourse, if chance threw them into the company of those whom they considered worldly, caused nothing but aversion in the minds of those for whom they were intended. When they distributed tracts, dropping them by night into good men's letter boxes while they were asleep, their tracts got burnt, or met with even worse contumely; they were themselves also treated with the ridicule which they reflected proudly had been the lot of true followers of Christ in all ages. Often at their prayer meetings was the passage of St Paul referred to in which he bids his Corinthian converts note concerning themselves that they were for the most part neither well-bred nor intellectual people. They reflected with pride that they too had nothing to be proud of in these respects, and like St Paul, gloried in the fact that in the flesh they had not much to glory.

Samuel Butler would probably not have understood the spiritual fervour that may have been present, in terms of their capacities, in some or many of those later fruits of Achaia. We may add to his account of what such Evangelicals were like in the early days of Lord Palmerston's ministry the non-fictional picture drawn by the Reverend T. Mozley of what seems to be much the same kind of people at Oxford in 1830 or so. A clergyman of the Established Church for many years, Mozley was brought up in Evangelical views, and later wholeheartedly removed himself from them. 'For many years of my life, my chief religious conclusions had been of a negative character, one continual revolt against the hollowness, flimsiness, and stupidity of "Evangelical" teaching.'[1] His tutor at Oriel when he went up in 1826 was John Henry Newman and he married Newman's sister.

'St Edmund Hall was then the headquarters of the Evangelical system' (elsewhere Canon Mozley refers to it as 'the cave, the den, of the "Evangelical party"'.) 'It is difficult to convey an idea of the very low position it had in the University; and it is even painful to recall it, for it was religion in the form of a degradation utterly undeserved.'[2]

It was to be a burning and shining light in the surrounding darkness, and that it entirely failed to be. The society was formed by selection. It consisted of young men who had shown early ability, and some interesting form of goodness; who made a profession and aspired to the ministry, but whose immediate relatives were too poor to send them to an ordinary college. A benevolent friend, a good uncle, or a society, had taken compassion on them, and

[1] Mozley, *Reminiscences*, vol. II, p. 311.
[2] *Ibid.* vol. I, p. 24. Mozley did not mean that the Evangelicals did not deserve contempt but that religion did not deserve the Evangelicals.

sent them to St Edmund Hall, where spirituality and economy were said to be combined. Thus all the circumstances and signs of failure were here concentrated in one focus. All were poor, struggling men, starting with the fixed idea that they were out of society, which, it was a comfort to think, was too worldly, and wicked a thing to be coveted, or envied.

These Edmund Hall men could be known anywhere. They were either very shabby or very foppish. They all had the look of dirt, which perhaps was not their fault, for they had dirty complexions. How is it that goodness, poverty, and a certain amount of literary or religious ambition produce an unpleasant effect on the skin? There must have been something in the air of the spot, which certainly was a dark hole. In those days the University sermons were occasionally preached at St Peter's, adjoining St Edmund Hall. The undergraduates of the Hall felt it their own ground, and took early possession of the front rows of the gallery. I shall not say who it was—but he became a very distinguished Prelate—proposed that before the opening of the church door there should be arranged a row of basins of water, with soap and towels, on the book ledge before the front row, with the admonition to wash and be clean.[1]

Having no secular literature, no great matters to talk about and very little indeed of what is now called Biblical literature, these men gossiped, gossiped, gossiped, from morning to night, running about from room to room in quest of somebody to talk with and something to talk about.... As the St Edmund Hall men divided their time between self-contemplation, mutual amusement, and the reading of emotional works; studying no history, not even critically studying the Scriptures, and knowing no more of the world than sufficed to condemn it, they naturally, and perforce were driven into a very dangerous corner. This was invention. Their knowledge was imaginary. So too was their introspection, their future, sometimes even their past. All precocity is apt to take this form. The quick ripening mind, for lack of other matters, feeds upon itself. These young men had been reared on unsubstantial and stimulating good; on pious tales, on high-wrought death-beds, on conversations as they ought to be, on one-sided biographies. Truth of opinion, they had always been told, was incomparably more important than truth of fact.[2]

There are striking similarities in those accounts given by two very different men, if there is perhaps a certain spiritual shallowness oddly common to the two. George Eliot's description of the Evangelical character of a time midway between Canon Mozley's and Butler's

---

[1] This sounds like Samuel Wilberforce, an intimate friend of Mozley's.
[2] *Reminiscences*, vol. I, pp. 242 ff.

seems to corroborate the part in which they agree. It is probably truer, certainly more kindly.

The time of *The Sad History of the Rev. Amos Barton* is 1837 or so. *The Pickwick Papers* have just been completed—the immense sale of which an Evangelical clergyman of the story thinks 'one of the strongest proofs of original sin'. Mr Barton is the curate of Shepperton, a quiet town with the usual High Church incumbents too, and dissenters round about. The incumbent some years before him, still well remembered, was one of those easy-going excellent old gentlemen of the pleasant eighteenth-century type, in fact that Mr Gilfil who 'smoked very long pipes and preached very short sermons'. The Reverend Mr Barton, 'quite another sort of clergyman', as curate is paid eighty pounds a year, the vicar pocketing the remaining thirty-five pounds ten brought in by the living, and with six children is constantly, in spite of all his wife's efforts, under a harassment that needs no explanation. Mr Barton is a man of about forty. 'A narrow face of no particular complexion—even the small-pox that has attacked it seems to have been of a mongrel, indefinite kind—with features of no particular shape, and an eye of no particular expression.' He is exceptional perhaps in only one respect: he is '"superlatively middling, the quintessential extract of mediocrity'. His father was a cabinet-maker and deacon of a dissenting chapel.

Mr Barton sniffs too much and has bad teeth. He has a temper, laughs at criticisms of himself that other people think damaging, and has no tact and a waning congregation. He is a man of earnest and sincere religious belief and is conscientious and hard-working. He preaches extempore, once in a while, and badly, and at best his sermons are likely to be on subjects of no possible interest, or even comprehensibility, to his hearers. There is one 'extremely argumentative' sermon on the Incarnation, 'which, as it was preached to a congregation not one of whom had any doubt of that doctrine, and to whom the Socinians therein confuted were as unknown as the Arimaspians, was exceedingly well adapted to trouble and confuse the Sheppertonian mind'.

Amos Barton is also 'an affectionate husband, and, in his way, valued his wife as his best treasure', though he is not a man whose sensibilities are sufficiently refined to have had Mrs Barton, 'a lovely woman; a large fair, gentle Madonna', destined to them by pre-established harmony.

We are told too that Mr Barton's grammar is none too correct, although, as he is middling in everything, it is not really very bad. He 'had not the gift of perfect accuracy in English orthography and syntax, which was unfortunate, as he was known not to be a Hebrew scholar, and not in the least suspected of being an accomplished Grecian. These lapses, in a man who had gone through the Eleusinian mysteries of a university education, surprised the young ladies of his parish extremely.... The persons least surprised... were his clerical brethren, who had gone through the mysteries themselves.'[1] Barton's pulpit and cottage oratory alike showed, as a rule, 'praiseworthy intentions inadequately fulfilled', and in this respect as in others he would have made an excellent deacon of an Independent Church. 'He might then have sniffed long and loud' in the corner of his Chapel pew; 'he might have indulged in halting rhetoric at prayer-meetings, and have spoken faulty English in private life; and these little infirmities would not have prevented him, honest faithful man that he was, from being a shining light in the Dissenting circle of Bridgeport.'[2] 'Alas for the worthy man... who gets himself into the wrong place! It is only the very largest souls who will be able to appreciate and pity him—who will discern and love sincerity of purpose amid all the bungling feebleness of achievement.'

We may add to Amos Barton's credit, just the same, one remark the excellence of which perhaps George Eliot did not wholly realize. Thinking about 'having service in the workhouse while the church is being enlarged' he plans to ask the substantial Mr Oldinport. 'If he agrees to attend service there once or twice, the other people will come', Mr Barton says, and when he adds 'Net the large fish, and you're sure to have the small fry', he could not have uttered more succinctly the essence of the great Evangelical strategy, though Wilberforce and Mrs More would not have expressed it quite in that way.

We learn that Amos Barton is a Cambridge man.

[1] It should be said here for Amos Barton that some such lapses are likely to happen to anyone, as George Eliot's next sentence shows: '...the workhouse, euphuistically called "the College"'. Miss Eliot was Evangelically educated herself.

[2] Do we see early Evangelical training in that belief too, so like Wilberforce's? Amos Barton would not do for a Bishop Tomline but would make a good honest Joseph Butterworth, Robert Hall or John Wesley. A poor Sedgwick Whalley, he would be a worthy John Bunyan.

The unhappy episode of morning prayers and brief discourse for the paupers could be passed over except for some short sentences of peculiar informative value. Mr Spratt the master of the workhouse brings forward a small sinner aged seven. Mr Barton ascertains that this 'inveterate culprit' does not like to be beaten. 'Then what a silly boy you are to be naughty. If you were not naughty, you wouldn't be beaten. But if you are naughty, God will be angry, as well as Mr Spratt; and God can burn you forever. That will be worse than being beaten.' The evil boy or Child of Hell, the angry and burning God, the right simon-pure Evangelical tone of a certain kind of Evangelical, have a familiar sound, and it is no shock when we are told on the following page that Mr Barton's 'Christian experiences...had been consolidated at Cambridge under the influence of Mr Simeon'.

Barton's congregation is already falling off when it falsely appears, by a not wholly impossible artifice of the author's, that he has become infatuated with a designing woman and is neglecting his lovely and endlessly unselfish wife. Her death and his genuine grief mend the situation. When the vicar notifies him shortly afterwards that he must give up the parish, there is 'general regret among the parishioners.... Amos failed to touch the spring of goodness by his sermons, but he touched it effectively by his sorrows; and there was now a real bond between him and his flock.' The substantial parishioners are anxious to help the bereaved family, and the most substantial, Mr Oldinport, offers 'his interest towards placing the two eldest girls in a school expressly founded for clergymen's daughters'.

We happen to know a good deal about that school, at least as it was a few years before the two eldest Barton girls got there; in fact, a little-known school then, it may now be the most famous of its time. It was called the Clergy Daughters' School and established by the Party in 1823 to make sure no daughter of their poorer clergy would have to come under High Church teaching. In July 1824 the curate of the parish of Haworth in Yorkshire, not far from Cowan's Bridge where the school was, took two of his daughters there to enter them in it. In July 1825 the two girls, eleven and ten years old, were brought home, to die in a few days. Twenty-two years later a younger sister who had joined them at Cowan's Bridge published a bitter picture of the Clergy

Daughters' School and a more bitter picture of its proprietor and supervisor, the Reverend William Carus Wilson. When *Jane Eyre* came out in 1847 an Evangelically-reared and once truly religious, now happily emerged Gentile artist had conferred immortality on Carus Wilson twelve years before his death.

The handle turned, the door unclosed, and passing through, and curtseying low, I looked up at—a black pillar!—such, at least, appeared to me, at first sight, the straight, narrow, sable-clad shape standing erect on the rug: the grim face at the top was like a carved mask, placed above the shaft by way of capital.... His features were large, and they and all the lines of his frame were equally harsh and prim....

'Well, Jane Eyre, and are you a good child?'

Impossible to reply to this in the affirmative: my little world held a contrary opinion: I was silent.... What a face he had... what a great nose! and what a mouth! and what large prominent teeth!

'No sight so sad as that of a naughty child,' he began, 'especially a naughty little girl. Do you know where the wicked go after death?'

'They go to hell,' was my ready and orthodox answer.

'And what is hell? Can you tell me that?'

'A pit full of fire.'

'And should you like to fall into that pit, and to be burning there forever?'

'No, sir.'

'What must you do to avoid it?'

I deliberated a moment; my answer, when it did come, was objectionable: 'I must keep in good health, and not die.'

'How can you keep in good health? Children younger than you die daily. I buried a little child of five years old only a day or two since,—a good little child, whose soul is now in heaven. It is to be feared the same could not be said of you, were you to be called hence.'

'Mr Robert Brocklehurst', the black pillar (or 'black marble clergyman') continues to examine into his little victim's religious life and devotional studies.

'And the Psalms? I hope you like them?'

'No, sir.'

'No? Oh, shocking! I have a little boy, younger than you, who knows six Psalms by heart: and when you ask him which he would rather have, a gingerbread-nut to eat, or a verse of a Psalm to learn, he says: "Oh! the verse of a Psalm! angels sing Psalms," says he; "I wish to be a little angel here below;" he then gets two nuts in recompense for his infant piety.'

When the young Jane Eyre remarks that 'psalms are not interesting', Mr Brocklehurst sees that she has a 'wicked heart', and passing on to the subject of her deceitfulness, which he has been told about, he presents her with a characteristic Evangelical gift of value in that field.

Deceit is, indeed, a sad fault in a child; it is akin to falsehood, and all liars will have their portion in the lake burning with fire and brimstone....Little girl, here is a book entitled the 'Child's Guide;' read it with prayer, especially that part containing 'an account of the awfully sudden death of Martha G——, a naughty child addicted to falsehood and deceit.'

Speculation about Mr Brocklehurst's little boy, who has some appearance of being just a normal calculating little boy, would be fruitless. Mr Brocklehurst himself and the Clergy Daughters' School, or 'nursery of chosen plants', as he calls it, have some interest. In Charlotte Brontë's account the school was a tragic product of pietistic, doctrinaire and morbid concern for the soul and contempt for the fleshly habiliments, at least other people's. 'I have a Master to serve whose kingdom is not of this world', Mr Brocklehurst says; 'my mission is to mortify in these girls the lusts of the flesh.' Humility, a Christian grace, is 'peculiarly appropriate to the pupils of Lowood', Mr Brocklehurst believes ('Lowood' is Brontë's name for the Clergy Daughters' School); 'I, therefore, direct that special care shall be bestowed on its cultivation among them. I have studied how best to mortify in them the worldly sentiment of pride.' Miss Brontë was probably accurate about Carus Wilson's Evangelical contempt on behalf of his young pupils for food, cooking and sanitation. Neither does there seem to have been anything pleasant about the bathing in icy water in the almost unheated school building, the bleak march on winter Sundays to Wilson's unheated church two miles away (morning and afternoon services), the patronizing airs of his ladies and his incessant reminders to his pupils of their charity status. But except for a certain spiritual attitude such things could have been found at many schools in the period and are not pertinent to an examination of this wrestling Jacob, stigmatized pilgrim, the conductor of the Clergy Daughters'

School, as a greatly respected leader of the Evangelicals through the 1820's and many years after.

Is it possible that anything approaching the morbid fear or hatred of beauty and the flesh, the edifying grim pietism and the other truly grisly aspects of 'Robert Brocklehurst's' religion, could have been characteristic of the later Evangelicals? Carus Wilson and the Clergy Daughters' School were still in existence when *Jane Eyre* came out, and there was hurt and angry protest when they were instantly recognized. They were still in existence ten years later when Mrs Gaskell's *Life of Charlotte Brontë* appeared. An intelligent and scrupulous woman, Mrs Gaskell before publishing reviewed the facts. When the matter had been discussed with Miss Brontë, she had declared the portrait of Wilson and the school was true and exact. Mrs Gaskell's investigation convinced her that Miss Brontë was right. 'She saw only one side, and that the unfavourable side of Mr Wilson; but many of those who knew him, assure me of the wonderful fidelity with which his disagreeable qualities, his spiritual pride, his love of power, his ignorance of human nature and consequent want of tenderness are represented.'[1] In a second edition of *Jane Eyre*, furthermore, which also appeared in 1847, Charlotte Brontë went on in a foreword to a somewhat emotional vindication of an attack on false religion that her book seems to have contained. 'Self-righteousness is not religion.' 'To pluck the mask from the face of the Pharisee, is not to lift an impious hand to the Crown of Thorns.' The world finds it convenient 'to let white-washed walls vouch for clean shrines', and may hate him who dares 'to penetrate the sepulchre, and reveal charnel relics'. A little more serenity, or humour, would have kept Miss Brontë from one obvious error there, for whatever else can be said about Wilson he was no whited sepulchre but steadfastly of the same solid sable hue outside as in.

Two other Evangelical characters in *Jane Eyre* support opposition to a belief that the portrait of Wilson was deliberately overdrawn. The superintendent of Lowood School, 'Miss Temple', does what she can, with love and courage, to mitigate her proprietor's grim bigotry. Mr Brocklehurst discovers that 'a lunch, consisting of bread and cheese, has twice been served out to the girls during the past fortnight. How

[1] Elizabeth Gaskell, *The Life of Charlotte Brontë* (New York, 1857), vol. 1, pp. 54, 64, 72.

is this? I look over the regulations, and I find no such meal as lunch mentioned. Who introduced this innovation? and by what authority?' Miss Temple admits her responsibility. 'The breakfast was so ill-prepared that the pupils could not possibly eat it; and I dared not allow them to remain fasting till dinner time.' Mr Brocklehurst's reply (as well as his other remarks that have been cited) could be taken as gross caricature by someone who has not read the Evangelical literature, but by no one who has.

Madam, allow me an instant.—You are aware that my plan in bringing up these girls is, not to accustom them to habits of luxury and indulgence, but to render them hardy, patient, self-denying. Should any little accidental disappointment of the appetite occur, such as the spoiling of a meal . . . the incident ought not to be neutralized by replacing with something more delicate the comfort lost, thus pampering the body and obviating the aim of this institution; it ought to be improved to the spiritual edification of the pupils, by encouraging them to evince fortitude under the temporary privation. A brief address on those occasions would not be mistimed, wherein a judicious instructor would take the opportunity of referring to the sufferings of the primitive Christians; to the torments of martyrs; to the exhortations of our blessed Lord himself, calling upon his disciples to take up their cross and follow him; to his warnings that man shall not live by bread alone, but by every word that proceedeth out of the mouth of God; to his divine consolations, 'if ye suffer hunger or thirst for my sake, happy are ye.' Oh, madam, when you put bread and cheese, instead of burnt porridge, into these children's mouths, you may indeed feed their vile bodies, but you little think how you starve their immortal souls!

We should note that Miss Temple's Evangelicalism must have stood searching tests to have qualified her as the superintendent of this school.

A second clergyman in *Jane Eyre*, St John Rivers, who gives his life to the conversion of the heathen, is also Evangelical (Charlotte Brontë probably did not know any other kind of clergyman), but remarkably unlike Mr Brocklehurst. He is 'a very good man', 'untiringly active'; 'great and exalted deeds are what he lived to perform'. Tall and fair, with blue eyes and a Grecian profile, he is truly able, with a first-rate brain; though apparently a Cambridge man (and if so surely a disciple of the Old Apostle) he is 'an accomplished and profound scholar', which we are told by George Eliot and others was not always, or often, the case with the Cambridge Evangelicals. But for all that, he is also remarkably like Mr Brocklehurst. St John Rivers is 'a good and great man', 'faithful, firm and devoted, full of energy, and zeal and truth'. But it is the supreme truth for him that 'this world is not the scene of fruition', and on that foundation, in the scheme of the Evangelicals the basis of so much good and so much harm, he builds up his life and everyone else's so far as he can with a rigid, intolerant and icy 'idealism'. The unforgivable thing about *Jane Eyre* to its 'serious' critics of 1847 was probably not Edward Rochester's oaths or attempted bigamy or Jane's deficiencies of maidenly reserve. It was her declining St John's offer to her to go out with him, an Evangelical missionary's wife, against the Gentile world, to marry in Rochester a man who is rather less of an Evangelical than Sam Weller.

In Carus Wilson's position of high esteem in the Party, round the time of Wilberforce's retirement and for thirty years after, there is more than is to be seen at a glance. There is even more than appears in his great felicity in stating the hardships of the rich, the folly of indigent discontent when no one's real riches are here below, the certainty that a shop closed on Sundays will bring its owner double profits, the virtual certainty that Sunday boaters will be drowned, and such Evangelical tenets. Well concealed under his sable hue, sombre utterance and sombre manner he had those other qualities that enabled the Evangelicals to make so deep an imprint on the social fabric of the English nineteenth century. For one thing he altogether lacked the Evangelical qualities so much cherished by Wilberforce's generation, the playfulness, jocularity, mirthfulness and 'apostolic joy' that with a proper suavity and elegance of manner constituted the signs of a happy religion not methodistically unsuited to the great. Not even to his firstfruits of Achaia, of whom Wilson was one of the most eminent, could the Old Apostle hand on his every virtue. But under that gaunt and grisly exterior, said Carus Wilson's defenders against Brontë and Mrs Gaskell, there was a strong wish to do good wherever possible that was the product of a warm love for his deserving fellow human beings.

As those defenders were undoubtedly right, it is fortunate that the record in the case of Carus Wilson is very rich. Like his great (earthly) master, Wilson lived in a region where, with warm Christian affection and great determination, he wished others to move also; and his methods of inducing them to do so leave some grounds for suspecting that it was not in his young pupils of the Clergy Daughters' School that he should have studied how best to mortify the worldly sentiment of pride. We do not possess any surviving account of Wilson's actual conversation, except for those given by Charlotte Brontë, if they are accounts of it; but there are hundreds upon hundreds of surviving accounts of the operations of his mind in written form, in the pages of his juvenile and other periodicals and his more formal written works. The serious student of moral thought in the early Victorian period misses any single one of those thousands upon thousands of pages at his risk.

A peculiarly Evangelical section of the Evangelicals' immense literary output came from a passion for the morbidly detailed contemplation of 'the deathbed scene'. This was a constant object of thought and utterance with nearly every member of the Party whose words have been preserved, the intelligent as well as the vulgar. 'I know of nothing so interesting', Hannah More wrote to Sir William Weller Pepys, 'as the closing scenes of a champion of righteousness'.[1] With its dreadful fascination and its strong support in precedent (the early Puritan literature abounding in such episodes) the deathbed scene was the sole subject or close to it of many and many a widely circulated work of the day. There are few Evangelical biographies or memoirs that do not contain many examples. They may be divided into three sections: the long drawn-out description of pious deceases, the deaths of both pious and impious children, and the deaths of profane swearers, blasphemers, Sabbath-breakers and infidels, in obdurate callousness or vain remorse. In the sub-section describing the deaths of celebrated infidels the chief subjects were Paine, Gibbon, Hume and Voltaire. Accounts of their horrified deaths, in agonies of fear and tardy repentance, were very popular. They were widespread and implicitly believed, even by the more intelligent of the Party such as Mrs More, Wilberforce and Bishop Porteus. Similar fantastic and vicious tales of the death of any notorious freethinker were accepted as wildly as they were fabricated. On the Evangelical premises such demises were obligatory. 'Heard of John Wilkes's death', Mrs More's journal says; '—awful event! talents how abused! Lord, who hath made me to differ; but for thy grace I might have blasphemed thee like him. In

[1] *More*, vol. II, p. 42.

early youth I read Hume, Voltaire, Rousseau, &c. I am a monument of mercy, not to have made shipwreck of my faith.' 'I have this day had an awful admonition—heard of the death of Mr Cadell, my bookseller for twenty-eight years, only a few years older than myself! born in the same village! In many respects we were alike prosperous, and went on with great amity in all our literary concerns....He was a useful man to literature. His friends Gibbon, Hume, Robertson— where are they?'[1]

The *New Times* quoted one such account 'widely circulated among the lower classes of society' and attributed to 'the celebrated Hannah More'.

DEATH BED OF TOM PAINE

[This narrative is preceded by a vicious account of Paine's life, of the kind recommended by Porteus to Mrs More back in 1792 as 'interesting and authentic'. He defrauded a public office in London, was dismissed from his next position for loose and immoral conduct with his employer's wife, and played a disgraceful and wicked part in France. In America he never failed to get drunk daily and lived in brutal violence and detestable filthiness. This went on from bad to worse, for 'during the whole of the week preceding his death, he never failed to get drunk twice a day'. The author of this piece, probably not Mrs More—such works could as naturally be attributed to her as Psalms to David—goes on to quote 'a Dr Manly's account'.]

During the latter part of his life, he would not allow his curtains to be closed at any time, and when it unavoidably happened that he was left alone, by day or by night, he would scream and halloo till some person came to him....He would call out during his paroxysms of distress, without intermission, 'O Lord help me! God help me! Jesus Christ help me!' &c. repeating the same expressions without the least variation, and in a tone of voice that would alarm the house. Two or three days before his death, when he was constantly ex-claiming the words above-mentioned, Dr Manly said to him, 'What must we think of your present conduct? Why do you call upon Jesus Christ to help you? Do you believe that he can help you? Do you believe in the divinity of Jesus Christ?—Give me an answer as from the lips of a *dying man*.' Paine made no reply; but to a Lady, who constantly visited and relieved him on his death-bed, after asking her if she had read one of his works, and being answered that she thought it the most wicked book she had ever seen, and had therefore burnt it, he replied, 'That he wished all who had read it had been equally wise;' adding, '*if ever the Devil had an agent upon earth, I AM THAT MAN!*'

[1] *More*, vol. III, pp. 56, 183.

Satan's Grand Instrument

On the 8th of June, 1809, died this miserable reprobate, aged 72 years, who, at the close of the eighteenth century, endeavoured to persuade the common people of England to think that all was wrong in that Government, and that religion, which their forefathers had transmitted to them. For the sake of England and humanity, it is to be wished that his impostures and his memory may rot together!!

That account was compiled chiefly from a 'Life' of Paine by a certain Cheetham (New York, 1809), who Paine's real biographer Sherwin rather temperately says 'exclusive of his being a treacherous apostate, was an illiterate blockhead'. During his last illness Paine was hounded by numbers of religious people, either from a sincere wish to act in a Christian way toward him or from the kind of religiosity represented by the *New Times*'s account. His surgeon Manly explicitly denied that he changed his deistic views.[1]

The 'delightful' or 'edifying' accounts of family deaths or deaths of friends that were avidly circulated among the Evangelicals are still more representative of the fascination of illness and dissolution than instances of belated repentance and dread on the part of famous 'infidels'. There is hardly an Evangelical biography or collection of Evangelical letters, if any, that does not contain an example or many examples. It would be supererogatory to offer more than the tiniest selection, which will be a single specimen, the shortest known, and taken from the best. 'I, and indeed all of us have been, for near three weeks, closely engaged in another triumphant deathbed scene', Hannah More wrote in 1792, in a letter primarily rejoicing over still another such scene taking place nearby in Bath at the same time, that of the death of Bishop Horne ('a more delightful or edifying death-bed cannot well be imagined'). 'Two such dying beds, so near each other, are not easy to be found.'[2] The current scene is that of a cousin of Wilberforce.

Miss H——. . . acquired in the near views of death and eternity, a sort of righteous courage, an animated manner, and a ready eloquence, which were all used as means for awakening and striking others. This extraordinary change was manifested in various ways during the eighteen days in which she was given over, but shone out with complete lustre the last night of her life.

[1] W. T. Sherwin, *Memoirs of the Life of Thomas Paine* (London, 1819).
[2] *More*, vol. II, pp. 325–6.

It may be more profitable to consider the behaviour exhibited in her last hours, as the make of her mind particularly exempted her from the charge of enthusiasm...her head was never more clear, nor her judgment more sound. When I expressed my concern that her sufferings were prolonged, she said she saw clearly the wisdom of that dispensation; for that if she had been taken away in the beginning of her illness, she should have wanted much of that purification she now felt, and of those clear and strong views which now supported her. She once observed, that it was a strange situation to be an inhabitant of no world; for that she had done with this, and was not yet permitted to enter upon a better. In the night on which she died, she called us all about her, with an energy and spirit quite unlike herself. She cried out with an animated tone—'Be witnesses all of you, that I bear my dying testimony to my Christian profession. I am divinely supported, and have almost a fore-taste of heaven: Oh! this is not pain but pleasure!' After this, she sunk into so profound a calm, that we thought her insensible. We were mistaken, however; for she had still speech enough to finish every favourite text I began: and to show how clear her intellects still were, when I misquoted, she set me right, though with a voice now scarcely intelligible. To perfect *her* faith, and to exercise *ours*, it pleased her heavenly Father to try her after with one hour of suffering, as exquisite as ever human nature sustained; and I hope I shall never forget that when, in order to save myself the pang of seeing her un-utterable agonies, I wrapped my face in the curtain, I heard her broken inarti-culate voice repeatedly cry, 'Let patience have its perfect work—Though he slay me, yet will I trust in him—Thy will be done.' This, with a fervent ejaculation to be kept from temptation, and the powers of darkness, she repeated till her strength failed. Her prayer was heard; and her last hour was so peaceful, that we knew not when she sunk to her everlasting rest.

Two little things are worth recording, merely to show how consistent she was: for I am anxious to rescue such a death-bed from the imputation of enthusiastic fervours. She desired, if the physicians thought it might be useful for any future sufferer, that she might be opened; which was accordingly done. The other instance was, that early in the night, when I saw the pangs of death approaching, I had prevailed on her afflicted sister M—— to quit a scene she was so little able to bear. H—— begged to see her, and said she should like M—— to see her die. I represented to her how unfit her shattered nerves were to go through it; and that if she should fall into fits, what should I do with both? She was convinced in a moment, begged she might not come, and only desired I would explain to the woman that her sister was doing her duty by staying away; that she did it because it was right, and not because she liked it.

'Instead of fearing that this last scene should be too affecting', Hannah More wrote, 'I am only dreading (such is the levity of my nature) that it will depart from my memory before it has done its errand on my heart.'[1]

This topic could be adequately set forth, if it has not been done now, from the writings of Mrs More alone, or indeed from those of nearly any of the articulate Evangelicals, even in the early period, the outstanding exception being William Wilberforce. The Evangelicals were engrossed with such scenes in an inconceivable degree. Burials naturally were as fascinating. 'If you could for a moment doubt my account', Miss Patty wrote to Hannah More about the funeral of one of their schoolmistresses in the Cheddar Valley, 'I would add, that the undertaker from Bristol wept like a child, and confessed, that without emolument, it was worth going a hundred miles to see such a sight.'[2]

The youthful deathbed scene was almost a special province of several juvenile publications. The later century saw a large development of such periodicals, many of them of a peculiarly Evangelical flavour, such as *The Band of Hope Review and Sunday Scholar's Friend*, *The Child's Bethel Flag, or Star of Hope*, *The Christian Child's Faithful Friend, and Sabbath Companion*, *The Child's Visitor and Pleasing Instructor*, *The Church Missionary Juvenile Instructor*. A particularly typical magazine of the kind during the Wilberforce period is *The Child's Magazine and Sunday Scholar's Companion* (1815; New Series January 1821), a little sheet that in some issues gives the impression of dealing solely with deathbed scenes of young children. The limitations of space that prevent doing justice to *The Child's Companion; or, Sunday Scholar's Reward*, a small monthly published for the Religious Tract Society and naturally of a pronounced Evangelical character, are particularly mortifying. Some of the pieces of the unknown authors of *The Child's Companion* reach a high level of artistry. It offered Evangelical instruction in many fields.

'*Joe.*—No; I can't be happy with swearing, drinking people, who break the Sabbath.' 'A fine fellow you are to talk in this way,' replied Ned Smith, with a sneer and an oath; and so saying, he pushed Joe, basket and all, into the ditch on the side of the road.

[1] *More*, vol. II, pp. 327–30. [2] *Ibid.* p. 441.

461

I am sorry to say that James was a boy who loved play better than his book.... He also only cared about pleasing himself, and used often to teaze those boys who read their bibles.

Samuel Jones was a very different boy. He rejoiced that the holidays were coming, because he longed to see his dear mother, who was a widow, and also his beloved brothers and sisters.... Samuel loved his bible; he would often go from the play-ground to read it....

Which of these two boys am I most like?

I asked some little boys whether play was a good thing or a bad thing. Several of them said, at once, 'A bad thing, Sir.'[1]

It is pleasant to be able to add that the worthy and benevolent gentleman who asked that question and was recognized at once does not hold play to be invariably a bad thing.

In hundreds upon hundreds of such little articles, or in published juvenilia, such as *The Dangers of Dining Out; or, Hints to Those Who Would Make Home Happy*, the evils of the age, or what seemed to the Evangelicals and other moralists to be its evils, were combated, often in a harmless or even beneficial way. As a rule the opening sentence or so of these works shows the nature of the whole adequately.

Georgiana had from infancy been accustomed to early rising; a morning walk with her dear father was amongst her chief gratifications, and her well-known tap at his study-door, seldom failed to call forth her indulgent parent ready equipped to accompany her.

How much time they lose, dear papa, she observed, who waste these pleasant hours in bed....

Very true, my love.[2]

The non-Evangelical works of this kind, which are likely to be instructive yet pleasant, may be recognized by their failure to get on to eternal themes, or of course by their lax High Church or infidel morality or doctrine. In Mary Lamb's *Stories of Old Daniel* (a fine example of almost pure pagan thinking) the informer is openly regarded as shameful, we learn that education and integrity are what ennoble man, not titles and wealth, and after Old Daniel has told his tales to the village children 'as amusement' they run off—on a Sunday evening—to play

[1] *The Child's Companion*, April 1824, p. 112; January 1824, p. 20; October 1826, p. 289.
[2] *Georgiana and her Father*, by the author of Little George (London, n.d. (*c.* 1825)).

on the green with merriment, as if they were animals (this in the very year of Hannah More's *Coelebs*).[1]

But three titles of *The Child's Companion* sound the true note of a large part of the Evangelical literature, substantial enough in the Age of Wilberforce and increasing greatly after it: *Death of an Infant Scholar, The Child's Funeral, You Are Not Too Young To Die*. One of the most important sub-sections of the Evangelical letters in this domain, in the post-Wilberforce period, dealt with the youthful deathbed to the explicit end of terrifying children with threats of a vengeful God. 'Who can dwell with everlasting burnings?' we remember Mrs More demanding; and if, as she tells us, even a philosopher cannot answer that question, still less can a little child. In this field the Reverend William Carus Wilson was without a peer and if he had had one few people would care to know him. Wilson was a 'moderated' Calvinist with a deep passion for the horrors of the infernal abyss, lacking in both the intelligence and goodheartedness of Newton and the dynamic triumphant radiance of his master Charles Simeon. When he was denied ordination by his own bishop because of excessive Calvinism, the Old Apostle had to resort to Bishop Mansel, held in reserve for such emergencies, to get him ordained, and lectured him on the double folly of being so rigid and letting it be known to an early nineteenth-century prelate professionally ill-equipped to cope with theological niceties.[2]

Wilson's vigorously dismal, actively morbid intellect was perfectly suited to shape the deathbed scene into a peculiar speciality. In the business of frightening little children into being Evangelical little children he was a prodigious master; his relentless and righteously ferocious hands must have planted a religious terror in the minds of thousands of youthful Englishmen. His ample means enabled him, in addition to contributing strongly to the Clergy Daughters' School and other Evangelical enterprises, particularly the London Jew and Church Missionary Societies, to conduct incessantly, for years, *The Friendly Visitor, The Visitor's Friend*, and *The Children's Friend*, three little spiritual penny dreadfuls written (apparently almost wholly by himself) to further the regeneration of the poor and the young, the first two

[1] *Stories of Old Daniel or Tales of Wonder and Delight* (London, 1808); *Continuation of the Stories of Old Daniel, etc.* (London, 1820).
[2] *Simeon*, p. 417.

designed especially for district visiting. The more morbid literature of the general type was about equally divided between delightful deaths as of Evangelicals, and shocking deaths, of disobedient children, radicals, philosophers, truant Sunday scholars, Sunday boaters, profane swearers, tobacco-smoking children and other castaways. Wilson excelled in both categories, 'well authenticated accounts of early piety' being nearly as fascinating to him as scenes of horror. A superb example of the former group appeared in February 1826 in *The Children's Friend*. It is fortunately short enough to be quoted in full.

The Sabbath

The little boy had a silk-worm. It was his daily work to feed this worm on mulberry-leaves; but when Saturday night came, a doubt arose in his mind, whether it was lawful to feed it on the Sabbath-day. So just as he was going to sleep, he sent his sister with a message to his mother, to know whether God would be angry, if he should feed it on that day; adding, that he would keep himself awake till the answer came.

He did so; and when he was told he might feed, but not play with the worm, he said, 'I thought so: for I know, when I was a little baby, and not able to speak, I was fed every day; and therefore I thought that the worm should be fed too.' And then he fell quietly asleep.

This little boy died before he was seven years old; having left many proofs behind him, that God's grace had made him ready for heaven.[1]

On the whole, well authenticated accounts of early impiety had a more profound appeal to Wilson. While in his hands juvenile piety was not invariably mortal, juvenile impiety had only one termination. The hopelessly remorseful dissolution of children seems in particular never to have been far from his thoughts; over that theme he brooded, no doubt with the horrified exultation of the saved person. The 'black marble clergyman' was as sable spiritually as the garments in which Charlotte Brontë pictured him; the qualities of his grim fancy make Mrs More look like a simple countrywoman.

In *The Child's First Tales*, Ben goes skating on the Sabbath and is drowned, Sam goes skating against his mother's wishes and is drowned.

---

[1] *The Children's Friend*, vol. III, pp. 42–3. Silkworms were very popular as pets in those days. They could be fed lettuce leaves for three days after birth but after that had to have mulberry leaves.

Satan's Grand Instrument

A Sunday boating party runs foul of a barge; the screams of the women are heard, seven are drowned. It could not have been expected that Wilson would neglect this old Evangelical favourite, which appears in many forms. Basil Woodd tells it as an experience barely avoided by his own son, who refused to go on a fatal boating party. It was so cherished that it graduated at an early point from fancy to fact. In 1774 the Reverend Rowland Hill was begged not to go to Richmond to preach, 'because a party of young men had hired a boat, and were coming down the river with the determination to draw him through the water. His feelings may be conceived, when informed the boat was upset, and that the poor misguided enemies of his ministry had all entered into the presence of their Judge in another world'.[1] (It is not certain Hill's feelings can be conceived, still less that Carus Wilson's could have been.)

Wilson's classic piece of this kind is *The Burnt Bible*, a small work telling the actual 'sad history' of Daniel Rutherford, who at twelve was a good steady boy in school but who fell away. Wilson lists the steps of his decline. Daniel first becomes careless, and second commits absence from school. 'Nay, what was worse, he told falsehoods to hide the real reason, which very often was his going off to rob birds' nests on the Sabbath day!' He then wanted to become a doctor, and while working from morning till night as a carpenter's apprentice he learnt his Latin books from night till morning. That kept him from the house of God and was the third step in his fall. The fourth was his meeting and associating with 'wicked men, the disciples of Tom Paine the infidel'; and 'the rest of poor Daniel's history is so full of horror that I scarcely know how to repeat it'. He went on (in brief) from one degree of sin to another, and finally dared in company with his wicked friends to kindle a fire and burn the Bible. He died in horrible fear and remorse and his soul fled... 'Alas! Whither?' Mrs More's question about Mr Cadell's deceased friends was very often on Carus Wilson's lips.

A good general collection of Wilsoniana is in the two series of *The Child's First Tales, Chiefly in Words of One Syllable*, the first of which appeared some time before 1828. These *Tales*, which may very likely contain all the harmful attitudes that it is possible to take with children, are a perfect statement of Mr Wilson's kind of religion and morality.

[1] Sidney, *Life of Rowland Hill* (New York, 1835), p. 103.

30

BFV

He had not made up his mind on one important matter, which would have interested Charlotte Brontë if she saw it.

> But those who wor-ship God, and give
> Their pa-rents hon-our due,
> Here on this earth, they long shall live,
> And live here-aft-er too,

says one hymn, and another repeats the sentiments expressed by Mr Brocklehurst to the young Jane Eyre:

> There is an hour when I must die,
> Nor do I know how soon 'twill come;
> A thousand children, young as I,
> Are called by death to hear their doom.[1]

In general the point of view and doctrine are sound and represent Carus Wilson at what may be described as his best. A few fragments are cited.

Where do you think that boys who do not do as they are bid must go when they die?

Now, Jane was a good girl....Oh! she was so hap-py! But she would not have been so if she had not been good at school.

You need not care what your lot is in this life, if you can but get to hea-ven, when you die.

Oh, how sad it would be if you should go to hell when you die. You would not wish to go there, I am sure.

Men who get drunk will not go to God when they die. They will go to hell.

Do but look at that bad child. She is in the pet. She would have her own way. Oh! how cross she looks. And oh! what a sad tale I have to tell you of her. She was in such a rage, that all at once God struck her dead....And where do you think she is now?[2]

Look there! Do you not see a man hang by the neck? Oh! it is a sad sight. ...He stole some hens and ducks, and was sent to goal [sic] for six months. When he was let out, and got home, he went on in his bad ways. And he stole some sheep. So the judge thought it was high time to hang him. And there you see him hang.[2]

And so you do if you are looking at the cut illustrating that little story.

[1] Second Series, pp. 70, 84 (in the story called *Bad Boy*). [2] *Ibid.* pp. 47, 6.

Satan's Grand Instrument

The impression should not be given that Wilson's pen touched no other Evangelical themes. In stating the canonical view of the problem of poverty and riches in the Christian life he was eminent perhaps even above Mrs Hannah More. On that matter he wrote with the authority usually granted to his station and his profession: a rich man, he could write about poverty without bitterness or rancour and was familiar with the vexatious cares of affluence, and a priest, pastor and district visitor, he knew the problems of poverty too and the appropriate doctrines of Scripture. His thinking on wealth and its acquisition was particularly useful in the field of Sabbath observance—where it is true he was considerably indebted to the principles of argument established by Mrs More in her refutations of the French philosophers. One of the most frequently urged hortatory points here was the argument from interest. To honour the Sabbath will invariably be financially profitable. 'My friends, whatever of prosperity has been vouchsafed to my brothers and myself', a speaker at Exeter Hall said,' I unhesitatingly attribute, under God, to that honoured father's instruction and example, who would not break the commandment to "Keep holy the Sabbath Day".' C. L. Balfour's *The Mill Owner, and How He Was Ruined* tells how a wealthy mill proprietor broke down from worry, strain and overwork—he worked on Sundays, 'no one ever saw him in the house of God'—and lost his mind. 'His mind', his physician said 'has had no Sabbath.' He recovered, but his wife died and he had nothing left but a shattered constitution and was a pauper to boot. It is odd it did not occur to this author and his admirers that so far as anything in his story goes the mill-owner would have been all right if he had taken Mondays off. A similar work is *The Wealthy Draper and the Bankrupt Sabbath-Breaker*. The wealthy draper dies suddenly and is found to be bankrupt. The cause, though a little mixed, was primarily his Sabbath violations. 'He usually spent the sacred day with his accounts and ledgers, and in drinking and card-playing. I have marked the history of not a few Sabbath-breaking masters, and have generally found that *sooner* or *later*, a blight has fallen upon them, their circumstances or their families.'

In Wilson's little works on the subject he states the worldly advantage to be gained by keeping the Sabbath in a more explicit way. It was his belief, based apparently on fact, that a merchant who closes his shop on Sundays is almost certain to do twice as much business. *The Friendly Visitor* printed a good deal of exhortation to that effect.

To encourage us to give up business on the Sabbath, let us see what God has done for those who would not work on that day. A baker made up his mind not to bake on Sundays, though a great part of the support of his family came from the business which he did on that day. At first, some of his customers left him, and he became poor; but still he would not break the Sabbath. His friends persuaded him to go on doing what he felt to be right. He did so. God blessed him, and at last he had a larger business than he ever had before.

Various of Carus Wilson's publications abound in such rather simple proofs.

A miller used to work his mills, and sell flour on the Lord's Day. But these words, 'Remember that thou keep the Sabbath-day,' were always coming into his mind, and this made him unhappy. So he gave up Sunday work, and would not serve his customers on that day. They were angry, and went to other millers. The next week, many of them came on Saturday night, and were served; and in a short time as many as he had before came back to him, and he was a thousand pounds richer than he had been before.

A man used to keep open his shop on the Sunday. The clergyman of his parish often spoke to him about it, but he used to say, 'Why, I can't afford to shut my shop, for I sell more on Sunday than all the other days of the week put together!' At last, he felt how wrong he was doing, and shut his shop. About six months after, the clergyman of the parish met him, and asked him how he had got on since he had not done business on the Lord's Day. He said, 'Sir, to tell you the truth, I have taken more money in the six months since I shut up my shop, than I did in any one year before since I was in business.'

A poor man was told by his young master to carry some coals on Sunday. The poor man said he would take them on Saturday night, but he could not break the Sabbath. 'Very well,' said the young man, 'if you do not carry that load tomorrow, you need not come on Monday.' 'I can't help it,' said the man; 'I had better offend my earthly than my heavenly Master, and I can't break his command.' Monday came, and the poor man went out to try to get work. He saw his young master, who asked him why he was not at work; and when he told him why, he said that he need not take any notice of what had passed, and asked him where he had learnt to keep the Sabbath? The poor man gave him a tract about the Sabbath. He read it, and got good from it. After this, the young man, his father, and mother turned to God. So we see that good may be done to others by our keeping God's day holy.

A person in New York found out, for twenty-five years, that *all* the merchants there who opened their shops on Sundays, failed, instead of getting richer.[1]

The right Christian practice of a wealthy man, in theory, was clear too to Wilson. In *The Friendly Visitor* he describes such a one, in the beginning only a good sort of person, who reading 'the 28th of Matthew' suddenly realizes he has not been doing his part in God's work. From then on,

when he filled his bosom with the golden sheaves, his harvest joys were unspeakable. Now he exulted in the smiles of a gracious Providence, because he had learned to make those smiles subservient to the glory of his Master—to the upbuilding of the church—to the advancement of his own eternal interests. No longer did he make his benefactions a mere matter of custom or convenience. He acted on principle. His exertions were the result of deliberate design—of a well arranged system. To do good was his leading object—an object to which other things were made subservient. And with him, it was as much a matter of calculation and provision, how much he should attempt to do for the Saviour's cause, as how much he should expend to support his family. This man held on his way.... When he died, it was an easy thing to settle his estate. It had been sent on to heaven, and turned to eternal gold.[2]

In Carus Wilson's firm accents, as may have been noticed, there are more than a few traces of a warm-hearted emotional sentimentality. His trumpet, in other words, sounded no uncertain note—as John Newton quoted about another—but it sounded a good many rhetorical ones. It is not to be supposed that William Carus Wilson's estate was sent on to heaven. A decent part of very many Evangelicals' gold was devoted to religious purposes, a large part of some, but generally the Evangelical gold was not eternally transmuted. While that might only mean that Wilson's principle was so lofty that practice could hardly come up to it, he does seem to have been remiss even in very worldly things. There is evidence that in the matter of personal adornment and rich attire, especially of the young, especially of the lower orders, for instance, he was very severe. 'A love of fine clothes will grow more and more; and a poor child, if she can-not get what she wants, may be led to pick and steal to get fine clothes.'

[1] *The Friendly Visitor*, vol. XXI, pp. 86–8.   [2] *Ibid.* vol. XX, p. 95.

> How proud we are! how fond to shew
> Our clothes, and call them rich and new,
> When the poor sheep and silk-worm wore
> The ve-ry cloth-ing long be-fore.[1]

But it is not certain that he applied such standards of plainness in female costume to people of elevated social station, such for instance as his own. At Lowood School—or so we are told by Charlotte Brontë—the Reverend Mr Brocklehurst is shocked at the adornment, even by nature, of the charity girls.

Suddenly his eye gave a blink, as if it had met something that either dazzled or shocked its pupil; turning, he said in more rapid accents than he had hitherto used:—

'Miss Temple, Miss Temple, what—*what* is that girl with curled hair? Red hair, ma'am, curled—curled all over?' And extending his cane he pointed to the awful object, his hand shaking as he did so.

'It is Julia Severn,' replied Miss Temple, very quietly.

'Julia Severn, ma'am! And why has she, or any other, curled hair? Why, in defiance of every precept and principle of this house, does she conform to the world so openly—here in an evangelical, charitable establishment—as to wear her hair one mass of curls?'

'Julia's hair curls naturally,' returned Miss Temple, still more quietly.

'Naturally! Yes, but we are not to conform to nature: I wish these girls to be children of Grace: and why that abundance? I have again and again intimated that I desire the hair to be arranged closely, modestly, plainly. Miss Temple, that girl's hair must be cut off entirely: I will send a barber tomorrow: and I see others who have far too much of the excrescence.'

'I have a Master to serve whose kingdom is not of this world', Mr Brocklehurst continues; 'my mission is to mortify in these girls the lusts of the flesh; to teach them to clothe themselves with shame-facedness and sobriety, not with braided hair and costly apparel.' It was a bad moment for him to have picked for that homily—as described by Miss Brontë—for he is interrupted by the entrance into the school room of other visitors, the ladies of his own family.

They ought to have come a little sooner to have heard his lecture on dress, for they were splendidly attired in velvet, silk, and furs. The two younger of the

---

[1] *The Child's First Tales*, Second Series, pp. 67, 97.

trio (fine girls of sixteen and seventeen) had grey beaver hats, then in fashion, shaded with ostrich plumes, and from under the brim of this graceful head-dress fell a profusion of light tresses, elaborately curled; the elder lady was enveloped in a costly velvet shawl, trimmed with ermine, and she wore a false front of French curls.

Of course Wilson may have done his best, even if that was a true picture of General Neville's daughter (herself author of *A Mother's Sermons for her Children*) and the young Wilson ladies. There are reforms that are harder to accomplish than giving liberty to Africans and getting missionaries into India.

Perhaps it is wrong to feel that those little narrations describing the advantages of Sabbath observance, brought forward by this unworldly priest so explicitly as factual, and so patently manufactured, with every mark of his far from inept fictional style, show in their simple way the very perfection of the belief that the chosen person may for his own virtuous ends employ any device at all.

Like Mrs More, Carus Wilson was closely informed about the daily life of the poor. His stories show the rich experience of long years of district visiting. Old Alice Gilbert's 'employment, when very young, was tending sheep'. Old Gilbert suffered 'much persecution from her family, none of whom, at that time, feared God'. It was she who speaking of her dread of meeting her sister Jowett 'who could not resist upbraiding her in the street' uttered one of Wilson's best sayings: 'I never came out of a hot furnace without leaving some dross behind.' 'About this time, her kind minister, Mr Spencer, visited her, and found her sitting over the fire crying. He enquired, "What is the matter, Gilbert?" She replied, "I cannot help crying, because I cannot love my Saviour better." He smiled, and said, "Tell me, Gilbert, who can?" "Thank you, sir; my mind is now more happy".' 'She lived a life of joy and peace in believing, which it was delightful and very instructive to witness. She abounded in short, pious ejaculations.'

On one occasion, her daughter Mary greatly desired to go to the races, with another young woman, contrary to the wish of her mother; who, after pressing her most warmly, and exhorting her not to go, went upstairs and prayed. In about half an hour, Gilbert came down, and on finding her daughter returned, she said, 'Ah! Mary, are the races over already?' 'No, mother; but you were right, I ought not to have gone; and when I was there, every one, I thought, looked at me, as if I had no business there.' She never afterwards went to the races, or any other vanity.

At another time, two of Gilbert's other daughters set their minds on going to the races, but their mother remonstrated with them, and prayed for them. They dressed themselves, and she then said, 'I have entreated you not to go, and have prayed for you; I can do no more, but will continue in earnest prayer.' She then went to a little prayer-meeting, and her daughters set off for the races. But before they had proceeded far, a neighbour invited them into her house, and telling them they could better employ their time, she persuaded them to allow her to teach them to chevin. They did so; and, with the first shilling they earned at their new employment, they bought their mother a pair of pattens, and then returned home.[1]

A small piece of Wilson's called *Practical Religion* deals with the problem of infidel relatives who have come to visit. 'Two important questions, dear reader. What answer can conscience give?' Wilson begins, the questions being 'What have they seen in thine house?' and 'What do ye more than others?'

It may be that ungodly relations have been staying under thy roof; have they beheld those holy fruits of spirituality and consistency of conduct that your profession of godliness warranted them to expect?...Was the Sabbath kept as strictly as if you had been alone; or were your servants' time and Sabbath privileges at all interfered with by extra provisions for the body on that holy day of rest? Did you induce your relatives to go with you to the house of God, or did you break the Sabbath by worldly compliance, and forsaking the sanctuary through their being worldly and gay? and did you, with affection and earnestness, plead with them for their own souls' sakes to seek the Lord, and beseech them to be reconciled to God...?...If the ungodly visit us, and see nothing in our houses, more than in their own—if they hear us, in public, cry against a worldly spirit, and in our dress, furniture, table, and domestic intercourse, shew no difference to themselves, how can they give us credit for not being of the world, even as Christ was not of the world?...Oh, let us all be awake to the importance of our example and influence with unconverted relatives![2]

Reading that exhortation such a one as Sydney Smith might feel that Carus Wilson's method would at least make certain the ungodly relatives had been seen for the last time.

---

[1] *The Friendly Visitor*, vol. XX, pp. 65–9.   [2] *Ibid.* pp. 91–2.

Satan's Grand Instrument

Simple pieces such as *Cottage Piety* and *Poor Hester, a True Story* show
The Friendly Visitor at its best in its kind of spiritual poetry and drama.

In the row of very poor houses to which we went, one was distinguished by
its very neat garden, and its cut hedge of evergreen box. Here will be daisies
and polyanthuses in abundance, in a few weeks; and carnations and lavender,
for those who live till midsummer to gather them. Ah! frail flowers! yet
there are frailer things that you outlive. It is not only the yew of a thousand
years, and the venerable oak, that laugh to scorn the mightiness of man; but
the lowly crocus will spring up for fifty years together in the same spot, when
he that first set it and his children are gone, and their place knows them no
more.
I was thinking of how short a time old Hannah had to live.

But her greatest trouble was yet to come. When the weather was very cold,
it was quite sad to see how much she suffered, when for days together nobody
came in to kindle her little fire. But it so happened, that one freezing morning
a neighbour did take pity on her, and made up a comfortable blaze, and then
put the room to rights, and went away. The poor little boy had not seen any
thing he liked so well for many a day; and as his bed-ridden mother could not
hinder him, he got out of bed, and went to warm himself, and play by the
fire. In one moment his little thin bedgown was in flames; and there lay the
poor crippled woman, not able to move, and there was her miserable baby
burning—her only child—and the door was shut, and no one came to help.
Oh! if any mother reads this true story, let her think what that mother's
feelings must be, and let me solemnly remind her of that awful place where
there is a worse burning—the vengeance of eternal fire. How must those
parents feel when they meet those children whom their bad precepts and
worse examples have brought there. Then the wretched parent shall be as
unable to help as poor Hester was, and He who is now willing to save, will
close his ears against the sad cry.
But to go on with my story. At last some neighbours heard the poor
mother and the child shriek, and came in. But it was too late to save him. He
died the same night. Many people came in to look at him, and to help put
him in his little coffin, and amongst others his cruel father, but he took little
notice of the poor, sad mother.[1]

Such works may be found in any volume at all of Carus Wilson's
writings that the reader may be able to come across.

[1] *Ibid.* pp. 97, 52–3. This piece in the usual place of Carus Wilson's leading article
is signed with the initials 'E.H.' If it is not his it is very close to his manner.

VI

—My mission is to mortify in these girls the lusts of the flesh. Lord, do thou remove the things that are obstructing the advance of some of my friends toward spiritual things. May I be endeavouring in all things to walk in wisdom to them that are without...labouring for the spiritual improvement of others.

The spiritual 'conceit' bitterly noted by the *Anti-Jacobin Review* is plainly indicated in many of those Evangelical followers of whom any evidence remains; it is to be seen on careful scrutiny even in the more civilized, intelligent and humane of the leaders almost without exception. It is more open, less disguised by good manners and good taste, in the more dynamic and confident of the elect, Richard and Rowland Hill, Simeon and his manifestly saved disciples, John William Cunningham and William Carus Wilson. Such people, probably also some of the early unaccommodated divines, made no attempt to conceal the gulf by which the awakened person is separated from the unawakened. In some of the more civilized Evangelicals this Evangelical highminded-ness would no more be noticed, on superficial acquaintance, than the fact of a puritan reformation would be noticed by anyone looking around him in St Giles's in 1830. No one could guess it on meeting Hannah More with her bright, quick intelligence, wit and fondness of fun, her poise and good manners, or the frail, crippled, half-blind little man with such unmistakable Christian loving-kindness, seraphic, not on his way to Heaven but there already. It was present just the same, and different in no fundamental way from the pious highmindedness of Dr Haweis, or of Dr Hawker who presided over the Gospel Tract Society with its committee of twenty-four saved gentlemen. It is seen in men of the most genuine Christian love and perhaps held by them most strongly if most quietly. John Newton's religion was a Calvinism so liberal as to be unique in this period if not in all periods. Like Henry Venn he was fond of saying he did not preach Calvinism but Christianity. It is with sorrow and pity he points out that without the Gospel the Africans obviously cannot be saved. To his mind a man can even make his way to the Cross without Calvin. But what non-Evangelical roads in the Church of England lead to the Cross? Who can be saved without the second birth? In Wilberforce's journals and diaries, even as printed by his sons, we see again and again that (through the period of his leadership) the Evangelical rightness was as wholly a basic part of his religious belief, politic and good-hearted as he was, as of any other Evangelical's.

Held implicitly by individual members of the group, in a more firm and unquestioning way as they more closely realized the perfection of the Evangelical character, this highmindedness, as the (High Church) Reverend Lewis Way noted, is still more manifestly a formal cause of Evangelicalism itself. It is more to be seen in the public life of the Evangelical Party than in the private lives of its servants.

We are not concerned here with that large-scale 'compliance with the ways of the polite world' that has been noted and this matter has no connection with trivial and vulgar rewards. Wilberforce, for years in a unique position of towering eminence, for hundreds of thousands of people the symbol of righteousness, 'the conscience of England', constantly receiving tributes of admiration and gratitude from the civilized world such as few other men have ever heard, was not vain or conceited at his accomplishments. Thomas Scott was not proud of the unprecedented sale of his *Family Bible*, Newton not consumed with vanity that he had been the human agent of the conversion of so many useful nominal Christians. There may even be some fashion in which one could say Hannah More was not proud of the unparalleled success of her writings and the Old Apostle not vain at the swarming of the young Cambridge men to his Sunday evenings and the part they were playing in the spiritual life of the country even before his death. But in their knowledge that the truth had made them through grace acceptable for salvation while others who were not Evangelicals were not acceptable, in their knowledge of the kind of religion and morality that England had to have, there was a certainty, and a consequent exaltation, that together with their manifest and exclusive closeness to Deity served them for a righteousness and led them to trust themselves and despise others.

That the perfection of the Evangelical character of this age is represented by Charles Simeon will probably be granted by any serious observer of it; the Evangelical of that day at any rate who would not agree would be too far off centre to have the right to speak. Sir James Stephen observes that had not the Established Church abandoned one of Papistry's most characteristic features we would surely have had a St Charles. Out of his many services, all distinguished by overwhelming vitality and boundless Christian assurance, of the most robust, dynamic 'highmindedness', one in particular, of the first importance to the cause, could only have been conceived and carried through by an awakened, reborn man standing in the most elevated and conscious way on an eminence above the world's votaries. That was Simeon's triumphant collection and use of Evangelical wealth to buy the way of proved, successful Evangelical clergymen into positions of strategic usefulness. In that extraordinary Church of England, to the outsider universally so admirable and in particulars so incomprehensible—*Ecclesia Anglicana stupor mundi*—large numbers of livings were commodities, to be bought and sold like so many Africans by any person who had the means and the will. After being for some years the dominant trustee of John Thornton's funds left for the same purpose, Simeon began in the 1820's to devote his own money and whatever other funds he could get hold of to 'the purchase of Livings (which I commit immediately to Trustees in perpetuity), that in them may be preached those doctrines which have produced so happy an effect on my own soul'.

It contributed in the most felicitous way to the success of that project that while the Party's leading clergymen of the early period—Foster, Romaine, Scott, Newton, Cecil, Joseph Milner and no doubt more—were no respecters of persons and had clearly in mind the truth that the chief preparation for Christian grace and duty is a humiliation, a broken and a contrite heart, a poverty of spirit, that 'consorts ill with the love of gold', there nevertheless gathered round the standard of Evangelicalism, gradually at first and then rapidly, larger and larger numbers of the well-to-do, the comfortably well-off, the pleasingly substantial, the wealthy, and as time went on the affluent and the immensely rich. Mrs More is able to write again and again, with discreet exultation, of the 'ample wealth', 'handsome competence', 'great affluence', 'vast fortune' and the like of incoming converts as the Evangelical ranks swell with power. As Evangelicals these peers, country gentlemen, traders, financiers and inheritors of vested wealth were well aware of 'the vanity of all earthly pursuits, possessions, enjoyments, and distinctions' (Thomas Scott), and knew thoroughly and believed, though not in the degree in most cases that Wilberforce thought they should have done, that their affluence had no more than been committed to their stewardship. The constitution of the Established Church was such that that stewardship could be utilized, with no possible legal interference, to displace Orthodox incumbents and introduce Evangelical incumbents. By the conversion of the properly substantial and properly situated people, it was possible (1) to secure lectureships, by nomination of the founder, by nomination of certain liveries and other institutions, and by election of the seat-holders; (2) to secure chaplaincies the appointment to which was in the hands of officers, or heavy subscribers, of hospitals, asylums and other benevolent institutions; (3) to acquire the right of presentation to churches by building them; (4) to purchase advowsons or next presentations; and (5) to collect and establish in trust sums for the accomplishment of such purposes, chiefly for the purchase of advowsons and their establishment in a systematic and permanent way.

What can be said of the Christian righteousness of Simeon's dynamic, vital, greatly helpful course of action? There was no recorded objection from any single Evangelical of the day; and so far as is known, Charles Simeon was untroubled by doubt or uncertainty, any faintest tinge of uneasiness or a single questioning. It was not so clear to Evangelical antagonists. Simeon's purchasings were done on a large, business-like, legally organized scale, with the openly stated purpose of stuffing into the church clergymen whose religious views were in every way that could be assured those of the purchaser: at first Simeon himself, later a financial trust in no position of church authority and opposed to the religious views of the great majority of the clergy. It can at least be said for this traffic that it occurred to no one to conceal it. The cause and the circumstances imperatively and simply demanded that Orthodox parishes, in particular 'key' parishes, be filled with truly religious incumbents. To an unaccustomed ear it sounds slightly odd to hear Simeon speaking of his 'buyings', his 'purchases', his 'treaties', the interposings of Deity to 'forestall' for him and prevent 'the payment' 'out of his own pocket', in the service of 'our common Lord, who gave His own life a ransom for us'. To the mind of some, the organized use of great wealth to purchase 'spheres' of religious influence, the consolidation of the purchased commodities into a legal body and its preservation 'in perpetuity' were strikingly unlike the spirit of Christianity and good churchmanship. There were soon those pointing out that there is a notable offence called simony, after one Simon who 'regarded spiritual functions as a marketable commodity' (A. T. Robertson), that 'Simon' and 'Simeon' are the same word and that such an offence might be a sin without being a crime. In an elaborate attack on Simeon's Trust years later it was pointed out that the seventeenth-century Puritans had a similar practice, attempting to constitute certain feoffees in trust for purchasing livings, that was put down by Laud, who described them as 'main instruments for the Puritanic faction to undermine the Church'.[1] About Simeon's whole scheme there was 'a taint of corruption'. 'There is a canker in the vitals of this confederacy which must destroy it. There is the contact with "the accursed Thing, the wedge of gold, the Babylonish garment, the 200 shekels of silver," which must bring a plague upon the congregation.'[2]

It was all clear and good to so shining a vessel as Simeon. 'I wrote to Dr Kilvington, whom I had never met, to ask some assistance...thinking he might possibly give me £500, and behold he gave me nearly £8000! And now that I am again engaged to the amount of above £10,000 a gentleman, whom I never saw but once, and then only for half-an-hour, has died and left me...£9000....Oh, what a Master He is!...On both these occasions He has just interposed (as indeed He has on several other occasions) to forestall and prevent the payment out of my own pocket; so that I am still as strong as ever to prosecute the same good work. Who needs prove to *me* the providence of God?'[3]

Simeon seldom agreed with his adverse critics, and would have disagreed with them on the present issue if he had ever given them a second thought. We are dealing here not with ordinary but superlative Evangelical practice. It seems the truest kind of indication of the extreme highmindedness of this kind of Evangelical, to be seen as each eight or ten thousand pounds comes in and he goes on increasingly— 'How evidently is God with me in this good work!'—that his success was a certain, unmistakable proof of the Divine approbation. The *Memoirs* of Mrs Sarah Hawkes mentions a warning of Richard Cecil (one of the superior Evangelical clergymen) about the danger of mis-

[1] W. D. Willis, M.A., *Simony, etc.* (London, 1865), pp. 132–3.
[2] *Ibid.* pp. 180–1.　　　　　　　　[3] *Simeon*, p. 604.

taking the workings of the imagination for the teaching of the Spirit.[1]
It is hard to avoid the thought that the Reverend William Huntington,
S.S. (Saved Sinner), a partly-demented religious quack of the day, may
have had precisely Simeon's attitude, on the basis of precisely those
clear, bright notions that John Newton wrote about, when the wealthy
widow of the Lord Mayor Sir James Sanderson was so foolish as to
marry him.

In a recent book about Simeon it is suggested (though not 'high-
mindedly') that 'the quality of genius' in his 'ecclesiastical statesmanship' 'resided in his ability to solve the problem by which he found
himself confronted'. The chief problem was the problem of continuity.
There was no trouble in 'recruiting and training a supply of Evangelical
clergy', or in 'finding Bishops willing to ordain' Evangelical clergy.
'By 1814 the demand for pious curates had outstripped the supply;
besides, a man's friends could usually find him something sooner or
later.' Simeon's purpose in buying livings was 'to secure continuity
of teaching'. 'No congregation could thrive if subjected to violent
alternations of religious guidance or misguidance.' 'Simeon, in fact,
inherited the Thornton policy and applied it, no doubt with keener
strategy, but to the same honourable end.'[2]

There is another way of looking at what Simeon was doing, and it
appears to be simpler. Back in John Thornton's time no one ever
troubled to say Thornton had any object whatever but that of getting
Evangelical clergymen into livings with the explicit purpose of keeping
High Churchmen out. A violent disruption of continuity—it would
seem—was the only purpose of acting at all. John Thornton and
Charles Simeon too could have secured continuity of teaching by the
simple step of minding their own business. But no genius in ecclesiastical statesmanship is needed to see that it would be continuity of a
teaching opposed to Charles Simeon's teaching, thus wrong.

That there was no trouble in recruiting a supply of Evangelical clergy
was due solely—when the Reformation had got to the point where there
was no trouble—to the powerful efforts described in the present study;
but before 1815 when Ryder became Bishop of Gloucester there was

---

[1] *Memoirs of Mrs Hawkes*, edited by Catherine Cecil (Richard Cecil's daughter),
(London, 1837), p. 100.
[2] Charles Smyth, *Simeon and Church Order* (Cambridge, 1940).

a great deal of trouble in finding bishops willing to ordain Evangelical candidates. It was even necessary sometimes to fall back on Henry Bathurst. Obviously if there had not been the greatest trouble in getting proper benefices for successful Evangelicals Simeon would not have exerted himself at all. The mention of curates and the observation that 'a man's friends could usually find him something' are far beside the point. No one was concerned with 'something' or curates. Neither Thornton's money nor Simeon's was spent to provide young Evangelicals with berths in the church. As everybody connected with it in those days said quite openly, it was spent to put strong, tested Evangelicals into 'useful', 'key' benefices. Simeon did not buy costly livings at Bath, Cheltenham and such fashionable resorts, and in other strategic spots, to launch young men on an Evangelical career.

A simple and conclusive case occurring so frequently that Simeon specifically warned his trustees about the error of securing continuity when it did was when there was a presentation to a living where the curate had been teaching, perhaps for years, and was endorsed by the parish. 'Whenever there is a good Minister, there will be, if any, a good Curate', he wrote to one of his trustees: '...consequently *in their view* he will be the fittest person to present: and therefore petitions will be made in his favour. From every place I have had petitions upon petitions; and for fit persons too. But where then is my knowledge of persons, my judgment, and my right of patronage, and my conscience, if I too readily, and without extreme vigilance comply with them? I must not only do *well,* but the *best* that I can *possibly* do; and I must spare no pains to effect this. It is on this account, that in my dying charge to my Trustees I have particularly guarded them against being influenced by *petitions for Curates.*' 'They must be particularly on their guard', the dying charge says (Simeon had regarded himself, Evangelically, as a dying man from the time of his conversion at the age of nineteen), 'against petitions from the parishes to be provided for, whether on behalf of a Curate that has laboured among them, or of any other individual.'[1] The deciding factor is neither the wishes of the parish nor the continuity of teaching, but is one thing solely: the new incumbent shall be the best available Evangelical who is peculiarly fitted for the Evangelical necessities and opportunities of the living.

[1] *Simeon,* pp. 746–8.

Of the one kind of continuity in which there was the most genuine and passionate interest, the continuity of the Evangelical acquisition of church power and the spread of true religion to play its part in the reform of the nation, Charles Simeon is the sole judge. 'I would please all men, but it should be *for their good* to *edification*; and how to do that, I must judge for myself.'[1] Where there is dissatisfaction with the presentation, 'a dissatisfied man says in fact, "I will take the Patronage into my own hands; and neither God nor the proper Patron shall have anything to do with it; or if the Patron presume to think and act for himself, I will quarrel with him on account of it." Such a person as this is not the proper person to consult or to follow.' (It is clear that those remarks are not intended to apply to the patronage of High Church patrons.)

'I live in a region in which I would have you also move', Simeon wrote to an erring friend.[2]

There is a true religion, and there is an obligation to impart it. If you do not wish to move in my region, you shall move in it just the same. It is right that you should do so, for I know it to be right, and my friends Dean Milner and William Wilberforce and Hannah More know it, and the Lord President of the Council, the Chancellor of the Exchequer, the Governor-General of India, and all who are Israelites indeed and stigmatized pilgrims, wrestling Jacobs and already half-beatified saints of the Lord.

An odd indication of the Evangelical rightness and at the same time one of the strongest indications of a basic honesty in all matters apart from Evangelical matters is what Wilberforce did when confronted with the two unmistakably good men he knew who made the Evangelical highmindedness impossible on any consistent reasonable foundation. That William Pitt remained a citizen of the Gentile world, in the malign grasp of Tomline Bishop of Lincoln, reduced him to uncomprehending silence in the face of a circumstance that on Evangelical principles could not exist but that he clearly saw existing. In such a case, what lessons of time and experience furnish a guide to belief? Pitt's 'regard for truth was greater than I ever saw in any man who was not strongly under the influence of a powerful principle of religion.' It did not amount merely to a relative goodness, as that statement could

---

[1] *Ibid.* pp. 748-9.   [2] *Ibid.* p. 617.

indicate, but to a distinguished moral integrity. What then—as virtue cannot exist without true religion—was its source? 'He appeared to adhere to it', Wilberforce's statement continues, 'out of respect for himself, from a certain moral purity which appeared to be a part of his nature.'[1] A still more deeply mystifying impossibility was furnished by Wilberforce's friend, neighbour and collaborator in the Abolition fight and many other Evangelical projects, William Smith, M.P., of Clapham, member for Norwich. 'What a lesson does he give to evangelical Christians!' the diary says, in 1823. 'I am never with him without thinking of talis cum sis, utinam noster esses, not with a party feeling, but from Christian love. I never forget his principles, and grieve over them.'[2] That too could not be, for Smith was a Unitarian. The principles over which Wilberforce grieved denied the very basis of true religion, the divinity of Jesus Christ. Would you were ours! There is nothing more to be said. How can it be explained that one without grace has a natural goodness, and one who denies the divinity of Jesus is manifestly a good man, when all goodness comes from the Evangelical religion? An unresolvable difficulty must be left unresolved; and Wilberforce had the distinguished moral integrity to see that this was one.

The Evangelicals were right, others wrong, and that that conviction is not intellectually demonstrable—can, in fact, and must be held, as even Wilberforce did, in the face of plainly true contradictories—is all the more cause to hold it unreservedly. Reason, Charlotte Elizabeth says, is a fool. The superior spirituality of Evangelicalism is not arrived at or held by argument. It rests on a stronger foundation: the internal knowledge, not opinion but infallible certainty, of becoming a new man, the 'great change'. Truth cannot be known by those who have not experienced that change. The Reverend Mr Fanshawe may have walked humbly with his God and lived a blameless life as a High Church priest for thirty years, but until he had entered upon his second life he was living in darkness.

What else than such a possession of exclusive truth could have allowed the Dean of Carlisle to tell us that if it had not been for Joseph Milner's conversion, after he had been for years a clergyman of the Established Church, the populous town of Hull might have con-

[1] *Private Papers*, p. 69.   [2] *Wilberforce*, vol. v, p. 161.

tinued in the dark irreligious state in which he found it, and thousands might have died without ever hearing the glad tidings of the Gospel properly stated? Milner did not mean that every High Church clergyman in Hull was an immoral man. Let every single one of them be of a decenter cast: they are still not citizens of Charles Simeon's 'Christian world'. So long as they follow the lead of Bishop Marsh they are confirmed castaways.

What other point of view would allow the Evangelicals, and foremost among them here *the Evangelical clergy*, to speak as they constantly did of their brothers in the Established Church?—False prophets and ravening wolves, the scribes and Pharisees of the day, perfect blanks in the creation,[1] fat bulls of Bashan, priests walking in darkness, pastors who would neither save their flocks nor be saved themselves, idol shepherds, unconverted clergymen. In Mrs More's neighbourhood they were emissaries of Satan and in Cambridge it was held that eighteen hundred years before they would have opposed Our Saviour himself. Against them was openly and repeatedly directed that most offensive of all expressions of contempt and hatred, Rowland Hill's call to truly religious persons: 'Come ye out from among them' ('and be ye separated, saith the Lord, touch not the unclean thing, and I will receive you').[2]

Without that consciousness of exclusive spiritual knowledge and merit how could it have been possible for men and women so intelligent to think of themselves as favoured and watched over by the Almighty when others who thought of themselves as Christians were not? For them so wholeheartedly to believe in those preposterous 'providences' that in many cases so evidently involved serious harm to innocent people and that so obviously happen in the lives of all people? How could it have been possible, without that conviction, for Charlotte Elizabeth to know unquestioningly that she was immortal until she had done the work for which God had chosen her? For Charles Simeon to believe that the luxuriousness of his establishment was not more than God approved of? That in Cambridge there were one hundred and ten, no more or less, certainly chosen and sanctified Christians? That at Cambridge in 1811—in the richest, most spectacular of all providences—

---

[1] *Joseph Milner*, vol. VIII, p. 421.

[2] II Cor. vi. 14. It was Hill's 'favourite text': Sidney, *Life of Rowland Hill*, p. 104.

God slew Augustus Henry Fitzroy third Duke of Grafton (a Unitarian), just as He would suddenly strike dead a little girl in the pet, so that Silly Billy could be elected Chancellor of the University, so that William Wilberforce could come to stay with Isaac Milner, so that Isaac Milner, in such grave dereliction of his duty that he was forced to get a royal dispensation, could absent himself from a cathedral chapter in Carlisle, so that he could be present at a Senate in Cambridge, so that Charles Simeon's evening lectures would be saved from the mere nominal Christian hostility of the Bishop of Ely?

If Bishop Dampier had fallen from his horse and been killed the day before that Senate meeting, how unhesitatingly would Charles Simeon have believed it was a direct act of Omnipotence on behalf of his acceptable servant Charles Simeon![1]

What other than a highmindedness so exalted could have allowed Isaac Milner to remind the Second Anniversary Meeting of the Cambridge Auxiliary of 'the memorable 12th of December, 1811, when, with my Lord Hardwicke in the chair, the Cambridge Auxiliary Bible Society was first formed with so much harmony, and so universal a concurrence'?[2]

What other principle of belief could have allowed Wilberforce to enter in his private journal the trust that his illness was an act of God to save him from going to the House where his vote for repressive measures might have offended the liberals who were supporting him on Abolition? How else could it have been possible for Isaac Milner—for all his bluster and indolence and gluttony and hypochondria one of the most decent and intelligent of the Evangelicals—to believe that God deliberately withheld his light from Joseph Milner and allowed him to be an unconverted minister walking in darkness, bringing to his people the false doctrine that leads to eternal death, until he had been chosen for those places of influence for which the Corporation of Hull would not have chosen a truly religious man? How could it have been possible for such men as Milner and Wilberforce so soberly and gratefully to think of the Almighty as acting on their behalf with a clear view

---

[1] 'Thomas Rogers…may perhaps be forgiven for suspecting the hand of Providence in the death of the Bishop of Ely's hostile examining chaplain a few hours before the examination'. (J. D. Walsh in *Church Quarterly Review*, Oct.–Dec. 1958, p. 505).

[2] *Isaac Milner*, p. 586.

to expediency and worldly contrivance? Joseph Milner providentially was not converted until he had been elected to influential positions in Hull. His conversion before that time would have prevented his election, for the Corporation would not have chosen a truly religious man. William Wilberforce was providentially not converted until after his election for Yorkshire. His conversion before that time would have prevented his election, for as a religious person he could not have stooped to the corrupt practices necessary to elect him. How could such men in perfect sincerity and innocence of heart attribute that wily calculation to their God, if they had not firmly believed that truth resides solely in Evangelicalism? It could no more be doubted than the salvation of Charles Simeon and St Paul.

On their premises and as truly religious and moral men and women of Christian lovingkindness, how could the Evangelicals refrain from enforcing the Evangelical truth on men and women in darkness with all their power? The Evangelical rightness is about no trivial matter; it concerns life eternal. The attitude toward life and death that led Dr Samuel Parr to be a Whig was not significant. The attitude that led him to oppose the Bible Society and the Missionary Society, deny the necessity of a personal conversion and stand out against all elements of Evangelical reform, was a fatality. Without suspecting it Dr Parr was an emissary of Satan. Mrs Siddons the Tragic Muse, without an equal in her dangerous profession, was a respectable woman. If asked she would have said she was a Christian. But Mrs Siddons, no particle more than a good sort of person of a decenter cast, knew no more about true religion than a rabbit. She was no more a Christian than Pitt's dire tutor. What is a true Christian's duty toward such people?

Mere nominal Christianity is 'little better than Heathen ignorance' and involves 'greater guilt', 'savages are not more ignorant of His glory and love than are nominal Christians'; truly religious people and no others are assured of salvation through liberty. Liberty is the right to choose true religion. For their own immense good, in the most important matter of their lives and regardless of their wishes about it, those people who are perishing must exercise that right. The Evangelicals' attitude toward their kind of freedom is precisely that of Jean-Jacques Rousseau toward his. It is so valuable that those who do not wish to be free must be forced to be free. If they cannot be taught, persuaded and led, they must be driven. That is not to diminish them but to enlarge them. It is done for their good to edification. Charles Simeon himself tells us.

An out-of-the-ordinary illustration of 'highmindedness' is provided by the two leading Evangelical biographies, the 'official' lives of Wilberforce and Hannah More, which happen to be also two of the chief Evangelical documents of the later period. They contribute to the impression that with a great advance in true religion of the clergy and the middle and higher ranks there had also been changes in the Evangelicals. *The Life of William Wilberforce* published in 1838 by his second and third sons, Robert Isaac, Vicar of East Farleigh and late fellow of Oriel College, and Samuel, Rector of Brighstone, has particular interest as indicating that some years before his death Wilberforce may already have felt himself a stranger in his own house.

CHAPTER 12

FRANKENSTEIN; OR,
THE MODERN PROMETHEUS

I

The *Christian Observer*'s review of Robert Isaac and Samuel Wilber-force's life of their father began immediately after it came out, in the issue of June 1838. The editor 'could not permit a single month to go by' without placing the young Wilberforces' title page on his list; he therefore squeezed in two or three pages of a forty-page review the rest of which appeared in September and December.[1] This first instalment thus served only as a hurried introduction to the notice of 'those already popular and highly-appreciated volumes' with 'their delightful and valuable contents'. It had no comment except of a general nature, such as the statement that Zachary Macaulay, who 'did not live to read the memoir of his beloved friend', furnished most of the materials apart from Wilberforce's diary and journals, and it seems certain that in June the *Christian Observer* had not read the book. They knew without reading that its contents would be delightful and valuable.

By September it had been read, in so far as its nature permitted it to be done in so short a time by so simple-hearted a reader. We come then to the beginning of one of the strangest reviews ever published. For a while the writer struggles with the incomprehensible conflict, the dimensions of which he never grasps, between what he is reading and what he knows to be the truth, his natural feeling of reverence for the great leader heightening his feeling of the impossibility of Wilberforce's sons doing what they seemed to have done. In this struggle simple piety and Christian ingenuousness prove unequal to the task, and the reviewer gives up, in disappointment and bewilderment.

'We will not waste much letter-press in critical remarks', he says, on the early page on which he prematurely calls the *Life* 'this delightful

[1] *Christian Observer*, 1838, pp. 403–5, 567–94, 774–84.

and instructive work'. But there are points so little to be expected in a *Life of Wilberforce* that even a wholly unsuspecting reviewer could not miss them. 'We have certainly here and there observed a remark which seems to indicate that the biographers, highly as they venerate the character, and honour the intentions, of their revered father, do not always enter heartily into some of his opinions and measures.'[1] The references to the Bible Society, for example, are nearly always 'an apology for their father's being a member of it'. It is not obligatory on everyone, of course, to approve of the Bible Society, and as the biographers 'both, we believe, were members of Oriel College', they could well have gathered much there to make them think their father and the Bible Society were in the wrong. But if they were not in sympathy with it, would they not be under a compulsion to minimize their father's devotion to it—a devotion surely recorded in many documents in their possession? 'We should ourselves have anticipated that his journal, diary, correspondence, speeches, and conversation would have afforded a larger relative proportion of remark, connected with this Society... than we find in these pages.' It may not be so, the reviewer continues (it is unquestionable, of course); but here the biographers appear to assume the character of a 'reluctant witness'.

There is one mild protest at the statement that at twelve Wilberforce was a good person by virtue of a 'baptismal seed', which no Evangelical would think, and at one point a sharp protest. Wilberforce had learned 'at this time, probably from Doddridge', the sons say apologetically, to view the Eucharist rather as an act of self-dedication than as a means of grace. An Evangelical writer in the *Christian Observer* could not be expected to pass that over. There is no reason to think Wilberforce had learned his view of the Eucharist from a dissenter, the reviewer points out, but in any case Doddridge's view was thoroughly Scriptural. 'Knowing, as we do, Mr Wilberforce's opinion on these subjects, we regret that his biographers should interweave their own hypotheses with his history.' 'We could have spared these editorial interjections of Oxford-tract doctrine.'[2]

From that point on, there is silence about Robert Isaac and Samuel Wilberforce. The whole last section of the review is given to quotation and a discussion of the useless controversy over the relative eminence

---

[1] *Christian Observer*, 1838, pp. 568, 569.   [2] *Ibid.* p. 588.

of Wilberforce and Thomas Clarkson in the campaign for the Africans.

The uncertain tone of that review, the puzzled protests, the hints at stronger differences than are brought into the open, the references to sinister effects of a horrid contamination to which the young Wilberforces were exposed at Oriel, with the reviewer's complete failure to take stock of the work as a whole and perceive what hob its authors were playing with the facts of their father's life, show a pathetic and understandable bewilderment. It seems clear that as late as 1838 it was not generally known to the Evangelical world that the sons of their revered leader, brought up in the heart of Evangelicalism, had gone over to High Church. That their doctrine was befouled in some particulars was evident to the *Observer*; to apprehend that they had altogether put from their hearts the true religion of those resolute people who fought so stoutly against 'nominal Christianity' was beyond them. How could it not be? For one thing, through the years in which he must have been at work on the *Life of Wilberforce* and in the year of its publication, Samuel Wilberforce was accepting repeated preferment from or through his father's cousins the Sumners that would hardly have been offered by such Evangelicals, in such times, to a High Churchman even if he was Wilberforce's son—preferment so lavish that when in 1845 he was made Dean of Westminster and in that year too nominated Bishop of Oxford by Sir Robert Peel he had at the age of forty held every office in the church short of an archbishopric. A powerful Evangelicalism had done much for this son of Wilberforce, whose adherence to High Church from his Oxford days or earlier had been well dissembled.[1] If it had been known in 1838 to the *Christian Observer*, a forewarned and forearmed reviewer, unpuzzled and resolute, could have pointed out many unbelievable things in the *Life of William Wilberforce*.

Under such circumstances, it would seem that Robert Isaac and Samuel might have disqualified themselves as biographers of their father. No matter how gifted in conciliation and accommodation Wilberforce was, he had never compromised in a single instance on

---

[1] 'He was a Churchman, and a High Churchman, from the first', his biographer Ashwell says (Canon Ashwell and Reginald Wilberforce, *The Life of Bishop Wilberforce*, vol. I, p. 54).

what he felt to be true religion. How could a High Churchman write about him with sympathy, understanding, and appreciation of his wonderful achievements? The most elementary moral principle, one would think, required those two young clergymen to turn over their great mass of materials to Venn, Dealtry, Goode, Vaughan, Cunningham, Carus, Carus Wilson or any esteemed Evangelical author who should be named by the Old Apostle. Or is it possible that some secret circumstance here required them to do nothing of the sort? Far from disqualifying themselves, Robert Isaac and Samuel appear to have kept at least one other from writing their father's biography. As early as 1820 John William Cunningham, a much esteemed Evangelical author, was in correspondence with Isaac Milner about such a project, 'with which Mr Wilberforce was acquainted, and of which he approved'.[1] It appears from so explicit a statement that Wilberforce's sons were not only not reluctant to write the *Life* but determined that no one else should do it.

That brings up a possible procedure that at first sight seems morally indefensible. It had at least seemed very immoral to Wilberforce. When his beloved young friend John Bowdler, a dedicated Evangelical, died in 1815, he resented with his gentle indignation that Bowdler's father, a High Churchman, hurried to write his biography to prevent an Evangelical one. In doing so, John Bowdler the Elder laid down canonically the simple principle on which such a book should be written: to leave out of it every document, incident and word that would allow a reader to know the truth. Apart from the objections that a scrupulous person might raise to such a performance, a considerable difficulty remains in this case. It is not impossible (as John Bowdler showed) to write such a 'biography' when the subject is an unknown young man. But Wilberforce not only had some claim to be held the leading moral and religious citizen of the world: it had been a matter of knowledge for thirty-five years that he was the Evangelical leader. Apart from moral considerations even, it would seem an utter impossibility to write the life of such a man on the Bowdler principle—or at least it would seem to require a resoluteness and skill hardly to be looked for in two ordinary young clergymen. Unless such an act can

[1] *Isaac Milner*, p. 713. (There seems no reason for Miss Milner's not telling the truth in such a matter.)

be thought of as dictated by some hidden and imperative necessity (a possibility that should be kept in mind), it would also seem to require a perhaps truly unusual degree of moral effrontery.

With the reservation noted, all difficulties are removed, at least in part, by our realizing that Robert Isaac and Samuel were not ordinary young clergymen. The method of John Bowdler *in toto*, but on a much larger scale and with greatly superior thoroughness and subtlety, was their method. The object of their biography was to record Wilberforce's Christian character and achievements in so far as it could be done while concealing his Evangelicalism; and that object was attempted so thoroughly that not only his leadership of the Evangelical reform campaign but the campaign and the Evangelicals too are coolly deleted from his life. There were people still living who knew more about that than Wilberforce's sons did; they had taken part in it;[1] but so far as the general public and posterity were concerned and so far as calculation and adroitness could manage, no reader who did not already know better was to know that Wilberforce had been anything but a Christian senator, the parliamentary leader of Abolition, a supporter of the missionaries and a good member of a non-controversial Established Church. As that naturally could not be done without suppressing the greater part of their father's life's work, the unsuspecting reader is left wondering, at the end of the five volumes, at occasional references to a moral reform of the country and letters congratulating Wilberforce on his prominent part in it. That God had called him to reform the morals of the country is recorded, so is his organization of the Proclamation Society of 1788; beyond that a few scattered and trivial references to the Bettering, Bible and Vice Societies and a few more.

The method of Robert Isaac and Samuel was (1) to omit all parts of letters and of the diary, journal and memoranda that presented Wilberforce's life in a way that could not be misinterpreted or misunderstood;[2]

[1] It may have significance that although Wilberforce died in July 1833 the *Life of Wilberforce* did not appear until immediately after the death of Zachary Macaulay in May 1838.

[2] The statement is made without an examination of the manuscripts and the present writer is aware of Professor Coupland's statement in the preface of his *Wilberforce* (1923), made after an examination of a part of the diary, that 'virtually nothing of interest or importance' in the diary was left unquoted. Sir Reginald Coupland's book is well-informed and able. He was interested, however, in Wilberforce's political life

(2) to print without explanation hundreds of passages that could not be left out without crowding their pages with asterisks or explained without revealing the truth (this is done many times when such passages are meaningless to the general reader); (3) to print ingenuously without explanation scores upon scores of Wilberforce's statements of clear Evangelical meaning that a general reader would take simply in an ordinary sense; (4) to take all advantage, often ingeniously, of ambiguous statements that would naturally be misunderstood; (5) to say as little as possible, or nothing at all, about episodes that could not be narrated without defeating the writers' purpose (the Blagdon Controversy is mentioned in only two sentences); (6) to describe so deviously as to conceal his motives episodes in which Wilberforce played a prominent Evangelical part; and (7) as much as possible to avoid explicit falsehoods by a deft manipulation of half-truths.

The constant Evangelical practice of using ordinary words in a specifically Evangelical sense helped greatly in these difficult procedures. For example, if Mrs More had complained to Wilberforce during the Blagdon Controversy that the *Anti-Jacobin Review* was representing 'all Evangelical men' as opposed to government, Robert Isaac and Samuel could not have printed the sentence. But Mrs More wrote 'all serious men'; and that could be printed, without explanation, her clear statement of the truth left absurd or unintelligible to an ultimate audience. There was no danger that they might understand it. In 1818 Wilberforce dined at Gloucester House, where he sat next to Lord Stuart, the diary says, 'and talked a little seriously with him, for which the Duke thanked me afterwards'.[1] An earlier entry takes us back to the Cheddar Valley. Visiting Mrs More, Wilberforce met 'Dr W, the true picture of a sensible, well-informed and educated, polished, old, well beneficed, nobleman's and gentleman's house-frequenting, literary and chess playing divine—of the best sort....' This is Whalley, of course, Mrs More's unfortunate champion. 'I hope', Wilberforce adds, 'beginning to be serious.'[2] Dr Whalley had then

and does not appear to have been concerned with the peculiar nature of the sons' biography. How large a part of the diary he examined is not stated. In any case the clear facts make a hypothesis of repeated omissions unavoidable.

[1] *Wilberforce*, vol. IV, p. 375.
[2] *Ibid*. p. 149.

been a clergyman of the Established Church, and a good Christian clergyman according to his lights if not Wilberforce's, for nearly forty years. A little earlier the diary records Wilberforce's dining with the Reverend Legh Richmond, author of *The Dairyman's Daughter*. 'It is just twelve years since he became serious from reading my book on Christianity.'[1] That did not mean Wilberforce thought Richmond had stopped being flippant.

In addition to that felicitously deceptive use of the Evangelical language, the biographers crowded their pages with delicate little devices that give a wholly false impression, in many cases entirely in Wilberforce's words, without the actual statement of any deliberate untruth, as an inimical biographer of Sir Thomas Fowell Buxton could do (to take a homely example) by quoting a sentence from one of Buxton's letters: 'Give my love to my secretary' and not adding that Buxton's secretary was his daughter.[2] Looking back over his life, in the 1820's, and listing his many blessings, Wilberforce cites his associates, who show 'above all, the wisdom of selecting religious men for friends'.[3] The unbriefed reader would assume that the Bishop of Lincoln, for instance, was included in that category. An analysis of the eighty to a hundred friends named in the five volumes shows what Wilberforce meant—in fact what Wilberforce said. Apart from Joseph John Gurney a Quaker, William Smith a Unitarian, his cousin Lord Carrington a mere nominal Christian if he was not an Evangelical, his friend William Pitt ensnared fast by Tomline, perhaps his friend Henry Bankes, they are all Evangelicals. No informed person could believe he thought Tomline was a 'religious man.' A similar misdirection is accomplished when we are told that Wilberforce cultivated 'more and more the company of those who lived habitually in the fear of God'. An American editor of Wilberforce's *Correspondence* tells us unashamed that Wilberforce became a member of 'that noble band who formed the brightest constellation that has ever adorned the moral firmament', and proceeds to name the others: Newton, Venn, Milner, Thornton, Grant, More, and Cecil. Those names occur in the *Life of Wilberforce*, but there is no indication that they were a noble band, or a band, and none that Wilberforce had any connection with them except that of friendship

[1] *Ibid.* vol. III, p. 421.   [2] *Buxton*, p. 274.
[3] *Wilberforce*, vol. V, p. 113.

493

or acquaintance.[1] The expression 'those who feared God' or something like it in fact becomes one of the Wilberforces' favourite pseudonyms for the Evangelicals. 'Came off to Teston, to see the Middletons and Mrs Bouverie. How much better is this society! I will endeavour to confine myself more to those who fear God.'[2] 'This was a friendship', the biographers say about his early acquaintance with Hannah More and her sisters, 'which his increasing desire of intercourse with those who feared God led him at this time especially to cultivate.'[3] It could be said in various ways. 'This tranquil state of feeling was henceforth fostered by a system of greater domestic intercourse with the friends whose principles he valued.'[4]

We are told that Wilberforce had 'certain topics carefully arranged before he entered into company, which might insensibly lead the conversation to useful subjects'.[5] It was not certain topics and useful subjects, but one certain topic and one useful subject.—His mother was 'not possessed at this time of those views of the spiritual nature of religion, which she adopted in later life'.[6] It was not possible for the writers to name the views. In his old age the agriculturalist Arthur Young 'found his chief pleasure in such society as that which he continually found in Mr Wilberforce's house'.[7] It could not be explained that Young, a peculiarly intense Evangelical, found no pleasure at all but in Evangelical society and no other society continually in Wilberforce's home if Wilberforce could help it. The *Life* is necessarily packed with such deceptions. 'I rejoice (we rejoice)', Wilberforce wrote to Lady Olivia Sparrow, 'to hear Lady Mandeville is going on so well.'[8] Instead of no explanation, a simple commentary could have been given here. It was not that Lady Olivia's daughter was going on so well in health, or with her needlecraft, or with her Oriental studies, but in Evangelical religion, to which she too, an object of Hannah More's sincere solicitude, had been converted. The 'we' does not mean the Wilberforce family. 'I (we) rejoice in Lady Lindsay and Co.'s going-

---

[1] *Correspondence of William Wilberforce* (2 vols., Philadelphia, 1841). The editor's name is not given. The English edition was edited by Wilberforce's sons the biographers, without that statement.

[2] *Wilberforce*, vol. I, p. 234.　　　[3] *Ibid.* p. 237.
[4] *Ibid.* p. 372.　　　[5] *Ibid.* vol. II, p. 104.
[6] *Ibid.* vol. I, p. 5.　　[7] *Ibid.* vol. IV, p. 244.　　[8] *Ibid.* vol. V, p. 235–6.

on', Wilberforce wrote to Lord Muncaster about his daughter and son-in-law.[1]

'Lord Harrowby rode over to see me, and I walked and sat with him, and he with me at my four o'clock dinner afterwards', the diary says for 10 September 1825; 'very clever, and entertaining as always. Talked for an hour or more with Lord Sandon. The dear Bishop quite happy, and on good grounds.'[2] That pleasant if puzzling little passage too must be printed and left as it is, without comment. It could not be explained without making it understood. The Earl of Harrowby, an Evangelical of the inner circle, for many years Lord President of the Council and twice offered the premiership, was close to the throne and outstanding in government. Nothing need be added to make the point that it was important his son should be Evangelical. Wilberforce did not talk to Lord Sandon about Walter Scott's novels. Even after his retirement he had no hours to throw away. Lord Sandon, second Lord Harrowby, was a leading Evangelical through a large part of the nineteenth century. Still less could the biographers point out what the cryptic concluding sentence meant. The dear Bishop was Harrowby's brother Henry Ryder, until 1826 the only Evangelical bishop. When Wilberforce wrote that sentence in his diary, Ryder had just been translated from Gloucester to Lichfield and Coventry, with an enlarged Evangelical usefulness that constituted good grounds indeed for happiness. Bishop Tomline might have been happy, contemplating his finances for instance, but not on good grounds.

'Miss W—— consulted me lately about the point of duty respecting her attending her parish church. I urged it, on the ground of the prayers composing the chief purpose of social worship.'[3] How should an innocent reader construe that point of duty? Can a communicant's duty to attend her parish church come into debate? Miss W—— was an Evangelical (the biographers might have explained), her incumbent a High Church clergyman. Should she attend an Evangelical, wherever the nearest one was to be found, or should she attend a dissenting but 'evangelical' minister inside her parish? We might note that Wilberforce, who had often done both, is now (1825) advising Miss W—— to attend a mere nominal Christian.

In 1807 John Thornton the Younger brought Reginald Heber to

[1] *Ibid.* vol. IV, p. 86. [2] *Ibid.* vol. V, p. 253. [3] *Ibid.* p. 252.

congratulate Wilberforce on the second reading of the Slave Trade Bill. 'Heber had entered the room with a strong suspicion of his principles', the *Life* says, a note adding that Heber knew Sir Richard Hill and 'imagined that his sentiments, which he deemed disaffected to the church, were shared by Mr Wilberforce.'[1] If Heber left the room imagining they were not he was deceiving himself as much as the Wilberforces were trying to deceive us. The only views of Sir Richard Hill that could be considered disaffected were his Evangelical views. To share them did not require one to share his unaccommodated Calvinism, tasteless devotional manners or crude lack of expediency. Mrs More thought Sir Richard 'very agreeable, and very pious',[2] and in the respect of being Evangelical he and Wilberforce were indistinguishable. But while the passage is deliberately false it contains no outright falsehood, and nothing obliged the biographers to point out that Wilberforce, Hill, Heber's friend John Thornton and every other man they name as present at that meeting except the Unitarian William Smith—Henry Thornton, Granville Sharp, Robert Bird, Zachary Macaulay and Charles and Robert Grant—was also a prominent Evangelical.

When Charles Simeon, establishing his Bible Society auxiliary at Cambridge in 1811, calls on Wilberforce for help the young biographers are in a bad spot. At this time Simeon was the best known Evangelical clergyman and the most disliked by the Orthodox. Any connection with him would be as unmistakable a sign of Evangelicalism as with the Bible Society itself. In this doubly tricky situation Robert Isaac and Samuel rise to one of their finest achievements. The whole Cambridge affair is introduced in a single superb sentence. 'A few extracts from [Wilberforce's] letters written at this time to Mr Simeon exhibit some of those secret links by which all through his long public life he was connected with the efforts of religious men in every quarter.'[3] Could it be more suavely implied that Wilberforce was interested in the Bible Society only because of others, that his support was merely a part of his public life and that Simeon's religious quarter was not his? This is a particularly cool sentence in the *Life* of a man who was a founder of the Bible Society and quite possibly the originator of it, a lifelong

[1] *Wilberforce*, vol. III, p. 298.   [2] *More*, vol. IV, p. 230.
[3] *Wilberforce*, vol. III, p. 559.

member, officer and heavy contributor, a constant attendant of its committee for many years and its most faithful, beloved and revered Anniversary speaker.

Probably the Wilberforces' most brilliant feat, however, was scored in connection with the attack on the Evangelicals led by Lord Sidmouth in 1811. They have been giving the false impression that their father's concern about the Sidmouth bill was on behalf of the Methodists and dissenters only. It was because of such a concern, we are told, that he wrote to William Hey of Leeds. 'From his early connexion with the Methodist body' Hey 'would enter into all the bearings of the question.'[1] That simple statement is second to nothing in the *Life of Wilberforce* for consummate adroitness. The attention of the reader could hardly be more deftly directed away from Wilberforce's Evangelicalism, and his objection to the bill as an attack on the Evangelical clergy, than by pointing out that Hey's early Methodism would enable him to realize the danger. And it is true Hey had an early connection with the Methodists. It was so early that in 1811 he had been an Evangelical member of the church for thirty years.

All this was accomplished with such grave competence that even the reader who knows something about Wilberforce is likely to realize only slowly that no division in the church was known to Robert Isaac and Samuel and no movement for national reform beyond Wilberforce's original declaration, his memorandum for and against publishing *Practical Christianity*, and quite mystifying references to a 'moral improvement' of the nation. No religious campaign was known to these biographers, no controversy except over Abolition and the missionaries, no neutral party in parliament. An already informed reader only could suspect that Wilberforce had ever differed from the heads of the church, had had opposition within it, had been the leader of any party, or that there had been any party. In Robert Isaac and Samuel's five volumes there is no mention of a 'school of Mr Wilberforce' or a 'Clapham Sect', under those names or any other. In the official life of the Evangelical leader the words 'Evangelical', 'Evangelicals' and 'Evangelical Party' do not occur.[2]

[1] *Ibid.* vol. III, p. 508.
[2] The word 'evangelical', 'evangelically' is used eight times, never with an understandable reference to a particular religious group.

The use of omissions, ambiguities and half-truths is given up for a simpler method only once. *Practical Christianity*, we are told, was 'addressed in the first instance to his personal acquaintance', it was 'devotional, not controversial', it 'spoke the language of no sect or party'.[1] The only assumption that would allow those statements to be thought of as errors is the assumption that Robert Isaac and Samuel had not read their father's book.

Perhaps it is allowable to pay *The Life of William Wilberforce* the qualified respect due a masterpiece of any class, particularly as like *The Shepherd of Salisbury Plain* its class consists of itself alone.

II

There is a possible explanation of the *Life of Wilberforce* that attributes love and respect for their father to the biographers, and an understandable if bad motive. It is reasonable enough to allow the hypothesis to be advanced that the whole unfortunate nature of the *Life* came from a scrupulous filial piety. For a reason apart from their dislike of Evangelicalism the young Wilberforces could not allow anyone else to write their father's life and had to do some such thing as they did to the best of their capacities. The evidence for that view is a kind of final commentary on the Evangelicalism of Wilberforce's last years.

In 1831 an unwise investment for his eldest son cost Wilberforce so much that he gave up his establishment and spent the remaining two years of his life alternately with Robert Isaac and Samuel. 'They were intensely devoted to him', Professor Coupland of All Souls says, 'and he was intensely fond and proud of them and their vocation.' An extraordinary statement follows. 'It did not trouble him that they had moved away from his own Evangelical standpoint.'[2] When Sir Reginald Coupland adds, 'He had always been broadminded in those matters', it is made more extraordinary. 'Those matters' were not a matter for broadmindedness. Wilberforce had never thought tolerantly about the people who attacked the true religionists so harshly. He had no more lax an attitude toward Gifford, Tomline and other High Church antagonists than toward Cobbett and Paine.

[1] *Wilberforce*, vol. II, p. 203.
[2] R. Coupland, *Wilberforce* (Oxford, 1923, pp. 506-7).

It may be true nevertheless that he was not troubled by his sons' apostasy from the religion they had learned in his home. The available evidence in fact seems to point that way. But it could only be true if he had followed them away from the Evangelical Party. There is a considerable amount of evidence supporting the belief that perhaps by 1830 Wilberforce had himself gone over to High Church.

He had believed for some years that in the course of the Evangelical Reformation the state of morals and religion among the upper and middle classes had improved greatly. In parliament improvement was particularly noticeable. In old Sir Richard Hill's day, back in the 1780's when he was introducing his Evangelical measures, the mention of a religious theme was the signal for hearty mirth. Not so thirty years later. 'To those who observe the signs of the times, the prospect is very encouraging', Wilberforce wrote to Hey in 1813, about the fight to introduce the missionaries into India. 'We were mercifully favoured by Providence in our parliamentary contest, and when I consider what was the state of the House of Commons twenty-five years ago, and how little it would then have borne with patience what it heard not only with patience but acceptance during the late discussions, I cannot but draw a favourable augury for the welfare of our country.'[1] His biographers are probably right in claiming that 'his own personal influence had been a powerful instrument in gaining this result. Never had he been able to bring forward in the House so openly his own religious principles; never had they been more respectfully received.' 'It must be a satisfaction to you to have observed', Joseph Butterworth wrote to Wilberforce when he retired, 'that the moral tone of the House of Commons, as well as of the nation at large, is much higher than when you first entered upon public life; and there can be no doubt that God has made you the honoured instrument of contributing much to this great improvement'[2] (a condition that was in Southey's mind when he wrote at the same time 'That House will not look upon your like again').[3]

The improvement in the Commons was a token and earnest of the whole, the greatly bettered moral tone of the nation at large. In 1818 Wilberforce lamented the retirement of Thomas Babington from

[1] *Wilberforce*, vol. IV, p. 125.
[2] *Ibid.* vol. V, p. 240.   [3] *Ibid.* p. 238.

32-2

parliament. 'The Almighty, however, can carry on his purposes by His own instruments', he wrote to Hey; 'and when I see in every part of this country new proofs presenting themselves of the diffusion of true religion, and of its blessed effects in promoting a spirit of active beneficence and warm sympathy for the instruction of ignorance, and above all the promotion of Christian knowledge, my spirits rise again.'[1] 'Depend upon it...we are getting forward. The standard of public opinion is rising under the influence of an improving body of clergy.'[2] 'Not the least pleasing feature he had noticed as he passed on, was the improved religious character he traced among the clergy. "I hear, thank God, a highly satisfactory report of it; it is solid and Scriptural, not fanatical or tinctured with partiality. A fault by the way which I never so well understood as of late years".'[3] In 1832 in a letter to Samuel he describes a discussion with Dr Rennell, Dean of Winchester. 'He holds the great degeneracy of these times. I, on the contrary, declared to him that, though I acknowledged the more open prevalence of profaneness, and of all the vices which grow out of insubordination, yet that there had been also a marked and great increase of religion within the last forty years.'[4] In the middle and upper ranks, the Evangelical Reformation ('within the last forty years') has made great progress, though insubordination still leads to profaneness, infidelity, atheism and all vices, which openly flourish in the lower orders (where Methodism had its chief results).

At the same time there were many signs of Wilberforce's increasing attachment to the formularies and discipline of the church. This is a far step from the early Evangelicalism that had always been little concerned with ritual and concerned greatly, in many of its clergy and laity wholly, with the preaching of Jesus Christ and Him Crucified. '...at Jay's,' the diary says in 1825, 'where I greatly wished to go, but thought it wrong.'[5] He had not thought so in the days when he and Mrs More attended Jay's Independent chapel in Bath, before the Blagdon Controversy, at least constantly enough to rouse comment. 'I found that so much use was made of my going to Jay's', he writes from Bath to Thomas Babington, in November 1799, 'that I have kept away.'[6] 'L. off to Birmingham to hear Hall preach to-

---

[1] *Wilberforce*, vol. v, p. 8. [2] *Ibid.* p. 318. [3] *Ibid.* p. 281.
[4] *Private Papers*, p. 279. [5] *Wilberforce*, vol. v, p. 258. [6] *Ibid.* vol. II, p. 351.

morrow; I should have liked it, but thought it wrong. In attending public worship we are not to be edified by talent, but by the Holy Spirit, and therefore we ought to look beyond the human agent.'[1] This is in 1822. Robert Hall, a Baptist, was one of the celebrated preachers of the age. Wilberforce had not always been of his later opinion. 'After much doubt, resolved and went to hear Hall at meeting', the diary says for 13 May 1804. '...He seemed to labour with a sense of the weight and importance of his subject. Truly evangelical also.' 'All of us struck with him. Simeon with us—his first hearing of Hall.'[2]

It was in 1825 that Wilberforce advised Miss W—— to attend her parish church 'on the ground of the prayers composing the chief purpose of social worship'. The Wilberforce of thirty years earlier had not thought so, when he and Henry Thornton went out of their parish week after week to hear Thomas Scott at the Lock Chapel, following him in the afternoon into the City. It seems likely we should accept his sons' statement, again of 1825, that 'this ardent love for the Liturgy grew manifestly with his years'.[3]

These are all steps, and large steps, away from Evangelicalism and toward adherence to the Regular, Orthodox or High Church point of view.

His education of his sons also has some interest. While it is not a subversive act for a Cambridge man to send three sons to Oxford, and Mrs More was happy to learn from correspondents there that along the Isis and the Cherwell true religion was now flourishing, the pertinent Evangelical circumstances, his position and the University of Cambridge's in the Evangelical world, seem to make Wilberforce's act an extraordinary one. How could the beloved sons of the commander, who had gone to Evangelical tutor after Evangelical tutor, not be sent up to the second Evangelical capital? In the 1820's there had been great changes since the days when Isaac Milner set out single-handed to make Queens' an Evangelical stronghold and Simeon fought his way against every kind of opposition. Milner was dead and Jowett gone in 1821 but Simeon, Farish and the others, triumphantly carrying on the work of Reformation Protestantism, were at their peak. No one at Oxford compared with them. In many colleges the young Evangelicals multi-

[1] *Ibid.* vol. v, p. 140. [2] *Ibid.* vol. iii, p. 186.
[3] *Ibid.* vol. v, p. 259.

plied and throve. Cambridge produced five out of six of the leading Evangelicals of their generation.

It is true that up to Oxford during these years went the sons of Sir Robert Peel, John Gladstone, William Manning, Sir James Graham, Sir Thomas Baring, Mrs Mary De Quincey and Benjamin Harrison of Clapham Common, with John Henry Newman who had been converted by an Evangelical schoolmaster. But those men were neither of the inner Clapham group nor among Wilberforce's closest associates outside it. From Cambridge in this period, after Rowland Hill, Venn, Wilberforce, Villiers, Babington and Gisborne, came Richmond, Robinson, the Sumners, Vaughan, Sargent, Marsh, Carus, Carus Wilson, Hodson, Buchanan, Martyn, Overton, the Noels, Silly Billy, Bishop Ryder, Lord Harrowby, the Cunninghams, Dealtry and many more, and to Cambridge went the sons of Richmond, Robinson, Vaughan and Carus Wilson and of John Venn, Elliott, Parry, Charles Grant, the Hoares, the Thorntons and Lord Teignmouth, all of the Clapham group and the inner circle. Furthermore to Cambridge went the sons of every one of Wilberforce's closest friends: Macaulay, Babington, Gisborne and Stephen. Wilberforce's sons were the sole exception, and when Robert Isaac, Samuel and Henry Wilberforce went up to Oxford, moreover, they did not matriculate from St Edmund Hall, the headquarters of Evangelicalism, but from Oriel, at that time its direct theological opposite. 'In the Evangelical scheme [the Provost of Oriel, Whately] saw nothing but a system of dogmas framed to create a groundless self-confidence, and to foster spiritual pride.' 'To Whately...the Evangelical system as presented at Oxford was below contempt.'[1]

Another statement in Coupland's book brings evidence about Wilberforce's change of religious connection. While he was not troubled at his sons' 'estrangement', Coupland says, it was perhaps as well 'he could not know that, when they came to write his biography, they would be constrained to make excuses for his sympathy with Nonconformists'.[2] Any constraint under that head is to be seen in the *Life of Wilberforce* only in its suppression of Wilberforce's activity in societies admitting dissenters, which came primarily, or wholly, from the biographers' determination not to describe his activities as an

[1] Mozley, *Reminiscences*, vol. I, pp. 23–4. [2] Coupland, *Wilberforce*, p. 506.

Evangelical. No doubt Robert Isaac and Samuel had little (or no) sympathy with dissenters. But they were not thereby caused any difficulty in writing the *Life*, for Wilberforce himself had no more.

The point has more importance than immediately appears, in trying to estimate a possible change in the nature of the Evangelical Party in the late 1820's and the 1830's and what Wilberforce thought of it. As a body the Evangelicals were happy to join with dissenters in the reforming societies, and in doing so were opposed to the Regular churchmen. The general assumption of a religious sympathy and close union transcending formal church adherence seems to have come entirely from that circumstance. It is quite unwarranted so far as the Evangelical leaders of Wilberforce's period are concerned, and Wilberforce was no exception.[1] One of his most important qualifications as commander was that by fortune, training and acquired tastes he was a cultivated eighteenth-century English gentleman. The easy and polished manners and manifest good breeding that gave the true tone of the English upper classes were important to him. But those were qualities that dissenters had no interest in. Of course Wilberforce was not blind to the merits of the leading dissenters, or to their usefulness, and undoubtedly respected them. He would have disagreed strongly nevertheless with Wesley's instructions to his ministers that they should be no more concerned to have the manners of a gentleman than of a dancing-master. The record is quite clear here. Wilberforce loved dissenters with Christian love, but he did not like them.

In 1818 the abolitionists were considering the possibility of having an agent with Castlereagh at Aix la Chapelle, suspecting that in Castlereagh they did not have a trustworthy advocate. Wilberforce felt that neither he nor James Stephen could do it but that the Reverend

---

[1] 'I was yesterday drawn by the pressing instances of some Clapham ladies to witness a feast given to the children of Miss Wilkinson's schools. This lady is a Baptist, and I believe of the Sabbatarian sort, but is rather in high esteem among our religious folks at Clapham, who are moved by her active benevolence to recede a little from their accustomed antipathy to Dissenters' (Zachary Macaulay; *Life and Letters*, p. 222). Henry Venn to his son John Venn: 'The melancholy account you send me, of a Dissenting minister coming amongst your people, is certainly a very heavy trial; yet be not discouraged! This is a trial all the pastors of Christ meet with. Your conduct is to be the same as theirs has been—to warn your people against this device of Satan' (*Venn*, p. 299). Many more such testimonies could be cited.

Thomas Clarkson seemed 'formed by Providence for the purpose'. 'He would be regarded as half Quaker, and may do eccentric things with less offence than you or I would', he wrote to Stephen.[1] 'Then to meeting of the British and Foreign School Society, Lord Ebrington in the chair', the diary says for 9 June 1820. 'Quite a Dissenting appearance, I must say; but being there, and arriving an hour too late, I thought it would be rude to come away, so I staid.'[2] In 1826 he went with Joseph John Gurney to the Quakers' meeting. 'We all came away thankful that not Quakers.'[3] 'Mr Lancaster came to the door', the diary notes in 1802, 'and I too lightly asked him to come in; but when in, treated him kindly.'[4] 'Of Olney I hear but a very melancholy account', he writes to Hey in 1809. 'It is indeed an awful instance of mercies slighted and privileges abused. I suspect also from what I have heard, that some of the former ministers of the place, like my excellent friend Mr Newton, not being quite enough on their guard respecting dissenting, and Dissenters, has been not unproductive of evil.'[5]

'"Southey", he said, whilst the account of Dr Coke's visit to America in Wesley's Life was being read to him, "never could have seen the Doctor. I wish I could forget his little round face and short figure. Any one who wished to take off a Methodist could not have done better than exactly copy his manner and appearance. He looked a mere boy when he was turned fifty, with such a smooth apple face, and little round mouth, that if it had been forgotten you might have made as good a one by thrusting in your thumb. He was waiting once to see me in a room, into which some accident brought Bankes. The Doctor made I suppose some strange demonstration, for he sent Bankes to Milner's room, saying in amazement, 'What extraordinary people Wilberforce does get around him.'"[6] At one time during 1808, his sons tell us to illustrate the 'shades of character and feeling' to be found in his constant throng of visitors, he was talking with a 'starched little fellow whom he was anxious not to disgust', when, Wilberforce's own account of it goes on, 'Andrew Fuller was announced—a man of considerable powers of mind, but who bore about him very plainly the vestigia ruris. Not a moment was to be lost. So before he came in

[1] *Wilberforce*, vol. v, p. 3. [2] *Ibid.* p. 57.
[3] *Ibid.* p. 270. [4] *Ibid.* vol. iii, p. 66.
[5] *Ibid.* p. 422. [6] *Ibid.* pp. 389–90.

I said to my little friend, "You know Andrew Fuller?" "No, I never heard his name." "Oh then you must know him; he is an extraordinary man, whose talents have raised him from a very low situation." This prepared the way, and Andrew Fuller did no harm, although he walked in looking the very picture of a blacksmith.'[1] 'He was often amused', his sons tell us, 'by these harmless incongruities.'

Another simple little sequence of references is eloquent on this point. In January 1812 Wilberforce was uneasy about the prospect of war with the United States; '...yet honest Butterworth's correspondents say that we need not heed the war cry.' In May 1812 Wilberforce mentions James Stephen's going to see Bellingham the condemned assassin of Perceval to try to bring him to repentance. 'He found honest Butterworth trying to get admittance.' In October of the same year he wrote, about the elections, 'Honest Butterworth's success reminds me of "Them that honour me, I will honour"'.[2] This is unhappily more than a little like one of Hannah More's condescending characters of the upper class ('He entered into conversation with the Shepherd in the following manner: "Your's is a troublesome life, honest friend, said he."')

Of course Wilberforce meant nothing unkind (as the saying is) by such turns of speech, but they do not give the conviction that he thought of dissenters as he did of his Evangelical friends. Joseph Butterworth, the Methodist lay leader, was intelligent, virtuous and even substantial, a Member of Parliament and a leading supporter of the societies, Fuller was a man of piety and intellect and this was that Dr Coke who was Wesley's right-hand man, devoted his life and his large fortune to Wesleyanism and died at sea on a missionary voyage. Wilberforce might once in a while in a playful way say 'honest Macaulay', but he would not say 'honest Pitt', 'honest Lord Harrowby' or 'honest Bishop Barrington'. He always spoke in such a fashion about dissenters with the exception of his friends Joseph John Gurney and William Smith, in whose case the spiritual eminence, enlightenment, benevolence and manifest temporal consequence as a pilgrim would have made such an attitude ridiculous.

[1] *Ibid.* p. 389.
[2] *Ibid.* pp. 5, 27, 65. ('A friend just told me, that an honest Baptist in his neighbourhood had been neutralized by Lord William Russell's driving to him in Leather Lane, with his coach and four, and outriders, &c.' (vol. III, p. 189).)

This is not to argue that such sentiments were held by all, many or few members of the Established Church, but merely to point out that they were Wilberforce's sentiments.

Wilberforce liked good manners, sweetness, gentleness, refinement and taste. He had never believed that true religion is incompatible with the characteristic good qualities of the upper classes, or felt at home with the assured vessels, the rough old Calvinists like Hawker, Haweis and the Hills. He did not like the familiarity with Deity that appeared to be a constant aspect of the assured vessel. He had frequently deplored the lack of manners of some of the Evangelical clergy, even so able and respected a one as Thomas Scott. He had complained humorously about the looks and bearing of some of the Evangelical candidates for Holy Orders who were sent to him for help. What would he have thought, feeling increasingly the importance of the Liturgy rather than the preaching, if at the same time that he saw the High Church party becoming seriously religious he saw the Evangelical Party sinking into a rigid, hard and mannerless pedantry and coming increasingly to be composed, in its articulate, dominant members, of the later Hawkers and the new Carus Wilsons—of people, that is, who to his mind would be of the 'dissenter type'? What would he have thought of the distressing creatures in the dark recesses of St Edmund Hall and the equally unsoaped Simeonite dwellers of the Johnian labyrinth...his own college?

In the *Life* there is a strange sentence describing the constant pressure Wilberforce was under, round 1822, to spend time on multitudes of projects that seemed to many of his associates to keep him from important matters. 'He was himself the last to perceive that the diffusion of his time in minor occupations was but the tax he paid for being the centre of a great moral system, and that his multifarious intercourse with men of all classes formed the ramifications of that power which gave an impulse to the age.'[1] If the young Wilberforces with some realization of that power had no full understanding of what their father had done through his leadership of the Evangelicals, and knew that some years before his death he had given up all spiritual kinship with the Evangelicals to turn to the High Church religion, it could have seemed to them impossible that his biography should be written in any other way.

[1] *Wilberforce*, vol. v, pp. 153–4.

III

Until they became known as 'the school of Mr Wilberforce'— and by some antagonists even later—the Evangelicals were known as 'Methodists in the church'. Taking the term 'Methodist' (without prejudice) to mean what the great generally meant by it—which was stated with youthful violence in the Reverend Mr Fellowes's polemics—it was a false and in some instances deliberately false designation of the Evangelicals of the early period. The Party's indignation at it was justified. But with allowance for Fellowes's rhetorical exuberance, a good deal of what he said would have been thought by High Church to refer accurately to the outward appearance, manners and inner being of William Carus Wilson. Years later in a work called *Pages from a Private Diary* that appeared in the *Cornhill Magazine* there was a short notice of 'the hideous Clapham School religion, from which "muscular Christianity" helped to deliver us'. 'Its outward symbol was black kid gloves, and its passwords were many, perhaps the most odious being the word "engage". When a clergyman called, it was quite customary for him to say, "Shall we engage?" and then and there you were expected to let him hale you into the presence of your maker.'[1] In addition to the instant image of Carus Wilson that it brings to any candid mind, that sort of thing is in the category of what the *Anti-Jacobin Review* meant by 'the whine and cant of the tabernacle'. It would be a noteworthy historical irony if a charge made so wrongly at the beginning of the period was coming at the end of it to have some truth in it.

The Reverend Legh Richmond owed his conversion to *Practical Christianity*, made Wilberforce his daughter's godfather, named his second son after him and had for him what in a pagan would have been an idolatrous devotion. 'It was not the tie of ordinary friendship, nor the veneration which, in common with multitudes, I felt for the name of Wilberforce, which induced me to give that name to my child; there had, for many years past, subsisted a tie between myself and that much-loved friend, of a higher and more sacred character than any other which earth can afford.'[2] It is a little pathetic that Richmond's ardent attachment was one-sided. 'Legh Richmond, though an excel-

---

[1] *Pages from a Private Diary* (4th impression, London, 1899), pp. 47–8.
[2] Grimshawe, *Memoir of Richmond*, p. 26.

lent man,' Wilberforce wrote to Samuel in 1829, after Richmond's death, 'was not a man of refinement or of taste.' It is possible he may have used the expression 'excellent man' to describe a good, even truly religious, man he did not really care much for; Carus Wilson was 'an excellent man' too. 'I entirely concur in your censure of Richmond's commonplace, I had almost termed it profane, way in which he speaks of the Evil Spirit. This falls under the condemnation justly pronounced by Paley against levity in religion.'[1]

Of course Wilberforce had respect for Richmond's accomplishments. The author of *The Dairyman's Daughter* (a moral tract with a circulation far beyond any of Hannah More's) and the tireless and greatly successful missionary to England was not a mediocre Evangelical. In the same way he would have had some respect for Amos Barton. It would not have been enough to make him a member of Barton's congregation, or encourage him to stay a member of his religious party. He did not think the admirable clergyman was necessarily without refinement or taste and had no need of a classical education. Plainly not all Evangelicals could have the polished suavity and elegance of Bishop Barrington any more than his wealth and high birth. But the later Evangelicals whom he saw around him, and particularly the clergy, seem in more than individual instances to have had increasingly little or no regard for qualities that he cherished.

Their 'dissenter-like' qualities were accompanied by an increasing puritanical strictness and senseless rigour, by hardening doctrinaire convictions defying humaneness and good thinking, and with many evidences of the later Evangelical 'highmindedness'. We have had a glimpse of the first in the total abstinence and anti-tobacco societies. It is most noteworthy in one of the later Evangelicalism's most harmful legacies to the nineteenth century, its creation of a Sabbatarianism not to be found in the early days of the Evangelical Reformation. That the Sunday was intended to be a venerated symbol of man's designed and proper unhappiness here below, this side Jordan, was not the belief of even the doughtiest champions among the older clergy. On 10 April 1798 the Eclectic Society took up a question proposed by Basil Woodd: 'What is the obligation of the Christian Sabbath?' 'As to the strictness of its observance,' Woodd said in introduction, 'I wish to have a line

[1] *Private Papers*, p. 243.

pointed out whereby we may steer clear on the one hand of Judaising, and on the other of too much license.' In William Carus Wilson's prime Judaizing was good enough. When he was six years old his clerical predecessors did not believe so. 'The Sabbath was designed for all men to whom the Gospel comes—to slaves and men in all circumstances', said Henry Foster, John Thornton's pastor. 'I have an idea that there is a liberty which men may take with a good conscience, which would be called by some a violation of the Sabbath.' 'As to the matter of observance,' the Reverend J. Davies said, 'I should say that whatever appears not to hinder personal religion, or the devotion of others, or public worship, seems allowable.' 'It seems manifest', said 'the Rev. Professor Farish, a visitor from Cambridge' (who on this occasion adds once more to his Christian as well as to his humane and civilized stature), 'that Christ meant to relax the strictness of the Sabbath.' 'Christianity is mild and accommodating.' 'The Sabbath is …of perpetual obligation, though not in its strictness.' Cecil, Pratt and Thomas Scott agreed, no one disagreed, and a group of clergymen who had a better right to stand for the Evangelical priesthood cannot be named.[1]

Two striking instances of this change in the Evangelical Party send us back again to Hannah More. There was one canonical Evangelical view that she really seems not able to go through with in spite of conscientious efforts. This is the view that poor and rich alike are appointed by Deity to enjoy the blessings and endure the hardships of their respective stations and that people living in the greatest indigence and degradation can be just as virtuous and happy as the well-to-do, in fact, having greatly less of trial and temptation, are much better off. Mrs More tries faithfully, and often, with this doctrine, but her heart is not in it. It may have had some connection with her failure to pay more than lip-service that—as Thomas Scott's son said of him—she had been 'conversant with humble scenes'.

Even in *The Shepherd of Salisbury Plain* there is an example of Mrs More's real thinking in this matter. After the church service, back at the hovel, where the Shepherd is beginning in his usual way to catechize his family, we come to an important part of the Evangelical accommodation: rather than a firm adherence to the principle of the

[1] *Eclectic Notes*, pp. 41-7.

blessings of indigence we have a satisfactory reconciliation of the two worlds. Mr Jenkins the good curate comes in with the happy news that old Wilson, his clerk, has died ('I know you will be sorry to gain any advantage by the death of a neighbour'). He has always intended that the Shepherd should succeed to his place. Mr Johnson now broaches his plan of establishing a Sunday school and making the Shepherd the master of it—'with your good Minister's leave and kind assistance', Mrs More adds quickly, having already in 1794 run into some little difficulty in setting up Evangelical religious institutions in High Church parishes. For honest Mary the Shepherd's wife Mr Johnson will endow a small weekly school of which she shall be the mistress, 'and employ her notable turn to good account, by teaching ten or a dozen girls to knit, sew, spin, card, or any other useful way of getting their bread'. The Shepherd is to move at once into the clerk's house, Mr Johnson paying the difference in rent, and Mr Jenkins is sure that his wife's father, who has already sent two blankets to honest Mary, will help a little toward buying some of the clerk's old goods.

Mrs More sees her difficulty here at once and is adroit in disguising it, but there is some awkwardness just the same. 'I am not going to make you rich but useful', Mr Johnson says. '"Not rich, Sir?" cried the Shepherd; "how can I ever be thankful enough for such blessings?" ...Here he and Mary looked at each other and burst into tears. The gentlemen saw their distress, and kindly walked out upon the little green before the door, that these honest people might give vent to their feelings.' '"If I were a king,"' Mr Johnson tells the Shepherd, '"and had it in my power to make you a rich and a great man, with a word speaking, I would not do it." "...I have...never attempted or desired to set any poor man much above his natural condition...".' But there is no getting away from the evident facts that the Shepherd did not really like his desperate, degrading and debasing indigence but on the contrary is overcome with gratitude to those who release him from it, and furthermore that no one, including Mrs Hannah More, thought he should like it.[1]

There is a fine statement of her actual thinking in a later tale called *The Delegate* (1817). This tract is not so rich as *The Shepherd of Salisbury Plain*, but it shows nevertheless, if not in art in doctrine, that a quarter-

[1] *Stories 1818*, vol. II, pp. 60–6.

century later Scanderbeg's sword still had Scanderbeg's arm. James Dawson is a Spitalfields weaver. He as well as his worthy wife has been industrious, prudent and saving, 'cutting off all unnecessary indulgences, and governing his whole behaviour in small things as well as great ones by an habitual religious principle'. But the race is not always to the swift, Mrs More points out, and 'so is not bread always to the man of understanding. In the common course of events, Providence usually blesses honest industry with success [of course Mrs More means success suitable to one's 'natural condition']; but the whole history of the world proves that outward prosperity is no certain mark of God's favour. Indeed, were this universally the case, we should want one of the strongest arguments for a future state.' (That contention, not originated by Mrs More, was gravely advanced by much more intellectual people, but in employing it Mrs More has no equal.) Dawson and his wife are severely ill, and then become partakers 'in the general distress with which it has pleased Divine Providence to visit this country during this last year'. In the course of the winter they burn all their furniture. His wife burst into tears—

and said, 'Oh, James, our creditable bed, which I had so much pleasure in buying with the money I saved in service, that I might have something to bring into the common little stock, that I fear must go next.' He took her by the hand, saying, 'I hope not, Sarah; but even if that should be our sad case, we shall be no worse off than our blessed Master was, who had not where to lay his head.... As we are not just now, through the decline of trade, allowed to labour for the meat that perisheth, let us labour more assiduously for that which endureth to eternal life.'

'Our clock', said Mrs Dawson, 'is already gone', and she wept as she spoke. 'True, my dear Sarah,' replied her husband; 'but if we are deprived of the pleasure of counting time, we are not debarred from the advantage of meditating on eternity, in which time will be soon swallowed up.'

James Dawson suddenly reflects that one of the worst effects of sorrow and sickness is that they are apt to make one selfish; he has not visited their equally impoverished neighbour, Mrs Brown, a 'widow gentlewoman, who had seen better days', since breakfast. Mrs Brown and the Dawsons, neither able to afford a fire, 'though it was now the coldest season of the year', help one another by having one 'alternately in each other's rooms', 'Mrs Dawson kindly undertaking the little cookery for them all. This worthy couple treated this afflicted woman with a delicacy which religion only could have taught them; for in her present destitute situation, they never forgot that she had been their superior.'

Having done what they could for Mrs Brown, the Dawsons return to their own room and sit down cheerfully to their 'scanty dinner' of potatoes and water. As Dawson is saying grace they are interrupted by the entrance of a couple of smart-looking dashing young men who are radical Reformers, one indeed a delegate. They had overheard the grace, 'and when they beheld the banquet over which it had been pronounced, they burst out into a brutal laugh'. Mr Dawson is proof against their democracy and atheism. 'You will soon sing another note', said the delegate. 'Your potatoes cannot last forever.' '"Sir," replied Dawson, "they are already exhausted. You see there the end of our stock."' Their visitors retire, baffled. '"You have one comfort, however," said the stranger, "though your food fails, your beverage is likely to hold out. If the rain continues as it has done the last ten months you won't want drink."'

Another knocking is soon heard, and in come Dawson's excellent minister and a benevolent gentleman who has been relieving the distresses of the Spitalfields weavers. Dawson has heard that people have talked of raising a subscription. '"*Talked*," said the gentleman, "why it is *done*: we have gone from house to house among the rich to raise money, and among the poor to distribute it. . . . We attribute the general patience and subordination of our people to the religious instruction which so many of them attend."' They depart leaving only 'a small present relief', but in a quarter of an hour arrives a lad with a large covered dish, 'and, before they had time to ask any questions, he stepped to the door and brought in a pot of porter; then uncovered the dish, which contained a large smoking beef-steak. All this, which seemed to come by magic, really came from the cook's shop next door, sent by the two gentlemen. Speechless, they carried all into Mrs Brown's chamber. Reader! if a heart of flesh makes a part of thy anatomy; if impiety and jacobinism have not turned that heart to stone, thou wouldst have had its best feelings excited, hadst thou beheld this plentiful supper, cheerfully devoured by this little grateful party.'[1]

In other stories too of Mrs More's there are characters living in

[1] *Works* (1830), vol. III, pp. 79–95.

abject destitution and squalor who seem to escape when the chance comes, virtuous and happy as they are, without a moment's regret and to no one's surprise. Carus Wilson and in general his contemporaries would not have forgotten that no usefulness can be accomplished by having good Evangelical workmen gladly give up their potatoes and water for indulgence and shameful indulgence.

It is a really sobering circumstance that the later Evangelicals believed Mrs More's writings for the humble fell short of being of a 'decidedly religious character'. The Religious Tract Society 'while they rejoiced in the wide diffusion of Mrs More's tracts, regretted that they did not contain a fuller statement of the great evangelical principles of Christian truth', and in reissuing them actually corrected their doctrinal laxness. That such people were blind to the consummately calculated usefulness of her writings is in itself a sharp commentary on the later period. An unexpected observer, the mathematician Augustus De Morgan, who investigated some of this editing thought the Society's conductors were hardly honest, either in their rewriting Mrs More without notice to their readers or in their secretary's defence, that they had not announced their reprints as exact reprints.[1]

The official biographies of Hannah More and Wilberforce are outstanding examples of 'highmindedness' in themselves. Even with their manifold deceptions they are two of the indispensable Evangelical documents of the post-Wilberforce generation. In neither was it only a matter of suppressing in a concealed way vital facts that seemed objectionable to the writers. More honest in that phase of their art than the Wilberforces, William Roberts tells us openly that in printing Mrs More's letters and journals he 'constantly suppressed' her 'severe animadversions' and her thought that 'often broke out in the language of becoming indignation against the manners of those who were raising altars to her genius'. That burnt offering to the Evangelical conception of best interests included also 'many of the reflections and animadversions of a sternly virtuous complexion, but which fell with great weight upon passing events and existing characters'.[2] But Roberts did not tell his readers that he went much beyond such editing. 'She calls Sir

[1] Augustus De Morgan, *A Budget of Paradoxes* (Open Court Edition, Chicago, 1915), vol. I, pp. 192–5.
[2] *More*, vol. II, pp. 5, 6.

Thomas Acland in one of her notes to me "the recreant knight of Devonshire",' Marianne Thornton says, 'which Roberts thinking uncivil I suppose, has altered into "the excellent and amiable Sir T. Acland"—two words that playful woman never used in her life. Somewhere else she began to me "When I think of you I am gladerer and gladerer and gladerer", which he, thinking bad English has done into "I am very glad".' Miss Thornton closed that sharp paragraph with a little-Evangelical but splendid judgment: 'Now if such an oaf as that will write a book at least he should be honest.'[1]

But men who act by the Evangelical principle of highmindedness believe unquestioningly that in such dissimulation (for instance), which is permitted to converted persons because of their superior spiritual merits, they are being honest. 'Regard for truth' forced William Roberts to say that passages in Mrs More's plays were objectionable and that possibly her hatred of everything French might have been excessive (though he did not point out that Mrs More had never been in France). But when he refers to her 'pious frauds', by which in this instance he means the seductive, otherwise 'vulgar', style in which she decked out her exhortations, and tells us 'she was a woman of business in all the concerns of humanity...and had a sort of righteous cunning in dealing with different cases',[2] he wholly approves. It was honest in Mrs More. In the Rector of Blagdon it would not have been.

Marianne Thornton's Recollections indicate that the Wilberforces used this Evangelical method too. Her wish that she and her correspondent Patty Smith 'were rich enough to buy up his father's life and burn it, out of love for the great old Man', she writes, after mentioning that 'dull Robert' had been at her home, came from the belief that 'you might as well put a mole to talk about an eagle' as to think 'such a creature as that can appreciate or describe that winged being and all his airy flight'. Robert Isaac however is not to be blamed for his 'measured calculating un-Wilberforce[d] like tone', as 'nature has made him a thorough Spooner from Birmingham'. In fact the only way to do justice to those qualities of Wilberforce would be through his letters, and they 'were like his talk with one foot on the step of the

[1] E. M. Forster, *Marianne Thornton*, p. 148. Acland voted wrong on Catholic Emancipation.
[2] *More*, vol. IV, pp. 313–14.

carriage and one off, desultory thoughtless, loving, and often nearly unintelligible. It is a sad loss that he never, or rarely at least, gave his mind to a letter, for I know not how else he is to be described...so I am afraid when I read his life I shall want to burn it.'[1]

Probably Wilberforce's formal letters were not all desultory thoughtless. But in *The Life of Wilberforce* every letter is coherent, composed literary and formally correct barring a few obvious slips. As even in transcripts of manuscript passages reproduced in facsimile in their own book Robert Isaac and Samuel deviate from their text, apparently just to improve Wilberforce's words, it seems indicated that their rewriting may have been constant and considerable. Taken with their overall plan and the Roberts principle, this even adds up to the possibility that in the two important Evangelical documents we are not certain we are reading the words of Hannah More or Wilberforce at any point where untrained, inexperienced editors far below them in spiritual merit, intellect, judgment and taste thought their expressions should be improved. In the process of removing from the records of Hannah More without specific notice to his readers every trace of severity, indignation, sternness and strength of feeling, no doubt also every expression that seemed to him maliciously witty, every outspoken thought that was impolite, every sharp criticism except those directed against manifestly evil people, William Roberts turned a lively, emotional, imaginative and very articulate woman into something that suited his own respectable mediocrity, even going so far as to correct harmless expressions of the most esteemed serious writer of the age. The Wilberforces almost certainly did something of the kind to their father.

In explaining the 'estrangement' of Robert Isaac and Samuel, Marianne Thornton offers a comment on their bringing up and home influences. 'I have often wondered what could be the fault in their education which has occasioned them to miss the positions that such children of such a father ought to have held. He loved them so much and was so anxious for their real welfare, and much as he was occupied with public business he really never neglected them. They were proud of belonging to him, but on that account rated themselves too highly, thinking everyone should be at their disposal because their names were Wilberforce. This idea they got from their mother as well as many

[1] E. M. Forster, *op. cit.* pp. 147–8.

penurious ways which I fancy came from the Spooners being of Jewish extraction.'[1] It seems unlikely that dull Robert's being a Spooner from Birmingham explains the nature of the *Life of Wilberforce*. Marianne Thornton did not like Barbara Ann Spooner Wilberforce. Neither did anyone else, apparently, except perhaps Wilberforce. But other Birmingham people seemed to be good Evangelicals, and it was not disqualifying to be of merchant and banker stock, as Wilberforce himself and all the Thorntons show us. There is no apparent reason for thinking of Robert Isaac's measured, calculating and un-Wilberforce-like qualities as Jewish rather than, for instance, Evangelical. Carus Wilson was measured, calculating and assuredly un-Wilberforce-like and in his veins ran the blood of the Percys. It is not certain, furthermore, that dull Robert was as dull as Marianne Thornton thought he was, or that in tacitly ascribing the whole composition of the biography to him she did not underestimate the share of his younger brother.

Several contemporaries and later writers who discuss the Wilberforces make independently a rather odd statement that (in effect) no matter how they conducted themselves in later life they always acted on principles they had learned in their youth. From a reading of Wilberforce's letters to Samuel, Canon Ashwell says, 'It will at once be seen that Samuel Wilberforce was indeed his father's son'.[2] 'Whatever his faults, [Samuel] was true to the teachings of the Clapham Sect', Telford says in a work called *A Sect that Moved the World*, which also asserts that how well the Clapham group 'laid the foundations is shown by the lives of their children'.[3] It is not absolutely clear what those statements were intended by their authors to mean, but they seem in a regrettable unintended way to be right. Wilberforce was deeply concerned to train his children to be faithful and devout servants of God. There must be few known instances of a public figure whose life was so crowded who gave so much of his time, with the greatest love, to bringing up his children in righteousness. Six hundred letters were preserved that he wrote to Samuel during his school and university days. But somehow, and it is hard to credit this wholly to Barbara

[1] Forster, *op. cit.* p. 146. This passage must have been written close to the time of publication of the *Life*, certainly before Samuel was made Bishop of Oxford.

[2] Canon Ashwell and Reginald Wilberforce, *The Life of Bishop Wilberforce*, vol. I, p. 3. [3] John Telford, *A Sect that Moved the World*, pp. 187, 198.

Ann Spooner of Birmingham, Marianne Thornton's assumption of a fault in their education seems to be warranted. The future Bishop of Oxford and Winchester should have learned many things in his home beyond the supple expediency and facile opportunism that even the sober *Dictionary of National Biography* says earned for him the name Soapy Sam. The Society for the Suppression of Vice was one of Wilberforce's two failures.

'What a strange fatality has attended the eldest sons of the Clapham Sect! Henry [Sykes Thornton] and Tom Babington expatriated and W. W.[ilberforce] excluded from respectable society. I am sure in this world some such stunning events are needed to remind us that this is not our true home.'[1] There were other, quieter, fatalities beyond those Marianne Thornton named. In giving preferment in his dioceses it was noticed that Bishop Wilberforce 'showed a decided preference for men of good family, good figure, and good social qualities'. 'Whatever speculative faith the "Evangelicals" of that period had in their theory of salvation', Canon Mozley observed, 'their highest success generally was to make their sons clever men of the world.'[2] Perhaps the deep-lying fault of the Evangelical educational system was what was wrong with Evangelicalism itself.

There is some pathos in the departure from the Protestant Reformation ranks of so many of the sons of the leaders—in the prominent Evangelical families or among those sons and daughters of the Evangelicals who were to write their names in England's records, almost all. They were brought up with Christian love and confidence that they would take their place in the front line. Tom Macaulay's first task was to be the indexing of the *Christian Observer*. 'Macaulay described to [Robert Isaac and Samuel Wilberforce] his father's extreme disappointment when he declined the important service for which he had been destined and educated, the long desired Index of the 'Missionary Register', or whatever the name of the father's periodical.'[3] It was hardly the service for which Thomas Babington Macaulay had been either destined or educated, but Zachary had so counted on his doing it that the run of the *Observer* has no Volume 21, which had been reserved. The Mores especially were fond of Tom Macaulay from his early years,

[1] Forster, *op. cit.* p. 213.
[2] Mozley, *Reminiscences*, vol. I, pp. 350, 107.   [3] *Ibid.* p. 107.

and he 'always felt kindly toward Mrs More' even when he could not accept her religious and other views. Thomas De Quincey too was a favourite of the Mores. They had his picture 'hung over the drawing-room chimney-piece', and Miss Sally More believed he 'could be a bishop if he wanted to'.[1] In their university days, or before, or after, the children of the Clapham inner circle and the Evangelical directorate elsewhere, and the children of the lesser known or unknown Evangelical families who were also to become eminent Victorians, depart steadily, for High Church, Roman Catholic Church, or no church: Macaulay and De Quincey, the sons of Babington and Gisborne and Stephen, the four sons of Wilberforce, the three daughters of Patrick Brontë, Marian Evans who called herself George Eliot, John Henry Newman; the son or sons of Charles Grant, Lord Teignmouth, Buxton, saintly Lady Emily Pusey, Benjamin Harrison, Sir James Graham, John Gladstone, Sir Robert Peel and William Manning. Charlotte Elliott remained an Evangelical, and Marianne Thornton in her un-orthodox way. Sir Thomas Baring's son remained an Evangelical and became Bishop of Durham. Of great wealth, excessively severe with High Church clergymen of his see who did not hold with Evangelical views, Bishop Baring can stand as a symbol of this transformation of the Evangelical Party in one aspect into its complete opposite. It was opposed to episcopal tyranny in the early days.

The evidence on all sides, from a variety of witnesses, seems strong that as the Age of Elegance, in so many ways vicious, barbarous and unchristian, is dying, thanks to William Wilberforce and his associates more than to any other citizens of this present world, and is gradually succeeded by the Bleak Age, the Evangelical Party is slowly reconsti-tuted by a different kind of Evangelical. There is continued progress of Protestant Reformation religion in the upper ranks for a time, and felicitous individual examples to the contrary; but it is hard to doubt that from the 1820's on there swarm into the Party increasing and eventually dominating numbers of a kind of Evangelical that Wilber-force for one did not like. As means come more and more to be taken for ends, leaders become less important, followers more; genuine beliefs harden into doctrinaire convictions and once heartfelt truths become shibboleths. Great moral societies grow into huge moral bureaux,

[1] *De Quincey Memorials*, vol. II, p. 78.

good parish priests become platform preachers, organizers and religious executives in 'the bustle of the religious world', and as the need of a classical training in the Evangelical priest vanishes, those aspects of breeding, education and good manners that were important to Wilberforce, Hannah More, Sir Thomas Baring, Lady Middleton, Bishops Barrington and Porteus, Lady Southampton and Lady Harcourt are not important at all.

It was only twelve years after Wilberforce's death, in 1845, that Sir James Stephen, the son of Wilberforce's brother-in-law, exclaimed, writing to his wife who was as much as himself born and bred in the direct centre of the Evangelical inner circle, 'Oh where are the people who are at once really religious, and really cultivated in heart and understanding—the people with whom we could associate as our fathers used to associate with one another. No "Clapham Sect" nowadays!'[1] If there was no Clapham Sect nowadays, people of taste and culture and intellectual interest whom the son of James Stephen and his wife Jane Catherine granddaughter of Henry Venn could enjoyably live with, who was there? There was still an Evangelical Party and a large one. What was it if it was not a Clapham Sect? In Marianne Thornton's Recollections again, there is a sudden brief flash of illumination. 'Mrs Wilberforce was a religious woman but lived much with a lower set of people 'professors' as they would have called themselves—who had a great deal of pious phraseology, and some of them not a very high standard of morality. I think that these sort of people unjustly disgusted her sons with "evangelicals" and made them turn to a more gentlemanly school in the Tractarians at Oxford who were just rising into notice when the three younger Wilberforces went there.'[2]

Who were that crew of Evangelical professors whom Mrs Wilberforce lived much with? Where did they come from? How did they get into the home of a man who, in Marianne Thornton's opinion particularly, differed so much from them? Did more and perhaps many more of the Evangelicals live much with 'these sort of people'? Or were they coming to be a significant element in the Evangelical Party? Miss Thornton may have been right in believing that these characters of a lower sort with pious phraseology and some of them not a very

[1] *Letters of the Rt. Hon. Sir James Stephen* (London, 1906), p. 87.
[2] Forster, *op. cit.* p. 146.

high standard of morality 'disgusted' the young Wilberforces. Was it 'unjustly'? Able young men and women over England who had been brought up in the best Evangelicalism were repelled during these years by something. Mrs Wilberforce's particular lower set of 'professors' could hardly at the same time have lived much with the Brontës in the Yorkshire moors, the many young Evangelicals at Cambridge and Thomas De Quincey down in Mrs More's country. But they would have had something to do with Wilberforce's attitude. It was just 'these sort of people' he did not like.

In 1818 a belated 'Gothic' tale appeared in London, not much read nowadays but often referred to by its title, the work of a girl who was the daughter of two of the great counter-Evangelicals of the age and wife of another. Mary Wollstonecraft Godwin Shelley's *Frankenstein; or, The Modern Prometheus* is the story of a young man who triumphantly creates a giant being, to find he has brought into existence a situation of monstrous danger that he has no control over. To take Wilberforce as a Frankenstein would be fanciful. But it would not be outrageously fanciful if England's danger was that the Age of Wilberforce might become the Age of Carus Wilson, the Evangelical accommodation live on to become the Victorian compromise.

IV

General Oglethorpe, whom Mrs More had been delighted to meet in her fashionable London days, as one of three living people who had been mentioned by Pope, had shot snipe in Conduit Street, but he had seen no such changes in England as Mrs More had seen by some years before her death. Above all, the important change. 'It is a singular satisfaction to me that I have lived to see such an increase of genuine religion among the higher classes of society.'

The lax, callous old century was on its last legs by the time of William IV and Adelaide. Earth had not been made heaven, as Mrs More wisely pointed out it was not designed by Providence to be. There was still sin, vice and profligacy. People still played cards and on Sunday too, and the Sabbath was violated in other ways. There were assemblies, poor people drank too much gin, the name of God was taken in vain and women adorned themselves with paints and jewels. There was still blasphemous literature and cruelty to animals. The Society for the Suppression of Vice had not really succeeded in doing very much. It was one of Wilberforce's two failures. But in so many walks of life and in so many areas of human conduct, what signs of improving morals and manners, more earnestness, greater spirituality! Manners that were objected to in 1785 only by the strictest moralists were impossible by 1830 in any society of even moderate respectability. The rips, rakes, bucks, fops, bloods, Corinthians and gaming hells were dying fast, the Mrs Billingtons, Lady Jerseys and Lady Conynghams were not paraded and celebrated. If the current Lord Sandwich appeared in Cambridge he did not openly bring his mistress along with him, illicit affairs of the great were not the subject of public knowledge and ribald amusement, and if there were still Harriette Wilsons they did not publish their memoirs. The fox-hunting three-bottle absentee parsons were mostly gone and their starving curates who galloped from pulpit to pulpit, and with them the merely Whig or Tory bishops, cunning intriguers like Tomline, and many, perhaps most, of the mere secular-trade clergy. There was no more vulgar or obscene clerical poetry in magazines, the last lottery had been held, bear-baiting and bull-baiting were almost things of the past, and Faro's Daughters, the barbarity of public executions and the frank use of the English speech and matter-of-fact references to the biological and physiological parts and functions.

The Victorian Age escaped a heritage it could easily have had. If Wilberforce (or some equally perfect leader) had not been chosen to reform his country and if the Methodists had remained in their status of 1800 (and there is no sign that they became a powerful reforming force), there could have been more sporting duchesses, more objectionable royal mistresses and continued lurid scenes at the Brighton Pavilion. The obscene prints and objects could have gone on openly displayed in the shop fronts and sold in young ladies' schools, and the *Town and Country Magazine* could have continued its open lubricities. The ladies of the opera could have gone on appearing in their gauze-covered nudity and the ladies of fashion in their shameless aping of the ladies of the French Revolution, and the ladies of the town could have continued their operations, so eloquently described for us, in the front boxes and the theatre bars.

When the veteran Evangelicals looked about them at the social scene in the early 1830's even, how could they have failed to think with exultation that the moral labours they had taken part in had had (humanly speaking) some considerable effect? In many respects what had happened in England coincided very closely with the aims of the great campaign—in some respects so closely that if the Evangelicals had been able to reconstitute the moral status of the country with a word speaking they could hardly have done more. They were opposed to the theatre and the prize ring, and England waited long years for the successors to Goldsmith and Sheridan, Belcher and John Jackson. They were opposed to music, and music was represented between 1830 and 1880, we are told, by the surely modest names of John Field and William Sterndale Bennett.[1] They were opposed to plain and blunt language in works of literature, and we have the reticences and pruderies of Dickens with his sexless heroes and next-to-personless heroines. In his portrait of Becky Sharp as one making her living by her 'wits' Thackeray achieved a discreetness that William Roberts could hardly have wanted to improve on, while complaining that not since *Tom Jones* had an English writer dared to picture a real man, and we have that other Victorian fiction and poetry in which sometimes can be made out under the thick shell of obligatory prudence the smouldering fires of passion and indiscretion.

Above all, at the court in the 1830's the most scrupulous decorum prevailed, and there could not have been a greater change. The queen, though an alien, could have been formed by Hannah More, including her hatred of the Reform Bill. In the days of George IV it was impossible for the ladies of the court to be *décolleté* enough, under Queen Adelaide they could not be *décolleté* at all. No clergymen were invited to Adelaide's state balls or dancing soirées and when Mrs Blomfield appeared at her first drawing-room in 'a train of rich immortal velvet' the queen was kept from a severe rebuke only by the thought that Mrs Blomfield's husband the Bishop of London was a successor of the apostles.[2] The mistress of the robes was the leading Evangelical of exalted rank, the Duchess of Gordon, the 'religious duchess' whose predecessor in the title had been the 'sporting duchess', a trend seen also

---

[1] *Early Victorian England*, Oxford University Press, London, 1934, vol. II, p. 251.
[2] Dr Doran, *Lives of the Queens of England of the House of Hanover*, vol. II, pp. 433–4.

in the religious eminence of Lords Grosvenor and Cholmondeley whose predecessors had been celebrated figures in actions for criminal connection. There could have been successions in kind to Lord Sandwich and the Barrymores and the Marquises of Hertford. It is true that at the court swarmed the nine illegitimate children of the king and Mrs Jordan, the Fitzclarences, whom *Figaro* referred to off and on as 'the degenerate bastards making a dead set at the Exchequer'. But at least Mrs Jordan had died in neglect at St Cloud, and it was known to everybody that her relationship with the Duke of Clarence had been as close to a marriage as could be between a royal prince and a commoner. And the Evangelicals handsomely repaid the Marchioness of Conyngham for her gift of the princely see of Winchester to Charles Richard Sumner, by conferring on her a distinguished status (even if perhaps it could not be guaranteed as a permanency). 'It is curious', remarks the editor of Greville's *Journal* of the visit to England of Madame du Cayla ('the best thing about her seemed to be the magnificent pearls she wore,' Greville wrote, 'though these are not so fine as Lady Conyngham's') 'that in 1829 the last mistress of a King of France should have visited England under the reign of the last mistress of a King of England.'[1]

No one walking the streets of London would have noticed any change, or at least any change for the better. If the success of Evangelicalism had no other index the reformers would have been heart-sick indeed. In 1823 the Reverend Haldane Stewart surveyed the metropolis with dread. Infamous houses abounded, young men were exposed in broad daylight to the allurements of the harlot, the prisons were filled with offenders, many of them boys. There were prize-fights and there was 'low gambling' (even in such a passage, from an Evangelical clergyman of standing, a well-known and devoted servant of the Church Missionary Society, there is apparently the Evangelical distinction between low gambling and high gambling). In the neighbourhood of London the fairs exhibited 'scenes of wickedness that cannot be thought of without horror'. The Sabbath was continually violated and corrupted, 'more polluted than any other day', with newspapers, travel, amusement and riotous debauchery lasting from the Saturday night. Although in no age had there been 'such extensive exertions to

[1] Greville, *A Journal of the Reigns of King George IV and King William IV*, vol. 1, p. 215.

spread true Christianity throughout the earth', in no late age had there been 'a more open avowal of the principles of infidelity'.[1] 'We are really at a loss where to begin upon a subject so full of horrors as the present state of London', the *Christian Review and Clerical Magazine* said in January 1828. There were over 6000 public houses, 'besides wine-vaults, coffee houses, and oyster saloons', and it was a compounding of the horror, five years after Haldane Stewart, that the Sabbath was still 'more polluted than any other day', with drunkenness, gambling, prize-fighting, prostitution, filthy obscenity, ribald profaneness, and ruffian violence.[2] As late as Victoria's accession in 1837 the *Christian Penny Magazine* pointed out that the 1830's had seen an increase of crime, Roman Catholicism and gin-drinking. In 1815 there were said to be fifty thousand prostitutes in London, or forty thousand, or thirty thousand. The estimated figure in 1835 was eighty thousand,[3] and it was believed that by the middle of the century all the prostitution societies combined, from the earliest down through the Maritime Female Penitent Refuge, for Poor, Degraded Females, the London Society for the Protection of Young Females, the London Preventive and Reformatory Institution and many others, might have helped perhaps fourteen or fifteen thousand women.[4] There seemed to be something wrong with the Evangelical method.

But the moral condition of England was not to be measured by the streets of London. Over the length and breadth of the land (and far beyond) those thousands upon thousands of moral and religious auxiliaries, and associations, and penny societies, and branches of all descriptions, those multitudes of the respectable and substantial, noble and influential, *those who count*, publicly manifesting by word and example their dedication to good morality, righteous living and vital (Protestant Reformation) religion! The first-fruits of Achaia, the noble patrons and patronesses, presidents and lady presidents, vice-patrons, vice-presidents, governors and treasurers and those respectable and devout members of ten thousand committees! The tract distributors

[1] James Haldane Stewart, *The State of the Metropolis* (London, 1823).

[2] *The Christian Review and Clerical Magazine*, January 1828, pp. 1–28.

[3] *The Refuge* (London, 1835), p. 173. This was the publication of the Maritime Female Penitent Refuge, for Poor, Degraded Females.

[4] J. Beard Talbot, *The Miseries of Prostitution* (1844), pp. 68 ff.

and tract writers, agents and Scripture colporteurs, pamphleteers, editors of those huge society reports and periodical records, collectors, informers, purchasers of obscene articles, ladies indefatigably 'at work' for the Bible Society and the Church Missionary Society, the missionaries to England and those ardent supporters who met them everywhere and got them into pulpits in the face of the hostile bishops, and all the labourers for the hundreds upon hundreds of branches of many societies in every county, for the suppression of vice, for the female penitentiaries, the provincial Magdalen Hospitals and Refuges for the Destitute, the Dorcas societies, for the London Jew Society, for temperance, for total abstinence, for 'educating' the poor and the Irish and the Africans and the Newfoundlanders, for the local Strangers' Friend societies, for that great society *of an aggressive nature* that visited poor people district by district *from house to house and from room to room*— by the time of Wilberforce's death so numerous and so widespread that it is easy to see all England as a dichotomy of exhorters and exhorted. By Evangelical devotion and incomparable leadership those plans of national reform that Hannah More had heard Wilberforce and Lady Middleton talking over had grown into a giant movement for the land's regeneration.

If in such a movement in the course of forty years what were once implementing devices had engrossed all interest and the pressing necessity that created the final objective they once served had disappeared, it would be simple for the first leaders to fade from view with the first objects. As Wilberforce's kind of Evangelicalism was transformed, the Evangelical Party had soon forgotten what it was like thirty years earlier and how it came into being ten years before that. By the 1840's it seemed to some perhaps that the truly religious in large numbers had formed themselves spontaneously into huge organizations for enforcing virtue and piety, and others were content with a simpler explanation that is always right. On 31 October 1848, in St Ann's Blackfriars, Edward Bickersteth, preaching the Church Missionary Society's Jubilee Anniversary sermon, described their rise to power. 'But God raised up the men, both at home and abroad, and fitted them for His own work. Its first preacher, the venerable commentator, Thomas Scott; its most efficient secretary for twenty-two years, my beloved and departed friend, Josiah Pratt...; the departed

Venn, who modelled the rules under which we have acted; these, with others dear to us all, and our lay brethren, Grant, Wilberforce, and Admiral Gambier, laid the foundations.'[1] In that hardly surpassable example of the art of blindness the coupling of the last two names in particular was a matchless triumph. It was only fifteen years after Wilberforce's death that those words were spoken, so close to the pulpit where Thomas Scott in the year 1801 described with such wisdom and insight the effects that a successful Church Missionary Society could have beyond its 'more immediate objects'. In the same years Sir George Stephen was pointing out that Wilberforce really had little to do with the actual passing of the Emancipation Act of 1833 and Sir James Stephen was pointing out that the Bible Society had failed to convert the world. Barely more than a decade after the commander's death the more immediate objects have always been the only objects.

When that has happened, it is reasonable to believe it was all the work of the clergy, and as there had been no other outstanding leaders in England, in the way of Protestant Reformation Christianity, the Methodist leaders become, humanly speaking, the founders. 'God then gave a glorious revival', Bickersteth wrote, in 1846, 'in the time of the Wesleys and Whitfield'.[2] If the Stephens and Bickersteth had begun their Evangelical career twenty years earlier they would have known better. Thomas Scott and John Newton knew better, and Richard and Rowland Hill and many another. Until the 1840's there is no statement by any Evangelical about the quickening of the religious spirit of their period that does not describe it as beginning round the time of Wesley's death, 'a marked and great increase of religion within the last forty years'.[3] Probably it is only on the assumption that the glorious revival

---

[1] Birks, *Memoir of Bickersteth*, vol. II, p. 400.

[2] *Ibid.* p. 347.

[3] 'The revival of religion in the present day' (Grimshawe (1828) in *Memoirs of Legh Richmond*, p. 2); 'It is no small praise to the age in which we live, that religion begins at length to assume the pre-eminence which its high claims and heaven-born character demand' (*ibid.* (1828)); 'the great revival of true religion which took place in this country about the close of the last century...' (William Goode jun. (1828), in *A Memoir of the late William Goode*, p. 47); 'the sun and the moon are scarcely more different from each other than Cambridge is from what it was when I was first Minister of Trinity Church; and the same change has taken place through almost the whole

was the work of the clergy that Bickersteth could have thought of himself as a follower of Wesley and Whitefield. Somehow the Church Missionary Society came into being, and somehow Scott, Newton, Pratt, Venn (and Edward Bickersteth) got where they were through natural or divine processes. The young Wilberforces' biography probably helped. It may even have been more widely known in the 1840's than is now apparent that Wilberforce was to be counted with those who were fat bulls of Bashan and cumberers of holy ground only a few years earlier when he gave form, life and power to the Evangelical Reformation.

It has helped too since that these events were only described by ecclesiastics. One example is enough. In 1886 a long-standard work on 'The Evangelical Revival'[1] was published by Canon Overton, a well-known and, judging from the tone and spirit of the book, kindly and honest church historian. All the Evangelical laity, it tells us—to take only a few of many similar statements—were 'in strict subordination to the clergy'; 'there is hardly a single layman who can be said to have attained the position of a leader of the first rank in the Revival'; 'the great instrument in the Revival was preaching'; 'the laity were debarred from using, nor do they seem to have desired to use, the main instrument by which the effects were produced'; 'none of [the Evangelical clergy] were by any means disposed to submit to lay dictation'; 'Romaine, Venn and others declined to be dazzled even by the glamour of a Countess'; 'a very short chapter will suffice to sketch the leading laity who took a part in the Evangelical movement'; 'the work of *Foreign Missions* received an immense stimulus from the Evangelical Revival'; Brougham's statement that Wilberforce was 'the head, indeed the founder, of a powerful religious sect...of course, is absurd'. 'William Wilberforce gave in his adherence to it'; 'two noblemen will complete the list of those laymen who can by any stretch of the term be

land' (Charles Simeon (1824) in *Simeon*, p. 593); 'I am astonished at the sight of evangelical advancement which my eyes behold' (Thomas Robinson (*c.* 1811) in Vaughan, *The Rev. Thomas Robinson*, p. 280).

[1] *The Evangelical Revival in the Eighteenth Century*, by John Henry Overton, Canon of Lincoln and Rector of Epworth (1886). The inclusion of Wilberforce, Lord Teignmouth and others of their generation shows that Canon Overton was not concerned only with the eighteenth century.

called leaders of the Evangelical Revival' (here Lord Dartmouth and of all people Lord Teignmouth are added to John and Henry Thornton, Wilberforce and William Cowper...a total of six laymen of whom three were dead by 1801 and a fourth by 1815).

It is not possible to miss the Evangelical achievement more completely, Canon Overton's misunderstanding being made absolute by his belief that Evangelicals and Methodists were indistinguishable and fought side by side. The Party laity converted many of the clergymen, educated many of them, got nearly all of them into pulpits (except for which they could have done nothing), forced more than one of them to be tactful and politic Evangelicals, and worked with all their might to get them into strategic church positions. They were thought of with the greatest respect by the clergy and clearly dominated the Evangelical Party, and so interested observers remarked again and again. Canon Overton's statement comes closer to being true of Wesley's and Whitefield's Methodists and is obviously not true of Lady Huntingdon's Connexion, as Lady Huntingdon was not a clergyman. It is an astonishing error to hold that there was hardly a single layman who had the position of a leader of the first rank in the Evangelical Movement. If it had not been for the scores upon scores who have been named in the present work (with many who have not been named)— the peers and peeresses, merchants, industrialists, financiers, Members of Parliament, East India and other magnates—the Evangelical clergy would have done nothing of national proportions. There were four great instruments of Evangelical reform that were more important than the preaching: the proselytizing, the societies, the money and the written propaganda. All of them were 'used' by the laity far more than by the clergy. Even the preaching was done very powerfully, perhaps most powerfully, by Hannah More, Mrs Sherwood, Charlotte Elizabeth and their colleagues, and the most influential religious book of the age was written by William Wilberforce, a Member of Parliament. (If the belief advanced in the present book is right, there was still another instrument of reform that was the most useful of all, the Abolition campaign.) The Evangelical clergy (it is surely not offensive to say) were exceedingly happy to submit, in practical matters, to the lay dictation of such laymen, and not one of them but was happy indeed to be dazzled by any number of glamorous Evangelical countesses, not to mention marchionesses and duchesses. The importance of the work of foreign missions was not that it received an immense stimulus from the reform campaign (which is true), but that it gave an immense stimulus to it. Brougham's statement about Wilberforce was right. Before him there was no Evangelicalism. That he was its St Paul was not questioned during his lifetime and is unquestionable. The simple thought that Brougham, a man of great ability, was there at the time might have led Canon Overton writing sixty years later to stop and ponder.

In 1808 Sydney Smith knew who the head of the Clapham Church was and who the prime movers of the Church Missionary Society were. In 1814 even Madame de Staël knew. 'Le même avocat de l'humanité, M. Wilberforce, est en Angleterre à la tête de l'établissement des missionnaires qui doivent porter les lumières du christianisme dans l'Asie et dans l'Afrique.'[1] But soon after Wilberforce's death he had become politically the liberator of Africa and religiously the parliamentary sponsor of the missionaries. He 'opened the door to the Gospel, through the East and the West Indies', Bickersteth approvingly sums up his work.[2] When the Church Missionary Society itself has forgotten what he had done, of all notion of this dedicated man's accomplishment *etiam periere*, the *Anti-Jacobin* might have said, *ruinae*.

If Wilberforce was the originator of the Bible Society and of the Church Missionary Society and with Margaret Gambier Lady Middleton thought of Abolition as a part of the reform of England, designed as much to free the English as the Africans, it would hardly be possible to doubt that no other man of his day, Wesley included, had so great an effect, for better and for worse, on the spiritual life of his country. He attempted a heroic civic task with unyielding courage and as great virtue as a man could have and successfully lead such a cause in such an age. Sir James Stephen was right about one thing, for the wrong reason. Wilberforce did reach a social and political eminence never before attained by any man who owed nothing to birth, to party or to the sword. He did it by leading his Evangelicals—and with them very many others—to do as much as could humanly be done of a task that was so heroic as to be impossible: to reform the manners and morals of a society while disturbing no element of its socially immoral structure.

---

[1] *Appel aux Souverains* (1814, in *Dix Années d'Exil*, à Londres, 1821), p. 276 (376).
[2] Birks, *Memoir of Bickersteth*, vol. II, p. 383.

It seems not to have been God's will that placing the Bible in every hand, leading the crusade to free the Negroes and forcing the admission of the missionaries into India should do away with crime, vice, infidelity and sin in England. But to bring a substantial part of those who count into playing prominent parts for virtue and religion would do much, and it would do much to bring together in that task thousands upon thousands of English men and women in every walk of life and in every part of the land who would otherwise not count. The 'historical mission' of the Evangelicals was to create a 'serious' respectable public and organize it into a coherent active group. So far as the life of their country is concerned, the vital function of the great Evangelical societies, lead-horses pulling the Evangelical cart, was simply to come into full existence. They could go on to 'more immediate purposes', if they wished, after they had done that. But when the archbishops and remaining recalcitrant prelates gave up their impossible opposition to the Church Missionary Society in 1841 they were less than Johnny-come-latelys. By the time they came in the work was all over.

There were extraordinary demonstrations of respect and reverence in many far-off places, tributes of gratitude such as had perhaps been given to no other Englishman, when Wilberforce died on 29 July 1833. It was a matter of course that he should be buried in Westminster Abbey, and never before, so far as anyone could say, had parliamentary business been suspended, an 'unequalled mark of public approbation', for members to attend the funeral of a man who had not held office. By his concern for the next world he had done much in this: declining all honours his country could give he was given the highest.

His sons emphasized the testimony of his achievements to the assurance 'Godliness has the promise of the life that is as well as of that which is to come'. 'If ever a man drew a prosperous lot in this life, he did so, who has been here described.' Strangely little described in the biography that ends with those words, the prosperity of Wilberforce's life was probably understood by few people who attended that ceremony in the Abbey on August 5. The only public statement of something like the truth seems to have been made in the *Christian Observer*, five years after his death. He achieved many things in Parliament, the writer says, and was 'the liberator of Africa'; but 'that which most impressed our minds, upon looking back at his life and times, is the extraordinary degree in which he was the instrument in the hands of God, of promoting that blessed revival and extension of religion in this and other lands, the effects of which will doubtless be felt to remote posterity'.[1]

In 1833 also, a few weeks after Wilberforce's death, the useful and honoured life of Hannah More came to an end. The great pioneer and veteran of the moral campaign was in her eighty-ninth year.

Toward the end of her life Mrs More was the victim of a doctrinaire act that she might have been spared. In 1827 she had lived alone at Barley Wood for eight years, so feeble in health that through that period she had been downstairs only once. She had known for some time that her old Evangelical servants were plundering her, but was willing to put up with it for the sake of living her last days in peace. The situation was not uncommon. She herself described in 1825 how Soame Jenyns had philosophically assigned £300 a year to cover such losses. Charles Simeon was 'robbed' by his coachman and Wilberforce's cousin Lord Carrington, examining the affairs of William Pitt, whose household consisted of himself, his niece, staff and guests, found that in one month Pitt had bought 3800 pounds of meat. But Evangelical friends, learning of the 'nightly festivities' in which after Mrs More had retired her old retainers (the coachman had been with her eighteen years, the 'ringleader' twenty-six) regaled themselves with game or turkey, the finest pastry and rum, brandy or gin,[2] pointed out to Mrs More that if she condoned such conduct she could be thought of as a 'patroness of vice' (Roberts). As all eight of her staff were involved it did not seem possible to replace 'the serious servants' with 'honest ones', and they forced the famous old woman to close up the home where her four sisters had died and she had lived alone since 1819, well looked after barring the peculation. So Mrs More, kept indoors by her physicians for years because she was badly susceptible to severe weather, was bundled out on a bitter April day, in a splendid act of pious pedantry, and forced to make a new home at the age of eighty-three.

She spent the remaining years of her life in Clifton (in a house of

[1] *Christian Observer*, June 1838, p. 404.
[2] *Correspondence of Sir William Weller Pepys*, vol. II, p. 223. They were considerate enough to withdraw to the coach-house when they had in a band of music.

Dr Sedgwick Whalley's), up to some months before her death still receiving the hordes of visitors who came steadily, as many as eighty whom she had never heard of in a week, to pay homage to the most revered spokesman for morality and religion in Christendom. There was no other private person then living to whom people came in such a way, from the Continent and America and all parts of the Empire, simply to pay their respects and express their Christian gratitude. They saw a frail old lady with sparkling black eyes, dressed in the rich costume of the eighteenth century, no High Church ornament but not meagre either, the wit and polish of her conversation not abated, who seemed to the later Evangelicals to relish the courtly language, savouring even of flattery, of an age that in the 1830's was unbelievably remote. Here Mrs More would show her visitors her playbills, mementoes of a mere nominal Christian youth, her collection of heathen idols sent by admirers from many heathen parts, and her works translated into forty languages she could not read. She died on September 7, 1833. Her will left most of a substantial fortune to some sixty Evangelical institutions not one of which had been in existence when she wrote the manifesto of the Evangelical Reformation, three years before the death of John Wesley.

It is a pity if an Evangelical biographer's conception of his art kept Hannah More, as seems possible, from being honoured by a remote posterity as one of the memorable English letter-writers. This could be prominent among the many losses we owe to the point of view from which William Roberts, with idolatrous veneration, reduced Mrs More to his level for our good to edification. For that he will have to answer at the day of judgment.

As we take a reluctant leave of Hannah More we might remember two items in the history of the author of *The Way To Plenty*. One is that she was fond of telling how calling on the Macaulays in Clapham Common she was met at the door by a pretty, fair-haired little boy who said to his aged visitor, 'My parents are not at home, but if you will come in, I will give you a glass of fine old spirits'. Thomas Babington future Lord Macaulay, aged three, had been reading *Robinson Crusoe*. The second is a valuable testimony that toward the end of her life, the purest austerity of her dogmatic Evangelicalism weakened, Mrs More sank into useless benevolence. In one of those dreadful winters shortly before she left Barley Wood a visitor found her weeping, not at the famine of the bread of eternity but at the helpless suffering and degradation of her poor neighbours in the face of the pitiful destitution that England in those days allowed so many of her inferior orders to be in. It seemed as if Mrs More had come to feel there was a bond, of some good natural kind, between her and the wives and children of the Mendip miners, as if they and Hannah More and William Wilberforce, the sick strangers and poor degraded females and persons imprisoned for small debts, the Evangelical duchesses and the black marble clergyman of Casterton Hall, perhaps even the idol shepherds walking in darkness, were all suffering and struggling human beings together. It is a duty rather than a right to hope—but it would have to be within some non-Evangelical scheme—that those tears atoned for *The Shepherd of Salisbury Plain.*

SELECT BIBLIOGRAPHY

Unless noted the place of publication is London.

I. CONTEMPORARY WORKS

ADAMS, ROBERT. *The Religious World Displayed.* 3 vols. Edinburgh, 1809.

(BERNARD, SIR THOMAS.) *Life of Sir Thomas Bernard, Baronet.* By the Rev. James Baker, his Nephew, 1819.

(BICKERSTETH, EDWARD.) *Memoir of the Rev. Edward Bickersteth, late Rector of Watton, Herts.* By the Rev. T. T. Birks [and his wife, Bickersteth's daughter]. 2 vols., 1851.

A Biographical Dictionary of the Living Authors of Great Britain and Ireland. 1816.

?BOWDLER, MRS HARRIET, ed. *The Family Shakespeare.* Printed by the Cruttwell Press, Bath, for Hatchard, Piccadilly. 1807.

BOWDLER, THOMAS [her brother, the Elder; 1754–1825], ed., *The Family Shakespeare.* 1818.

(——) *Memoir of Thomas Bowdler (the Elder).* By [his nephew] Thomas Bowdler [the Younger; 1780–1856]. [To remove from Shakespeare 'that which is indecent and offensive' 'was attempted some years since by one of Mr T. Bowdler's nearest relatives in respect of twenty of the best plays'.]

BRONTË, CHARLOTTE. *Jane Eyre.* 1847.

(——) *The Life of Charlotte Brontë.* By Elizabeth Gaskell. 1857.

(BUXTON, SIR THOMAS FOWELL, Bart.) *Memoirs of Sir Thomas Fowell Buxton, Bart.* Edited by his son, Charles Buxton. 2nd ed., 1849.

CECIL, RICHARD. *Remains of the Rev. Richard Cecil* [with a Memoir by his wife]. 1811. 13th ed., 1849.

(——) *Memoirs of Mrs Hawkes, late of Islington; including…extracts from sermons and letters of the late Rev. Richard Cecil.* By Catherine Cecil. 1837.

CHADWICK, EDWIN. *Report on the Sanitary Conditions of the Labouring Population of Great Britain.* 1842.

CHARLOTTE ELIZABETH [Browne Phelan Tonna]. *The Works of Charlotte Elizabeth.* 2 vols. New York, 1844 (7th American ed., 1849).

(——) *Personal Recollections.* Continued to the close of her life. 4th ed., 1854.

(——) *Memoir of Charlotte Elizabeth.* By Lewis Hippolytus Joseph Tonna. In *Works of Charlotte Elizabeth,* ed. 1849 (vol. 1).

Bibliography

(CLARKE, EDWARD DANIEL.) *The Life of Edward Daniel Clarke.* [By William Otter.] 2 vols., 1824.

COLLINS, WILKIE. *The Moonstone.* 1868.

(COLQUHOUN, PATRICK.) *A Treatise on the Police of the Metropolis.* By a Magistrate. 1796.

Correspondence, see Wilberforce, William, *Correspondence.*

COUPLAND, R. *Wilberforce. A narrative.* Oxford, 1923.

DICKENS, CHARLES. *Bleak House.* 1853.

Eclectic Notes; or, Notes of Discussions on Religious Topics at the Meetings of the Eclectic Society, London. During the years 1798–1814. Edited by John A. Pratt. 1856.

ELIOT, GEORGE. *Scenes of Clerical Life.* 1857.

(GAMBIER, ADMIRAL LORD.) *Memorials, Personal and Historical, of Admiral Lord Gambier.* By Georgiana, Lady Chatterton. 2 vols., 1861.

(GOODE, WILLIAM.) *A Memoir of the late William Goode.* By the Rev. William Goode, jun. 2nd ed., 1828.

GUNNING, HENRY. *Reminiscences of Cambridge.* 2 vols., 1854.

(HAWKES, MRS.) *Memoirs of Mrs Hawkes, late of Islington; including . . . extracts from sermons and letters of the late Rev. Richard Cecil.* By Catherine Cecil. 1837.

HAWKSTONE. *A Tale of and for England in 184– .* 1845.

HAZLITT, WILLIAM. *The Spirit of the Age.* 1825.

(HILL, SIR RICHARD, Bart.) *The Life of Sir Richard Hill, Bart.* By the Rev. Edwin Sidney, A.M. 1839.

(HILL, ROWLAND.) *The Life of the Rev. Rowland Hill.* By the Rev. Edwin Sidney, A.M. 1834.

Isaac Milner, see Milner, Isaac.

JONES, WILLIAM. *The Jubilee Memorial of the Religious Tract Society.* 1850.

Joseph Milner, see Milner, Joseph.

LE FANU, JOSEPH SHERIDAN. *Uncle Silas.* 1864.

(MILNER, JOSEPH.) *Works of the late Rev. Joseph Milner.* Edited (with Memoir) by Isaac Milner. 8 vols., 1810.

(MILNER, ISAAC.) *The Life of Isaac Milner.* By his Niece Mary Milner, author of 'The Christian Mother'. London and Cambridge, 1842.

More, see below, *Memoirs of . . . Mrs Hannah More.*

MORE, HANNAH. *Collected Works.* 11 vols., 1830.

—— *Stories for the Middle Ranks of Society, and Tales for the Common People.* 2 vols., 1818.

(——) *Memoirs of the Life and Correspondence of Mrs Hannah More.* By William Roberts, Esq. 4 vols., 1834.

Bibliography

(MORE, MARTHA.) *Mendip Annals: or, A Narrative of the Charitable Labours of Hannah and Martha More in their Neighbourhood. Being the journal of Martha More.* Edited, with additional matter, by Arthur Roberts. 1858.

NEWTON, JOHN. *The Works of the Rev. John Newton, late Rector of the United Parishes of St Mary Woolnoth and St Mary Woolchurch Haw, London.* From the last London edition. 6 vols., New York, 1810.

PALEY, WILLIAM. *The Works of William Paley, D.D.* 6 vols., 1830.

(PORTEUS, BEILBY.) *Life of the Right Rev. Beilby Porteus.* By Robert Hodgson. New York, 1811.

Private Papers, see Wilberforce, William, *Private Papers.*

Public Characters. Published by Richard Phillips, 1798 onwards.

RICHMOND, LEGH. *Annals of the Poor.* 1814. The chief of the five stories collected in this work, the most widely published religious book of the age, were:

The Negro Servant. The Christian Guardian, May, August, 1809.

The Dairyman's Daughter. Ibid., February, March, May, August, 1810; March, 1811.

Jane, the Young Cottager. Ibid., September, December, 1811; April, May, 1812; February 1813; May 1814.

—— *Recollections Relative to the Dairyman's Daughter. The Christian Guardian*, March, September, 1815; March, April, 1816.

(——) *A Memoir of the Rev. Legh Richmond.* By the Rev. T. S. Grimshawe. 1827, 4th ed., 1828.

(ROBINSON, THOMAS.) *Some Account of the Reverend Thomas Robinson.* By Edward Thomas Vaughan. 1816.

ROGERS, SAMUEL. *Recollections of the Table-Talk of Samuel Rogers.* 2nd ed., 1856.

SCOTT, THOMAS. *Theological Works, Published at Different Times.* Buckingham, 1805 (1807, etc.).

(——) *The Life of the Rev. Thomas Scott.* By John Scott. 1822.

SHERWOOD, MRS. *The Works of Mrs Sherwood.* 13 vols., New York, 1835. [Volumes 9–12 contain, in 2174 pages, Mrs Sherwood's moral tale *The Lady of the Manor; being a Series of Conversations on the Subject of Confirmation, intended for the use of the Middle and Higher Ranks of young Females.*]

Simeon, see below, *Memoirs of the Life of the Rev. Charles Simeon.*

(SIMEON, CHARLES.) *Memoranda of the Rev. Charles Simeon.* By Matthew Morris Preston. 1840.

(——) *Memoirs of the Life of the Rev. Charles Simeon.* Edited by the Rev. William Carus. London and Cambridge, 1847.

STEPHEN, SIR GEORGE. *Antislavery Recollections.* 1854.

STEPHEN, SIR JAMES. *Essays in Ecclesiastical Biography.* 1849.

—— *Letters of the R. Hon. Sir James Stephen.* 1906.

Stories 1818, see More, Hannah, *Stories for the Middle Ranks of Society.*

(TEIGNMOUTH, LORD.) *Memoir of the Life and Correspondence of John Shore Lord Teignmouth.* By his son Lord Teignmouth. 2 vols., 1843.

TOMLINE, GEORGE. Bishop of Lincoln. *Elements of Christian Theology.* 2 vols., 1799.

—— *The Refutation of Calvinism.* 1811.

(TRIMMER, MRS SARAH.) *Some Account of the Life and Writings of Mrs Sarah Trimmer.* [By her children.] 2 vols., 1814.

TROLLOPE, MRS FRANCES. *The Vicar of Wrexhill.* 1837.

(VENN, HENRY.) *The Life and a Selection from the Letters of the late Rev. Henry Venn.* By the late John Venn and the Rev. Henry Venn. From the sixth London edition. New York, 1855.

WATSON, RICHARD. *Anecdotes of the Life of Richard Watson, Bishop of Landaff*: written by himself at different intervals, and revised in 1814. Published by his son, Richard Watson, Prebendary of Landaff and Wells. 1817.

WATTS WILKINSON. *Memoir of the Rev. Watts Wilkinson.* 1842.

(WHALLEY, THOMAS SEDGWICK.) *Journals and Correspondence of Thomas Sedgwick Whalley, D.D., of Mendip Lodge, Somerset.* Edited by the Rev. Hill Wickham. 2 vols., 1863.

WILBERFORCE, WILLIAM. *A Practical View of the Prevailing Religious System of Professed Christians in the Higher and Middle Classes in this Country contrasted with Real Christianity.* 1797.

(——) *The Life of William Wilberforce.* By his sons Robert Isaac Wilberforce and Samuel Wilberforce. 5 vols., 1838.

(——) *The Correspondence of William Wilberforce.* Edited by his sons Robert Isaac Wilberforce and Samuel Wilberforce. 1840. [Revised and enlarged from the London edition. 2 vols., Philadelphia, 1841.]

(——) *Private Papers of William Wilberforce.* Collected and edited by A. M. Wilberforce. 1897.

(WOODD, BASIL.) *Memoir of the Rev. Basil Woodd.* By S. C. Wilks. 1831.

YOUNG, ARTHUR. *Enquiry into the State of the Public Mind Amongst the Lower Classes.* 1798.

(——) *The Autobiography of Arthur Young.* Edited by M. Betham-Edwards. 1898.

II. LATER WORKS

ABBEY and OVERTON. *The English Church in the Eighteenth Century.* 2 vols., 1878.

Bibliography

BALLEINE, G. R. *A History of the Evangelical Party in the Church of England.* 1908.

BARING-GOULD, S. *The Evangelical Revival.* 1920.

BREADY, J. WESLEY. *Lord Shaftesbury and Social-Industrial Progress.* 1926.

BRILIOTH, YNGVE. *The Anglican Revival.* 1925.

BRYANT, ARTHUR. *The Age of Elegance.* 1950.

BUTLER, SAMUEL. *The Way of All Flesh.* 1903.

CANTON, WILLIAM. *The Story of the Bible Society.* 1904.

—— *A History of the British and Foreign Bible Society.* 5 vols., 1904–10.

CARUS-WILSON, HERBERT, and TALBOYS, HAROLD I. (editors). *Genealogical Memoirs of the Carus Wilson Family.* Hove, 1899.

CHURCH MISSIONARY SOCIETY. *The Centenary Volume of the Church Missionary Society for Africa and the East. 1799–1899.* 1902.

Clapham and the Clapham Sect. Published by the Clapham Antiquarian Society. Clapham, 1927.

(DALLAS, ALEXANDER R. C.) *Incidents in the Life and Ministry of the Rev. Alex. R. C. Dallas.* By his Widow. 1871.

EDWARDS, MALDYN. *After Wesley.* 1935.

(ELISABETH, DUCHESS OF GORDON.) *Life and Letters of Elisabeth, Last Duchess of Gordon.* By the Rev. A. Moody Stewart. New York, 1868.

FORSTER, E. M. *Marianne Thornton. A Domestic Biography.* 1956.

HAMMOND, J. L. and BARBARA. *The Bleak Age.* 1934.

HARLAND, MARION. *Hannah More.* 1900.

HENSON, H. H. *Sibbes and Simeon.* 1932.

HOLE, CHARLES. *The Early History of the Church Missionary Society for Africa and the East to the end of A.D. 1814.* 1896.

JAPP, ALEXANDER H. *De Quincey Memorials.* 2 vols., New York, 1891.

LIDDELL HART, B. H., editor. *The Letters of Private Wheeler.* 1951.

(MACAULAY, ZACHARY.) *Life and Letters of Zachary Macaulay.* By his Granddaughter Viscountess Knutsford. 1900.

MEAKIN, ANNETTE M. B. *Hannah More. A Biographical Study.* 1911.

MOULE, H. C. G. *Charles Simeon.* 1892.

—— *The Evangelical School in the Church of England.* 1901.

MOZLEY, T. *Reminiscences Chiefly of Oriel College and the Oxford Movement.* 2 vols., Boston (U.S.A.), 1884.

OVERTON, J. H. *The Evangelical Revival in the Eighteenth Century.* 1886.

Pages from a Private Diary. 1899.

REYNOLDS, J. S. *The Evangelicals at Oxford 1735–1871.* 1953.

(ROSE, GEORGE.) *Diaries and Correspondence of the Right Hon. George Rose.* Edited by The Rev. Leveson Vernon Harcourt. 2 vols., 1860.

RUSSELL, GEORGE W. E. *Collections and Recollections.* 1898.
—— *An Onlooker's Note-book.* 1902.
—— *Seeing and Hearing.* 1907.
—— *A Short History of the Evangelical Movement.* 1915.
SEELEY, M. *The Later Evangelical Fathers.* 1879.
SMYTH, CHARLES. *Simeon and Church Order.* Cambridge, 1940.
STIRLING, A. M. W. *The Ways of Yesterday.* 1930.
STOUGHTON, JOHN. *Religion in England from 1800 to 1850.* 2 vols., 1884.
TELFORD, JOHN. *A Sect that Moved the World.* N.d., *c.* 1906.
THOMAS, GILBERT. *William Cowper and the Eighteenth Century.* 1935.
(VINE HALL, JOHN.) *An Autobiography of John Vine Hall.* Edited by the Rev.
　　Newman Hall. 1865.
WAY, HERBERT L. *History of the Way Family.* Privately printed, 1914.
(WILBERFORCE, SAMUEL.) *Life of Samuel Wilberforce.* By A. R. Ashwell and
　　Reginald Wilberforce. 3 vols., 1880–2.
WILLIS, W. D., M.A. *Simony.* 2nd ed., 1865.
WILSON, P. W. *William Pitt, the Younger.* 1930.

III. THE BLAGDON CONTROVERSY

*The Controversy between Mrs Hannah More and the curate of Blagdon, relative to
　　the conduct of her teacher of the Sunday School in that Parish, with the original
　　letters and explanatory notes.* By Thomas Bere, curate of Blagdon. London,
　　1801.
A letter to the Rev. T. Bere, rector of Butcombe. By John Boak, rector of
　　Brockley. Bristol, 1801.
*A letter to the rev. Thos. Bere, rector of Butcombe, occasioned by his late unwarrant-
　　able attack on Mrs Hannah More. With an appendix, containing letters and
　　other documents relative to the extraordinary proceedings at Blagdon.* By Sir
　　Abraham Elton, bart. Bath, 1801. (The appendix has a separate pagina-
　　tion, and is headed: A letter from the rev. Dr Crossman, rector of Blag-
　　don, to the rev. Sir Abraham Elton, bart.)
*Expostulatory Letter to the reverend Sir Abraham Elton, bart., in consequence of his
　　late publication addressed to the rev. Thomas Bere, rector of Butcombe.* Bath,
　　1801. [? By the Reverend William Shaw.]
*An appeal to the public on the controversy between Hannah More; the curate of
　　Blagdon, and the rev. Sir A. Elton.* By Thomas Bere, rector of Butcombe.
　　Bath, 1801.
*A statement of facts relative to Mrs H. More's schools, occasioned by some mis-
　　representations.* Bath, 1801. [? By Dr Charles Moss.]

Bibliography

An address to Mrs Hannah More, on the conclusion of the Blagdon Controversy. With observations on an anonymous tract, entitled a statement of facts. By Thomas Bere, curate of Blagdon. Bath, 1801.

The Blagdon Controversy, or short criticisms on the late dispute between the curate of Blagdon and Mrs Hannah More, relative to Sunday schools, and Monday private schools. By a layman. Bath, 1801.

Suggestions respecting a plan of national education with conjectures on the probable consequences of nondescript methodism and Sunday schools; in a letter addressed to his grace the archbishop of Canterbury. By William Shaw, B.D., rector of Chelvey. Bath, 1801.

The something wrong developed; or free remarks on Mrs H. More's conventicles, &c., seasonably addressed to the Blagdon controversialists; and inscribed to the bishop of Bath and Wells. Bristol, 1801.

The force of contrast, or quotations accompanied with remarks, submitted to the consideration of all who have interested themselves in what has been called the Blagdon Controversy. Bath, 1801. [By Thomas Drewitt, curate of Cheddar.]

Imposture exposed in a few brief remarks on the irreligiousness, profaneness, indelicacy, virulence, and vulgarity of certain persons who style themselves anti-Jacobin reviewers. By Josiah Hard, esq. Cambridge, 1801.

Animadversions on the curate of Blagdon's three publications...with some allusion to his Cambrian descent from 'Gwyr ap Glendour ap Cadwallader ap Styfnig,' as affirmed and set forth by himself in the twenty-eighth page of his appeal to the public. London, 1802. [By the Reverend Thomas Sedgwick Whalley.]

Truths respecting Mrs Hannah More's meeting houses, and the conduct of her followers: addressed to the curate of Blagdon. By Edward Spencer, apothecary, Wells. Bath, 1802.

Illustrations of falsehood, in a reply to some assertions, contained in Mr Spencer's later publication. By Thomas Drewitt, curate of Cheddar. Bath, 1802.

An alternative epistle addressed to Edward Spencer, apothecary. By lieut. Charles H. Pettinger. Bristol, 1802.

Elucidations of character, occasioned by a letter by the rev. R. Lewis, published in the Rev. T. Bere's address to Mrs H. More; with some remarks on a pamphlet lately published by Edward Spencer of Wells. By John Boak. Bath, 1802.

Seasonable hints to the younger part of the clergy of the church of England occasioned by the relative increase of libertinism and the antinomian heresy, the timely close of the Wansey and Blagdon Controversies, and the reported suppression of Methodist conventicles in the diocese of Salisbury. By John Duncan, D.D. Bath, 1802.

Bibliography

The Life of Hannah More, with a critical view of her writings. By Rev. sir Archibald MacSarcasm, bart. [By William Shaw, rector of Chelvey.] Bristol, 1802.

Candid observations on Mrs H. More's schools, in which is considered their supposed connection with methodism. Recommended to the attention of the public in general, and particularly to the clergy. By the rev. ——, rector of ——. Bath, 1802. [This has been attributed to Wilberforce.]

The Force of contrast continued, or extracts and animadversions. With occasional strictures on the contraster and others of Mr Bere's opponents, and observations on the effects of Mrs H. More's schools. To which is added a postscript on the editors of the British Critic. Respectfully submitted to the consideration of those who have interested themselves in the Blagdon Controversy. By a friend of the Establishment. [? The Reverend E. Crosse.] Bristol, 1802.

IV. THE SOCIETIES

(a) Medical

A General State of the Corporation of the London Hospital. 1799.

An Account of the Nature and Intention of the Lock Hospital, near Hyde-Park-Corner. 1802, 1805.

Vaccine Pock Institution. The Report on the Cow-Pock Inoculation. 1803.

Names of the Governors of Christ's Hospital. 1806.

List of the Governors of St Bartholomew's Hospital. 1806.

Plan of the Universal Medical Institution. 1811.

Short Account...of the New Rupture Society. 1811.

Reasons for Establishing and Further Encouragement of St Luke's Hospital for Lunatics. 1817, 1819, 1836.

Royal Jennerian Society for the Extermination of the Small-Pox. 1817.

The City of London Lying-in Hospital. 1817.

The Fifteenth Report of the Institution for the Cure and Prevention of Contagious Fever in the Metropolis [this is the same institution as the preceding]. 1817.

The History of the London House of Recovery. Printed for the Society for Bettering the Condition of the Poor. 1817.

City of London Truss Society for the Relief of the Ruptured Poor. 1818, 1822.

General State of the London Hospital. 1818 (etc.).

Report of the Bethlem Building Committee. 1818.

The Royal London and Westminster Infirmary, for the treatment of cutaneous diseases. 1819.

Account of the Lying-in Charity. 1820.

Annual Report of the Royal Humane Society. 1820.

Bibliography

A List of the Governors of St Thomas's Hospital Southwark. 1820.

Fifteenth Annual Report of the London Infirmary for Curing Diseases of the Eye. 1820.

London Vaccine Institution. 1821.

The Asylum for the Cure of Scrofulous and Cancerous Diseases. 1822.

List of Governors and Plan of the City Dispensary. 1822.

The Royal Metropolitan Infirmary, for sick children, in memory of Princess Charlotte. 1823.

An Account of the Infirmary for Asthma, Consumption and other diseases of the Lungs. 1827.

Fifty-third Annual Report of the Royal Humane Society. 1827.

Seventh Report of the Committee of the Seamen's Hospital Society. 1828.

The Thirtieth Report of the London Fever Hospital. 1832.

List of Governors [of the London Fever Hospital] from 1802–1831 who have given more than ten pounds. 1832.

Royal Universal Infirmary for Children. 1835.

Fourteenth Annual Report of the Royal Free Hospital for the Destitute Sick. 1839.

National Truss Society for the Relief of the Ruptured Poor. 1842.

Fourth Annual Report of the Orthopaedic Institution; or Infirmary for the cure of Club-Feet and other Contractions. 1843.

Laws of the Westminster Medical Society. 1848.

Rules and List of the Present Members of the Society for Improving the Condition of the Insane. 1854.

(b) Philanthropic, Religious, etc.

Rules, Orders, and Regulations, of the Magdalen Hospital. 1787.

An Account of the Institution of the Lock Asylum. 1796.

Reports of the Society for Bettering the Condition and Increasing the Comforts of the Poor. 1796, etc. These reports were issued irregularly, chiefly by Sir Thomas Bernard, with many incidental publications. The thirty-ninth Report, 1816.

An Account of the Rise, Progress and Present State of the Society for the Discharge and Relief of Persons Imprisoned for Small Debts throughout England, 1799, 1808 etc.

Report of the Committee of the Society for Carrying Into Effect His Majesty's Proclamation Against Vice and Immorality for the year 1799. 1800.

Report of the London Society for the Suppression of Juvenile Prostitution. N.d., apparently early century.

The Constitution, and Laws and Regulations of the Asylum. 1801.

A Brief Account of the Lock Asylum. 1802, 1805.

Bibliography

Proposal for Establishing a Society for the Suppression of Vice. 1802.

Reports of the School for the Indigent Blind. 1802.

Address to the Public from the Society for the Suppression of Vice. 1803.

Part the Second of an Address to the Public from the Society for the Suppression of Vice. 1803.

The Charter and Bye-Laws of the Royal Institution of Great Britain. 1803, 1806, etc.

The Friendly Female Society. 1803, 1838.

The Nature, Design and Rules...of the Benevolent, or Strangers' Friend Society. 1803, 1806, 1812, 1813, 1819.

Address to the Public from the Society for the Suppression of Vice, Part the Second. 1804.

An Account of the Nature and Present State of the Philanthropic Society. 1804, 1814, 1816, 1823, 1824.

Statement of the Proceedings of the Society for the Suppression of Vice. 1804.

Plan of the Ladies' Charitable School of St Sepulchre, London, King Street, Snow Hill. 1805.

Proposal for forming a Society for Promoting the Civilization and Improvement of the North American Indians within the British Boundary. 1806.

Rules and Orders of the Schools Belonging to St Anne's Society. 1808.

An Abstract from the Account of the Asylum or House of Refuge. 1809, 1812.

By-Laws and Regulations of the London Female Penitentiary. 1809.

Juvenis. Cursory Remarks on a Recent Publication etc. [i.e. the above]. 1809.

Narrative of the Reverend Joseph Samuel C. F. Frey, Minister of the Gospel to the Jews. 1809.

The First (etc.) Report of the Committee of the London Society for Promoting Christianity Amongst the Jews. 1809 (etc.).

The Fourth Report of the London Female Penitentiary. 1811. The 34th, 35th Report of the Committee. 1841, 1842.

An Account of the Origin and Object of the Society for the Diffusion of Knowledge upon the Punishment of Death, and the Improvement of Prison Discipline. 1812.

Eighth Anniversary Meeting of the Sunday School Society. 1812.

First (etc.) Annual Report of the National Society, for Promoting the Education of the Poor in the Principles of the Established Church. 1812 (1822, etc.).

The Interesting Proceedings of The Meetings of the Norfolk and Suffolk Auxiliary Bible Societies. 1812.

Occasional Reports of the Society for the Suppression of Vice, no. VI (1812), no. VII (1816), no. IX (1822).

Rules of the Christian Tract Society. 1813.

Bibliography

The Fund for Mercy: or, An Institution for the Relief and Employment of Destitute and Forlorn Females. 1813.

Report of the Provisional Committee of the Guardian Society. 1815, 1816.

Reports of the British and Foreign School Society. 1815, 1818. Seventeenth Report of the Society. 1822.

Report of the Committee for Investigating the Causes of the Alarming Increase of Juvenile Delinquency in the Metropolis. 1816.

Third Report of the Society for... Prison Discipline. 1816.

First (Sixth) Annual Report of the Society for the Promotion of Permanent and Universal Peace. 1817 (1822).

Second (Eighth, Ninth, Tenth, Twelfth) Report of the Committee of the Guardian Society. 1817 (1827, 1828, 1832, 1838).

The Second Annual Report of the Loan Society. 1817.

Address from the Committee of the Society for Superseding the Necessity of Climbing Boys. 1818.

List of the Proprietors and Life Subscribers of the London Institution. 1818.

The First (Second) Report of the General Wesleyan Methodist Missionary Society. 1818 (1819).

The Ladies' Royal Benevolent Society. 1818.

The Committee for the Relief of Distressed Seamen. 1818.

Account of the Society of Friends of Foreigners in Distress for the year 1819. (1820, 1823, 1828).

General State of the Marine Society. 1819, 1831.

Report of the Committee of the East-London Irish Free Schools etc. for the year 1820. 1820.

Rules Proposed for the Government of Gaols... by the Society for the Improvement of Prison Discipline and the Reformation of Juvenile Offenders. 1820.

Fourth Report of the Committee of the City of London Society for the Instruction of Adults. 1820.

A List of the Governors of the Magdalen Hospital. 1821.

Eighth (etc.) Report of the Committee of the City of London National Schools. 1821 (1832).

The Society for Superseding the Necessity of Climbing Boys. 1821.

Third Annual Report of the Committee of the Merchant Seamen's Auxiliary Bible Society. 1821.

Committee Appointed to Manage a Subscription for the Purpose of Affording Nightly Shelter to the Houseless and Temporary Relief to the Destitute during the Winter of 1821–2. 1822.

The Committee for the Relief of Distressed Districts in Ireland. 1822.

The Irish Society of London, etc. 1822.

Bibliography

A Short Account of the Magdalen Hospital. 1823.

The Report of the British and Irish Ladies' Society for Improving the Condition and Promoting the Industry and Welfare of the Female Peasantry in Ireland. 1823 (1825).

The Society for Educating the Poor in Newfoundland. 1823.

First Annual Report of the Committee of the Society for Educating the Poor of Newfoundland. 1824.

First (Second, Third) Annual Report of the Gospel Tract Society. 1825 (1826, 1827).

Proceedings of the Society for Educating the Poor of Newfoundland. 1825, 1827.

Report of the Society for the Suppression of Vice. 1825.

A Brief Account of the City of London School of Instruction and Industry, for the benefit of children of the indigent poor. 1827.

An Appeal on Behalf of the Philo-Judaean Society. 1827.

Annual Reports of the British and Foreign Bible Society. Twenty-third Report, 1827; Thirtieth Report, 1830.

The First Report of the Philo-Judaean Society. 1827.

Objects and Address of the Society for the Prevention of Cruelty to Animals. 1829.

Reports of the Church Missionary Society.

Proceedings of the Church Missionary Society.

The Church Missionary Society Record. 1830 onwards.

The Report of the Provisional Committee of the Metropolitan Female Asylum. 1830.

The Society for the Relief of Distressed Widows. 1830.

A Statement of the Proceedings of the Western Committee for the Relief of the Irish Poor. 1831.

The First Public Meeting of the London Temperance Society. 1831.

A Report of the Proceedings at the Annual Meeting of the Association for Promoting Rational Humanity Towards the Animal Creation. 1832.

District Visitors Record. 1832 (etc.).

(First) Report of the British and Foreign Temperance Society (formerly the London Temperance Society). 1832. Second, Third, Fourth Annual Reports, 1833–5.

Proceedings of the Labourers' Friend Society. 1832. Second, Third Annual Reports, 1833–4.

Report of an Extra Meeting of the Society for the Prevention of Cruelty to Animals. 1832.

Fourth Annual Report of the Childrens' Friend Society (formerly known as The Society for the Suppression of Juvenile Vagrancy). 1834.

Twelfth Report of the Westminster Asylum. 1834.

Bibliography

The Animals' Friend. 1835.

Fiftieth Annual Report of the Benevolent, or Strangers' Friend Society. 1835.

First Report of the Established Church Society. 1835.

Rules and Regulations of St Peter's Proprietary School. 1835.

St Anne's Society Schools etc. 1835.

First (Third) Annual Report of the New British and Foreign Temperance Society. 1837 (1839).

First Annual Report of the Aborigines Protection Society. 1838.

Tenth Annual Report of the Maritime Female Penitent Refuge, for Poor, Degraded Females. 1839.

The Jubilee Volume of the Church Missionary Society. 1849.

Report of the British Anti-Tobacco Society. 1853, 1856.

Seventeenth Annual Report of the Home and Colonial Infant School Society. 1853.

Report of the Committee of the Church of England Education Society. 1854.

Jubilee Volume of the Monthly Tract Society. 1888.

Fifth Annual Report of the Working Men's Religious Tract Society. N.d.

INDEX

The names of works are followed by their authors in parentheses.

Index

Barclay, Robert, 89, 241 n. 2, 342, 351, 357, 389 n., 405
Barclays, the, 236 n., 281, 429
Barham, first Baron (Sir Charles Middleton), 2, 74, 77, 101–2, 494
  supports Evangelical societies, 9, 87, 89, 241 n. 2, 260, 270, 343 n. 2, 349, 355, 360
Barham, second Baron, 10, 355, 360
Barham, T. F., 389 n.
Baring, Charles Thomas, Bishop, 502, 518
Baring, Sir Thomas, 91, 324, 502, 518, 519
  supports Evangelical societies, 88, 241 n. 2, 270, 343 n., 357, 360
Barley Wood, 288, 422, 531, 532
Barnard, Lord, 256
Barnes, Mr (Tutor of Queens'), 291
Barrett, Elisabeth, 6
Barrington, first and second Viscounts, 31
Barrington, Shute, Bishop, 31, 32, 210 n., 235, 286, 422, 505, 508, 519
  and Blagdon Controversy, 197, 199
  supports Evangelical societies, 85, 88, 236, 238, 241 n. 2, 246, 248, 256, 264, 279, 342 n., 344, 357, 359, 429, 432
Barry, Lady Lucy, 280
Barrymore, Earls of, 17, 261, 523
'Barton, Rev. Amos', 449–51, 508
Bath, Countess of, 269
Bathurst, Henry, Bishop, 247, 256, 264, 278, 279, 296–7, 480
Baxter, Nadir, 389 n.
Beadon, Richard, Bishop, 40, 209, 226–7, 308 n., 314
Beaufort, Duchess of, 10, 83, 102, 153, 195, 241 n. 2, 324, 358, 360, 416
Beaufort, seventh Duke of, 256, 272
Beaumont, Sir George, 346
Bedford, Duchess of, 416
Bedford, fifth Duke of, 94
Bedford, sixth Duke of, 247, 256, 306
Behn, Aphra, 41
Bell, Andrew, 397–8
benevolence, Evangelical, 81, 104–5, 140, 153–4, 167, 178–9, 229–32, 237, 238–41, 243, 259, 318, 322, 324, 341, 350, 382, 397–9
  imputation of corruption in, 370–2

Benevolent Society, see Strangers' Friend Society
Bennett, William Sterndale, 522
Bentham, Jeremy, 345, 346
Bentinck Chapel, 273, 426
Bere, Thomas, 182, 188, 193, 196–203, 208–11, 213–20, 222, 227–8, 232, 258
Berkeley, Norborne, 219
Bernard, Sir Thomas, 87, 88, 89 n., 91, 238, 248, 356, 358, 403
Bernard, Viscount, 270 n.
Bernard, Viscountess, 10
Berridge, John, 29, 65, 175, 289
Bertazzi, Baptista, 431
Bessborough, third Earl of, 248
Bettering Society, 70, 88, 98, 235, 243, 334, 343, 344, 345, 347, 358, 359, 360, 491
Bevan, David, 236 n., 405, 429
Bevan, R. C. L., 241 n.
Bevan, Sylvanus, 236 n., 241 n. 2, 342 n., 405, 429
Bexley, first Baron, see Vansittart, Nicholas
Bible, An Introduction to the Study of the (George Tomline), 311
Bible Commentary (Thomas Scott), 396 n., 475
Bible Society, British and Foreign, 56–7, 80, 233, 234, 240, 244–5, 261, 263, 264, 265, 274, 275, 317, 322, 335, 342, 360, 395, 526
  auxiliaries of, 72, 89, 94, 98, 246–54, 256, 258–60, 280, 282, 285, 316, 329, 333, 336, 343, 347, 387–8, 394, 400
  Cambridge auxiliary, 7, 258, 295–7, 301, 303–11, 315–16, 484, 496
  ladies in, 248, 249, 258–9, 525
  opposed, 8, 31 n., 97, 255–8, 276, 279, 295–301, 304, 308–11, 315–16, 363, 369, 485
  in Russia, 252–3, 254, 259
  Wilberforce and, 70, 72, 98, 243, 245–8, 250, 252, 302–5, 307, 311, 316, 488, 491, 496–7, 529
Bible Society, History of the (John Owen), 249, 254
Bickersteth, Edward, 153–4, 240–1, 274, 323, 387–8, 403, 424–5, 525–7, 529

Index

Biddulph, T. T., 195, 272
biographies, Evangelical, characteristics of, 403, 419
Bird, Elizabeth, *see* Wilberforce, Elizabeth
Bird, Hannah, John and Judith, 72 n.2
Bird, Robert, 496
Birks, T. T., 154 n., 403, 425
bishops, general tendencies of the, 31–2, 38–40, 83, 85, 244, 250, 256, 264, 272, 276, 279
Black, Alexander, 359
Black Giles the Poacher (Hannah More), 138–9
Blackstone, Sir William, 34
Blacow, Richard, 272–3, 276
Blades, John, 236 n., 342, 356
Blades, Joseph, 389 n.
Blagdon Controversy, 33, 47, 180–3, 187, 188, 192–3, 194, 196–233 *passim*, 234, 258, 285, 492
Blagdon Controversy, The ('A Layman'), 213
Blake, William, 344
Blandford, Marquis of, 39
blasphemy, 18, 26, 71, 85–6, 364, 429, 431, 457, 521
Bleak Age, The (B. and J. L. Hammond), 324, 441–2
Bleak House (Charles Dickens), 318–19
Blessington, Countess of, 345
Blind, School for the Indigent, 334, 343, 344, 359, 400
Blomfield, Bishop Charles and Mrs, 522
Boake, John, 193–4, 208, 221, 222
Bolton, Lord, 256
Bootle, Edward, 349
Boringdon, second Baron, 256
Bosanquet, Samuel, 90, 353
Boscawen, Mrs, 90, 101–2, 109, 349
Boucher, Jonathan, 160–1, 162, 395
Bouverie, Bartholomew, 236, 354
Bouverie, Mrs, 9, 90, 101, 349, 494
Bowdler, Harriett, 7 ('a maiden lady'), 534
Bowdler, John (sen.), 347, 490–1
Bowdler, John (jun.), 490
Bowdler, Thomas, 346, 347
Bowdler, Thomas (the younger), 534

Bowles, John, 16, 169, 346
Bradney, Joseph (sen. and jun.), 389 n.
Braybrooke, second Baron, 256
Brenton, Admiral Sir Jahleel and Captain Edward Pelham, 359
Bridges, George, 236 n.
Bridges, John, 358
Bridgewater, Duke of, 157
Bristol, Evangelical fervour at, 272
Bristol, fourth Earl of (Bishop of Derry), 27, 425
Bristol, fifth Earl of, 236, 254, 303, 305, 358
British Critic, 182, 210
'Brocklehurst, Robert', 283, 452–6, 466, 470
Broglie, Duchesse de, 372–3
Brontë, Anne and Emily, 6, 518
Brontë, Charlotte, 6, 324, 451–7, 464, 466, 470, 518
Brontë, Rev. P., 282, 308 n., 451, 518
'Brook, Miss Mabel', 320, 323
Brougham, Lord, 347, 527, 529
Brownlow, Earl, 85 n., 342, 358
Buccleuch, Duchess of, 241 n. 2, 342 n., 358
Buccleuch and Queensberry, fourth Duke of, 256
Buchanan, Claudius, 272, 277, 279, 284, 502
Buckingham, first Marquis of, 247, 256
Buckle, Henry Thomas, 6
Budd, Henry, 96 n., 271, 429
Bulkeley, Lord, 89, 235, 256, 349, 358
bull-baiting, 15, 112 n.2, 327, 521
Bunyan, John, 450 n.
Burdett, Sir Francis, 346, 347
Burgess, Thomas, Bishop, 256, 264, 279, 429
Burke, Edmund, 101
Burn, Andrew, Major-General, 247
Burn, Edward, 271, 277
Burney, Charles Parr, 358
Burney, Fanny, 344
Bury, Lady Charlotte, 92, 312, 439
Butcombe, 202, 222
Butler, Rev. Samuel, 308 n., 346
Butler, Samuel, 6, 324, 455–7

Index

Index

Cumberland, Duke of (brother of George III), 256, 261

Cumberland, Duke of (son of George III), 314, 343

'cunning, Evangelical', 7, 10, 181, 183, 187, 216, 392, 407, 430–1, 514

Cunningham, Francis, 502

Cunningham, John William, 271, 308 n., 402–3, 429, 474, 490, 502

Cure for Melancholy, A (Hannah More), 139–40, 406

Curling, Jesse, 236 n., 241 n. 2, 342 n., 356

Dairyman's Daughter, The (Legh Richmond), 493, 508

Dallas, A. R. C., 422–3

Dampier, Thomas, Bishop, 8, 85, 276, 286, 296–8, 300, 484

Dance, George, 91, 345

dancing, 15, 17, 364, 398, 430, 442, 443–4

Darnley, Countess of, 10, 359

Darnley, Earl of, 85 n., 237, 248, 256, 354, 360

Dartmouth, Countess of, 359

Dartmouth, second Earl of, 2, 9, 51, 102, 260, 528

Dartmouth, third Earl of, 360, 432

Dartmouth, fourth Earl of, 256

Daubeny, Charles, 161, 172–6, 395

Davies, J., 509

Davy, Humphry, 41

Deacon, John, 356, 389 n.

Deaf and Dumb Children, Asylum for, 334, 343, 400

Dealtry, William, 271, 309, 342 n., 490, 502

death, Evangelical preoccupation with, 457–61, 463–6, 473

death penalty, 42–3

Society concerned with, 335, 345, 347, 349, 351

de Courcy, Richard, 160

Deerhurst, Lord, 347

Delegate, The (Hannah More), 251, 510–12

democracy, Evangelicals and, 112, 133, 134, 202

See also lower orders

De Morgan, Augustus, 513

De Quincey, Mrs, 59, 64, 288, 317, 502, 520

De Quincey, Thomas, 6, 59, 288, 502, 518, 520

Derby, Countess of, 249

Derby, Earl of, 256

Derry, Bishop of, 256

Desart, Earl, 281

Devonshire, Duchess of, 60, 90–1

Devonshire, fifth Duke of, 90–1

Dickens, Charles, 19, 241, 318–19, 325, 326, 445, 522

Dikes, Thomas, 271

dissenters,

relationship of with Evangelicals, 5, 63, 162, 169–70, 177, 243, 246, 271, 275, 503

relationship of with Methodists, 62, 286–8

See also Methodism

District Visiting, 240–1, 259, 324, 464, 471

Society for Promoting, 338, 342, 360

Doddridge, Philip, 488

Downshire, Marquis of, 256

Doyle, Sir J., 256

dress, 15, 437–41, 469–71, 521

Drewitt, Thomas, 208, 222

drink, 17, 23, 25, 177, 328, 404–6, 430, 442, 508, 520, 524, 525

Drummond, Henry, 241 n. 2, 342 n., 356

Dublin,

Archbishop of, 256, 277, 280–1

Lord Mayor of, 281

du Cayla, Madame, 523

Dudley and Ward, Earl of, 17, 256, 345, 347

Dunmore, Earl of, 256

Dunstanville, Lord de, 88, 241 n. 2, 282, 344, 349, 358

Dynevor, Lord, 88, 241 n. 2, 358

Eardley, Lord, 90, 241 n. 2, 344, 349, 356

East India Company, 261, 265, 366

Charter Bill, 94, 275

Ebrington, Lord, 241 n. 2, 504

Eclectic Review, 94

Eclectic Society, 52, 265, 444, 508

Eden, Sir R., 256

Edgeworth, Maria, 344, 346

Edinburgh Review, 41, 44, 83, 298, 363–4, 374, 432

Index

Edwards, Edward, 271

Edwards, Jonathan, 289

Egmont, Earl of, 241 n. 2

Egremont, third Earl of, 10, 28, 29 n., 90, 353 n., 356, 360

Eldon, first Earl of, 96–7, 142 n., 270, 286, 342, 344, 347, 376

Eliot, Edward, 72 n.2, 88

Eliot, George, 6, 30–1, 324, 402, 448–51, 455, 518

Ellenborough, first Baron, 276, 286, 347, 430–1

Elliott, Charles, 9, 236 n., 237, 265, 269, 358, 389 n., 429, 502

Elliott, Charlotte, 237, 518

Ellis, George Agar, 359

Elton, Sir Abraham, 196–200, 208, 211–14, 219 n., 222, 227, 396

Ely, Bishop of, 33, 200

Erskine, first Baron, 86 n., 286

Esdaile, William, 389 n.,

Established Church,

    clerical corruption or laxity in, 11, 17–19, 29, 30, 37, 129, 249, 261

    Evangelical relations with, 5, 6, 10, 29–31, 34–5, 48, 63–4, 80, 85, 117, 156–7, 162–8, 171, 208–9

    'nominal' Christianity in, 2–4, 9, 17, 29–40, 42, 44, 58, 63–4, 80, 97, 99–101, 104, 115–20, 162, 165–6, 178–9, 188, 200, 207, 271, 275–6, 296 n., 350, 387, 391, 403, 416, 449, 475, 484–5, 489, 493, 495, 521

    preferment in, 31–2, 33, 37–40, 61–2, 292, 310, 446, 489, 517, 523

    See also High Church

Etherington, Sir Henry, 256

Evangelical and Pharisaical Righteousness Compared (Charles Simeon), 299

Evangelical Revival in the Eighteenth Century, The (John Henry Overton), 527–8

Evangelicalism

    eminent supporters of, 6, 9–10, 87–90, 235–7, 241 n. 2, 247–8, 256, 260, 270, 279–82, 342–60 *passim*

    misconception concerning, 7–9, 218

    reforming methods summarized, 4–11

two types of, 6, 324–6, 518–20, 525

    See also institutions *and* language

Exeter, Dowager Marchioness of, 241 n. 2

Exmouth, Admiral Viscount, 237, 359

Falmouth, first Earl of, 256

Fanshawe, W., 64, 482

Fantom, Mr, History of (Hannah More), 124, 125–6, 128, 151, 153, 154, 350 n., 412

Faraday, Michael, 347

Farish, William, 271, 289, 295, 297, 305, 306, 309, 408, 501, 509

Farnham, Lady, 280 n., 359

Farnham, Lord, 280 n., 358

Fatal Falsehood (Hannah More), 102

Fauntleroy, Henry, 345

Fellowes, Robert, 156, 176–9, 204, 507

Female Education, Strictures on... (Hannah More), 161, 395

Female Sex, Duties of the (Thomas Gisborne), 439

Ferrers,

    fourth Earl of, 126

    Evangelical Earl, 126, 241 n. 2, 270

Field, John, 522

Figaro in London, 313–14, 315, 321–2, 403, 404, 427–8, 441, 523

Finch, General Edward, 270 n.

Finch, Lady Charlotte, 349

Finch, Lady Harriet, 236

Finch, Lady Maria, 236

Fisher, John, Bishop, 256, 286

Fitzgerald, Lady Mary, 9, 90, 349, 359

Fitzwilliam, second Earl, 58–9, 256

Flaxman, John, 345

Fletcher, John, of Madeley, 46, 278

Florio (Hannah More), 103

Flower, Sir Charles, 342 n., 355

Foley, Lord, 256

Foreigners in Distress, Society of Friends of, 335, 343–4, 359

Forster, E. M., 397, 514 ff.

Forsters, the, 351, 427

Fortescue, Countess, 236

Foster, Henry, 74, 75, 93, 165–6, 170 n., 245 n., 444–5, 476, 509

Foster, John, 94–6

Index

Index

Index

Index

Leven and Melville, Earl of (Lord Balgony), 235, 247, 342 n., 349
Leveson-Gower, Lord, 256
Lewis, Matthew Gregory, 345
Lichfield and Coventry, Bishop of, *see* Ryder, Henry
Liddell Hart, B. H., 401
Lifford, Lady, 280
Lifford, Lord, 280–1
Lilford, Lord, 236, 241 n. 2, 359
Lindsey, Theophilus, 159
Lister, Daniel, 90
Listowel, Earl of, 10
Liturgy, The Excellence of the (Charles Simeon), 301
Liverpool, second Earl of, 61 n., 112, 256, 270, 286, 298, 356
livings,
    competition for wealthy, 37–8
    Evangelical acquisition of, 2, 8, 71, 80–1, 92–3, 96, 116, 159–60, 162–3, 165–6, 170, 188, 277, 368, 371, 476–7, 479–81, 528
    plurality of, 33, 40
Lloft, Capel, 347
Lloyd, Thomas, 295
Lock Hospital and Asylum, 8, 73–4, 98, 330, 333, 343, 345, 360, 501
Lockett, J. G., 359
London Female Penitentiary, 8, 25, 61, 335, 336, 344
London Fever Hospital, 238 n., 331, 347, 353
London Jewish Society, 70, 238 n., 276, 281, 329 n. 1, 335, 342, 353, 355 n., 358, 360, 369, 400, 402, 406, 426, 463, 525
London Tavern, 244, 246
Long, Beeston, 353
Lorton, Lieut.-General Lord, 281, 355, 360
Lothian, Marquis of, 256
Loughborough, first Baron, 92, 188 n.
lower orders, Evangelical attitude to, 29, 45–8, 52–3, 84, 132–3, 167–8, 239, 278, 323–4, 327–41 *passim*, 394, 407–8, 412, 431–4, 469–70
    See also under More, Hannah, *and* Wilberforce, William

'Lowood' School, 282–3, 324, 452–5, 470
Lowth, Robert, Bishop, 39
Lubbock, Sir John, 354
Ludlam, Thomas, 172–3
Ludlam, William, 173
Luther, Martin, 175

Macartney, Countess, 241 n. 2, 359
Macaulay, General, 359
Macaulay, Thomas Babington, 6, 288, 317, 347, 502, 517–18, 532
Macaulay, Zachary, 288, 370–1, 372, 402, 403, 412, 491 n. 1, 503 n., 505, 517, 532
    close friend of Wilberforce, 6 n., 38, 107, 317, 389, 487, 496, 502, 505
    supports Evangelical societies, 96 n., 241 n. 2, 246, 269, 355, 429
Machiavelli, Niccolò, 45
Mackintosh, Sir James, 107, 267–8, 345–6, 347, 376, 381, 383
Mackworth, Sir Digby, 248, 359
Maddock, H. J., 271
Magdalen Hospital, 98, 333, 343, 346, 347, 352, 359, 401
Magdalene College, Cambridge, 289
Maitland, Ebenezer, 88, 342 n., 359, 389 n.
Maitland, E. F., 270 n.
Maitland, John, 270 n., 343 n., 359, 389 n.
Maitland, Robert, 88, 389 n.
Majendie, Henry William, Bishop, 40
Maltby, Edward, Bishop, 347
Malthus, Thomas, 346
Manchester, Duchess of, *see* Mandeville, Viscountess
Manchester, fifth Duke of, 247, 256
Mandeville, Viscount, 359
Mandeville, Viscountess, 236, 241 n. 2, 359, 494
Manly, Dr, 458–9
Mann, Sir Horace, 247
Manners, General, 270 n.
Manners, Lady Robert, 9, 235, 241 n. 2
Manners, Lord Robert, 270 n.
Manners of the Great..., Thoughts on... (Hannah More), 98–9, 100, 103–4, 106, 159
Manners Sutton, Charles, Archbishop, 40, 64, 235, 279, 286, 298, 308

Index

Moray, Earl of, 256

Mordaunt, Dowager Countess, 241 n. 2

More, Hannah, 11, 31, 55, 70, 118, 156–8, 264, 268, 280, 288, 324, 356, 390–3, 403–4, 415, 422, 435, 437, 439, 441–3, 445, 463, 474, 481, 501, 518, 528

    background, 76–7, 101–2, 219

    literary fame, 98–9, 101–2, 123–4, 135–6, 159, 194, 235, 395–6, 475, 508, 513, 515

    and ruling class, 60–1, 83, 98–104, 111, 127–9, 148, 150, 194–5, 229, 232, 272, 302, 312, 315, 326, 343, 394, 399–400, 412, 450, 476, 505, 509, 519, 520, 522

    and lower orders, 19, 47, 81, 105, 121, 123–30, 131, 134–55 passim, 179, 188–95, 221–2, 227–32, 238, 251–2, 304, 322, 350 n., 379–80, 396, 398–400, 405–6, 416, 467, 471, 509–13, 533

    and 'nominal' Christians, 30, 35, 99–102, 104, 120, 391, 483

    and Blagdon Controversy, 106, 180, 182–3, 188, 192–3, 196–224, 226–9, 232, 234, 258, 492

    and slavery, 106, 109–11, 112, 379, 385, 399–400

    friendship with Wilberforce, 59, 60, 77, 92–3, 103, 105, 106, 109, 141, 151, 154, 161, 163, 171, 187, 189, 194, 196, 197, 220, 226, 232, 258, 312, 394, 396 n., 492–4, 496, 500, 525

    on deathbed scenes, 457–61, 465

    schools started by, 7, 71, 105–6, 123, 135, 141, 152, 154, 182, 188–99, 203, 208–11, 216, 219, 221–2, 226, 228–32, 251, 397–8, 510

    societies supported by, 236, 240, 241 n. 2, 274, 349, 395, 429

    death, 531–2

More, Hannah, Life and Correspondence of (William Roberts), 513–15, 532

More, Hannah, Life of (William Shaw), 208, 218–20, 232, 486

More, Martha ('Miss Patty'), 43, 135, 189 n., 192, 207 n., 221–2, 229, 387, 393

    and the Blagdon Controversy, 197, 201, 217

    and the schools, 105, 141, 154, 188, 195, 230–1, 304, 397–8, 461

More sisters, the, 101, 103, 105, 158, 187, 204, 219, 317, 397, 494, 517–18

Morier, J. P., 344

Morley, Countess of, 10

Morley, first Earl of, 10

Morritt, Mr, 37

Mortlock, John, 241 n. 2, 355

Morton, Dowager Countess, 10

Mosley, Sir Oswald, 359

Moss, Charles, Bishop, 40, 195, 197–200, 203, 209, 213–15, 226

Moss, Charles, jun., Chancellor, 195, 197–203, 209 n., 213–15, 226, 228

Mount-Charles, Lord, 61

Mountnorris, Earl of, 280, 359

Mount Sandford, Earl of, 359

Mozley, T., 97, 447–8, 517

Muncaster, first Baron, 75

Muncaster, second Baron, 37, 87, 495

Murray, Lady Caroline, 236

Murray, Lady Catherine, 9

Murray, Sir George, Vice-Admiral, 278

Murray, Sir J., 256

Nailsea, 141, 191, 196, 230

Napoleon Bonaparte, 246, 273, 372, 427, 442

Nares, John, 347

Nares, Robert, 345

Neave, Sophia, 389 n.

Negroes, Society for Religious Instruction to, 334, 337, 344, 347

Neild, James, 350

Nelson, Horatio, Lord, 41

Nepean, Major-General Sir Evan, 237, 282, 359

Nero, Emperor, 127, 133, 379, 380

Neville, Major-General, 279, 359, 471

New Times, 458–9

Newfoundland Society, 72, 262, 335, 342, 360, 400, 525

Newman, John Henry, Cardinal, 6, 295, 447, 502, 518

Newman, R. W., 270 n.

Newton, John, 3, 31, 110, 173, 177, 245 n., 262, 326, 369, 403, 444–5, 476, 479, 526–7

Index

Perceval, Lady Elizabeth, 236, 241 n. 2
Perceval, Spencer, sen., 286–7, 296, 298, 346, 368, 505
Perceval, Spencer, jun., 441
Percy (Hannah More), 102, 103, 159
Peterborough, Bishop of, 204
Petty, Lord Henry, 347
Phelan, Captain, 423
Philanthropic Society, 89–91, 98, 235–6, 243, 333, 343, 345, 347, 389 n.
philanthropy, *see* benevolence
Phillips, Sir Richard, 347
Philpotts, Henry, Bishop, 142 n.
'Pindar, Peter' (Dr John Wolcot), 19, 158, 180
Piozzi, Mrs, 203, 223
Pitt, William, 36, 41, 74, 100 n., 131, 162, 264, 266, 347, 531
  and the Church, 38, 40, 92–3, 210, 223–6, 235, 292, 481, 493
  friend of Wilberforce, 3, 71, 73, 76, 91–3, 112, 116, 117, 157, 199, 210, 223–6, 268, 481–2, 493, 505
Pitt, William Morton, 87, 88, 235, 349, 356
Place, Francis, 113, 345, 346
Plumer, Lady, 241 n. 2
Plumer, Sir Thomas, 90, 236, 343 n., 344, 349, 355
'Plymley, Peter' (Sydney Smith), 368
Political Register, 180–2
Polwhele, Richard, 159, 162, 168, 215
poor, the, *see* lower orders *and* poverty
Pope, Alexander, 102, 520
Porter, Jane, 11, 19
Porteus, Beilby, Bishop, 8, 106, 210 n., 247, 266, 457
  and Evangelicalism, 31, 85–6, 160, 163, 166, 196, 235, 244, 246, 264, 279, 519
  and Blagdon Controversy, 183, 197, 199, 201, 203, 213–16, 218, 222–3, 226
  and Hannah More, 102, 103, 121, 123–4, 126, 134, 151, 157, 158, 458–9
poverty, 16, 42, 140–1, 146–8, 187, 230–1, 251, 400, 533
Powell, Baden, 346, 347
Poynder, John, 270, 359, 389 n., 427, 429
Poynder, Thomas, sen., 359, 389 n.
Poynder, Thomas, jun., 389 n.

Practical Piety (Hannah More), 395
Practical View of the Religious System of Professed Christians... (William Wilberforce), 115–22, 123, 160, 172, 235, 245, 396 n., 493, 497–8, 507, 528
Pratt, John H., 403
Pratt, Josiah, 52 n. 2, 251, 403, 429, 444–5, 509, 525, 527
  and C.M.S., 264, 271, 279, 280, 281, 282, 284
Prayer Book and Homily Society, 335, 342
preferment, *see under* Established Church
Pretyman, Bishop, *see* Tomline
Price, Sir Charles, 236 n., 342
pride, spiritual, 63, 386–8, 390–3, 409, 417, 454, 457, 474–6, 478–9, 481–6, 502, 508, 513, 514
Priestley, Joseph, 218, 223 n.
Prince Regent, *see* George IV
prison discipline, Society concerned with, 335, 345, 347, 349, 351
Proclamation Society, *see* Vice and Immorality
prostitution, 15–16, 21–2, 23–5, 71, 327, 348, 374, 521, 523
  societies concerned with, 24, 335, 340, 346, 347, 363, 392, 429–30, 437, 524
Protestant Dissenting Ministers Bill, 285–8
Public Characters, 18, 38–40, 47
Pulteney, General Sir James, 269
Puritanism, Evangelical tendency to, 5–6, 162–3, 324–5, 404, 508
  attacked, 16, 169–70, 174, 177, 179–83, 200, 210, 211, 369–71, 434, 436, 478
Pusey, Edward Bouverie, 6, 353 n., 518
Pusey, Lady Emily, 6 n., 241 n. 2, 353 n., 518
Pusey, Philip, 6 n., 88, 89, 235, 236, 241 n. 2, 342, 343 n., 344, 349, 353 n.

Quakers, 244, 309, 342 n., 345, 346, 350, 351, 372, 379, 405, 429, 493, 504
Queen Mab (Percy Bysshe Shelley), 288, 428
Queens' College, Cambridge, 290–1, 295, 501

Radnor, Admiral Earl, 87, 88, 102, 241 n. 2, 344, 349, 356, 359
Radnor, Lady, 102

562

Index

Index

Index

Index

Truman, Hanbury, Buxton & Co., 241 n. 2
Truslow, John, 32–3
Turner, Mr, of Belmont, 219, 223 n.
Turner, Sharon, 90
Two Shoemakers, The (Hannah More), 137
Two Wealthy Farmers, The (Hannah More), 135–6, 152
Tyrwhitt, Thomas, 91, 347

Uncle Silas (Sheridan Le Fanu), 445
Unitarians, 91, 94, 159–60, 244, 286, 484, 493
United States, 252, 396 n., 439
Unsexed Females, The (Richard Polwhele), 159
Unwin, Mary, 349
Uxbridge, Earl of, 256

Valentia, Viscount, 280, 281
Vansittart, Mrs, 358
Vansittart, Nicholas (Lord Bexley), 270 n., 342 n., 481
  and Evangelical societies, 10, 56, 89, 241 n. 2, 269, 270, 275, 306, 309, 343 n., 344, 357, 360
Vansittart, Sophia, 241 n. 2, 349, 358
Vaughan, Edward Thomas, 134, 173, 272, 280, 403, 490, 502
Venn, Henry, 34, 98, 326, 389 n., 403, 422, 503 n., 519
  and Calvinism, 55, 110, 172, 474
  and 'nominal' Christians, 63, 391
  and Wilberforce, 76, 77, 493, 502
  attitude to wealth, 51–2, 53, 57–9, 527
  on Simeon, 289, 293, 294
Venn, Henry (son of John), 34 n., 403, 490, 502
Venn, Jane Catherine, 519
Venn, John, 34 n., 299, 309, 389 n., 391, 403, 502, 503 n.
  and Evangelical societies, 265, 368–9, 444–5, 526–7
Vernon, George, 358–9
Vernon, Lady, 241 n. 2
Vernon, Lord, 241 n. 2, 256
Vesci, Viscount de, 281
Vicar of Wrexhill, The (Frances Trollope), 402–3, 445

Vice, Society for Suppression of, 5, 8, 27, 84, 238 n., 288, 334, 345, 347, 360, 363, 372, 407–8, 433–4
  branches, 435–6
  Wilberforce and, 26, 70, 96 n., 246, 428–32, 435, 491, 517, 521
Vice and Immorality, Society for Carrying into Effect His Majesty's Proclamation Against, 15, 27, 333, 347, 363, 369
  Wilberforce and, 3, 70, 83–8, 234–5, 432, 491
Victoria, Princess and Queen, 1, 10, 524
Village Politics (Hannah More), 123–4, 126–9, 137, 148, 228, 356
Villiers, J. C. (third Earl of Clarendon), 88, 241 n. 2, 344, 356, 502
Voltaire, François Marie Arouet de, 427, 457–8

Waldegrave, Lady, 312
Wales, Prince of, *see* George IV
Wales, Princess of, 17
Walker, Samuel, 282
Watson, Joshua, 90 n., 347, 353
Watson, Richard, Bishop, 40, 296 n., 310
Watts, Isaac, 137 n.
Way, Drusilla, 440
Way, John Raymond, 426
Way, Lewis (Evangelical), 72 n. 2, 271, 358, 388, 405, 426, 437, 440
Way, Lewis (High Churchman), 294, 388, 475
Way, Thomas, 426
Way of All Flesh, The (Samuel Butler), 324, 445–7
Way to Plenty, The (Hannah More), 142–4, 218
wealth, Evangelical attitudes to, 5, 9–10, 32, 49–53, 56–9, 61–2, 66, 68, 79–81, 83, 94, 120, 181, 209, 236 n., 293–4, 298, 326, 371, 386, 399, 409–16, 418, 425–6, 467–9, 476–80, 483, 485, 508
  See also ruling class
Weare, William, 442
Weavers Company, 165–6
Wedmore, 195
Wellington, Duke of, 256, 266, 273, 344, 373, 427

Index

Index

DATE DUE

~~███████~~			
MAY 2 2 2000			
GAYLORD			PRINTED IN U.S.A.